Benjamin West

Books by Robert C. Alberts

The Most Extraordinary Adventures
of Major Robert Stobo

The Golden Voyage: The Life and Times
of William Bingham 1752–1804

The Good Provider: H. J. Heinz and
His 57 Varieties

Benjamin West: A Biography

Benjamin West

A BIOGRAPHY

Robert C. Alberts

HOUGHTON MIFFLIN COMPANY
BOSTON 1978

Library of Congress Cataloging in Publication Data

Alberts, Robert C
Benjamin West: a biography.

Bibliography: p.
Includes index.
1. West, Benjamin, 1738–1830.   2. Painters — United
States — Biography.
ND237.W45A6   759.13 [B]   78-17241
ISBN 0-395-26289-5

Printed in the United States of America
V 10 9 8 7 6 5 4 3 2 1

The lines from "Epistle to Be Left in the Earth" from
NEW AND COLLECTED POEMS 1917–1976, Copyright ©
1976 by Archibald MacLeish, are reprinted by permission
of Houghton Mifflin Company.

To the memory of dear friends

Richard Hudson Klemer
George Porter Paine
John Irwin Scull
Richard Joseph Simon
Ruth Mering Simon
Joseph Grange Smith

"I pray you,
        you (if any open this writing)
Make in your mouths the words that were our names."

Archibald MacLeish,
"Epistle to Be Left in the Earth"

Contents

Illustrations

Unless otherwise stated, the picture is
by Benjamin West. Dimensions are in inches.

Grouped following page 78

Introduction

OF BENJAMIN WEST it was said in 1975, "His career was the first great success story in the history of American art. Few subsequent successes — even by today's standard of international celebrity — have matched the immensity of his." It was said of him in 1973, "Benjamin West, a paramount example of the American success story, led a life so remarkable for its propitious circumstances that it reads like a work of fiction." West's life does indeed have elements of good fortune and early success that would seem to belong in a romantic novel rather than in a documented biography. In 1753 he was a fifteen-year-old prodigy, the youngest of ten children of an innkeeper in a village west of Philadelphia, painting his first awkward portraits for a pound or two each. Seven years later, as the first American-born art student in Italy, he was a favorite of worldly Roman society. Visiting England on his way back to America, he met Joshua Reynolds and Richard Wilson, who persuaded him to show two of his pictures in an exhibition. They created such excitement that he decided to settle in London. He was soon England's most popular painter, became a friend and companion of King George III, and worked with him to found the Royal Academy of Arts. He welcomed Charles Willson Peale as his pupil and so established in London what has been called the first effective American school of art, to which later came virtually every other American artist of consequence who painted before 1820 — artists who would influence and sometimes dominate the trends of English art. All this happened by the time West was thirty, with the best fifty years of his life and work ahead of him.

Such a man obviously deserves at least one new biography in every generation. It is one of the anomalies of American and English letters that the biographies have not appeared — none in the 158 years since West's death in 1820. John Galt, the Scottish romantic novelist, wrote a life in West's old age that is unique, invaluable, adulatory, incomplete, and unreliable. A 115-page adaptation of Galt's work appeared in 1900 that added nothing at all in the way of ideas or information, save for several major misinterpretations of Galt's text. James Thomas Flexner produced an important eighty-page section on West in his *America's Old Masters* in 1939. In it he declared that a complete listing of the works in which West is mentioned would fill a volume, and he deplored as "amazing" the lack of a biography and *catalogue raisonné*. The critic Hilton Kramer has described West's position in American art history as "relatively obscure," called it "astonishing," and added, "We cannot quite explain this reluctance to accord West the generous attention his achievements warrant."

One reason is undoubtedly the long period, lasting from about 1830 to perhaps 1938, when West's paintings were ignored or ridiculed and cited as all that was meretricious in art. Even as his work had been overpraised in West's lifetime, so it was undervalued for more than a hundred years after his death. The collapse of West's reputation and its resurgence in recent years is a subject of some importance in a West biography; it is covered in the last chapter of the present work.

In the past several decades there has been a reassessment of much eighteenth and nineteenth-century art that for several generations had been considered wrong and bad. John Canaday has described this shift in values in a trenchant and amusing paragraph:

> It is a little comical to see the dilemma in which critics and art history teachers find themselves when confronted with their revived victims. Over a period of several decades we had a marvelous time explaining why these paintings were so bad that they were hilarious, why you must not under any circumstances admit to feeling any respect for them. It is a hard act to follow when it becomes necessary, as it is now, to explain to your reconditioned audience why these same paintings are good — or if not good, at least important and interesting and not all that funny.

West is foremost among those whose work has thus been revalued, furthered by a recent succession of brilliant essays on his work by American and European critics. Allowance is at last being made for his inferior pieces, which is a right due any artist or writer. Respect is now being paid to some of his other works for their importance as documents or their influence in the development of modern art. And the corpus of his best work contains pictures that it is impossible not to like and admire, including, in the words of a modern critic, "long-neglected minor works that come like revelations in their variety and freshness."

West has also had a long-overdue reassessment as a person. This began in the 1920s with the publication of an abridgment of the diary of his fellow artist Joseph Farington (1747–1821). Readers of the eight volumes (covering the years 1793–1821) come upon a West who was a quite different man from the West who had always been depicted as cold, colorless, pompous, inarticulate, and even a bit obtuse. The much longer unpublished Farington diary, first made available in 1951 in typescript at Windsor Castle and in the Print Room of the British Museum, carried the reappraisal still further. In its 7261 pages (seven microfilm reels), West's vanity and blunders emerge with embarrassing clarity; but so, too, do his sound knowledge of the techniques of painting, engraving, and teaching, his courage under savage attacks from his quarreling colleagues in the Royal Academy, his capacity for friendship, good conversation, and shrewd observation, his decency and kindness, and his generosity to his colleagues and to young beginners.

The complete Farington diary, whether judged as art history, or social history, or for its sheer readability, is one of the treasures of English arts and letters. Scholars working in special fields and on biographies of several artists have used it to good purpose — Jules David Prown, for example, in his two volumes on John Singleton Copley, and Alexander Fineberg on William Turner; but it is still a relatively untapped resource on the later Georgian period, when English art was at its height. Farington was West's associate through a period of fifty-six years, five of them as his opponent and twenty as his closest friend. For a biographer of West his diary, with its eleven columns of indexed references and its many pages of new material on West, is priceless. The unpublished Farington manuscript is the sole or main source of a number of episodes here related in full for the first time, among them the number and fierceness of the quarrels among English artists of the period; the Venetian Secret swindle perpetrated on the leading members of the Royal Academy; and the classic struggle for control of the Academy, with its elements of rage, jealousy, and humor — indeed, of high comedy. A score of fine artists flourished in England between 1763 and 1820, the years West was in London, and their work is part of the world's inheritance; but (except for Reynolds) they have been shadowy figures, one scarcely distinguishable, as a person, from another. In Farington they come alive as rounded, three-dimensional human beings, breathing, working, playing, fighting — especially fighting: Hoppner and Lawrence, Fuseli and Flaxman, Constable and Turner, Copley and Beechey and Angelica Kauffmann, and West himself. With them stand the supporting characters: the English eccentrics, the titled patrons and collectors, the prelates of the Anglican Church, the notorious William Beckford of Fonthill; the waspish Horace Walpole of Strawberry Hill; hard-drinking James Boswell at fifty-two, at the height of his fame; a surprisingly likeable George III, his homely queen, and their brood of thirteen unhappy princes and princesses. With the recent revival of interest in Georgian art and the disclosure of such rich material in Farington, one may hope that the Farington diary will soon be annotated and published in full.

Except in a few instances where an eighteenth-century flavor seemed desirable in a short passage, I have modernized and corrected the punctuation and spelling of all quoted material of the period. I have used Gilbert Stuart's plea for West's help, however, exactly as he wrote it in 1777, since it somehow seemed improper to change it. West himself, like so many of his contemporaries, was a wretched speller — so bad that his errors, if not corrected, would distract the reader and sometimes obscure the sense.

There is much direct discourse in this work, but I have invented none of it and have made no changes other than to drop words, as indicated. John Galt interviewed and quoted West at length. Other associates recorded conversations in their letters, diaries, and memoirs. Farington and William Dunlap are the richest sources for such quoted discourse; others will be recognizable in the Bibliography. These writers may have improved some of the dialogue they recorded, but they were there at the time and this is what they said, or heard and recalled, or were told by their contemporaries. One may question the accuracy of a conversation West recounted to Galt in his old age, thirty or forty years after the conversation took place; but West had told these stories many times before, they were crystallized in his mind, and we must assume that this was what he thought at the time, or remembered, or at least wished to remember, in later years.

Notes and sources appear on pages 417–475, keyed to the text by page number and an identifying phrase. West's pictures reproduced or mentioned in the text are grouped alphabetically under his name in the index. My acknowledgments to the people and the institutions to whom I owe a deep measure of gratitude appear on pages 403–407.

ROBERT C. ALBERTS

May 15, 1978

Benjamin West

1

The Death of Kings

Mr. West's readiness to give advice and assistance to artists is
well known. Every morning before he began to work he received
all who wished to see him. A friend of mine called at his house
the day after his death. His old and faithful servant, Robert
[Brunning], opened the door, and said, with a melancholy shake
of the head, "Ah, sir! Where will they go now?"

CHARLES ROBERT LESLIE
1834

THE OLD KING DIED at Windsor Castle on January 29, 1820, in
the sixtieth year of his reign. He had been blind, totally deaf, un-
shaven and long-bearded, intermittently out of his mind, living in a
world of fantasy in which he talked for hours on end to persons long
dead. He lay in state for two days and was buried in a nighttime
ceremony in St. George's Chapel, Windsor, where lay his queen and
Edward IV and Henry VIII and Charles I. On the day of the funeral,
merchants locked their shop doors, business ceased, and some citizens stayed at home and closed their shutters.

Many years earlier the young king had asked Benjamin West how
old he was, and when he heard that they were within four months
of being the same age, he had laughed and said, "Ah! Then when I
die, West, *you* will shake in your shoes." West's sons, Raphael and
Benjamin Junior, tried to keep the news of the king's death from
their father, asking visitors not to discuss the subject and omitting
all reference to it when they read the newspapers to him. He was
not deceived. If he did not hear that the servants of the Royal
Academy had been put into mourning for George III, or that his
own exhibition of pictures in Pall Mall had been closed, he must
have guessed it when the great bell of St. Paul's tolled on the day
of the funeral, three hours in the morning and three hours in the

evening. "I am sure that the King is dead," he said, "and that I have lost the best friend I ever had in my life."

He was eighty-one years and four months old when George III died, and he was a last survivor, with the architect George Dance, of the thirty-six original members of the Royal Academy. His mind was active and alert, though he tended to forget Mr. Dance in speaking of himself as the last of the foundation members of the Academy, and there had been a bit of confusion when he assumed that the celebration of the Academy's fiftieth anniversary in 1818 was being held in his honor. He sat musing and dozing in his arm-chair in the front drawing room, where he could receive visitors, and he talked occasionally of retouching some of the pictures in his gallery. He planned another picture the size of *Death on the Pale Horse*, 14 feet, 9 inches by 26 feet, which he always referred to as "my great work," and he even made a beautifully finished draw-ing on the subject, *Peter's Denial of Christ*. Jane Porter, author of the immensely successful romances *Thaddeus of Warsaw* and *Scottish Chiefs*, begged as a precious relic a brush he had used in painting one of his religious canvases. He sent her three worn brushes he had used in painting the *Pale Horse*.

Mrs. Benjamin West, Junior, who was running the household, complained that Mr. West never talked to her or her husband about his professional or even his domestic concerns, managing every-thing himself, and to a friend she "mentioned many particulars respecting her husband and herself and their situation with Mr. West." The many particulars, unfortunately, were not preserved for posterity. Both sons felt that their father's mind was wandering, but Sir John Hayes, the family physician, said privately, "I think that is owing to his not feeling an interest in what they say, for when I speak to him he is attentive and clear in his replies." A second physician, Dr. Edmund Baillie, had been called in; he de-clined all practice other than that of attending consultations, but he agreed to call on Mr. West twice a week, charging two guineas the visit, later lowered to one guinea. (He had charged the king thirty guineas and traveling expenses for twice-weekly calls at Windsor that he must have known were pointless.) Mr. West com-plained that the doctors did not understand his disorder; he "made use of stronger expressions than usual for him" in declaring his dissatisfaction with the medicines prescribed; and he reported that he did not feel as well since Dr. Baillie began to attend him as he had before. Dr. Baillie, a plainspoken man, told his patient that he understood his disorder very well, had seen two hundred such cases, and added, "Mr. West, you are a man of sense and must be aware that decay is natural at your age."

John Galt, the Scots journalist, called at 14 Newman Street with galley proofs of the second volume of his *Life, Studies and Works of Benjamin West, Esq., President of the Royal Academy of London, Composed from Materials Furnished by Himself*, but the old gentleman was too infirm to give them serious attention, or even to correct the date of his wife's death, wrong by three years. Joseph Farington, *éminence grise* of the Royal Academy, called to sit and talk with the friend and colleague he had met fifty-seven years earlier in the painting room of the landscape artist Richard Wilson. No one, including Mr. West, knew that Mr. Farington since July 13, 1793, had been keeping a diary in which he recorded daily events, gossip, opinion, rumors, conversations, and the activities of his associates; or that the diary, the handwritten equivalent of more than 7000 typed pages, would lie forgotten until discovered in 1921 in a mahogany case in a lumber attic in Sussex; or that, when published (in part), it would provide an incomparable account of life in England's golden age of art and artists. That evening Mr. Farington wrote in his diary, "Mr. West was much disposed to conversation, but his articulation was so bad that with my deafness, I could understand but little of what he said."

As the days passed, Mr. West lost his appetite; he could not bear "animal food" and lived mainly on sago and custard mixed with a teaspoon or two of brandy. Joseph Farington and other officers of the Royal Academy, "in consequence of Mr. West being in this alarming state," discussed who was to succeed him as president. They agreed that the choice would certainly fall upon Sir Thomas Lawrence, who was on his way home from the continent after many months of painting the monarchs, statesmen, and generals of the alliance that had defeated Napoleon.

John Thomas Smith, keeper of the prints at the British Museum, was the last known caller on the old gentleman. He found him in the front drawing room, lying on a sofa that he was now using as a bed. A volume of Fra Bartolomeo's drawings lay open on a small settee within his reach, so that he could conveniently turn the pages from his pillow. Four days after that visit, at 12:30 A.M. on March 11, 1820, Benjamin West died.

Thomas Lawrence, arriving in England on March 30, called the death "a national calamity." A cast was taken of the artist's right hand one hour after his death, curved as in holding a brush, and for a time it was revered as a sacred relic of the world of art. A poet published in one of the newspapers an elegy that ended:

> *Those who best know his generous, social mind,*
> *Replete with all that's manly, good and kind,*

While they his Virtues prize, — his merits scan,
Admire the Painter and revere the Man;
And, long as friendship warms the human breast,
Shall Memory sacred hold the Name of WEST.

Joseph Farington urged the Royal Academy to conduct a funeral ceremony "graced by the presence of persons of Rank and Distinction, agreeably to the common usage of this country on occasions where particular respect is meant to be done." Accordingly, the Academy held a public funeral, acting with the consent of the family and under a proclamation of King George IV. The body lay for one evening and throughout the night in the Royal Academy at Somerset House, where it was viewed by the members only. Charles Robert Leslie, one of the last of a score of distinguished artists who had studied under West, described the scene in a letter to his sister in Philadelphia.

> [The funeral] was arranged exactly on the plan of that of Sir Joshua Reynolds. An apartment on the ground-floor of the Academy was hung and carpeted with black, the daylight entirely excluded, and the room lighted by a number of tall wax-candles, placed at regular distances on the floor, around the coffin, which was covered by a pall and lid of black feathers. Against the wall, at the head of the corpse, hung a hatchment, bearing the family arms. No one remained in the room, excepting Robert [Brunning], West's old servant, who had sat up there all the preceding night. My feelings were greatly affected by this scene.
>
> The company who were to attend the funeral assembled in a large upper room, where they were provided with black silk scarves and hatbands, the Academicians wearing long black cloaks. It was interesting to see persons of different ranks and different nations, and of well-known different political sentiments, meeting on this occasion, and uniting in the last tribute of respect to a man of genius.

More than sixty mourning coaches, arranged by rank, their horses covered with black velvet, made up the funeral cortege on March 29. The coaches included those of the lord mayor of London, an archbishop, three dukes, two marquises, nine earls, and four bishops. Many others "of Rank and Distinction" were too old, infirm, or ill to attend the service, or were in the country, and they sent surrogates in their coaches; their absence was noticed and deplored by persons who remembered that such a thing had not happened at the funeral of Sir Joshua Reynolds in 1792. Among the other mourners were James Henry Henderson, the family solicitor, who thereafter would submit to the West sons a bill of £700 for legal services on the estate and for assistance in conducting the funeral negotiations; Henry Fauntleroy, West's banker and broker, who four years later would be hanged for forging documents in handling his clients' accounts; and the poet-essayist-editor Leigh Hunt, grandson of Mrs. West's brother, who had referred to his granduncle West as "a wretched foreigner," but whose newspaper said on this occasion, "The world has seldom possessed a better man, and not very often a greater artist."

The hearse was drawn by six black horses, moving at a slow pace along the Strand through an immense concourse of spectators on closed-off streets, through the Temple Bar, and on to St. Paul's Cathedral. The senior city marshal and attending officers in full dress met and arranged the procession at the Great Western Gate. Preceded by church dignitaries, the eight pallbearers, one of them Richard Rush, the American minister to Britain, another the banker Sir Thomas Baring, carried the coffin to the choir. The body of Academicians, Associate Members, and students of the Royal Academy followed two by two according to seniority. Mr. Farington, tired by the preparations of the past eighteen days and afraid of catching a cold in the unheated church, had returned home in his coach.

The Reverend, the Honorable Dr. Gerald Valerian Wellesley, brother of the duke of Wellington, had volunteered to conduct the service, and did so, according to John Galt, who was present, "in a very impressive manner." Since it was Passion Week (and perhaps because there had been a question about Mr. West's baptism and Quaker antecedents), the usual chanting and performance of music could not take place, but by special permission one anthem was sung by the boys of the choir. During the service the pallbearers carried the body through the vault door and down into the southwest section of the crypt, known as "Painters' Corner." There it was lowered to its place under the pavement, at the head of Sir Joshua Reynolds' grave. The service was concluded under the dome of the cathedral, while the sexton in the crypt below, at the proper moment, dropped some earth on the casket. The mourners returned to Somerset House in the same order of procession and there partook of cakes and wine.

So died and was buried Benjamin West, who was born in humble circumstances in an obscure Quaker village in eastern Pennsylvania, who landed in England at age twenty-four, a stranger without friends or influence, and who within five years was the friend and protégé of the reigning monarch and almost a member of the royal household. His pictures were respected, even revered; women sometimes wept or swooned, and men removed their hats and spoke in hushed voices, in the presence of some of his later works. On two continents his former students spoke of his kindness and generosity in the help he had given them. Of him a twentieth-century painter-critic would say, "No other artist of any land at any time has ever so completely influenced and dominated the art of his country."

2

"A Fire in My Breast"

I will now tell my little readers about BENJAMIN WEST, the great painter; who was an honour to his country while he lived, and will be long remembered now he is dead.

GERRITT VAN HUSEN FORBES,
The Life of Benjamin West,
The Great American Painter,
Written for Children,
New York, 1837

AMONG THOSE who accompanied William Penn on his second voyage to America in the autumn of 1699 was a couple from the parish of Long Crendon in Buckinghamshire: Thomas West, a cooper, and his wife Rachel Gilpin, daughter of a Cromwellian soldier who became a noted Quaker minister. They brought with them two of their three sons, leaving the youngest, John, age nine, with relatives to finish his education at the Quaker school at Uxbridge.

Penn had received a royal grant of more than 28 million acres — rich forested land measuring some 300 by 130 miles — where he established a colony, a Christian state on the Quaker model, known as Pennsylvania, and a town named Philadelphia at the junction of the Delaware and Schuylkill rivers.

John West completed his education at Uxbridge, worked for a time as a cooper, and joined his parents and brothers in Delaware County in 1714, when he was twenty-four. Two unusual circumstances marked his journey to America. He had been a Quaker — every person born of Quaker parents was a member of that religious fellowship at birth — but he did not carry with him a certificate of transfer, which meant that he was not in good standing with the Society of Friends when he left England. And he left behind him a wife who, pregnant with their first child, died a few months later in bearing a son. With his father's consent, the child was reared in England by his mother's parents, eventually becoming a watch and clock maker in Reading. Fifty years would pass before John West saw Thomas, his firstborn.

John West, widower, met and in 1720 married Sarah Pearson, the seventh of ten children of a Quaker couple, Thomas Pearson, a mason, and wife Margery, both of whom had come from England to Pennsylvania in 1683. Sarah Pearson, too, had been a birthright Quaker, but now for some unknown reason — an indiscretion, a dereliction, or a considered action held contrary to Quaker beliefs — she had been "disowned," read out of meeting. The marriage ceremony, of course, was not conducted according to the rules of the Society of Friends, and so the children of John and Sarah Pearson West, of whom there were ten, were not registered at meeting and were not Quakers. The point is an important one, for Benjamin, their youngest child, was widely believed to be a Quaker, and stories were later told — some of them by Benjamin — about his family's problems, in and out of meeting, with a son who followed the frivolous pursuit of painting pictures.

John West has been variously called a tinsmith, cooper, hosier, sailor, and innkeeper, but only his innkeeping is a matter of record in America. In 1733 he was living in Chester, where, on May 29, he applied for a tavern license: "Humbly showeth that your Petitioner has taken to ffarm [lease] the house, with the Appurtenances, where James Trego Lately Dwelt on the Green, near the Courthouse in Chester, where a house of entertainment hath been for some time and is now kept." He was given the license he desired. A year or two later he was listed as a taxable in Springfield Township, some ten miles west of Philadelphia and six miles north of Chester, where his wife's father had originally settled. There he rented a three-story mansion of cut stone on the high road to Chadd's Ford and operated it as an inn. In a first-floor room in the southeast corner of the building Benjamin West was born on October 10, 1738.[1]

In August 1743, when Benjamin was almost five, his father applied successfully for a new tavern license, attesting that he "has Rented a Comoudyas house & all other Conveanances there and to belonging for a house of entertainment on the Roade Leading from Darby to Springfield & from thence to Conistoga [in Lancaster County on the Susquehanna River]; which is of late much fre-

---

[1] The building still stands in its original location, now on the campus of Swarthmore College.

quented by the Dutch waggons, to the number of 40 or 50 in a Day." It is not known whether the West inn was a "stage stop" or a less elegant "waggon stop," but in either case it gave Benjamin a childhood full of excitement and activity. There were the immigrants traveling west, pale from their six-to-ten-week ocean crossing and their rough journey in a springless coach or wagon; most of them Germans; many of them redemptioners sold at auction to work for a term of years as indentured servants to pay their passage; all of them recently sworn by signing their names or putting their marks to three oaths: to be faithful to King George II and to abjure the Pope and the doctrine of transubstantiation. There were the Lancaster County farmers driving to the great Wednesday and Saturday market in Philadelphia, stopping to "bait" their horses at the inn, cursing a road that overturned or mired or broke the axles or wheels of their carts and wagons; the wagoners who ate at the inn and slept on the floor of the kitchen or taproom in winter and under their vehicles in the wagon yard in summer; the drovers of cattle, sheep, swine, and turkeys; the prosperous Lancaster lawyers, merchants, landowners, and public officials on their way to and from their weighty affairs in the city. Any boy in the years between four and eight, and especially the youngest of ten children, would have devoted himself doggedly to following his elders, and so would have been scolded for being constantly under foot — by his brothers and sisters, by the kitchen help, by the chambermaids when they carried the slop jars down the stairs in the morning and the hot coals in the warming pans up the stairs in the evening. The stable, barn, and bullock pen would have been a source of constant interest, filled as they were with ever-changing hostlers, cattle, carriages, and horses.

A celebrated Quaker preacher had prophesied at Benjamin's birth that he was destined to have an extraordinary future, but the child waited until June of 1745 to give the first sign that the prophecy was true. The story is one that has charmed generations of children; Nathaniel Hawthorne told it in one of his books for young people, and it has appeared in new children's books as late as 1947 and 1967. E. M. Ward, member of the Royal Academy, made a painting of the incident and John Sartain produced an engraving after the painting that hung in nurseries on two continents. As Benjamin told John Galt, and Galt retold it in his biography, one of his married sisters came with her infant to spend a few days with her parents. One day when the baby was asleep in the cradle, Mrs. West and her daughter stepped outside to the house garden, leaving Benjamin to watch the child and brush away the flies.

After some time the child happened to smile in its sleep, and its beauty attracted his attention. He looked at it with a pleasure which he had never before experienced, and observing some paper on a table, together with pens and red and black ink, he seized them with agitation, and endeavoured to delineate a portrait; although at this period he had never seen an engraving or a picture, and was only in the seventh year of his age.

Hearing the approach of his mother and sister, he endeavoured to conceal what he had been doing; but the old lady observing his confusion, enquired what he was about, and requested him to show her the paper. He obeyed, entreating her not to be angry. Mrs. West, after looking some time at the drawing with evident pleasure, said to her daughter, "I declare he has made a likeness of little Sally," and kissed him with much fondness and satisfaction.

At this, Benjamin was encouraged to say that he would make pictures of the flowers his mother held in her hand, if it would give her any pleasure, "for the instinct of genius" (Galt said) "was now awakened, and he felt that he could imitate the forms of those things which pleased his sight."

In the course of the summer, Galt continued:

A party of Indians came to pay their annual visit to Springfield and being amused with the sketches of birds and flowers which Benjamin showed them, they taught him to prepare the red and yellow colours with which they painted their ornaments. To these his mother added blue, by giving him a piece of indigo, so that he was thus put in possession of the three primary colours.

West often told the story at London dinners. Europeans were fascinated by American Indians, and West, who had a legitimate interest as an artist in attracting public attention and knew it as well as any man of his time, made the most of being the only painter in England who had grown up among savage red men. Delaware and Conestoga Indians were certainly present in Eastern Pennsylvania at the time, and they traveled and lived in peace among the Quaker communities.[2]

The next story has been told and retold many times, but John Galt told it first and no one has told it better.

---

[2] Some cynics of the period claimed that the Quakers lived in peace with the Indians because there were fifty miles of Scotch-Irish Presbyterians between them and the untamed Shawnees.

His drawings at length attracted the attention of neighbours; and some of them happening to regret that the artist had no pencils,[3] he enquired what kind of things these were, and they were described to him as small brushes made of camels' hair fastened in a quill. As there were, however, no camels in America, he could not think of any substitute, till he happened to cast his eyes on a black cat, the favourite of his father; when, in the tapering fur of her tail, he discovered the means of supplying what he wanted. He immediately armed himself with his mother's scissors, and, laying hold of Grimalkin with all due caution, and a proper attention to her feelings, cut off the fur at the end of her tail, and with this made his first pencil. But the tail only furnished him with one, which did not last long, and he soon stood in need of a further supply. He then had recourse to the animal's back, his depredations upon which were so frequently repeated, that his father observed the altered appearance of his favourite, and lamented it as the effect of disease. The artist, with suitable marks of contrition, informed him of the true cause; and the old gentleman was so much amused with his ingenuity, that if he rebuked him, it was certainly not in anger.

In 1744 John West rented an inn at Newtown Square, north of Springfield. A year or so later, "Mr. Pennington, a merchant of Philadelphia," who was related to the Wests, paid his yearly family visit.[4] Though a Quaker, young Mr. Penington was "a man of pleasant temper and indulgent dispositions." Impressed by his little cousin's drawings of birds and flowers in colors extracted from roots, herbs, and barks of trees, he sent him a box of paints and brushes, several prepared canvases, and six engravings by an artist Galt called "Grevling," who may have been Hubert François Gravelot, or Simon Gribelin, or (it has been suggested) Giovanni Guercino. They were the first engravings and the first real paint and brushes he saw, and he saw them with transports of joy. For several days he stayed home from school, secretly spending his time in the attic combining two of the engravings into one composition, until apprehended when the schoolmaster inquired into his whereabouts. West exhibited it many years later in his gallery in London; he

---

[3] In the eighteenth century, and in poetic use well into the nineteenth, pencil meant a brush of hair or bristle used by artists to lay on colors, especially a small brush for fine work.

[4] This was Edward Penington (1726–1796). He was to have a distinguished career as a judge; he would build one of the finest houses in Philadelphia, become a member of the American Philosophical Society, attend the Continental Congress of 1774, and spend time in jail during the Revolution as a Loyalist.

would tell visitors with emotion that it had "inventive touches of art which with all my subsequent knowledge and experience I have not been able to surpass."

When Penington made another visit to the West household a few days later he was so highly pleased with the effect of his present that he obtained permission to take Benjamin with him to Philadelphia. The boy, now in his ninth year, had never been there, and it was "a circumstance most grateful to my feelings — indulging the hope of seeing some pictures in the city." When Penington gave him more materials "for making pictures in oil," he attempted "a landscape, in which were ships, cattle, and other things which I had [become] accustomed to see." Before the work was finished, Samuel Shoemaker, "an intimate friend of Mr. Pennington," came to see the nine-year-old prodigy at work.[5] He said that a few days earlier he had met a stranger on the street carrying an oil painting. He introduced himself, asked to see it, and found it to be "a landscape of considerable merit, and painted by the person in whose hands the picture was." The artist's name was William Williams. He had recently settled in the city and "appeared to possess a powerful mind and a great love of painting." Shoemaker had given him a commission for a landscape. When it was dry enough to be moved safely, he said, he would bring it and the painter so that Cousin Benjamin might see both. West described the meeting and his long association with Williams in a lengthy letter he wrote in 1810, discovered in the 1960s:

> The palpitation of joy which this conversation produced in my mind when I became certain of seeing it was what I can never forget, nor did hours ever pass slower away than those which intervened until I saw the picture, which in a few days was brought to Mr. Pennington's. I believe the blush of joy which overspread my face on the picture being first exposed to view attracted the attention of those present even more than the picture itself although a work of considerable merit: it being the first picture I had seen except the small essays I made in the country, and the one I was then attempting in oil.

Williams continued to regard Benjamin while Penington and Shoemaker were examining and commending his landscape. To Pening-

---

[5] Samuel Shoemaker (1725–1800) was Penington's brother-in-law. He was a successful Quaker merchant and lawyer, a member of the American Philosophical Society, and became treasurer of Philadelphia and its mayor in 1769 and 1771. A Loyalist, he would flee to London, where West would befriend him.

ton he then said, "I am of opinion, Sir, that this youth has the sensibility proper for the studying of painting." He turned again to Benjamin and asked him if he had ever read the lives of any of the great masters of painting. Benjamin replied that he had never heard of such lives and that he had never read any account of great men except those in the Bible, which his parents directed him to read and remember. Williams said that if Mr. Penington permitted it he would lend the boy several books of that nature.

He gave Benjamin two volumes, both of them standard but out-of-date works important to eighteenth-century English classicism. One was John Dryden's 1695 translation of a long critical and philosophical work in Latin verse by Charles Alphonse du Fresnoy, *De Arte Graphica — The Art of Painting, with Remarks.* The other volume, by the English painter Jonathan Richardson, was either *An Essay on the Theory of Painting* (1715) or the 1719 work commonly known as *Two Discourses.* West declared, "Those two books were my companions by day, and under my pillow at night," but it is difficult to believe that he understood more than a small part of the high-flown language and aesthetic theories he found there. He learned from Fresnoy that he should study the sculpture of ancient Greece, without whose guidance "all is nothing but rash and blind barbarity"; to abhor the Gothic, the Baroque, and the debased naturalism of the Dutch and Flemish genre painters; and, in his studies, to make a careful selection and raise nature to a higher ideal plane. In creating universal ideal types, he was to follow a measured relationship between all parts of the human body:

> *"Learn then from Greece, ye youths, Proportion's law;*
> *Informed by her, each just position draw."*

Under that law, "the sole of the foot is the sixth part of the figure in length"; "the longest toe is a nose long"; "the two outmost parts of the teats, and the pit between the collar bones of a woman make an equilateral triangle," and so forth.

Children do have, however, a remarkable ability to absorb ideas from books that are far beyond their experience and comprehension. From Fresnoy and Richardson, then or a few years later, West seems to have ingested elements of the enduring artistic philosophy that shaped his thinking and his career. Richardson taught him, "A painter ought to be a title of dignity, and understood to imply a person endued with such excellencies of mind and body, as have ever been the foundations of honour amongst men." Young West, in fact, became so imbued with the nobility of his chosen profession that he seems to have become, for a time, a little prig. His parents, perceiving "a great change in his conversation," attributed it to the predestination that had been revealed at his birth. When a schoolfellow showed up with a saddled horse to take him to a neighboring farm on a half-holiday — an occasion to be enjoyed and celebrated — Benjamin refused to ride behind him, because he had resolved never to ride behind anybody. The boy obligingly allowed him to take the saddle. When the boy revealed that he was about to become a tailor's apprentice, Benjamin announced that he intended to become a painter and that a painter was the companion of kings and emperors. In the words that followed, Benjamin dismounted and said, "You may ride by yourself, for I will not ride with one willing to be a tailor."

When he saw some wide poplar boards at a cabinetmaker's shop near his home, he asked for and was given six short pieces on which to make drawings. On these he drew six heads in ink, chalk, and charcoal and gave them to "Mr. Wayne, a gentleman of the neighborhood," who the next day rewarded him with a dollar for each. It was the first money he received for his work as an artist. A short time later he had his first of a long line of patrons, a young Dr. Jonathan Morris, who gave him "a present of a few dollars to buy materials to paint with." [6]

The other events of these early years are difficult to date and put into a sequence, partly because of the Galt-West tendency to emphasize precocity by making everything happen at the earliest possible age. It is recorded that when he was twelve Benjamin was attending a log schoolhouse in Newtown Square; there existed at one time a copybook filled with drawings of animals and birds which, according to legend, he had given to a schoolmate named Williamson as compensation for help with his arithmetic. He had instruction during these years from a Mr. Hide, a German artist who had painted in London, and he spent several weeks in the home of "Mr. Flower . . . who possessed some taste in painting." [7] Flower had lost his wife a short time earlier, and to rear and educate his children he had imported an English governess, "a lady eminently fitted for the trust." Arriving in the household a few days before Benjamin, she took a liking to him, frequently including him as one of her pupils

---

[6] Isaac Wayne (1699–1774), one of the large landowners of the area, was the father of "Mad Anthony" Wayne, hero of the American Revolution. Jonathan Morris (1729–1819) had studied medicine under Dr. John Bard in Philadelphia, continued his training in New York, and settled at Newtown Square in 1751.

[7] Samuel Flower, a justice of the peace in Chester County in 1745, was co-owner with his father-in-law of an iron furnace and of rich iron-ore deposits. He would become a relative of the West family by marriage in 1761.

and, in reading aloud from translations of the classics, gave him his first formal knowledge of Greek and Roman history and legends.

In March 1749, Benjamin's sister Rachel had married John Levenus Clarkson, a member of the prominent De Peyster family of New York and "a gentleman who had been educated at Leyden and was much respected for the intelligence of his conversation, and the propriety of his manners." Clarkson's brother Matthew became a successful merchant who four times served as mayor of Philadelphia. Either as a vendor or as a publisher, or both, he advertised and sold engravings. With the heart of the city only ten miles away and rides easily obtained from the vehicles stopping at or passing his father's inn, Benjamin now frequently went to stay with his sister. On these visits he came to know William Williams better. "My attention," he said, "was directed to every point necessary to accomplish me for the profession of painting: this often brought me to the house of Williams." That artist, long forgotten but today a subject of heightened interest among art historians, was then in the early years of a career that was to produce some excellent portraits and portrait groups, including what were probably the first "conversation pieces" executed in the American colonies.

Williams was twenty-two years old in 1749, though Benjamin thought him much older. He had been born in Bristol, England, where he attended grammar school and where, he told West, his greatest delight had been to visit an elderly artist who painted heads and small landscapes in oil. From this experience, he said, he conceived a passionate desire to become a painter. He was "disposed of" to the sea by his father as an unwilling apprentice seaman, his master being an American captain in the Virginia trade. Williams jumped ship in Norfolk on his second voyage and made his way to the West Indies. There he hoped to work his passage to an American city where he might become a painter. He was shipwrecked on the Moskito Coast of Nicaragua and, if his story is accepted, spent some two years as a castaway there with the Rama Indians. He managed to reach Philadelphia in 1745, where he taught the art of drawing, designed stage scenery, ornamented ships, cleaned, repaired, and varnished old pictures of value, did lettering, sign painting, and gilding, gave lessons in the flute (hautboy, German, and common), and practiced "painting in general." He must have been at least moderately successful, for at one time he made an investment of "upwards of a hundred pounds" in stage scenery, and he collected prints from the works of eminent painters as part of biographical material he was assembling on their lives. He lent the manuscript of his "Lives of the Painters" to Benjamin, who devoured it as he had devoured Fresnoy and Richardson. He also told young West about a book he was writing, titled *Mr. Penrose: The Journal of Penrose, Seaman*, which he said was based on his own experience as a castaway. "He was an excellent actor in taking off character," West said. "He often to amuse me, repeated his adventures amongst the Caribs and Negro tribes in the West Indies." He addressed a tribute to West in his twelfth year, a poem, that was published in one of the daily papers and was much admired.

As West's first practical instructor in the techniques of painting, Williams would have shown the untrained boy how to handle and care for the bladders that held the pigments, how to lay the ground on a canvas, how to hold a palette, how to set up the colors on a palette, the way to use the different brushes in applying paint to a surface, how to rest the maulstick against the painting to support the wrist when precision of touch was required. "Most undoubtedly," West said, "had not Williams been settled in Philadelphia I should not have embraced painting as a profession ... It was to his books and prints that I was indebted for all the knowledge I possessed of the progress the fine arts had made in the world ... The Lives of the Painters ... lighted up a fire in my breast which has never been extinguished."

3

The Practising Artist

Nor let the muse forget thy name, Oh West.
Loved youth with virtue as by nature blest!
If such the radiance of thy early morn,
What bright effulgence must the noon adorn?
Hail sacred genius! may'st thou ever tread
The pleasing paths your Wollaston had led.
Let his just precepts all your works refine.
Copy each grace, and learn like him to shine.

FRANCIS HOPKINSON,
The American Magazine,
September 1758

WHEN BENJAMIN WEST was seventeen, his friend Samuel Flower — the neighbor with the motherless children and the English governess — recommended him as a portrait painter to George Ross, a prospering young Lancaster attorney with whom Flower had a business and social relationship.[1] Ross looked at some of the likenesses West had made in Newtown Square and invited him to come to Lancaster to paint his portrait and that of his wife. West made the visit and painted three-quarter-length portraits of Ross, his wife Ann, and his younger sister, Catherine Ross. He was still having certain difficulties affixing arms to torsos in a natural relationship, but the three portraits show a vast improvement in technique and skill. It may be assumed that they were recognizable likenesses and were well received, for the sphere of his celebrity, he said later, "was greatly enlarged."

---

[1] George Ross (1730–1779), son of an Episcopal minister, Crown prosecutor in Cumberland County, became a member of the First and Second Continental Congresses, a signer of the Declaration of Independence for Pennsylvania, and an eminent jurist.

Lancaster was the westernmost and largest inland town in the American colonies, lying on the Conestoga River sixty-five miles west of Philadelphia. It had been settled by Quakers, Episcopalians, Scotch-Irish Presbyterians, and later in swelling numbers by German Lutherans, Dunkards, Mennonites, Amish, and Moravian Brethren. They took a rich countryside and by intensive cultivation made it the most productive agricultural area per acre in North America. West extended his visit to the town for some twelve months of 1755–56, and he painted a sizable number of portraits there (seven, possibly eight of which are now identifiable).

One of the notable men of Lancaster was a master gunsmith named William Henry. He had been apprenticed at fifteen, on his father's early death, to a rifle maker in the town, and in 1750, when he was twenty-one, he set out to make arms on his own account. His company became armorer for the Pennsylvania forces attached to General Braddock's disastrous expedition in 1755 against the French at Fort Duquesne and three years later for the successful march led by General Forbes. Henry was an enthusiastic student of scientific experiment and a gifted deviser of labor-saving machinery. He was devoted to the extraordinary notion that a steam engine might be mounted in or on a vessel to propel it through the water, and in 1763, some twenty-four years before John Fitch and forty-four years before Robert Fulton, he would launch a paddle-wheel steamboat on the Conestoga River. (It failed.)

West took up residence in the Henry household on East King Street in 1756 and painted the newly married couple: Ann in three-quarter length, seated, holding a book, wearing a low-cut blue dress that accentuated her long neck; William standing, half-length, wearing a fashionable powdered wig and lace cuffs, holding one of his Pennsylvania rifles in his left hand.

Henry's formal education had ended at fifteen and he had never traveled beyond the Colonies, and yet he was aware of one of the prevailing aesthetic dogmas in Europe. He knew that producing portraits was considered an unworthy artistic pursuit and that painting morally uplifting historical subjects should be the goal of an artist as talented and promising as West. He conveyed these ideas to his young guest and suggested that the death of Socrates was a suitable topic for creating an elevating moral effect. Who, asked West, was Socrates? From a bookshelf Henry took volume four of a work by the French historian Charles Rollin: *The Ancient History of the Egyptians, Carthaginians, Assyrians, Babylonians, Medes and Persians, Macedonians and Grecians.* He showed West the engraved frontispiece: Socrates in prison surrounded by guards and disciples, in the act of reaching for the hemlock poison.

West made a sketch and showed it to Henry, who "commended it as a perspicuous delineation of the probable circumstances of the event, and requested him to paint it." He would be happy to try, West said, but observed that he would not be able to do justice to the figure of the slave who presented the poison, because the slave should be naked and he had painted only fully clothed figures. Without answering, Henry sent for one of the workmen in his shop. A handsome young man entered, bare from the waist up, and Henry said, "There is your model." West realized that he "had only to look into nature for models which would impart grace and energy to his delineation of forms." The finished picture, he said, "attracted much attention."

While *The Death of Socrates* was never actually "lost," it disappeared from view and was not located by the art world until 1952, when James Thomas Flexner, after a search of more than ten years, found it (and the copy of Rollin's *Ancient History*) in the parlor of a direct descendant of William Henry who lived in Nazareth, not far from Lancaster. Flexner observed in the soiled, faded picture that West's description of the episode was correct in one point: The slave was naked to the waist. He marveled that the young artist, working in rural Pennsylvania in 1756, should have painted such a picture: Not only that it was a history theme, not only that he painted it so well, but that he introduced elements of composition that foreshadowed, "although very crudely, one of the basic conceptions of the more sophisticated neo-classical painting" that West later helped to popularize in Europe.[2]

Socrates attracted the attention of Dr. William Smith, provost of the College of Philadelphia, who was in Lancaster to advise the inhabitants on the proper curriculum for a public grammar school they proposed to establish. A graduate of the University of Aberdeen (1747), an ordained Anglican priest, Smith had gone to New York as a tutor and there became known for his writings on the kind of educational institution best suited to the needs of a new country. Benjamin Franklin had persuaded him to join the faculty of the Philadelphia Academy and Charitable School (of which he was a founder and board president) as teacher of logic, rhetoric, and natural and moral philosophy. When the academy became the College of Philadelphia in 1755, Smith, at twenty-eight was made its first provost.

---

2 "The arches are placed parallel to the picture plane with the figures set against them in a straight row as in a bas-relief. No European conceived of this approach until Jacques-Louis David painted *The Oath of the Horatii* in 1785, nearly thirty years later." John Wilmerding, *The Genius of American Painting,* 1973, p. 67.

If young West would attend the college, Smith said, he would give him a special course that "to a certain degree" would acquaint him with classical literature and "the taste and character of the spirit of antiquity . . . requisite to a painter." West accepted the offer and over the next year spent an undetermined number of evenings taking Dr. Smith's specially designed course, staying with his sister Rachel and her husband and continuing to paint portrait commissions. Smith "did not impose upon him those grammatical exercises of language which are usually required from the young student of the classics, but directed his attention to those incidents which were likely to interest his fancy, and to furnish him at some future time with subjects for the easel." Whatever it did for West as an artist, the course did not remedy his deficiencies as a speaker and writer of the English language. He could express himself clearly and vividly, but his pronunciation of polysyllabic words was faulty and his spelling was a matter of comment, even in an age when spelling was often more ingenious than correct.

Smith introduced West to four young men "whom he particularly recommended . . . as possessing endowments of mind greatly superior to the common standard of mankind." The provost was prophetic. The four were Francis Hopkinson, later the statesman, poet, musician, and composer; Joseph Reed, who, among other accomplishments, became adjutant general of the Continental army; Jacob Duché, who served as chaplain of the Continental Congress before going over to the British; and Thomas Godfrey, who "gave the most promising indications of an elegant genius for pathetic and descriptive poetry." The young men would sit under a clump of pines near the upper ferry of the Schuylkill River, four of them fishing while Godfrey lay in the shade and read aloud his verses as he composed them. West painted a portrait of Godfrey, now lost, and made a drawing of Hopkinson. When Godfrey, a watchmaker's apprentice, published an unsigned poem, "The Temple of Fame," in a Philadelphia newspaper and Dr. Smith expressed admiration for it, West revealed that the author was their friend Godfrey. Smith thereupon obtained Godfrey's release from his indenture and persuaded the governor of the colony to give him a commission as an ensign in the Pennsylvania militia.

On the occasions when he returned to his home at Newtown Square, West spent time walking about the countryside with Dr. Jonathan Morris, his first patron, now his friend and companion. Years later he wrote nostalgically to Morris from London of the delight he remembered of the "injoyment of the many pleasing and happy hours I have spent with you in those rural and inocent juvenal amusements," and again, "of the morning of my life, when inocently sporting on the banks of those refreshing streems which lie in the shady groves that are in the nabourhood of Newtown." West was again in Lancaster in the spring or early summer of 1756, drilling with young Anthony Wayne alongside of a militia regiment raised by Colonel Isaac Wayne to protect the frontier against Indian attacks that followed the defeat of Braddock's army. Samuel West, six years older than his brother Benjamin, was a captain in the regiment and later served in the 1758 Forbes campaign. But word was received in Lancaster that Sarah West was gravely ill, and Benjamin (and presumably his brother) hurried to Newtown Square. He arrived a few hours before his mother died. He did not return to Lancaster or the military life, but instead, in August 1756, moved to Philadelphia to stay and make his career as an artist.

Philadelphia was a city of 2300 houses and of almost 15,000 people in 1753 — far behind London in size but still one of the largest cities in the British empire, and second only to London in its wealth and culture. The houses were substantial, of stone and red brick with white marble steps and trimmings, much of the furniture brought from England. The rich merchants and ship owners lived on Water Street, facing the Delaware River, but some of them were now building baronial mansions several miles to the east along the Schuylkill. The tower, belfry, and bell of the State House had been finally erected in 1753, some twenty-two years after the groundbreaking. The bells of Christ Church had been installed in 1754; the Pennsylvania Hospital, finest in the American Colonies, was completed the following year (its cornerstone inscription written by Benjamin Franklin). Politically, commercially, and socially, this was the leading city in the Colonies. It was the principal seaport, though the ocean was a hundred miles distant. (On one October day in 1754 there were 117 large ships at dock in the Delaware.) It was also the principal stopping point between New York and Virginia, between north and south. A regular stage line was started up in 1757 between Philadelphia and New York, and with the improved roads the ninety-mile journey could be accomplished in two days. The slave auctions were held at the London Coffee House, each subject, man, woman or child, standing on the head of a cask for display to the purchasers.

Visitors to Philadelphia remarked that this was a city where great sociability prevailed among all classes; everybody spoke to everybody else, and everyone immediately recognized a stranger. Most residents lived at the same place, and often in the same building, where they carried on their business. People dressed according to their station and occupation; tradesmen wore leather aprons and hired women wore short gowns that revealed the ankles. Elderly gentlemen carried gold-headed canes. Toward the close of a summer day the young people of the city, and especially the females, would dress up neatly and sit on the front porch or steps, while the young males would stroll up and down the street, pausing now and then to talk.

Philadelphia was a city in which much of the wealth and almost all the power were concentrated in a dozen or so families. The members of these families were enlightened and educated, and they were eager to do what was best for Philadelphia and eastern Pennsylvania. To that end, they appointed their sons, grandsons, brothers, brothers-in-law, uncles, nephews, and cousins to the important political and administrative offices. Sometimes it was necessary to appoint such a relative to hold two or three positions at the same time. Among the great families were the Allens, Shippens, Whartons, Hamiltons, Clymers, and Willings. Naturally, there was a pattern of intermarriage among the leading families.

West fitted easily into this society; he had acceptable manners and a pleasing appearance to go with his talent. According to William Dunlap, one of his students in London several decades later, he "possessed a fine form, and a face as fair as artists paint angels, or lovers their mistresses. At the age of fifty, he was remarkable for comeliness; and it is presumed that . . . his appearance [when young] must have been very prepossessing . . . He was about five feet eight inches in height, well made and athletic . . . His eye was piercing." A physician's report in 1763 described his "very fair complexion." An English courtier wrote, "He stood so straight that he seemed taller than he was." Other observers said that his manner was composed, controlled, and temperate. Though he was not a Quaker, he seems to have become imbued with some of the Quaker moral principles, perhaps most of all with George Fox's precept: "Be still and cool in thy own mind and spirit." He suffered recurrent attacks of "rheumatisms and joint pains," but his skill as a skater indicates that these were not disabling.

During the several years he lived in Philadelphia, West chanced to see, and to remember that he saw, Colonel Washington, commander of the small Virginia forces trying to repel French and Indian attacks, and he struck up an acquaintance with young William Howe, commander of an English regiment of foot. Colonel Howe was an ardent ice skater, and the two met and skated together on one or the other of the many ponds in the city. West, an expert skater, selected a partner and showed the colonel "The Philadelphia

Salute," a figure Howe remembered years later. In this complicated affair,[3] he and his partner approached each other on their forward right outside edge, thus creating the first curve of a serpentine outline. While executing this part of the move, they passed each other face to face and doffed their hats in greeting. Each skater then completed the final curve of the serpentine. The effect was something like a bow in a minuet or a salutation in a square dance.

In October 1757, Dr. William Smith founded *The American Magazine,* using it to enlarge his audience, express his literary and political views, and attack the opinions and policies of his former patron, Dr. Franklin. In the February 1758 issue appeared a long poem signed "Lovelace" and titled "Upon Seeing the Portrait of Miss xx —— xxx by Mr. West." The second of the six stanzas describing the beautiful Miss xx —— xxx reads:

> *The enlivened tints in due proportion rise;*
> *The polished cheeks with deep vermillion glow;*
> *The shining moisture swells into her eyes,*
> *And from such lips nectareous sweets must flow.*

The editor, presumably Dr. Smith, prefaced the poem by saying, "The lady who sat, the painter who guided the pencil, and the poet who so well described the whole are all natives of this place and very young." The lady has not been identified. It has been supposed that the poet was Francis Hopkinson, or Thomas Godfrey, or Joseph Shippen III, or a mysterious Mr. Hicks. In the December issue of the same year, Hopkinson addressed a poem to John Wollaston, the prolific itinerant English artist who, after training in London under a drapery painter and working in New York, was spending some months in Philadelphia before going out to India as a clerk for the East India Company. Several of West's portraits done in this period show a strong Wollaston influence, most strikingly in the heavy-lidded, slanting, almond-shaped eyes. Hopkinson expressed in rhymed couplets the delight and wonder he felt at watching "the amazing conduct" of the hand of "famed Wollaston," and in his tribute to West, "loved youth with virtue as by nature blest," he advised him to follow the master's pleasing paths and just precepts.

> *So shall some future muse her sweeter lays,*
> *Swell with your name, and give you all his praise.*

---

[3] As described by Dick Button, world figure-skating champion.

West found no lack of commissions in Philadelphia. His fee was now two and a half guineas for a head, five for a half-length. He painted Rebecca Moore Smith, Dr. Smith's wife, and Dr. Smith himself in his black robe with white ministerial bands, his right hand raised in an oratorical gesture. (The portrait was a present from the artist.) He painted Ann Inglis and her sister Mary, and a very homely Elizabeth Peel (with slanting almond-shaped eyes), and pretty Jenny Galloway when she was thirteen, ten or eleven years before she married Colonel Joseph Shippen, dressing her in satin and lace and a garland of flowers. He made a drawing of a young lady (legend has it that Anthony Wayne introduced them) named Elizabeth Shewell. She was pretty, fifteen years old, the second daughter of Robert Shewell, a prosperous merchant, and Elizabeth (Barton) Shewell. A Mr. Cox ordered a portrait of his daughter, but West persuaded him to commission a historical subject instead; Mr. Cox received a canvas containing no fewer than forty figures, titled *The Trial of Susanna by the Young Daniel.* He painted a portrait of Benjamin Franklin's thirteen-year-old daughter Sarah. Dr. Franklin did not much like the picture, though he seems to have taken it with him in 1757 when the Pennsylvania Assembly sent him to England. He suggested to his wife Deborah that she have John Hesselius paint another portrait of Sally.

In a supreme effort of his early career, West painted Thomas Mifflin, the fourteen- or fifteen-year-old son of John and Elizabeth Mifflin. He dressed Thomas in the color he liked best: breeches and coat of rich dark blue broadcloth, with a blue velvet collar. He stood him against a brown wall with vines and a receding stretch of blue-green trees and water. Master Mifflin has been hunting. He grips a standing Pennsylvania rifle at the muzzle; his powder horn is slung over his shoulder; his dog is retrieving a bird in the water; and three birds — a female duck and possibly two sandpipers — lie on the ground. ("Young West," said critic William Sawitzky, "was no forerunner of Audubon.") It is acknowledged to be the finest portrait West painted in America.[4]

West's career took an upward turn when he met William Allen, called "the Great Giant" and known to be the richest man in Philadelphia. He was a merchant in his middle fifties, educated at Cambridge in England and trained in law in London. He had been a member of the Provincial Assembly, a member of city council,

---

[4] Thomas Mifflin became a member of the first Continental Congress, Washington's aide-de-camp, quartermaster general of the Continental army, a member of the 1787 Constitutional Convention, and first governor of the new state of Pennsylvania.

mayor of the city, Grand Master of Free Masons, and progenitor and financier of the State House construction. He was now chief justice of Pennsylvania (he gave his annual salary of £120 to charity), a leader in the American Philosophical Society, a trustee of the College of Philadelphia, and owner of the land on which he laid out the town of Northampton, later renamed Allentown. He was sponsoring in the 1750s an expedition to find the Northwest Passage out of Hudson Bay. Allen had married a sister of James Hamilton, governor of Pennsylvania, and his patronage gave West access to Hamilton's picture gallery at his "Bush Hill" estate on the Schuylkill. It was a somewhat meager collection, but it was still considered to be the best in America.

West began to work in 1758 to realize an ambition he had felt since he first saw William Williams' paintings, engravings, and books: to go to Europe, and especially to Italy, there to see with his own eyes the great works of art in their original state. There were no art schools in America, no art galleries, no proper art supplies, few teachers of art, few private collections of pictures, few books on art to read. The only work for an artist in America was painting portraits. If he could get to Europe he could study art in the presence of the old masters and learn to paint pictures on great moral themes.

When he was offered some portrait commissions in New York in 1758, he decided to go, double his fees there, and save money for the European journey. Before he departed he painted an "auto-miniature" — a self portrait done in water color on a small oval piece of ivory. He presented this work to Miss Elizabeth Steele, a young lady living a few doors down the street whom he had been courting; one report is that he smuggled it to her, as Mrs. Steele had forbidden him to call. Rebecca Steele, in fact, afraid that her daughter might elope to Swede's Church, where runaways were married, had taken precautions to keep the young people apart. Sixty years later West was shown his self-portrait by Elizabeth Steele's son-in-law. He examined it carefully and said, "We were very much in love with one another, and the old lady, her mother, whose memory I honor, did not like my intended profession." And then, "This is not a bad picture for one who had never seen a miniature."

He did not like New York, finding the society there "much less intelligent in matters of taste and knowledge than that of Philadelphia." He missed the college, the library, his friends, and the elevated conversation he had known. New York society, he felt, was devoted wholly to mercantile pursuits, "a disposition to estimate the value of things, not by their utility, or by their beauty, but by the price which they would bring in the market, almost universally prevailed . . . The population of New York was formed of adventurers from all parts of Europe, who had come thither for the express purpose of making money, in order, afterwards, to appear with distinction at home." He worked for eleven months in New York, producing portraits, copying pictures and engravings, and working at the problem of painting the lights and shadows of a man reading by candlelight. In the eleventh month he had accumulated enough money for a round-trip passage to Italy and a very short stay in that fountainhead of art. He undertook to paint a portrait of a Mr. Kelly, a New York merchant, after which he intended to return home and sail for Europe.

While West was thus engaged in New York, young Colonel Joseph Shippen in Philadelphia, having retired from military service after the glorious victory over the French and Indians, was planning a pleasure trip to Europe. As became a Shippen, he decided to combine pleasure with a profitable "mercantile adventure." He and one of his brothers each put up £750 with which to buy a cargo of sugars for shipment to England, and they made the rounds of uncles and cousins to increase the size of the investment. Cousin William Allen invested £1000 for his son John, on the condition that Colonel Shippen look after John on a tour of Europe. He had seen the vice and luxury of Europe, he said, and was very sensible that the two young men would go through a fiery trial in the many temptations that were too predominant there, but he trusted Colonel Shippen as "a sober, virtuous, sensible young man." Shippen, who was twenty-seven, was reluctant to spend so much time in Europe when he should be starting a business career, but one did not oppose William Allen lightly. Cousin William, moreover, agreed to pay two-thirds of the joint expense of the tour. By April the investment in the cargo was £7000. On William Allen's advice, the port of destination was changed from London to Leghorn.

Hearing of these plans, Provost William Smith called on Mr. Allen and suggested that Benjamin West be allowed to go on the trip. Mr. Allen agreed to persuade his partners to make this painless benefaction to the cause of art. He decided privately, moreover, that he would make a financial contribution to help the young man, and that he and Brother James Hamilton should have Mr. West paint copies for them of the old masters. Dr. Smith conveyed the splendid news in a letter to New York.

West dutifully finished the portrait of Mr. Kelly, who paid his ten guineas and then asked the artist to carry and personally deliver a letter to his agent in Philadelphia. When West presented the letter a few days later, the agent read aloud what Kelly had written.

He desired that a present of fifty guineas should be given to Mr. West to help him defray the cost of his projected journey and studies abroad.[5]

In the weeks before the vessel sailed, West called on friends to bid them farewell. He visited William Williams, who gave him an acrostic poem on the name *West* that predicted future greatness for the young artist. He spent some time with William Henry, who had come from Lancaster on a business trip. With William Allen and James Hamilton he discussed the old masters he was to copy for them in Italy. From important people in Philadelphia he collected letters of introduction to important people in Florence, Rome, and London. He made no attempt to see Miss Steele, for now he wished to marry nineteen-year-old Elizabeth Shewell, the girl whose portrait he had drawn four years earlier. In the charming phrase of a Shewell descendant, "some love passages had occurred between the young people," and Betsy promised to wait for him until he returned from his journeys.

William Allen wrote on April 5, 1760, to Messrs. Jackson and Rutherford, merchant-agents in Leghorn, asking them to procure for his son and Joseph Shippen letters of credit and recommendation to the several cities they would visit. He had written, he said, to Horace Mann, English minister at Florence, whom he had known at Clare Hall, Cambridge. After asking Jackson and Rutherford to send him some silk cloth, anchovies, and Parmesan cheese, he wrote:

> In this vessel comes a passenger, a Mr. West, a young ingenious painter of this city, who is desirous to improve himself in that science, by visiting Florence and Rome; but being unacquainted how to have his money remitted has lodged with me one hundred pounds sterling, which I shall remit to Messrs. David Barclay and Sons [in London] upon his account. I beg therefore you would give him a credit for that sum and take his bills for the amount; and should be further obliged to you for any kindness you show him, as he has among us the character of a very deserving young man.

Edward Shippen accompanied his brother Joseph, John Allen, and Benjamin West to Gloucester on the Delaware, where they boarded their vessel, and he reported to his father in Lancaster, "He is in a good vessel and has a cheerful and obliging captain." The *Betty Sally*, Captain Sneed, twelve carriage guns, twenty men, sailed out

---

[5] Kelly's £50 was the equivalent of about £1000 in modern times.

of Delaware Bay and past Cape Henlopen on April 12, 1760. In this voyage the venerable critic E. P. Richardson sees an act of profound importance to American art, both in fact and in symbol. Talents (he has written) had appeared in America too great to be contained within the limits of colonial life. West was carrying out the great task of American painters of that time: to transcend the narrow boundaries of the colonial portrait tradition, to enlarge the imaginative field of subjects that painting could deal with, and eventually to take some part in the great movements of neoclassical and romantic idealism that dominated the cultural climate of the next seventy-five years.

4

An American in Italy

From all accounts he is like to turn out a very extraordinary person in the Painting Way, and it is a pity such a genius should be
cramped for want of a little cash.

WILLIAM ALLEN,
Philadelphia,
August 10, 1761

THE *Betty Sally* had a fast but stormy thirty-day voyage across
the Atlantic, with "strong gales of wind and very rough seas almost the whole way." John Allen was seasick most of the time, but
the three young men found each other good company and were
(Shippen wrote home) "extremely hearty and well, having lived very
happily together on our short passage . . . [Captain Sneed] has behaved to us like a gentleman." The Seven Years War was in its fourth
year in 1760, and the Mediterranean was infested with French priva-
teers and Algerian pirates, a fact that the Shippens did not mention
in Philadelphia "because the underwriter would exact an unreasonable premium on the voyage back if they knew it." A privateer
chased the *Betty Sally* into Gibraltar on May 10, "contrary to our
intention," where it put in for safety and to take on water. A Captain Michael Kearny boarded the vessel and questioned the master.
If he did not know it, Captain Sneed now learned that Britain had
embargoed shipment of certain goods to Italy and that his vessel
and cargo were subject to confiscation for engaging in illegal trade.
After a short conversation, however, Kearny passed the ship without examining its papers or asking its destination, though, under
British maritime law, prizes of war became the property of the
captors. West learned that Kearny was related to the Allens and
that he considered them "the best of friends that I ever had in the

world." That generous act, West said, tended to confirm him in his liberal opinion of mankind.[1]

Captain Kearny sought out John Allen and invited him to visit his frigate, the *Terror*, with his friends and to dine in company with the governor of Gibraltar, his staff, and the principal officers of the fortress garrison. Because of these "great civilities," received during a two-week wait for a convoy to be formed, Allen, Shippen, and West were treated as distinguished persons during the voyage across the Mediterranean. One day out of Gibraltar, Captain Medows of the *Shannon* and Captain Pownall of the *Favourite*, the warships escorting the convoy, invited the three Americans to finish the voyage as passengers in their vessels. They declined, but every day when the weather was fair they dined on board one ship or the other.

The convoy arrived in Leghorn on June 16. Because of its stop in Gibraltar, the *Betty Sally* was quarantined for fifteen days, during which time those aboard could not go ashore, dared not come closer than three yards to visitors, and did not send letters because "they would have to be smoked in such a way as to render them unfit to be sent any distance." When their confinement ended, the three young men were taken as guests into the home of Robert Rutherford of Messrs. Jackson and Rutherford. The merchant partners, showing West "a degree of attention beyond even their general great hospitality," gave him letters of introduction to various personages in Rome, including the famous antiquarian, Cardinal Alessandro Albani. Leghorn was a "traiding town" with one very long straight street and one very large wide square. Shippen described it as a "well-built clean city" with "no great curiosities" other than a larger-than-life-size marble statue of the grand duke, shown with the bronze figures of four slaves chained to his pedestal.

Shippen had business to transact in Leghorn.[2] "Benny West," he said, was impatient to get to Rome "for his improvement" and cashed part of his letter of credit and made his farewells. Jackson and Rutherford placed him in the care of a French courier who was on his way to Rome; if he followed the usual route, he journeyed through Siena and Viterbo. There had been little foreign travel in Italy since the outbreak of war in 1756, and West, introduced by the

---

[1] For further comment on this episode, see Appendix I.

[2] He was disappointed at the "indifferent market our sugars have come to here," clearing only 15 percent profit, but he dispatched the vessel in July with a £734 cargo of brandy and wine that made up "a very respectable voyage of it." He authorized Captain Sneed, if captured by pirates, to pay a ransom equal to two-thirds of the cost of the vessel and cargo, or at full cost if taken near the American coast.

courier as an American artist who meant to study in Rome, created something of a sensation in the towns through which he passed. The sight of an American was an uncommon event; the idea that an American could paint was astounding.

They reached the outskirts of Rome on the morning of July 10. While the horses of the post chaise were being watered and fed at an inn, West walked on alone. The road led to an elevated point from which he looked out over the fields and hills and vine-covered architectural ruins to see a thrilling sight: the dome of St. Peter's, the principal and largest church of the Christian world. A broken milestone told him he was eight miles from the capital. He sat on the milestone, heard a bell behind him, and turned to watch a peasant dressed in shaggy skins herding a few goats from the ruins of a fallen building. While gazing across the wasteland of the *Campagna*, he dwelt on solemn, melancholy thoughts appropriate for such an occasion: on the romantic antiquity of Rome, the evidence of decay and decline he saw around him, the progress of civilization, the great cycle of human affairs, the glorious future of America, "where all was young, vigorous and growing."

They descended the long slope to the Porta del Populo and rode down the Corso to the dogana, or customhouse, which had been the hall of Emperor Antoninus Pius. Their luggage was carried inside for inspection for contraband. The courier, it may be assumed, gave an officer a small present to keep him from tearing things apart for such nonsense and to stamp their health certificates. He then led his charge to a lodging house, almost certainly in the Piazza di Spagna area. That was the gathering place of artists, and it contained the principal hotels, lodging houses, banks, and shops that served the English. It was, moreover, relatively clean and the quietest and safest section of the city, perhaps because it was under the royal jurisdiction of the Spanish ambassador at Rome. West had scarcely washed when a young gentleman was shown to his room. He introduced himself as Thomas Robinson, an Englishman who was spending some months in Rome. He had heard that Mr. West, a young American Quaker, had come to study the fine arts in Italy. Mr. West must have dinner with him that afternoon. Mr. West accepted, and in a gentle fraud practised the rest of his life, he permitted, if did not encourage, the belief to persist that he was a Quaker.[3]

---

[3] Thomas Robinson, a Cambridge graduate, the same age as West, was described by Horace Walpole as "a very agreeable, pleasing young man . . . possessed of solid though not eminent parts." In March of the following year, he was elected a Member of Parliament; in 1770 he succeeded his father as the second Baron Grantham and entered the House of Lords.

In the course of the meal, Robinson asked West what letters of introduction he carried. When West told him of the recommendations given him in Philadelphia and Leghorn, he expressed pleased surprise. Most of the letters, he said, were addressed to particular friends of his, and he was engaged to meet them that very evening at the home of Mr. Crispigné, another Englishman, a collector of art, who had long resided in Rome.[4] Naturally, Mr. West would accompany him.

Robinson conducted West to Crispigné's house that evening and put him on exhibition at a typical Roman *conversazione*. To those few who had not already heard it, he revealed the extraordinary news. Mr. West was an American and a Quaker. He was an artist, self-taught, who had obtained his first colors from Indians. He had come to Rome to study the fine arts.

Robinson took his guest into an inner apartment to introduce him to one of Rome's wealthiest and most powerful men. He was seated, for he was sixty-eight years old and almost totally blind. Cardinal Albani, once a dashing young soldier and diplomat, was the nephew of Pope Clement XI, a cardinal from the age of twenty-nine, a great and knowledgeable collector of art and classical antiquities, an archeologist, imperial ambassador in Rome, librarian of the Vatican, and protector of the Holy Roman Empire, in which post he presided over the German congregation in Rome. He had sold several collections — Pope Clement XII bought one in 1734 to found Rome's first museum, the Capitoline — but in 1760 he still possessed one of Europe's finest accumulations of art treasures. Some of it was housed in the Palazzo Albani (now the Palazzo del Drago), near the Quirinal in the heart of Rome; most of it was at the cardinal's suburban estate, the Villa Albani, which stood just outside the Salarian Gate on the northeast edge of Rome.

Cardinal Albani had weighty affairs on his mind in the summer of 1760. He was a patron of the German critic Johann Joachim Winckelmann, his librarian, who lived in the upper quarters of the Palazzo, who was helping him to furnish the villa and was writing a book that promised to revolutionize modern theories of art. The cardinal was also a patron of the German artist Anton Raphael Mengs, who was painting a ceiling fresco in the villa in the "new style," according to precepts laid down by Winckelmann. Albani was completing very expensive additions to his villa — two Grecian temples and a ruin contrived of ancient fragments. Vittoria, his

---

4 Crispigné, of whom little is known, may have been Claude Champion de Crispigny, created a baronet in 1805, died in 1818 at age eighty-three.

elder daughter by his favorite (and last) mistress, the Contessa Francesca Cheroffini, was of an age to marry and he needed to raise a substantial sum of money to provide her dowry. When he was not otherwise engaged, he performed the services of a paid agent in supplying Horace Mann with information on the doings of the English Jacobites in Rome.

West stood before the blind cardinal. Robinson said, "I have the honor to present a young American who has a letter of introduction to your eminence, and who has come to Italy for the purpose of studying the fine arts." Albani, assuming that an American might be an Indian, asked, "Is he black or white?" He was told that the American was very fair. Albani was astonished. "What!" he cried. "Is he as fair as I am?" Onlookers suppressed their mirth, for the cardinal's complexion was a deep olive.

The cardinal asked West to come closer. Moving his hands over his face, he expressed admiration for his features and the shape of his head, exclaiming in Latin, "Ah, fair young man! Handsome fellow!" He asked questions about his life in America, which Robinson translated. The onlookers asked more questions. A spirited discussion followed, not a word of which West understood. While Signor West obviously was not an Indian, he was still an American and therefore must have received the education of a savage. What would be the effect on his primitive mind when he first saw a great work of art? What would he say or do, for example, at his first sight of that supreme achievement of ancient art, that foremost work among all the ornaments of Rome, the statue of the Greek god Apollo at the Vatican? It was agreed that the whole company would assemble the next morning, drive to the Vatican with Mr. Robinson and his protégé, and find out.

When the party ended, two stories went forth to Roman society. One told of the experiment that was to be conducted that morning at the Vatican. The other reported the cardinal's query, "Is he as fair as I am?" It gave rise to a sardonic catchphrase popular for some years: "As fair as the cardinal." Robinson explained to West the trial to which he was to be put. It is probable that he told him he would see the Apollo Belvedere, and that he and West devoted some concentrated thought to what he would say when he saw the statue.

Thirty or more of the city's most magnificent carriages gathered at the appointed hour, the assembly now having grown to include "the principal Roman nobility" and "some of the most erudite characters in Europe." The Apollo — found at Frascati in 1455, an early Roman Empire imitation in marble of the 350–320 B.C. Greek original in bronze, acquired for the Vatican by Julius II — stood in the Belvedere courtyard enclosed in a cabinet, a few feet from the Laocoon. West was placed facing it; the spectators arranged themselves on each side. The keeper opened the doors.

Johann Winckelmann had written of the Apollo Belvedere, "The eternal spring of youth covers the perfect manliness of his body . . . If a God should be pleased to reveal himself in such a shape, all the world would worship at his feet . . . Here they would find the sun embodied in human shape," and again, "I forget all else over the sight of this miraculous work of art, and assume a more exalted position myself in order to be worthy of this sight." The American artist Washington Allston, when he saw it in 1803, would describe the experience as "a sudden intellectual flash filling the whole mind with light and light in motion." In five years James Boswell, having reached Rome on his grand tour, would write in his journal, "Apollo, baddish knees." West regarded the figure, the exemplar of manly beauty, the first Greek god adopted by the Romans. He was naked except for a chlamys draped over his left arm. The right forearm and the left hand, which had held a shield, had been restored. A fig leaf had rather recently been applied to the private parts. His face, with its Greek profile of forehead and nose in an almost straight line, was expressionless, impersonal, neuter. "My God!" West exclaimed. "How like it is to a young Mohawk warrior!"

Robinson translated. Some of the Italians were puzzled — perhaps as puzzled as a Mohawk warrior would have been; others were mortified at having their Apollo compared to a savage. They asked Robinson, and Robinson asked West, to explain. He described the education of the young Mohawk brave, his skill with the bow and arrow, his fine physique developed by his active life. "I have seen them often," he said, "standing in that very attitude, and pursuing, with an intense eye, the arrow which they had just discharged from the bow." Robinson translated the explanation. Someone — probably Cardinal Albani — indicated his approval. The others now expressed delight and agreed they had seldom heard a better comment on their Apollo.

As the capital of a mighty empire, Rome had been a metropolis of two million inhabitants. Now, in 1760, it was a city of 180,000. Only one-fifth of its former area was occupied; the rest was wasteland or in gardens and vineyards, with here and there the villa of a prince or cardinal standing out in the desolate countryside. Every foreign visitor was conscious of the melancholy state of ruin and decay about him. Great public buildings had been stripped of their marble for reuse in other construction or for burning in the lime kilns. The Colosseum was crowded with cattle sheds, the Arch of Septimus Severus lay buried to half its height in rubbish, the Roman Forum was used on Thursdays and Fridays for a cattle market, the Tiber was awash with the city's garbage. The streets churned with mud in wet weather and with clouds of dust when dry; their only illumination at night was an occasional lamp or candle burning before a madonna. The outer walls of the public buildings, the entrances, corridors, staircases, and courtyards, were defiled with noxious filth. Beggars everywhere displayed their sores and deformities. Dr. Johnson's friend, Hester Thrale Piozzi, found the appearance of the city "mean and disgusting"; the artist John Flaxman was disappointed, for the streets were narrow and dark, the ruins of the ancient buildings on a smaller scale and less striking than he had been led to expect from the prints of Giovanni Piranesi.

There was no industry, little commerce, and little agriculture. One-third of the city's population were ecclesiastics or were employed in the huge papal bureaucracy at the city's 250 churches, 23 seminaries, 45 convents, or the 3 papal palaces. The sixty or seventy cardinals who ruled the city were considered in Rome to rank with kings; they traveled in a retinue of handsome red carriages, taking precedence over everyone else in the streets. The principalities of Italy had been torn by centuries of dissension, war, and foreign rule; the Papal States, which encompassed Rome, Bologna, Ferrara, Ancona, and Ravenna, were among the poorest and most backward in Europe, and they were about to begin three years of bad harvests and starvation. It was the policy of the cardinals to pass over vigorous young men and elect elderly Popes who would hold the office for only a few years and not make trouble by introducing change or reform.

And yet Rome was recognized as the most attractive, agreeable, and stimulating city in Christendom. It was a city of pleasant sounds, of church bells by day and of the fountains in its squares by night. It had long been the capital of the artistic world, but now the greatest of all displays of classic and Renaissance art had been enhanced by the treasures recently unearthed at Paestum, Herculaneum, and Pompeii. The Romans paid friendly attention to strangers, especially to the British, and any decently dressed person with manners could gain access to pleasant social circles. Things were inexpensive — rooms, meals, carriages, the theater, cafés, servants, guides — and while everyone expected to be tipped, a copper coin of the smallest denomination would suffice. The public spectacles were free: the nightly promenade on the Corso, the religious processions, the elaborate fireworks displays from the Castel Sant'

Angelo, the eleven-day pre-Lenten carnival, when St. Peter's dome was illuminated with 6000 fire lamps. The young women were known for their grace and beauty, and while unmarried daughters were strictly controlled, Roman wives exercised an extraordinary degree of social freedom. It was a city of good nature and tolerance, a free port of ideas; nowhere else in Europe had the Jews such freedom of movement and conscience as in papal Rome. It was possible to meet notable people here from the other cities of Europe and to share their interest in art, archeology, religion, or history. The genius of the place, West said in retrospect, was such that accomplished strangers often felt themselves endowed with new qualities.

West accompanied Robinson to a high mass at St. Peter's, expressed horror at "the spectacle of beggary" in the piazza before the church, and was moved when a beggar to whom he had given a copper coin searched him out some moments later and held out several smaller pieces, explaining that she had asked him for a farthing and he had given her a twopenny piece. Someone introduced him to the artist Pompeo Batoni, who was then, at fifty-two, at the height of his reputation as a painter of religious pieces, classical allegories, and portraits, especially portraits of sovereigns (twenty-two of them in all) and of young Englishmen who wanted a commemorative painting of themselves against the background of the Colosseum or the Laocoon. "When I went to Rome," West marveled in 1814, "the Italian artists of that day thought of nothing, looked at nothing, but the works of Pompeo Batoni." He told of their meeting. Batoni, very elegant, received him in his painting room. "And so, young man, you come from America. How far is it?"

"Three thousand miles."

"Three thousand miles from the woods of America to become a painter. You are very fortunate in coming to Rome at this time, for now you shall see Batoni paint. There — stand right there." He dipped his brush in the color, put the finishing touches on the canvas before him, uttering sounds of delight as he worked, stepped back, and said, "Go, young man. Now you can say you have seen Batoni paint. Evviva Batoni!"

One evening Robinson took him to call on Gavin Hamilton, a man of growing consequence as a painter, archeologist, and dealer and collector's agent in old masters and classical sculpture. Hamilton was described by a contemporary as "a man of very pleasant manners and respectable character." Born thirty-seven years earlier to a family of Scottish lairds in Lanarkshire, educated at the University of Glasgow, he had journeyed to Rome before 1748 to study art and had stayed there. He, too, painted portraits of members of the British colony in a Roman setting, and he had distinguished himself in 1758 with a painting depicting James Dawkins and Robert Wood in the act of "discovering" the ruins of Palmyra in Syria in 1751. (In the absurd artistic convention of the eighteenth century, both men were shown wearing Roman togas.) In his journeys to distant churches in search of old masters for his English clients, Hamilton commonly took along an artist who would paint a replica to leave with the priest and his congregation. He knew everyone in Rome: Batoni; Giovanni Piranesi, who was then working on his large copperplate engravings of the buildings and monuments of Rome; Mengs, the professor of painting at the Capitoline Museum, who was doing the ceiling at the Villa Albani; Winckelmann, Mengs' preceptor.

Hamilton befriended West, spent time with him at the Caffè degli Inglesi, and (since he conveyed his enthusiasms to other young artists in Rome) undoubtedly talked to West about his own work. He was then engaged on what he called "my great plan in life" — a series of six (later fourteen) large pictures illustrating Homer's *Iliad* and *Odyssey*, done in the new or "true" (neoclassical) style. He was painting the first of these in 1760, *Andromache Bewailing the Death of Hector*, and had sketched the second, *Achilles Bewailing the Death of Patroclus*. He intended to make small pictures of each work in color and then seek a patron to commission a large version at £50 per figure, which would take three years to complete and from which an engraving would be made. Hamilton was one of the first artists to understand the full possibilities of making first-rate engravings from his pictures and of using them as a source of income, a stimulus to sale of his works, and a means of enhancing his reputation throughout the Continent. West was to take that procedure to England and use it to achieve unprecedented results.

Robinson took West to call on Cardinal Albani at his villa, showing him elegance on a scale far beyond anything he had ever seen. A large garden lay before the palace, very formal in the Italian style, with terraces and balustrades, fountains and canals, graveled walks and sheared hedges that formed a pattern of circles, diamonds, and bowknots — a garden, young Boswell would say, "spread like a periwig." The Palladian facade had High Renaissance embellishments, with a loggia behind nine columned arches under nine second-story windows. A flight of dazzling rooms known as the *Galleria Nobile* displayed statues, portrait busts, funerary urns and vases set in niches, in recesses, on pedestals; mosaic and relief sculptures on walls lined with the richest polychrome marble;

sconces and chandeliers holding hundreds of tall candles; seventeenth-century Italian drawings; and paintings by, among others, Raphael, Perugino, and Vandyke.

Mengs' *Parnassus,* not yet finished, was on the ceiling of the Grand Salon. It showed the naked Apollo, life-size, in the center of a fresco measuring almost 10 by 20 feet, his laurel-crowned head forming the apex of the pyramidal composition favored in neoclassical scenes. On either side of him were the nine muses in appropriate poses. The *Parnassus* was already the talk of Rome. Admirers asserted that the work would reflect the noble simplicity and calm grandeur prescribed by Winckelmann's rules. Opponents held that it was a collection of painted statues.[5]

Cardinal Albani remembered West when he ran his hands over his face. Anton Mengs, who had recently moved into the villa with his family, made an appearance. He was interested in West, and when he asked to see one of his drawings, West agreed to produce some of his work. In the carriage on the way to the hotel, however, he confessed that the drawings he had brought with him from America had excited little attention. He was fully aware, he said, of his deficiencies in drawing, arising from his lack of anatomical study and of opportunity to draw unclothed models. He proposed, therefore, that he paint Robinson's portrait and submit that to Mengs instead of a drawing. Robinson, who was having his portrait painted by Mengs at the time, agreed.

When West finished the picture, Robinson suggested that they quietly put it to the test of public taste and judgment without revealing the name of the artist. Mr. Crispigné was about to give one of his semiannual grand assemblies, to which were invited "all the nobility and strangers in Rome, the most eminent for rank, birth and talents." With Crispigné's concurrence, the portrait was hung on that occasion. The guests assumed it was Mengs' portrait of Robinson, and — Mengs not being present — offered frank comments on the work. Thomas Jenkins congratulated Robinson on having obtained a portrait on which Mengs had used his colors as ably as he drew. Nathaniel Dance agreed that the color was better than Mengs usually produced, but felt the drawing was below his

---

[5] Art histories still call *Parnassus* the first manifesto of neoclassicism in painting, though there has been a trend to award that distinction to Gavin Hamilton's earlier, though less celebrated, historical pictures. Winckelmann's biographer writes, "[The Apollo's] face is as saccharinely sweet as that of any calendar Jesus, while his physique approaches Winckelmann's ideal of the hermaphrodite." (Wolfgang Leppman, 1971.)

standard.[6] West, seated on a sofa nearby, heard these observations with mixed pleasure and anguish. When Crispigné identified West as the artist, the Italians ran to embrace him. Mengs, when he saw the work, graciously allowed that it had merit, and he indicated that he would be willing to have West attend his classes.

At the height of his triumph in Rome, West became seriously ill. His inflammatory rheumatism flared up and he became feverish and listless; he had constant pain in his legs, was unable to sleep, and could not work. Several physicians in consultation concluded that he must remove himself from the unwholesome summer heat and malarial air of Rome. They so advised Robinson, and Robinson persuaded him to follow their advice. On August 20, only forty days after his arrival, West left Rome to return to Leghorn.

Robert Rutherford welcomed him again into his house. John Dick, the British consul at Leghorn, arranged for him to use the Imperial Baths, and he and his wife treated him "with great partiality." With rest, quiet, mineral baths, and sea bathing, West made a quick recovery. Joseph Shippen wrote from Rome to express his and John Allen's regrets that the plan to meet there had been thwarted. "We proposed ourselves a satisfaction," he wrote, "in having your company with us in viewing the palaces and paintings, etc., here. But I am much more sorry for the disagreeable occasion that obliges you to leave this place, where you was fixed so happily." He also had a favor to ask. John Murray, the English minister resident at Venice, "to whom Mr. Allen and I are under many obligations for the civilities received from him," had commissioned an artist to paint a representation of the four parts of the world, but it could not be finished "for want of knowing the particulars of our Indians to distinguish America." They had agreed to furnish Mr. Murray with a drawing of an Indian warrior in his proper dress and accoutrements with his squaw. Would Mr. West be so kind as to paint the figures on canvas and give it to Mr. Rutherford to send to Mr. Murray? "It would be best that each figure be at least 18 inches high that the particularities of the dress may be plainly dis-

---

[6] Jenkins, an English artist, art dealer, banker, and sometime partner of Gavin Hamilton, had a workshop in the ruins of the Colosseum. He was accused of charging his competitors with being Jacobites and of "forging" antique sculptures by replacing missing parts of genuine torsos from a store of miscellaneous heads and limbs, some of which were antique. He is remembered for his observation, "The English have no value for statues without heads."

Nathaniel Dance was an early painter of history pictures, all but one of which have been lost. It is possible, however, that his younger brother George Dance, an architect, was meant. Both were in Rome at this time.

tinguished. The warrior's face should be painted and feather in his head. He ought to have his gun and tomhawk and spear but no dog with him as he is supposed to be going out to war." West took the request seriously, painting a picture he called *The Savage Chief Taking Leave of His Family on Going to War.* (It has disappeared but is known through an engraving by Bartolozzi.)

West left Leghorn in late autumn to return to Rome and resume his studies. About the time he was leaving, William Allen in Philadelphia was entertaining the principal members of the government at dinner. He read aloud to the company a letter received that day from Messrs. Jackson and Rutherford in Leghorn, telling the story of West's success with Mr. Robinson's portrait. Mr. Allen supposed that Mr. West's money must now be pretty far reduced. "I regard this young man as an honor to the country," he said, "and as he is the first that America has sent to cultivate the fine arts, he shall not be frustrated in his studies, for I have resolved to write to my correspondents at Leghorn to give him, from myself, whatever money he may require." Governor James Hamilton, moved by this declaration, said with equal animation, "I think exactly as you do, Sir, but you shall not have all the honor of it to yourself, and therefore, I beg that you will consider me as joining you in the responsibility of the credit." Several of the other gentlemen present added their names to the support of the young artist, including Samuel Powel, son and heir of "the rich carpenter" who had built more than ninety houses in Philadelphia. Benjamin Franklin wrote from Philadelphia to friends in England: "After the first cares for the necessaries of life are over, we shall come to think of the embellishments. Already some of our young geniuses begin to lisp attempts at painting, poetry and music. We have a young painter now studying at Rome."

5

"The American Raphael"

To an Englishman the remembrance of a journey in Italy is however often more delightful than that of any other country, for no
where else is his arrogance more patiently endured, his eccentricities more humourously indulged, nor the generosity of his
character more publicly acknowledged.

BENJAMIN WEST,
on leaving Italy,
July 1763

WEST WAS IN ROME from late autumn of 1760 to midsummer of
1761. He drove himself to study and master "the most glorious
productions of ancient and modern art" before the time came to
return to America. For hours he lay on his back on the cold floor
of the Sistine Chapel, gazing up at Michelangelo's story of Genesis
from the creation to the flood. In a large sketch book he copied
The Deluge in brown ink and black chalk, and then several details
from *The Last Judgment*. He drew the *Apollo Belvedere*, the *Farnese Hercules*, and the marble frieze of the *Ara Pacis Augustae*. He
studied Michelangelo's *Moses* and *Pietà*, the *Laocoon*, the horsemen
on the Quirinal, a *Sleeping Faun* in the Barbarini Palace, the *Venus*
and the *Dying Gladiator* in the Capitoline Museum. By night he
was in demand as a social curiosity, and by day he was "in a constant state of high excitement," reeling from palace to church to
museum like a wine lover going from tavern to tavern trying to
taste every vintage. The young man who had seen relatively little
art, and most of that portraits, was now suddenly immersed in an
overwhelming quantity of great pictures, sculptures, and architecture. One civilization was piled atop an earlier in Rome, one period
followed another: pagan and Christian, Gothic and Renaissance,
baroque and rococo.

With the simplicity of his education, his inexperience and his enthusiasm, he was torn by what he saw. The poverty, filth, and disease, alongside the splendor of the nobility, shocked him. A "theocratical despotism," he said, "overspread the whole country like an unwholesome vapour." Art had fallen into a "lamentable state" in Italy; the pictures and statues were almost all religious, and they glorified the Catholic saints, the Virgin Mary, and the powerful princes of the church. With his American Quaker background in a Protestant land, he saw this as the use of art "to inflame bigotry, darken superstition, and stimulate the baser passions of our nature." And yet as works of art they were irresistible, and as religious icons they conveyed the intensity of feeling with which they had been created. In the common people of Rome he saw "the forms and graces of the human character in all their genuine dignity."

West was now being taught by Anton Mengs, for he had entered that artist's classes at the Capitoline Academy, where he was professor of painting. Mengs, ten years older than West, a child prodigy, had endured rigid training as a court artist at Dresden and was now acknowledged (by everyone but the artist Pompeo Batoni) as the most famous painter working in Rome. His friend Casanova de Seingalt described him as eccentric, stubborn, and cruel and said, "He always got up from the table drunk, but when he dined out he had the good sense to drink only water." His wife Margaretta, Casanova wrote, was "pretty, virtuous, very scrupulous in performing the duties of a wife and mother, and very submissive to her husband . . . [She] had the patience to serve as his model for all the nudes he had occasion to paint. She told me one day that her confessor had ordered her to obey her husband in this respect, for otherwise he would have taken another model whom he would have enjoyed before painting her and so would have sinned." Their friend Winckelmann was elated for a time when, physically attracted to Margaretta, he announced the discovery that he could love a woman. Mengs encouraged him, but "in this predicament, virtue came to my aid," wrote Winckelmann, and he was able to control his passion.

The English artist James Northcote, who studied in Rome some years later, described Mengs as a teacher. "It is usual in Passion Week," he said in his Devon accent, "for the tapestries made from Raphael's cartoons to be exhibited under the circular piazza in front of St. Peter's . . . Now I remember once seeing Mengs come along with a whole train of his pupils to see these tapestries. He marched on before with a ridiculously pompous air, and they walked behind him . . . moving as he moved; if he made a step, so did they, and when he stopped, they stopped, always carefully keeping the same distance." West may have accepted such treatment with good grace, or he may have escaped it as a special student. In either case, he admired Mengs and in 1763 called him "my favourite master." He and Gavin Hamilton were among the few English-speaking artists in Rome who became a part of the Albani-Winckelmann-Mengs circle and were disciples in the international group — Danes, Swedes, Germans, French, Russians, Poles — in the Mengs School.

Mengs was a tireless worker, though a slow and uncertain one, and he approached his art with the utmost seriousness of purpose. His *Reflections on Beauty and Taste,* published in German in 1762, is a work of some profundity, and at least one of its precepts is still quoted: "When drawing always think about color, and when painting always think about drawing." West was in the hands of the most sophisticated artist he had met — indeed, one of the most sophisticated of his time. Somewhere in Italy in this year, and presumably as a member of the Mengs School, West learned those technical skills that an older painter can teach a younger: how to grind pigments in the European manner; increase luminosity in the red by painting it over white; improve the shadows of flesh tints by glazing — the application of a thin layer of transparent paint; and add emphasis, richness, or denser quality of surface by impasto — loading on paint with the palette knife. He learned how to find the depth of reflections in water by means of a formula; to use a formula for finding the true directions of lines in perspective when there is no vanishing point; to rely on color instead of converging parallel lines on the horizon to create perspective.

West was young and receptive, and he was prepared to absorb with ready aptitude, under Mengs' tutelage, the ideas and doctrines of neoclassicism then being formulated in Rome.[1] From Richardson and Fresnoy he had already learned the painter's obligation to impart morality and religion, both in art and in life. He knew that the high purpose of art was not to please or amuse but to instruct — to exalt the mind, he said, and "to assist the reason to arrive at correct moral inferences by furnishing a probable view of the ef-

---

[1] The eminent British critic Ellis K. Waterhouse has developed the thesis that Mengs' influence on neoclassical art has been exaggerated, since he was not in Rome when most of the artists he is supposed to have influenced were there. He is incorrect, however, in his statement on West, which he bases on incomplete information in Galt. He says that West was absent from Rome for eleven months following his first departure in August 1760, "and, by the time he was back in Rome, Mengs had already left for Spain." West went to Rome in late autumn of 1760 and stayed until midsummer of 1761. Mengs did not leave for Spain until August 1761.

fects of motives and of passions." Now he learned the refinements
of the rules under which neoclassical works were to be painted, as
laid down by Winckelmann and practised by Mengs. The artist
should abjure the baroque and rococo styles that had dominated
painting through the first half of the eighteenth century, for they
were insincere, frivolous, unnatural, and degenerate. Painting in
the True, the Correct Style, he should follow the interpretations of
nature made by the ancient Greeks and Romans, especially as revealed in Greek sculpture, mankind's supreme artistic achievement.
He should strive to depict ideal, universal types rather than individual human beings, so that they might serve as models by which
beauty could be judged. "The only way for us to become great and,
if possible, inimitable, lies in imitation of the Greeks," Winckelmann stated. Since the laws of beauty were eternal and immutable,
he had drawn up a set of codified rules to follow. ("The navel is
markedly indented, especially in female figures, where it is drawn
in an arch and occasionally in the shape of a small semicircle pointing downward or up... Of the testicles, the left is always larger,
as is the case in nature.")[2]

The painter's human forms should resemble statues or figures on
a mezzo-, alta-, or bas-relief or classical frieze, arranged parallel to
the surface, showing no motion, animation, or feeling. He must
emphasize the simplicity and discipline of clear, sharp line and
outline rather than linear pattern and the effects of color; his color
should be cold, muted almost to a monochrome, and applied with
a perfect smoothness. Faces should be impassive, even in action,
and even under stress, for expression produced distortion, detracted
from beauty, and was inappropriate in depicting lofty themes and
heroic virtue. "The most eminent characteristic of the Greek
works," Winckelmann said, "is a noble simplicity and calm grandeur [edel Einfalt und stille Grösse] in gesture and expression."
Passion should not be shown for a quite logical reason: the ancients
properly believed that deities of every degree possessed power that
rendered exertion unnecessary, and accordingly always represented
them as sublimely calm and composed.

The Correct Artist, finally, was not to draw or paint anything
that concerned what was going on about him. He was advised to
turn his eyes from the present, ignore genre scenes, and try to improve society by depicting actions of heroism, self-sacrifice, or civic

---

2 Critics have pointed out that Winckelmann saw few Greek original marbles
and almost none from the great period of Greek art. His theories were founded
on the study of Roman copies that had far less vigor, less muscle and sinew, than
the robust originals.

virtue taken from Biblical texts or Greek and Roman history and mythology. Allusions to present-day events could be suggested by allegory, with the viewer making the association and drawing his own inferences, aided by an explicit descriptive title to the picture (*Sextus Pompeius Consulting Erictho before the Battle of Pharsalia*).

Such was the philosophy of a school of art whose leading exemplar in England came to be Benjamin West. Neoclassical theories dominated European art until the end of the eighteenth century and a little beyond. In the nineteenth century the term *neoclassical* changed to *pseudoclassical,* and the works of neoclassicism were ignored or passionately despised. Only in our own past decade or so has neoclassicism again been analyzed and seriously discussed as an art form. Present-day art historians and critics have described it not only as a style of art but as a whole intellectual climate and way of thought; as a new attitude toward visual reality and a new interpretation of tradition; as a protest against the insincerity and sophistication, the empty virtuosity and brilliance of the rococo; as a movement of revolutionary character and serious purpose rather than simply a revival of antique forms — a *risorgimento* of the arts that took place in a period of great intellectual excitement. "It is impossible for us to comprehend today," E. P. Richardson has written, "how vivid, fascinating and important the dream of Greece and Rome was to men in the later eighteenth century... The past was... a tool of liberation, the key to the future."

It must be a matter of continuing regret that several generations of painters turned their backs on what was going on about them and produced works that seemed to date from earlier ages. But as Hugh Honour declared in 1968, "When we try to understand the art of the late eighteenth century it does not matter very much which aspects seem most appealing now or which seem true or false by present-day standards. What matters is whether our conception of the whole... corresponds to what the artists thought and believed themselves."

Mengs had advised West, when he completed his studies in Rome, to go to Florence "and observe what has been done for Art in the collections there." He should then go to Bologna and study the works of the Caracci family, proceed to Parma and examine attentively the pictures of Correggio, and go on to Venice and view the productions of Tintoretto, Titian, and Veronese. "When you have made this tour," Mengs told him, "come back to Rome and paint a historical composition to be exhibited to the Roman public, and the opinion which will then be formed of your talents should

determine the line of our profession which you ought to follow."
In midsummer, 1761, however, as West wrote to his patrons in
Philadelphia, "the heats began again to bring on my rheumatism
pains" in an attack more serious than the first. His friends in Leghorn, hearing of the recurrence of his illness, recalled him to that
city so that they might supervise his treatment. He stayed four
months in Robert Rutherford's home, most of the time in bed. He
was soon cured of his fever, but his left leg was now badly swollen
with an infection, and there was the threat of an open abscess
above the ankle. A surgeon advised him to have it operated on,
his friends concurred, and the operation was performed in Leghorn.
When several months passed without any signs that the wound
was healing, Rutherford wrote to ask the advice of his friend Sir
Horace Mann, British minister to the grand ducal court in Florence.
Mann advised that he be taken to Florence to consult Angelo Nannoni, the eminent surgeon of the Hospital of Santa Maria Nuova.
West traveled the sixty-five miles to Florence late in November
1761 and took lodgings with an Italian-born English painter named
Ignazio Hugford, whose house lay "over against" the Pitti Palace.

Dr. Nannoni, in his forty-sixth year, was famous for his methods
of treating wounds and for his work in surgery. His six-page case
history on West begins with a short biographical note on the patient, a history of his "rheumatisms and joint pains," and the observation that he brought from America to Italy "a very delicate
complexion which corresponded to a very fervid temperament." [3]
Finding a deep abscess between the achilles tendon and the external
malleolus (the bony protuberance on the outside of the ankle), Dr.
Nannoni decided to operate. "The pain was excessive," West told
Joseph Farington almost fifty years later, adding, "I can bear pain."
For some days Nannoni treated the wound with tepid liquid irri-
gations and dry dressings of balls of lint. He then operated again,
waiting for a day with clean air, "because, alas, in the treatment of
this wound I had observed how much cloudiness and humidity
acted in promoting and increasing bad fermentations." He found
still more abscesses, operated a third time, and dressed the wound
twice daily with myrrh and wine.

During the intervals between operations, West had a frame made
to fit over his bed in such a manner that he might paint and draw;
he produced several portraits but "principally studied the human

---

3 *Memorie Di Chirurgia*, Siena, 1774. See Adrian W. Zorgniotti, M.D., "Benjamin West's Osteomyelitis: A Translation," *Bulletin of the New York Academy of
Medicine*, August 1973, pp. 702–07.

figure." By this means, he said, he triumphed over every pain of body, severe paroxysms of sickness, and oppression of mind. He was almost four months in Dr. Nannoni's care, "lodged in a most deplorable condition," confined to his chamber and mostly to his bed "without being able to stir out and to see anything," alone in a foreign country whose language he did not speak well, "and in such pains that brought me nearer to Death's door than I ever have been yet." Horace Mann visited him often and showed him "marked attentions" and "extraordinary kindness... which I shall always have a most grateful remembrance of."

Nannoni performed a fourth operation on February 14, 1762. "Every ulcerated cavity abolished itself," he recorded, "and scar appeared.... Mr. West, triumphant by our surgery, fully recovered his health after a very complicated illness... [His] leg remained very thin. This did not prevent him from walking freely."

West spent more than two months in his room recovering his strength. On May 11 he wrote one of his infrequent letters, this time to make a dutiful report to his friend Joseph Shippen. He was happy that Colonel Shippen had returned safely to Philadelphia and that the several copies he had made for Governor Hamilton had arrived in good condition and been judged worthy to be hung in the governor's house. "I hope I am now perfectly cured," he wrote in giving a long account of his illness. "Thank God my patience and good constitution have got the better at last." He acknowledged orders received for copies of some of the great masters from John and William Allen and Governor Hamilton, but he was unable to set a price for these works, because he was so much indebted to his worthy patrons. He felt obliged to point out, however, that any single one of the large pieces might take him more than two or three months to copy — especially Guido Reni's *St. Michael*, where the figures were half again as large as life. He submitted to their consideration, therefore, whether the price they suggested as payment would not be too small.

During his convalescence he was carried into the Boboli Gardens behind the Pitti Palace, and he began to visit the grand duke's gallery (the Uffizi) and the Pitti. "I went very slowly picking up," he wrote to Colonel Shippen. "I... found myself unable to apply closely to my work for a long time, notwithstanding all the inclination and longing I had to do so. Every time I sat down to the slightest studies, though but for a quarter of an hour, there came a giddiness and feverishness upon me that forced me to leave off."

About this time there arrived in Florence a young woman, Angelica Catherina Maria Anna Kauffmann, who was traveling south with her father at a leisurely pace. She was not yet twenty-two, a native of a Swiss town on Lake Constance, and as a child of twelve she had revealed a precocious talent as a painter. Having achieved a modest reputation in copying pictures, decorating churches, and painting portraits, she now planned, under her father's guidance, to make a broader career as an artist. Indeed, she was on her way to Rome to paint a portrait of Johann Winckelmann, commissioned to do so by a Swiss admirer of the German critic. But she also had a fine voice, and it was thought that she could as well make a career as a singer. She spoke three languages fluently — French, German with an amusing Saxon accent, and English with the romantic charm of the continental inflections.

West and Angelica Kauffmann met in Florence, where (he later said) he gave her the first lessons she had "in the principles of composition, the importance of outline, and likewise the proper combinations and mixtures of colors." They made portraits of each other. With a few sure lines West drew the head and shoulders of a beautiful young woman of character. Angelica worked in pastel. She dressed her subject in fact or in imagination in a last-century costume — plain jacket buttoned to the throat, slashed sleeves, a square linen collar with lace edging. He wears his own hair, lightly powdered. His gaze is candid, his countenance open and without guile — a face oddly at variance with the worldly visages usually seen with that costume. Angelica Kauffmann seemed to see West as a sensitive, intelligent, romantic young man, too sweet and innocent to get along in a rough world, too gentle to bear pain and suffering, too artless ever to plan a career or to push himself forward. Charles Willson Peale, who came to know West intimately four years later, declared that Miss Kauffmann set her cap for West. If she did, he remained faithful to Betsy Shewell, the girl back home to whom he was pledged. Some observers have felt regret and a sense of loss that a marriage did not take place.

West began to copy Titian's naked *Venus of Urbino* in the Uffizi for William Allen when, "just as it was dead colored in, the fire broke out in the gallery and put everything there in confusion and stopped the work of copying there for some time." He would have proceeded to Rome and resumed his studies there, he wrote to Colonel Shippen, except that two more months must pass before the end of the unhealthy Roman summer season.

> As I had a very favorable opportunity of passing that interval in a journey to Bologna, Parma, and Venice, I resolved to embrace it, considering those places, for different merits, as much the object of a student's attention as even Rome itself, in a certain de-

gree. I also considered, that while I was thus not losing my time, I should be improving my health, which . . . required such exercise and change of air, after so long and cruel confinement, and such close application as I had given the whole summer.

The "very favorable opportunity" arose when Henry Matthews suggested that he and West visit the Lombardy cities and Venice together on the tour Mengs had suggested. Matthews, manager of the Jackson and Rutherford office for more than twenty years, had resigned a year earlier and was now employed in Florence as an advisor on objects of art to John Udney, a collector who later became British consul at Venice. West described Matthews as "one of those singular men who are but rarely met with in mercantile life, combining the highest degree of literary and elegant accomplishment with the best talents for active business. He was not only confessedly one of the finest classical scholars in all Italy, but, out of all comparison, the best practical antiquary, perhaps, then in that country." West went first to Leghorn to consult Jackson and Rutherford on his finances. He had received £60 from John Allen before or during his illness, but he now had only £10 remaining in his account. In withdrawing this amount he was given the happy news that Mr. Allen and Mr. Hamilton had each sent an additional £150 to his credit. He discreetly sounded out Jackson and Rutherford on the propriety of Matthews' proposal, "who were pleased not to disapprove of it, but on the contrary favored us both with the kindest and most honourable letters of recommendations for all the places where we were to go in."

They first visited Bologna, the city of towers and arcaded streets and fine food, the center of the Bolognese eclectic painters Guido Reni, Domenichino, Guercino, and the Caracci family. West, who "carefully inspected every work of celebrity to which he could obtain access," would have seen the unusual treasure preserved in a convent and visited by all strangers: a portrait of the Virgin Mary painted by St. Luke. He was much taken with Guido Reni's *Saints Peter and Paul*, which was a reserved picture kept in the last chamber of the Zampieri palace, covered with a silk curtain. He was mortified when he was refused permission to make a copy. (The English engraver Robert Strange had also been recently refused.) West studied the picture, retired to a neighboring street, painted a part of the picture, returned to compare and correct it and to memorize another part, and so continued in and out of the palace until he had completed an accurate copy. He and Matthews then traveled to Parma, where West began a copy of Correggio's celebrated *St. Jerome and the*

Holy Family, but, because of a recurrent touch of his illness, had not time to finish it. From Parma they went on to Mantua, Verona, Padua, and Venice.

They stayed for some weeks in Venice, their longest sojourn. The city-state had a pre-Lenten carnival lasting six months and 135,000 inhabitants who worked only when they could spare the time from their pleasures. It had as many as 60,000 visitors in a year, each of whom marveled that here, now, in the middle of the eighteenth century, existed the one unchanged metropolis that, except for modern dress, looked exactly as it had looked in centuries past. Venice was the city of great art and artists, of the three Bellinis, Carpaccio, Giorgione, Titian, Vecchio, Bordone, Bassano, Veronese, Tintoretto, and now, in modern times, Tiepolo, Canaletto, and Guardi.

While in Venice West painted a portrait of Lady Northampton, wife of an English diplomat, in the character of a madonna with her child, which, Robert Rutherford reported to Philadelphia, gained great applause and earned the artist fifty zeccheni.[4] He visited a palazzo on the Grand Canal near Santa Chiara to call on John Murray, the British resident (minister) in Venice, for whom at Shippen's behest some seven months earlier he had painted the *Savage Chief Taking Leave of His Family*. Murray treated him with "particular kindness," West wrote to Colonel Shippen, "and made my stay there much longer than I ever imagined," which he attributed to the kind report Allen and Shippen had made on him during their visit. He painted a half-length portrait of Murray, for which he received forty zeccheni. Dr. John Morgan of Philadelphia, the "father of American medicine," visited Venice a year later with his friend Samuel Powel, and he found that Mr. Murray and the ladies of his house "entertain great opinion of Philadelphia from the accounts which Mr. Shippen and Mr. Allen as well as Mr. West have given them of it. The ladies in a jocose way talk of making a party to come over to Philadelphia in the way of a visit to see the country — which we promise when they do to make a party to meet and conduct them thither."

In painting Murray, West presumably did not know that he was in the company of a thoroughly wicked man, one of the master libertines of his time, and one who was pleased to debauch young travelers to Venice. Lady Mary Wortley Montagu, who was living

---

[4] Sequins; this Venetian gold coin was still in use as late as 1919, when it was worth about $2.25.

alone in Venice in her old age, called Murray "a scandalous fellow in every sense of that word ... not to be trusted to change a sequin, despised by this [Venetian] government for his smuggling, which was his original profession, and always surrounded with pimps and brokers who are his privy councellors." One of Lady Mary's grievances was that Murray would not send her the English newspapers he received; she moved to Padua to escape his persecution and was convinced that Murray would "plunder my house when I die." His friend Casanova described Murray as a man of wit and learning who looked like a fine Bacchus painted by Rubens. Casanova also called him a prodigious lover of women, drinking, and good eating, reported that he had a penchant for seducing nuns, and added with distaste that he entertained his friends by giving erotic exhibitions with Ancilla Campioni, one of his mistresses. Murray had arranged for his sister (acidly described by Lady Mary as "a Beauteous Virgin of forty") to marry an eighty-two-year-old widower in order (it was said) to obtain control of the man's wealth and collection of art. The widower was Joseph Smith, retired British consul at Venice, who had inherited a fortune from his late wife and was one of Murray's fellow libertines.

West also met Richard Dalton in Venice, a man of unusual power and importance. Dalton was ranging about Europe in search of works of art for His Majesty George III of England. He was an artist, one of the first in England to draw and engrave the masterpieces of ancient Greece and Rome. He had traveled to Greece in 1746 as a draftsman for the earl of Charlemont; his engravings of the Parthenon and the Erechtheum were the first ever published. When young George III ascended the throne in 1760, he appointed Dalton (who was rumored to be his half-brother) to the posts of librarian and keeper of pictures in the royal household. Dalton was in Venice looking at the collection of Joseph Smith, who, no doubt to the mortification of Murray and his sister, was now eighty-seven. At the time of West's visit, Dalton had bought or was about to buy for £20,000 Smith's collection of books, gems, cameos, Italian and Dutch drawings, and most of his pictures, including 53 paintings and 150 drawings by Canaletto, more than 30 Zuccarellis, Pietro Longhi's choice *The Morning Levée,* and three works considered of lesser importance: Rembrandt's portrait, *Young Man in a Turban,* his *Rabbi with a Flat Cap,* and Vermeer's *Lady at the Virginals,* then thought to be by van Mieris. It was to be the most important single purchase the king ever made.

"Mr. Dalton," Rutherford reported to Philadelphia, "became very fond of Mr. West, and having received faculty from the King to distinguish such of the [?artists] of most merit as he met with in Italy, actually ordered Mr. West to paint a small composition for his Majesty." He also insisted that West should visit England and arranged to meet in Rome and travel with him on the journey.

West left Venice, a lamb apparently unscathed by wolves, and returned to Florence, where he completed his interrupted copying of Titian's *Venus*. He then hastened on to Rome "to make as much as possible of the short time that remained for me there," arriving in January 1763, having been away twelve months longer than he had expected. He stayed in Rome about four months. Gavin Hamilton was there, but Mengs was gone, having departed for Spain in a burst of glory, conveyed in a Spanish warship especially sent to fetch him. Thomas Robinson was gone, too, having returned to England to enter the diplomatic service. But Angelica Kauffmann was still there, painting what was to be universally greeted as a fine portrait of Winckelmann, who admired her greatly. "My portrait is being done by a rare person," he wrote. "I think she can be considered a beauty, and, as far as singing is concerned, she ranks with our best virtuosi." Nathaniel Dance, the English artist, then twenty-eight, fell in love with her; she seemed to encourage what would have been a good match, but the artist John Thomas Smith described her as a coquette:

> She was ridiculously fond of displaying her person, and being admired; for which purpose she one evening took her station in one of the most conspicuous boxes of the Theatre, accompanied by Nathaniel Dance and another artist, both of whom, as well as many others, were desperately enamoured of her ... While she was standing between her two beaux, and finding an arm of each most lovingly embracing her waist, she contrived, whilst her arms were folded before her on the front of the box over which she was leaning, to squeeze the hand of both, so that each lover concluded himself beyond all doubt the man of her choice.

Winckelmann wrote the following year, "Every Englishman who comes to Rome wants his portrait taken by Angelica." Goethe described her in his Italian journal: "She is very sensitive towards all that is beautiful, true and tender, and also incredibly modest."

Cardinal Albani had sold his collection of drawings — some thirty folio volumes — to James Adam, another of George III's agents, for £3500, plus an under-the-table present to the Contessa Cheroffini, Albani's mistress, who had persuaded him to accept the offer. Thus Albani raised the required dowry for their daughter

Vittoria, and thus Vittoria was able to marry the wealthy Marchese Guiseppi Lepri and live unhappily ever after.[5]

West renewed these acquaintances and resumed his study of Roman treasures. This time he concentrated on Raphael, whose works eighteen months earlier had not much interested him, and on improving his knowledge of ancient costumes by studying cameos with his friend Joseph Wilcocks, author of *Roman Conversations,* "a man of singular attainments in learning" whom he had first met at Crispigné's famous 1760 party of the portrait. The Abbé Peter Grant, a Scottish priest who was in charge of the Scots mission and a member of the Scots College in Rome, took him to St. Peter's on St. Peter's Day (when the Pope himself said the high mass), placing him in an advantageous position among the ecclesiastics. Behind them was a Scot who had arrived that morning with the intention of converting the Pope to Presbyterianism. As the host was raised he boomed out in a thick Scots accent, "O Lord, cast not the church down on them for this abomination!" The priests around them looked pleased, thinking his outburst was a manifestation of zeal produced by the effects of the ceremony.

West's health remained tolerably good, a development he attributed "more to the exercise I have had in traveling about than to any amendment in my constitution." For his patrons he made a copy of the Guido Reni *Herodias with the Head of St. John* in Cardinal Corsini's palace in Rome. He finished *Cimon and Iphigenia,* the picture Dalton had commissioned for George III, and he used it to fulfill Mengs' charge: "Paint a historical subject to be exhibited to the Roman public." It was a scene from the First Story of Day the Fifth in the *Decameron,* when young Cimon, rich and handsome but an uncouth and hopeless dullard, sees the beautiful and lightly clad Iphigenia asleep in a dell and is so transformed by love that he becomes the sprightliest and most accomplished man on the Isle of Cyprus. Rutherford dutifully described the picture for his friends in Philadelphia:

> His figures are half size. Iphigenia has two female attendants who sleep as soundly as herself, and in the background at a proper & respectfull distance, lies stretched her drowsy squire: Cymon and two little loves are the waking figures. He [is] fixed in stupid amaze on the beauties of Iphigenia, and they looking

---

[5] She married in 1764 and, in what became a celebrated scandal, later asked for a divorce, claiming that the marriage had not been consummated and explaining further that she loved another man, who turned out to be a eunuch.

like two little rogues who in spight of their tender age begin to know what's what. I am assured by good authority that this performance has been much admired by the judges at Rome.

In Rome he also painted, and perhaps exhibited in an incomplete state, a work titled *Angelica and Medoro*, based on a sentimental episode in Ludovico Ariosto's long narrative poem, *Orlando Furioso*.[6] Both paintings were more romantic than neoclassical; neither did much to exalt the mind or assist it to arrive at correct moral inferences; but they so enhanced West's reputation that he was elected a member of the academies of Florence and Bologna and was given the freedom of the Academy of Rome. For the first time the phrase "the American Raphael" was heard in reports sent out of Rome.

During these happenings, West received a letter from his father suggesting that, since the war between England and France had ended, he should return home by way of England. There he should call on Thomas, his half-brother, a watchmaker in Reading, the son John West had never seen. A trip to England accorded with Richard Dalton's proposal, but now Dalton wrote that he was unable to meet West in Rome or to accompany him to England, for his movements had become too irregular and depended too much on business over which he had no control. He suggested that they meet in London, and he promised to be of such use to him there as lay within his power. West was racked by indecision. He wanted to visit England, but he was reluctant to go by sea because it would be a five to six weeks' voyage; he felt too weak to make the three- to four-week journey alone by land; and he had a dread "of being laid up again at every return of the summer if I persisted to stay at Rome, where ... my studies required me to stay." For help he turned to Daniel Crispin, a friend in Rome. "Honest Crispin" first advised him in the strongest terms to go at once to England and not to lose so fine an opportunity, especially since his health was in danger in the Roman climate. He then produced a friend, Dr. William Patoun, a Scottish physician "of considerable learning and some taste in painting" who had spent many months in Rome, was now ready to return to his home in Richmond, and "was pleased to offer me his company." Thus, Rutherford wrote to Colonel

---

[6] Medoro, a Moorish youth of low birth but great beauty, page to Agramante, king of Africa, is wounded. Angelica comes upon him, dresses his wounds, falls in love, jilts Orlando, and elopes to Cathay, where, in his wife's right, Medoro becomes king. This event causes Orlando to go mad with grief.

Shippen, perhaps with just a touch of weariness, "means were found at last to quiet him."

West accepted a letter of introduction from Thomas Jenkins to the English landscape painter Richard Wilson and set out with Patoun for Florence, arriving there on or about the first of June 1763. The obliging Dr. Patoun waited while his companion made a side trip to Leghorn "to pay my respects to the worthy gentlemen there." He spent three days with his friends and benefactors, during which time he supervised the shipment of three copies he had painted for the Allens and Hamilton. (Rutherford thought the *Venus* "the most beautiful, most exact and best I ever saw, of a great many I have seen.") In a letter to Colonel Shippen, West asked one favor: "That on the arrival of the case in which the three copies are, they may be carefully taken out, and the case fastened up again, as it is full of things I am desirous not to have seen, as they are little particulars belonging to painters." He added: "I am very sensible of my own wants in regard to painting, and it will be the labor of my whole lifetime to supply them. Your useful hints upon this subject I take in the kindest part; and for the friendly intentions you have, I value them as much as if they came from Mengs himself." He obtained letters of recommendation from Jackson and Rutherford for use in England, drew the last £150 credit he had with the house, made his farewells, and returned to Florence. In Parma, he and Dr. Patoun each worked at copying the St. Jerome. When West was elected to the Academy of Parma, the local duke expressed a wish to see the young Quaker-American artist. Introduced at court by the chief minister, he did what he had heard was the practice observed at the court in England; he kept his hat on during the entire audience. The courtiers were shocked, and the duke, who attributed the breach to the young man's Quaker principles, was delighted.

The two men proceeded by way of Genoa, Turin, Savoy, Lyons, Paris, and Calais. West was exhausted in Paris — too tired to stay for the opening of the Salon and "little inclined to pay attention to the works he found there." During his short stay he happened to run upon an acquaintance he had met in Italy, a Scot named Robert Mackinlay. Twenty-six years later, in April 1789, Dr. Mackinlay wrote from Clydesdale to request a small favor for a young Scots artist who was visiting London for the first time. He recalled their earlier meetings:

> I beg leave to repeat some incidents in our acquaintance which
> commenced at Rome soon after your arrival from Pennsylvania,

your journey to Parma, your colouring after Correggio soon procured you the admiration of your brother painters at Rome. We met again at Paris; you was then thinking of returning to your own country, when I ventured my opinion and advice to settle in London.

I have never forgot your modest answer: "What would you do among the Reynolds and Ramsays?" I said ... that you would make your way with Honour and Eclat amidst all the painters not in London only, but everywhere else.

6

A Fine View of London

Mr. West is arrived from Italy with a great character as a painter.
I had the pleasure of a good deal of his company and of introducing him to Mr. Penn.

SAMUEL POWEL to
George Roberts, from
London, September 1, 1763

WEST AND DR. PATOUN landed at Dover on Saturday afternoon,
August 20, and set out for London without taking time for dinner. They got as far as Canterbury that night. Observing the English
scene from a seat on top of the coach, West was struck by the rough,
free-for-all manner of the children at play and by the English
coaches on the post road, "so uniformly well furnished and the
horses and harness so handsome." The next afternoon they reached
Greenwich, home of the famous Greenwich Naval Hospital, Greenwich Park, Royal Observatory (Flamsteed House), and, in the crypt
of the parish church of St. Alphege, the tomb of General James
Wolfe, hero four years earlier of the victory over the French at
Quebec. During the stop there, one of the passengers mentioned
the fine view one might see from a hill not far away. West decided
to leave the coach, take in the view, go the rest of the way on foot,
and meet Dr. Patoun in London. He ate his first dinner in England
in "a mean tavern," walked to Shooters Hill, and there marveled
at the extensive view of London, the Thames and the plain of
Essex, a sight he forever after remembered as the most magnificent
he had ever seen. He walked down Shooters Hill Road to the heart
of London and at the junction of Piccadilly and the present Lower
Regent Street took a room at the White Bear Inn, a house busy with
coaches going to and from west and southwest London. His first
call the next day was on Coutts and Company, bankers, No. 59 the

Strand. He settled in lodgings at 19 Bedford Street, a handsome broad avenue, a favorite locality of artists, that lay off the Strand between King Street, Covent Garden, and Maiden Lane.

The coincidence seems too neat to be credible, even allowing for West's extraordinary luck, but the records bear it out: Four of his American friends and leading patrons were in London at the time of his arrival. Provost William Smith was working with John Jay in a successful joint effort, with royal permission, to raise money for the College of Philadelphia and King's College, New York. Chief Justice William Allen was in England, among other reasons, to express American grievances against British economic policies and to oppose the newly levied duty on American sugar. Lieutenant Governor James Hamilton was conferring with the proprietors of Pennsylvania, the Penns, whose deputy he was, on ways to resist attempts to make Pennsylvania a Crown Colony and thus free it from Penn control and ownership. Samuel Powel was on one of his grand tours, bearing letters to King George III, the King of Sardinia, the Pope, and Voltaire, with the last of whom he carried on a spirited discussion on whether dogs have souls. These men received West "with joy and triumph." The meeting was more than a pleasant occasion. They had influential commercial and professional connections in London; they were being received in the homes of high-ranking army and naval officers they had entertained in Philadelphia; and they introduced their young protégé to these lofty circles. Samuel Powel took him to call on Thomas Penn, the founder's second son, who now dominated the family's holdings in America.

During his first week in London, West called on the renowned Richard Wilson in his rooms at Covent Garden over the north arcade of the Great Piazza. He may have been somewhat apprehensive, for Wilson's sharp tongue, irritable temper, and rough manner were well known. Born in Wales forty-nine years earlier, Wilson had come to London at an early age, distinguished himself as a portrait painter, and then in 1749 set off for Italy. Influenced by the works of Poussin and Claude, he renounced portraiture and devoted himself solely to landscapes, and in so doing became the father of the British school of landscape painting. He returned to England six years later. On West's arrival he was with his favorite pupil, Joseph Farington, the sixteen-year-old son of a well-to-do Lancashire family that had paid Wilson fifty pounds for two years of instruction. (It was a fateful meeting for both young men, for Farington was to play a leading role in West's career.) West presented his letters to Wilson. They talked for some time, no doubt of Thomas Jenkins, with whom Wilson had traveled to Rome and shared an apartment in the Piazza di Spagna for two years, and of Anton Mengs, who had admired Wilson's landscapes so much that he painted a portrait of Wilson in exchange for one of his Roman scenes. West asked Wilson to look at two paintings he had brought to show him: his *Angelica and Medoro* and *Cimon and Iphigenia*. There had been a recent scandal in London art circles; a George James had acquired two works in Rome painted by Baigio Rebecca and had showed them in London as his own. Now Wilson studied West's two works. "If you painted these pictures," he said, "remain in England. Stay here. If you did not, get away to America as fast as you can."

Wilson was one of the organizers, with Joshua Reynolds, of the Society of Arts, which had been founded in 1754 to arrange a public exhibition of the members' works and to raise money for the relief of indigent artists. The Society operated a drawing academy off St. Martin's Lane, and West, probably at Wilson's suggestion, arranged to study there when he returned from some trips he intended to make in England.

He journeyed first to Hampton Court Palace on the Thames above London, mainly to see the celebrated Raphael cartoons King Charles I had bought on the advice of Rubens — seven of the ten drawings done for Pope Leo X, who sent them as designs to the Flemish artisans making tapestries for the Vatican. He next traveled to the town of Windsor in Berkshire, on the Thames twenty-three miles west of London. There he climbed the hill to look at Windsor Castle, the chief residence of British sovereigns since the time of William the Conqueror; inspected the Chapel of St. George and its royal mausoleum; and walked on the north terrace, with its commanding view over the river to Eton and across the Thames valley and 60,000 acres of royal forest. If the royal standard was flying from the Round Tower, he might have seen the young king at his prayers in the Chapel or walking on the terrace, for George III was quite accessible to his people.

West continued on to Oxford, Blenheim Palace, Corsham Court in Chippenham, with all its Italian and Flemish old masters, and Bath. William Allen had taken up residence in Bath, and West remained there about a month, which meant that he had found a portrait commission or two. On his roundabout return to London he visited Salisbury Cathedral and four great Wiltshire country houses: Stourhead, built earlier in the century in the Palladian style; the William Beckford house at Fonthill; Inigo Jones' Wilton House, with its renowned "double cube" room and its collection of Vandyke portraits; and Longford, the earl of Radnor's Elizabethan country seat. At Reading he stayed a week with Thomas West, his half-brother, twenty-three years older than he.

Back in London, West attended classes at St. Martin's Lane Academy and let it be known that he would take portrait commissions. General Robert Monckton, a hero of the Battle of Quebec, in which he was wounded, and commander of the army that in 1762 had taken the island of Martinique from the French, called on him and commissioned a full-length portrait; he brought visitors to West's painting room who also ordered portraits. Dr. Patoun, his traveling companion, introduced him to his friend Joshua Reynolds. Wilson and Reynolds laid aside their distrust of each other long enough to join in urging West to exhibit the Monckton portrait and his two subject pictures at the April 1764 show of the Society of Artists in the Spring Gardens gallery.

The winter of 1763–64 was unusually cold and, to the delight of some of the citizenry, London's lakes froze over. West was walking one morning in St. James's Park when he saw a crowd lining the canal to watch the ice skaters. He stopped to observe them and, seeing a person who rented skates, chose a pair and spent some time on the ice. As he was unbuckling his skates, a gentleman who had been watching him approached and volunteered some information. "I perceive, Sir," he said, "you are a stranger and do not perhaps know that there are much better places than this for the exercise of skating. The Serpentine River in Hyde Park is far superior, and the Basin [Round Pond] in Kensington Gardens still more preferable. Here, only the populace assemble. On the Serpentine, the company, although better, is also promiscuous. But the persons who frequent the Basin in the Gardens are generally of the rank of gentlemen, and you will be less annoyed among them than at either of the other two places."

West was not averse to skating in better company, and the next day he bought a pair of skates in Piccadilly and proceeded to Kensington Gardens. He made a few trial turns on the ice and glided out into the crowd, performing in his best American manner. He stopped when a gentleman called to him by name. It was none other than Colonel William Howe, who some months earlier had returned from the siege and capture of the Spanish city of Havana, Cuba. "Mr. West," said the Colonel, "I am truly glad to see you in this country, and at this time. I have not heard of you since we parted on the wharf at Philadelphia, when you sailed for Italy, but I have often since had occasion to recollect you. I am, therefore, particularly glad to see you here, and on the ice, for you must know that, in speaking of the American skaters, it has been alleged that I have learnt to draw the long bow among them. But you are come in a lucky moment to vindicate my veracity." He called over some of the young noblemen who were with him, introduced West, and requested him to perform the Philadelphia Salute.

West protested that he was too long out of practice to perform such a difficult move, but he agreed to attempt it. After a few trials he did the Salute successfully and to great applause. The young noblemen later talked of his talents as a skater with such praise and in such places that in the course of a few days "prodigious crowds of the fashionable world, and of all descriptions of people, assembled to see the American skater." West seems to have trained a partner, for the *Morning Herald* of February 4, 1764, reported, "There never was a more brilliant exhibition than Hyde Park afforded on Sunday — Ministers, Lords, Commons, all on the ice. Of the Commons Mr. West the celebrated painter, and Dr. Hewitt were the best. They danced a minuet on their skates, to the admiration of the spectators." [1]

On January 27, 1764, William Allen wrote to Benjamin Chew in Philadelphia:

> My Lady Juliana Penn called upon us to go and see our Country man Wests painting. [2] He is really a wonder of a man and has so far outstripped all the painters of his time as to get into high esteem at once, whereas the famous Reynolds was five years at work before he got into vogue, as has been the case with all the others who generally drudged a longer time before they had anything of a name. If he keeps his health he will make money very fast, he is not likely to return among us so that you will not be able to have Mrs. Chew and your little flock painted.

West was indeed weighing the possibility of staying permanently in England, and he could not come to a decision. He considered the advantages and disadvantages of the courses he might follow.

First, he could return home, as he had originally intended to do. There he would have no rivals, and he might become the founder of an American school of art. But this would undoubtedly mean that he would have to spend the rest of his life painting portraits — and, as he told one of his students, "I am not friendly to the indis-

---

[1] William Dunlap, one of West's American students, skated with West two decades later and pronounced him "the best, though not the most active, then on the ice."

[2] Juliana, fourth daughter of the first earl of Pomfret, married Thomas Penn in 1751, retaining her title as Lady Juliana.

criminate waste of genius in portrait painting." There was no taste and no market for the Grand Style in America and no public buildings of the scale necessary to hold such works. It meant, however, that he would be happily reunited with his family and with Betsy Shewell.

Or, secondly, he might stay in London. Here he could paint just enough portraits to make a living and spend the rest of his time on really important work, on history painting, which no one else in England seemed to be doing. But this meant that he would have to abandon Betsy or ask her to wait still longer for him. She was now almost twenty-three, an attractive young lady of a good family, and she had already been waiting for him for almost four years.

Or, thirdly, he could return to Philadelphia, marry Betsy, and bring her back to London. That would mean two sea voyages of four to twelve weeks each. It also meant that he would have to cancel or try to postpone commissions he had accepted, and he would have to take the chance of re-establishing himself in London, with a wife, after a long absence.

He sat down with Judge Allen and Dr. Smith and asked for guidance. They gravely discussed his problems and considered the alternatives. They deplored the loss, if he stayed in England, of the contribution he could make to American art and the distinction he could bring to Philadelphia, but they urged him, nonetheless, to stay in England and prosper. They advised against making the trip to America. Interest, even excitement, had been generated about Benjamin and his work. This he might lose in an absence of several months. It was quite possible that he might return to a London no longer interested in the oddity of a colonial country boy who had once consorted with Indians and studied art in Italy.

Allen and Smith offered a fourth course of action. It was a bit unusual, but it was logical. Miss Shewell should herself cross the ocean and marry Benjamin in London. Some respectable, responsible older person, of course, would accompany her. The assurances of Judge Allen, Governor Hamilton, and Dr. Smith would certainly satisfy her family and all Philadelphia that Benjamin's intentions were upright and that Miss Shewell's honor would be protected.

West agreed to the proposal and a battery of letters went off to Philadelphia. Confident that Betsy would concur, he chose suitable quarters for a married man, moving in April from Bedford Street to Castle Street in Leicester Square. Reynolds was a neighbor, and the aged William Hogarth, whom West saw as "a strutting, consequential little man."

In April, the Society of Artists of Great Britain (which had split off from the Society of Arts) opened an exhibition in its room at

Spring Gardens, Charing Cross, showing paintings, sculpture, and architectural designs. A first exhibition in 1760 had been, according to a press account, "crowded and incommoded by the intrusion of a great number whose stations and education made them no proper judges of statuary and painting and who were made idle and tumultuous by the opportunity of a show"; but that problem was solved by charging a shilling for the catalogue and admitting no one who did not have a catalogue. The quality of much of the work in the 1764 exhibition was poor and drew sharp criticism in the press, though the Hanging Committee had tried to place the worst pieces in the darkest corners. West's portrait of Monckton excited no comment, but his *Angelica and Medoro* and *Cimon and Iphigenia* caused something of a sensation. "These are much admired," Horace Walpole wrote in the margin of his catalogue, and then added how much he disliked them. A correspondent sent some verses in French to the *Public Advertiser* eulogizing "Mr. West, a celebrated painter in Castle Street, Leicester Fields, known in Italy by the name of the American Raphael," and beginning with the line, "Thou who canst make the canvas live . . ." The editor invited readers to submit translations into English. Several were printed, one in Latin, but the whole subject was dropped when another correspondent pointed out that the verses were not original, having been written some fifty years earlier by Antoine Houdar de la Motte, a French poet, and dedicated to Bernard de Fontenelle, another French poet. Still another correspondent observed that he would have to see more of Mr. West's work before he could use the phrase "the American Raphael" without blushing.

One day that spring West received a visit at Castle Street from a tall, portly man with a magnificent presence who introduced himself as the Reverend Dr. William Markham, headmaster of Westminster School. Markham, known as one of the best classical scholars of his time, though an indolent one, had become interested in West and his work. His interest grew with acquaintance, and he introduced West to his friends — among others, to Dr. Samuel Johnson, Samuel Dyer, one of the luminaries of the Johnson circle, and Edmund Burke, for whose only son Markham was godfather. (West had met Burke's brother, a Benedictine monk, at Parma.) One of the trustees of Westminster School was Charles Watson Wentworth, Marquess of Rockingham, and it was presumably through Markham that he became aware of West. Rockingham offered the young artist "a regular, permanent engagement" of £700 a year to paint historical subjects for his mansion at Malton in Yorkshire. This was a flattering and tempting offer from a man who within a year would be head of the government (with Burke as his private secretary), and it was an enormous sum of money; a frugal artist could live a year on £50. West declined the offer after again consulting William Allen. Judge Allen advised him that he should not confine himself to serving one patron — and especially not one who was a Whig and an opponent to the king.

In due course West received the long-awaited replies from America. Elizabeth Shewell agreed to leave home, family, and country, cross the Atlantic, and trust herself to Benjamin's care. The news caused a stir in Philadelphia. Colonel Shippen conveyed the information to Robert Rutherford in Leghorn on June 28:

> I understand [Mr. West's] reputation is in so high esteem that he is now employed by many of the nobility and people of the first fashion, so that I fear we shall never see him in this country again. In consequence of this great prospect of making a handsome living he has just sent over for a young lady of this town, Miss Shewell, to whom he had paid his addresses before he left this country, and has retained the strongest affection for her ever since. She is now embarking for London under the care of Mr. West's father, who is also going over at his son's request.

Elizabeth Shewell and John West were accompanied by Elizabeth's maid and by her cousin, Matthew Pratt, twenty-nine, a Philadelphia portrait painter. Pratt longed to study in Europe, preferably under the aegis of so successful a painter as Mr. West. Records of the journey are sparse. Pratt later wrote in an "autobiographical memorandum" for his family: "June the 24th I took my departure from Phila in company with Miss Betsy Shewell, and Mr. John West, Father to the famous Benjn West, bound to London . . ." Miss Shewell wrote in the margins of *A Pocket Almanak for the Year 1764*: June 24, "Left Philadelphia and all friends," and August 6, "Landed at Gravesend and came to London."

Betsy delivered letters she carried from her fiancé's friends in Philadelphia, one of them from Provost William Smith. When Benjamin asked his father what he thought of the appearance of London after the long absence, the old gentleman replied, "The streets and houses look very much as they did; but can thee tell me, my son, what has become of all the Englishmen? When I left England, the men were generally a portly, comely race, with broad skirts and large flowing wigs; rather slow in their movements, and grave and dignified in their deportment. But now they are docked and cropped, and skipping about in scanty clothes like so many monkeys."

In the language of the day, Benjamin West was united to the

object of his affections on September 2 in the church of their parish, St. Martin's-in-the-Fields. English weddings of that time were almost invariably small, quiet, family affairs with no festivities and only a few friends and relatives present. (It was felt that the bride should not be subjected to the curious and speculative stares of the public.) The curate, P. Dixon, conducted the service. Matthew Pratt gave away the bride; he and Thomas Lamar, a friend, signed the marriage register as witnesses. Matthew Pratt wrote in his autobiography: "In a few weeks after our arrival, I had the pleasure of officiating, as father in the marriage ceremony ... in joining Miss Shewell to Mr. Benjan West as a wife ... to the entire satisfaction, of all their friends and relatives." The words *to the entire satisfaction of all their friends and relatives* are important, for a legend was to develop in the next century that Elizabeth Shewell's family violently opposed the marriage; that her brother Stephen confined her in his house in Philadelphia; that he then sent her to the house of their sister Mary (Mrs. Abraham Bickley) at Pen Rhyn; and that Elizabeth climbed from her bedroom window down a rope ladder and, with the help of three prominent citizens, eloped by proxy with John West and Matthew Pratt.

The reputed source of that tale was the venerated William White, rector of Christ Church in Philadelphia, organizer of the Protestant Episcopal Church in America, and bishop of Pennsylvania. It was handed down in a letter written on February 17, 1887, by Thomas F. Shewell of Bristol, Pennsylvania, a family descendant. According to Shewell's letter, Bishop White was entertained during a diocesan visit in 1833 at the house of Dr. Joseph Swift, grandson of Elizabeth West's brother Joseph. During the evening Mrs. Swift persuaded him to talk of the events on the evening of June 24, 1764. When West's friends learned that Elizabeth had been locked in her room, Thomas Shewell wrote,

> they determined, in the Bishop's words, that "Ben should have his wife," sending to Miss Shewell by her maid, concealing under her dress, a rope ladder, with a note saying that they would cause the vessel to drop down to Chester, sixteen miles, to obviate suspicion, and that on a given evening they would have a carriage round the corner at eleven o'clock at night, and if she would use the ladder to reach the ground, they would safely convey her to Chester and put her on board the vessel.
>
> The plan was entirely successful. The lady entered the carriage with two of the gentlemen, while one rode outside with the driver. The roads were abominably bad, and the eloping company only reached the vessel at daybreak, and the weary night came to an end ...

During the whole course of the story, the venerable Bishop
spoke with great animation, and seemed to relish the adventure,
saying, "Ben deserved a good wife, and, old as I am, I am ready
to do it again to serve such worthy people."

The party, Thomas Shewell wrote, consisted of Benjamin Franklin,
Francis Hopkinson, and Bishop White. "I have thus endeavored,"
Shewell's letter continued, "to give you the statement as related to
me by Dr. Swift, as the story of the Bishop. Mrs. West was the first
cousin of my grandfather, Robert Shewell."

The story was picked up by the lighter social historians, improved
with interesting variations and appropriate dialogue ("It's us, lass!
Ben West's friends. We're here to get ye onto a packet that leaves
tonight for England!"), and was made a dubious but persisting part
of the West annals. The Shewells, it was said, never forgave or
communicated with their daughter or her husband.

The historian Charles Henry Hart scoffed at the elopement story
in an exchange of letters published in 1908:

> Permit me to state a few undeniable facts that stamp the story on
> its face as absurd and well-nigh impossible if one will but for a
> moment reflect and consider the period when it must have oc-
> curred, the social conditions of the time and the distance that
> then . . . existed between extreme youth and matured manhood.
> In 1764 . . . Bishop White, the mainstay of the legend, *was a boy
> of 16*, Francis Hopkinson a young man of 27, and Dr. Franklin
> *within two years of threescore*. Fancy, then, Benny Franklin of 58
> having a tryst with Billy White of 16, and taking him by the
> hand to lead him to help in an elopement, with Frank Hopkin-
> son of 27 as an accessory. Does anything have to be added to this
> picture to show that it is the baseless fabric of a dream?
>
> If it does, I am in a position to add it. I knew intimately for
> twenty years before their deaths Miss Rebecca White, the grand-
> daughter, and Miss Elizabeth Nixon, the grand-niece, of Bishop
> White. . . . These ladies were each 28 years old when the Bishop
> died in 1836, and they had held the closest possible relations to
> him. I interrogated both of them as to this episode in the Bish-
> op's life, but neither of them had ever heard a word of it from
> him; and yet such a story would have been of the first interest to
> two young and romantic girls, and the Bishop the very man to
> have entertained them both with it, had it really occurred.

Mr. Hart might also have pointed out that Elizabeth's parents,
Robert and Elizabeth Barton Shewell, were alive and well in 1764
and would hardly have permitted their son Stephen to lock up his
sister Elizabeth. And that Matthew Pratt, though an accessory in

the "elopement," painted portraits of Elizabeth's parents in 1768, after he returned to America. And that Benjamin West corresponded with his brother William, a farmer in Upper Darby, by sending his letters in the care of Joseph Shewell, one of Elizabeth's brothers. Those who are reluctant to give up such a romantic story, on the other hand, might point out that Franklin was indeed in Philadelphia in June 1764, and that after returning to England he twice called on Mrs. Benjamin West (on the 9th and 14th of February 1765).

Benjamin and Betsy were not alone on their honeymoon; they were accompanied by John West and Matthew Pratt. Pratt wrote:

> After the ceremony in the church, we visited all Mr. West's relatives; viz: Old Mr. West's sister, then living at Marlborough, near Thames in Oxfordshire. And Mr. Thomas West's family at Reading in Berkshire, who is a very respectable member of the Society of Friends, etc.
>
> After spending some weeks in our journey visiting Windsor Castle, Oxford, and all that was worth going to see in the country, we returned, to the city, where Mr. Benjn West had a very elegant house, completely fitted up, to accommodate a very large family, and where he followed his occupation, in great repute, as a Historical and Portrait painter.

John West stayed for some time with his sister at Marlborough, and then with his son at Reading, and then with Benjamin in London, traveling from one to another as his inclination led him. West agreed to take Pratt into his studio as a pupil and assistant and, in fact, gave him several rooms in his house. In Pratt's words, West "rendered me every good and kind office he could bestow on me, as if I was his father, friend and brother." Pratt stayed with West for two and a half years and in that time painted an attractive pair of portraits — the earliest known of Elizabeth, one of the earliest of Benjamin. Elizabeth is revealed as a handsome woman with regular features, brown hair, lambent brown eyes, and a very serious expression.

Pratt also painted a group portrait, a "conversation piece," that through two centuries has charmed and amused those who have seen it. First shown at the 1766 exhibition of the Society of Artists under the title *The American School*, the painting depicts five young artists in West's painting room. One of them shows a completed drawing on blue paper to West, while the others stop their work to watch and listen. The painting has been called "leggy," and Matthew Pratt, seated on the Chippendale chair at right, is disproportionately small in scale, but it is a captivating and unforgettable work and is now generally included among early American masterpieces. (It was much admired and much exhibited throughout the Bicentennial year 1976.)

Pratt was the first of three generations of young American artists who were to pass through Benjamin West's studio. During the next fifty years they would cross the Atlantic and go straight to West for help and guidance. He fed them, housed them, lent them money, introduced them to patrons, found them work and commissions, encouraged them, and imbued them with pride in their profession. He lent them paintings from his collection to study and copy, and, in a day when there were no public galleries in London, used his considerable influence to gain them entry to see the royal and private collections. He hid nothing from his students at a time when some artists, including Joshua Reynolds, locked the paints-cupboard so that students could not see their materials. "He had no secrets or mysteries," said his pupil William Dunlap. "He told all he knew . . . Every American was as a brother to him, and his open doors and open heart ever received them as such."

7

"In Britain's Bosom"

I have (God be praised) past through the many dangers of the seas and am now at my studies with Mr. West who gives me encouragement to persue my plan of painting and promises me all the instruction he is capable of giving.

CHARLES WILLSON PEALE
to John Beale Bordley,
London, 1767

WEST HAD ARRIVED in England at an opportune time; conditions were propitious for support of the arts. The country was at peace after seven years of war against France, and the treaty signed in 1763 enlarged the empire, enriched it, and opened the way for worldwide commercial expansion and accumulation of wealth. Discoveries and improvements made since 1750 were changing British life: in science, medicine and health, agriculture and breeding of livestock, construction and manufacturing, and — a newly coined word — in technology. A little of the wealth was filtering down to the working classes. A laborer could earn fourteen shillings a week in the cities in 1764; a craftsman — a jeweler, chair carver, maker of optical instruments, an arcanist, modeler, or colorist in the porcelain trade — could make one pound to four pounds. The prevalence of drunkenness among the laboring poor had been diminished by the sobering effects of the new Protestant creed of Methodism; also by a high tax on gin and restrictions on the sellers. Louse-borne disease was being reduced, without conscious intent to do so, with the introduction of iron beds and washable cotton bedclothes instead of unwashable wool. Both the health and the appearance of the people were greatly improved when cheap cotton garments replaced wool and leather. Older people could remember that in the reign of George I not one person in 500 wore stockings, but now everyone wore them.

English social conscience was becoming more liberal and enlightened. Fear of witchcraft was recognized as a superstition and the laws against it were unused. Very few reputable physicians now consulted the stars in making a diagnosis or performing an operation. The scandal of unwanted babies being put out to die in a ditch — contrasted to the care given them by the church in France — was producing reforms. A number of state-supported orphanages had been founded, and while the death rate among the children was unfortunately very high, work was being found for the survivors down to the age of six, by which they became productive, learned a trade, and were kept out of trouble. Hospitals had been established on the newest principles of nursing care and medical science; some of them held that baths were not weakening, that two patients might be placed in the same bed together only if they had the same disease, and that a woman lying-in should have a bed to herself. The English penal code was one of the severest in Europe, with more than a hundred felonies punishable by death; but its effects were ameliorated by the refusal of juries to convict, even in the face of clear evidence against the defendant. Many persons under sentence of death, moreover, had a choice of being deported to the American colonies. The characteristic sense of British fair play was such that no person condemned to death could be forced to choose deportation to America if he preferred to hang. There were between 14,000 and 15,000 black slaves in England, but the feeling against slavery was so strong that many believed it would be abolished within a decade.

One-tenth of England's 6.1 million people lived in London. (Everyone said "Lunnun.") Toll roads built and maintained by turnpike companies had increased travel and were bringing the capital closer to the rest of the country. A person with ten shillings could take a coach in Birmingham in early morning and be in London, 115 miles away, that same night. Mail coaches were actually traveling 12 to 14 miles an hour. Back country manners and fashions were much improved by this increased contact with London.

London was different from Rome and Paris in many ways, and most noticeably in that it had no great boulevards and its palaces and large public buildings were few in number and not well sited. New Street, however, had been built to speed the flow of livestock to the Smithfield Market, and congestion was now being further eased by tearing down the city's old gates: Aldgate, Moorgate, Ludgate, Bishopsgate — all but Temple Bar. A second bridge had been completed over the Thames at Westminster in 1750 — the first in 500 years; London Bridge had been widened in 1757; and a third bridge was now going up between them at Blackfriars.

When the inhabitants were not rioting to protest some loss of privilege or to support some political firebrand like Jack Wilkes, London was an orderly city. It was expanding rapidly across open fields toward the outlying hamlets of Chelsea, Knightsbridge, Marylebone, Belgravia, Paddington, and Hackney; and, except for the growth in the marshy areas south of the Thames, the development was nicely planned around garden squares, with solid brick houses on well-designed streets. Under the Westminster paving act of 1762, numbers were placed on shops, jutting doorsteps were removed, and streets were being rebuilt with sidewalks, curbs, and gutters, to the great satisfaction of those on foot, who needed protection against careening carriages, coaches, wagons, and carts. Casanova, who arrived in London about the same time as West, was shocked to see Englishmen turn toward the street when they urinated, instead of toward the side of a building as on the Continent.

In several of the fine city parks, one could buy milk from milkmaids tending their grazing cows. For several hours each day the parks were reserved for adults, with children and servants in livery excluded. London was a noisy city, but it had the best lighting in Europe, and probably in the world. Street lamps were filled with oil as a municipal service and the cotton wicks lighted each day before sunset. (Londoners laughed at the German prince who, visiting the city for the first time, thought it had been illuminated especially for him.)

To match these civilizing changes, England had a new king, its first young monarch in a hundred years and the first Hanoverian born in England speaking without a German accent. "We were so weary of our old King," Dr. Samuel Johnson wrote in a letter, "that we are much pleased with his successor, of whom we are so much inclined to hope great things, that most of us begin already to believe them." George III was handsome, popular, and progressive. He painted a little, loved music and played several instruments, wrote anonymous articles on advanced agricultural practices, and was eager to advance the arts and sciences. He had, for example, recently given a pension of £300 a year to Dr. Johnson, whose political views opposed his own; and he had intervened to award a prize of £20,000 to John Harrison, son of a carpenter, for developing a marine chronometer — an instrument for determining longitude at sea. For many years the only pictures of any importance painted in England had been done by foreigners — by Lely, Holbein, Vandyke, and Kneller, among others — and even now, except for William Hogarth, the only English artists of any consequence were painting portraits. Art circles had great hope that the young king would support the fine arts, and especially the arts of the orders higher than "face painting." Every artist dreamed of obtaining the great prize, the key to fame and fortune: the king's favor and patronage.

West fitted smoothly into the life of a London artist. He was happy in his marriage, his painting, and his teaching and got along well with his patrons and fellow artists. With all his varied activities, he gives the impression in the years between 1764 and 1768 of a hard-working, competent, rising young artist, ambitious, idealistic, full of vitality, who knows exactly where he is going and what he intends to do with his life.

On April 8, 1766, he and Elizabeth became the parents of a son, whom they christened Raphael Lamar, the middle name after the friend who had attended their wedding. A few months earlier West had become a director of St. Martin's Lane Academy and a member and director of the Society of Artists, now incorporated under a royal charter. He and Richard Wilson were appointed to hang the pictures of one of the Society's spring exhibitions. As West told the story years later, it was a memorable year for bad paintings, probably because of the large number of beginners.

> When the pictures were all up, Wilson, with an expressive grin, began to rub his eyes, as if to clear them of something painful. "I'll tell you what, West," said he after a while, "this will never do. We shall lose the little credit we have. The public can never stand such a shower of chalk and brickdust."
>
> "Well, what's to be done? We can't reject any pictures now."
>
> "Since that's the case, then we must mend their manners."
>
> "What do you mean to do?"
>
> "You shall see," said Wilson after a pause, "what India ink and Spanish liquorice can do." He accordingly dispatched the porter to the colourman and druggist for these reformers, and dissolving them in water, actually washed nearly half the pictures in the exhibition with this original glaze. "There," said he, " 'tis as good as asphaltum — with this advantage: that if the artists don't like it, they can wash it off when they get the pictures home."

The paintings, West added, looked all the better for the treatment.

He made two drawings to illustrate his friend William Smith's *Expedition against the Ohio Indians*, published in London and Philadelphia in 1766. He painted portraits of, among others, Dr. Oliver Goldsmith, Lady Diana Mary Barker, Governor James Hamilton, Mrs. Thomas Hopkinson (mother of Francis), and the Reverend Dr. William Markham. Through Dr. Markham he met two high churchmen and painted their portraits: Dr. Thomas Newton, bishop of Bristol, and Dr. Richard Terrick, bishop of London; and he did a double portrait of the two older sons of Dr. Robert Hay Drummond, archbishop of York. The quality and style of his portraits and the reception they received were such that West clearly could have devoted the rest of his career to that profitable work — perhaps repeating the same stock subjects dozens of times, as did Allan Ramsay, with his portraits of George III, and John Hoppner with Pitt the Younger, and Joseph Nollekens with his busts of Charles James Fox. Perhaps he might reach that point, as did Joshua Reynolds, where he would paint a face in four and a half hours, turn the rest of the portrait over to his drapery painter and other assistants, and produce 120 portraits a year. Had he confined his attention chiefly to portrait painting, the English critic William Roberts asserted, he would have ranked well with the greatest masters of the English school. But West was determined to paint history pictures, even though, as he wrote to a friend, it was everywhere believed that this was "a department of art that would never be encouraged in this kingdom." Whatever his motivations, he was rejecting a safe and comfortable future to search for new ideas and artistic growth.

He displayed two history subjects in the Society of Artists exhibition of 1765, and in the following year showed two neoclassical history pictures painted on speculation to demonstrate to the public what he could do and intended to do. One was *The Continence of Scipio,* which shows the Roman general in the act of renouncing his right to a beautiful captive slave girl and returning her to her fiancé. The other, *Pylades and Orestes Brought as Victims before Iphigenia,* depicts the moment when Orestes and his devoted friend Pylades, captives of the barbarians of Tauris, stand before the maiden priestess Iphigenia for judgment. She is about to sacrifice them to Diana, according to the Tauric custom, when Orestes recognizes Iphigenia as his long-lost sister, who he believed was dead. All three escape to Greece. (Nothing could be more alien to modern taste than such moralizing story-telling pictures; but through several centuries of western art, and especially during the emphasis on history subjects in the last third of the eighteenth century, every educated person and lover of art had, as part of his cultural training, a knowledge of and interest in the episodes of history, mythology, the Bible, classical tragedy, and moral allegory.) The two paintings were sensationally successful, possibly, as the critic Grose Evans suggests, because of the eighteenth-century Englishman's longing for a share of the great classical tradition of art. "The great crowd of the year," it was said during the Spring Gardens gallery exhibition "is about Mr. West's pictures."

West had first exhibited *Pylades and Orestes* at his home. According to James Northcote, West's contemporary, the painting attracted unusual attention, "as any attempt in history was, at that period, an almost unexampled effort.... His house was soon filled with visitors from all quarters to see it; and those amongst the highest rank, who were not able to come to his house to satisfy their curiosity, desired his permission to have it sent to them; nor did they fail, every time it was returned to him, to accompany it with compliments of the highest commendation on its great merits." West's servant gained upwards of thirty pounds in tips for showing the picture, Northcote said, but no one ever asked the price of the work or offered West a commission to paint any other subject. "Indeed, there was one gentleman so highly delighted with the picture, and who spoke of it with such praise to his father, that he immediately asked him the reason he did not purchase, as he had so much admired it, when he answered, 'What could I do, if I had it? You would not surely have me hang up a modern English picture in my house, unless it was a portrait.'" When *Pylades and Orestes* was returned from the exhibition unsold, a nobleman's steward, a Mr. Geddes, bought it for 100 guineas. (Professional men were commonly paid in guineas rather than pounds.) Mr. Geddes expressed indignation at the public apathy and at the want of spirit or judgment among those professing to be connoisseurs, who could suffer such a work to revert to the painter.

During the 1766 exhibition, West was the subject of another poetic effusion that must have embarrassed him, or should have if it did not. A rhymster who signed himself "An Impartial Hand" began a pamphlet by saying that before he climbed the stairs to see the paintings —

> Sly Malice pluck'd my sleeve and did assure
> That most above were modern, mean and poor,
> But West and Genius met me at the door:
> Virgilian West, who hides his happy art
> And steals, through nature's inlets, to the heart,
> Pathetic, simple, pure, through every part.

Several pages of flattery then followed the lines:

> Thou long expected, wish'd for stranger, hail!
> In Britain's bosom make thy loved abode,
> And open daily to her raptured eye
> The mystic wonders of thy Raphael's school.

West's second American student arrived in 1766. He was Abraham Delanoy, twenty-four, son of a New York purveyor of lobsters and pickled oysters; another West student described him as a man of mild manners, awkward address, and unprepossessing appearance. About the same time came West's old friend from Philadelphia, Francis Hopkinson. He was now a practising lawyer, collector of customs at Salem, New Jersey, and a not very successful manufacturer's agent; he was also an accomplished composer of songs and occasional poetry, a public performer on the harpsichord, and secretary of the Library Company of Philadelphia. Still a single man, he was seeking political preferment through the influence of English friends and relatives. He stayed part of the winter of 1766–67 with the Wests and wrote enthusiastically to his mother of their hospitality. ("I live with them in a manner perfectly agreeable to myself.") Dr. Franklin was "very kind" to him. "I am very happy in his good company. He made up a party the other day. Mr. and Mrs. West, Mrs. Stevenson [Franklin's landlady], Miss Stevenson, one Miss Blunt and myself. We all went down the Thames in a boat and spent the day at Greenwich most agreeably. We dined on whitings and white-bate, a most delicate little fish, and returned by water and moonlight in the evening."

Hopkinson was a competent artist, specializing in crayon pictures, especially portraits, and the design of official seals, heraldic devices, and banners, and there is evidence that he took some training from West while in London. When he sailed for home, West presented him with a gift for the Library Company. It is still there in its original wooden box with a sliding top, bearing a label written by Hopkinson: "A Woman's Hand from an Egyptian Mummy: presented to the Library Company of Philadelphia by Mr. Benjamin West, formerly of this City, but now of London, Historical Painter, November 1767."

On February 13, 1767, a well-dressed stranger appeared at West's door on Castle Street. He was an American, Charles Willson Peale of Maryland, and he wished to see Mr. West. He had, in fact, stepped off a ship that morning and had spent his first hours buying some proper English clothes: a light blue half-dress suit, gloves, shoes, black stockings, and a beaver hat.

West read the letter he presented. He would have welcomed Mr. Peale as an American, he said, even if he had carried no letter of recommendation, and would have given him all the assistance in his power. A letter such as this one, however, from Mr. William Allen of Philadelphia, was the most powerful he could have brought. He was at Mr. Peale's service.

Peale gave the reason for his call. He was an artist who had received very little in the way of instruction, and he would welcome Mr. West's guidance and advice. He was twenty-six years old (three years younger than West) and had set up a business as a saddler, but of late he had become a portrait painter. He had left a wife and infant son in Maryland and, with the financial help of some Maryland gentlemen, was in England to study painting, under Mr. West if possible. In the course of the next several hours he met Mrs. West and the child, Raphael, admired the works he saw on the easels and walls about him, and, at West's request, posed for the hand on a portrait of Governor Hamilton of Pennsylvania. He was to stand with his right hand resting on the table. He did so, he later said, "with all possible steadiness," but he was faint from the rigors of an eight-week ocean crossing, and in time he began to turn pale and falter. West hurried him into the fresh February air and he recovered.

Did he have lodgings? Perhaps he would like to take a room in the neighborhood just vacated by one of his pupils, Mr. Delanoy, who had returned to America. The two men went to a nearby house but found Delanoy still there; he had been unexpectedly delayed, he said, in his departure. West had cause, Peale felt, to be displeased at not being informed of this development, but he simply replied that Mr. Delanoy was welcome to visit him during the delay and copy a picture so that he might have a work to exhibit in New York. Lodgings were found for Peale in Silver Street, at Golden Square. (Delanoy returned to New York, where another West student later found him "consumptive, poor, and his only employment sign painting." He was the first artist to advertise that he had been taught by Benjamin West.)

Peale became at once a full-time member of "the American School." In a letter to his leading patron in Maryland he wrote that he was hard at work with West.

> I have been to see Reynolds and [Francis] Cotes who are called the best painters and in my humble opinion Mr. West's work exceeds them all by far. He paints a great deal of History latterly and is excessively fond of it and there is no other eminent in that way at present which leaves a great opening for him. He has two pieces ready for the Exhibition . . . They are painted in a masterly style and in a different manner from common oil painting, which gives great luster and strength to the colouring — a method of art no painter here else knows anything of. Mr. West is intimate with the best miniature painter [and] intends to borrow some miniature pieces for me to copy privately as he does nothing in that way himself.

West had learned that his new pupil needed to make money from his painting as soon as possible, and he knew that there was a demand for portraits in miniature in London and employment for any artist who mastered the technique.

Peale fitted himself into West's daily routine, observing everything, copying pictures in West's collection, preparing canvases, painting drapery, posing for figures or parts of figures. As the weeks passed, he revealed more of his unusual background. His father had died in 1750, when Charles was eight. His mother found work as a seamstress, sent Charles to a charity school, and signed him to an eight-year apprenticeship with a saddler just before he turned thirteen. On completing his apprenticeship he married and set himself up as a saddler and harness maker in Annapolis. He taught himself watch and clock repairing, metalworking and silversmithing, added upholstering in partnership with a chairmaker, and became active in radical anti-British politics. When he saw some paintings on a business trip to Norfolk, "the idea of making pictures" took possession of his mind. He began by painting signs and advanced to portraits, after giving the artist John Hesselius one of his best saddles with all fittings in return for being permitted to see him paint a portrait. At a paint dealer's shop in Boston he heard the name of John Singleton Copley, Boston's best portrait painter. He called on Copley, introducing himself "as a person just beginning to paint portraits." Copley received him "very politely," allowed him to examine "a considerable number of portraits, many of them highly finished," and lent him a work to copy. On a by-trip to Newburyport, during the excitement following the passage of the Stamp Act, he met with and worked for the Sons of Liberty, making emblematical designs that showed "with what unanimity of detestation the people viewed the odious acts of Parliament." In the fall of 1766, a group of Maryland gentlemen subscribed eighty-three pounds, obtained a free passage, and collected letters of introduction so that Peale might study painting for one year in England. He sailed in December on a boat that was returning with a consignment of stamped paper nullified by repeal of the hated Stamp Act.

In London, Peale applied himself to learning the whole art of painting; he was not content, he said, "with knowing how to paint one way, but engaged in the whole circle of arts, except at painting in enamel. And also at modeling, and casting in plaster of Paris." He even "made some essays" in the art of mezzotint — engraving on copper by scraping away parts of a uniformly roughened surface.

Perhaps to hearten his pupil after the loss of an inheritance he had expected to claim in England, West painted Peale's portrait. It shows an extraordinarily handsome young man with a strong, straight nose, his face half-shadowed, in the act of pausing, brush in hand, to examine what he has done and what he should do next. Painted without expectation of payment and with no need to flatter, it is one of West's finest portraits.

In their conversations at dinner or during the long hours of work, the teacher and the pupil would certainly have talked about John Copley — Peale about his visit to the artist's studio the summer before, West about his odd association with a Copley painting hanging in the April 1766 exhibition of the Society of Artists. The picture — Peale must have seen it among Copley's "highly finished" works in Boston — was a portrait of Copley's sixteen-year-old half brother, Henry Pelham, offspring of his widowed mother's second marriage. On or before September 10, 1765, Copley sent it to a friend in London, R. G. Bruce, a ship's captain. Bruce showed the picture to Lord Buchan, a fellow Scot. His lordship, Bruce reported to Copley, "showed it to the most eminent conniseurs, then gave it to Mr. Reynolds, who sent it with his own paintings to the Exhibition." It was identified only as the performance of a young American, and it created a stir among the artists who saw it before opening day. Some held that the identification was mistaken and that it must be the work of Joseph Wright, a portrait painter in Derby who, exhibiting that year for the first time, had two strong works in the show.

West saw and studied a remarkable painting.[1] A young man, dressed in a black suit, yellow waistcoat, and white collar, shown in profile against a red drapery, is sitting at a plain mahogany table. A half-filled glass of water rests on the table before him. Looped over the fingers of his right hand is a gold chain, at the end of which sits a pet squirrel eating a nut. It was a deceptively simple bravura piece in which every component was calculated to demonstrate the artist's skill in composition, realistic detail, and the qualities of the various surfaces — textiles, water, glass, the table top, fur, hair, the skin of the beautifully painted hand. It has been supposed that West at once recognized the work as American because of the American pine on which the canvas was stretched and because of its American squirrel, the easily trained Southern Flying Squirrel (*Glaucomys volans*). It is known that he sought out Captain Bruce, obtained the name and address of the artist, and promised to write to him.

---

[1] It has been called the first American picture expressly painted — as far as is known — for exhibition in Europe. It appeared in the same exhibition with Pratt's *American School*.

THE DEATH OF SOCRATES, ca. 1756. West's first "history picture," a crude pre-
cursor of European neoclassicism, was painted for his early patron, William Henry,
gunsmith and inventor in Lancaster, Pennsylvania. *Private collection.*

THOMAS MIFFLIN, 1758-59. This work, acknowledged as West's finest American portrait, was once attributed to various other artists, including John Wollaston and John Singleton Copley. Mifflin, here shown at age fourteen or fifteen, became a hero of the Revolution and first governor of Pennsylvania. *The Historical Society of Pennsylvania.*

WILLIAM ALLEN, 1763. In this portrait West tried to suggest the qualities of a rich Philadelphia merchant, chief justice of Pennsylvania, trustee of the College of Philadelphia, and founder of Allentown. Allen generously supported West during three years of study in Italy. *Private collection in England.*

APOLLO BELVEDERE. West made this drawing during his stay in Italy, 1760–1763. The Romans considered their *Apollo* a supreme artistic achievement. They regarded young West as an uneducated natural child of the New World. Accordingly, they had placed him before the statue, waiting breathlessly for his response. *Friends Historical Library of Swarthmore College.*

Benjamin West: ANGELICA KAUFFMANN. The two met in Italy and did portraits of each other. A beautiful Swiss girl of twenty-two, talented as a painter and singer, fluent in three languages, Miss Kauffmann became the rage of Rome and London. The critic Anthony Pasquin said of her, "She is perhaps the most fascinating woman in Europe." *Friends Historical Library of Swarthmore College.*

Angelica Kauffmann: BENJAMIN WEST. West had just recovered from a nearly fatal illness when Angelica Kauffmann drew this idealized portrait. There is testimony that she set her cap for West and hoped to marry him. He gave her art lessons but was faithful to Betsy Shewell, his fiancée back in Philadelphia. *National Portrait Gallery, London.*

ANGELICA AND MEDORO, 1763-64. This romantic work excited such attention in Rome that West was hailed as "the American Raphael." It depicts an episode in Ariosto's *Orlando Furioso. University Art Gallery, State University of New York at Binghamton.*

THE REVEREND DR. WILLIAM MARKHAM, ca. 1771, well-to-do headmaster of Westminster School, later Archbishop of York and preceptor to King George III's two oldest sons. Dr. Markham became interested in West and introduced him into influential English circles. *The National Portrait Gallery, London.*

PYLADES AND ORESTES BROUGHT AS VICTIMS BEFORE IPHIGENIA, 1766. This is one of two pictures West painted in 1766 under the rigid tenets of neoclassicism. It was sensationally successful in London. The priestess is about to sentence these captives to death, not knowing one of them is her long-lost brother. *The Tate Gallery.*

AGRIPPINA LANDING AT BRUNDISIUM WITH THE ASHES OF GERMANICUS, 1766–68. West's most-admired neoclassical work was painted for Archbishop Robert Hay Drummond. This is probably the preliminary sketch West did for Dr. Drummond, who so admired the finished picture that he had West show it to the king. *Philadelphia Museum of Art, the George W. Elkins Collection.*

CHARLES WILLSON PEALE, 1767-69. Peale was one of the first in a long and distinguished line of American artists who studied under West in London. *New-York Historical Society.*

Matthew Pratt: BENJAMIN
WEST, 1765. A Philadelphia
portrait-painter, Pratt went to
London expressly to study under
West, whose reputation as a successful artist was spreading in
the American colonies. *Pennsylvania Academy of the Fine
Arts.*

Matthew Pratt: ELIZABETH
SHEWELL WEST, 1764-65.
Pratt accompanied Miss Shewell,
his cousin, from Philadelphia
to London. In this first known
portrait of her, she is revealed
as a composed and poised young
woman with a pretty heart-
shaped face. *Pennsylvania
Academy of the Fine Arts.*

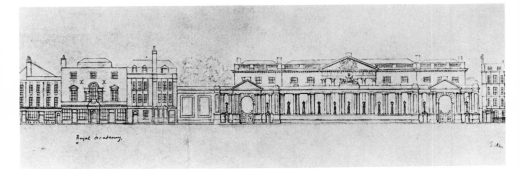

Unknown artist: THE SOUTH SIDE OF PALL MALL shows the first location of the Royal Academy of Art, 1768–1779. The section is now occupied by a row of stately clubs.

THE DEPARTURE OF REGULUS, ca. 1767. This was the first picture West painted for George III. He gave it three main points of interest: Regulus returning to certain death in Carthage rather than break his parole; his friends who have begged him to stay in Rome; his beautiful wife swooning in anguish. *By permission of Her Majesty Queen Elizabeth II.*

SELF-PORTRAIT, 1770–71. West, a prospering artist in London, not yet thirty-three, has come a long way from his beginnings in rural Pennsylvania. He will soon produce his most famous works and become history painter to the king. *National Gallery of Art, Andrew W. Mellon Collection.*

MRS. WEST AND SON RAPHAEL, ca. 1768. In the fashion of the time, West "quoted" an old master in modeling this portrait of his wife and son on Raphael's *Madonnna della Sedia* in Florence. *Reynolda House, Winston-Salem, North Carolina.*

Matthew Pratt: THE AMERICAN SCHOOL, 1765. One of the earliest and most popular of American conversation pieces, this awkward but pleasant work shows West standing, while Pratt, seated on the Chippendale chair at right, listens to his critique. The three other students cannot be identified. *The Metropolitan Museum of Art.*

THE CRICKETERS, 1763. West met William Allen, "the principal of my patrons," in London in 1763, and painted two of his sons in this fine, little-known conversation piece. Shown left to right are James Allen, Ralph Wormeley of Virginia, Andrew Allen, and Ralph Izard and Arthur Middleton, both of South Carolina. The picture, in a private collection in England, has been owned continuously by descendants of the Allen family.

THE GOLDEN AGE, 1776, shows three generations of an Old Testament family. The critic E. P. Richardson wrote in 1975: "It is impossible not to admire in a small picture such as this West's skill as a composer, and his beautiful use of light to create a poetic mood of stillness and contentment." *The Tate Gallery.*

KING GEORGE III, 1779. The king wears the ribbon and star of the Garter and holds the plans for repelling the French fleet off the coast of England. Of this portrait, exhibited in 1780, Horace Walpole wrote, "There is a signpost by West of his Majesty holding the memorial of his late campaign, lest we should forget that he was at Coxheath when the French fleet was in Plymouth Sound." *By Permission of Her Majesty Queen Elizabeth II.*

A VIEW IN WINDSOR GREAT PARK, no date. West did a number of Windsor Park scenes. Since there was little market for landscapes in eighteenth-century England, he did them as "fancy pieces"—works painted solely for the artist's own pleasure. Gainsborough admired his painting of trees. *By permission of Her Majesty Queen Elizabeth II.*

QUEEN CHARLOTTE, 1779. This was the king's favorite portrait of his queen. West twice had to rearrange the children in the background (see detail) when the number rose from eleven to thirteen. He made the queen prettier and taller than she actually was. *By permission of Her Majesty Queen Elizabeth II.*

A detail from QUEEN CHARLOTTE.

Above:

THE DEATH OF GENERAL WOLFE, 1770. This early application of the principles of history painting to reportage of a current event "excited a great sensation" and led to Europe's first best-selling print. The picture has been called "the first Pietà of nationalism." *The National Gallery of Canada, Ottawa. Gift of the Duke of Westminster. 1918.*

Left:

Guiseppe Ceracchi: BUST OF SIR JOSHUA REYNOLDS, 1788. Sir Joshua, President of the Royal Academy, objected to contemporary dress in sculpture and history painting done in the grand manner, and he tried to dissuade West from using it in *The Death of Wolfe. Royal Academy of Arts.*

UNA AND THE LION, 1772. West extended history painting to subjects taken from early English literature—in this example, from Spenser's *Faerie Queene*. Una, the heroine personifying Truth (and perhaps Protestantism), sets out to rescue her royal parents, who are being besieged by a dragon; she is protected by this charming lion. *Courtesy of the Wadsworth Atheneum, Hartford.*

Paul Sandby: THE RIVER FRONT OF OLD SOMERSET HOUSE. From 1771 to 1779 the Royal Academy was domiciled in the original Somerset House, built ca. 1547 by Edward Seymour, Duke of Somerset, "the Protector."

COLONEL GUY JOHNSON, 1776. Johnson succeeded his uncle and father-in-law, Sir William Johnson, as superintendent of Indian Affairs in North America in 1774. He and the Mohawk chief (thought to be Joseph Brant) led the Iroquois in frontier warfare against the Americans during the Revolution. *National Gallery of Art, Andrew W. Mellon Collection.*

WILLIAM PENN'S TREATY WITH THE INDIANS, 1771. West's second great popular success came soon after his *Death of Wolfe*; the engraving sold even more widely than that of *Wolfe*. West's father stands in the group at left (with lighted face); his half brother is recognizable as the figure just left of Penn. *The Pennsylvania Academy of the Fine Arts.*

THE ARTIST'S FAMILY, 1772. John West and his eldest son, paying their first visit to Mrs. West on the birth of her second child, sit in silent meditation before offering up a prayer. Young Raphael stands at the left, the artist at the right. Charles Robert Leslie, West's pupil, called the picture "a happy treatment of The Ages of Man." *From the collection of Mr. and Mrs. Paul Mellon.*

John Singleton Copley: THE COPLEY FAMILY, 1776–77. The artist, who had never painted a composed group in America, did this ingenious composition some two years after arriving in England. Copley stands behind Richard Clarke, his father-in-law. His son, the future Lord Lyndhurst, embraces his mother. *National Gallery of Art, Andrew W. Mellon Fund, 1961.*

Johann Zoffany: THE ACADEMICIANS OF THE ROYAL ACADEMY, 1771-72. The members are grouped under candlelight in the Life School in Old Somerset House. Angelica Kauffmann and Mary Moser are represented by portraits on the wall. *By permission of Her Majesty Queen Elizabeth II.*

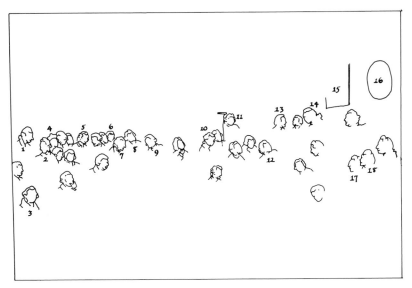

KEY
1. Giovanni Cipriani; 2. Benjamin West; 3. Johann Zoffany; 4. a visiting Chinese artist; 5. Paul Sandby; 6. John Richards; 7. Francis Newton; 8. Sir William Chambers; 9. Sir Joshua Reynolds; 10. Francesco Bartolozzi; 11. Richard Wilson; 12. Francesco Zuccarelli; 13. Edward Penny; 14. George Michael Moser; 15. Angelica Kauffmann; 16. Mary Moser; 17. Joseph Nollekens; 18. Richard Cosway.

Thomas Malton: THE STRAND FRONT OF NEW SOMERSET HOUSE, 1780. The Royal Academy moved into "the Fine Rooms" of William Chambers' Somerset House in 1780. An arch in the Palladian facade (right, between the carriages) led from the Strand to the entrance hall. The Fine Rooms have recently been restored as they were in the early nineteenth century. From Thomas Malton's *Picturesque Tour through the Cities of London and Westminster, 1792.*

George Scharf: ENTRANCE HALL OF THE ROYAL ACADEMY, SOMERSET HOUSE, 1836. The hall, about 25 feet square, leads to the elliptical staircase and the stairwell used to hoist pictures to the galleries above. The Academy still owns the casts, including the huge Hercules in the rear. *British Museum.*

Gilbert Stuart: PORTRAIT OF BENJAMIN WEST, 1780–81. Stuart worked five years in West's studio (1777–1782), and his first success as an exhibitor came with this first of two portraits he painted of his teacher. *National Portrait Gallery, London.*

Copley first heard from returning travelers that his picture was a triumph in London, that Joshua Reynolds and Benjamin West admired it, and that West would do anything in his power to help the artist and intended to write to him. On October 13, 1766, in the first contact of what was to be a fateful association, Copley wrote to West:

> This testimony of your goodness . . . has my most grateful acknowledgments . . . It would [give] me the greatest pleasure imaginable to have . . . a letter from one of whom I entertain so high an opinion, as an artist engaged in the same studies with myself, and esteem as my countryman, from whom America receives the same luster that Italy does from her Titiano and Divine Raphael.
>
> It seems almost needless to say how great my desire is to enter into a correspondence with you, as it is very obvious that the pleasure and advantages would be very great on my side.

He asked West to receive his next picture, as "I have no friend else that I am certain would give themselves the trouble of sending it to the exhibition, unless you would be kind enough to take that trouble upon yourself."

In the meantime, Bruce had written to Copley on August 4, the two letters crossing. He reported on the extraordinary acclaim the *Boy with a Squirrel* had received. "I have begged Mr. West to be copious in his criticisms and advices to you. Mr. Reynolds would have also wrote to you but his time is too valuable . . . Mr. West seems sincerely disposed to be your friend. Mr. Reynolds is too busy and too great a man to be active for you, though he is also much disposed to serve you." Reynolds had praised the picture:

> He says of it, "that in any collection of painting it will pass for an excellent picture, but considering the disadvantages [I told him] you had laboured under, that *it was a very wonderful performance.*" "That it exceeded any portrait that Mr. West ever drew." "That he did not know one painter at home who had all the advantages that Europe could give them, that could equal it, and that if you are capable of producing such a piece by the mere efforts of your own genius, with the advantages of the example and instruction which you could have in Europe, you would be a valuable acquisition to the Art, and one of the first painters in the world, provided you could receive those aids before it was too late in life, and before your manner and taste were corrupted or fixed by working in your little way at Boston . . .

With his own letter, Bruce enclosed one from West to Copley — a letter notable for generous sentiments, artistic perception, and ingeniously creative spelling. West assumed that Copley, as a painter who had made great progress in the art, would be most interested in comments on his work from those in the profession, "and as I am here in the midst of the painting world, I have the greater opportunity of hearing them." He explained at length the general critical opinion, and his own, that the *Boy with a Squirrel* had too hard a line, too great a precision in the outline of the figures and objects depicted. He advised Copley to send over another painting in his care and "you may be sure it shall have the greatest justice done to it." Like Reynolds, he urged Copley to study in Europe. "Nothing is wanting to perfect you now but a sight of what has been done by the great masters, and if you could make a visit to Europe for this purpose for three or four years, you would find yourself then in possession of what will be highly valuable. If ever you should make a visit to Europe you may depend on my friendship in any way that's in my power to serve." Copley replied on November 12. He would endeavor, he said, to avoid too great precision in the outline of the next picture he sent over.

> In this country as you rightly observe there are no examples of art, except what is to be met with in a few prints indifferently executed, from which it is not possible to learn much . . .
> It would give me inexpressible pleasure to make a trip to Europe . . . I was almost tempted the last year to take a tour to Philadelphia, and that chiefly to see some of your pictures, which I am informed are there. I think myself peculiarly unlucky in living in a place into which there has not been one portrait brought that is worthy to be called a picture within my memory, which leaves me at a great loss to guess the style that you, Mr. Reynolds, and the other artists practice.

While these letters were being exchanged, West proposed Copley as a Fellow of the Society of Artists; he was elected in September 1766, the honor being slightly clouded by the recording of his name as William Copeley. In February 1767 Copley shipped a second picture to West, a portrait titled *Young Lady with a Bird and Dog* (now generally known as *Mary Warner*) and suffered through a five-month delay before he could learn how it was received. "Mr. West did it all justice," Bruce wrote him, "having the principal direction of placing the pictures." The reception was mixed; the execution was admired but the subject — an unpleasant, simpering child with a head too large for its body — was "universally condemned." Bruce wrote:

Mr. Reynolds . . . says "your drawing is wonderfully correct, but that a something is wanting in your colouring." I begged him to explain it, that I might communicate it to you, but he told me "that it was impossible to convey what he meant by words, but that he was sure (by what you have already produced) he could make you instantly feel it by example, if you was here." . . .

Mr. West seems much your friend, and would be useful to you if you come to Europe. He is making great progress in History-Painting, and produced some capital pieces this year. He is at the same time a very agreeable amiable young man . . .

The artists depend on another exhibition from you next year. They already put you on a footing with all the portrait painters except Mr. Reynolds. If you have been able to attain this unassisted at Boston, what might you not achieve in Europe?

West wrote a long and earnest analysis of the second picture. He had been delayed in answering Mr. Copley's last letter, he began, because he had "been so much engaged in the study of his business, in particular that of history painting, which demands the greatest care and intelligence in history imaginable." He thought Mr. Copley's *Young Lady* was the better in execution, though not in subject.

Your picture is in possession of drawing to a correctness that is very surprising, and of coloring very brilliant, though this brilliancy is somewhat misapplied, as for instance, the gown [is] too bright for the flesh, which overcame it in brilliancy. This made the [artists] criticise the shadows of the flesh without knowing from whence this defect arose; and so in like manner the dog and carpet [were] too conspicuous for accessory things, and a little want of propriety in the background.[2]

These were criticisms he would not make if Mr. Copley's pictures were not "very nigh upon a footing with the first artists who now paint, and my being sensible that observations of this nature in a friendly way to a man of your talents must not be disagreeable."

I hope I shall have the pleasure of seeing you in Europe, where you will have an opportunity of contemplating the great productions of art, and feel from them what words cannot express. For this is a source the want of which (I am sensible of) cannot be

---

[2] Alfred Frankenstein in *The World of Copley* comments: "The defects of one era often become the virtues of another, and our own time relishes precisely the same quality of emphasis in a painting that struck West and his contemporaries as a serious flaw. The 20th century believes, as Henri Matisse once put it, that every part of a picture must work as hard as every other part."

had in America; and if you should ever come to London my house is at your service, or if you should incline to go for Italy, if you think letters from me can be of any service, there are many at your service.

The *Boy with a Squirrel* had been returned to Reynolds' studio; Captain Bruce reclaimed it and took it to West's, "where I think it had better remain as a specimen till you arrive yourself to dispose of it... I wish it was convenient for you to paint your next exhibition picture at the house of Mr. West, where you would be very welcome, and where you would receive some assistance. I should think your business at Boston could not, at any rate, suffer much by a year or two's absence, and the expense would not amount to much."

In 1767 Copley seemed very much disposed to go to Europe. He was sobered by the reception of his second picture; it told him that he must study the old masters and receive personal instruction if he was to stand in the front rank of the great artists of the age. His next letter, undated and unaddressed, could have been written only to West or Captain Bruce:

> Subjects are not so easily procured in this place. A taste for painting is too much wanting to afford any kind of help; and was it not for preserving the resemblance of particular persons, painting would not be known in this place. The people generally regard it no more than any other useful trade, as they sometimes term it, like that of a carpenter, tailor or shoemaker, not as one of the most noble arts in the world. Which is not a little mortifying to me. While the arts are so disregarded I can hope for nothing, either to encourage or assist me in my studies but what I receive from a thousand leagues distance. Be my improvements what they will, I shall not be benefitted by them in this country, neither in point of fortune or fame.

To West he wrote, "Your friendly invitation to your house, and your offer to propose me as a member of the Society, are matters which I shall long remember."

8

The Visible Instrument

Gentlemen,

An Academy, in which the Polite Arts may be regularly cultivated, is at last opened among us by Royal Munificence. This
must appear an event in the highest degree interesting, not only
to the Artists but to the whole nation.

> JOSHUA REYNOLDS,
> inaugural address on the opening
> of the Royal Academy,
> January 2, 1769

ROBERT HAY DRUMMOND'S GRANDFATHER was Robert Harley, Lord Oxford, lord high treasurer under Queen Anne, one
of England's greatest collectors of books and manuscripts, and be-
getter of the Harleian Library in the British Museum. Jonathan Swift
mentioned Robert Drummond's birth in 1711 in his *Journal to Stella;*
the poet Matthew Prior escorted him when he was six to Westminster School. After graduating from Christ Church, Oxford, he made
a four-year grand tour of Europe, from which he returned (his uncle
reported to Swift) not only "untainted but much improved." He
rejected a career in the army to take holy orders; Queen Caroline
made him a royal chaplain. In 1753 he appeared before the Privy
Council to defend a bishop and two companions charged with having drunk the health of the Stuart Pretender, and when he obtained
their acquittal, George II remarked, "He is indeed a man to make
a friend of." He preached the sermon at the coronation of George
III and Queen Charlotte in 1761 and became the young king's lord
high almoner (distributor of the royal alms). When he was made
archbishop of York the same year, Horace Walpole observed that
he was "a man of parts and of the world" and "a dignified and accomplished prelate." His Grace had humor and an affable manner;
his hospitality was generous and convivial.

Here, obviously, was a sophisticated man of wealth, power, and influence — a man who could choose his company with discrimination from a large circle, who had no reason to spend evenings with anyone who bored him. It speaks well for Benjamin West that the archbishop took a liking to him and his work and frequently invited him to dinner. (It was common practice in the eighteenth century, in all levels of society, for a man to spend a social evening in company without his wife.) His Grace from time to time brought up a subject that certainly was not displeasing to West — the fame that persons and families might achieve by patronizing the arts.

One evening Archbishop Drummond spoke of an episode in Roman history that he felt would make a splendid picture: an example of courage, conjugal devotion, and noble conduct in the face of injustice and tyranny. He sent one of his sons to his library to fetch volume three of the *Annals* of Tacitus, and from it he had the son read — probably by sight translation — the pathetic story of Agrippina. As the wife of Germanicus, who was the nephew and adopted son of the Emperor Tiberius, she accompanied her husband on his military campaigns in Germany, and when his legions mutinied, she distinguished herself for bravery. Germanicus had such success in Germany that Tiberius, fearing him as a possible rival, ordered him to a distant post in western Asia, where he died in his thirty-fourth year. Agrippina and her friends were convinced that he had been poisoned by order of Tiberius. Tacitus described the arrival of Agrippina with her husband's ashes at Brundisium (Brindisi) on the Adriatic:

> As soon as the fleet was seen on the horizon, not only the harbour and the adjacent shores, but the city walls too and the roofs and every place which commanded the most distant prospect were filled with crowds of mourners, who incessantly asked one another, whether, when she landed, they were to receive her in silence or with some utterance of emotion . . . The fleet slowly approached, its crew, not joyous as is usual, but wearing all a studied expression of grief. When Agrippina descended from the vessel with her two children, clasping the funeral urn, with her eyes riveted to the earth, there was one universal groan.

Agrippina returned overland to Rome and there called for justice; an inquiry was held but it never determined the cause of her husband's death.[1]

---

[1] Tiberius exiled Agrippina and her children to an island off the coast of southern Italy, where she died in A.D. 33, possibly at Tiberius' command. Her son Caligula succeeded Tiberius as emperor; her daughter became the mother of the Emperor Nero.

Drummond proposed to West that he paint this scene, commenting on it at some length to convey an idea of the way he thought the subject should be treated. West returned home in a state of excitement and immediately began to make a sketch for the picture. Working with subdued colors, mostly blues and grays, he chose that moment when Agrippina, followed by her attendants in procession, her head bowed, her children clutching her robe, lands on the wharf at Brundisium. He modeled his figures on those in an ancient frieze he had seen at the Uffizi Gallery in Florence, a fragment from the *Ara Pacis* monument in Rome. Across the background he placed architectural elements dominated by the palace of the Emperor Diocletian at Spalato (present-day Split) on the Dalmatian coast, which he knew from Robert Adam's recently published book on that subject. West recalled a drawing Gavin Hamilton had made in Rome on Agrippina's arrival at Brundisium, and from it he borrowed some details. His treatment of the whole, however, was considerably more daring and ambitious than Hamilton's.

The next morning he carried his sketch to Archbishop Drummond's palace. His Grace, West said, "was equally surprised and delighted to find his own conception so soon embodied in visible form," and he requested him to execute the picture without delay.

West proceeded to paint a trial version, oil on paper, later mounted on canvas, about 13-1/2 by 19 inches in size. *The Landing of Agrippina at Brundisium with the Ashes of Germanicus* was a considerable advance over any history painting he had done, and it was his first work truly in the neoclassical style according to the precepts of Winckelmann and Mengs. Some modern critics believe it to be a good deal more than that. James Flexner calls it the first complete expression of a type of neoclassicism that was to spring up all over Europe. To Allen Staley it is a picture important not only because it stands as a major early monument in the rise of neoclassical taste, but also because West's concern with the accurate reconstruction of past events anticipated what was to become a leading obsession of nineteenth-century painting. Frederick Cummings writes of it, "His concern was to recreate not only the air of antiquity but its actuality. He achieved this through the techniques of research and archeological investigation and applied the knowledge gained to the re-creation in his art of the apparatus of antiquity." A modern viewer who knows who these people are, what they are doing and why, may feel in this picture a haunting sense of place and time. E. P. Richardson believes that "the grandeur and solemnity of the conception strike an observer today, as they did in the eighteenth century. The color is excellent, the chiaroscuro interesting." Robert

Rosenblum holds that the picture has the quality of "almost a photographic image on an event in Roman history."

Archbishop Drummond was pleased with his finished *Agrippina* and with the favorable response of those to whom he showed it. The earl of Exeter, with his consent, commissioned West to paint a replica. The engravers Valentine Green and Richard Earlom began the long, slow work of producing a print. And Drummond used the picture as the basis for a campaign to raise 3000 guineas in subscriptions so that the artist could forego the "drudgery" of portrait painting and devote his talents to historical subjects. His Grace was chagrined by the cool reception his proposal met with; he could raise only £1500 from patrons, and so he and the others who had exerted themselves in the undertaking for Mr. West agreed to drop it. The failure to support the work of living genius, Drummond felt, cast a stigma on the country and the age; he declared that he would now seek the patronage of the king, in the hope that his example might create a taste for the fine arts in Britain.

The time was not propitious to approach the king; he was sorely troubled by the problems of governing a riot-prone country. He had ended decades of rule by the Whigs, but now, having unwillingly recalled William Pitt as first minister, he found that Pitt had poor health and never appeared at court. He was at the height of his war with John Wilkes, author of seditious libels against him. Wilkes had been expelled from Parliament, fled to France to escape imprisonment, and now was back in London, re-elected to Parliament, the idol of the street mobs, again publishing his libels. In 1768 the king's troops put down a London riot with bloodshed, loss of life, and added public outrage because the troops were Scots. In addition to all this, the American Colonies were challenging the authority of king and Parliament, and what was even worse, their challenge was being supported by influential Englishmen.

Archbishop Drummond was a leading member of the party out of favor at court, but he relied in his approach on his personal relationship with the king and on the king's love for the arts. George III spoke and wrote three languages fluently; he was widely read and was collecting a library that eventually would total 67,000 volumes and become the glory of the British Museum. The architect William Chambers had tutored him in the understanding of architecture; the artists George Michael Moser and Joshua Kirby had taught him drawing and perspective. Drummond also relied on his knowledge that the king's taste in art very closely resembled his own; they both favored history paintings that inculcated in the viewer a greater respect for virtue, morality, and courage, and a deeper love of country.

He went to court at the earliest opportunity, and when it was his turn to have the king's ear, told him the story of Benjamin West and his splendid painting *Agrippina.* The king, his curiosity aroused, said he would send for the artist and his picture. Drummond conveyed the happy news to his protégé, and very shortly thereafter a Mr. Barnard, one of the king's retainers, called on West and requested him to attend the king the next morning with his picture. Barnard lingered long enough to describe his master. The king, he said, "was a young man of great simplicity and candour of disposition, sedate in his affections, and deeply impressed with the sanctity of principle; scrupulous in forming private friendships; but when he had taken any attachment, not easily swayed from it, without being convinced of the necessity and propriety of so doing."

Charles Peale remembered and recorded something of the excitement of that day and of West's departure the next morning. Everyone, of course, whatever his ambitions, hoped to attract the king's attention at court; that was the best of all possible roads to recognition and preferment.[2] But a private audience was a rare and special privilege for any subject, and especially for an artist, whose future depended on patronage in high places. West was attired in court dress. He had somewhere procured and was wearing a sword, one chosen very carefully, because, as he explained to Peale, it was essential that he seem "to belong to the higher orders of society." He carried his *Agrippina,* securely wrapped, under his arm. Someone — Barnard or Drummond — had clearly instructed him in the etiquette to be followed in the presence of the king. His Majesty was always to speak first, and he always chose the subject of conversation. One's first sentences were accompanied by "May it please Your Majesty." One might then say "Your Majesty" several times, after which it was permitted to say "Sir." One did not say "Sire," for that was a mistranslation of the French *Sieur.* The queen was also to be addressed as "Your Majesty" and then as "Ma'am," pronounced "Mawm." Both were always to be addressed in the third person, never as "you." One never disagreed with or contradicted Their Majesties, and they were never to be touched, except if they extended a hand to be kissed. One always remained standing,

---

[2] Richard Dalton, the king's agent in Italy, had clearly indicated that he would obtain the monarch's favor for West, and he had commissioned him to paint a small picture for the king. Dalton had returned to England and to his post as librarian and keeper of pictures in His Majesty's household; but there is, curiously enough, no report of any significant association between Dalton and West in England, no evidence of help given, and no record of the picture West painted for the king.

no matter how long. If there was a crowd in the room, all conversation ceased when the king entered, and voices were to be kept thereafter at a whisper. The king determined the length of a conversation or an audience; when the time was up he would bow or say, "I will not detain you longer." When departing, one kept the face toward the king, never turning the back, continuing to bow while retreating, until out of the room.

West presented himself at Buckingham House, at the head of St. James's Park, and was ushered into an anteroom, where he unwrapped his picture and waited. This was the former town residence of the dukes of Buckingham, which the king had bought in 1762 and was furnishing with pieces he was buying or was transferring from the other palaces, chiefly on the advice of William Chambers.[3] The king entered and after a few words of greeting and inquiry, he spent some time looking at the picture, silently but, West felt, with apparent satisfaction. He was a rather tall man, well formed, weighing almost 200 pounds. His complexion was ruddy, his eyebrows blond, his expression open, and he moved with some grace and dignity. He was the fortunate possessor of a feature much valued in the eighteenth century, a well-turned sturdy leg that "filled the stocking." He had a slight speech impediment, or rather, "a hurry of his utterance," and he commonly ended his sentences with a quick "What? What? What?" or "Eh? Eh?" West was to notice that he pulled at his eyebrows when he was perplexed.

Was the picture in the proper light? the king asked. West replied that the light was perhaps not the most advantageous, if it please Your Majesty. The king conducted him through several apartments in search of a better light, chose a place, called the servants, and actually helped them to move the picture. He looked at it again for some time. He then left the room, indicating that West was to wait.

He returned with the queen and presented West to her. Charlotte was small, young (twenty-three), and very plain; she was thin and pale, and she had a wide mouth that has been passed down to many of her descendants. She had been a princess from a minor north German duchy, Mecklenburg-Strelitz, and she was pregnant with the fifth of the fifteen children she was to bear the king in the first twenty-two years of her marriage. West thought that her manner

---

[3] It stood on the site of and was later incorporated into Buckingham Palace. The king disliked nearby St. James's Palace, calling it "a dust trap," and he used it only for conducting business and for state occasions. He closed down Hampton Court permanently because of his unhappy memory of the quarrels there between his father and grandfather.

was gracious. As she examined the picture, the king observed that the subject had seldom been properly treated. West replied that it was indeed surprising that Poussin had not done so. The king proceeded to tell the queen the story of Agrippina, dwelling at last on the circumstance that Mr. West had produced the sketch overnight. He turned briskly to West and said, "There is another noble Roman subject which corresponds to this one, and I believe it also has never been well painted. I mean the final departure of Regulus from Rome. Would it not make a fine picture?"

West may or may not have heard of Regulus before that moment, but he agreed that it was undoubtedly a magnificent subject. "Then," said the king, "you shall paint it for me." He rang a bell and ordered an attendant to bring the seventeenth volume of Livy's *History of Rome*. Archbishop Drummond, he said to the queen, had made one of his sons read to Mr. West, but "I will read to him myself on the subject of my picture." He then translated the epic tale of patriotic Roman courage and heroic martyrdom. Marcus Atilius Regulus, Roman general and consul in the First Punic War, at first successful against the Carthaginians, was defeated in 255 B.C. and taken prisoner. When he was sent to Rome on parole to negotiate a peace or an exchange of prisoners, he urged the Senate to reject both proposals, even though it meant that he must return to Carthage and certain death, and he refused the pleadings of family, friends, and the senators to break his parole and stay in Rome. On returning to Carthage, he was put to death by torture. The king commanded West to return with the sketch as soon as possible. When he departed, West felt that he had experienced "something that might be described as friendliness."

He prepared a sketch for *Regulus Leaving Rome*, Charles Peale posing for Regulus at the moment of his departure with the Carthaginian envoys to a ship in the harbor. He went again to Buckingham House, placed his work on a chair, and waited. The king entered and at a glance said, "Ah, West, I see you have chosen the Doric order for the buildings. That is my favorite order of architecture." They discussed the picture at length, West being restrained by the rule that the monarch was not to be contradicted in any expression of opinion. The king led him to what was called the Warm Room in one of the principal apartments and there showed him a space on a wall, 7 feet, 4 inches by 10 feet, that the picture should fill. West could not have failed to see that there were two other empty matching panels in the room.

During the months he was painting *Regulus*, West was invited from time to time to spend the evening at Buckingham House, where the king often detained him as late as eleven o'clock. They reviewed the fifty-odd drawings he made for *Regulus* and spent much time discussing the best way to promote the study of fine arts in England. George III was a young man with no intimate friends (he had recently broken with Lord Bute, his mentor); he had vexing cares on his mind, with new and worse problems arising every week, with politicians nibbling away at him throughout the day. He seemed to find pleasure in the company of this American artist of his own age, a free common man with an exotic past, whose chief concerns were to elevate the artist to a position of dignity and to use art as a vehicle for improving mankind.

The newspapers at that time were carrying stories about dissension in the Society of Artists, and in one of their conversations the king asked West what was happening. There was a great deal to tell, and West, as a director, was well able to tell it. The meetings of the Society were torn by arguments and animosities — over the right to the best places for hanging pictures, the distribution of tickets to the exhibition, the way funds were to be spent, and, above all, who was to control and run the Society. Unfortunately, there were not proper restrictions on the number and qualifications of those who could join, and the organization had risen to an unmanageable 211 members. The newer artists, some of them with little talent, had formed a cabal to take control from the very men who had founded the Society and were its most distinguished ornaments. (The cabal claimed that it represented a majority of the membership and that the Society was being run by a "tyrannical faction" of twenty-four self-perpetuating directors who refused to retire or be replaced.) The rebels were so obnoxious that Richard Dalton, the Society's treasurer, wrote of "malicious dark spirits" at work in the Society and resigned his office. At the latest meeting, a large majority had voted for a law that would require the election of eight new directors annually. This the incumbent directors were refusing to obey.

The king deliberated a while on this information and then told West that he would gladly serve as patron to any new association of artists that would be better suited to improve the arts in peace and harmony. West hurried with this earth-shaking news to his friends in the artistic community. A group of unhappy Society members had been meeting secretly in the fall of 1768 at the home of Joseph Wilton, a sculptor, and West made his report to them. It developed that the king had voiced pretty much the same views to William Chambers, the architect, who had dominated the Society since its founding but was now facing a rebellion. A committee of four was appointed to find ways to take advantage of the king's proposal: West, Chambers, George Michael Moser, and

Francis Cotes. Chambers had a Swedish background; had traveled to China, obtained the patronage of the king's mother, built for her the famous pagoda in Kew Gardens, wrote *A Treatise of Civil Architecture,* tutored the king when he was Prince of Wales, and designed the magnificent state coach used at the king's coronation.[4] Moser was an elderly Swiss-born medalist and engraver who had come early to England; he was the country's best chaser in gold, a close friend of Joshua Reynolds and one of the principal figures of St. Martin's Lane Academy. He spoke English with considerable difficulty.[5] Cotes, a rival of Reynolds, had just painted the queen and two of the princesses.

At the king's request, the four prepared a paper describing the dissension in the Society and its causes. All four signed it and carried it to the king; Cotes presented it for the committee. His answer, West recalled, was "gracious and approving." He asked them to act in secrecy, for fear that some political use might be made of the matter. Events moved fast in the next two months.

October 8, 1768: Seven members of the cabal called a meeting at the Castle Tavern in Covent Garden to choose a slate of directors to be put forth "who will consider the general interests of the Society."

October 18: At a general meeting of the Society, the cabal removed the president and sixteen directors, replacing them by others from their own numbers. They removed Francis M. Newton as secretary and as president elected their own man, Joshua Kirby, the expert on perspective. West was one of the eight directors retained in office, but word was circulating that these would be replaced at the next election.

November 10: West and the seven other retained directors signed and sent a letter of resignation to the Society. In a second letter to Joshua Kirby they wrote that they had the highest regard for him, but that "the ungenerous treatment which we ... have met with from the Caballers, and their obstinacy in still continuing to insult us ... render it impossible for us to continue in office with any degree of decency." All eight members were marked "expelled" on the Society's books.

November 28: The four-man committee presented to their fellow artists a memorial to be sent to the king. It solicited His Majesty's "gracious assistance, patronage and protection" in executing a "use-

---

[4] The coach was featured in June 1977 in the procession celebrating the twenty-fifth anniversary of Queen Elizabeth's accession to the throne.

[5] He is remembered for interrupting Oliver Goldsmith with the words, "Stay, stay, Tochtor Shonson is going to say something!"

ful plan" for "establishing a society for promoting the Arts of Design," being sensible that every establishment of that nature "must
be ineffectual without the Royal influence." The two principal
objectives were to found an academy for use of students in the arts,
and to hold an annual exhibition "open to all artists of distinguished merit." It was felt that the profits of the exhibitions would
make the academy self-supporting and even permit distribution
"somewhat in useful charities"; but it was hoped that if the profits
were too small, His Majesty would "not deem that expense ill-
applied which may be found necessary to support so useful an
institution." Benjamin West signed the memorial first and twenty-
one other artists followed.[6] Chambers carried the document to the
king, who told him he regarded the welfare of the arts as a matter
of national concern and promised to be a patron, protector, and
supporter of the new endeavor.

On the king's order, Chambers began to draw up an "Instrument
of Foundation" setting forth the principles, rules of conduct, and
by-laws of the proposed organization. It was to be named The Royal
Academy of Arts in London. Membership was limited to forty
Royal Academicians: painters, sculptors, and architects, men of
fair moral characters, of high reputation in their several professions,
at least twenty-five years of age, and not members of any other
society of artists established in London. The king would name the
original forty members; thereafter vacancies would be filled once
each year by election from among the artists who had exhibited.
A president was to be elected annually. There was to be an elected
secretary (paid sixty pounds a year); a treasurer appointed by the
king; part-time staff professors for a school; and an elected keeper,
who would supervise the classes, manage the servants, provide the
living models, and "be constantly at hand to preserve order and
decorum," especially among the students. Classes were to be free
to the students. New laws and regulations, and expulsion of any
member who became "obnoxious," must first be approved by the
king.

West proposed that engravers be admitted to full membership,
but in the debate that followed, the consensus, expressed most
forcefully by Richard Dalton, was that engravers were merely

---

[6] One of those who signed was Miss Angelica Kauffmann, who had come to
London as the protégée of the wife of the profligate ambassador John Murray.
Lady Wentworth (she retained her premarital title) had declined to accompany
her husband when he was transferred from Venice to Turkey, and, returning to
London and Charles Street, she brought Angelica with her, promising that she
would make her fortune in England. Angelica had joined the Society of Artists
and was becoming a favorite of the artistic and fashionable world.

mechanics, working in an inferior branch of the arts that was purely imitative and required no powers of thought or conception. The motion to exclude engravers was passed, and the engravers were in a fury of anger at the slight. (They remained so for the next fifty years.) Robert Strange, one of the best and one of the angriest, wrote in a fierce pamphlet in 1775, "It is a justice due to the ingenious Mr. West to acquit him of having had any share in this proceeding. This gentleman warmly opposed the motion: he entered into the merits of the profession. But his endeavours were to no purpose, and the measure was carried against him."

Chambers "seemed inclined to be president" of the Academy, according to West's later recollection, but he was an architect and there was general agreement that the president should be a painter. Joshua Reynolds had stayed aloof from both the Society and the secessionists and had attended none of the meetings at Wilton's house. His pre-eminent position in English art, however, was such that he was the almost unanimous choice, if he was willing to accept and if the king approved him.

December 7: Chambers carried the Instrument of Foundation to the king, who reviewed it line by line, approved it in principle, and suggested several particular changes. He asked that nominations for members, officers, and staff be given to him on the morning of December 10. He disliked Reynolds and had refused to buy his pictures or give him portrait commissions, but he acceded to the artists' wish that Reynolds become the first president. In the blank space left for the name of the treasurer he wrote that of William Chambers, Esquire.

December 9: Some thirty artists were summoned to a dinner meeting at Wilton's house, where they were to receive the Instrument of Foundation, make the nominations, and welcome Joshua Reynolds as their president. In the course of the day, however, George Moser and his colleague, Edward Penny, called on West in a state of perturbation. Chambers had sent them to bring Reynolds to the meeting, but now for some reason they could not comprehend, he had decided not to attend.

West went immediately to 47 Leicester Square. He found that Reynolds was reluctant to become involved in the affair and that he was surprised and dubious that it had progressed so far. Joshua Kirby, he said, had assured him that there was no truth to the rumor that a new organization, a rival to the Society of Artists, would be successfully founded. Kirby, indeed, had just declared to his members in his inaugural address that the king intended to support the Society and would visit its annual exhibition. Reynolds had concluded, therefore, that it would be unwise to join a group that had no royal sanction for what it was doing — that was acting on a delusion which would come to nothing.

West spent some two hours telling Reynolds all that had been done to create the Academy and trying to persuade him to go to the meeting. He at last prevailed on him to order his carriage, make an appearance at Wilton's, and see for himself whether Kirby or West was correct. They arrived very late. When they entered the crowded room, the artists hailed and welcomed Reynolds as their president. He seemed to be much affected by their reception and thanked them for their approbation. Then he declined to accept the office; he wished first to ask the advice of his friends Edmund Burke and Dr. Samuel Johnson. The company was greatly disappointed — especially West and Cotes, who the next morning were to have presented a complete list of officers to the king.

December 10: The final Instrument of Foundation was presented to the king at St. James's Palace; it was inscribed on both sides of two very large sheets and bore the names of thirty-six Royal Academicians, Joshua Reynolds appearing first, Benjamin West second, Thomas Gainsborough seventh. Ten were foreign-born. Two women were named: Angelica Kauffmann and Mary Moser, painter of flower pieces and daughter of George Michael Moser.[7] The king wrote at the end of page four, "I approve of this plan; let it be put in execution. George R."

West and Cotes made their excuses to the king and asked for more time in which to name the officers. A fortnight later, having consulted Dr. Johnson and Mr. Burke, Reynolds accepted the presidency, and the names of the officers and staff were sent to the king for approval. Newton became the secretary, Moser the keeper, West one of nine visitors (part-time staff professors).

In the course of these events, West finished his *Regulus* and went to Buckingham House to present it. While the king and queen were studying the picture, one of the pages announced that Mr. Joshua Kirby was without, waiting His Majesty's command. The king consulted the queen in German about the propriety of allowing him to enter at that moment, West remembering just enough of his Pennsylvania Dutch to understand that they ordered the visitor to be admitted. Oddly enough, he had never met Kirby, despite the

---

[7] A critic observed that Miss Moser was admitted to the Academy "by painting a sublime picture of a plate of gooseberries." She and Angelica Kauffmann were the only women Academicians for the next 150 years, until the early 1920s, when several women became Associate Members. It was understood that Miss Moser and Miss Kauffmann would not actually attend Academy meetings, for that would be indelicate. They would send in their vote for members and officers by mail or by proxy.

respect expressed for him in the letter of resignation signed on November 10, and he was pleased at the opportunity to become acquainted with a man whose writing on art he admired. As he recalled the story years later, Kirby had continued to use a freedom of manner he had enjoyed as the king's tutor, and now he blundered into an indiscretion.

The king directed Kirby's attention to *Regulus*, which was leaning against a chair, and asked his opinion of it. Kirby praised the work highly, commending especially the perspective, and asked who had painted it. The king introduced West. Kirby said, "Your Majesty never mentioned anything of this work to me." A look of displeasure crossed the king's face, but he remained silent. Kirby asked, "Who made this frame?"

West, a bit uneasy at this development, mentioned the name. Kirby said somewhat sharply, "That person is not Your Majesty's workman." He named the king's carver and gilder. "It ought to have been made by him."

The king said, not unpleasantly, "Kirby, whenever you are able to paint me a picture like this, your friend shall make the frame."

Kirby said to West, "I hope you intend to exhibit the picture." West replied that it had been painted for His Majesty and the exhibition of it must depend on his pleasure. He had intended, however, to ask permission for that purpose.

George R.: "Assuredly, I shall be happy to let the work be shown to the public."

Kirby: "Then, Mr. West, you will send it to my exhibition."

George R.: "No, it must go to my exhibition — the Royal Academy."

It was the first time poor Kirby heard that name. A few days earlier he had assured Reynolds and the Society of Artists that no such institution was to be formed. Now he turned pale, begged to be excused, bowed, and departed.

The first General Assembly and dinner of the Royal Academy was held on January 2, 1769, at its temporary headquarters at the southeast end of Pall Mall, in large rooms that had served as Lambe's auction house, then as Richard Dalton's print-warehouse, and now were owned by the Crown. It was a festive occasion. The Academy was safely launched and much work had been accomplished in a few weeks' time. The schools were operating.[8] The Council had

---

[8] The first class of seventy-seven students included Joseph Farington, Richard Cosway, Thomas Banks, John Yenn, John Flaxman, Francis Wheatley, and John Downman, West's pupil.

met no fewer than four times, and it had already drawn up rules for upholding the artistic integrity of the institution. ("No needlework, artificial flowers, cut paper, shell work, or any such baubles should be admitted," nor any picture without a frame.) An admission charge of one shilling, unfortunately, would have to be made for admission to the exhibitions "to prevent the rooms from being filled by improper persons."

Joshua Reynolds, now president of the Royal Academy and entitled to put the initials P.R.A. after his name, presided. He declared the Royal Academy open and delivered an inaugural address intended "to make and prove art a matter fit to occupy cultivated and serious minds" — the first of what was to become a notable series of discourses. Unfortunately, he was a timid speaker handicapped by deafness, an injured upper lip, and a Devonshire accent, so that only those in his near vicinity could hear what he said.

One may conclude that the foundation members at that historic meeting were pleased at what they had accomplished. An association was now in being that would raise the profession of the artist to the position of respectability, dignity, security, and honor to which his talents entitled him in a civilized nation. He was now supported by an imposing institution, by a visible instrument for direct negotiation with patron and public. His level would be raised professionally, financially, socially.

There was no need, moreover, and little opportunity in this association for the unseemly intrigues and internal quarrels, the sordid and vulgar love of power, the narrow prejudices and cold calculations that had disrupted its predecessor. Control by the king and the limitation to forty members would keep out troublemakers. Paul Sandby wrote to Sawrey Gilpin in 1770: "We shall by the regulation avoid the disagreeable circumstances of that numberless body being divided in opinion easily alarmed and easily worked into tumult by the insinuation of artful men."

There must have been especially strong emotions among those few who were largely responsible for creating the Academy.

King George was pleased with what he was already calling "my Academy"; it would make him known as "The Father of Fine Arts in England."

George Michael Moser had reason to be proud of his accomplishment in setting up the schools so quickly. Beginning with nothing, he had been able to do so only by appropriating the equipment at St. Martin's Lane Academy. He explained that it no longer needed its casts, figures, lamps, easels and so forth, and acted so rapidly that the staff and the students there did not realize what they were giving up. He promised them free use of the Royal Academy schools; then said they would have to subscribe a guinea for each student; then promised that the equipment would be returned or paid for. These were only oral promises, however, and he never kept them. When the St. Martin's Lane group began another school in Maiden Lane, Moser thoughtfully arranged for one of the models to keep him informed of the activities there.

Richard Dalton was pleased because he had managed to deny membership in the Academy to the engraver Robert Strange, a person he detested, even though to do so he had been obliged to exclude all the other engravers in England. He had succeeded, moreover, in selling his print-warehouse property, on which he had suffered serious financial losses, to the Crown at a good price for use by the Academy.

William Chambers had three reasons to be pleased. He had revenged himself on the malcontents who had thrown him out of the Society of Artists, and, by writing a provision against dual membership in the Academy and any other association of artists in London, he had dealt the Society itself a blow from which it would never recover. He had managed to keep James Stuart and Robert Adam, his leading competitors, from membership in the Academy, thereby curtailing their opportunity to display their work in London. He felt he should have been chosen as president, for, as he would tell Swedish authorities in a successful effort to obtain a knighthood, the whole Academy "was planned by me and was completed through my efforts." As treasurer of the Academy, however, and as its liaison officer with the king, he could dominate the institution, direct its private affairs and finances, and control Mr. Reynolds, the nominal head. He had made a point of telling His Majesty about Mr. Reynolds' unwillingness to accept the presidency of the king's Academy until he could ask the advice of Dr. Johnson and Mr. Burke. The name of Edmund Burke was anathema to the king.

Joshua Reynolds was pleased because he had so successfully maintained his contacts with both of the rival groups until he saw clearly which was to have royal support and would prevail; because he had successfully made the presidency of the Academy a condition for joining it; and because there had been a strong hint that if he took the presidency he would be knighted. Moreover, three of his dangerous competitors — George Romney, Robert Edge Pine, and Benjamin Wilson — had been kept out of the Academy. Members of the Society of Artists were making the most outrageous charges against him of duplicity and betrayal, and the papers were printing them, but that was a small price to pay in terms of the results achieved.

Benjamin West was especially pleased. He was happy that his boyhood dream of a society in which artists spoke as companions of kings was being realized, and that he had helped his sovereign to create an association, a fellowship, within which the best artists of Great Britain could work with one another in harmony and happiness, with good will and warm friendship. "The breast of every professional man," he said, "glowed with the warmth and energy of genius at the establishment of the Royal Academy, and at the pleasing prospect it held out in the higher department of art — historical painting."

9

A Star Ascendant

I have embarked in Historical painting — by which means I have removed that long received opinion that that was a department in the art that never would be encouraged in this Kingdom. But I can say I have been so far successful in it that I find my pictures sell for a price that no living artist ever received before.

BENJAMIN WEST to
John Green in Philadelphia,
September 10, 1771

CHARLES PEALE was West's close associate through a period of twenty-five months in 1767–69, working daily in the painting room, making himself useful about the house in London. West began to call him "the ingenious Mr. Peale"; on one occasion, when he was conducting some visitors through his gallery and their attention was distracted by hammering, he explained that the noise came from his young countryman, Mr. Peale, "who, when he is not painting, amuses himself by repairing my locks and bells." When West threw away a small broken palette, regretfully because it was his favorite, Peale mended it, and West used it the rest of his life.

Peale's money ran low at the end of 1767 and he made plans to return home while he still had enough to buy his passage and a store of painter's supplies not available in America. West advised him to stay six months longer to complete his studies, offering to give him free board. Shortly thereafter Peale's American sponsors, having heard good reports of his progress, sent him an additional thirty pounds. This, with miniatures he began to paint for a jeweler, enabled him to extend his visit by a little more than one year.

While living in London, Peale called on Benjamin Franklin, interrupting him in an amorous dalliance with a young lady but staying, at the doctor's invitation, to discuss art, clocks, inventions, experiments, and British mistreatment of Americans. On hearing of still another repressive British act in America, Peale resolved never to remove his hat when the king's carriage passed and not to take any new English clothes back with him when he departed. He discussed the matter of English-American relations with West and (as their later correspondence indicates) found in him a frank and open advocate of American rights.

Peale also called on Miss Angelica Kauffmann, who was living with her father on Golden Square, and was received in her painting room, where she was working on portraits of several persons of distinction. (An observer wrote of her at this time, "She shared — with hoopskirts of extra magnitude, headdresses of superabundant floweriness, and shoe-heels of vividest scarlet — the privilege of being the rage.") Angelica and the artist Nathaniel Dance were engaged when she left Italy, "pledged to each other to marry" (in Joseph Farington's words) "by every possible declaration. But when he was in this state of confidence, she without explanation or anything preceding it shut her door against him." It was generally assumed that, having met Joshua Reynolds, rich and distinguished, forty-five and a bachelor, she set out to win him as a husband. She painted his portrait, posing him before a bust of Michelangelo, and found him, she told her father, "one of my kindest friends, and is never done praising me everywhere." But Reynolds had no intention of marrying. On learning this, Miss Kauffmann, in November 1767, married the wealthy young Count Frederick de Horn of Sweden, who was visiting England and was thought to be the next Swedish ambassador. It was a dreadful mistake, for when the real Count de Horn arrived in England, Angelica's husband turned out to be an imposter, a one-time servant in the real count's household, and a bigamist. She paid him £300 to leave England.

Peale was never really happy in England; he worked himself too hard, he was lonely, and he was poor. He went several times to the entertainments at Ranelagh and Vauxhall gardens, but he found little enjoyment there and regretted the time taken from his studies. It might have been different, he felt, if his wife Rebecca had been with him, for "the mere novelty of sights was soon satisfied when not aided by the converse of a good friend." West arranged for him to see some of the great private art collections in London, but he went to only one or two; he could not afford the tips that had to be passed out to the haughty liveried servants.

He sailed for home on or about March 6, 1769, some six weeks before the opening of the first Academy exhibition, having obtained free passage through the generosity of a friend. He wore no new English clothes when he left, but he carried a large case of painter's supplies. West gave him as a farewell present an elaborate model's throne — a chair that moved up and down, swiveled, and rolled about on casters, mounted on a dais a foot and a half high. Some scores of America's most renowned citizens were to sit in that chair for portraits painted by Charles Peale and his children — called "the greatest dynasty America has known in the fine arts."

To match the gift, Peale traveled to the town of Derby outside Philadelphia and painted a portrait of William, West's brother. He sent it to London as "a present to my Master," with the request that the friend who received it should show it to West without disclosing the identity of the subject, "in order to test the likeness." Peale's style and skills had improved with his training. He had overcome his provincial awkwardness and learned the painterly mechanics and techniques; he ignored the grandiloquent theories of neoclassical painting and within three years was producing the first of his American masterpieces. In 1775 he named his second child, his first daughter, Angelica Kauffmann Peale.

The first annual exhibition of the Royal Academy opened in the Pall Mall gallery on Wednesday, April 26, 1769, with 136 works of art, almost 80 of them by Academicians, two of them by Benjamin West. The exhibition lasted one month, 8 A.M. to 7 P.M. daily, was viewed (in Horace Walpole's words), "by a very crowded and brilliant rout of persons of the first position," and the journals of the day observed that the encouragement given to the new Academy was already visible in the works of genius there exhibited. The show produced a handsome £700 in admissions, and two days before the closing it was honored by a visit from the royal family.

One of West's pictures was an almost life-size representation of *Venus Lamenting the Death of Adonis.* The other was his *Regulus,* which produced a stir even greater than that caused by his *Agrippina* the year before. *Regulus* was a different, new, disturbing kind of painting for an audience accustomed to many portraits with a scattering of landscapes and allegories. The shock it produced, the cumulative effect of the twenty-one pictures he had exhibited at the Society of Artists in his five years in London, his role in founding the Royal Academy, the patronage of the king, the constant mention of his name in the press — these raised West close to the top rank among artists in Britain. The king paid him £420 for *Regulus*[1] and ordered companion pieces for the other two panels in the Warm Room, one of them to be *Hannibal Brought When*

---

[1] About $23,000 in 1970 money, before the burst of inflation in the 1970s.

Nine Years Old, by His Father, Hamilchar, to the Altar of Jupiter, Where He Swears Eternal Enmity to the Romans. Valentine Green, the finest engraver in England, was engaged to make a mezzotint of *Regulus.* David Garrick, the finest actor, told his friends that he greatly admired the picture. Francesco Zuccarelli, R.A., landscape painter, exclaimed, "Here is a painter who promises to rival Nicolas Poussin." Johann Zoffany, R.A., portrait painter, who was not very friendly with Zuccarelli, replied tauntingly, "A figo for Poussin. West has already beaten him out of the field."

In what was called "a token of their grateful sense of His Majesty's favor to them," the Academicians gave an entertainment on June 6, the king's official birthday. The facade of their building in Pall Mall was decorated with a new art form: paintings on translucent paper with lamps of various colors placed behind them. West did the section on the left side, depicting Sculpture as a female figure standing on a rock of marble, holding in one hand an antique bust and in the other a chisel and mallet. All this was received by the populace (and presumably by the king) "with astonishment and delight." Joshua Reynolds presided at the dinner. He was now Sir Joshua, having been knighted following a threat in February to resign as president of the Academy. The knighthood was not unexpected but was a blow to William Chambers. He recovered neatly, however; Sweden gave him its Order of the Polar Star for his work in creating the Royal Academy, and he persuaded George III to let him assume the rank and title of knight in England.

In 1769 West acquired a country house at Hammersmith, on the Thames above London, and as a consequence moved his house and studio from Castle Street in London to smaller (but more genteel) quarters on Panton Square. To his old patron Dr. Jonathan Morris in Lancaster he wrote:

> As this is the part of the world my department in life has fixed me, I have endeavoured to accommodate and settle myself in a domestic life with my little family which consists of my Dear Betsy, her little boy, a servant or two — one house in the country four miles distance from town where Betsy and her little boy stay eight months in the year, and another in London where I carry on my painting. And by that I get exercise of coming into town and going out to them every day. By which I secure my health in good state, which otherways would be impossible by reason of my close application to studies.

One of his servants was James Dyer, a trooper in the Horse Guards who left the military life to enter West's service and remained in it for almost fifty years. Dyer posed from time to time as a figure model in the Academy schools, took care of the two saddle horses West now owned, and, mounted on one of the horses, attended his master on sketching excursions in Windsor Forest. Elizabeth West was a good manager of his household. She read a great deal, amused herself by writing poetry, and kept several spaniel dogs for which she had a special fondness.

West is shown briefly but pleasantly in 1769 through the eyes of another visiting American artist — Henry Benbridge of Philadelphia, twenty-six years old, distantly related by marriage to Mrs. West. He had spent some four years in Italy — the first American to study there after West — where he received instruction and advice from Pompeo Batoni. He arrived in England in December 1769 in a splash of publicity engineered by that master publicist James Boswell, who had commissioned him to go to Corsica and paint a full-length portrait of Boswell's hero, the Corsican patriot Pasquale Paoli. Benbridge visited the Wests, of course, and from them collected a two-year accumulation of mail they had been holding for him. To his mother he wrote of "the kind reception I met with from Mr. West and his wife, who insisted upon my eating at their house, and were very sorry they could not accommodate me with a room, having but a small house of only two rooms on a floor, every one of which is occupied." He took lodgings on Panton Square for thirty-five shillings a week, painted a portrait of Benjamin Franklin (which West "approves of and thinks it very like"), and exhibited in the spring show of the Society of Artists. Mr. West, he wrote, "intends to decline portrait painting and to follow that of history, which will enable him to recommend me much stronger, than if he was in the same way with myself." Benbridge sailed for America (and a successful eighteen-year career in Charleston, South Carolina) in July 1770, bearing a letter of introduction from West to Francis Hopkinson. "You will find him an ingenious artist and an agreeable companion," West wrote. "His merit in the art must procure him great encouragement and much esteem. I dare say it will give you great pleasure to have an ingenious artist residing amongst you."

It is not known how West came upon the idea of painting *The Death of General Wolfe,* his most famous work. He may have discussed it with General Robert Monckton when he was painting his portrait in 1764, or with his skating companion, Colonel William Howe, both of whom had been at Quebec, Monckton as senior brigadier and second-in-command under Wolfe. In any event, this was one of the inspirational stories of the time, an epic chapter that kindled a spirit of pride and patriotism in even the most stolid

Englishman: How James Wolfe, stalemated for three months in his siege of the French army at Quebec in 1759, led his troops up a path in the cliffside; how he met and defeated a superior number of French on a plain outside the city walls; how he was twice wounded, then struck fatally, and at the moment of victory died in the arms of his officers.

The subject had been painted three times before. Edward Penny, now professor of painting at the Royal Academy, had produced two versions in 1763 and 1764, neither of which attracted much critical applause or public attention. Young George Romney had painted a *Death of General Wolfe* in 1763 and entered it in a competition for historical paintings held by the Society of Artists. The judges cited him for second prize, but the decision was reversed and the award given to another artist, Romney receiving a special premium of twenty-five guineas "as an encouragement to merit." (John Romney, a son, charged in a memoir of his father that Reynolds used his influence to deprive him of the award.)

In studying the subject, West had several crucial decisions to make. For one thing, contemporary accounts did not agree on who was present at the death scene. The best evidence was that Wolfe expired in a tent attended by only two junior officers and a surgeon's mate. Such circumstances did not make for dramatic effect; they would have to be improved on, even at the expense of the realism West wanted to achieve, even with a loss in the historical correctness called for by the rules of neoclassical painting. No one would be inspired by a picture of Wolfe dying in a tent like an ordinary man.

He would, moreover, have to develop a different approach in painting this subject. The neoclassical style, the flat-plane, bas-relief effect of the *Agrippina* and the *Regulus*, their chaste academic severity, muted colors, and repressed emotion, were not right for this scene of violence and excitement.

There was, finally, the matter of costume. He would have to violate a basic principle, not only of neoclassicism, but of the Grand Style — that is, of the adaptation of neoclassicism Sir Joshua Reynolds was imposing on English art. He could not "generalize" the dress of Wolfe and his officers with classical garments to show that this was an event worthy of the ancients; he could not avoid contemporary details that would soon make the picture out of date and out of style. This would have to be what was called contemptuously "a breeches and waistcoat piece." The problem, the danger, would be to show modern dress — British uniforms — and still achieve the sense of heroic grandeur demanded by the canons of neoclassicism and Reynolds' Grand Style. It was exactly there that

Romney and Penny had failed in their earlier modern-dress pictures of the death of Wolfe.[2]

He began with a sketch in which he chose the conventional composition of three pyramids. He placed Wolfe in the center group, stretched out on the ground as in a seventeenth-century Pietà, his body in the pose of any traditional *Lamentation* or *Deposition of Christ*. On Wolfe's face he showed an expression of anguish taken from Charles Le Brun's engraved *Passions,* the academic textbook for depicting strong emotions. These "quotations" from religious and classical art would convey to the viewer the response that was expected of him. Directly behind Wolfe he placed Colonel Isaac Barré, and above Wolfe, holding a huge half-furled flag, Lieutenant Henry Browne of the Louisbourg Grenadiers. On the right he placed two grieving figures: General Wolfe's servant and a tall grenadier, his hands clasped. In the group at the left he showed General Monckton and Colonel William Howe, his green coat contrasting with the red of the other uniforms. (Browne was actually present at the death scene; Monckton and Barré at that particular moment were lying wounded on another part of the field; Howe was in the rear with the reserves.) In the foreground he painted with particular care a brown-skinned, breech-clothed Indian brave (though there were no Indian braves with Wolfe's army), watching contemplatively to see how a great English chief died. In the distance he depicted a running soldier, waving his hat, carrying a French flag, excitedly bringing the news of a French retreat. This figure he borrowed from the versions by Edward Penny, who, as a painter of minor sentimental pieces, would no doubt feel pleased and flattered to be "quoted" in this way. In the background he showed massed and milling soldiers, a spire of Quebec City, the masts of British ships standing in the St. Lawrence, swirling smoke, menacing black clouds, and a patch of sunlight in the sky.[3]

---

[2] For a more detailed discussion of this issue, see Appendix II.

[3] There has been some gossip down through the years that West demanded money from officers to include them in the picture, and that the demand accounted for the presence of some persons who are shown but were not there, and the absence of some who deserved to be shown but were not. The charge seems to have first appeared in 1901 in *The Siege of Quebec* by Arthur Doughty and G. W. Parmalee, which says (Vol. II, p. 314) that West asked John Hale of the 47th Regiment for £100 for the privilege of appearing in the picture. I have been unable to find any contemporary evidence that West was charged with making such a demand — and certainly nothing to support the statement of one modern art historian: "West [let] it be known that any officer who had been on the Heights of Abraham on that fateful occasion could proffer himself as a model and be ensured of immortality by the payment of a mere hundred pounds." Farington, the greatest of gossips, certainly would have mentioned such a devel-

West painted the full picture (5 by 7 feet) in late 1769 or early 1770. His house was thronged by students, visitors and friends, and word soon spread that Mr. West was working on a major battle piece with everyone in modern dress. The king let his views be known: he did not wish to buy the picture, he had been informed that the dignity of the subject was impaired by the characters in modern military costume, and he personally thought it quite ridiculous to exhibit heroes in coats, breeches, and cocked hats. Another patron who disapproved of West's proposal was Archbishop Drummond. As West told the story, "His Grace was apprehensive that, by persevering in my intention, I might lose some portion of the reputation which he was pleased to think I had acquired by his picture of *Agrippina* and [by His] Majesty's of *Regulus*." Drummond called on Joshua Reynolds to discuss this disturbing development and to ask his opinion on what should be done.

Reynolds was committed to the principle that obtrusion of modern dress into a history painting in the Grand Style would degrade the work and introduce a vulgarizing innovation into the Academy. In his *Third Discourse*, delivered to Academicians and students at the same time that West was at work on his picture, he affirmed that the artist must separate "modern fashions from the habits of nature."

> The whole beauty and grandeur of the art consists, in my opinion, in being able to get above the singular forms, local customs, particularities . . .
>
> The painter . . . must divest himself of all prejudices in favour of his age or country; he must disregard all local and temporary ornaments, and look only on those general habits which are everywhere and always the same; he addresses his works to the people of every country and every age, he calls upon posterity to be his spectators . . .
>
> Here, then . . . we must have recourse to the ancients as instructors.

Reynolds and Drummond decided that they should call on West together and remonstrate. According to West, Dr. Drummond in-

---

opment in his diary if he had heard it, and a body of artists who sought to ruin West in the years 1801–06 would have used it against him. To believe such a charge, one would have to read the situation backwards and conclude that the picture was famous before it was painted. On the contrary, realistic history painting was little known in England before 1770, the picture was an uncertain gamble, it was subject to possible ridicule, and its success was quite unexpected.

formed him of the object of their visit, after which Sir Joshua "began a very ingenious and elegant dissertation on the state of the public taste in this country, and the danger which every attempt at innovation necessarily incurred of repulse and ridicule." He concluded by urging West earnestly "to adopt the classic costume of antiquity, as much more becoming the inherent greatness of my subject than the modern garb of war." West listened to him "with the utmost attention," but he could perceive no logic in Reynolds' reasoning — "only a strain of persuasion to induce me to comply with an existing prejudice — a prejudice which I thought would not be too soon removed."

> When he had finished his discourse . . . I began by remarking that the event intended to be commemorated took place on the 13th of September, 1758 [1759], in a region of the world unknown to the Greeks and Romans, and at a period of time when no such nations, nor heroes in their costumes, any longer existed. The subject I have to represent is the conquest of a great province of America by the British troops. It is a topic that history will proudly record, and the same truth that guides the pen of the historian should govern the pencil of the artist. I consider myself as undertaking to tell this great event to the eye of the world; but if, instead of the facts of the transaction, I represent classical fictions, how shall I be understood by posterity! . . .
>
> I want to mark the date, the place, and the parties engaged in the event; and if I am not able to dispose of the circumstances in a picturesque manner, no academical distribution of Greek or Roman costume will enable me to do justice to the subject.

West asked his visitors to withhold their judgment and to return when the picture was finished. He was so profoundly impressed with the friendship of their intercession, he said, that if they did not approve of it, he would consign it to a closet, regardless of his own view.

In due course, West called on Drummond and fixed a day for him to come with Reynolds to see the finished work.

> They came accordingly, and [Reynolds] without speaking, after his first cursory glance, seated himself before the picture, and examined it with deep and minute attention for about half an hour. He then rose, and said to His Grace, "Mr. West has conquered. He has treated his subject as it ought to be treated. I retract my objections against the introduction of any other circumstances into historical pictures than those which are requisite and appropriate; and I foresee that this picture will not only be-

come one of the most popular, but occasion a revolution in the art." [4]

On June 21, 1770, nine months before the picture was to be put to the public test in the Academy exhibition, West wrote to Peale, "I have had much sickness since you left this place — so as to deprive my making use of the pencil for six months and more — but at present I enjoy good health and am at work on a second picture for His Majesty... I have painted a picture of the death of Genl Wolfe, that has procured me *great* honour."

A happy development during these months was the removal of the Academy schools and administration offices from the building in Pall Mall (where the exhibitions were still to be held) to Old Somerset House. This rambling mansion standing between the Thames River and the Strand had been built in the mid-sixteenth century by the mighty Edward Seymour, Duke of Somerset, known to history as the Lord Protector. It had been the residence of several queens and the scene of magnificent ceremonies and entertainments under the Stuarts, but now for the past seventy years it had been shuttered in some parts and little used in others. Seven large rooms of the royal apartments were repaired and altered under William Chambers' direction for the Academy's school of drawing, the library, council room, hall for the Monday night lectures, and lodgings for the keeper. The school opened in January 1771, being described in the press as "the most superb of any in the world and the best stocked with casts after the antique." The king's brother, the duke of Cumberland, attended the opening ceremony; President Reynolds "took the lecturer's chair for a few minutes to expatiate on the indulgence His Majesty has shown to the arts by conferring on them such honor."

The 1771 exhibition opened in Pall Mall on April 29. From the

---

[4] No other passage in Galt's biography has been so severely condemned as this one. Critical comment has run a gamut from ridicule to scorn and even fury at West's presumption. At its kindest it has accused "poor Galt" of a flight of the imagination. In 1800, however, when Galt was twenty-one and still unknown in Scotland, an article on West in *The Port Folio* affirmed the main point of Galt's account. Dr. James Beattie had recently attacked West's use of modern dress in *The Death of Wolfe*. The unknown author of the *Port Folio* article responded: "Does Dr. Beattie think ... that Mr. West should have wrapped the limbs of his Wolfe, his Moncton, and the other figures of that painting, in the blue, red, and yellow blankets of Florence, or in the seraglio trappings of Rubens?... I know that Sir Joshua Reynolds was persuaded to think so before he saw the picture; but the greatest men are obnoxious to error; and I know that when he did see it ... he needed no arguments to induce him to change his opinion."

first day, *Wolfe* was a sensational success. The public stood in long lines to get into the gallery to see it. William Pitt, who had placed Wolfe in command of the army that captured Quebec, came to see it. "His Lordship," the press reported, "placed himself before the piece and examined it with great attention," while those in the gallery awaited his verdict. "Upon retiring he pronounced it well executed upon the whole, but thought there was too much dejection, not only in the dying hero's face, but in the faces of the surrounding officers, who, he said, as Englishmen, should forget all traces of private misfortunes when they had so grandly conquered for their country." David Garrick visited the gallery at an early hour in order to study the picture close up and undisturbed, but he found a crowd already gathered around it. Everyone made way for him, and the actor enchanted the company by lying in Wolfe's posture before the picture, "displaying in his features the exact countenance depicted by the artist." He then showed how Wolfe should have been painted, assuming the expression of joy the dying general surely had felt when he heard the words, "They run! They run!" and replied, "Now God be praised. Since I have conquered I will die in peace." The audience applauded enthusiastically. These events were covered by the press; publicity created success, and success created more publicity.

Beyond that, the work genuinely stirred the public imagination. It was like no other modern picture Englishmen had seen. It made the viewer feel that he was present at and a part of a great historic event of his time, that he was an accessory with others in a tragic but inspiring occasion. And it came precisely at a time when Englishmen were prepared to accept a work glorifying English heroism, sacrifice, and victory. Even Horace Walpole had a kind word for the picture, with reservations. He wrote in his catalogue, "Fine picture, though there is too little concern in many of the principal figures, and the grenadier on the right is too tall."

Lord Grosvenor bought the picture for £400, and the king, expressing his chagrin at having rejected it, said to West, "But you shall make a copy for me." West made a repetition, for which he received £350, and he obtained commissions from the king to paint two other notable death scenes, that of the Theban general Epaminandos and of the fearless and faultless French knight, the Seigneur de Bayard. He made at least four other repetitions of *Wolfe*, one of them for Monckton, one for the German Prince of Waldeck (for which he received £250), and one for himself. On the Waldeck copy he placed a pair of moccasins on the ground beside the Indian, for Henry Laurens, merchant from South Carolina, had pointed out to him that an Indian warrior never went into battle in his bare feet. John Boydell, London alderman and print publisher, commissioned William Woollett to engrave *Wolfe*. The print appeared five years later; it broke all records in sales and was copied by the best engravers in Paris and Vienna. Woollett made almost £7000 on that one print, Boydell made £15,000 selling it, and West received a sum in royalties that has never been revealed. The three men created a new popularity and demand for history paintings and a vastly broadened market for prints taken from those pictures. They gave the artist and the engraver a new source of income and in some measure freed them from sole dependence on the private patron.

If there were any doubts that West meant what he said about modern costume in works of art, or that he would continue in his new style, or that he could match his great success with another picture of comparable rank, the doubts were settled within the year.

When Thomas Penn asked West to paint a scene commemorating his father's settlement in Pennsylvania, West responded by choosing an event that happened, or may have happened, in 1682. Late in November of that year, according to legend, William Penn met the chiefs of the Delaware, Susquehannock, and Shawnee tribes at the Indian village of Sachamexing (now called Shackamaxon). There they exchanged certain Indian lands for certain English goods and agreed on a treaty, "pledged without an oath and never broken," under which whites and Indians would live in peace and friendship. Working on a canvas about 6 by 9 feet, West showed some three dozen Quakers and Indians in a parley. He placed the figures in two main groups on a straight frontal plane, with Penn in the center, his arms outstretched, balancing and uniting them. Triangular groups at each lower corner led the eye to the central figures. Penn was a vigorous man of thirty-eight in 1682, but West showed him as a portly figure considerably older, presumably on the premise that anyone making a historic treaty should look like a man of solidity and substance.

In painting *William Penn's Treaty with the Indians*, West drew heavily on his childhood memories. He showed the huge elm tree near which the Shackamaxon meeting was held and under which he had played as a boy. He painted the brick houses he had seen when he was young, and the shadbelly clothes worn by the elderly Quakers of that day. (Both were anachronisms, coming some seventy years after the treaty.) Among the Quakers he portrayed his father and his half brother. For the Indian braves, squaws, and children he drew upon a number of Indian garments he had collected. "The great object I had," he said, "was to express savages brought into harmony and peace by justice and benevolence, by not withholding from them what was their right and giving to them what they were in want of, and as well as a wish to give by that art a conquest that was made over native people without sword or dagger."

William Penn's Treaty with the Indians when he Founded the Province of Pennsylvania in North America first appeared in the 1772 Academy exhibition. It was immediately acclaimed. The subject and the figures were quite new in European art. The picture told a story with gestures, facial expressions, and stage properties that anyone could read. In his catalogue Horace Walpole wrote, "This picture... has good drawing and great merit. The contrast of simplicity between the Quakers and the Indians has great effect." John Opie, R.A., called it "a consistent and *good prose picture.*" Later critics have pointed out that the work aroused a response in the hearts of people and that it was admired for emotional rather than intellectual reasons.[5]

By June 1775 John Hall produced an engraving in the same 19- by 24-inch size as that of the *Death of Wolfe.* Sales were heavy and continuous. Over the next two centuries, *Penn's Treaty* was reproduced in every conceivable and some inconceivable ways: on china platters, gravy boats, vegetable dishes, tin trays, bed quilts, window curtains, lamp shades, candle screens, letterheads, hand-blown glass, tavern signs, banknotes, cast-iron stove plates, medals, and Christmas cards. It was the only picture that hung in most Quaker homes in both England and America; the Friends customarily gave an engraving of it as a wedding present. The English critic Roger Fry, his sensibilities offended at seeing it so often, called it "that detestable picture." The American critic Wesley Frank Craven declared, "It is as indelibly impressed on the American mind as Washington's crossing of the Delaware." The historian Frederick B. Tolles calls it one of our national icons: "There he stands under the great elm at Shackamaxon, portly and benignant, the Founder of the Quaker Commonwealth, eternally dispensing peace and yard goods to the Indians."

---

[5] The critic John Canaday has written, "A charming painting... The locale and the participants are sufficiently picturesque to approach genre painting, although West was only following his own precedent in presenting another recent historical event in appropriate factual terms rather than allegory... There is a certain — rather engaging — naiveté about it. But it is an honest picture, more original than it looks today."

West was now at the full tide of success. He was favored in August 1772 with a second son, Benjamin, for whom Benjamin Franklin agreed to be the godfather. In the same year, George III appointed him historical painter to the king, with an annual stipend of £1000.

"The American War"

I have been introduced to Mr. West, and have made some acquaintance with him. He is of very genteel behaviour, and seems
greatly partial to Americans; at least he is much pleased with
visits from them. He speaks very highly of Mr. Copley's merit,
and declared to me, that in his opinion, he only wanted the advantage of studying proper masters to be one of the first painters
of the age.

GULIAN VERPLANCK in London,
to his brother in New York,
February 26, 1773

ON NOVEMBER 24, 1770, John Copley resumed his correspondence with West. He apologized for not having written for two
years and for having sent no pictures to the 1769 and 1770 exhibitions. He had not forgotten his friend, he said, and had not neglected
his work, but his hands were tied; his time was so entirely engrossed in painting portraits that it was not in his power "to prosecute any work of fancy." Certain obstructions, moreover (they
were an infirm mother, his marriage in 1769, the birth of a child,
his portrait commitments) stood in the way of the visit to England,
but "they shall not prevent it finally. I will make all give way to
the predominant passion of cultivating our art."

West had been hearing of Copley's proposed trip for four years,
and now his answer, while polite, was brief and somewhat distant.
He felt that Europe "will every way answer your expectations." He
hoped to see Mr. Copley in London and would be happy to render
any service that lay in his power. Despite his coolness, West had
lost none of his admiration for Copley's work. To a Bostonian
whose young son wished to become a painter, he wrote that the
boy should draw from nature "and advance himself as Mr. Copley

has done, and he will find himself equal to the first in Europe." His beginning in America, he added, "was the most fortunate circumstance that could have happened to me. My having no other assistance but what I drew from nature (the early part of my life being quite obscured from art), this grounded me in the knowledge of nature; while had I come to Europe sooner in life, I should have known nothing but the receipts of masters." (The father sent a copy of the letter to Copley.) A visitor to London wrote, "I saw one of [Copley's] portraits at Mr. West's. It was of a woman and a very ordinary one, and yet so finely painted that it appeared alive. West was lavish in its praises, pointed out its beauties, the natural fall of the arm and hand, the delicate manner in which the light was carried through the whole, and many other things which I forget. In short, he said Mr. Copley would make no small figure in the world of painters." [1]

Two years passed. In December 1772, Jonathan Clarke, Mrs. Copley's English brother, called on West to discuss the long-delayed European tour. Once again West gave his advice, both to Clarke and in a long letter to Copley. Mr. Copley and his wife, he wrote, could live genteelly in Rome for £100 a year, one-fifth the cost in London. Mr. Copley would be wise to travel alone, however, leaving Mrs. Copley in Boston, so that he could devote himself single-mindedly to his studies. His journey to Italy was rather to finish his study than to begin it, and eighteen months or two years would be sufficient time. He should go directly from Boston to Leghorn, "as it will save a good deal of trouble and some expense." West would send Copley letters of introduction to a friend in Leghorn and to another in Rome. He listed the artists and art works Copley should study in pursuing "the higher excellences in the art."

Copley was torn by indecision. He weighed desire against duty, artistic growth against love of family, the praise of his peers in London against lack of appreciation of his genius in Boston, the risks of an uncertain future abroad against financial security at home. And then in the fall of 1773 the rising tide of events took over and helped him to make his hard decision.

His father-in-law, Richard Clarke — a nephew of Governor Thomas Hutchinson — was a wealthy Tory merchant. He was also, in November 1773, one of five agents of the East India Company for tea consigned to Boston with a tax on it of threepence a pound. When Clarke refused to resign his agency, the Sons of Liberty

---

[1] The portrait is thought to be that of Mrs. Humphrey Devereux, mother of John Greenwood, the American artist and art dealer who was living in London. Copley exhibited that portrait at the Society of Artists show in 1771.

massed outside his house in Boston, pounded on his doors, broke his windows, and threatened him and his sons with a tar-and-feathering. The Clarkes fled to Castle William, a fortress in the harbor, where they stayed for some months under the protection of British troops. They asked John Copley to represent them in Boston, and he agreed.

Copley was one of the few men both sides would trust. He had Tory affiliations, but his background was Whig — his widowed mother had owned a tobacco shop on Long Wharf — and he was a friend of some of the radicals; he had painted portraits of Samuel Adams, John Hancock, and Paul Revere. He had taken no sides, voiced no public opinions, in the conflict. He was a peaceful man, even a timid one; he hated violence and dreaded civil war; and he was now in the open arena attempting to mediate the differences of two irreconcilable forces. Steeling himself, he called on the radical leaders to advise a course of compromise and moderation. Samuel Adams, one of the shrewdest revolutionaries in the long history of revolutions, made no promises.

The tea ships arrived and their cargo — 342 chests worth £18,000 — was thrown into the bay. In retaliation, Parliament closed and blockaded the port of Boston and sent three British regiments to occupy the city. The other colonies poured gifts of food into Boston. Paul Revere departed for the capitals of the southern colonies with an account of Boston's response to the British coercion, and plans were laid to call a General Congress in Philadelphia in the autumn.

Copley's position between Loyalists and Rebels had become intolerable, and he decided to escape it by making his long-delayed study trip to Europe. He sailed alone on June 10, 1774, leaving his family behind in safe care. He carried a weight of worries with him. If the trip to Europe failed in its purpose, he would lose time and money; and if it was thought that he was fleeing the country as a Loyalist, he would lose his reputation in Boston and perhaps his landed property as well. (He owned three houses, a barn, an orchard, and some twenty acres of rural land on Beacon Hill, a considerable distance from downtown Boston.)

He arrived at Deal on July 9 after a safe and easy passage of only twenty-nine days, and at once his spirits rose. He was impressed by the "surpassingly beautiful" countryside, the friendly people, the neatness of the houses, the food on the road ("double refined sugar, the best Hison tea, and all things in proportion"), and the transportation in a post chaise, a comfortable and "genteel" public conveyance that took him to London, the entire cost of the seventy-two-mile trip amounting to only three guineas. Arriving on a Sunday evening (as West had eleven years before him), he was enchanted with London ("this superb city . . . really an astonishing city").

He put up at the New England Coffee House and the next morning called on Jonathan Clarke, his brother-in-law. There he spent some hours writing to his half brother, Henry Pelham ("I am now beginning that correspondence from which you will no doubt receive much pleasure") and to his wife Susannah. It seems that every respectable American took pains on arriving in London not to look provincial; Copley at once "procured some things to be decent in" and, accompanied by Clarke, he called "to see my friend Mr. West." It was a happy meeting. West was eager to hear the latest news from America, Copley to talk of art and artists, to see West's pictures, to discuss his trip to Italy. Copley found in West "those amiable qualities that make his friendship both desirable as an artist and as a gentleman." West took him and Clarke to meet Sir Joshua Reynolds, where "we saw a very large number of his portraits and a fine collection of other masters." Copley the next day had "the superlative pleasure" of visiting the Royal Academy with West: the facade was magnificent, the collection of statues was very fine, the students "had a naked model from which they were drawing." The following day West took him to Buckingham House, "where I beheld the finest collection of paintings I have seen, and, I believe, the finest in England." There he saw "Mr. West's *Death of General Wolfe,* which is sufficient of itself to immortalize the author of it." To Henry Pelham:

> Mr. West when I first came would have had me lodge at his house, but was just preparing to move to his new house and could not accommodate me;[2] but had this not been the case I should have declined it; but he desired I would always come to dinner when I was not engaged, with the same freedom as I should at home. Indeed, he is extremely friendly and I am under great obligations to him.

West found him lodgings a few doors down the street: two first-floor rooms and a small room to powder in, "very genteel, for which I pay a guinea a week."

He stayed in London for six weeks. Reynolds had him to breakfast and took him to see Rubens' celebrated ceiling at Whitehall Palace. He dined at least twice with Governor Hutchinson, who

---

2 West moved in 1774 to 14 Newman Street, off Oxford Street several blocks east of Oxford Circus, where he had a large house in a newly developed neighborhood.

had left Boston one week before him, replaced by General Thomas Gage; there were twelve Bostonians in the company the second time and they dined on "choice salt fish." Hutchinson and Clarke took him to see Greenwich Hospital and Greenwich Park, Vauxhall Gardens, and the yacht that had brought Queen Charlotte from Mecklenburg to her state marriage in England. ("Here such a profusion of rich ornament presented itself as cannot be described.") He tendered his letters of introduction and was "invited to dine almost every day." He was offered several commissions to paint portraits but had resolved to reject all such opportunities until he had seen Italy, unless they came from the king or queen.

Copley was grateful for the kindness and courtesy he met with in England, referring to these characteristics several times in his letters. He was a reserved man who was accustomed to giving only the required civility to strangers, and he was astonished at "how friendly those people are into whose acquaintance I have fallen." There was, he said, "a great deal of manly politeness in the English. There is something so open and undisguised in them that I can truly say exceeds rather than falls short of my expectations."

He was enraptured at his first sight of major works of art, but on studying them closely he was a little disappointed in what he saw, because he had expected so much more. Close acquaintance with the masterpieces fortified him in his belief in his own competence. "The works of the great masters," he informed Pelham, "are but pictures, and when a man can go but a very little beyond his contemporaries, he becomes a great man. The difference between Raphael, Titiano, Angelo and the common run of moderately good artists is not so great as one would imagine from the praises bestowed on those great men."

As an artist seeking to improve himself, he was most deeply interested in those pictures that contained two or more figures or groups of figures, since he had had almost no experience in creating such works.[3] The difficulties of painting a composition with multiple figures had worried him, but now he advised Pelham, "I find ... the means by which composition is attained is easier than I thought it had been. The sketches are made from life, and not only from figures singly, but often from groups. This you remember was [what we] have often talked of, and by this a great difficulty is removed that lay on my mind."

---

[3] Of the American paintings reproduced in the first (or American) volume of Jules Prown's *Copley,* 308 are single portraits; 6 contain two figures (mother and child, husband and wife, a pair of sisters); and 1 (the Gore children) has four figures arranged side by side.

By a stroke of what appeared to be great good luck, Copley found a traveling companion to accompany him to Rome. He was George Carter, an Englishman, forty-five, a painter, an experienced traveler who spoke some French and Italian — "a very polite and sensible man," Copley wrote, "who has seen much of the world . . . agreeable in every respect." They took the packet boat out of Brighthelmstone (Brighton) on August 29, reached Dieppe in eleven hours, and were in Paris by September 2. "I know not how it happens," Copley wrote to Pelham, "but I believe there is something in the air of France that accelerates or quickens the circulation of the fluids of the human body, for I already feel half a Frenchman." By this time he was beginning to realize that George Carter was not the prize he had thought. They quarreled. Carter kept a journal of the tour, and he set down in incisive terms the worst that he could say about Copley.

> This companion of mine is rather a singular character; he seems happy at taking things at the wrong end; and laboured near an hour today to prove that a huckaback towel was softer than a Barcelona silk handkerchief . . .
> My agreeable companion suspects he has got cold upon his lungs. He is now sitting by a fire, the heat of which makes me very faint; a silk handkerchief about his head and a white pocket one about his neck, applying fresh fuel, and complaining that the wood of this country don't give half the heat that the wood of America does.

In the European custom, Carter expected to be asked each morning how he had slept, and to return a serious reply. "He has never asked me yet, and we have been up an hour, how I do, or how I have passed the night: 'tis an engaging creature." On another occasion, Carter wanted to ride and Copley to walk (or vice versa) and they stood in a rain shower arguing about it.

> We had a very warm altercation, and I was constrained to tell him, "Sir, we are now more than eight hundred miles from home, through all which way you have not had a single care that I could alleviate; I have taken as much pains as to the mode of conveying you, as if you had been my wife; and I cannot help telling you, that she, though a delicate little woman, accommodated her feelings to her situation with much more temper than you have done."

Mr. Copley had some strange ideas about the future of the American colonies: "My companion is solacing himself, that if they go on in America for an hundred years to come, as they have for an hundred and fifty years past, they shall have an independent government: the woods will be cleared... art would then be encouraged there, and great artists would arise." Carter was embarrassed by Copley's traveling attire:

> He had one of those white French bonnets which, turned on one side, admit of being pulled over the ears; under this was a yellow and red silk handkerchief, with a large Catherine wheel flambeaued upon it, such as may be seen upon the necks of those delicate ladies who cry Malton oysters. This flowed half way down his back. He wore a red-brown, or rather cinnamon, great coat, with a friar's cape, and worsted binding of a yellowish white: it hung near his heels, out of which peeped his boots: under his arm he carried the sword which he bought in Paris, and a hiccory stick with an ivory head. Joined to this dress, he was very thin, pale, a little pock-marked, prominent eye-brows, small eyes, which, after fatigue, seemed a day's march in his head.

The two parted without regret in Rome. Though he kept no journal, Copley had the final word. To fellow artists he later described Carter as "a sort of snail which crawled over a man in his sleep, and left its slime and no more."

Copley took lodgings across the street from Gavin Hamilton, "from whom I have received many proofs of friendship," and set out on a program of studying, copying, and sightseeing. He painted an Ascension in the manner of Raphael and a double portrait of Mr. and Mrs. Ralph Izard of Charleston, South Carolina, posed elegantly at a carved Italian table and against a background that showed a classic column, a Greek vase, a statue of Orestes and Electra, a richly brocaded curtain, and an Italian landscape containing the Colosseum.

When his wife wrote him that conditions were so bad in Boston she would like to leave, Copley urged her to join him in London, and now for the first time he decided to settle in England. ("I cannot think of going back to starve with my family.") Hamilton assured him that he would be "better established than West, because he [West] could not paint such portraits as those of Mr. Izard and Lady, and portraits were always in demand."

After seven months in Rome, Copley conceived a way to shorten his stay; he invested a considerable sum in large plaster casts of certain sculptures, including the Laocoon, and shipped them to London, where he would "always have the advantage of drawing from them." He went to Parma to make a commissioned copy of

Correggio's *St. Jerome,* and there in late June 1775 he learned that England and the Colonies were at war. To his wife he wrote:

> If I am not mistaken, the country which was once the happiest on the globe, will be deluged with blood for many years to come. It seems as if no plan of reconciliation could now be formed; as the sword is drawn, all must be finally settled by the sword. I cannot think that the power of Great Britain will subdue the country, if the people are united, as they appear to be at present. I know it may seem strange to some men of great understanding that I should hold such an opinion, but it is very evident to me that America will have the power of resistance until grown strong to conquer, and that victory and independence will go hand in hand.

On July 28, still in Parma, he learned for the first time not only that his wife had sailed but that she and three of their children were safe in London.

Copley finished his work in Parma and then traveled almost 800 miles in sixteen days to join his family in early October. Richard Clarke and his sons had fled Boston by way of Canada and were also in London. Copley and his father-in-law took a house together on Leicester Square, Clarke becoming a permanent member of the household. There, at the age of thirty-seven, John Copley set out to make a new career.

Although he concentrated on portrait work, he planned to achieve a higher glory as a history painter. He suffered a grievous blow when, on opening the crates from Italy, he found his casts shattered to bits; it was a loss he regretted the rest of his life. The artist-dealer John Greenwood was delegated by the floundering Society of Artists to solicit his continuing membership in that body, but Copley elected instead to exhibit at the Royal Academy, and in November 1776, in competition with twenty-one other candidates, he was elected an Associate Member, the probationary rank that could lead to full acceptance as an Academician. (He was the first American so elected.) West used his considerable influence to get him portrait commissions and introduced him at court. The two men were close professionally and personally, and Susannah Copley and Elizabeth West shared their friendship, the families dining together from time to time at 12 Leicester Square and at the Wests' handsome new house at 14 Newman Street. Newman Street had been laid out from the north side of Oxford Street in the past few years, when the houses were built; the north end looked onto open fields and hills, and from the windows there one could see as far as the garden wall of Middlesex Hospital. West now had a large establishment (acquired on a ninety-nine-year renewable lease) with room for an attached gallery he planned to build. The gallery would house his growing collection of art objects, and it would serve as a model to show others how pictures should be hung and lighted.

The relationship of Copley to West was not, of course, that of a pupil to a teacher, nor of a disciple to a master. Copley was not an inexperienced beginner, nor a penniless visitor without friends; he was as old as West, he was a mature and successful artist, and in his heart he felt he was the better painter. The relationship was one in which West supplied and Copley accepted some guidance and encouragement; in which Copley returned respect and deference. West was clearly proud, as an American, to have another such American with him in London — an artist with a remarkable talent, and an artist who would not be his competitor. Copley was a portrait painter. West, as the king's history painter, had no need to spend what he called "anxious, laborious hours in becoming a fashionable painter of vacant faces."

Copley painted West's portrait during this early period. He did so in what is sometimes called his American manner: a half-length figure in a natural pose, realistic and honest, without flattery or superficiality, against a plain background, showing the personality, character, and appearance of the subject. As a matter of fact, most of Copley's English portraits done before 1800 had the same qualities, though it has been charged that his move to England weakened or ruined him as an artist. (West has sometimes been blamed on the ground that he lured Copley to England.) Mrs. Seymour Fort, Mr. and Mrs. Robert Hyde, Mrs. Montresor, Mrs. Hooper, Admiral and Mrs. Gayton, Henry Laurens, John Adams, and a dozen other portraits, all painted in England, are among his finest works. They escape the faults, moreover, that are sometimes found in Copley's American portraits: badly proportioned bodies and limbs, standard poses, and repetitive pictorial devices.

Every ship from America brought news of spreading violence in what came to be called "the American War." In June 1775 the British suffered 1000 casualties in the battle to take Bunker Hill, overlooking Boston; General William Howe, West's skating companion, led the assaults. In 1776 Howe abandoned Boston rather than attack General Washington's forces on Dorchester Heights, taking some 1000 Loyalists with him in his ships, young Henry Pelham among them. In July the Second Continental Congress declared the Colonies to be independent states, free of ties to Great Britain. General Howe, in command of 32,000 trained, disciplined, and well-armed troops, supported by an immense fleet of warships and transports, captured New York. At the end of 1776 Benjamin Franklin arrived in Paris as a commissioner, sent to persuade France to lend money and join the war against Britain.

The war was unpopular in Britain: The young people were pro-American, officers resigned their commissions rather than fight against Americans, and some of the country's most powerful political figures — among them William Pitt, Edmund Burke, Charles James Fox, the earl of Shelburne, and John Wilkes — were demanding that Parliament make concessions and withdraw the army. When Burke delivered his "Speech on Conciliation" in 1775, only two-thirds of the members supported the king in the vote that followed.

West's position was a peculiar one. The king had befriended him, visited him in his painting room at Windsor Castle, called him in private by his Christian name, and spent as much as a half day at a time talking with him while he was painting. And yet West was sympathetic to the American cause, and while he did not parade his republican views, he did not deny them. He was frank in his exchange of letters with Peale, which were no doubt reviewed by His Majesty's censors, since Peale was now not only a soldier in the Continental army, but also a zealous patriot in politics in Pennsylvania, the one state that was having a class revolution internally as well as a civil war with Britain. "The present commotions between this country and its colonies," West wrote to Peale two months before Concord and Lexington,

is a subject I could dwell long on, but prudence and the times will not permit my saying any thing on that head — as what I might say would have but little weight in the scale of opinions. If it would, I should stand forth and speak it boldly, though it were at the risk of my all.

As opposition and differing in opinion in regard to the right of taxing America, seems to be hastening to a crisis, I hope my countrymen will act with that wisdom and spirit which seems to have directed them as yet, and be the means of bringing about a more permanent union than has been for these some years past between that country and this.

Measures taken here relative to America show but little knowledge of that country ... and should measures with you be as wrongly advised as with us, both countries are for some time undone, and which if pursued must finally break those extensive outlines of British Empire which those colonies alone must have procured her.

Some of the Loyalists who had fled to England were not pleased to see a man of West's views receive His Majesty's favor, and mutterings were heard that Rebel sympathizers in London were using West to convey information to the king.[4] The king did indeed discuss the war with West, partly to check on the information he was getting from overly optimistic Loyalists in New York and London. Joseph Farington recorded such a conversation told him by West in 1799. A report reached the king that Philadelphians had rebelled against the Continental Congress and raised the king's standard.

> West was one day with the King when he came from Court to dinner, and His Majesty mentioned the circumstances and asked West if he corresponded with any persons in America and had heard of it. West told His Majesty that a Quaker was lately arrived from Philadelphia and was with him the day before, and he asked the King when the Standard was raised. The King said the day mentioned was June 25. West observed that the Quaker left Philadelphia July 1st and knew nothing of such a circumstance.

The queen was present at that conversation. The next day West had occasion to go to Buckingham House to transact some business for her.

> When he had done it, she asked him if he was engaged that morning. He said not. She then told him to go into her closet with her which he did and found the King sitting there. The King began to talk about America. He asked West what would Washington do were America to be declared independent. West said he believed he would retire to a private situation. The King said if he did he would be the greatest man in the world.
>
> He asked West how he thought the Americans would act towards this country if they became independent. West said the war had made much ill blood but that would subside, and the dispositions of many of the chiefs, Washington, Lawrence [Laurens],

---

[4] Almost 100,000 American Loyalists — more than 3 percent of the population — fled the country, some 6000 to 7000 of them to England, most of the others settling in Canada. For the most part they left voluntarily. Usually they had supported the king when the British troops commanded the area in which they lived, and they departed when the troops departed. Lewis Einstein, in *Divided Loyalties* (1933), likened the exodus to that of the Huguenots from France. The Loyalists have been credited (or charged) with holding Canada loyal to the Crown in the War of 1812. James Truslow Adams attributed the rapid decline in taste and cultivation in the United States in the nineteenth century in part to the disappearance of the country's conservative and educated class in 1775–83, which might have been a counterweight to the crude, brawling folk of the western frontier.

Adams, Franklin, Jay, were favorable to this country which would soon have a preference to any other European nation. During this conversation the Queen was much affected and shed tears.

The American Loyalists were for the most part unhappy exiles. They subsisted on small pensions paid by the Crown, complained of high prices and mismanagement of the war, and made their loneliness worse when they scattered to the outer counties where living was cheaper. Curiously, their identity as Americans was reinforced by British attitudes toward "the insurgents." Samuel Curwen, a former judge of Admiralty at Salem, now one of the early Loyalist refugees in London, where he received a £100 annual grant, wrote in his journal:

> It is my earnest wish the despised Americans may convince these conceited islanders, that without regular standing armies our continent can furnish brave soldiers and judicious and expert commanders, by some knock-down irrefragable argument. For then, and not till then, may we expect generous or fair treatment. It piques my pride, I confess, to hear us called "our colonies, our plantations," in such terms and with such airs as if our property and persons were absolutely theirs, like the "villains" and their cottages in the old feudal system, so long since abolished, though the spirit or leaven is not totally gone, it seems.

Despite his sympathy for the Rebel cause, West gave comfort and help where he could to these exiled countrymen. One such was Isaac Hunt, who had married Mary Shewell, Elizabeth West's niece by her brother Stephen. Hunt, a lawyer, had been manhandled by a Philadelphia mob for preaching Loyalist sentiments and had fled to England by way of the West Indies, presumably on one of his father-in-law's ships used to carry on trade during the Revolution. Two years later Mary Shewell Hunt joined her husband with their three young children. West gave them shelter at 14 Newman Street and intervened personally at court to have Isaac Hunt put on the pension list. (Their son, the poet-editor Leigh Hunt, born in England in 1784, never forgave the United States or his grandfather Stephen Shewell for treatment his parents had received.)

A leading spokesman among Loyalists in London was Samuel Shoemaker — he who in 1747 had introduced young Benjamin (age nine) to William Williams and so produced his "palpitations of joy" at first seeing a real oil painting. Shoemaker had left Philadelphia with the occupying British army when it evacuated the city in 1778 and was charged with treason, his estates confiscated. West entertained him at his house on Park Street in Windsor on a pleasant October weekend and managed to obtain for him a private audience with the king, queen, and several of the princesses. Shoemaker wished that some of his violent countrymen could have had such an experience; they would certainly be convinced that George the Third had not one grain of tyranny in his composition, and that he was not, could not be, that bloody-minded man they so repeatedly and so illiberally called him. It was impossible; a man of his fine feelings, so good a husband, so kind a father, could not be a tyrant.

Another refugee was the Anglican clergyman Jacob Duché, a boyhood friend, who had married Francis Hopkinson's sister. Duché had been so zealous for liberty in 1774 that he was made chaplain of the Continental Congress. In 1777, however, after being imprisoned by the British forces occupying Philadelphia, he experienced a change of heart, wrote a letter to Washington advising him to begin peace negotiations with the British, whether Congress approved of it or not, and fled to England to escape a charge of treason. (His property was confiscated, but his family was given enough money to follow him.) When Duché published two volumes of his sermons, dedicated to Lady Juliana Penn, West contributed a frontispiece engraving for each volume.

From these and other refugees, West learned what was happening to his friends and patrons back in Philadelphia. His cousin Edward Penington, the Quaker merchant who had given him his first box of paints and brushes, openly opposed resistance to Britain and was arrested and exiled from Philadelphia for some months. William Allen, a mild Loyalist who advocated compromise rather than rebellion, resigned his judicial positions and, at seventy-two, retired to England. James Hamilton, another patron, was arrested as a Loyalist, held prisoner for a year, and was then released, heartbroken and without office or influence. George Ross, who had persuaded him to paint in Lancaster, was a signer of the Declaration of Independence. Thomas Mifflin, subject of his finest American portrait, was one of the youngest and most radical members of the Continental Congress; he distinguished himself in the early battles and in August 1775 became quartermaster general of the Continental army. William Henry of Lancaster was appointed armorer of Pennsylvania and assistant commissary general of the United States. Joseph Reed, one of his boyhood companions on the banks of the Schuylkill, was a true hero of the Revolution, at the center of great events as a member of the Continental Congress, president of the Pennsylvania provincial congress, General Washington's military secretary, and an adjutant general who saw action at Long Island, Trenton, Princeton, Brandywine, Germantown, and

Monmouth. William Smith, provost of the College of Philadelphia, adopted the name "Candidus" to write against the "ruinous, delusive and impracticable" idea of separating from England; when the Pennsylvania radicals seized his college, he retreated to Chestertown, Maryland, to establish another. Francis Hopkinson, another close boyhood friend, was author of satirical pamphlets against the British, a member of the Continental Congress, and a signer of the Declaration of Independence.

One of those at court who disapproved the king's intimacy with an American commoner of known or suspected rebel convictions was William Schaw, Lord Cathcart. He was a young Scottish baron who had distinguished himself in America as a cavalry officer and there married the daughter of the Loyalist lieutenant governor of New York. (Lord Cathcart was the brother of the beautiful Lady Graham, subject of Gainsborough's portrait masterpiece.) In a story recorded by Benjamin Silliman,[5] Lord Cathcart one day asked West, in the king's presence and in a loud voice, if he had heard the war news that morning. West replied that he had not seen the papers. Cathcart said, "Then, sir, let me inform you that His Majesty's troops in South Carolina have gained a splendid victory over the rebels, your countrymen. This, I suppose, cannot be very pleasant news to you, Mr. West."

West replied, "No, sir, that is not pleasant news to me, for I never can rejoice at the misfortunes of my countrymen."

The king had not appeared to notice the conversation, but now he turned and said to West, "Sir, that answer does you honor." To Lord Cathcart he said, "Sir, let me tell you that, in my opinion, any man who is capable of rejoicing in the calamities of his country, can never make a good subject of any government."

Lord Cathcart was not converted by this rebuke. As his influence increased at court in the early years of a long and distinguished career, he and his wife worked persistently to end West's influence with the king and to stop the allowance paid him from the king's privy purse.

---

[5] Silliman was founder of the Yale Scientific School and the *American Journal of Science and Arts,* and first president of the organization that was to become the American Association for the Advancement of Science. He heard the story from West in 1805.

The American School:
1777–1781

West wiser than Reynolds and was in fact as to goodness what
Sir Joshua seemed . . . He gave positive while the other only neg-
ative instruction . . . By nature West was the wisest man he ever
knew.

MATTHEW HARRIS JOUETT,
notes of a conversation
with his teacher,
Gilbert Stuart, 1818

*J*OSEPH WHARTON, JR., forty-two years old in 1776, a member of the great Philadelphia Quaker mercantile family, was in
England through much of the American Revolution. He saw his
friend West frequently and, in fact, posed for one of the figures in
The Destruction of the French Fleet at La Hogue, which West exhibited in 1780. And he was present at an encounter of some significance to American art.

As Wharton told the story to the American artist Thomas Sully
in 1810, he was with several other Americans dining with West
when a servant announced that a man at the door wished to speak
to Mr. West. West said, "I am engaged," but after a pause added,
"Who is he?" The servant replied that the man said he was from
America.

West left the table at once, and on returning said the caller was
a young man who claimed to be known in Philadelphia. He asked
Wharton to "go and see what you can make of him." Wharton
went out, saw "a handsome youth in a fashionable green coat," and
questioned him.

"You are known in Philadelphia?"

"Yes, sir."

"Your name is Stuart?"

"Yes."

"Have you no letters for Mr. West?"

"No, sir."

"Who do you know in Philadelphia?"

"Joseph Anthony is my uncle."

Wharton had had business dealings with Anthony, a well-to-do merchant, and he at once asked Stuart to join the company.

Gilbert Stuart, the son of an emigrant Scottish snuff grinder, had been reared in Newport, Rhode Island, where he taught himself to paint portraits and to play several musical instruments. He entered the studio of a Scottish artist who took him to Edinburgh; the Scot died in 1772, leaving Stuart penniless. He worked his way back to America as a seaman and there for several years painted portraits in Newport and Boston. Joseph Anthony, his mother's younger brother, joined with several patrons to lend him passage money to England. He arrived in the autumn of 1775.

Stuart had hoped to study under West, but because of pride, or shyness, or perversity, he lived a hand-to-mouth existence in London for almost a year without writing or calling. Benjamin Waterhouse, a boyhood friend he had counted on for companionship and help in London, was in medical school in Edinburgh. Joseph Anthony had fled to a Pennsylvania farm to escape the turmoil of the Revolution and declined to send money. Waterhouse returned to London in the summer of 1776 to find Stuart in a cheap room with one painting on his easel, a portrait for which he had collected the fee but seemed unable to finish. Waterhouse obtained decent lodgings for him with two of his female cousins and, though poor himself, several times rescued his friend from debtors' prison. He got Stuart a ten-guinea portrait commission, given as an act of charity, which he finished, and another which he could not finish. He collected a half guinea each from his fellow medical students to have Stuart paint a portrait of a loved professor. Stuart spent the money but could not be persuaded to begin the portrait. Waterhouse had to beg the money from an uncle to repay the students; the episode caused him "inexpressible unhappiness and mortification, which brought on me a fever." When Stuart finally called on West, he had one article of decent apparel: a fashionable green coat.

Now the young man told of his long desire to see Mr. West and of his great wish to improve himself in the arts, to all of which (according to Joseph Wharton's account) West listened "with kindness and attention." He requested Stuart to bring something he had painted; it is not certain that he did so. For some days he seems to have spent his time simply observing what was going on in West's studio. What profession, West finally asked, did he intend to follow? Stuart replied that he had not yet made up his mind, but he was thinking of becoming a musician. Did he suppose, West asked, that he could compete with London's musicians? Should he not fix on one particular instrument, practice under a first-rate teacher, and then set out to succeed?

Several days later Stuart was passing St. Vedast's Church in Foster Lane when, seeing a crowd at the church door, he asked what was taking place. He was told that it was a competition for an organist. He asked to be heard, was taken to the organ-loft, and performed so well that he was given the post at thirty pounds a year. West suspected the story until he saw the written appointment. On being convinced that Stuart was not deceiving him, he still doubted that the young man would persevere in the duty more than a few weeks.

Stuart quit or was relieved of his post three months later. By Easter of 1777 he was in desperate circumstances. He had used up his stock of good will with his few friends in London; West was the only person he could turn to for help. Unwilling to call at 14 Newman Street, he composed a letter, a statement of need, a plea for rescue:

> Sir
>
> The benevolence of your disposition encourageth me, while my necessity urgest me to write you on so disagreable a subject. I hope I have not offended by takeing this liberty my poverty & ignorance are my only excuse Lett me beg that I may not forfeit your good will which to me is so desireable. Pitty me Good Sir I've just arrived att the age of 21 an age when most young men have done something worthy of notice & find myself ignorant without bussiness or freinds, without the necessarys of life so far that for some time I have been reduced to one miserable meal a day and frequently not even that, destitute of the means of acquiring knowledge, my hopes from home blasted & incapable of returning thither, pitching headlong into misery, I have this only hope I pray that it may not be too great (to live & learn without being a burthen. Should Mr. West in his abundant kindness think of ought for me I shall esteem it an obligation which shall bind me forever with grattitude with the greatest humility
>
> Sir
> Yours at Com^d
> G C Stuart

Dr. Waterhouse (who may have persuaded Stuart to write the letter) seems to have called on West at this same time and, in his own words, "laid open to him his (Stuart's) situation, when that worthy man saw into it at once, and sent him three or four guineas." Two days later West dispatched his servant to find and bring Stuart to him; he offered employment in copying at one-half guinea a week, with the freedom to continue his own painting. Stuart accepted and at once took a room near 14 Newman Street.

Stuart was at a moment of profound change in his life and art. For the first time he was able to work under proper conditions. He now had facilities important to any artist: adequate supplies and equipment, large rooms, models to draw from, other pictures to study, books to read, a place to display his work. He had discipline and guidance, and he received reassurance and his first recognition. He was transformed from a lonely outlander to a participant at a sophisticated center of English painting, in rooms busy with comings and goings, gossip, ideas, and, despite West's consistently grave demeanor, a good deal of merriment. As West's assistant he met some of the personages of the day, informally and often: the officers and artists of the Royal Academy, West's patrons and visitors and those who sat to him for portraits, officials of the court at Windsor, American agents and expatriates.

Having decided to take a chance with this unstable young man, the Wests went to extraordinary lengths to nurture him. "I was welcomed with true benevolence," Stuart said in his old age, "encouraged and taken into the family, and nothing could exceed the attentions of the artist to me — they were paternal." He poked fun at West in his later years, but when an acquaintance called West a fool, assuming that Stuart would agree, he turned on the man with a savage rebuke.

Early in their association, West was inspecting a new instrument that had been left with him, a camera lucida.[1] He showed it to Stuart; Stuart let it fall, and the mirrors (or the lens) cracked into pieces. He stood with his back to West, looking with despair at the broken instrument, bracing himself for the outburst that must follow. West, after a pause, said only, "Well, Stuart, you may as well pick up the pieces."

Stuart responded well to such treatment. He settled down and directed his untamed energies into hard work. He seems to have developed a coltish infatuation for Elizabeth West (14 years older than he), with a consequent improvement in his manners. Under West's sponsorship, he showed a *Portrait of a Gentleman* at the Academy exhibition in the spring of 1777; West was on the Hang-

---

[1] An optical device that projects an image of an external object on a screen or other flat surface so that its outlines may be traced.

ing Committee that year and gave it good space. West obtained permission for Stuart and one companion to see the royal collection on a Saturday afternoon. Stuart's one-sentence letter to Waterhouse fairly bursts with excitement:

> Friend Benjamin
>> By no means disappoint me, but be at my lodgings precisely at three o'clock, to go to the Queen's Palace.
>>> Yours,
>>> G. Stuart

Waterhouse long remembered that "we found nothing to equal the collection at the Queen's Palace." [2]

West had begun a series of major portraits of the royal family, all of which appeared in the annual Royal Academy exhibitions in the years 1777–1784. He first painted Queen Charlotte, three-quarter length, seated on a sofa, a tatting shuttle in her hand, her ten-year-old daughter Charlotte, the Princess Royal, standing, holding a length of brocade between them. There was a saying in art circles, "We judge no painter, living or dead, by his portraits of royalty," but this work (for which he received £157) is a competent, pleasant and reasonably honest one. (Walpole called it "bad, and too old for the Queen.") The king admired it and kept it in his private retiring chamber at St. James's. Eleven other pictures followed: the king, two more of the queen, the king and queen together, and the Prince of Wales and the other children at various ages, singly or in groups. The most remarkable of these was the 1779 full-length portrait of the queen, standing on a beautifully painted "Turkish carpet," a spaniel at her feet, her crown on a table beside her. In the background, on the south front terrace at Windsor Castle, are grouped her thirteen children (two more were born later). The picture took several years to complete, and it had to be revised from time to time when another prince or princess appeared. This was the king's favorite royal portrait; he hung it in the room where every morning he had breakfast with the queen. [3]

---

[2] Waterhouse went shortly thereafter to Leyden in the Netherlands to continue his medical studies (he lived there in the same house with John Adams, then American minister) and did not see Stuart again until many years later in Boston. In 1780 he returned to the United States, where he became a founding professor of the Medical Department of Harvard University and in 1800 introduced Dr. Jenner's smallpox vaccine into the United States.

[3] George III's fifteen legitimate children by one wife, unaccompanied by bastard half brothers or sisters, has been called a record for European royalty.

Stuart advanced from copier to student to full assistant, and he worked on the royal portraits as drapery painter and "finisher" of those lesser parts sketched in by the master. West had introduced two new subjects into British art: scenes from early English literature, beginning with Spenser's *Faerie Queene*, and episodes from Saxon history. The first Saxon piece, painted in 1778, was magnificently titled, *William de Albanac presents his three daughters (naked) to Alfred the Third, King of Mercia, with the following words, "Here be my three daughters, chuse to wife which you list; but rather than you should have one of them to be concubine, I would slay her with my own hand."* [4] In addition to working on such pieces, Stuart, like anyone else present, often served as a model for figures or parts of figures. When West was painting *The Battle of the Boyne*, he put on a suit of armor and lay for hours on the floor as the slain duke of Schomberg. "Are you dead?" West called when he had finished. Stuart, having lost sensation in both legs from the weight of the armor, moaned, "Only half, sir."

One of the frequent callers at West's home and studio in the years 1778–80 was William Williams, his first teacher, the man who in Philadelphia some twenty-five years earlier had lighted the fire in his breast that had "never been extinguished." Williams' two sons had been killed fighting for American independence and his second wife had died. Alone in the world and almost fifty, he had accepted the invitation of a Bedfordshire gentleman of means to return to England and settle down with him and paint on his country estate. Williams had earlier called on West with his friend in 1776, passing through London on his way to Bedfordshire. His benefactor, unfortunately, had died within eighteen months, and now Williams was living alone in London. He often called at 14 Newman Street and sat smoking his pipe while West was painting. West assumed that his friend was poor, but Williams refused offers of money and occasionally added to his collection of engravings. When painting *The Battle of La Hogue*, West employed him as a model, making him the half-naked, fierce-visaged, struggling seaman in one of the boats. "I was of some service to him in London," West said, "but of a sudden missed him from town." Becoming apprehensive, he inquired among the engravers and learned that Williams was indeed very poor, was losing his eyesight, and had moved to Bristol "to claim some provision that was due him from the parish."

---

[4] The picture was destroyed by fire in 1816. George Washington owned a print of it that hung in the family dining room at Mt. Vernon during his lifetime.

Another American artist appeared on West's doorstep in the spring of 1778, asked to become his pupil, and was taken in. He was Ralph Earl, twenty-seven, just arrived from Connecticut, where he had painted some remarkable portraits in a stiff, awkward, realistic manner. Earl was a living refutation of a guiding principle of West's life and art: that next to genius and industry, virtue was the best qualification a painter could have. Earl was likeable, good-natured, and full of humor; he has lately been reassessed as one of the most gifted of eighteenth-century American painters; but he was somewhat deficient in virtue. He had deserted a wife and two children in Connecticut. At the outbreak of the Revolution his father raised and commanded a body of patriots; Earl refused a commission in the unit and was disinherited. He was taken before a Committee of Safety, refused to cooperate with it, and was released on his promise to leave Connecticut. Instead he joined the colony's Friends of Government (Tories). Learning of Rebel plans to attack British forces on upper Long Island, he and his friends sent a messenger thirty miles by boat to warn them. The Rebel attack was repulsed. He was summoned again before the committee and would have been executed save for his father's high rank. He again promised to quit the colony and this time managed to get to England disguised as a servant of the quartermaster general of Burgoyne's army, to whom he had been furnishing intelligence information. He committed bigamy by marrying an English girl; he was a heavy drinker and a spendthrift; and the quality of his art rose along with the quantum of his sinning.

Earl studied under West for four or five months in 1778, then leaving to strike out on his own. A year or two later, somewhat chastened, he returned to the warmth and orderliness of West's studio and was received without reproach. While continuing his studies and working under West, he took portrait commissions on his own and exhibited at the Royal Academy. He was one of the assistants who spent the summers and autumns in the West house at Windsor.[5]

John Trumbull, twenty-four, late colonel in the American rebel army, appeared in London on July 13, 1780, bearing a letter of intro-

---

[5] Earl sailed for America with his English wife in April 1785, after two and a half years in West's studio. He decided, injudiciously, to go first to Worcester, Connecticut, where he ran into a hornets' nest of recrimination and legal action from his first wife and her relatives. He fled to New York to begin his most creative years in a third phase of his career. He died in 1801, age fifty, having destroyed himself, according to William Dunlap, "by baleful intemperance." One hundred thirteen of his portraits have been identified, ninety-six of them signed. *Roger Sherman* and *Mr. and Mrs. Oliver Ellsworth* are his best-known works.

duction to West from Benjamin Franklin, then American plenipo-
tentiary to France. Trumbull was the son of one of the principal
supporters of the American rebellion, the governor of Connecticut.
On graduating from Harvard College in 1773, he had decided that
he might become a painter. Mr. Copley had commended his work,
but Trumbull was not altogether sure that a career as a professional
painter was suitable for a gentleman and a college graduate. At the
outbreak of the Revolution he offered his services to the army. He
saw and sketched the Battle for Bunker Hill from a distance, won
General Washington's attention with his ability to draw maps, and
served as the general's second aide-de-camp for nineteen days.
When the papers came through that made him a colonel, they were
dated seventy-five days later than he expected, and he thus felt
that his honor as an officer required him to resign his commission.
He resumed his study of painting.

Trumbull's friends urged him to seek artistic instruction in
France and at the same time conduct there a business speculation
(the nature is unknown) in which they would all share the profits;
they raised the funds to pay for his journey. A British offical in
Boston who knew Benjamin West intervened to say that he should
study under that artist, and, concealing nothing of Trumbull's military past, obtained the British government's permission for him to
do so, provided he did not commit even the smallest indiscretion,
avoided all political activity, "and pursued the study of the arts
with assiduity."

Trumbull sailed from New London to France in May 1780 in an
armed French merchantman loaded with sugar and coffee from
Santo Domingo. He called on Franklin and John Adams in Paris,
saw his prospects for a business speculation collapse with disastrous
American losses in the war, and decided to proceed at once to
London, traveling by way of Ostend. He sent word of his arrival to
Lord George Germain, secretary of state for the Colonies, and then
went to see Mr. West. The next day a body of American Loyalists
called on Lord George. They were led by Joseph Galloway, once a
delegate to the First Continental Congress and speaker of the Pennsylvania Assembly, who had gone over to the British during their
occupation of Philadelphia; he was now the Loyalist spokesman in
London, an able pamphleteer, and an enemy of Benjamin West. He
and his colleagues informed the secretary of the arrival of John
Trumbull, a Rebel, and protested his presence in England. "You are
late, gentlemen," Germain said sardonically. "Mr. Trumbull arrived yesterday at three o'clock, and I knew it at four. My eye is
upon him, but I must observe to you, that so long as he shall attend

closely to the object of his pursuit . . . he shall [not] be interrupted."
The Loyalists were not reconciled to that decision.

Trumbull wrote:

> I presented the letter of Dr. Franklin to Mr. West, and of course
> was most kindly received. His first question was, whether I had
> brought with me any specimen of my work, by which he could
> judge of my talent, and the progress I had made; and when I
> answered that I had not, he said, "Then look around the room,
> and see if there is anything which you would like to copy."
>
> I did so, and from the many which adorned his painting-room,
> I selected a beautiful small round picture of a mother and two
> children. Mr. West looked keenly at me, and asked, "Do you
> know what you have chosen?"
>
> "No, sir."
>
> "That, Mr. Trumbull, is called the Madonna della Sedia, the
> Madonna of the chair, one of the most admired works of Raphael.
> The selection of such a work is a good omen. In an adjoining
> room I will introduce you to a young countryman of ours who is
> studying with me. He will show you where to find the necessary
> colors, tools, etc., and you will make your copy in the same
> room."

The young countryman who had the privilege of a private painting
room was Gilbert Stuart. Trumbull found him in his working
clothes: "He was dressed in an old black coat, with one-half torn
off at the hip and pinned up, and looked more like a beggar than a
painter." With Stuart's help, Trumbull prepared his materials and
proceeded to his work.

> When Mr. West afterwards came into the room, to see how I went
> on, he found me commencing my outline without the usual aid
> of squares. "Do you expect to get a correct outline by your eye
> only?" "Yes, sir. At least I mean to try." "I wish you success."
> His curiosity was excited, and he made a visit daily, to mark
> my progress, but forebore to offer me any advice or instruction.
>
> When the copy was finished, and he had carefully examined
> and compared it, he said, "Mr. Trumbull, I have now no hesita-
> tion to say that nature intended you for a painter. You possess
> the essential qualities. Nothing more is necessary but careful and
> assiduous cultivation."

With this encouragement, Trumbull for the first time seriously applied himself as an art student, "allowing little time to make myself
acquainted with the curiosities and amusements of the city."

From that time forward he was in daily contact with Stuart, his complete opposite in background, education, and personality. They played duets together on the flute. Stuart once astonished him by asserting that he not only read books but remembered what he read, and by giving an example: "Linnaeus is right. Plato and Diogenes call man a biped without feathers. That's a shallow definition. Franklin's is better: 'A tool-making animal.' But Linnaeus's is best: 'Homo: — animal mendax, rapax, pugnax.'" Trumbull once brought him a drawing for criticism. Stuart turned it this way and that and then said in a perplexed tone, "Why, Trumbull, this looks as though it was drawn by a man with one eye." Trumbull was offended by the remark but was mollified when he learned that Stuart did not know he had lost most of the vision in his left eye in a childhood accident. Because of his monocular vision, West imposed an "injunction" on Trumbull: He should paint only small pictures; he should represent even the largest scenes with great precision on canvases not more than 25 by 30 inches, thus avoiding distortion of the subject.

Stuart painted directly on the canvas without first drawing the figure or object; he could never, Trumbull observed, "exercise the patience necessary to correct drawings." [6] West assembled his son Raphael, Stuart, and Trumbull and said to them, "You ought to go to the Academy to study drawing, but as you would not like to go there without being able to draw better than you do now — if you will only attend I will keep a little academy, and give you instructions every evening." Trumbull and young "Rafe" applied themselves with diligence and became adept draughtsmen; Stuart lost his patience and gave it up.

"I used very often to provoke my good old master," [7] Stuart said in later years, "though, heaven knows, without intending it . . . I was a giddy foolish fellow then." He was in West's painting room one day with Trumbull and began to lecture on the painting standing on the easel, a portrait of a child, and on West's "way of making curly hair by a flourish of his brush, thus, like a figure of three." Did Trumbull wish to learn how to paint hair? "There it is, my boy! Our master figures out a head of hair like a sum of arithmetic . . . We may tell how many guineas he is to have for this picture by simple addition."

---

[6] "Drawing the features distinctly and carefully with chalk [is a] loss of time. All studies [ought] to be made with brush in hand. [It is] nonsense to think of perfecting oneself in drawing before one begins to paint." Stuart in 1816.

[7] West could not have been more than forty-eight in the context of this statement.

How much the sum would have amounted to I can't tell, for just then in walked the master, with a palette-knife and palette, and put to flight my calculations. "Very well, Mr. Stuart," said he — he always *mistered* me when he was angry . . . "Very well, Mr. Stuart! Very well, indeed!"

You may believe that I looked foolish enough, and he gave me a pretty sharp lecture without my making any reply. When the head was finished there were no figures of three in the hair.

On another occasion West asked Stuart to complete a portrait that had to go out in two days, adding that Stuart's work on it "will do well enough." Stuart promised to finish it the next morning.

He never came down into the painting-room, at the bottom of the gallery, until about ten o'clock. I went into his room bright and early, and by half-past nine I had finished . . . That done, Rafe and I began to fence, I with my maulstick and he with his father's. I had just driven Rafe up to the wall, with his back to one of his father's best pictures, when the old gentleman, as neat as a lad of wax, with his hair powdered, his white silk stockings and yellow morocco slippers, popped into the room, looking as if he had stepped out of a bandbox. We had made so much noise that we did not hear him come down the gallery or open the door.

"There you dog," says I to Rafe, "There I have you! And nothing but your background relieves you!"

The old gentleman could not help smiling at my technical joke [that is, the double meaning he gave to the word *background*], but soon looking very stern, "Mr. Stuart," said he, "is this the way you use me?"

"Why, what's the matter, sir? I have neither hurt the boy nor the background."

"Sir, when you knew I had promised the picture . . . should be finished today, ready to be sent away tomorrow, thus to be neglecting me and your promise! How can you answer it to me or to yourself?"

"Sir," said I, "do not condemn me without examining the esel. I have finished the picture, please to look at it."

He did so, complimented me highly, and I had ample revenge for his "It will do well enough."

On the afternoon of November 20, 1780, West received alarming news in a letter hand-delivered from the Brown Bear, a lock-up house opposite the police station on Bow Street. It came from John Trumbull. Late the night before, a police officer had come to his rooms in York Buildings with a warrant to arrest John Steel Tyler, a former American army officer with whom Trumbull shared lodgings. (Colonel Tyler, forewarned by a friend, had fled to France that same evening.) The police officer also had a warrant to secure the person and papers of John Trumbull for examination. Trumbull, under arrest, his letters impounded, had spent the night at the Brown Bear with "bloods, bullies and pimps," guarded by an armed officer. At eleven o'clock the next morning he was taken across the street, under guard, through a crowd of curious idlers, and examined by three police magistrates. They read the customary statement that he was under no compulsion to answer and then questioned him about the suspicious language in three letters they read aloud. They did so in a style "so offensive to my feelings" that he burst out with a forceful statement.

> You appear to have been much more habituated to the society of highwaymen and pickpockets, than to that of gentlemen. I will put an end to all this insolent folly by telling you frankly who and what I am. I am an American. My name is Trumbull. I am the son of him whom you call the rebel governor of Connecticut. I have served in the rebel American army. I have had the honor of being an aid-du-camp to him whom you call the rebel General Washington. These two have always in their power a greater number of your friends, [their] prisoners, than you have of theirs. Lord George Germaine knows under what circumstances I came to London, and what has been my conduct here. I am entirely in your power; and, after the hint which I have given you, treat me as you please, always remembering that as I may be treated, so will your friends in America be treated by mine.

He said further that he was protected by the assurances he had received from the British government before leaving America and by the general amnesty that had been offered to all Rebels by the Peace Commission in October 1778. He had come to England for the sole purpose of studying painting under Mr. West, who could inform the magistrates how he had passed his time these past four months. He demanded permission to write to Mr. West. "I half feared that I had said too much," he observed later, "but I . . . was immediately, and ever after, treated with marked civility, and even respect."

He was taken to Bridewell Prison at Tothill Fields, where he spent the night *"in the same bed with a highwayman."* The next day he was questioned again and then was remanded with a writ of incarceration, on suspicion of the Crime of High Treason committed within His Majesty's Colonies and Plantations in America. The news of his arrest caused (in Trumbull's words) "extreme anxiety" to Mr. West. "His love for the land of his nativity was no secret, and he knew that the American loyalists . . . were outrageous [*sic*] at the kindness which the king had shown to him, and still continued. He dreaded also the use which might be made to his disadvantage of the arrest for treason of a young American who had been in a manner domesticated under his roof, and of whom he had spoken publicly and with approbation."

In these circumstances, West also had to consider the possible effects on his other American students, including Earl and Stuart. The newspapers were carrying stories of the arrest, and though they were not unsympathetic, they spoke of a letter in Trumbull's possession from William Temple Franklin, grandson and secretary of that intriguer and archenemy of England in Paris, Dr. Franklin. With the normal fears of a man in such a delicate situation, West must also have considered the possibility, however quickly discarded, that Trumbull could be provably guilty of planned, organized espionage under the cover of his art studies — or at least could have been indiscreet in what he had said in his letters to France and America.[8]

It was not a good time to be associated with an American accused of spying, or to take steps to defend one. The British people were indignant at the hanging of Major John André as a spy on October 2. The American cause, moreover, had never looked so hopeless as it did in 1780; British leaders were predicting a quick end to the war, and pro-American, antiwar protests by the Whigs, while still strong, were unusually subdued. Charleston, South Carolina, had fallen to the British in May with the loss of 5500 men and immense military stores. General Horatio Gates had been defeated and disgraced at Camden, South Carolina, with the loss of one-third of his army. The defection of General Benedict Arnold to the British side had been revealed in September. The American economy was bankrupt; the Continental supply system had collapsed; Washington's meager army had little real support from the people.

West put on his hat and went immediately to Buckingham House, where he requested an audience with the king. He was admitted. Asking and receiving permission to speak, he began by explaining why he had come. He was naturally concerned, he said, that the arrest of one of his students for treason might involve his own character and diminish His Majesty's kindness to him. He declared that Mr. Trumbull's behavior had always been exemplary and that his devotion to his painting had left no time for political intrigue.

---

[8] Trumbull's latest biographer, Irma Jaffe (1975), believes it is "just possible" that Trumbull, Tyler, and two others were involved in a scheme relating to the impending war between Britain and Holland in the West Indies.

He pointed out that several years had passed between his leaving the American army and his arrival in England. He pledged himself for the young man's good disposition and conduct.

The king listened attentively. He said, "West, I have known you long and have conversed with you frequently. I can recollect no occasion on which you have ever attempted to mislead or misinform me, and for that reason you have acquired my entire confidence. I fully believe all you have now said, and assure you that my confidence in you is not at all diminished by this unpleasant occurrence. I am sorry for the young man, but he is in the hands of the law, and must abide the result — I cannot interpose. Do you know whether his parents are living?"

West replied, "I think I have heard him say that he has very lately received news of the death of his mother. I believe his father is living."

"I pity him from my soul!" The king was silent for a time, and then added, "But, West, go to Mr. Trumbull immediately, and pledge to him my royal promise that, in the worst possible event of the law, his life shall be safe." [9]

West went from the king to see Lord George Germain and the American Benjamin Thompson, undersecretary of state, the future Count Rumford. They assured him that as soon as the noise subsided a little, Mr. Trumbull would be released. He hurried to Trumbull in Bridewell Prison with this reassuring information and found him comfortably situated in one of the rooms of the keeper's house, a nicely furnished parlor on the ground floor, about 20 feet square, with a bureau (folding) bed, for which he paid one guinea a week. Trumbull said that Sir Sampson Wright, one of the magistrates, had sentenced him to Clerkenwell Prison, apologizing as he did so for the poor conditions and the bad company he would find there, and explaining that the anti-Catholic Gordon rioters the previous June had destroyed most of the prisons in London. When Trumbull sent a note of remonstrance to Germain at being placed "in such detestable companionship," his lordship sent word that Mr. Trumbull might choose any prison in England, from the Tower down, in which to be confined.

He had learned by inquiry that fees in the Tower were quite excessive, and so he had chosen Bridewell, where he had been pleased by the quiet (it lay behind Buckingham House toward Pimlico) and

---

[9] "The favor which was thus done to me by the king, in promising me pardon, if I should be brought to trial for treason and condemned, merits my grateful remembrance." Theodore Sizer, ed., *Autobiography of Colonel John Trumbull*, p. 70.

by the "civility and kindness" of Mr. Smith, the keeper, who, having served as butler to the duke of Northumberland, "had the manners of a gentleman." Trumbull had his meals sent in from a nearby public house, "what I choose to order and pay for." He was allowed two pennies a day for food; these he gave to the turnkey for brushing his hat and clothes and cleaning his shoes.

Undoubtedly relieved by what he saw and what he heard from Trumbull, West asked his friend what he could send him to soften his tedious confinement. Trumbull requested his painting equipment and materials and asked if he might borrow the "beautiful little Correggio" he had been copying — the *St. Jerome* West had copied in Parma seventeen years earlier. Gilbert Stuart took these to him. Stuart came often, bringing him other articles he needed, poking fun at him as "Bridewell Jack," and painting his portrait. (The head only; Trumbull added the body, the background, and bars on the window.)

Trumbull spent seven months in Bridewell Prison. He finished his copy of *St. Jerome*. He drew from a male model and sent work to the Academy's 1781 spring exhibition. He had a number of visitors, some of them important persons interested in his case. John Lee, a barrister of eminence and a member of Parliament, informed him that he could not force a court trial or release on bail because the act of habeas corpus had been suspended for the duration of the war, which meant that "proof was unnecessary and justification useless." Charles James Fox, leader of the Whig opposition, came, commiserated, lamented that he could not act because he was not on speaking terms with any of the ministers, and advised him to write to Edmund Burke, to whom he would speak on the matter. Burke came in May in response to Trumbull's letter. He said he would press the case with the ministers, and if he failed with them he would bring it before Parliament as an act of injustice which their honor obliged them to redress.

The ministers were now disposed to release Trumbull with conditions. His case was an embarrassing one: His status under the law was not clear, and public pressures were being brought to bear — from, among others, Governor Trumbull's bankers in Amsterdam, Messrs. John de Neufville and Son. In June a writ of discharge under bail was issued by the privy council. Trumbull was enjoined to leave the country within thirty days, and he was to post bond of £400. Trumbull raised £200 of that amount; West and Copley went surety for £100 each. Trumbull stayed ten more days in London, recovered all his papers except several of his more indiscreet letters to his father, and then took ship for Amsterdam, where he would find money to buy his passage back to America.

Joseph Galloway, the Loyalist leader in London, was not consulted about the release, which he deplored as further evidence of the British wish to conciliate the Rebels. West observed the omission and concluded that Galloway's influence had ended.

In the autumn of 1781 the war in America took a sudden and surprising turn against the British. There was public apprehension in Britain when it was learned that the army in Virginia commanded by General Lord Cornwallis was penned up on a peninsula between two rivers, attacked on land by a force of French and Americans and from the sea by a fleet of twenty French line-of-battle ships. In November an English packet boat returned to Dover from Calais, where, under a flag of truce, it had delivered a passenger of state. It brought back with it a French newspaper with a full account of the surrender on October 19 of General Cornwallis and his entire force of 7200 men — the bulk of the British field army in America.

More than a few Englishmen — some of them in high places — were jubilant. The strongest supporters of the war in America no longer had the will to continue the fight. On December 4 the guilds of London, in a Grand Remonstrance against continuing the war, told the king: "Your armies are captured. The wonted superiority of your navies is annihilated. Your dominions are lost."

The government fell and the Whig opposition, pledged to end the American War, took office. When it became apparent that Britain was defeated, the king drafted a declaration resigning the crown "with much sorrow" to the nineteen-year-old Prince of Wales, "whose endeavours for the prosperity of the British Empire he hopes may prove more successful." The king told West privately that he intended to abdicate and go to Hanover, the home of his ancestors, and he expressed a desire that West should accompany him. But he did not send the declaration to Parliament and it was heard of no more.

West was with the king when he received from his new ministers a box containing the speech from the throne he was to read granting American independence. He should have been pleased, he told West, if the Americans had remained under his government, but since it was otherwise, he hoped they would be happy in their new state and that they would not change it for a worse. He wished them no ill.[10] West and John Copley were in the House of Lords

---

[10] Virtually everyone who has written of this episode has described it as happening when the king received word of the American Declaration of Independence. It is obvious, of course, that George III could not have wished the

on December 2, 1782, when George III, reading in a halting and embarrassed manner, without his usual impressive delivery, recognized the independence of the United States of America. Copley returned home to resume work on a portrait he was painting of Elkanah Watson, an American then in London. The picture showed a ship in the background. "He invited me into his studio," Watson wrote in his *Memoirs*, "and there with a bold hand and a master's touch, he attached to the ship the stars and stripes. This was, I imagine, the first American flag ever hoisted in Old England."

Americans happiness in their new state in 1776. The error owes to a misinterpretation of West's account made by his young student, Samuel Finley Breese Morse. Joseph Farington, who heard the story from West on July 13, 1813, clearly identifies "the acknowledgment of American Independence" in 1782.

The Peace Commissioners

I did not ask favours or receive any thing but cold formalities from ministers of state or ambassadors. I found that our American painters had more influence at court to procure all the favors I wanted, than all of them.

JOHN ADAMS,
in recollections
of his experiences
in London in 1783–84

THE AFFAIRS of the Royal Academy, in the meantime, had been going well. The organization began to pay its own way in 1780, free for the first time from annual deficits that had to be made up from the king's privy purse; and in the same year it moved all its activities into handsome new quarters. The king had commissioned William Chambers to demolish Old Somerset House (where the Academy's schools had been held) and to rebuild on the site a vastly enlarged new Somerset House for the Royal Academy, Royal Society, Society of Antiquaries, and several government departments. The massive hewn-stone building was hailed as the finest public structure in London, one of the greatest pieces of civic architecture in England, and "a monument of the taste and elegance of His Majesty's reign." Horace Walpole wrote acidly to his friend William Mason, "It is quite a Roman palace and furnished in perfect taste as well as boundless expense. It would have been a glorious apparition at the conclusion of the great war; now it is an insult on our poverty and degradation."

The Academy's rooms fronted the Strand on the right (west) side of the building. The ground floor contained an entrance hall graced by casts of Greek and Roman statues, the porter's lodge, and to the right the Academy of Living Models. The mezzanine floor held administration offices. The first floor (European enumeration) had an anteroom that served also as a library, the Antique Academy (more casts), and the Council Room, its ceiling showing five panels painted on canvas by West (*Air, Earth, Fire, Water,* and *The Graces Unveiling Nature*) and four oval panels by Angelica Kauffmann (*Design, Colouring, Composition, Invention*). On the top floor were an anteroom, the living quarters of the keeper, and the Great Room or Assembly Hall, 53 by 42 feet, 32 feet high, lighted from above by clerestory windows set high up under the roof on all four sides. The four stories were served by a steep elliptical staircase of eighty-three steps; pictures were hoisted up the well of the staircase.[1] The Academy held its highly successful 1780 exhibition in the new galleries, Reynolds showing four pictures, Gainsborough sixteen, and West nine, including his first four royal portraits, *The Battle of La Hogue,* and *The Battle of the Boyne.*

Even in the larger galleries the pictures were hung, in the manner of the day, from floor to ceiling, the frames touching. Every year there were anger, heartache, and rebellion over placement, artists feeling their works deserved to be hung "on the line" in the Great Room, at or near eye level; they were outraged when they were skied to a position too high to be seen or were relegated to one of the lesser rooms.

John Downman, a Welsh associate member who called West "my most beloved teacher" was on bad terms with Academy officers because they persisted in treating his portraits as drawings (he worked in chalk and oil) and invariably hung them in poor light in a lower room; in 1782 he sought a guarantee that his pictures would be hung in the Great Room and was refused.[2] A year later Gainsborough wrote to the Academy Council stating exactly how he wished his pictures to be hung, sending an accompanying sketch and the threat that if they were not so hung "he never more whilst he breathes, will send another picture to the Exhibition. This he swears by God." The Hanging Committee acceded to his demand,

---

[1] Dr. Samuel Johnson, recovering from an illness, boasted that he felt so well he could run up the steps of the Royal Academy without stopping. The Academy remained in Somerset House for fifty-seven years. It moved in 1837 to a wing of the new National Gallery on Trafalgar Square and in 1869 to Burlington House in Piccadilly, where it abides today. On each remove it carried away its casts and its ceiling panel pictures by West and Kauffmann. In the 1970s Britain's Department of the Environment restored the former rooms of the Royal Academy, Royal Society, and Society of Antiquaries at Somerset House.

[2] In the 1920s Downman's oil and chalk portraits became popular and began to command high prices.

but the following year they rejected a similar notice and removed his eight pictures from the wall to be returned to him. Gainsborough never again exhibited at the Academy.

Art was now fashionable; indeed, there was almost a "picture mania," and the leading portrait painters were flooded with commissions. Many of the "most distinguished nobility," James Northcote, R.A., observed, "were now proud to come forward as patrons of the arts." The arts were splendidly benefited in 1785 when the twenty-three-year-old Prince of Wales attended the Academy dinner held the night before the opening of the spring exhibition. The prince's best friends and closest rakehell associates were the king's worst political enemies, and London buzzed with the news that the king, on being escorted through the exhibition, passed by a full-length portrait of his oldest son without a word and with his eyes averted.

The newspapers began to cover art news in detail in these years, and much of London's steady hum of gossip now concerned artists and their relationship to one another and to their patrons. Sharp, witty, and often malicious *ripostes* were seized upon and repeated in coffee houses, at dinner tables, and in the press. Because of his elevated position, and perhaps because he almost never introduced his fellow artists into the select intellectual company of the Literary Club, Joshua Reynolds was a favorite subject of satiric humor and gossip. His constant experiments with asphaltum and other glazes were causing his pictures to crack and deteriorate alarmingly, and a wit observed that Sir Joshua's subjects lived longer than their portraits. The story went the rounds of the lady who, when her head was finished, told Sir Joshua she would return to sit for the painting of her hands (which she believed to be very fine); he innocently replied that he would not give her so much trouble, as he commonly painted the hands from his servants. Reynolds, who did not like the landscape painter Richard Wilson, said pointedly in Wilson's presence at an Academy dinner, "Yes, Gainsborough is certainly the best landscape painter of the day." Wilson responded, "He is also the best portrait painter."

Wilson was now the Academy's librarian at fifty pounds a year, having been given that position as an act of charity to keep him from starving. Students heard and passed down to younger students stories about this old, irascible, grotesque character. When he visited the celebrated Falls of Terni outside Rome in his youth, he stood silent for a time, admiring the great volume of water falling some 650 feet, and then exclaimed, "Well done, water, by God!" He and an acquaintance were invited to visit a gentleman's house.

When they approached it, Wilson turned to his companion and inquired, "Are there any young ladies?" The answer was "Yes." He asked, "Do they draw?" and was told that they did. "Then," said Wilson, "good morning to you," and turned back. When the king sent Richard Dalton to him with word that 100 guineas was too high for a landscape he had painted on order, Wilson replied, "Tell His Majesty I do not wish to distress him. I will take it out at one guinea a week." Stories about Joseph Nollekens, the eccentric, miserly sculptor, were also passed about. He was adept at the old practice of pretending to cut away whenever the sitter pronounced a nose too large or a lip too pouting; he would allow a little stone dust to fall from his hand while moving his rasp or striking his chisel, until the sitter cried "Stop! stop! Don't cut away too much, that will do very well. Now, sir, don't you see how it has been improved?" When modeling the bust of a lady of high fashion, Nollekens requested her to lower her handkerchief in front. The lady objected and asked him simply to follow the general form, with which he was sufficiently acquainted. He was heard to mutter, "There is no bosom worth looking at beyond the age of eighteen."

West showed two pictures at the 1781 exhibition, neither of which produced much comment, but he was singled out for praise as the subject of a half-length portrait by Stuart. The gallery was hung with a dozen portraits by Reynolds and Gainsborough, but the critic of the *St. James's Chronicle* wrote, "An excellent portrait of Mr. West; indeed I do not know of a better one in the room." It was the first public notice Stuart had received, and he was undaunted by the critic's error in calling him E. F. Stuart. Like an author blissfully reading over and over his first printed piece, he stood for hours beside his picture, watching the viewers, listening to their comments. West was finally moved to approach him and say, "You have done well, Stuart. Now all you have to do is go home and do better." To his other students West said, "It is no use to steal Stuart's colors: if you want to paint as he does you must steal his eyes."

Stuart did sensationally better the following year with his memorable *Portrait of a Gentleman Skating* — the life-size figure of William Grant, a trim, handsome Scot from Congalton, black-clad, his arms folded, skating gracefully on the Serpentine in Hyde Park. The portrait — apparently Stuart's first attempt at a full-length — was painted in West's studio, and surely it was West who, thinking back twenty years, suggested that the skaters in the distant background should be doing the Philadelphia Salute. Against it in his catalogue

Horace Walpole, usually so sparing in his praise, wrote "Very good." Years later Stuart observed that he was "suddenly lifted into fame by a single picture."

West advised Stuart that he now should set out as a portrait painter in his own right. West's friend, Nathaniel Dance, concurred. "You are strong enough to stand alone," he said. "Take rooms. Those who would be unwilling to sit to Mr. West's pupil will be glad to sit to Mr. Stuart." Dance had recovered from a broken heart over Angelica Kauffmann and married a Mrs. Dummer of Hampshire, a rich, beautiful, and amiable widow. He changed his name to Dance-Holland, achieved a baronetcy, and stopped painting pictures. He gave Stuart all he wanted of his studio supplies, and when Stuart modestly took only a palette and a few brushes, he sent him much more. Mrs. John Hoppner, wife of a young rival portrait painter, wrote at the close of the 1782 exhibition, "Stuart has taken a house, I am told, of £150 a year rent, in Berners Street, and is going to set up as a great man." If Stuart so intended, he changed his mind, for he took a house at 7 Newman Street.

West and Stuart seem to have practised a kind of reciprocity. The St. James's Chronicle critic poked fun at them in May 1782: "Mr. Stuart is in partnership with Mr. West, where it is not uncommon for wits [to commission pictures] they do not . . . want, because they are told by Mr. West that Mr. Stuart is the only portrait painter in the world; and by Mr. Stuart that no man has any pretensions in history painting but Mr. West." [3]

West's next American student came to him with a strong recommendation from Benjamin Franklin. He was Mather Brown of Boston, who was descended from generations of Puritan clergymen, beginning with the formidable Richard, Increase, and Cotton Mather. Copley had been on terms of close friendship with Brown's mother and grandfather and had painted fine portraits of both. Brown's mother died before Mather was two, and he had been reared by her maiden sisters, one of whom, some time after his twelfth year, took him to young Gilbert Stuart in Boston, "the first person who learnt me to draw." As a teen-age itinerant miniature painter and wine salesman, Brown made enough money to provide for his aunts and to pay for three years of study in Europe. He carried a letter from his grandfather to Franklin in Paris, arriving in 1781; Franklin wrote such a glowing introduction to West that

---

[3] One Stuart subject, possibly referred to him by West, was Lord Grantham, who as Thomas Robinson in 1760 had introduced West to Cardinal Albani.

West gave him instruction "gratis, in consequence of the recommendation of Dr. Franklin." Brown also presented letters from his aunts to Copley, "who is particularly kind to me, welcomed me to his house, and lent me pictures." He studied briefly under Copley, but since that artist had little time to spend with students, he worked hard and seriously under West, for whom (according to his obituary fifty years later) he had a lifelong admiration that amounted "to idolatry." In January 1782, not yet twenty-one, he entered the Royal Academy schools, the first American to attend, and in the exhibition that spring he had a *Portrait of a Gentleman.*

"I will let them see if an obscure Yankee boy cannot shine as great as any of them," he wrote his aunts in 1784.

> I have just removed into a very elegant house, where I have genteel apartments for my pictures, and cut a respectable appearance which is of great consequence for one of my profession. My rent is 25 guineas pr. Ann. and I have laid out this week as much more for furniture. My name is elegantly engraved on a brass plate on the door, and I board myself with the help of a lodger in the house as cheap as I can. I am just entering the world, and have all the good wishes of my friends, and hope to get Business.

West, Copley, Stuart, and Brown were joined by still another American student in 1784. John Trumbull, pining in America for the artistic life of London, went to his father when news of the preliminary peace treaty was received in Connecticut and proposed that he return to his studies in England. Governor Trumbull proposed that he follow the leading profession in a republican government, that of a lawyer. John Trumbull explained to his father that a lawyer's career was passed in the midst of all the wretchedness and meanness of life, devoted as it was to extricating rogues from the consequences of their villainy. He wished, rather, to receive such honors and rewards as the ancients, particularly the Athenians, had bestowed on their artists. Governor Trumbull replied, "My son, you have made an excellent argument, but... you have omitted one point... Connecticut is not Athens." He bowed and left the room and, Trumbull said, never afterwards interfered in his choice of a career.

Trumbull arrived in London in January 1784, made immediately for 14 Newman Street, was "kindly received," and happily resumed his studies.

In April 1783, four months after the signing of the Preliminary Peace Treaty in Paris, Charles Willson Peale wrote to West to give a report on the state of the arts in the new country and on his own progress as an artist. Even while in military service he had been busy with portraits, especially in miniatures, "because they are portable and therefore could be kept out of the way of a plundering enemy." The continual increase in paper money, however, meant that he scarcely received half his price in real value. He had heard with pleasure that Mr. West was "still raising in reputation and constantly employed in the Historical line, that with honors you have riches, which I hope will continue to you in a long life with every other happiness." He asked West to sell for him a full-length portrait of General Washington, which he proposed to ship "by some of our public ministers which I expect will be sent to the Court of London, by which means it may go duty-free."

West replied on June 15. He felt "great delight" at the prospect of seeing "a whole-length portrait of that greatest of all characters, *General Washington* ... that phinominy among men." He wished to "congratulate you and my countrymen in general, on the event of the Peace and the fortitude they have shown during the unhappy war. Their wisdom and unshaken perseverence enroll them forever among the greatest charactors of antiquity." He forwarded a request for art services by an English publisher who "will make you the recompense you may require." And he continued:

> I have now a favor to ask for myself, which is that you would procure me the drawings or small paintings of the dresses of the American army, from the officers down to the common soldier, riflemen, etc. etc. — and any other characteristic of their armies or camps from which I may form an exact idea, to enable me to form a few pictures of the great events of the American contest.

Some seven weeks later, to make sure that Peale received his request, he wrote again, describing and elaborating on "my intention of composing a set of pictures containing the great events which have affected the revolution of America." He revealed that he meant to produce the whole undertaking himself, thereby increasing his profit and maintaining complete control. "This work I mean to do at my own expense and to employ the first engravers in Europe to carry them into execution, not having the least doubt, as the subject has engaged all the powers of Europe, all will be interested in seeing the event so portrayed."

Peale replied to the first letter on August 25, writing a description of the attire frontier riflemen would wear, with "powder horn and shot pouch of the Indian fashion, with wampum belts, small round hats of bucks tail and sometimes feathers. Very often these shirts were dyed brown — yellow — pink and blue black color according to the fancies of the company." With Pealesian practicality he obtained a hunting shirt and leggings from an acquaintance and sent them along by Dr. Caspar Wistar "who has the merit of being an admirer of the fine arts in spite of a Quaker education." Peale wrote again on December 10. As subjects he suggested *The Meeting of the Committee of Congress with General Howe on Staten Island* and *The Taking of the Hessians at Trent Town.* General Joseph Reed, he said, was carrying his portraits of General Washington and General Nathanael Greene to London to have plates engraved. ("Your advice would oblige me.") General Reed (West's boyhood friend) had been "meritoriously active and he can inform you of many matters which you may want to know."

West's first effort in the American Revolution series was *The Peace Commissioners in 1782,* a group portrait of the seven persons at the signing of the preliminary peace treaty: Franklin, Adams, Jay, Henry Laurens, William Temple Franklin (secretary of the American Commission and Dr. Franklin's grandson), and the British commissioner, Richard Oswald, with his secretary, Caleb Whitefoord. He began late in 1783 with an oil sketch 28-1/2 by 36-1/2 inches in size. Adams and Jay were both in London in the winter of 1783–84, after the signing of the final agreement, the Treaty of Paris in September, and both posed for West. He spent a considerable amount of time with Adams and his young son John Quincy. Adams described one episode in reminiscences he wrote in 1813:

> Mr. West asked of their majesties permission to show me and Mr. Jay the originals of the great productions of his pencil, such as *Wolfe, Bayard, Epaminondas, Regulus,* etc., etc., etc., which were all displayed in the Queen's Palace, called Buckingham House. The gracious answer of the king and queen was, that he might show us "the whole house."
>
> Accordingly, in the absence of the royal family at Windsor, we had an opportunity at leisure to see all the apartments, even to the queen's bedchamber, with all its furniture, even to her majesty's German bible, which attracted my attention as much as anything else. The king's library struck me with admiration...
>
> We gazed at the great original paintings of our immortal countryman, West, with more delight than on the very celebrated pieces of Vandyke and Reubens; and with admiration not less than that inspired by the cartoons of Raphael.

Copley procured a place for Adams in the House of Lords to hear the king's speech on the opening of Parliament. He obtained it from the earl of Mansfield, lord chief justice, whom he had painted, and whose constant refrain during the Revolution had been, "My Lords, if you do not kill him [John Adams], he will kill you." Now the Gentleman-Usher of the Black Rod roared out in a very loud voice, "Where is Mr. Adams, Lord Mansfield's friend?" "This," West remarked to Adams, "is one of the finest finishings in the picture of American Independence."

West next painted Henry Laurens, who was in England from time to time in 1783 as a kind of unofficial American minister. Dr. Franklin, however, presented a problem. West had not seen him for some eight years, and there seemed little chance that he would come to England. "You can tell me," Franklin wrote in August 1784, "whether my appearance in London may not be offensive to some whom I ought not and do not desire to offend any farther"; but his health at seventy-seven was such that he decided not to make the journey. West must have considered traveling to Paris, but instead he asked the help of his friend Caleb Whitefoord, whose portrait he would also have to paint. Whitefoord brought him a letter from Franklin, a portrait bust of Franklin, and a portrait painted in 1781 by one of West's students. This was Joseph Wright, son of Patience Lovell Wright, the wax modeler, proprietor of a London waxwork museum. West borrowed Wright's portrait and adapted it for *The Peace Commissioners.*[4]

Temple Franklin sat to West on a visit to London in August 1784, thus completing the five American faces. Unfortunately, the British commissioner, Richard Oswald, refused to pose for West, either because he was conscious of his extreme ugliness, or was disinclined to be immortalized on the occasion of his country's great defeat, or both. There was no contemporary portrait of Oswald on which to draw, and he died on his estate in Scotland in November 1784. West therefore could not finish the picture, and he abandoned it. It hangs today in the Du Pont Winterthur Museum in Wilmington, Delaware, in its incomplete state, one of the country's most-reproduced pictures, the right side blank, the left side showing the figures of Jay, Adams, Laurens, and the two Franklins.[5]

---

[4] Wright had traveled to Paris with a letter of introduction from West to Jean-Baptiste Marie Pierre, court painter to Louis XVI. He had painted the Franklin portrait there, made a number of replicas, and then embarked for America, bearing a letter of introduction from Franklin to George Washington.

[5] It is important to remember that West was painting the *Signing of the Preliminary Treaty in 1782*, since some historians have mistakenly assumed that he was painting the signing of the final treaty in 1783, which had a different cast of characters. Professor Richard B. Morris, for example, is amused in *The Peace-*

Years later, in 1817, West paid a social call on John Quincy Adams, who was about to conclude his service as U.S. minister to the Court of St. James's and return home to become President Monroe's secretary of state. They talked of the unfinished *Peace Commissioners*, which Adams remembered having seen in 1782, as a boy of fourteen, when his father posed for the work. He expressed a desire to see it again, and West the next morning obligingly sent it to his residence. On his voyage home, Adams wrote of the picture in his diary, and in so doing made a minor contribution to a subject on which little is known: To what extent were the famous English portraits of that time true resemblances? "The most striking likeness in the pictures," Adams wrote, "is that of Mr. Jay. Those of Dr. Franklin and his grandson . . . are also excellent. Mr. Laurens and my father, though less perfect resemblances, are very good."

West abandoned not only *The Peace Commissioners* but the whole series on the American Revolution as well. It is not known when he decided to do this — whether before, during, or after his work on the peace treaty picture; nor do we know his reasons for making that decision. He may have come to the considered but somewhat belated conclusion — or may have been advised — that it would be most unwise and in bad taste for the king's history painter to produce a series of pictures and engravings glorifying a war in which Britain had wasted £100 million and suffered a shattering defeat at the hands of rebellious subjects. At the least, he could embarrass his friend and patron; at the worst, he could lose his standing at court, his annuity, and his largest market for pictures.

The presence of John Trumbull in his studio certainly had an influence on his decision. Trumbull had moved smoothly into the position Stuart had held. He had a passion for accuracy in such details as dress, weapons, and architecture that pleased West. He was painting by day at West's house and drawing by night at the Academy school. In the summer of 1785, he said, "I finished, for Mr. West, a copy of his glorious picture of the battle of La Hogue, on cloth, a few inches larger on every side than the original. This work was of inestimable importance to me." (The copy was "retouched and harmonized by Mr. West," who enlarged and completed the picture and, in 1806, again retouched it.) On finishing

---

makers (pp. 435–36) that West "perpetuates an historical image which is incorrect in two particulars" — that is, neither Laurens nor Temple Franklin was present at the signing in 1783. Both were present, of course, at the 1782 scene West was painting.

his first London portrait he "had the vanity" to take it to show to
Reynolds, who, the moment he saw it, said in a quick, sharp tone,
"That coat is bad, sir, very bad. It is not cloth — it is tin, bent tin."
Trumbull wrote, "The criticism was but too true, but its severity
wounded my pride, and I answered (taking up the picture), 'I did
not bring this to you, Sir Joshua, merely to be told that it is bad.
I was conscious of that, and how could it be otherwise, considering
the short time I have studied? I had a hope, sir, that you would
kindly have pointed out to me, how to correct my errors.' I bowed
and withdrew, and was cautious not again to expose my imperfect
works to the criticism of Sir Joshua."

In the autumn of 1785, Trumbull began to think seriously about
painting the Revolutionary War subjects West had abandoned.
With West's blessing, he began with two early events: the death
of General Warren at the Battle for Bunker Hill, and the death of
General Montgomery in the American attack on Quebec. Both
pictures were painted in West's studio.

> When the Bunker's Hill was pretty far advanced, he said to me
> one day, "Trumbull, will you dine with me tomorrow? I have
> invited some of our brother artists, and wish you to be of the
> party."
>
> He received his friends in his painting-room, where by his di-
> rection my picture was standing in an advantageous light.
> Among the guests was Sir Joshua Reynolds, and when he entered
> the room he immediately ran up to my picture — "Why, West,
> what have you got here? — this is better colored than your works
> are generally." "Sir Joshua" (was the reply) "you mistake — that
> is not mine — it is the work of this young gentleman, Mr. Trum-
> bull. Permit me to introduce him to you." Sir Joshua was at least
> as much disconcerted as I had been by his *bent tin;* the account
> between us was fairly balanced.

West turned over to Trumbull not only his subject matter but also
his full concept of producing a series on the American Revolution.

> Mr. West witnessed the progress of these two pictures with great
> interest, and strongly encouraged me to persevere in the work of
> the history of the American revolution, which I had thus com-
> menced, and recommended to me that I should have the series
> engraved, by which means not only would the knowledge of
> them, and of my talent, be more widely diffused, but also, in
> small sums from many purchasers, I should probably receive a
> more adequate compensation for my labor than I could hope
> from the mere sale of the paintings, even at munificent prices. He

proceeded to detail to me a history of his own method, and of his success in the publication of the engravings from his history of England, and explained to me, with the kindness of a father, all the intricacies of such an enterprise — the choice of engravers, printers, publishers, etc. etc.

Since Trumbull wished to devote all his time and attention to his studies, West procured for him an Italian artist living in England, Antonio di Poggi, "of very superior talents as a draughtsman, and who had recently commenced the business of publishing"; he would handle the engravings and publication of the pictures.

In February 1785 the Wests gave a dinner party for Mr. and Mrs. John Copley, Henry Pelham (Mr. Copley's half brother), and Jonathan Clarke (Mrs. Copley's brother). Among the other guests were Mr. and Mrs. Joseph Farington and Valentine Green, the engraver, and Mrs. Green. Mrs. West that morning had bought two fowls, two soles, six lobsters, four dozen eggs, one dozen oranges, forty-six apples (she preferred American apples), six pounds of sugar, one-quarter pound of souchong tea, a pound of raisins, and a pound of almonds.

Copley had become so famous and prosperous that he now ranked close to West in London's growing colony of American artists, excelling West as a portrait painter, rivaling him in history pieces, and lagging behind only in having no entrée to the court, no power in the Royal Academy, and no band of loyal and admiring students. He had had three outstanding successes in the eleven years since his arrival in England. In 1776 he had exhibited at the Academy a dramatic and sensationally different picture of action and suspense he called *A Sea Boy Attacked by a Shark*. In 1781, after two years of hard work, he had finished an immense history painting: the fatal seizure of William Pitt, Earl of Chatham, in 1778, when he was addressing the House of Lords on a proposal to grant independence to the rebellious American colonies. He painted from life the heads of fifty-five peers who were, or could have been, present on that occasion, each dressed in his scarlet, gold, and ermine robes (though the lords were not so attired on the day Chatham was stricken). He exploited the picture skillfully. He solicited and sold 2500 subscriptions for a large engraving to be produced within four years, describing it in his prospectus as "the most arduous work of its kind hitherto undertaken in any capital country." And he exhibited the work, not at the Academy, but at the former gallery of the defunct Society of Artists in Spring Garden.

When William Chambers protested this in a letter as an improper "raree show," Copley released the letter, with his answer, to the press, which printed both with appropriate comment. *The Death of the Earl of Chatham* was shown a few days after the opening of the Academy exhibition; it ran for ten weeks, and some 20,000 people each paid a shilling to see it, as many as 800 in a single day. (The Academy's admission receipts had been £3069 in 1780; they were only £2141 in 1781.)

West had also conceived the idea of painting *The Death of Chatham* and had made considerable progress when he learned that Copley was working on the same subject. His son Raphael declared, "On the disclosure of their similar but separate plans Mr. West generously relinquished the object of his pursuit and left the field open to his adversary." A more impartial witness, Horace Walpole, wrote in his notebook:

> Mr. West made a small sketch of the death of Lord Chatham, much better expressed and disposed than Copley's. It has none but the principal persons present; Copley's almost the whole peerage, of whom seldom so many are there at once, and in Copley's most are mere spectators. But the great merit of West's is the principal figure which has his crutch and gouty stockings, which express his feebleness and account for his death. West would not finish it to interfere with his friend Copley.

As a much faster worker than Copley and with fewer figures to paint, West would certainly have produced his work first if he had continued with it. Whatever his reasons, he did not.

Copley produced his third outstanding success in 1784 with *The Death of Major Peirson*, based on Peirson's heroic resistance to a French attack in 1781 on the English island of Jersey. He again held his own exhibition, hanging the work in a gallery with a second showing of *The Death of Chatham*.

At the time of the West dinner party, Copley was working on two major pictures, with both of which West had been involved. One was a commission, arranged by West, to paint his first portrait for the royal family. The king had asked West to recommend an artist to paint his three youngest daughters, the Princesses Mary, Sophia, and Amelia. If West thought of Stuart, he rejected him, for Stuart hated to paint children, did not like to paint groups, preferred to paint only head-and-shoulders portraits, sometimes refused to finish his portraits, and occasionally insulted his sitters. West warmly recommended Copley, who, recognizing at once that this was an opportunity to improve his reputation and extend his influence, proceeded to the work with particular care. He painted the three children playing in a grape arbor, three spaniels frisking about, two scarlet parrots pecking grapes. Copley was, in West's words, "the most tedious of all painters." The sittings dragged on and on, Copley, in his usual manner, making a series of preliminary sketches, painting out and starting over, altering his design, matching every part of the face in light, shadow, and reflection with a tint on his palette, requiring hours and hours of the sitters' time. Mary, Sophia, and Amelia grew weary of posing, and according to court wits, so did the spaniels and the parrots. The children's attendants complained to the queen, the queen complained to the king, the king suggested to Mr. West that Mr. Copley be asked to speed up his work. West begged him to be patient, explained that Copley should be permitted to move at his own pace, and promised an exceptionally fine result. The king and the queen accepted the advice, and now the picture was nearing completion.

Copley's other work in progress was a large picture commemorating the British victory over the French and Spanish at Gibraltar in 1782. Copley and West had both sought the commission from the Corporation of the City of London. It was their first head-on competition, and Copley had won it for a fee of £1000 and a promise to complete the work within two years.

West was busy with his own work while Copley was achieving these triumphs. He showed nineteen pictures at annual Academy exhibitions in the four years between 1782 and 1785, only four of them portraits, the others works of major size and complexity. Ten of these he painted in a huge new venture he had undertaken for the king. West may have given Trumbull the series on the American Revolution because of his political discretion. He may have dropped his *Death of Chatham* for the same reason, as well as for his loyalty to Copley. But certainly a main consideration in both decisions was his commitment to paint three dozen or more pictures of monumental size, on religious subjects, for the king's new chapel at Windsor.

There had been virtually no public or church support of religious art in England since the Reformation in the sixteenth century. Parliament had further condemned and proscribed it in the time of Charles I. In 1773, West, Reynolds, and several other Academicians had suggested that surely, in these enlightened times, it must be possible to produce religious ornamentation that would not give offense in a Protestant country. They proposed that St. Paul's Cathedral be made complete by the addition of religious pictures,

for which Christopher Wren had left vacant large panels and com-
partments. Six artists had agreed to contribute pictures: Reynolds,
West, Nathaniel Dance, Angelica Kauffmann, James Barry, and
Giovanni Cipriani. Reynolds and West obtained the support of
Thomas Newton, dean of St. Paul's, but the bishop of London, Newton's superior, who had not been consulted, overruled him with the
pronouncement, "Whilst I live and have the power, I will never
suffer the doors of the metropolitan church to be opened for the
introduction of popery into it." The project to ornament St. Paul's
and to win church patronage of the arts died with those words.
West was the only artist to complete and exhibit the picture that
would have been hung in the cathedral: *Moses Receiving the
Tables.* In the Academy exhibition of 1779 he showed a small work
titled *St. Peter Denying Christ,* which he presented to the king as a
gift.

The subject of religious art came up again about this time in what
West called "some private and . . . familiar conversations" with the
king. They were discussing what subjects were best adapted to the
powers of painting. West suggested that scriptural subjects were
more congenial with true art than those taken from poetry.

> I gave this as my reason: The scriptural being wholly grounded
> upon truth, the painter had only to consult nature in her purest
> and simplest character, and make his representation perfect;
> whereas the nature of the poets was, in essence, a fiction; and
> the painter, to do justice to his author, must see it through the
> poet as a medium.
>
> The King was struck with these remarks, and as I saw that he
> coincided with me, I suggested that a series of pictures, giving a
> history of revealed religion from the fall of Adam to the atone-
> ment of Christ, would at once afford the best means of displaying
> the powers of the art, and of applying those powers to the noblest
> end.

The king commanded him to make some sketches to illustrate his
views, "which I accordingly did; and in these sketches I showed
that the whole history of revealed religion might be compressed
into thirty-five pictures." At an appointed time he called at the
palace with his drawings. He was startled to find in the room a
half dozen Anglican bishops who had been summoned to render a
judgment on the propriety of introducing ecclesiastical art into the
churches. The king explained his position. He did not feel himself
a free agent in the matter. He wished to see the churches of his
land adorned with works of art, illustrative of great events in the

history of religion, as the Bible itself often was illustrated with engravings. But as head of the Church of England, he would be bound by the views of its prelates. If the bishops approved, he intended to house thirty-five or more of Mr. West's religious pictures in a magnificent private chapel to be built on the open space known as Horn Court inside Windsor Castle.

The king then called on West to show the bishops his drawings, explain what they meant, and give his reasons for creating them in the way he did. West was not forewarned or prepared, but he rose to make his address. (It was, said James Northcote, to whom West told the story, "a thing that West was mighty capable of doing, for he was fond of talking.") He had divided his subjects into four "Dispensations," with pictures for each: Antediluvian and Patriarchal, Mosaical, Gospel, and Revelation. His thirty-five pictures began with *The Expulsion of Adam and Eve* and ended with *The Last Judgment* and *The New Jerusalem*. They were divided almost evenly between the Old Testament and the New. There were an *Annunciation* and a *Nativity*, but, out of deference to Anglican feelings, no saints and no *Virgin Mary and Child* as such.

The king kept smiling while West spoke, and at the conclusion he revealed the source of his amusement. "You see how well *he* understands these things," he said, "for whilst you bishops have been spending your time amongst heathen fables, he has been studying his Bible." Each bishop was given a piece of paper listing West's four Dispensations and thirty-five subjects and was asked to meet again to render a judgment.

At the second meeting, with West present, Dr. Richard Hurd, bishop of Lichfield and Coventry and tutor to the Prince of Wales and the duke of York, spoke for the bishops. They were of the unanimous opinion that the introduction of paintings into the chapel which His Majesty intended to erect would in no respect whatever violate the laws and usages of the Church of England. They were of the opinion that Mr. West's subjects, if properly treated, might be contemplated with edification, even by a Quaker.

And so West was instructed to make designs from his list of subjects. Later, with the king's assistance, he drew up an architectural plan for the new chapel, which was to be 95 by 50 feet in size.

West was now charged with the most ambitious commission ever awarded in English art. He had given up his series on the American Revolution and had lost his *Death of Chatham* and the commission to paint the British victory at Gibraltar; but he had his history of revealed religion, on which he expected to be working for years, perhaps for more than a decade. He was freed for all time from the need to solicit and paint portraits. His friendship with the king was strengthened by a common project on which the two spent pleasant hours. By his unique relationship with the court and the church, he had single-handedly worked a revolution in British art, reversing a 200-year proscription. The way was cleared for church patronage of the arts; English artists could now use religious subject matter that artists in other lands had always used. West had executed every detail flawlessly in a campaign, an achievement, that was to be the great mistake of his life.

13

Life at 14 Newman Street

It is impossible for two painters in the same department of the
art to continue long in friendship with each other.

SIR JOSHUA REYNOLDS
to James Northcote, ca. 1786

WILLIAM DUNLAP, eighteen, arrived in London in mid-June
1784 after a six-week voyage from New York. He first outfitted
himself with London-made clothes and then sent forward to Mr.
West the "recommendatory pictures" he had brought with him.
This done, he called on his father's friend, Effingham Lawrence, the
American sea captain who had arranged for him to become Mr.
West's pupil. Captain Lawrence accompanied him to 14 Newman
Street. Dunlap later wrote of his introduction to the household:

> The impression made upon an American youth of eighteen by
> the long gallery leading from the dwelling-house to the lofty
> suite of painting rooms — a gallery filled with sketches and de-
> signs for large paintings — the spacious room through which I
> passed to the more retired attelier — the works of his pencil sur-
> rounding me on every side — his own figure seated at his easel
> and the beautiful composition at which he was employed, as if in
> sport, not labour — all are recalled to my mind's eye at this dis-
> tance of half a century.

West was working on *Lear and Cordelia,* a picture commissioned
by Catherine II, Empress of Russia. He welcomed Captain Lawrence
as a friend, greeted Dunlap with the usual questions addressed to
one who has just finished a long ocean voyage from America, and
led them to the room where Dunlap's pictures had been deposited.
They first examined a copy he had made of Copley's *Sea Boy At-*

tacked by a Shark, done in India ink. (He had made a copy of *The Death of Wolfe,* but he had, "in the simplicity of my heart, preferred the copy from Copley, because I had done it better.") "I stood on trial," Dunlap recalled. West said, "This is very well..." (Dunlap's spirits rose) "...but it only indicates a talent for engraving." (His spirits fell.) Captain Lawrence untied a picture of Washington at the Battle of Princeton and unrolled it on the floor. West studied it and appeared to be pleased. "This," he said, "shows some talent for composition." Dunlap's spirits rose again. West looked at the figure of General Mercer in the background, dying in the same pose and with the same expression as his own General Wolfe, and he smiled. Said Dunlap, "I felt encouraged."

The two visitors were given a tour of the pictures in the painting room and gallery, many of them for the king's chapel at Windsor. Dunlap was most impressed by *Moses Receiving the Tables.* West directed them to No. 84 Charlotte Street, Rathbone Place, where rooms had been engaged in the home of Robert Davey, an artist — a painting room, a bedchamber, board, fire, and candles for one guinea a week. Dunlap unpacked, went to see the lions at the Tower of London, and returned to his rooms to make a chalk drawing from the bust of Cicero.

The Wests frequently had young Dunlap to dinner, and in these meetings they learned something of the young man's background. He was the son of an Irish officer in the British army who had married an American and retired from the service to run a store in the harbor town of Perth Amboy in northeast New Jersey. Dunlap had read omnivorously as a child despite the loss of vision in his right eye in an accident. After making some respectable ink copies of engravings, he began to read books on art, talked a great deal about the success of West and Copley in London, and aspired to go to England and be a painter. His parents, then living in British-occupied New York, sought an art teacher for him. Abraham Delanoy, a sign painter in Maiden Lane, was advertising that he had studied under West in London, and he offered to take the boy, but the Dunlaps had no confidence in his capacity and chose someone else. Dunlap began to draw portraits in India ink and crayon at three guineas a head. With the peace in 1783 he went to Philadelphia to study the pictures in Charles Willson Peale's gallery.

While spending that summer as the guest of family friends at Rocky Hill, near Princeton, New Jersey, he was taken to General Washington's headquarters nearby and (just turned seventeen) actually obtained the general's agreement to sit for his portrait. His several weeks of work stopped when the artist Joseph Wright arrived from Paris flourishing a letter of introduction from Franklin to Washington. Back in New York, Dunlap helped Delanoy complete a portrait he was having trouble with (it was Dunlap's first experience with oil paint), received artist's supplies in payment, and used them to paint a full-length portrait of Washington at the battle of Princeton. Seven months later, with the blessing of his indulgent parents, he was in London studying under Benjamin West.

West found him an unsatisfactory student. The young man began by delivering a portfolio of his drawings to Somerset House. They won him permission to enter the Academy school, but he never went back and never saw his drawings again — "I know not why — perhaps because I was too timid to ask Mr. West to introduce me or too bashful and awkward to introduce myself." He persuaded Captain Lawrence to permit him to paint a group portrait of his children but found that he was unable to complete it. He did learn to set a proper palette, did a few portraits of his other friends, copied West's *The Choice of Hercules,* and painted a scene from Ariosto with a ghost in it that West praised. He took another work to the master for criticism.

> He was at work in the room where I had first seen him, and his subject this time was a landscape, a scene in Windsor forest . . . He elucidated the doctrine of light and shadow by drawing a circle on an unoccupied canvas, and touching in the light with white chalk, the shadow by black, and leaving the cloth for the half-tint and reflexes [reflections]. He then pointed to a head in the room to show that this theory was there in practice, and turning to the landscape said that even the masses of foliage on the oak tree there represented were painted on the same principle. All this has long been familiar to every artist, and that this lesson was thought necessary is perhaps a proof of the little progress I had made in the rudiments of the art I professed to study.

He took another picture to West, a portrait he felt was by far the best thing he had done. "He gave it due praise, but observed, 'You have made the two sides of the figure alike — each has the same sweeping swell — he looks like a rolling pin.' . . . I took the lesson in silence . . . My habit of silence, in presence of those I considered my superiors, was very detrimental to me . . ." He occasionally met Trumbull in the studio and, when his painting room was not occupied, admired the two canvases he was working on: *The Battle of Bunker's Hill* and *The Death of General Montgomery.* But "Trumbull was awfully above me . . . I received neither advice nor instruction from him."

As time passed, Dunlap saw West only when he paid courtesy

calls, or visited his friend Raphael West, or was asked to dine. "He saw no proofs of my industry," Dunlap wrote, "and heard no good reports from Mr. Davey." He thoughtlessly moved into more elegant quarters without informing West. "Davey was not backward in communicating my change to West, and I presume, in assigning motives unfavorable." Despite his self-consciousness among his elders, Dunlap was overflowing with animal spirits and was a favorite among companions his own age. "The theatre — Vauxhall — parties on foot to Richmond Hill and on horseback to Windsor, and every dissipation suggested by my companions or myself, was eagerly entered into." One of his young friends was the master of a large house while his parents were away on a trip, and he was thereby able "to assemble us for mirth and midnight revelry ... I look back with astonishment at the activity of my idleness, and the thoughtlessness of the consequences with which I acted."

Raphael West, then in his nineteenth year, was one of those who shared in the mirth and midnight revelry. "Raefe helped me to do nothing," Dunlap wrote, "and I very frequently was a hindrance to his little application, by visiting the little room in Newman Street, at the head of the gallery ... His derelictions were probably charged up to my account where nothing appeared on the credit side ... I did nothing to satisfy the man who had it in his power to serve me. My follies and my faults were reported and exaggerated to Mr. West, and as he saw no appearance of the better self which resided in me (for there was a better self), he left me to my fate."

One day in August 1787 a ship's captain appeared at Dunlap's door and told him to prepare to leave at once; his father, having heard of his son's conduct, had booked a passage home. He sailed for New York after thirty-eight months of what he called "unprofitable idleness." He continued to paint in New York, especially in miniature, but he made an outstandingly successful career in other fields — as a prolific playwright, a translator of German and French plays for American production, a theater manager, a biographer, and as the first historian of the American theater. In his old age his theatrical friends raised $2517 for him with a benefit performance. He used the money to research and write a two-volume *History of the Rise and Progress of the Arts of Design in the United States* (1834) and became the American Vasari — the first American to bring to the world of art a curious, observing eye, a retentive memory, and a writer's persistence and skill in reporting what he had seen and heard about the artists of his country.

Raphael Lamar West was twenty when his friend Dunlap sailed for America. He had, it was said, "more talent than industry."

Dunlap believed he was "one of the best designers of the academy figure from life that England possessed," but felt that "he did not apply himself with the necessary industry to painting which ensures success. He painted a very little, played on the fiddle or hautboy [oboe] a great deal, and amused himself in the room sometimes occupied by Trumbull." He seemed, Dunlap thought, to be "discouraged by the overshadowing merit and fame of his father." Mrs. Papendiek, assistant keeper of the queen's wardrobe and reader, described Raphael in her memoirs:

> The eldest son, Ralph, was delightful. He had a fine, tall figure, with an expressive countenance, and invariably sat to his father for the portrait of St. John. His dress was simply elegant, which was striking amid the large cravats, curled hair, and other extravagant fashions set by the Prince of Wales ... Ralph and I were sworn friends. He came in and out of our house at pleasure, and his society was always agreeable to us all.

Raphael exhibited one large picture, *Prometheus,* at the Academy exhibition in 1782 (it hung near Stuart's portrait of Benjamin West), but his real function was to serve as his father's assistant. It was work he did not enjoy. When Trumbull endeared himself to West by making a copy of *The Battle of La Hogue,* he was simply completing a project that Raphael had started and then abandoned. In a few years Raphael would tell Joseph Farington that painting for his father caused him trouble with his bile; he wished he could simply be given £100 a year and left alone.

The Wests lived quietly but well at 14 Newman Street, in a manner befitting a family whose head was the king's history painter. Visitors were impressed by the master's collection of pictures, sculptures, and Italian engravings, and by the way they were displayed. The gallery, with two other rooms, made three sides of a garden, described by a visitor as "very small but elegant, with a grass plot in the middle and busts upon stands under an arcade.[1]

It had been an expensive house to buy and enlarge, and, with five servants, it was costing £1600 a year to maintain. Gilbert Stuart, recalling his early days there as an assistant, said: "When I had finished a copy of a portrait for my old master, that I knew he was to have a good price for, and he gave me a guinea, I used to think it hard — but when I looked on the establishment around me, which with his instruction I enjoyed, and knew it was yet to be paid

---

[1] West made the gallery available to William Wilberforce and Thomas Clarkson for early meetings in their campaign to abolish the slave trade.

for, I fully exonerated West from the charge of niggardliness, and cheerfully contributed my labor in return for his kindness."

No one has so well described 14 Newman Street as the poet-essayist Leigh Hunt, who as a small child was often taken there by his mother:

> The quiet of Mr. West's gallery, the tranquil, intent beauty of the statues, and the subjects of some of the pictures . . . made a great impression upon me. My mother and I used to go down the gallery as if we were treading on wool. She was in the habit of stopping to look at some of the pictures, particularly the *Deluge* and the *Ophelia,* with a countenance quite awe-stricken. She used also to point out to me the subjects relating to liberty and patriotism, and the domestic affections. Agrippina bringing home the ashes of Germanicus was a great favorite with her . . .
>
> As Mr. West was almost sure to be found at work, in the farthest room, habited in his white woolen gown, so you might have predicated, with equal certainty, that Mrs. West was sitting in the parlor, reading. I used to think that if I had such a parlor to sit in, I should do just as she did. It was a good-sized room, with two windows looking out on the little garden . . . The garden with its busts in it, and the pictures which you knew were on the other side of its wall, had an Italian look. The room was hung with engravings and colored prints . . .
>
> Mrs. West and my mother used to talk of old times, and Philadelphia, and my father's prospects at court. I sat apart with a book . . . I remember being greatly mortified when Mr. West offered me half-a-crown if I would solve the old question of "Who was the father of Zebedee's children?" and I could not tell him. He never made his appearance till dinner, and returned to his painting room directly after it. And so at tea time. The talk was very quiet; the neighborhood quiet; the servants quiet; I thought the very squirrel in the cage would have made a greater noise any where else. James the porter, a fine tall fellow, who figured in his master's pictures as an apostle, was as quiet as he was strong.

West commonly began his morning by seeing his students and the other young artists who came to him for advice and sat in his anteroom, each clutching a canvas. In his diary William Dunlap wrote: "Those who applied for his advice or instruction in the art over which he presided, freely received both, given with the kind, full, perfect wisdom of the sage, and the simplicity of the child . . . He told all he knew and added, 'Work, night and day, draw from the Antique, paint from nature. Study the masters, but copy nature.'" John Thomas Smith, the West student who became keeper of prints at the British Museum, observed that he "often, in the kindest manner possible, gave up whole mornings to the instruction of those students who solicited his opinion . . . I have frequently known him to correct their errors with his own hand." The roster of West's American students is well known — or at least the identity of those two dozen or so who made names for themselves. Only a few of his British students are known, on the other hand, though they must have far outnumbered the Americans. Smith believed, "There are very few artists now [1827] basking in the sunshine of patronage who have not benefited essentially by his generous and able communications," and he added, "To Mr. West's well known liberality I owe the best portion of the little knowledge I possess in the art of painting." James Northcote, R.A., historical painter, the source of some of the most savage attacks on West, said: "He was a learned painter, for he knew all that had been done in the art from the beginning; he is exactly what is called 'the schools' in painting, for he did everything by rule, and could give you chapter and verse for every touch he put on canvas. He was on that account the best possible teacher, because he could tell you why and wherefore everything was to be done."

The leading artists and patrons of the time moved freely in and out of the Newman Street gallery. To American visitors it was one of the places to go in London; they might collect their mail there, see a collection of old masters and West paintings, and perhaps talk to Mr. West himself. To the artists in the American colony, it was a place to meet, work, exchange ideas, and hear gossip.

Mather Brown was the new star of the American colony. Having completed his studies under West in 1784, he was enjoying a phenomenal popularity as a portrait painter of the realistic school. He received a royal appointment, painted a full-length portrait of the Prince of Wales, and moved to a splendid house on Cavendish Square, where he kept a servant in livery. He did a fine portrait of Thomas Jefferson (believed to be the first ever painted), became the favorite painter of John and Abigail Adams, and exhibited some thirty-four portraits at the Royal Academy between 1782 and 1790. An English correspondent expressed a sense of indignation: "Mr. West paints for the Court and Mr. Copley for the City. Thus the artists of America are fostered in England, and to complete the wonder, a third American, Mr. Brown of the humblest pretenses, is chosen portrait painter to the Duke of York. So much for the Thirteen Stripes — so much for the Duke of York's taste."

Gilbert Stuart returned frequently to Newman Street. He came on one occasion to paint a portrait of West, this time for John Boydell, publisher of engravings, who intended to exhibit portraits of fifteen of the country's leading painters and engravers. Stuart, at thirty, married in April 1786 the eighteen-year-old daughter of a Reading physician. He now ranked only slightly behind Reynolds and Gainsborough in popularity as a painter of portraits; he charged fifty guineas for a head-and-shoulders and claimed to be earning as much as £1500 a year. Dunlap, who observed Stuart's manner of living, remarked, "He was a stranger to prudence." He set up an elaborate establishment in New Burlington Street, began to dress, in the words of his daughter, with "extreme elegance," hired a French cook, and entertained lavishly. In order always to have company at dinner, he put up seven cloak-pins in his hallway and issued a standing invitation for any male friend to join him who called and found an empty pin. A person to whom he described this system asked what Mr. West thought of it. "He shook his head," Stuart said, "and observed, it would eat itself out. It did so . . . in about six months."

Freed of West's discipline and Mrs. West's motherly supervision, Stuart reverted to his earlier instability and went disastrously in debt. The collapse came late in 1787, when he fled to Ireland to avoid debtors' prison, taking with him his wife and their two infant children. In his last months in London he wrote to Elizabeth West, to whom, as a mark of gratitude and esteem, he had earlier made a gift of his first portrait of her husband. Would she please lend him the picture for a few days that he might make some alterations in it? She sent the picture to him. Some days later West was astonished to see his portrait on display in John Boydell's gallery. He asked how it came to be there. Boydell replied that Stuart had sold it to him. West reclaimed the picture and Boydell lost his money.[2]

West forgave that breach of faith. He regretted Stuart's departure and expressed the opinion that if he had stayed he would have become England's foremost portrait painter. When Francis James Jackson was appointed minister to the United States in 1809, West told him he would find there "the best portrait painter in the world, and his name is Gilbert Stuart." Ambassador Jackson became one of the most detested Englishmen ever to set foot on American soil, but he kindly repeated West's praise to Stuart when commissioning him to paint his portrait and that of his wife.

On January 1, Elizabeth West began to keep a daily record of her household expenditures for the year 1785. On the right-hand pages

---

[2] William Dunlap is the embarrassed and apologetic source of this story. He heard it from Joel Barlow, American poet, diplomat, speculator, and radical polemicist. Barlow heard it from Benjamin and Elizabeth West, with whom he was on intimate terms in the 1790s.

of her account book she listed the goods and services she bought, the date, and the prices paid. On the first left-hand facing page, in her own version of double-entry bookkeeping, she wrote "Rec'd of Mr. West... £100" and went on to record the names of guests who came to dinner, homes in which she dined or took tea, problems with the servants and tradesmen, and peregrinations of members of her family. She kept the record for five years and filled about 100 pages. The folio-size volume, bound in vellum and reposing in the Friends Historical Library of Swarthmore College, gives a remarkable glimpse into the daily life and habits of a well-to-do family in London in the ninth decade of the eighteenth century. It is also one of the very few documents before 1793 that penetrate into the personal life of the West family. Elizabeth West was not a dedicated record keeper; she tended eventually to record only the larger expenditures and made no more entries of cash received from Mr. West.

Entries for purchase of food, exactly itemized in the first years, are the most numerous. They reveal that the Wests and their guests ate well, with a variety of delicacies. In addition to the staples, Mrs. West bought oranges and lemons, melons and "asparagrass," cucumbers and radishes, grapes and plums, pears and raspberries and strawberries, salmon and lobster. She sometimes bought truffles, smelt, shrimp, tapioca, refined liquorice, and Golden Pippin apples. "Mr. West's March wine bill" — one might sense a certain asperity in the wording — was £26.12.9.

Clothing purchases include a ground-squirrel muff, six pairs of ribbed cotton stockings for Raphael, a pair of doeskin breeches for Raphael, kid gloves for Raphael, four cotton night caps for Mr. West, and "a pair of pumps in Windsor for myself, £0.13.0." Itemized household supplies include £16 for hay and straw for the horses. Purchased services include that of a farrier for the horses; 10 shillings a year for the lamplighter; Mr. Goddard for cleaning the clock and two watches; and a sweep to clean the kitchen chimney. (She tipped the boy one shilling sixpence.) The Wests bought that most famous of eighteenth- and nineteenth-century drug remedies, Dr. James's Powders, good for almost all ailments; bottles of magnesia, tincture of rhubarb, "1 box of analeptic pills," and "tincture for corns."

Entries that can be described only as miscellaneous are:

Bamboo cane with sword	£0.15.0
2 locks for dog collars	0. 1.0
Head by M[ichel] Angelo	0.12.0
To clean house at Windsor	0.10.6

1 pack cards	0. 2.4
Lost at cards, Mrs. Copley	0. 6.6
Shaving box for Raphael	0.10.0
36 tickets for the illumination	0. 7.6
An old man	0. 1.0
Went to play with Benny	0. 5.0
Gave Mrs. Duché for a poor woman	0.10.6
Easter offering	0. 5.0
3 tooth brushes, one comb	0. 2.0
To see the Learned Pig	0. 2.0

The Wests paid £20.18.0 to put skylights in the gallery, £8.10.0 to Mr. Jenkins the colourman, and £30 to send Benjamin, Jr., age sixteen, away to boarding school, delivering him there under the care of William, a manservant. In a six-month period in 1786 Mrs. West gave £33.14.0 to pay the bills of Mary Shewell Hunt, her unfortunate niece, and £5.5.7 to Isaac Hunt, her refugee Loyalist husband.

The Wests were book buyers. Among their purchases are *The Spectator* in eight volumes, Goldsmith's histories of Greece and Rome, Ovid's *Metamorphoses* and *Epistles,* Pope's Homer, Newton's Milton, Warburton's Shakespeare, Hester Lynch Piozzi's *Anecdotes of Dr. Johnson,* Cumberland's *Catalogue of Spanish Painters,* the first number of Johann Kaspar Lavater's *Physiognomical Fragments for the Promotion of Knowledge and Love of Man* (on the art of judging character from facial characteristics), the first volume of Joseph Strutt's *Dictionary of Engravers,* and the works in three volumes of West's friend, Thomas Newton, bishop of Bristol, who had died in 1782. The Wests' bill for newspapers in 1785 was £3.18.0. On July 3, 1789, they paid £0.2.5 for "America's Constitution."

Elizabeth West's nature is revealed in some of her entries. She is constantly giving Raphael and Benjamin, Jr., money out of her household funds, above their allowances. She "drank tea with Mrs. Green; from the treatment I then received, determined not to do so any more." Unlike her husband, she could spell correctly, writing such difficult words as *liquorice, raspberries,* and *rhubarb* flawlessly. She almost visibly restrains her disapproval when she puts down, "Mr. West lent Mr. Jn Samuel 20£ for which he did not take any note." She is annoyed by a tradesman: "Mr. Smith of Knightsbridge sent an oil cloth for the passage, which he has promised us the use of, till he has prepared the one for us, which has been bespoke three years past and which he has several times disappointed us of." In an age when it was the male prerogative and pleasure to buy the horses, she was given an extraordinary responsibility: "Paid for bay horse and settled account with Mr. Mitchell, £35.15.0. He agreed, Mr. Bromley and Raphael present, that if Mr.

W. does not approve of the horse that he will exchange him until he gets one that he likes."

Servants occupy much space in the account book. The wage was £16.16.0 per year for the ordinary manservant, about half that for the unskilled woman. (If the girl was young, the wage was commonly paid to her mother.) On April 5, 1785, Mrs. West "Discharged Robert Thrower from our service in consequence of his insolence"; the next day she rehired him "upon his promise of amendment and future good behaviour"; but on July 22, "Robert Thrower went away." She hired Elizabeth Peters, though her "character" recommendation was not quite satisfactory; two days later, "Discharged E.P. for misbehaviour." When Sarah Jenkinson left, on the other hand, she was given a present. On February 8, 1789, Mrs. West gave each of her three maids a new gown. She tried the common strategy used to retain servants and apprentices: "Deborah Moore came from Lady Argill's. Wages 9 guineas for the first year and if she remains with me till the expiration of the second year she is to have 10 guineas."

Sir Joshua Reynolds dined twice with the Wests, William Chambers once, John Trumbull three times at special dinners, and Mr. and Mrs. Joseph Farington six times. John Adams, first American minister to Great Britain, and Mrs. Adams called on the Wests one evening. Mrs. Adams dined once in a company made up of four members of the Copley family and Mr. Trumbull. Mrs. Adams brought her daughter Abigail to dine again, accompanied by Colonel William Stephens Smith, with whom young Abigail was about to embark on a disastrous marriage.

The Copley name appears more frequently than any other in the account book. Mrs. West records the death in the autumn of 1785 of Susanna Copley, age nine, "of a putrid sore throat," and two weeks later she records the loss of a second Copley child, Jonathan, three, of the same disorder. She seems to have dined and played cards a number of times with Mrs. Copley, perhaps when their husbands were at Academy dinners.

It is regrettable that Elizabeth West did not write more generously on more subjects, and that her account book covers only five years; but one is grateful for what she did commit to paper. Unfortunately, there are no entries on one household experiment she is known to have conducted. Longing for the taste of American corn, she sent to Philadelphia for seed and tried to grow it in her garden at Newman Street, but without much success. She continued to try, however, simply to be able to boil a few inedible ears, the smell of which reminded her of America and home.

*

The Royal Academy exhibition that opened in April 1785 marked a turning point in West's career. The turn came as the result of a slashing attack by the critic of the *Morning Post* on his three pictures. West answered the attacks and was caught up in an open quarrel that did him lasting harm as a person, an artist, and an officer of the Academy.

The *Morning Post & Daily Advertiser* was a folded sheet of four pages that appeared daily and sold for threepence. The *Post* editor had recently announced a new policy: He intended to rescue the arts "from such ignorant and prejudiced accounts as have heretofore been given in the public papers," and to accomplish this he had engaged "artists of ability and judgment" (unnamed) to review the arts. The new reviews began with the Academy's 1785 exhibition; they were the severest anyone had ever seen in England; and they were felt to be not only cruel but in poor taste. Copley and West were singled out for attacks even stronger than those made on other artists. The critic was John Hoppner, twenty years younger than Copley and West, a former Academy student. He was a busy and successful painter of portraits, but now he had taken on the additional work of writing art criticism for the *Post*.

Copley hung one work in the exhibition, *The Three Youngest Daughters of King George III*, the long-delayed conversation piece he was counting on to raise him to the forefront of fashionable portrait painters. It is considered a delightful picture today, though somewhat busy with detail; Watteau-esque, rococo, with an element of fantasy,[3] the daughters charming and believable, with almost none of the candybox cuteness of children as commonly painted by eighteenth-century English portraitists. Hoppner, who happened to have his own picture of the king's youngest daughters in the show, began his unsigned review, "So, Mr. Copley, is this the fruit of your long studies and labours?" and ended with, "Princesses, parrots, dogs, grapes, flowers, leaves, are each striving for pre-eminence and opposing with hostile force all attempts of our wearied eyes to find repose." Copley's hope for favor in high places died with the *Post* review. (A review, moreover, often determined whether a picture was engraved for sale of prints.)

Hoppner wrote that West's *St. Peter's First Sermon after Being Filled with the Holy Ghost* was "coldly conceived." In fact, he went on, all of Mr. West's works this year were "cold in the extreme. They have more the effect of having been wrought by *a machine*, than by a hand directed by a *glowing mind!*"

---

[3] Anthony Pasquin wrote of the picture, "It seems, at a distance, like a bed of tulips disturbed by the wind."

This we presume may be the cause of his pictures giving *now* so little satisfaction; or perhaps the public are become better judges. Whatever may be the cause, it is certain his productions are not held in the estimation they were wont to be; and was it not for *particular patronage,* we fear he would soon be in the situation of the despoiled St. James, who . . . was, from being covered with gold and jewels, at last reduced to the very *block* he was made of.

West's *The Lord's Supper* was "a mockery of the sacrament . . . a wretched performance . . . weak and unaffecting, affording no pleasure to a spectator of feeling." Since he had not the requisites of an exuberant imagination and penetrating judgment, Hoppner suggested, it would have been better if Mr. West had been totally unqualified for the arts, so that he could have followed some occupation where a mind and an intimate acquaintance with human nature were not wanted.

Of the several works Hoppner had in the exhibit, an anonymous critic wrote, "We consider this as the best whole length portrait in the room, excepting only the works of the president [Reynolds]. The figure has uncommon grace and animation of attitude, and the landscape is beautifully picturesque . . . We are glad to see a gradual improvement in the pencil of this ingenious artist, a progress from good to better, which will doubtless soon put him at the top of his profession."

Though Hoppner's reviews were unsigned, his association with the *Post* was well known; indeed, he was willing to have it known.[4] He freely admitted that he had written the reviews on Copley and West, denying only that he had written the praise of his own works. Academy officers burned with indignation and injured artists fumed with protest. One member declared that Mr. Hoppner "deserves the thanks rather than the censure of the public for so ably pointing out to them the beauties of his own performances and the defects of those of every other painter." West was especially free and outspoken in condemning Hoppner. He deplored the brutal treatment given the young artists, and he charged Hoppner with

---

[4] William T. Whitley, who first uncovered Hoppner's connection with the *Post* in his life of Gainsborough in 1915, writes with unusual vehemence of Hoppner's "inexcusable conduct." His comments on the pictures of that year, he says, "were not those of an artist but of a vulgar man attempting to be humorous." But the "unforgiveable feature of his criticism" was that he made use of the *Morning Post* to attack, anonymously, Copley, who was his rival, and West, who was his personal enemy.

ingratitude for favors he, West, had done him. In due course he received a letter:

> To Benjamin West, Esq.
> Historical Painter to his Majesty:
>
> Sir:
> As I have it from responsible authorities that you have been busy with my reputation, it becomes necessary that I should justify myself. I therefore give you notice that I shall publish in the course of this week a dispassionate statement of the obligations I have to you for a fancied benefit ill returned, in which I am boldly taxed with ingratitude.
>
>   J. Hoppner

Hoppner published in two numbers of the *Post* his dispassionate statement, "An Address to the Public," in which he launched a long and caustic attack on West, based on grievances dating back several years. His story was read by everyone in London, for the *Post* was an important paper, West was a public figure, and Hoppner introduced into his account the names of the king and queen.

John Hoppner's father was reputed to have been a German surgeon (never identified) who had come to England in the service of George II. (The name was originally Höppner.) His mother, possibly English, was a waiting woman or a domestic at the royal palace. As a "singing boy" at St. James's chapel school, Hoppner "had the run of the Royal kitchen." When he showed an early talent for drawing and crayon portraits, George III gave him an allowance of three shillings a week and encouraged him to continue his studies. West took a supervisory interest in the boy, apparently at the request of the king. These acts of favoritism led to the suspicion — which led to the rumor, which led to the widely accepted belief — that he was the king's bastard son, a belief Hoppner did not contradict and seems to have encouraged.[5] He was admitted as a student at the Royal Academy in 1775 and in 1780 began to exhibit there. In 1782 he won the gold medal for historical painting with a scene from *King Lear*. In that year he married Phoebe Wright, whom West had helped as a model, whose brother Joseph, now in America, West had taught, and whose mother, Patience Wright, West had helped and sponsored.

---

[5] In May 1795 Hoppner was introduced to the king to learn his wishes about a portrait he was painting of the Princess of Wales. According to John Yenn, R.A., who was present, the king did not act like a father; he failed to recognize Hoppner or recollect his name until it was mentioned by a page.

Patience Lovell Wright, an eccentric American republican, owned and ran a museum in which were displayed her amazingly lifelike waxwork figures of English notables past and present. Anthony Pasquin, the art critic, wrote, "Her house became the rendezvous for the Legislator and the Artist, and there I have often encountered the late Lord Camden, Dr. Franklin, Mr. Garrick, Samuel Foote, Dr. Dodd, Mr. West, Silas Deane, etc." Mrs. Wright did a bust of West, which she placed a short distance in her museum from her figures of George III and Queen Charlotte. Charles Coleman Sellers, her biographer, believes that West introduced her to the king and queen, who posed repeatedly for her.[6] They humored her eccentricities and for a time gave her quite extraordinary freedom at court. During the American War, however, despite West's warnings to be more discreet, she lectured the king so boldly on American rights that she was no longer admitted.

Somewhere in this course of events, Hoppner lost favor at court, including even his entrée to the royal kitchen. It has been suggested that his marriage to the daughter of Patience Wright offended the king, which might be a reasonable assumption if he was indeed the king's son. Hoppner's biographer cites a lawsuit in which a Joseph Walker charged that Hoppner's mother and one of the king's pages were collecting money from Walker on the promise to procure him, through their influence, a place in the customs house. Walker won a verdict of fifty pounds and costs, which would have created talk at court and would certainly have caused the disappearance of Mrs. Hoppner and her son. Still another possible reason given for the king's displeasure is a portrait painted by Joseph of his mother and exhibited at the Royal Academy, titled *Mrs. Wright Modelling a Head.* Since the head Mrs. Wright was modeling in wax was that of Charles I, which the English had chopped off in 1649, and the present king and queen were shown watching Mrs. Wright at work, a certain amount of scandalized press and private comment followed the showing of the picture.

Hoppner, in any case, was certain that he knew the reason for his dismissal: He blamed West, and he spread the whole story in the pages of the *Post.* It was only because of the repeated solicitation of his friends, he wrote in "An Address to the Public," that he was taking steps to clear himself "from imputations laid to me by men who have an interest in destroying my reputation." He would show "that those who are loudest against me are themselves acting

---

[6] He also points out that West and Patience Wright did portraits of a number of the same persons about the same time, and concludes that on occasion she may have shared sittings of subjects with West in his studio.

with the most *infamous duplicity*, and secretly labouring to destroy the reputation of their most intimate friends." In his criticism of Mr. West's pictures in the *Post*, he said, he only anticipated the public opinion. Mr. West, with a weak case against him, lived up to "his reputation for cunning" by adding ingratitude to his other charges. It was solely on Mr. West's advice that the king had "withdrawn his protection" from John Hoppner. Mr. West had confessed this to him in person, and he, of all people, could lay no claim to *gratitude*. "He would insinuate he meant through sufferings to have made me an artist; but I rather think he hoped when he threw me precipitately on the world, without interest, without money, and with more than myself to provide for, that I should have sunk under the weight of my distresses." West, Hoppner said, then came to him and declared that the king considered Hoppner to be "one of his family." His Majesty desired West, therefore, "to be watchful over my interests, and not to leave me a prey to want. Were I to describe the distresses I laboured under for some months it would appear that Mr. West had ill acquitted himself of the trust reposed in him." Lord Belgrave and Lord Grosvenor, however, took up Hoppner, and through them he came to know and paint the Prince of Wales, the duke of York, the Whig nobility, and others of "the Carlton House set" who were politically opposed to the king.

As he acquired reputation as an artist, he charged, West "became assiduous in his civilities," and in order to quiet suspicions that it was he who had been instrumental in causing Hoppner's misfortunes, "he took frequent opportunities of calling at my lodgings, and with the most consummate hypocrisy would exclaim, 'I have the pleasure to tell you that I have had a conversation with His Majesty, who inquired after you and gave me an opportunity of saying many things in your favour.'" Hoppner, however, was not deceived; he "perceived the snake in the grass and opposed *art* to *deceit*." On the day Their Majesties visited the Academy exhibition in 1784, he said, West brought him a message. It was the royal wish that he should paint the three youngest princesses.

> After complimenting me upon it, he said, "What makes it more flattering, it was by the Queen's own desire, which is much better than if it resulted from any application to her." This, however, he has since contradicted by industriously reporting that he was the person to whom I was indebted for this mark of their favour. But I believe there is . . . little truth in this tale.

He had learned, he went on, that Mr. West had been more than commonly industrious in propagating additional falsehoods about him. He desired the gentleman to take notice that he had thus far been dispassionate and temperate infinitely beyond what his injuries warranted. If he found that "he perseveres in his misrepresentation and hideous calumny, I shall be obliged to lay before the public a series of such facts as must convince the warmest of his friends that I wished not to chastise when there was any chance of amendment, and that, when I could overwhelm with confusion, I chose only to remonstrate."

If West defended himself in any printed statement against this paranoid assault, no record of it is known. Hoppner's biographers, William McKay and W. Roberts, attribute their subject's irritability, "of which there are many proofs," to his long-continued ill health. (He had "a weakness of the bowels," which he claimed to have cured by eating raw peppercorns, and chronic bilious and liver complaints.) Samuel Rogers, banker, poet, art patron, and diarist, who saw a great deal of Hoppner and thought him a genius, said in his *Table Talk*, "He had an awful temper — the most spiteful person I ever knew!"

In his "Address to the Public," Hoppner printed a most revealing exchange of letters with the Reverend William Peters, apparently so sure of his own rectitude that he could not see the harm they did his character. Peters, who was a painter, R.A., and chaplain to the Royal Academy, had heard from Hoppner the story of West's unkind treatment and, as befitted a chaplain, offered to defend and represent Hoppner in the Academy. But when Hoppner's pieces appeared in the *Post*, he wrote to him withdrawing the offer. He was distressed, he said, at "much unprovoked professional abuse against Mr. West" and others, considering it illiberal in Hoppner as an artist and unworthy of him as a man. Hoppner replied that Peters' conduct was "mean and unmanly," and as his friendship had been unsolicited, so the deprivation of it would be unregretted. Peters wrote back that he had been shocked at Hoppner's charges that West had oppressed him in a most heinous way, calumniated him to the king, and caused the royal protection to be withdrawn.

> On these accounts I did indeed, as you say, offer you my *unsolicited services*, but that in doing so I should have loaded [Mr. West], as you express it, with the *most degrading epithets*, I must tell you, Sir, it is not true ... In regard to Mr. West I now give you my opinion of him in a manner not so easily to be misunderstood: — that the more I have searched into him and known him, the more I have reason to respect him; and the manner of my speaking of him at Lord ——'s table ... was such as did honour to his head and his heart.

In his last printed letter, Hoppner set the record straight on the "degrading epithets" Peters had loaded on West at Lord ——'s table: "What you then said has not escaped my memory; the substance of which was that the presence of Mr. Copley was always dreaded at your meetings in the Academy, and that particularly when Mr. West rose to give his opinion, Copley immediately followed in opposition to it; but you added, 'And I must say this for Mr. West, he always bore it with great calmness and patience.'"

Before these unpleasantries, West had known little but praise, encouragement, and friendship. This was the worst of his few experiences with unkind criticism, and it was his first meeting with hatred publicly expressed. His early success, his continuous steady rise, the ever-present help of a friend in the right place, his position of power in the Academy and at court, had elevated him to a position where he invited attack. His faults, which up to this point had been overlooked or accepted, were now to be examined and charged against him. His motives had always been trusted, but now they would be questioned. He was no longer an engaging young American; he would be fifty in 1788, and thus subject to the pressures from disrespectful younger men who cared only a little, if at all, that he had once helped to found the Academy, had introduced neoclassicism and historical realism into English painting, and was the founder of historical engraving in England. In the nature of such things, the attack once made was easier to repeat; the words and phrases, once used, came more easily to mind, tongue, and pen. West was to hear the words *cunning* and *duplicity* again.

In his final side blow at Copley, John Hoppner had directed attention, as he intended, to a conflict more serious than his own — to that between West and Copley. West had been conscious for several years of Copley's almost reflexive compulsion to counteract him, though he resolutely separated Academy matters from personal affairs and continued to meet Copley socially. Other Academicians, of course, had observed and commented privately on the antagonism between the two men. Now it was common knowledge throughout London and Windsor, in art circles, in the City, and at court.

14

The Painter's Eye

The Queen was most brilliant in attire, and when she was arrayed Mr. West was allowed to enter the dressing room, in order to give his opinion of the disposition of her jewels, which indeed were arranged with great taste and effect.

FRANCES (FANNY) BURNEY,
Second Keeper of the Queen's Robes,
June 4, 1787,
the king's birthday

WEST SPENT much of his time at court in the five years following the Peace of Paris, and many working hours in the painting rooms he had been given in Windsor Castle and Buckingham House. They were pleasant and productive years. England was at peace with France and the former American colonies, and he no longer had to be on guard against accusations of sympathy for the American insurrectionists. Their Majesties were especially grateful to him for an unusual picture he painted after the deaths of their two youngest sons, Alfred in August 1782 and Octavius, the king's favorite child, in May 1783. (Octavius, the fourteenth child, died of an inoculation against smallpox. "There will be no heaven for me," the king said, "if Octavius is not there.") On a canvas 8 by 5 feet West painted *The Apotheosis of Prince Octavius*, a representation of four-year-old Prince Octavius being welcomed into heaven by two-year-old Prince Alfred under the protective wings of an angel and the gaze of two cherubs. After it had been shown at the Academy exhibition in 1784, the king gave Robert Strange a workroom at Buckingham House in which, under West's expert supervision, he was to make an engraving. Strange had been a fighting Scots Jacobite and an unrestrained critic of George III and of the Royal Academicians (save only his friend West) for having excluded engravers from Academy membership. When the engraving was completed in 1787, he presented 40 proof impressions to the queen and 100 impressions and the plate itself to the king. His Majesty asked West how he might reward Strange. (He had paid West £315 for the picture.) West observed that Strange was prospering, well provided for and in "respectable circumstances," and he reminded His Majesty that in the previous century monarchs had granted knighthood to able artists. The king approved the suggestion, proposed it to Strange, and told him to appear at St. James's Palace that same day to be knighted. The king, moreover, paid the £100 investiture fees himself and, saying he must not appear to give knighthood as a barter for property, presented West with two £100 notes to deliver to Sir Robert.

No knighthood was conferred on West, though the *Morning Post* informed its readers that it was a dignity "for which he has been panting these many years." Predictions that he was about to be knighted were made so often that in time — as early as 1792 — "Sir" was sometimes put before his name on the assumption that he must have been made a knight. It appears that the king offered to give West a knighthood and that he "firmly but respectfully declined the honor," doing so in the hope of attaining a higher title. A knighthood was not a hereditary honor; it brought no wealth or income with it; it cost a sizable fee; and one was addressed as "Sir," not as "Lord." William Henry, Duke of Gloucester, acting for the king, his brother, asked West if a knighthood would be acceptable, and West said "No" in a statement of some 180 words. No man, he began, had a higher respect for political honors and distinctions than he. He felt, however, that he had already earned greater eminence by his art than a knighthood could confer on him; and since the title would perish on his death, it could confer no dignity on his family. "But were I possessed of a fortune, independent of my profession, sufficient to enable my posterity to maintain the rank, I think that with my hereditary descent [1] and the station I occupy among artists, a more permanent title might become a desirable object. As it is, however, that cannot be." He spoke so explicitly, he said, that there might be no misunderstanding on the matter. The duke took him by the hand and said, "You have justified the opinion which the King has of you. He will be delighted with your words." Whatever the duke's interpretation of the words may have been, they would seem to indicate that West believed he should be made a baronet and given an income with the title. Raphael West

---

[1] West traced a branch of his family in an unbroken line to Roger, third Baron Delawarre, who distinguished himself in the wars of Edward III.

told Charles Robert Leslie, one of his father's students, that the king and West had an understanding: the title of baronet would be conferred when the revealed religion pictures were completed.

Miss Frances (Fanny) Burney, the queen's second keeper of the robes (and the author of the successful novels *Evelina* and *Cecilia*), described West as she saw him at court: a "very pleasing man, simple, soft-mannered, cheerful and serene." She observed a habit he had of speaking of his own work in the highest terms of praise and admiration: "Another man would be totally ridiculous who held such language about his own performances, but there is in Mr. West a something of simplicity in manner that makes his self-commendation seem the result rather of an unaffected mind than of a vain or proud one. It may sometimes excite a smile, but can never, I think, offend or disgust." And Miss Burney recorded the great moment at St. James's when, on the king's birthday, Mr. West was asked to enter the queen's dressing room and give his opinion of the arrangement of her jewels.[2] The queen was kind to Miss Burney, though she failed to see that her health was being harmed by persecution from the first keeper of the robes, a German dragoness named Mrs. Schwellenberg. Queen Charlotte, indeed, was noted for her occasional kindnesses. In one instance she saw that one of her ladies in waiting, who suffered from swollen legs and had been standing for hours, seemed to be in pain. They were alone together, and the queen said gently, "Madame, you may lean against the back of the chair."

The queen acknowledged an indebtedness to West for special consideration he gave to one of her protégés, Johann Heinrich Ramberg, young son of the king's physician in Hanover. Showing a talent for drawing, he had been brought from Germany in 1781, at eighteen, invited to court, and placed under West's tutelage to be trained as a history painter, privately and at the Royal Academy. Six years later Ramberg petitioned the king to support him during several years' study in Italy. The king, having observed that the young man's deeper interest lay in caricature and stage design, declined. West, apparently at the queen's request, interceded on Ramberg's behalf. The king assented on condition that West draw

---

[2] Miss Burney reported that the queen lost her first delight in wearing her jewels because of "the fatigue and trouble of putting them on, and the care they required, and the fear of losing them." Her most costly pieces were a stomacher she valued at £60,000 and earrings with three drops, the center drop of each costing £12,000.

up, and that Ramberg promise to follow, an itinerary and course of study in Italy.[3]

That West had a perceptive and not uncritical understanding of court life is indicated by an acute observation he made to his fellow artists who had never seen it. You could always tell the highest nobility at court, he said, by their being the most abject to those above them, more so than others who had nothing to gain in the game of royal ceremony. Their attitude toward the king and those of higher rank was one of profound humility. This was a matter of considered policy, for the higher they raised the highest person above them, the higher they raised themselves who were next in point of rank. "They had," said West, "a greater interest in the question."

The 1780s were West's most prolific and experimental years. Charles Ryskamp, in his introduction to Kraemer's *Drawings by Benjamin West and His Son Raphael Lamar West* (the 244-page catalogue of the 1975 Morgan Library exhibition), writes of his "immediate sketches" of this period:

> We find new and vigorous concepts of heroism and death, of horror and terror, and we discover new views of nature. Sketching from nature kept West from mannerism and pomposity in most of his drawing; as a result, the sketches of animals, trees, landscapes are outstanding examples of early romantic modes of art. From the 1780s on West drew in Windsor Great Park and Little Park, and was fascinated by ancient blasted trees, with only a few branches of leaves left on the gnarled and twisted stumps. Herne's Oak at Windsor, made famous in *The Merry Wives of Windsor*, especially attracted him and he drew it again and again. For the next forty or fifty years, to the time of John Linnell and George Richmond, and beyond, the parks at Windsor, and the ancient trees, would captivate English artists. In this way, as in so many others, we can see that in these drawings Benjamin West established new subjects for art and new ways of looking at these subjects.

West was completing four historical scenes commissioned by the first earl of Grosvenor after the success of *The Death of Wolfe*.[4]

---

[3] West's document, some 4000 words in length, first published in 1967, has been cited as the only written statement of West's views on art between his letters to Copley before 1774 and a discourse he delivered to the Royal Academy in 1792. It contains West's aesthetic creed, his theories on color, and a guide based on his own studies in Italy.

[4] *The Battle of La Hogue, The Battle of the Boyne, Cromwell Dissolving the Long Parliament,* and *The Landing of Charles II at Dover.*

In addition to the works on revealed religion, he was painting a set of eight other large pictures commissioned by the king. This was planned as a record of the victorious reign of Edward III, to be hung in the Presence Chamber at Windsor Castle.[5] (It had been redesigned and reconstructed by Edward to serve as a meeting place for his newly established Knights of the Garter.) Most of the subjects were from Jean Froissart's *Chronicle*, and the king (who was learned in heraldry) watched the progress of these works closely. West began by making a small study for each picture, in which he showed the details of costumes, weapons, banners, and armorial bearings. As he obtained new information, particularly on the armorial bearings, he found it necessary to depart from his sketch in painting the full-size canvas. West told Henry Angelo, a courtier, "In no instance, not even the most minute alteration that I made, ever escaped the vigilant memory of His Majesty. 'I perceive, West,' he would say, 'that you have altered this — aye — and that. It stood so-and-so. I thought you were wrong.' "

The king liked to hear the gossip of London — who was betrothed, married, pregnant, separated, quarreling, disinherited, in financial trouble — and West was well able to collect and retell such gossip. The king, for some unaccountable reason, had no real personal secretary. He frequently spent three hours a day signing letters and documents and then would go for a walk, perhaps in his "Windsor uniform" — blue with gold lace and red collar and cuffs. He would stroll for a time on the north terrace and return for three more hours of signing. He was troubled during these years by the misconduct of his brothers and his grown sons, who were bored by the suffocating dullness of the court and were forming alliances with actresses, other women of dubious morality, and ladies of the Catholic faith. The Prince of Wales, in addition to giving his support and companionship to his father's political opponents, had fallen in love with a Marie Anne Fitzherbert, a commoner, twice widowed, six years older than he, and a Roman Catholic, and he was threatening to kill himself if she would not marry him. (A virtuous woman, she inconsiderately refused to become his mistress.) He had, moreover, run up debts in the summer of 1786 to the colossal total of £270,000 — more than one-fourth

---

[5] *Edward the Third Embracing the Black Prince After the Battle of Cressy, The Installation of the Order of the Garter, The Black Prince Receiving the King of France and His Sons at Poictiers, St. George Vanquishing the Dragon, Queen Phillipa Defeating David of Scotland in the Battle of Nevilles Cross, Queen Phillipa Interceding with Edward for the Burghers of Calais, King Edward Forcing the Passage of the Somme,* and *King Edward Crowning St. Eustace de Beaumont at Calais.*

the annual civil expenditures of the realm. George III had need of disinterested companionship and distraction to relieve his mind of such burdens. He found them in the hours spent working with West on the architectural plans for the new king's private chapel of the history of revealed religion.

The five years following the Peace of Paris marked a broadening of West's activities, despite the preponderance of time given to the king's commissions. He was moving into the post of Reynolds' unofficial deputy at the Academy. He took a trip to Paris. He was now being consulted on attributions and prices of pictures and on quality of engravings. In 1779 he and G. Battista Cipriani had placed a valuation on 174 old masters in the collection of the late Robert Walpole at Houghton Hall. Sir Robert had urged Parliament to buy his entire collection, but the Empress Catherine of Russia acquired it at the price of £40,555 set by West and Cipriani — one of the six collections she bought between 1764 and 1779.[6] The sale of the Houghton Hall pictures made West a sought-after authority on art appraisals and led to a modest amount of discreet, gentlemanly buying, selling, and trading of pictures.

The trip to Paris took place in the early spring of 1785. On March 28 he went with John Quincy Adams, then serving as his father's secretary, to call on a Mr. and Mrs. Rucker and then to take a walk together in the Palais royal, during which they philosophized on the birth the day before of a son, the duke of Normandy, to Queen Marie Antoinette. Three days later he joined all the Adamses, Thomas Jefferson, and several others to go to the residence of the marquise de Lafayette. She had arranged reserved

---

[6] Gerald Reitlinger, in *The Economics of Taste: The Rise and Fall of the Picture Market, 1760–1960*, calls this "enormous transaction" a perfect cross-section of picture values in the late eighteenth century. The prices, he says, were set according to the "exalted ideas of Benjamin West," in most cases two or three times as much as the auction room maximum of the day; but "it is the proportional values that are interesting." West, according to the taste of the time, placed a high valuation (up to £600) on works by Pietro da Cortona, Eustache Le Sueur, Sébastien Bourdon, Francesco Albano, Pietro Mola, Carlo Maratta, and Jan van Huysum, among other now-forgotten masters. He disparaged the Dutch-Flemish genre paintings and valued Frans Hals' *Officer at a Window* at £40. (Andrew Mellon paid the Soviet government £35,000 for it in 1931.) He valued Rembrandt's *Portrait of Saskia* and *The Sacrifice of Isaac* by Abraham at £600 for the pair; a Giovanni Bellini *Holy Family* at £60 ("which was Benjamin West's way of saying it might be worth twenty"); and a dozen Vandyke portraits at £200 each. ("Here we come across a peculiar kink in West's mind. He was determined that full-length portraits, painted by the illustrious dead, should not be esteemed higher than modern portrait commissions.") Mr. Reitlinger's five pages on the Houghton Hall transaction form a sobering exegesis on the changing nature of taste, the fluctuations in artists' reputations, and the fallibility of human judgment in art.

seats for the group at Notre Dame Cathedral to see and hear the *Te Deum* honoring the child's birth. They rode through jammed streets to the cathedral and found their seats in a gallery that commanded the choir and from which they could clearly see the king, all his court, and twenty-five bishops. They returned to the Hôtel de Lafayette and drank tea with the marquise. Nothing more is known of West's stay in Paris — who accompanied him, whom he saw, why he went, how long he stayed.

West frequently saw the Adamses later that year when Mr. Adams was named minister to Great Britain. He called at their house in Grosvenor Square in September bursting with news and immensely proud. He had just bought a 4 by 6 foot dirt-and-wax-encrusted landscape painting at John Greenwood's auction house, paying (amid general laughter) 20 guineas. On cleaning the picture he discovered that it was a Titian, *The Death of Acteon,* and he had already refused on offer of 1500 guineas for it. He was rearranging his whole gallery to give the work the place of honor. The *Morning Post* featured the discovery, calling it an "indisputable and pre-eminent" Titian from the collection of England's Charles I, and said that Greenwood the auctioneer should change his name to Greenhorn. Paul Sandby, R.A., called it "the best picture in the country" and wrote to a friend in Dublin, "Half the town of vertu are crazy about a picture by Titian which Mr. West purchased for about £20 out of a lumber corner."

West entered a competition in 1786 to do an altarpiece for the new chapel at Greenwich Hospital, proposing to paint *St. Paul's Shipwreck at Malta* with fifty figures on a canvas 16 by 20 feet. In due course he learned that Copley had also entered a design and had been awarded the commission by the decision of John Montagu, Lord Sandwich, former first lord of the Admiralty. West decided to go over Lord Sandwich's head to reverse the decision in his own favor. He may have concluded that since (as everybody knew) Sandwich's administration was the most corrupt and incompetent in the history of the British navy, the Admiralty's decision needed to be rectified. Or he may have felt that in withdrawing his *Death of Chatham* and in losing the *Siege of Gibraltar* commission, he had conceded enough to Copley. Whatever his rationalization, he went either to Lord North (according to one newspaper) or to the king (according to another), who intervened to give him the commission. The *Morning Herald,* in reporting the change, opined that Copley "beyond all comparison is the superior artist." The person reversing the decision may have been influenced by knowledge that Copley was in deep trouble on his 18 by 25 foot *Siege of Gibraltar,* commissioned by the Corporation of

London in 1783 and promised for 1785. Now, in 1786, Corporation officers and eyewitnesses were complaining that the picture did not show the full action (West had proposed that he paint two pictures to meet that problem), and Copley was redesigning the work.[7]

The following year West was called on as an expert witness at a notable action brought by one picture dealer against another. The plaintiff was French-born Noel Desenfans (originally Des Enfans), a friend and frequent dinner guest of the Wests. He had been a dealer in lace, came to England to teach French, married one of his pupils who had £5000, became interested on his honeymoon in buying art, and (in the words of a contemporary) "by great industry and a little taste," established a going business as a picture dealer. Desenfans called by written invitation at the shop of a dealer named Benjamin Vandergucht to see a Nicolas Poussin that had just arrived from France, titled *La Vierge aux Enfants*. (The *enfants*, seventeen of them, were shown adoring the Virgin.) He pointed out to Vandergucht that in his opinion certain parts of the picture were not typical of Poussin. Vandergucht responded with the claim that Mr. West, on first seeing it, had been struck with admiration by its beauty and declared it to be the finest and most exalted Poussin in existence. On the strength of that impressive testimonial, Desenfans bought the picture for £700, obtaining a written warranty and giving Vandergucht permission to exhibit it publicly for the next six weeks. When some friendly critic advised him that the work was not by Poussin, Desenfans brought action to cancel the sale and recover his £700.

John Copley, subpoenaed by Desenfans' counsel, would not say that *La Vierge aux Enfants* was *not* by Poussin, but it was, in his opinion, an inferior picture. Vandergucht's counsel quoted from Lawrence Sterne: "Of all the cant in the canting world, though the cant of hypocrisy be the worst, yet the cant of criticism is the most tormenting." Thomas Gainsborough declared that if he had seen the picture in a dealer's shop on sale for five shillings, he would not have bought it. In cross-examination, Vandergucht's counsel said, "Mr. Gainsborough, I observe that you lay great stress on the phrase 'the painter's eye.' What do you mean by that?" Gainsborough's

---

[7] He finished it in the spring of 1791, six years later, and quarreled with the Corporation in an effort to have his fee increased from £1000 to £1500. He exhibited the work in a large tent in Green Park, not far from the Queen's House; when nearby residents objected to the crowds and made him move, the king (who had seen the picture in May) said, "Push it up nearer to my wife's house — she won't complain."

answer circulated around London that week: "The painter's eye is to him what the lawyer's tongue is to you."

When he was called, West said he had considerable difficulty in determining whether the picture was or was not a genuine Poussin. There was something of Poussin about it, he said, and yet it had defects he had not seen before in Poussin. The characters were gross, the Virgin's head was too large, the children's heads lacked the grace and correctness of a typical Poussin. And yet the features did have some Poussin qualities. On the other hand, he might have said some flattering things about the picture to Mr. Vandergucht, because he followed the practice of never condemning what he could not applaud. West's testimony was ridiculed in the press. The *Morning Herald* said he acted very much like an American Loyalist, ready to join in turn either the king or the Congress.

> Never yet was anything half so sceptical. "Turn it," says Mr. West to the man who had the picture in court, "a little towards me. And now from me. 'Tis very like Poussin. — 'Tis very unlike Poussin." — and thus was an alternate preponderation in favour of and against the picture kept up to the embarrassment of all who had ears to hear the witness and eyes to see the picture. Mr. West understands this sort of light and shade as well as anybody, and, like Polonius, can convert "a whale to a camel, and a camel to a weasel — yea, a black weasel."

The jury was out only briefly and returned a verdict for Desenfans.

Thomas Gainsborough died of cancer a few months later, in his sixty-first year. He was buried in the churchyard at Kew in a simple ceremony attended only by those named in a list he had made up some weeks before his death. West was a pallbearer with five other designated artists, including Reynolds, Chambers, and Bartolozzi. Reynolds and West served as Mrs. Gainsborough's friendly advisors on disposition of the estate, which included many drawings, partly finished portraits, and landscapes. They counseled her to hold these works against a rising market. The Gainsborough market, unfortunately, did not rise; it declined for landscapes and it collapsed for portraits, not recovering for another seventy years. Families of sitters would not redeem unfinished portraits, even though half the commission had been paid in advance. When 103 Gainsborough lots were sold in 1797, only 5 brought more than six pounds each. Two full-length finished portraits went for six pounds and four pounds, fourteen shillings, sixpence. *Mrs. Graham as a Housemaid* (now at the National Gallery, London) fetched four pounds, fourteen shillings. Within a few years after Gainsborough's death, styles in clothing completely changed. The women's towering coiffures and hoop skirts, the men's powdered wigs, embroidered waistcoats, wired coattails and buckled shoes, became absurd, ugly, and unfashionable.

In the autumn of 1788, a few months after Gainsborough's funeral, West (according to the *Morning Post* of January 13, 1789) painted a landscape at Windsor for the queen, and at her request, and for the edification of young Prince Adolphus, included a lion. When he saw the picture on West's easel, the king condemned the drawing of the lion; it looked like a dog, he said, not like a lion. West was hurt but of course held his tongue. "The King then deliberately took up a pencil and drew it through the figure, and then drawing a fantastic sketch showed it to the painter as a proper drawing of the animal." West, shaken by the experience, told the queen what had happened. She "informed him of the melancholy apprehensions" she had felt for some time that His Majesty's mind was disturbed. The account declared that West was the first person outside the royal household to observe the king's condition.

There had been no earlier indication of mental trouble. The king's health was good, his physique was robust, and he had stood up with admirable fortitude under severe political and family stresses in 1772 and in 1782–83. The year 1788 was one of relative calm, with few pressures that might unsettle him. There were indications that he had at last won the affection of his people, partly because his sober domestic life was in such contrast to the extravagant excesses of the Prince of Wales. But now he began to talk rapidly, incessantly, incoherently, especially late at night, and to utter coarse epithets and obscenities he had never been heard to use before. He could not sleep. His eyesight and hearing began to fail. The king tried for a time to maintain his daily routine and to keep the news of his illness from the public "to stop . . . any fall of the stocks." "The Queen," Fanny Burney wrote, "is almost overpowered by some secret terror." She dreaded spending the night with the king, changed her bedroom, locked her door, and kept a companion constantly with her.

In the middle of November the king lay in a coma for several hours and was thought to be very close to death, but he recovered some of his strength, though his mind was still afflicted. His physicians — seven of them — could not agree on a diagnosis, on treatment, or on the chances of recovery. The king's madness had symptoms quite unlike any madness they had known before, for there were intervals when he was perfectly lucid, self-controlled, and conscious of what he was experiencing. John Brooke, a recent biographer, believes that from the third week of November he was on the road to recovery, and that his "madness" thenceforth resulted largely from his struggle to escape the stern, even brutal command of his physicians. The worst of these was a well-intentioned tyrant named Francis Willis, a clergyman who operated a lunatic asylum on the theory that the patients responded best to relentless discipline and physical restraint. The Reverend Dr. Willis succeeded in removing the other physicians (who considered him a mountebank), assumed complete control of the sickroom, and confined the king in a straitjacket or strapped him in bed or tied him in a restraining chair when he resisted orders — if he refused to eat when he could not swallow, if he did not go to bed when he was too restless to sleep, if he threw off his bedclothes in a sweating attack, if he used improper language. The king once struck a page who was carrying out such an order; that night he sent for the page, took him by the hand, and begged his pardon. In one of the king's lucid moments, Willis explained that he was doing what Christ had done; he was healing the sick. The king replied sardonically, "Yes, yes, but he had not £700 a year for it."

West was several times with the king during his illness. On one occasion he called at Kew, where the king was confined to his bed. The queen entered and seemed to be displeased that he had been admitted. A few days later at Windsor the king sent for West, who found him with two gentlemen and the queen, with two of her ladies, looking over some silks. As he told the story to Farington, "The King began to speak of his illness and said it was owing to his not having taken the Queen's advice but that from henceforward he always would, that she was a good woman, etc. etc. This rambling and singular conversation caused the Queen to flutter among the silks and the attendants to feel very awkward. He finished by ordering West to go to the castle and he would come to him to see an experiment on the philosophy of colours."

The king's illness, at its worst, affected all who depended on or were associated with him. West's payments from the king's privy purse stopped — unfortunately, just at the time he took on the responsibility of supporting his half brother Thomas' destitute family in Reading. The Prince of Wales expected to be named regent, and the king's Whig opponents expected to become ministers in the regent's government. William Pitt the Younger, fighting to stay in power, adroitly produced a regency bill that limited the prince's authority and put the king's person and patronage in the hands of the queen. The bill was about to be voted on by Parliament when, in February 1789, in a remarkable victory of a strong constitution over misguided medical treatment, the king had what appeared to be a full recovery of his health and reason. He appeared in public to receive a tumultuous welcome and to witness rejoicing such as had not been seen in England in living memory. Dr. Willis, who was given credit for effecting the cure, cast a gold medal with his own name and face on one side and, on the other, the words, "Britons Rejoice, Your King's Restored 1789." [8]

By 1790 it was widely understood that West would succeed Sir Joshua Reynolds as president of the Royal Academy. Reynolds' last two years were neither pleasant nor easy. His eyesight was failing, his health was deteriorating, and he became involved in quarrels with the other Academicians. In considerable degree the quarrels were his fault, for he had grown irritable, he was stubborn, and he was frequently wrong. Feeling against him had been rising, partly because he was denying space to other artists by hanging so many of his own pictures at the annual exhibitions — eighteen of them in 1788. An anonymous member, during one critical quarrel, published twenty-nine pages of *Observations on the Present State of the Academy,* one sentence of which read, "Indeed, he had been so long in the habit of dictating from his gilded chair, and had been so continually flattered by the submission of those over whom he presided that, perhaps, he chose rather to hazard a falsehood, though degrading to his honour, than suffer a diminution of that

---

[8] In 1969, Dr. Ida Macalpine, a physician who had served as psychiatrist at St. Bartholomew's Hospital, London, and Dr. Richard Hunter, her son, a physician in psychological medicine at the National Hospital in London, co-authors of a history of psychiatry, together wrote a study of George III's malady. In their analysis they made the first serious examination of the doctors' carefully preserved notes and records and for the first time concentrated on the physical symptoms described therein. In what they call "a firm diagnosis of his disease in the light of present medical knowledge," they make the following observations:

George III suffered from a painful illness caused by faulty metabolism. It is a hereditary, Mendelian-dominant disorder. Its name is porphyria — a failure of the blood cells to convert porphyrin, a pigment contained in the hemoglobin of the blood. Porphyria attacks the nervous system, usually beginning in the autonomic system, then advancing to the peripheral nerves, then the cranial nerves, and finally the brain itself. At the height of the attack the patient is paralyzed and in agonizing pain. It is a physical, not a psychotic disease. George III's malady was not insanity, or manic depressive psychosis. His episodes of derangement were simply "the mutterings of a delirious mind temporarily disordered by an intoxicated person."

The Macalpine-Hunter diagnosis, now widely accepted, is of special interest in view of the charge of several art historians that George III chose and favored Benjamin West as court painter because he was of unsound mind.

dignity which was so dear to his pride." (It was believed that John Henry Fuseli, a candidate for election as one of the twenty Associates of the Royal Academy, helped to write the pamphlet.) West saw all this at first hand: the imperiousness of the young, the vulnerability of the man at the top, the glare of light concentrated on faults that heretofore had been accepted, the rancor that can be directed against one who has been too long in office.

Reynolds charged that the attacks against him were being engineered by "an infamous cabal," by "a low politic combination," and that the majority of the Academicians, either from weakness or malevolence, were ready to be led "wherever impudent boldness will undertake to direct them." There was some truth in what he said. An architect and sculptor named William Tyler, a "foundation member," led a revolt when Reynolds tried to force on the Academicians a professor of perspective who was not an Academician and whom they did not want. "Tyler was an odd man," the king said to West several years later. "How came he to be an Academician?" "When the Royal Academy was formed," West replied, "there was not a choice of artists as at present, and some indifferent artists were admitted."

At the general meeting in February 1790, when Reynolds forced the issue of appointing his choice as professor of perspective, he was insulted and humiliated before the entire membership. The next morning he resigned both the presidency and his seat in the Academy, writing a letter so heated that he later agreed to replace it with one more temperate. To the rejected candidate he wrote, "I cannot persuade myself any longer to rank with such beings."

Some of the members rallied to Reynolds' support, the newspapers expressed their indignation at the treatment given the dean of British artists, and the rebels had some sober second thoughts about what they had done. Reynolds rejected a request of the king, conveyed through Chambers, the treasurer, that he retain his seat as president, and he turned back an overture of reconciliation from the Academy. (He was enjoying himself writing a somewhat tedious defense of his conduct and a scathing attack on the low politic combination.) But the members in general meeting, instead of electing a new president, voted to send a kind of apology to Reynolds, and they appointed West and eight other artists to beg him to remain. Reynolds relented and took his chair again at the end of March. It was allowed that West behaved himself very well during this crisis in Academy affairs. He did not agree with Reynolds' conduct in the matter but at the same time felt he had been ill used.

The opposition, however, was quelled but not ended. Chambers scolded Reynolds roundly for removing a picture from the spring exhibition, "contrary to a positive law of the Academy ... and a stretch of power in you, which it will be difficult to justify." When Reynolds proposed that the Academy contribute £100 toward a monument to Samuel Johnson to be erected in St. Paul's, Chambers attempted to overwhelm the idea with ridicule. The proposal was carried on a motion of West, who supported it not so much out of respect for the memory of Dr. Johnson, but rather because he still nursed the battered hope that the erection of works of art in St. Paul's would "open a new field for the display of the abilities of our brethren." Chambers persuaded the king to veto the proposal.

Reynolds delivered his fifteenth and last discourse in December 1790 at a meeting that nearly became uniquely famous in the annals of art: One of the floor beams under the Assembly Room cracked and sagged, and if it had given way the flower of English art would have perished. (A member may have averted a disaster by calling out, with great presence of mind, "Gently, gently, or mischief will be anticipated!") Sir Joshua presided over his last meeting in July 1791. Four months later he again resigned from the Academy, this time pleading poor health. The members persuaded him to retain his post and to appoint a deputy to act for him until he recovered. He named West. He died in February 1792, in his sixty-ninth year. When his executors proposed that the body lie in state at the Royal Academy the evening before the funeral service and burial, Chambers, as surveyor at Somerset House, declared that he could not authorize such a precedent. West went directly to the king and obtained his consent and command "that that mark of respect should be shown." The Academicians wore mourning for Sir Joshua for one month.

Sir Joshua was buried in St. Paul's Cathedral with great pomp and circumstance, ninety-one carriages following in the funeral procession. (He had chosen St. Paul's himself because he felt Westminster Abbey was much too crowded and "resembled a stone cutter's shop rather than a Christian church.") The funeral cost £600, each Academician being assessed 30 shillings as his share. One newspaper complained of the "hauteur" and "miserable conduct" of the executors, who did not give the Academicians, after three hours of tedious waiting, so much as a glass of sherry. When Reynolds' art collection was placed on sale, the catalogue listed 70 Vandykes, 54 Correggios, 44 Michelangelos (most modern critics believe that Michelangelo may have left behind no easel pictures at all), 24 Raphaels, and 12 Leonardos. No fewer than 412 pictures were auctioned, and they brought an average of less than £25 each.[9]

The members of the Royal Academy attended a special meeting called for the evening of March 17, 1792, to elect a new president. John Copley put himself forward for the office, which some members thought was unbecoming of him. With William Chambers presiding, West was elected by a vote of twenty-nine to one, with no abstentions.

---

[9] Reitlinger, *Economics of Taste,* I, 9, III, 252. The flood of bogus old masters gave impetus a half century later to the pre-Raphaelite brotherhood of British painters. They recognized that pictures painted before the time of Raphael (1483–1520) were certain to be genuine, and thus a pure source of inspiration, because later generations thought them "barbarous," unworthy of being copied, and not worth forging.

Benjamin West, P.R.A.

Therefore, gentlemen, not on account of any personal merit on my part, but to do honor to the office to which you have so kindly elected me, I shall presume in the future to wear my hat in this assembly.

> BENJAMIN WEST, address
> to the Royal Academy,
> March 24, 1792

THE RESULT OF THE ELECTION was carried at once to the king, whose signed approval was read at a special meeting held at Somerset House on March 24, 1792. West's inaugural address as president was graceful and short — about 800 words. He paid tribute to the genius and "amiable dispositions" of his predecessor, Sir Joshua Reynolds, and to His Majesty, declaring that he had observed the bosom of every member "to glow with gratitude and loyal affection to our AUGUST FOUNDER, patron, and benefactor." He directed a prescient message to the leaders of what would come to be known as Britain's industrial revolution: Design acquired at the Academy, having spread itself through the various manufacturies of the country, "has given a taste that is able to convert the most common and simple materials into rare and valuable articles of commerce. These articles the British merchant sends forth into all quarters of the world, where they stand pre-eminent over the productions of other nations." He would strive as president to demonstrate his duty to his sovereign, his love for the Academy, and his zeal for the cultivation of genius and growth of universal virtue.

Within the month, in another attempt to heighten the dignity of the institution, West introduced the custom (still observed) of having the Academy porters wear red and gold braid gowns on formal occasions. In May he gave a dinner at his house for the entire body of Academicians, setting up tables in his large painting room. Peter Pindar, poet-critic, celebrated the event in the *Morning Post* with verse:

> *Full forty years to gain a name*
> *Unluckily has West been studying.*
> *Finding his brush despised by Fame,*
> *He tries the powers of beef and pudding.*

His first public test as president came with the opening of the annual exhibition, when he presided at the annual dinner of members and their guests and the next day welcomed the king and other royalty on their tour of the gallery.

Everything at the dinner went smoothly almost to the end. The usual toasts were drunk to the king (followed by three cheers), the queen, the Prince of Wales, the Princess Royal, the duke of York and the army, the duke of Clarence and the navy, prosperity to the Royal Academy (three cheers), and success to the next exhibition. But at the last moment, when the company was about to break up, James Boswell astonished those in charge of the carefully planned program by rising (perhaps unsteadily) and asking permission to say a few words. Boswell, whose biography of Dr. Johnson had appeared a few months earlier, was the Academy's newly elected secretary for foreign correspondence, one of the honorary posts Sir Joshua Reynolds had created to please his friends Dr. Johnson, Dr. Oliver Goldsmith, and Joseph Baretti. Boswell had succeeded Baretti, accepting in a letter written not only in the required Italian, but in two other languages as well. This was Boswell's first dinner and he had no occasion to speak, but he had something on his mind. He lamented that this was the first exhibition dinner the Academy had held without seeing in the chair "that excellent and eminent person of whom I cannot speak, and you cannot hear, without emotion." He observed that this was a day of anxiety for everyone in the room. The anxiety did not arise, he felt sure, because of any apprehension of deficiency in the respectable gentleman who was now presiding so worthily. It arose, rather, because the uncertainty attending every change created a degree of fear. No one could be quite sure — "I say it with hesitation and delicacy" — that the president would not, in a "variable temper," do things differently. Had that happened, everyone would have felt uneasy. He was pleased to observe with the highest satisfaction that the day of trial was happily over, that everything had gone well, and, what was particularly pleasing, that there was a numerous attendance of the particular friends of the ever-to-be honored Sir Joshua Reynolds.

West may have been annoyed, angered, or unnerved by this gratuitous insult, but the 1792 exhibition, which opened the next day, was a marked success, at least in the measurable terms of pictures hung (780, of which 654 were by nonmembers) and of total admission receipts (£2602). When the king came, West and the secretary received him at the first landing on the elliptical staircase and accompanied him through the gallery, followed by his entourage. His Majesty took his usual pleasure in identifying the portraits of those people he knew. He rarely made a mistake, but when he did, rather than appear to criticize the artist, he would say, "Lord ——— is difficult, very difficult, to paint." He had a retentive memory and could recall and talk about almost every important picture he had seen from the first year of his reign.

Boswell seems to have been made aware of some criticism for his unscheduled remarks, perhaps from the court, since he had inferentially questioned the king's judgment in approving West's election as president. At the next dinner of the Royal Academy Club, over which West presided, held at Freemason's Tavern, Boswell sang a "complimentary strain" he had composed in honor of President West. To a formal Academy dinner in honor of Queen Charlotte's birthday, which he was too ill to attend, he sent still another song. It was delivered to West at the head of the table. He read it and handed it to Richard Cosway, who was sitting nearby, and then to John Inigo Richards, the secretary. Richards appealed for a volunteer to sing it. A member or a guest performed and was rewarded with loud applause. Two stanzas, no worse than the other four, went:

> This is the Day,
> The Queen's Birthday,
> The very day, Sir, when,
> We'll drink and sing
> God Save the King
> And eke our own rare Ben . . .
>
> Then be it so
> For well I know
> Her Majesty will then
> Applaud the thing
> And tell the King
> How I respect rare Ben.

West found himself in the spring of 1792 at the head of an organization that had very substantial administrative responsibilities. Reynolds had left him a large, vigorous, successful operation. The Academy was now not only self-supporting, it had more than £16,-

000 in investments and was making an annual profit of around £400. It was contributing a modest amount each year for the relief of "decayed artists" or their distressed widows and children "on the donation." Mrs. William Hogarth was one such beneficiary, though her husband had died before the Academy was founded. There was talk, moreover, of setting up a pension plan for the forty members. The Academy was running an art school that in the past twenty-two years had accepted, without charge, 564 students (all males, of course), some 50 of whom had become Associate Members or Academicians. Until 1794 and the spread of war in Europe, it had provided allowances of £100 a year for three years, and 30 guineas travel expenses, for students to study in Italy. (Part of the money was given by the Dilettanti Society.) Art students before 1770 had still been a part of the craft-guild apprenticeship system, serving in a master's studio; now they had been raised to a professional level. Though Wilson, Gainsborough, and Reynolds were gone, a whole new generation of promising young students, Associates, and Academicians was coming up. Among them were Thomas Lawrence, twenty-three, the fourteenth of sixteen children of a bankrupt inn-keeper; Martin Arthur Shee, twenty-three, an Irishman from Dublin; and Joseph Mallord William Turner, seventeen, a rough young man, son of a barber, who had entered the Academy schools at fourteen and exhibited a water color at fifteen.

English art had risen with the improvement in the condition of English artists. London had become a recognized art center. Until the French Revolution and the war with France, British artists, through the sale of their engravings, initiated and dominated European artistic trends. England now had an institution to which it could turn for advice on matters relating to the arts, as it had been doing on coinage, public statues, copyright in sculptured models, and duties on imported works of art. In one document of the period the Academicians described their institution, grandiloquently but pardonably, as "a permanent monument of public utility and royal munificence."[1]

---

[1] "The Royal Academy was largely responsible for raising the status of artists above that of mere tradesmen or craftsmen; its banquets were attended by members of the royal family, by diplomatists and politicians — a far cry from the jovial carousers of the old artists' clubs... Its annual exhibitions gave artists the opportunity of studying each other's works and provided them with a shop window in which to show their performances, thus helping to free them from the old system of patronage and the tyranny of the picture dealer. Whereas the majority of pictures had formerly been painted to fulfil commissions, the Academy... opened up a much wider market." Hugh Honour, *Connoisseur's Complete Period Guides*, p. 837.

West now had to spend a considerable portion of his working day on Academy business. He was involved in correspondence, meetings, visits, supervision of the staff, awards of medals to the students, trips to Windsor to consult the king, and preparations for the annual exhibition and the two large dinners held in April and December. He told Joseph Farington that the interruptions were so frequent during the day that he had begun to do most of his painting at night, working from after teatime to midnight or later. With a strong light from his lamp (probably the new Argand burner), he could see, he said, as well as in daytime. He was aided by a new kind of eye glasses invented around 1776, possibly by his friend Franklin in Paris. He was hypermetropic — far-sighted — and when he painted wore what were called "double" or "divided" glasses.

Some of his problems were time-consuming but trivial. Lady Inchiquin, later marchioness of Thomond — she had been Mary Palmer, Reynolds' niece and heiress — complained that she was not accorded a private viewing of the exhibitions, and she blamed Mr. West. The Academy dinners were now important social occasions, with tickets much in demand, and time had to be spent pacifying those who were forgotten or denied. There were continuing complaints in letters to the newspapers and to the Academy about the unclothed Greek and Roman statues that lined the hall, staircase, and Antique Room, and especially about the stark naked giant-size *Farnese Hercules*. These were, one correspondent said, "the terror of every decent woman"; at the sight of them, another wrote, "a woman must forfeit her claim to decency." The proposal was made that women should be spared such dangers by having their own visiting day, with males barred. Young Thomas Lawrence created a minor problem when he petitioned to have his full-length portrait of Lady Manners hung in the center at the head of the Great Room. Joseph Wilton, keeper of the Academy, reported at a Council meeting that the students were behaving very rudely. They were throwing at each other the bread they were issued for erasing their drawings, wasting so much that the bill for bread was as high as sixteen shillings a week. Farington moved "that henceforward, no bread be allowed in the Academy for the students," which was solemnly and unanimously resolved. West observed that it would be productive of much good to the students to deprive them of the use of bread, for it would induce them to pay more attention to their outlines and learn to draw more correctly, when they could not be perpetually rubbing out.

On December 10, 1792, West delivered a first discourse to the assembled students. It was an unwise thing for him to do, for he laid himself open to unamiable comparison with the master he was following, the now-beloved Sir Joshua. West praised Reynolds at the start for daring "to break out from the confined notions of his predecessors" in British art; but he then took a liberal view in opposing the High Style that Reynolds for two decades had sought to impose upon British painting (*Lady Bunbury Sacrificing to the Graces, Miss Emily Pott as Thais*). Academy instruction, West said, should leave the student "perfectly free to that line and to that expression of art which the natural turn of his own genius shall lead him to embrace." More harm than good had been done, he said, "by the systems of those schools which, having their own ideas of excellence, have brought every genius to assimilate with them." A strength of genius, on the other hand, would always be apt to run wild if it was not brought under some regulations. The young artist must be in love with his art, or he would never excel in it. He must feel his profession to be not only honorable, but something more in its perfection than was common to mankind. Virtue, always indispensable, was of the first consequence in the life of the elegant artist, whose contemplations were, or should be, always sedate, and whose mind should always be tranquil and at home.

On December 10, 1793, West was unanimously elected to a second term as president of the Academy. To the assembled members he reported that he had talked with the king, who was graciously disposed to permit a celebration of the Academy's twenty-fifth anniversary, to be observed in such a manner as the members saw fit and to be paid for from Academy funds. James Barry, his Irish blood boiling, "spoke vehemently" against asking the king's permission on such a matter, which could set a bad precedent and end the independence of the institution. In the early evening of December 31, West presided over and addressed a twenty-fifth anniversary dinner. It was attended by almost the entire membership, of whom fifteen were founding members. Joseph Farington, having heard West talk of the dominant role he himself had played in founding the Academy, pointedly proposed a toast to Sir William Chambers "for his able and active conduct in planning and forming the Royal Academy." Five instrumentalists and four vocalists had been engaged to give a concert. Many members were irritated when they had to leave their seats to make room for the harpsichord, and most of the members were displeased — especially Mr. Boswell — when the music went on so long and so loud that conversation was impossible. West gave a full account of the dinner to the newspapers. Some weeks later a commemoration medal designed by Robert Smirke and struck by Thomas Pingo and Sons was distributed: four in gold to the royal family, sixty in silver to the Academicians and Associates. Lady Inchiquin complained that no medal was given to the Reynolds family.

At the meeting in February 1794, during which Associates were voted on for full membership, Thomas Stothard and Thomas Lawrence were elected. John Hoppner and Richard Westall were tied at fourteen votes each, which meant that West, as president, would cast the deciding ballot. He announced that in such cases, when the artists were of equal merit, he would always give the preference to seniority. Westall had been an Associate one year longer than Hoppner and so received West's vote. "Hoppner," Farington wrote, "is much mortified." He had lost in the first ballot to Lawrence, his rival in portraiture, eleven years younger than he, and in the second ballot to an inferior artist by the vote of West, a man he hated.

If he did not know it before, West soon became aware that he was responsible to a highly volatile body of men. They were, in varying degrees, proud, contumelious, quick to take offense, and prodigiously egocentric. They were of all ages and they differed widely in background — in nationality, social level, education, income, and talent. The Academy was a remarkably democratic institution for any time or country, and certainly for a class-conscious eighteenth-century society; it ignored "plebian origins" and judged a candidate solely for his ability as shown in his work. John Opie,[2] son of a carpenter, "The Cornish Wonder," the self-taught genius who came to London in 1780, was described by a contemporary: "His appearance was uncouth in the extreme, and the manner in which he sometimes conveyed his remarks to elegant females was captious, vulgar and coarse." But Opie had talent, he devoted himself to his art with extraordinary diligence, and in 1786 he was made an Associate, in 1787 a full member of the Academy, where his behavior at meetings was described as careless and contemptuous.

It was to be expected that these artists should quarrel with one another and with the Academy from time to time, but the amount and intensity of the quarreling in the early years of West's presidency, as revealed in Farington's diary, seem truly phenomenal. West, with his peace-loving Quaker background, his lack of experience in administering a complex organization, and his own ambitions, was no man to control the quarreling, and in time its full fury turned on him.

This is a sampling of the contentions that took place among

---

2 He pronounced his name *Oppy;* his friends called him Jan rather than John.

Academy members in the seven years between West's election as president and the year 1800.

May 10, 1793: When Fuseli hung a picture of a scene from *Macbeth* and Lawrence hung a picture of a scene from *The Tempest,* Fuseli charged that Lawrence had stolen his idea, inspiration, and figures. Lawrence said that his picture had been painted first and that if there was any stealing, it had been done by Fuseli. The art critic of the *Oracle* wrote, "These gentlemen may be perfectly easy: the figures are original neither to the one nor the other."

February 12, 1794: James Northcote told Hoppner that he was well aware of the unhandsome manner in which Hoppner had spoken of him.

April 27: Joseph Nollekens was angry that "some busts which he desired to exhibit were refused to be placed in the Council Room, in consequence of which he would not exhibit."

December 13: John Yenn and John Soane exchanged words when Yenn accused Soane of having spoken disrespectfully of the Royal Academicians and of the institution.

January 6, 1795: John Opie expressed surprise at William Beechey's raising his price to thirty guineas a head. He said that Beechey's pictures "were of that mediocre quality as to taste and fashion that they seemed only fit for sea captains and merchants."

May 2: Northcote said he was convinced that the Hanging Committee was determined not to have him considered as a portrait painter.

November 8: James Barry advised Thomas Malton, when defeated as an Associate, to bring an action against George Dance and William Tyler for declaring him not to be an architect, but only a draughtsman of buildings.

November 13: Copley said he would oppose the election of any more architects to the Academy, as he thought them useless members, and no more than two should be allowed.

December 31: The Academy Council denied a request from William Chambers "because his gross behavior to the Council and the Academy in general did not entitle him to any attention from them." John Richards declared that he had been unhandsomely treated by Copley when he refused to pay Copley some fees for hanging pictures, which Copley was not entitled to.

February 20, 1796: Hoppner derided the quality of Lawrence's work on a portrait of Lady Louise Gordon, causing the Gordons to ask Lawrence to make changes in it.

April 11: William Beechey wrote an "impertinent letter" to the Academy demanding his pictures and frames back; he would not exhibit them.

April 18: Northcote was alarmed that his pictures were not all being hung together.

April 23: A warm conversation took place between Hoppner and Fuseli "in which, without directly quarreling, they said many severe things on each other's work," Fuseli sneering at Hoppner's "cold flesh and hot backgrounds."

June 3: Yenn showed Farington some pointed verses at an Academy dinner "describing Soane as an architect destitute of merit."

January 2, 1797: Hoppner spoke with contempt of John Flaxman as a draughtsman. "I cannot draw," he said, "but I can draw better than Flaxman can, and his thoughts are all borrowed and purloined from a variety of things he has seen. He has nothing original about him."

February 1: Fuseli said Barry's head was filled with stuff retained by the memory and undigested. Robert Smirke agreed that his lectures contained very little information.

February 10: Yenn accused Farington of rigging an Academy election, at which Farington said, "You are very impertinent. This is the second time you have insulted me in the Academy," and "some little bustle ensued." George Dance said that Yenn's insolence was not to be borne and that some way should be found to put an end to it.

February 17: Beechey, an Associate, was defeated for election to full membership by Sawrey Gilpin, who painted animals. Beechey sent a letter to West resigning his seat in the Academy. West apparently decided to treat the letter as a personal one and to withhold it from the Council, and no more was heard of Beechey's resignation.

February 25: Beechey wrote three angry letters to Ozias Humphry accusing him of "having spoken to his prejudice as a puffer in the newspapers." Humphrey replied that it was Harry Tresham who said it.

December 15: Fuseli's behavior was so violent at one of West's lectures that a Colonel Smith, a guest, told him he thought he was among people whose profession would teach them to act like gentlemen, but he had found it otherwise.

July 21, 1798: Edmund Garvey observed to Farington how rude John Richards, the secretary, was to everybody who came near the Academy.

July 27: Barry refused in a passion to have any dispute with such a person as Richard Cosway. At this, Farington rose and declared that if the members would bear such an insult to one of their own body, no man who felt as a gentleman would attend their meetings.

January 28, 1799: Northcote charged that he was being excluded from office "by *favorites* being preferred."

April 2: Hoppner expressed indignation at the manner in which his pictures were being placed and threatened to withdraw them.

William Sandby, who wrote the first history of the Royal Academy in 1862, described the importance of the early Academy meetings, citing the twenty-fifth anniversary dinner as an example. "These social gatherings," he wrote, "had charms which the more stately Exhibition Dinner could not afford. The members met to know each other more intimately — to discuss freely, as friends and brothers in art, the prospects of the institution of which they formed a part, and the several matters in which their individual sympathies were concerned."

On a Sunday in May 1794, Robert Smirke, R.A., called on Benjamin West at 14 Newman Street. During the visit, West made critical remarks of some kind about Joseph Farington, his friend and sometime dinner guest, and about Farington's conduct in Academy affairs. The following Thursday, Smirke repeated the remarks to Farington, who, incensed at what he heard, wrote to West demanding an explanation or an apology or both. (No copy of his letter is known to exist.) He showed the letter to Smirke, Fuseli, and George Dance, who approved it, and he then sent it by a manservant to West's residence.

Farington was a man with whom West could ill afford to quarrel, for he was moving into a position of power in the Academy. A scion of an old Lancashire family of means, nine years younger than West, he had become one of the Academy's first students, after studying under Richard Wilson, whom he revered. He and his young brother George, a pupil of West's, had spent three years at Robert Walpole's Houghton Hall in Norfolk making tinted drawings for a book of engravings of the pictures there — the pictures that were later appraised by West and Cipriani and sold to Catherine the Great. Farington had then passed some months in the north of England and in Wales making landscapes and cityscapes; these were published quite profitably in folio as *Views of the Lakes, etc., in Cumberland and Westmoreland* and *Views of Cities and Towns in England and Wales.* He returned to London in 1780, took up residence at 35 Charlotte Street, Fitzroy Square, and in 1785 was elected an R.A. He held nothing but minor offices in the Academy, and he was only a landscape painter — indeed, what was even lower in the professional scale, a "topographical draughtsman" — but within a decade he was beginning to be thought of as a dominant figure in the Academy's operations. James Barry, who was "inveterate" against him, called him "Warwick, the King Maker." Northcote said in the 1830s, "How Farington used to rule the Academy! He was a great man to be looked up to on all occasions; all applicants must gain their point through him... His great passion was the love of power — he loved to rule. He did it, of course, with considerable dignity."

Farington achieved his power honestly and on merit. He was a handsome man of majestic presence, a shade under six feet tall. He had a flair for business and hard work, and within a few years would render great service in improving the Academy's financial affairs. Since he had no children and was under no pressure to support himself by painting, he was free to give time to the Academy. He had good social connections and was received by distinguished patrons of the arts. (His wife Susan Hammond was cousin to Horace Walpole.) He had tact, good judgment in most things, and a genuine wish to manage affairs from the background. And he was an ever-patient listener and counselor to any artist who sought his aid or advice — most notably in straightening out the affairs of Thomas Lawrence, who could not handle his money, and later in advising a troubled young landscape painter from Suffolk, John Constable, whom he sponsored as an Academy student on March 4, 1799. Farington had recently begun to keep a diary — one that, when revealed in the twentieth century, would affect the reputations of many artists, as well as other Englishmen, of his time.[3]

On receiving Farington's angry letter, West at once wrote to say that the charges in it were such that he could confute them only by an interview. If Mr. Farington and Mr. Smirke would come to his house at their convenience, "I have not the smallest doubt but that I shall convince you and him that those charges are not founded in what you conceive to be the facts." Farington wrote a second letter in which he apparently declined to meet with West. A few days later he dined with other members at the Academy Club, West presiding, and found the meeting "thin and not convivial." The next day, while he was at the Academy exhibition, West, Mrs. West, and another woman came in. If he did not cut

---

[3] He began to write it on July 13, 1793, with an account of a visit he had made that day with George Dance and Samuel Lysons, an eminent antiquary, to Strawberry Hill to see Horace Walpole, seventy-six years old, infirm, but mentally alert. Dance made one of his famous profile portraits of Walpole, and at four o'clock a neighbor, Mr. Berry, came to dinner with his two daughters, Mary and Agnes Berry, "esteemed and very accomplished women... handsome in their persons." It is pleasant to think that Walpole may have persuaded Farington to begin his diary.

the Wests, Farington seems to have looked the other way, for he "had no conversation with them." A few weeks later he declined an invitation to dine with his friend Sir George Beaumont, an amateur landscape painter, apparently because West was to be one of the guests.

West was in more serious trouble in a controversy involving the writings of his friend and admirer, Robert Anthony Bromley. The Bromley affair took place in 1793–94, during and just after the twenty-fifth anniversary celebration; it began over a trivial matter — whether the Academy would buy one of Bromley's books. The episode had comic overtones as it unfolded from day to day in all its convolutions, but the passions were real and the issues were serious ones that occupied the time and thoughts of some of the best artistic talent in England. The Bromley affair caused a split in the Academy, the members choosing sides between two groups of irreconcilables. It was, in fact, the first skirmish in what was to be a twelve-year war. West and Copley, as the central figures, were both grievously injured in the fighting.

The Reverend Mr. Bromley, rector of St. Mildred's in the Poultry and minister of Fitzroy Chapel, London, had published by subscription the first volume of a ponderous two-volume *Philosophical and Critical History of the Fine Arts, More Especially Painting.* On West's recommendation, the Academy subscribed for a copy and placed it in its Somerset House library. In that work, Bromley called Fuseli "a libertine of art" and ridiculed his "frivolous, whimsical and unmeaning subjects" by name, including his most famous work, *The Nightmare.* He lavishly praised one modern artist and one modern picture, and except for some kind words for James Barry's six historical murals in the Royal Society, praised no others. The artist was West, "that master who had introduced Britain to a taste in the historic line, which was very new to the acquaintance of her own artists." The picture was his *Death of Wolfe,* called "one of the most genuine models of historic painting in the world." Artists knew that Bromley was helping West to write his discourses. Some artists believed that Bromley was getting his ideas on art from West, and that his ideas on West and West's pictures came from the same source.

Fuseli, who was as talented a writer as he was a painter, twice had reviewed Bromley's book, both times unfavorably, declaring that it had hardly any claim to serious consideration other than its size, and that it contained scarcely a sentence that was not subject to censure. John Copley, whose *Sea Boy and the Shark, Death of Chatham, Death of Major Peirson,* and *Siege of Gibraltar* were not mentioned in the section on history painting, spoke up sharply against Bromley's praise of *Wolfe* as the one and only perfect historical picture. This, he said, was treason against the arts, against the artists of every age, and especially against the artists of Britain, living and dead.

At the general meeting called in December 1793 to discuss the twenty-fifth anniversary celebration, Copley rose immediately after the minutes were read to make a motion on Bromley's *History*: It was unworthy of a place in the Academical library and should be removed from the shelves "with marks of degradation and disgrace." Opie seconded the motion. The matter was debated "with great warmth" for two full hours. In order to get to the business of the evening, a member suggested that before they cast this kind of unprecedented obloquy on the volume, it would not be amiss for the members to read it. The logic of this proposition was so reasonable that no one could object, and further discussion was put off until the next meeting. A few days later, West offered a new thought; he pointed out that Bromley's book could not be removed from the library, since it had been bought by the king. An unreconstructed member wanted to know, "With whose money?"

Bromley responded to this attack by writing and circulating several very long letters to Fuseli, naming him as leader of a cabal whose aim was to crush his book in an attack that was as wanton as it was gross and bitter. He followed these with four similar letters to Copley, also privately circulated, whom he called "the first, and if possible the most vehement, but certainly the most virulent leader in the attack on my publication." His praise of West's *Death of Wolfe*, he said, "has been the ground work of all the faction which you have raised in the Academy, and of the abuse which I have received from that faction." He mocked Copley as "a painter from America who, before his arrival in this country, had sent hither a *squirrel* as the harbinger of his fame," and soon after his arrival, seeing a Vandyke for the first time, declared that his squirrel was every bit as good. He derided Copley for squeezing the last possible guinea out of *The Siege of Gibraltar* by unbecoming maneuvers, and he turned the knife by alluding to current accusations that the proofs of the *Gibraltar* engraving were not being distributed honestly. He attacked Copley for degrading history painting — for "descending from the dignity of the epic" and for introducing matter-of-fact scenes into the British school of history paintings — scenes "hardly a degree removed beyond portrait painting." As for *The Sea Boy and the Shark*, the water was too transparent, the boat did not tilt as it should, the boy was swimming in the wrong direction, and the anatomy and behavior of the shark were all wrong. "You have given us miserable violations of nature . . . For your own sake, I would advise you to put that picture in the fire."

Copley, deeply hurt, perhaps psychologically damaged by this assault, told his friends that Bromley's information about Vandyke and the squirrel could have originated only with West. He readied himself for two Academy sessions in February 1794. At the first of these, called to elect three Associates to full Academy membership, he again entered his resolution to remove Bromley's book; it was defeated by a vote of ten to five. At the meeting on February 20, called to discuss the medal commemorating the recent twenty-fifth anniversary celebration, Fuseli rose and began to make a statement on Bromley's book. West ruled him out of order, declaring that the Bromley matter was not on the agenda for that meeting. William Chambers supported West on the point. Copley rose to complain of attacks that were being made on him in newspapers and in circulating letters. He charged that the abettors of such proceedings (meaning West) were as guilty as the principal mover. William Hodges was opposed to debating the Bromley matter again. In Farington's words, he "rose with indiscreet warmth, and a violent altercation took place," during which Copley was criticized for his language.

Farington said that if Mr. Copley had used improper words, allowance should be made for a man injured by such attacks.

John Bacon said that if the business of the medal could only go forward, peace and order would be restored.

Farington objected; it could hardly be expected that harmony should prevail in a society where an injured man was not supported by his brethren. If Mr. Fuseli was prevented from speaking, those who espoused his cause would feel for his injury.

Bacon agreed that if Mr. Fuseli had new information on the Bromley matter, he should be allowed to present it.

West ruled that so long as Mr. Fuseli had no motion to make, he might state what had passed between him and the Reverend Mr. Bromley.

Fuseli recapitulated the whole unhappy story. William Tyler then moved that the subscription to Bromley's second volume be canceled. Smirke seconded him. The motion to cancel was passed by a vote of seventeen to four, five members abstaining. West, of course, did not vote. The members then further resolved that Mr. Fuseli had conducted himself properly in his remarks on Mr. Bromley's book.

Bromley responded to this defeat by publishing his letters to Fuseli and Copley in the *Morning Herald*, the first appearing on

March 12. Farington found it "filled with gross falsehoods and statements calculated to mislead," and he called the sixth letter, to Copley, "a composition of vulgarity and folly." The letters were printed at intervals throughout the spring and summer of 1794. In the meantime, Bromley brought out the second volume of his *History* in the middle of May, and in it he ran all his letters as a forty-two-page preface.[4]

The letters as published contained several passages in praise of West, "whose conduct always does him honor" and whose "amiable and just temper" caused him to extinguish the attempt to remove his book from the Academy library. "The firmness of his heart," he wrote, "will never suffer any compromise to supplant the reciprocities of friendship. In and out of the Academy, he is beyond your reach to shake the fidelity which will stand by the man who has stood by him. And in that chair which he so deservedly fills," etc., etc.

Bromley's books were merely tedious and pretentious, but his letters were spiteful even by the standards of normal eighteenth-century abusiveness. West's willingness to be identified with Bromley, to seem to support him, and to accept his fulsome praise, was a serious blunder. Combined with his other mistakes and misfortunes, it weakened his authority to preside over the affairs of the Academy.

Fuseli and Copley had told West that they intended to make an issue of Bromley's book. Farington and Sir Francis Bourgeois, R.A., had cautioned him against Bromley as an unworthy, mendacious man, and West later admitted ruefully to Bourgeois that he should have heeded their advice. His failure to do so, his unwillingness to divorce himself completely from Bromley the day after the first letter was circulated, demonstrates a curious blind spot in West's character. He seems to have had an imperfect understanding of how people felt when they were criticized, slighted, or pushed aside. He was apparently unable to see that when his friend Bromley praised his work extravagantly and ridiculed that of his colleagues, offense would be taken and resentment directed at him as well as at Bromley. West was a kind and generous person, as shown

---

[4] Part of Farington's quarrel with West had concerned a passage in Bromley's first unpublished letter to Copley "in which I am attacked." Farington's name, however, does not appear in the published letters, and the attack cannot be identified; Bromley may have deleted it from the original. Farington declined West's request to visit him because "from his account he only seemed desirous of it that he might disclaim all collusion with Bromley. That did not affect me but in a second degree; my charge was for what he said of me."

in scores of recorded actions, but in appearance and effect, many of the things he said and did in the 1790s could not have been more damaging if they had been motivated by malice.

He was insensitive, moreover, in praising his own pictures. He seemed to be sincere and even, in a sense, objective and impersonal in valuing his own work so highly, but he was at fault in not realizing how such self-praise appeared to others — what they would think, say, and write about it. They did indeed talk and write about it, and so his history is sprinkled with small embarrassments. He stands with a friend before his *St. Paul Shaking Off the Viper* and remarks, "A little burst of genius, sir!" To his Academy colleagues he says, "When my pictures come into the exhibition, every other painter takes his place as if a Royal sovereign had come in. Dukes and lords fall back into their places." He competes for the design of the anniversary medal, and Bourgeois tells him of a comment by Northcote: "He ought not to grasp at or expect every honor. The Academy has clothed him with a robe of velvet, but he should not struggle for every strip of ermine." Northcote says to William Hazlitt, poised with pen in hand, "West thought Wolfe owed all his fame to his picture; it was he who had immortalized Wolfe, not Wolfe who had immortalized him."

On June 2, 1795, Joseph Farington went to Cadell the bookseller and inquired about the second volume of Bromley's *History*. He was told that not one copy had been sold.

16

The Fall from Favor

Remarks are made at Windsor that the President does not go there as usual. He says it is to prevent that envy which arose from seeing him there so often and so noticed.

JOSEPH FARINGTON,
Diary, November 23, 1793

*W*EST HAD BEEN DISTURBED during the king's illness when he thought he saw a change in Queen Charlotte's manner toward him. After the king's recovery the queen's coolness became so marked that he knew he could not be mistaken; he learned that she deeply resented his having been so much with the king "when he showed symptoms of disorder." He delicately asked the king if he had done something to cause offense. The answer he received satisfied him that whatever the queen's feelings were, and for whatever reasons, the king was still his friend.

In the spring of 1794, however, he began to notice a change in the king's attitude as well. This became quite evident when he asked which day it would please His Majesty to name for visiting the exhibition, and His Majesty indicated that he did not care to attend. West carried this shocking news to William Chambers at his home in Hounslow, and the next morning the two men hurried to Windsor Castle. The king received them. West explained the harmful impression that would be created if His Majesty declined to make his usual visit. Chambers warmly seconded him. The king relented and set a date in April on which he would call at Somerset House.

There was now no doubt about what was troubling Their Majesties: they had been told that the Royal Academy was infested with democrats and that West was one of them, if not their leader. The charge was a serious one in 1794, even more so than earlier accusations of sympathy for the American Rebels. England was at war again with France, for the fifth time in the century, but this time France was a different and deadlier enemy, a republic with a people's army, an inflamed country with revolutionary goals far more sweeping than the capture of a strategic fortress, a sugar island, or a colony. The word *democrat* was now used in England to describe a subject who was disloyal to the crown, approved regicide, and was sympathetic to the aims of the revolution in France. The queen was implacably set against West. The king wavered; when he was with West he was friendly, as with an old and trusted associate, but when stories of West's subversive views were relayed to him, he was again critical and suspicious.

Most Englishmen had welcomed the overthrow of feudalism in France and her progress from the sixteenth into the late eighteenth century and the Age of Enlightenment. If not wholly sympathetic, they at least understood the reasons for the attack on the Bastille, the declaration of the Rights of Man, the constitution of 1791. The English, after all, had imprisoned and beheaded their king in 1649; they had deposed and exiled another in the Glorious Revolution of 1688. The poverty of the French masses, the economic stranglehold of the church, the idleness of an army of courtiers, the absolute power of the king, seignorial jurisdiction, sale of offices, pensions obtained without just title, the arrogance of the *noblesse* in refusing to pay taxes, the denial of rights and preferment to the lower orders, the denial of army commissions except to sons who had at least three generations of noble ancestry — all this called for drastic reform. Young William Pitt was not unfriendly to the goals of the Revolution as first set forth, but as prime minister he was more interested in internal problems and his own financial program than in the strange developments across the Channel. But something had gone terribly wrong in France. Instead of a constitutional monarchy or a democratic and egalitarian republic, the French now, in 1794, had a Revolutionary Tribunal controlled by bloody despots named Marat, Hébert, Saint-Just, and Robespierre. Instead of reform and the sovereignty of the people, they had the most autocratic government ever seen in a civilized country. Instead of the Rights of Man they had the Second Committee of Public Safety, the Law of Suspects, the Law of 22 Prairial, under which there could be no defense of those charged with conspiracy or treason — accusation meant automatic conviction, and conviction meant execution. In the course of defending itself against invasion, France was occupying, annexing, robbing, and brutalizing its neighbors. It had declared war against England in January 1793, and now it was promising to mount an invasion to free the English people from their oppressors. The French army, in the course of carrying liberty to oppressed people, dragged a guillotine behind it on its marches. In the month in which George III visited the Royal Academy, the Reign of Terror, eight months old, had just become the Great Terror. If the day he chose was an average day across the water in Paris, some 200 men and women, few of them nobles or even of the upper classes, were tried that morning in groups of thirty or forty, were convicted by a jury that did not leave the courtroom, and were driven that afternoon in carts to a public square, where they had their heads severed by a guillotine.

London was crowded with refugees, each with a story of the horrors that were taking place in Paris and throughout much of France.[1] French revolutionary doctrines and agents were also crossing the Channel. There were apologists in England, as in the United States, for mass executions in the name of progress and liberty. There were a few Jacobin clubs where the toast was heard: "Success to Rebellion, in the Cause of Freedom." In waging war, the Pitt government raised taxes, suspended the right of habeas corpus, and passed bills for the suppression and punishment of sedition (which soon came to mean any advocacy of parliamentary or social reform). The war, though young, was unpopular. The "British Royal Family and the Privileged Orders" (a phrase being used by revolutionaries and democrats) were alarmed at the temper of the people and the times.

Young Richard Westall, newly elected an R.A., dined at Lord Grosvenor's table and came back to report, "The Democratic disposition of members of the Royal Academy was mentioned." The earl of Harcourt, one of West's friends at court, gave "many circumstances" in telling West that it was the Academy library set who were charging him with being a democrat. (Presumably this meant the Academicians who had worked to remove Bromley's book.) Mrs. William Harcourt, he said, one of the queen's ladies-in-waiting, had defended West and silenced a lady who was endeavoring to set the minds of the princesses against him. West told Robert Smirke (who was also being charged with holding democratic ideas) that Nicol the bookseller had voiced his suspicions to Barnard, the royal librarian, and that Barnard had carried them to the king. Even Joseph Farington was assumed to be politically unreli-

---

[1] Many of the refugees congregated in Richmond. Some were royalists, some were constitutionalists, and they tried to avoid meeting each other in public places.

able. William Windham, Pitt's secretary at war, saw him in the gallery of the House of Commons during the debate on the habeas corpus suspension bill. To Nathaniel Marchant, A.R.A., he said that he supposed Mr. Farington was a democrat. Marchant told him he was quite mistaken; Mr. Farington was "a violent aristocrat."

Farington reported that West was not going so often to Windsor and that the courtiers were commenting on it. He recorded West's explanation — that he wished to prevent the envy that had arisen from his being seen there so often — but he was not deceived. Farington knew that the architect James Wyatt, R.A., had supplanted West in the king's favor. "Wyatt designed the decorations at Frogmore," he wrote, "for the entertainments given by the Queen. He was paid by the Queen, but the King was so well pleased with the effect of his designs that His Majesty presented Wyatt with a watch as a mark of his royal approbation." And again, "Wyatt considers the Queen as a very warm friend to him . . . Wyatt is always treated with great respect at Windsor. He always dines at the equerries table."[2] West would soon come to believe that Wyatt was the prime originator of the accusations at court that he held "French principles."

As an American, West was under double suspicion, for relations between Britain and the United States were near to a breaking point in 1794. The English government fully expected the Americans to honor their fifteen-year-old alliance with France and to give her material help against Britain, their former common enemy. Mr. Jefferson, the American secretary of state until the end of 1793, was devoted to the goals of the French Revolution and defended its excesses; his party was calling for support of France in her war against England. When President Washington sent John Jay to London in the summer of 1794 as special ambassador with instructions to settle the disputes between the two countries, King George was moved by the unexpected evidence of American goodwill. He took occasion to remind West of the prediction he, West, had made during the American War, that bad blood between the two countries would subside and a preferential relationship between them would be restored. The prediction, the king acknowledged, was well founded and his advice was good. The queen was present during the conversation — perhaps the king meant her to be — but she said nothing and simply flirted her fan in a gesture of contempt.

---

[2] Frogmore was a royal residence one mile southeast of Windsor Castle. Wyatt had designed the celebrated Pantheon in Oxford Street (destroyed by fire in 1793), was the leader of a burgeoning Gothic revival in England, and, as the king's surveyor general, was in charge of remaking Windsor Castle into a habitable royal residence.

One of the black marks against West, unquestionably recorded in government files, was his friendship with Thomas Paine, a man seething with radical ideas far ahead of his time. He corresponded with Paine, entertained him at Newman Street, and probably received him at Windsor. That had been in 1788, to be sure, before the French Revolution, before Paine's *Rights of Man* was proscribed in England, before he was indicted for treason in 1792, and before he fled to France to take a seat in the National Convention; but such chronological distinctions tend to be forgotten when charges of subversion are made. When West first heard that it had been reported to the queen that Paine lodged at his house while in England, he protested: He had seen Paine only three or four times in all, and when he first called at Newman Street he was accompanied by Edmund Burke.[3] West was also friendly with Joel Barlow, another pro-French American agitator, another American who fled England to seek political office in France's revolutionary government, another American author with a work proscribed in England (*Advice to the Privileged Orders in the Several States of Europe Resulting from the Necessity and Propriety of a General Revolution in the Principle of Government*).

Whispered charges against West were clearly being spread at court and in the Academy by persons motivated by rancor, jealousy, or prospect of advantage. At the same time, however, he gave them no lack of material with which to work, or even on which to base honest disapproval. His friends as well as his adversaries deplored his indiscreet enthusiasm for democracy in a country whose existence was being threatened by democrats. He retained a larger and longer faith in the ideals and accomplishments of the French Revolution than most other believers. And, unfortunately, he became involved in the Gillies affair.

Dr. John Gillies was a Scottish historian and classical scholar, a graduate of the University of Glasgow, who had written *A History of Ancient Greece, Its Colonies and Conquests.* West was looking for someone to fill the Academy post of professor of ancient history, to succeed Edward Gibbon, recently deceased. He approached Sir Joseph Banks, president of the Royal Society, and asked his opinion of Dr. Gillies. Sir Joseph's answer was favorable and, Dr. Gillies being in the room at the time, West suggested to him that he stand for election. Gillies agreeing, West supplied him with a list of Academy members to whom he should apply if he wished to get

---

[3] Farington called Paine "a fellow of discontented temper, fond of gin and water." Trumbull spoke of him "with aversion" and said he was "a man disposed by nature to disturb the peace and order of society."

their votes. Dr. Gillies asked Sir Joseph to write on his behalf to three of the members. Sir Joseph did, and West was in trouble.

Farington had breakfast with Sir Joseph and from him happened to hear what West had done. He explained to Sir Joseph that honorary professors had not formerly been chosen in that manner; that West should have consulted the other members of the Academy before he spoke to Dr. Gillies; and that it would reflect poorly on any man who obtained such a position by canvassing for it. Banks told Farington he would immediately send another letter to the three members he had written and recall his request to them. It was plain to him now, he added, that Mr. West was trying to curry favor with him, but his mind was made up on the subject of Mr. West and had been ever since learning of his conduct in political matters.

Unfortunately, the *History of Ancient Greece* was written with a strong Whig bias, and this was taken to mean that Gillies, like West, was a democrat. James Boswell "spoke violently against the pretensions of Gillies," declaring that he held democratic principles. He threatened to write a letter to West, to write a letter to the newspapers, and, if Gillies was elected, to resign his own professorship. He favored William Mitford, M.P., a classical scholar who had published the first volume of a projected five-volume *History of Greece*. Mitford had failed to graduate after several years at Oxford, but he could not be charged with holding democratic principles. He was so impassioned a monarchist and anti-Jacobin that his critics accused him of being unjust to the Athenians, in addition to having "a general negligence of dates."

The unfortunate Dr. Gillies called on Farington. He pointed out that his history of Greece had passed through many editions, whereas Mr. Mitford's had not. He said he would suffer serious injury if not elected, as people would suppose that the cause was suspicion of his holding democratic principles, as asserted by Boswell. In the meantime, the king sent word by William Chambers that he would not sanction the election unless it was unanimous, that he had never approved of the honorary professorships in the first place, and (with good common sense) that he would not allow such a small question to divide the Academy.

Farington feared that Gillies, if elected, might become a member of the Royal Academy Club, "which would be a strong objection with me." He had no desire to hurt Gillies, on the other hand, and so he proposed a face-saving solution to his colleagues: to elect nobody and, "out of delicacy," to leave the professorship open for several years. The proposal was accepted, and the office stood vacant for twenty-four years, until 1818, when William Mitford was finally elected. But in 1794, the sponsorship of Dr. Gillies, a man believed to hold democratic principles, caused another black mark to be placed beside the name of Benjamin West.

Over the next several years, West committed a number of small blunders, each unimportant in comparison to his troubles over Bromley and Gillies but all serious in their cumulative effect. He endured a storm of criticism and censure, a steady erosion of his powers as president of the Academy, and episodes that could only have caused him heart-scalding humiliation.

December 1794: At the annual election of officers, thirty members being present, West received twenty-six votes for re-election as president. Copley, Charles Catton (a foundation member and coach painter), Edward Burch (sculptor), and Mary Moser Lloyd (the flower painter) each received one vote. "A contention took place," Farington wrote, "about admitting the last name on the books [minutes] of the Academy. Barry supported the necessity of it. It was at last agreed to be omitted, as it was evidently intended as a joke, and if seriously she was not eligible." Though Barry seems the logical person to suspect, Fuseli (who was present) was popularly supposed to have cast the ballot for Mrs. Lloyd. To the merriment of London art circles (and to the enjoyment of Fuseli's biographers), he is also supposed to have said, "One old woman is as good as another."

February 1795: Shortly before the general meeting of February 10, which was called for the election of one new Academician, West received a letter of stern rebuke from young Thomas Lawrence and Richard Westall. They had been elected Academicians three months earlier; they had delivered their diploma pictures; why were they not summoned to the February 10 meeting to receive their diplomas and to vote on the new candidates? West wrote a letter of apology, the contents of which (now unknown) surprised Lawrence and enraged Westall. Farington raised the matter formally at the meeting. "West," he wrote, "was confused and made lame excuses." The balloting followed, John Hoppner being elected.

In a conversation held a few days later with John Boydell, engraver and print publisher, the king criticized West for saying that he, the king, had not signed the diplomas in time. West, he said, had given him, and he had approved, the election of officers for the year 1795, but West had not given him the diplomas to sign. What, he asked Boydell, could have been West's reason for the misrepresentation? Boydell could only suppose that West might have held the diplomas back to keep the new Academicians from voting in the February 10th election. (This did not make sense, since they were known to be opposed to the election of John Hoppner, West's enemy.) As Farington heard it from Boydell, "The King said that was probably the case, but he wondered after their long enmity that West should take an interest in [supporting] Hoppner's election. The King rather wondered at the Academy electing Hoppner, who had made himself obnoxious by abusing the members."

March 1795: Farington "strongly pressed the necessity" of having Academy business with the king "transacted...a more direct and becoming form than it is at present." Communication, he said, should be placed on a regular footing, by resolving that all business to be laid before him should be formally stated by the council in a document. The president should then be accompanied by the secretary or the treasurer when he visited the king to present the documents. West approved the idea "if it could be carried into execution in a manner satisfactory as to etiquette." Farington's recommendations were adopted. On a later curb of his powers, West "said he wished such a regulation had been made when the Academy was instituted, but he did not like to have the privileges of the President infringed while he was in the chair, as it might be a future cause of complaint."

June 1795: West served as chairman of a committee charged with erecting a monument to William Woollett (1735–1785), one of the outstanding engravers of the century. A design by the sculptor Thomas Banks, R.A., was approved and the work proceeded. Woollett's most famous and perhaps his finest engraving was the large battle plate after West's *Death of Wolfe.* West quite inappropriately directed that the engraving be listed by name in the inscription on the monument, apparently doing so after the text had been agreed upon, after the work was well advanced, and without putting the matter before the committee for a formal vote. Many of the subscribers to the monument, according to Farington, objected to the addition as "ridiculous and vain." At a committee meeting on June 10, motion was made to expunge the word *Wolfe.* West, in the chair, put the motion to a vote, and it was carried unanimously against him. The word was removed without difficulty, for Banks, foreseeing or forewarned of the protest, had only marked it in black letters instead of cutting it into the stone.

December 1795: John Flaxman, lately returned from Rome, showed Farington a printed copy of a letter he had obtained there, sent by West to the British commissioners of the treasury, relating to a petition to the commissioners from English artists in Rome. "This letter," Farington said, "wrote as from *himself, President of the Royal Academy,* and proposes his opinion on the subject, without referring to the Council of the Academy, so as to make it an Academical act. On this impropriety and on the *incorrectness* of the letter, Flaxman remarked."

November 1796: Copley wrote to West charging an irregularity in notifying members of business to be discussed at general meetings. West answered the letter and, according to Farington, gave the wrong reason for his procedure. West, Farington wrote, "is perpetually showing his ignorance of the Constitution of the Academy and its laws."

In the course of these events, Raphael West told Westall that his father was "busily employed" at Windsor writing a discourse on art to be delivered to the students at the next meeting. Raphael was embarrassed; he told Westall "he thought his father had better have left it alone, as it was out of his way." A good many of the Academicians agreed with Raphael, and they spent an extraordinary amount of time complaining of West's lectures and trying to devise ways to persuade or force him to stop them. His delivery was described as monotonous and without much energy or inflexion of voice; but "he never failed to make himself heard. Each sentence was so clear and articulately spoken that every person in the room might hear every word." Much of the criticism was directed at West's always naive and now out-of-fashion thesis that only a virtuous artist could be a great artist. In his December 1794 *Discourse* he had gone so far as to tell the students, "Without the guidance [of moral purpose], painting and sculpture are but ornamental manufactures; and the works of Raphael and Michael Angelo, considered without reference to the manifestations which they exhibit of moral influence, possess no merit beyond the production of the ordinary paper hanger." John Flaxman "spoke of West's last [1794] Discourse which he considered both for matter and delivery a disgrace to the profession and thought some means should be used to prevent him from delivering another." Westall "thought it would be prudent for the Council to pass a resolution 'That it is not necessary for a President to deliver a Discourse.' If such a motion failed in its effect, to follow it with another, 'That no Discourse should be delivered by the President which has not been approved by the Council.'"

West delivered his 1796 discourse. At the next Council meeting, when a routine request should have been made asking the president to print his lecture, Farington observed, "No notice was taken . . . of the President's Discourse. It seemed to be a general feeling amongst the Academicians to avoid anything that could seem to sanction it." A week or so later, Yenn returned from the Queen's House with a choice story, which Farington duly recorded:

> The King asked him if he was at the Academy on Wednesday the 10th. Yenn said he was. The King replied, "I suppose you had a good deal of Hack, Hack, Hack," alluding to West's pronunciation of the word Academy, which he pronounces *Hack*ademy. The King further said that West had given tickets to several persons about the Court. The whole expressed the smile of the King at West's pretending to turn orator.[4]

West was being unmercifully criticized and ridiculed in the public press in these years, and it is obvious that the attacks hurt him in the eyes of his colleagues, injured him in his professional practice, and pleased his enemies at court. The spirit of this age of revolution was such that art criticism was brutal and abusive beyond anything known to earlier or later generations. Nothing was sacred; the painter of a portrait and his subject were both derided as well as the picture itself, and even the royal family was mocked and scorned. (It is probable that no king and queen have ever endured such published vilification as George III and Charlotte, as expressed in prose, verse, and caricature.) A critic wrote of Thomas Lawrence's portrait of the queen, "Her Majesty's nose, indeed, appears sore from taking snuff, but that is not the fault of the painter." Another wrote of his *Portrait of a Gentleman,* "This I understand is the likeness of [Richard Payne] Knight and is repulsive in the attitude; it fills me with an idea of an irascible pedagogue explaining Euclid to a dunce." A critic called Domenico Pellegrini's portrait of Lord Spenser "a disgusting object" and his *Bacchante* "an indelicate and meretricious performance and can only be pleasing to tottering voluptuaries." Richard Westall's portrait of a young gentleman was as "puerile as the subject," and his *Minerva* was "all legs and thighs, like the late Sir Thomas Robinson." The *Morning Chronicle* described Juno in James Barry's *Jupiter and Juno* as a "drunken, clumsy whore just broke out of Bridewell," and Jupiter as her "Bedlamite patagonian paramour" whom she is embracing upon a "dunghill."

Two widely read critics of the time surpassed most others in their

---

[4] John Yenn returned from the court with a number of such damaging stories about West, all recorded in Farington's diary. It may be noted here that in 1805, at a moment of crisis in the Academy's affairs, it was revealed that Yenn had fabricated such a story, and he slunk from a general meeting of the Academicians in disgrace.

vituperation. One was John Williams, who used the name "Anthony Pasquin"; the other was Dr. John Wolcot, a former physician whose pen name was "Peter Pindar." One of the specialties of Williams-Pasquin was the personal attack based on physical features. He wrote of Hoppner's portrait of the young duke of Bedford that it looked "like a lounging pickpocket." Of Richard Cosway he wrote, "[He] is a miniature painter of merit, but where he possesses an ounce of capability, it is sicklied over with a pound of vanity . . . He is as mischievous as a monkey, and as illiterate as a Savoyard, and, though a contemptible animal in his person, he firmly believes that the first beauties of the nation are sighing for his favours." Of Copley he wrote, "To talk of any man possessing genius, who is so immoderately fond of money, is preposterous: the warm beams of genius thaw the icy altars of avarice, and to have genius, and be ungenerous, is impossible." West was the object of continuing assault by Williams-Pasquin and Wolcot-Pindar. Both had been admirers of Joshua Reynolds, and both were outraged, in some thousands of words, that the king had given commissions to West rather than to Sir Joshua. No development should be surprising, Williams wrote in 1794, "which is in any way dependent upon the caprice of hereditary power."

Wolcot, who wrote in a kind of satiric doggerel, was especially indignant when "George's idol, West," was chosen to succeed Reynolds. His most scathing attack he wrote in a long poem, "The Academic Procession to St. James's," in which he described West being knighted by the king:

> Behold once-Quaker-Benjamin be-knighted,
> Amid a moon-eyed host of wonderment!
> Now on his shoulder drops the magic sword:
> "Arise Sir Benjamin!" the Sovereign says.
> Happy the Knight ariseth at the word,
> And feels himself o'erwhelmed with Glory's rays . . .
> With Lords behold him talk — with Ladies chat
> Of sceptres, snuff, rebellions, and all that.

The investiture, of course, did not take place, but in what must appear to be a dishonest act, Wolcot ran the poem again in the 1812 edition of his works with a lame footnote appended: "Since the first edition, the Poet . . . finds himself mistaken; the ceremony did not take place."

Whatever the criticism, West seems to have borne it with admirable patience and equanimity; there is, at least, no record of any display of anger or complaint on his part, no sign of retaliation, and very few instances where he attempted to explain or defend himself. He was re-elected P.R.A. each December with only token opposition. He continued to manage the affairs of the Academy, calling frequently on the king with matters to discuss or papers to be signed, and the king never indicated that he wished West to be replaced. He presided over the Council sessions, the general meetings, and the annual dinners; he continued to present the medals and deliver an annual discourse to the students. And he turned out a prodigious amount of work.

In the first eight years of his presidency, 1792–1799, he exhibited seventy pictures. There were no more portraits of the royal family, but every year he added one, two, or more works to the seemingly endless series of Biblical episodes for the Windsor chapel. He painted four more pictures in the Edward III series for the Audience Chamber at Windsor Castle; a few portraits; a half dozen landscapes; some genre scenes (*Gentlemen Fishing, The Bathing Place at Ramsgate, The Washing of Sheep, A Drayman Drinking, A Harvest Scene, A Woman Selling Rosemary*); and two scenes from *King Lear* and *Macbeth* for John Boydell, who was commissioning illustrations of Shakespeare's works for a large Shakespeare Gallery he had built in Pall Mall. He also painted nine pictures for William Beckford, an important new patron; he was now producing historical, religious, and allegorical subjects for Fonthill Abbey, a castle Beckford was building twenty miles east of Salisbury.

In June 1797, West, accompanied by Trumbull and Dr. Edward Bancroft, went to the Salonière Hotel in Leicester Square to call on and, he hoped, to paint the portrait of a distinguished and honored visitor to England. He was Tadeusz Kosciuszko, Polish general and statesman, hero of the American Revolution, who had led the unsuccessful 1791–1794 fight for Polish independence from Russia. Severely wounded at Maciejowice, he had been captured and held prisoner for two years in Russia. Freed a few months earlier, he was spending some weeks in London before making a second visit to the United States.

General Kosciuszko, wearing a black velvet dressing gown, was reclining on a couch beside a low window looking out on a London scene. He was still suffering from a saber-cut on his head (bandaged with a black silk cloth), two stab wounds in his back, and a blow on his right thigh (also bandaged). The wounds had been given poor medical treatment in Russia; he could walk short distances with the aid of a crutch but otherwise had to be carried. At the time of West's visit he was making sketches from his window. He talked of his trip to America, where, he said, he hoped to find peace, and he asked for news of the mutiny of British sailors that was taking place at the Nore sandbank in the mouth of the Thames. He declined to pose for West or to allow him to draw or paint his portrait.

In the hall outside Kosciuszko's room West undoubtedly paused to make a quick drawing; on his return to Newman Street, he at once began a portrait.[5] He worked in oil on a small horizontal panel about 12 by 17 inches. He painted with richer, more brilliant colors than he customarily used, and, as was often the case with his first rapidly produced oil sketches, his brush strokes were surer, freer, bolder than those of his more carefully finished pictures. He placed Kosciuszko on the couch with St. Paul's and the Thames seen through a window framed by heavy scarlet draperies. He showed the general's crutch, his sketching paper and portfolio, a pile of books on the floor, and on a small table a sword of honor recently presented by the Whig Club of London. He depicted Kosciuszko in a moment of reverie, touching his head with a pensive gesture, on his face and in his eyes the expression of a hero who has seen the defeat of his army, the destruction of his country, and the loss of his own freedom. It is an astonishing picture for the year 1797, an obvious anachronism, a precocious anticipation of Byronic melancholy and mood-laden *Weltschmerz* — a prototype of pure romanticism that was not to flower until the second decade of the next century.[6]

With his remarkable ability to drop an old style and take on a new one — indeed, to paint in three or four styles at the same time — West had been experimenting for twenty years in a manner and with subject matter that later generations would identify with romanticism. He began in 1777 with *Saul and the Witch of Endor*, a scene from the *First Book of Samuel*: the witch, at Saul's request, summons up the spirit of Samuel, who foretells that Saul will be killed the next day and his army defeated in a battle with the Philistines. He began again in 1783 with one of the scenes intended for the king's chapel at Windsor, taken from the Last Judgment in the final chapter of the New Testament, titled *The Revelation of St. John the Divine*, commonly called the *Apocalypse*. He illustrated the passage from chapter 6, verses 7, 8.

---

[5] Richard Cosway, who was also refused permission to make a portrait, was reported to have sketched Kosciuszko through the keyhole of his door.

[6] West made a gift of one of his pictures to Kosciuszko, who gave it to Thomas Jefferson on his visit to the United States. It was sold in Boston in 1828 at the disposal of Jefferson's collection.

And when he had opened the fourth seal, I heard a voice of the fourth beast say, come and see. And I looked, and behold a pale horse, and his name that sat on him was Death, and Hell followed with him. And power was given to them over the fourth part of the earth, to kill with sword, and with hunger, and with death, and with the beasts of the earth.

He made a drawing and then a sketch in color, oil on paper, about 15 by 26 inches in size. Within that space, in a fury of movement, turmoil and color, he showed the Horsemen of the Apocalypse wreaking destruction on man and all living things. Wild lions spring on horses, a mother dies with her infant, a starving man grubs for roots, mysterious riders on gleaming chargers brandish swords, shoot arrows, and hurl bolts of lightning. West may have made a considered artistic decision to return to the tumult of Rubens' *Battle of the Amazons* and *The Lion Hunt*, but the completeness of the change seems to tell of shackles broken or of the release of a force contained in the artist during the decades of calmer works. *Death on the Pale Horse*, like the moody *Kosciuszko*, is a picture of protoromanticism.

Fiske Kimball, director of the Pennsylvania (now Philadelphia) Museum of Art in 1938, was one of the first Americans to give a detailed statement emphasizing the influence of West's work on the French romanticists. He wrote, "If the British school and West . . . were important in the formation of French classicism, we . . . find that he was equally in advance in the general development of Romanticism of figure painting. Here the great French manifestos were the works of Géricault and Delacroix at the Salon of 1827. Although we now recognize that French Romanticism had a long period of formation prior to this, prior even to 1800, it must be appreciated that in such a tendency the British were far in advance, with West in the van."[7] The assessment has been enlarged upon many times since 1938 and is now generally accepted by critics and historians of art.

West continued to experiment with romantic themes and subjects charged with emotion. He fell under the influence of Henry Fuseli's work and borrowed the technique Fuseli introduced into eighteenth-century art: that of creating a melodramatic effect by

---

[7] In Delacroix's journal appear the sentences, "Study the sketches of West" and "Borrow engravings of Trumbull and West." They were written in 1825 as marginal notes on one of his studies for *Death of Sardanapalus* and on a sheet of pencil sketches.

giving the principal figure the command of the horizon — foreshortening the figure from ground level and having it look down on the viewer, generally with burning eyes. He veered more and more, sometimes with unfortunate results, toward the romanticism of the wild and supernatural, of mystery and fear, where, in the words of Edmund Burke, "all is dark, uncertain, confused, terrible and sublime to the last degree." And he kept coming back again and again to his *Death on the Pale Horse,* painting a revised sketch in color in 1787 and another in 1802. He planned one day to develop the work into a picture of enormous size, as one of the crowning achievements of his life.

The first person to feel the impact of West's new *Sturm und Drang* was James Northcote. He had developed a nice specialty: a series each year of genre pictures, painted to a theme in identical size, with an uplifting moral, in the manner of a more modest *Rake's Progress* or *Harlot's Progress,* to be later sold as engravings by the minor print dealers. He entered sixteen pictures in the 1796 exhibition, ten of them in a story-telling sequence (*The modest girl and wanton fellow servant in a gentleman's house; The wanton revelling with her companions; The modest girl receives the honorable addresses of her master,* and so forth.) Having asked that they be hung all together and in a good space, he was "much mortified" to find that West's wildly dramatic, highly emotional, and brightly colored *Death on the Pale Horse* had been placed directly in the center of his series. He complained to Farington, who told him he thought his pictures were well hung and that "it had been the wish of the Committee to please'him."

The king, too, was disturbed by *Death on the Pale Horse.* He expected Biblical illustrations for the Royal Chapel at Windsor that were inspiring and comforting, but now he was getting turbulent episodes, daemonic figures, tortured gestures, horrific expressions, and apocalyptic scenes of final judgment, damnation, and death. The king had known horror at close acquaintance; he lived under the fear that he would know it again; and he was not pleased with what he called "Bedlamite scenes from the Revelations."

17

The Venetian Secret

What has reasoning to do with Art or Painting?

WILLIAM BLAKE
Annotations to Sir Joshua Reynolds'
Discourses, 1798

O NE OF THE DREAMS of painters throughout the eighteenth century was that of discovering the Venetian Secret — the unknown means by which the artists of Venice, Titian in particular,
achieved such beauty in the use of color. When he was in Venice in
1762, West had attempted to solve the mystery; he painted his subject first with pure primary colors and then softened them with the
semitints. For a time he believed that he had found the master's
method, but he soon changed his mind. He never forgot his dream,
however, and a third of a century later, in London in 1795–1797, he
was an easy mark for a clever swindler who convinced him, and the
other members of the Royal Academy as well, that he had discovered
the true secret of Venetian coloring.

Thomas Provis was an unlikely person to come forward with such
a happy discovery. He had never attempted to paint and he was a
lesser member of the king's household at St. James's Palace, holding
the post of sweeper[1] to the Whitehall Chapel Royal. He had a
plausible story, however, and an ingenious plan, and he understood
how human beings respond when invited to share a secret that
promises them profit or power.

Provis took his secret process first to the artist Richard Cosway,
who suggested that West was the proper person to approach. As
president of the Academy, West might make a trial of the Titian

---

[1] A verger; one who took care of the interior of a church building.

method, possibly recommend it to his colleagues, and work out
with them an appropriate recompense to the discoverer. Provis
opined that £50 would be adequate payment for revealing all he
knew. As interest in his story developed he raised the figure to £500,
then £600, then £1000, and finally dropped back to £600.

Provis called on West in December 1795 and revealed how he had
come into possession of the Venetian Secret. He had found it, he
said, in a volume of bound manuscripts acquired in Venice by his
grandfather, a ship captain named Morley, who had a vessel in the
East India Company service. A Signor Barri, a Venetian friend, had
pointed out to Captain Morley that certain pages contained the
secret of the lost color process. Unfortunately, Provis said, the
original manuscripts had been lost when his house in Ryder Street,
St. James's, was destroyed by fire. Happily, he had copied out everything in the manuscripts that related to painting. This he had done
because his twenty-year-old daughter, Mary Ann Jemima, "was
then practising that art." The girl was of a delicate constitution,
and the oil commonly used in painting affected her health, which
made the Titian process doubly desirable. (Oil was used as the
vehicle in the process, Provis explained, but it was purified to a
state like water.) He produced several specimens painted by his
daughter, and in them West saw, or thought he saw, some evidence
that they might hold the Venetian Secret. He agreed to make an
experimental painting. This would be done at Provis' home, where
there would be no interruptions.

Unfortunately, West took no one from the Academy with him
when he made the call. The experiment was not a success. On a
canvas prepared by Provis, and following the cryptic directions of
Miss Provis, he painted a head that turned out badly. When he
suggested that the ground on the canvas seemed not to be right,
Provis agreed, said that it was not the proper color, and asked for
time to prepare another canvas. West told him to send word when
it was ready. Hearing nothing for some weeks, he called on Provis
several times but never found him at home. In the meantime, he
finished a large work he had under way, a *Crucifixion* for St.
George's Chapel at Windsor.

It was not until the following October that West made the second
experiment. He drew a subject on a small canvas prepared by Provis
and again began to paint under Miss Provis' direction. He was excited by the result, for he showed it to a colleague, praised the secret
formula he had used, and declared that "a new Epocha in the art . . .
would be formed by the discovery." He painted the heads of his
sons Raphael and Benjamin on another small canvas and then proposed to conclude the experiment by testing the process on two

large canvases. He chose the subjects *Cupid Stung by a Bee* from Anacreon and *Cicero Discovering the Tomb of Archimedes*. By this time, of course, the news had circulated throughout London, in somewhat garbled versions, that West had discovered, or bought, or stolen the Venetian Secret. It was at this point that Provis produced his master stroke.

He went in an alarmed state to several Academicians and pleaded for protection against Mr. West, who he said was trying to rob him of a great discovery. According to the story he told, he had approached West with his secret formula for Titian's coloring. West had cautioned him that he must be careful to fix upon a person of candor, integrity, and great ability to make a trial of the process, and he offered himself as such a person. Provis trustingly revealed the secret to West, who, having tried it, thereafter avoided him with the excuse that other urgent business kept him from devoting any more time to the experiment.

At this, Provis became apprehensive, then suspicious, then indignant. He was now quite sure, he said, that West intended to paint pictures for the next exhibition "that he may come before the public *with the advantage of the process exclusively.*" (Farington's emphasis.) West, he added, had kept and hidden away his daughter's specimens. West had attempted to use the process in his *Crucifixion* but, needing more information, he applied again to the Provises, apologizing for his delay in seeing them. His daughter had painted several parts of *Cupid Stung by a Bee*, though West put only his own name at the bottom. It was clear that West was "endeavouring to *disclaim as much as he could* the information he had received," that he did not intend to form any plan for the Provises' benefit, and that he had violated his word by giving the secret to his son Raphael. He, Provis, had even heard that West was already claiming credit for the discovery, and, indeed, he had seen several boards and canvases at West's that had been prepared for the new process. In these circumstances, Provis said, he wished to call on the members of the Academy for advice and help. Rather than be cheated by West, he would make a gift of his process to the Academicians.

All this was discussed at a meeting of the Academy Club on January 6, 1797, West being absent. The general consensus, Farington reported, *"was that West was bound to propose the discovery as soon as he had made a trial of it, and not keep it back under any circumstances."* In the next few days the criticism spread and grew stronger. One Academician said that West had certainly trifled with Provis in an unbecoming manner. Another condemned his habit of adopting the thoughts of others and presenting them as his own, saying that if what Provis charged was true, he hoped West would be made an example of. A third told Farington he had heard of West's maneuvers and was afraid he would contrive to monopolize the secret. John Hoppner condemned West's conduct; in order to remove him from office he proposed to limit the Academy presidency to one term, "like the Lord Mayor." William Beechey, a true pragmatist, thought that West should have bought the secret from Provis and kept it to himself.

On January 11 Farington met Provis for the first time, two other Academicians being present with him in a three-hour session in which Provis told his story of betrayal by West. The three colleagues, quite convinced that West had acted improperly and "meant to have the *cream* of the discovery at the next exhibition," decided that a larger group should meet with Provis the following evening at Wright's Coffee House, hear his story, and consider in a body how best to handle the matter. Recognizing that attention was being diverted from the main question, which was the merit of the process itself, Farington told Provis, with more emphasis than logic, "that after the prevaricating accounts of Mr. West, the members of the Academy would require a more satisfactory proof than any yet produced of the nature of the secret."

Seven men met at Wright's Coffee House.[2] Richard Cosway, the eighth person invited, sent word that he would concur in any proposal the members might adopt, but he declined to meet with them before he had talked with West. He suggested that West himself should be brought into the business and the difficulties faced together. On hearing this, Provis asserted that he had had "such experience of Mr. West that he had not further desire to refer to him." He spoke at length on West's "deceptious conduct." As recorded by Farington:

> He always endeavoured to appear as owing as little as possible to them. While Miss Provis was communicating parts of the process to him he would affect to be inattentive, and the next time she came would tell her, as if discovered by himself, what she had before communicated to him, which, when she reminded him of, he would seem not to hear her. When Provis saw the head which West had begun of his son Raphael, he asked him how long *that* had been painted. West answered three months, thereby meaning to go back to a time beyond the last experiments made with Miss Provis. Provis, not crediting West, asked

---

[2] Farington, Hoppner, John Francis Rigaud, John Opie, Richard Westall, Thomas Stothard, and Robert Smirke, all R.A.'s.

his servant how long it was since West begun that head. The man replied, about ten days. Here, said Provis, I detected him in a lie.

The group, now known as "the Committee," decided they would meet again at Opie's home in two weeks, when Miss Provis would show them the process. If it had the qualities claimed for it, they would recommend that the Academy grant a joint annuity to the Provises for life. Provis told the Committee that if they wished to save time they might order canvases to be stretched, sized, and pumiced, the knots rubbed smooth, which, when an agreement was reached, he would prepare with his secret ground. The group dined together and had much "laughable conversation." The subject of their humor was William Blake and his "eccentric designs."

> Stothard supported his claim to genius, but allowed he had been misled to extravagances in his art, and he knew by whom [that is, Fuseli]. Hoppner ridiculed the absurdity of his designs, and said nothing would be more easy than to produce such. They were like the conceits of a drunken fellow or a madman. "Represent a man sitting on the Moon, and pissing the Sun out, that would be a whim of as much merit." Stothard was angry, mistaking the laughter caused by Hoppner's description.[3]

Westall complained the next day that he was suffering from having stayed out so late that night and that all through his short sleep he had dreamed of Provis' discovery.

West, in the meantime, had learned that Provis, without speaking of his apprehension to him, had been speaking a great deal about it to others, and he attempted to meet with his adversaries and defend himself. He asked Smirke to assemble Farington and Bourgeois so that he might speak on the Provis affair. The meeting was held at Smirke's home on January 17, and there for the first time West gave an account of his relationship with the Provises, detailing step by step what had actually happened. Farington wrote:

> West then concluded by saying he had stated all he had to offer on the subject, that he believed the discovery of the process would be of great advantage to the art, that for himself his career was run. He had only to endeavour to maintain his professional rank. His character, whatever it might be, was determined. That

---

[3] On February 19, 1795, West spoke warmly of the designs of Blake as works of genius and imagination, and he gave Blake's publisher a testimonial on the excellence of his drawings for Robert Blair's *The Grave*.

composition [not color] was his forte. He had selected Smirke
and myself for communicating his statement to others and should
say no more.

Farington and Bourgeois each related exactly what Provis had told
them, sparing no criticism of West and emphasizing the wide differences in the two accounts. After the meeting, both men agreed
privately that West's principal object had been to monopolize the
discovery so as to have an advantage at the next exhibition.

Some days later Farington read aloud a letter from West to the
full Committee. It had always been his intention, he asserted, to
make a fair report on the Provis discovery and to assist in benefiting
him. He would agree with the others to any proposal adopted for
a recompense, but he thought it must be done, not by the Academy
in the form of a lifetime annuity, but rather by the members themselves in a private subscription. He suggested that the Academicians might pay ten guineas each, giving security that they would
not communicate the secret until Provis had received £600. He
further suggested that Provis might prefer to set up a color shop,
by which means he could prepare canvases and colors for the
artists and still preserve his secret.

As the date for the demonstration drew closer, Provis announced
that he now had two new conditions. The Committee must pay
him twenty pounds before he would show the process, and he
would not reveal three secret "articles." He was not interested, he
said, in opening a color shop, though he would prepare grounds for
the members. He had decided to stain a gray color over the backs
of the canvases so that the process would be concealed. "Provis,"
Farington said with a new note of acerbity, "has raised his expectations much lately." A few days later he wrote, "West called on me
and showed me a letter which he has received from Provis full of
acknowledgements of error and groundless suspicion, and that his
daughter was always averse from his acting the part he had done
with regard to Mr. West."

The demonstration took place at Opie's house on January 30.
The six Academicians present signed "an agreement to make a
faithful report of process of painting to be disclosed by Miss Provis,
and not to communicate the mode of doing it." They were to be
allowed to see the process on payment of ten guineas each, three
guineas of which had to be paid before the demonstration began.
Miss Provis painted a head with white only on a dark ground, and
she glazed with colors a head and part of a landscape she had prepared in white. Opie declared that he was dissatisfied with what
he was seeing; he had known it all before. Stothard was alarmed;

he called it nothing but a glazing process. Hoppner, however, said the system was worth knowing, though he probably would never use it himself. Rigaud, Smirke, and Farington were still convinced that it was a discovery of great importance. Farington had a clerk draw up papers for subscribers to exchange with Provis. In his enthusiasm, Rigaud proposed that the process be denied to Academy students, because it would place a disadvantage on those who could not afford to pay the ten guineas.

On February 22 Provis took Farington and Smirke with him to collect West's ten guineas and to witness his bond guaranteeing secrecy, with a £2000 fine for breach of the confidence. When West hesitated because of some technical point involving his students, Provis angrily repeated his statements that West had stolen his secret for his *Crucifixion* and had given it to his son. West, "much agitated," denied both charges. Farington, thinking of John Trumbull, advised West that if any other person in his household had discovered the secret, he should be put on the same footing as the subscribers. John Trumbull, West said, may have learned it; he would speak to him. Farington offered to make Trumbull an exception to the rule against foreigners being included in the secret. (Raphael West and Trumbull did each pay their ten guineas and sign a bond of secrecy.)

From this point forward the Provises appear less and less often in the pages of Farington's diary. Miss Provis gave Farington several private lessons in the technique of using the Venetian process, assuring him that his landscapes had always been very much like those of the Venetian masters. During these lessons, Farington made an interesting discovery: Five years earlier Miss Provis had become mentally deranged and was placed for a time under the care of Dr. Willis. In May, Provis reappeared to announce that he was moving to a better residence on Portland Street and intended henceforth "to paint heads in close imitation of the Venetians which will be very fine indeed." And then no more was heard of Thomas and Mary Ann Provis.

The disillusionment, when it set in, was rapid. West decided that Provis' grounds were too cold and purple. Stothard announced that pictures done with the process "looked like enamel painting on earthenware — something not true." Thomas Daniell, R.A., complained of the way the Committee had handled the Provis affair and said he had known from the first that the dark ground would not do. The critics and reviewers of the 1797 exhibition agreed that the results of the new method were worse than those obtained by the old. Richard Cosway declared that West had been "used very ill about Provis' process." James Gillray, the celebrated English caricaturist, did one of his amusing engravings on the Provis affair, featuring Hoppner as one of the dupes. James Barry asserted, "Such a concurrence of ridiculous circumstances, so many gross absurdities, and such industrious folly in contriving for the publicity of a quacking, disgraceful imposture, is, I believe, unparalleled in the history of the art."

Thomas Lawrence castigated himself for his stupidity. "He had surrendered himself to Provis and his daughter," he told Westall, "as if he had never held a pencil, and afterwards was surprised at having done so to two fools who knew so much less than himself." Farington, the last to lose his faith in the Venetian Secret, said simply, "That is because he does not yet understand it."

Henry Tresham, R.A., was a combative young Irishman whose particular enemy, at a certain time, was John Hoppner. His vexation was such that he went to Sir Francis Bourgeois for advice: What should he do about Hoppner's insulting behavior? Where, Bourgeois asked, had the insult been given? Tresham replied that it was at one of the Academy meetings. Since it happened at the Academy, Bourgeois said, he must consider it like the free expression used in the House of Parliament and not like an affront given in a coffee house.

This nice distinction, observed rather closely by Academicians until a major blowup in 1803, explains the social intercourse the members kept up with each other throughout their quarrels in the Academy. Despite his animosity in the 1790s, for example, Farington visited West to see pictures he had received from France, and West called on Farington several times to take tea. Over the teacups Farington made a suggestion that West should not hesitate so long between the toasts, as he had at the last dinner. (That, West explained, was owing to Lord Mansfield engaging him in too much conversation.) On another visit West suggested that Farington give his moon a more spirited and silvery light in a landscape. ("This observation I found to be just.") Studying a series of views Farington had made in Wales, he urgently advised him "never to touch again upon a sketch made on the spot." He spoke frankly of the disappointment he felt in his plans for his sons. He had meant Benjamin to set up a company that would print his engravings, but Benjamin had no interest in the project.

There was, indeed, a gradual but perceptible change in Farington's attitude toward West after 1797; by 1800 he had become sufficiently well affected to address him as "West" rather than "Mr. West." He had good cause to moderate his earlier disapproval. He and his colleagues had obviously treated West with unjust and unkind suspicion in the Provis affair. He, Farington, was being attacked by Academy members who felt he had achieved too much power, and so he wished to reduce the number of his adversaries. He was finding, moreover, that West was good and interesting company. Scores of entries in his diary tell of hours spent in conversation; of anecdote and inside information West had picked up at court; of a "whimsical circumstance" about this or that personage, this or that event. West talked of his experiences on the Court of Governors of the Foundling Hospital, one of the enlightened new institutions of the century. He told of a series of lectures on electricity he was attending, delivered by a Dr. Hays, in which he learned the astounding scientific fact that "electric fire" traveled with a velocity of 1000 miles a minute. He told of a new, experimental engraving technique he and his son Raphael were working on, called *polyautography* (invented in 1796 by a Bavarian named Senefelder) and showed his first engraving done in the process: *Angel at the Tomb*. It involved taking an impression off a specially prepared stone slab, on which a design had been drawn in reverse with an ink or crayon of a greasy substance. (The process was soon renamed *lithography*.) [4]

The underlying reason for the change in Farington's attitude, however, lay in the growing interest he and West shared in running the affairs of the Academy. In a three-man committee with John Hoppner, they opened negotiations with William Pitt to have the Academy exempted from the 10 percent tax on income levied in the Assessed Taxes Bill of 1798. Pitt praised the Academy in one of his speeches for having supported a national school of art without any aid from the public funds; and in view of the depressed condition of the fine arts and the destitute situation of many artists, he included the Academy in the lower tax category of places kept for public entertainments, houses let for lodgers, and buildings licensed for the reception of lunatics. Their colleagues gave West, Farington, and Hoppner a formal vote of thanks. West and Farington worked with George Dance and William Tyler to examine and unscramble the financial records of Sir William Chambers, who had permitted no one else in twenty-five years to see his books and whose "manner of stating the accounts was such as was not easily understood," having in it "always something obscure." Sir William had died in March 1796, and after the death West found that he, as president, was now in sole and complete control of the funds of

---

[4] The first dated English lithograph is a reproduction after a pen drawing by West. It bears the date 1801 and was published with twenty-three other similar plates by Fuseli, Barry, and others in 1803.

the Academy, invested in the Bank of England. He had taken steps that resulted in a review of the institution's accounts back to its founding, appointment of perpetual auditors and a committee of trustees, and investment of the funds in the name of the Academy.

West and Farington were studying an ever-present problem, described by the secretary as "the indecent behaviour of the students, who show no respect to anyone," and they were serving together on committees to arrange the monuments in St. Paul's Cathedral and Westminster Abbey. To Farington and Northcote West confided that he thought he could buy for the Academy the duke of Orleans' collection of pictures, then up for sale in London. He had talked to the king, William Pitt, and Charles Long, joint secretary to the Treasury, asking for £40,000 and pointing out that "there would be a noble collection for young artists to refer to without being obliged to go to Paris . . . where with their studies they would suck in political opinions ill calculated for England." (The collection, however, was sold to three English private collectors.)

West and Farington worked hardest and longest on a project dear to both. On their way home from an Academy meeting at midnight: "I conversed with West on the Charity Fund of the Academy, and he expressed great willingness that something more should be done. He thought that if the solid fund is encreased to £10,000 it then might be left, and all over-plus receipts be applied to encrease the Charity Fund." A few weeks later: "West said the King is well convinced of the propriety of doing it . . . The tears came twice into West's eyes while he was speaking." The plan was to establish a full-fledged pension fund — to set up "an Academical provision for decayed members of the Academy and their widows." The rules were drawn up and discussed, and before they were submitted to the members for a vote, West cleared them unofficially with the king "so he would not cross out any portion after approval by a general meeting." The beginning pension was not to exceed £50 a year, provided the sum given did not make the Academician's annual income exceed £100. Widows were to receive £30. The king added two significant provisions: A widow should receive a pension only as long as she remained unmarried, and no member should receive a pension who did not exhibit regularly. It was decided that painters must not miss two consecutive exhibitions, and sculptors must not miss three. At the last moment the king inserted an exception: Any member past sixty might be excused from exhibiting if he so requested. The pension bylaw was approved at a general meeting, the king signed it on November 2, 1797, and the Academy embarked on one of its most effective, humane, and celebrated programs.

Two members — Barry and Copley — waged vociferous opposition to the pension plan. Barry demanded that the Academy use the pension fund money to buy a collection of old masters for the students to study, and that it build "an addition on the ground floor equal in size to the present exhibition room." Copley's reasons for opposing the plan are not clear, though the pattern of his conduct at this time suggests that he would object on principle to anything that West proposed or supported. He did speak out against the limitation of time for exhibiting, even if it were forty years, and he said he had known nothing of the pension fund until it was passed as a bylaw. He wrote a letter to West in which he threatened to "prepare a remonstrance" against the plan and present it to the king. West laughed and said he hoped he would do so, for then "he would be settled."

Farington had come around to one deeply held conviction. He saw a faction coalescing that meant to strip the power from those — including Farington — who were running the Academy. Their first objective was to remove West from the presidency and put their own man in office. He had led the opposition against West himself in the past, but now he believed that to replace him with any of the men being proposed would bring on new problems far worse than the old. "Much has been said about changing the President," he wrote after a meeting of the Academy Club. "I said it would be followed with difficulties which they were not aware of, that urged such a measure."

During these months James Barry changed from an Academy embarrassment to an Academy problem on which action had to be taken. He had never been an easy man to get along with, from 1772, when he was elected to the Academy, and especially from 1782, when he was made professor of painting. Edmund Burke, who had brought him penniless from Cork, introduced him to Reynolds, and liberally financed a five-year stay in Italy and France, patiently endured his angry reproaches for what Barry charged was lack of respect. Reynolds had said that it was a bad thing to hate any man but that he feared he did hate Barry, and that if so, he had much excuse. Barry would call on him, stay for dinner, and a day later send to the press a mocking attack on his art, his person, or "the poor mistaken stuff of his Discourses." Miss Ann Birch Cockings, head housekeeper of the [Royal] Society of Arts in the Adelphi, where Barry had painted his seven huge pictures for the Great Room, said of him, "His violence was dreadful, his oaths horrid, and his temper like insanity. The servants were afraid to go near him."

Much was forgiven Barry for his genius. Dr. Johnson admired

the grasp of his mind. Miss Cockings admitted that when he could be coaxed to talk his conversation was sublime. His critical writings were believed to be brilliant. His Adelphi pictures, which he began without a commission and with only seventeen shillings in his pocket, receiving only the expenses of canvas, paints, and models, living on bread and apples for seven years, were at once recognized as masterpieces.[5] But his writings had become defamatory, he had not exhibited a work at the Academy for more than two decades, and his conduct at Academy meetings had become a subject of increasing concern, discussion, and condemnation.

West was the object of Barry's strongest criticism, both in and out of the Academy. West told Farington of Barry's "brutal behaviour" to him at a committee meeting at St. Paul's and said he had "made a point of commanding his temper." Barry attacked West again in January 1799 in a lecture to his students (West was presiding) for not having acquired the pictures of the Orleans collection for the Academy. It was, West said, an unjust attack, the more so because he had informed Barry of the effort he had made to buy the Orleans pictures. In February he informed the students that there was £16,000 in the Academy treasury that should be laid out for their benefit in pictures. He had talked to Mr. West about this, he said, "who as usual was always mysterious." The students clapped at the severest passages, and Barry, at each round of applause, bowed. Northcote, who was in the audience, said that he "sunk his head in his great coat that he might not be known." One of Farington's students told him that the young men now thought that the Academy's property belonged to them. He added that outsiders were seeking and getting tickets "to hear Barry abuse the Academicians."

Matters came to a head when Barry wrote a pamphlet titled *A Letter to the Dilettanti Society*, in which he attacked the "mercenary cabal" that was running the Academy, ridiculed "this pension business," and restated his demands for a collection of pictures and an exhibition hall. Seven members met at the home of the sculptor Joseph Wilton, keeper of the Academy, and laid plans for dismissing Barry from his professorship, or expelling him as a member, or both. Wilton addressed a letter of complaint to President West and the Academy Council. He denounced Barry for making in his lectures "long digressions from the subject on which he is bound exclusively to discourse, in order to utter the most virulent

---

[5] They were called in 1974 "perhaps the finest single achievement in the grand style by a British artist."

abuse on the established Laws, the Acts and Government of the Academy, and calumniating its actual and even its deceased members. And also hinting to his auditors that the Academy's money was disposed of in a mysterious and secret manner in pensions for themselves." West read Wilton's letter aloud at the next Council meeting, and five other members (following an agenda prepared by Farington) added their evidence on Barry's reprehensible conduct. West asked for and was given authority to put the matter before the General Assembly.

The Assembly met on March 19, 1799, with twenty of the forty members, including Barry, present. West ordered that the minutes of the last Council meeting be read, which included Wilton's letter in full and liberal extracts from Barry's *Letter to the Dilettanti Society*. He asked for authority to appoint an eleven-man committee to investigate and report on Mr. Barry's conduct as professor of painting and as an Academician. Barry rose and "loudly and violently demanded a copy of the paper which had been read, said it contained impudent lies, which he could prove to anybody in half an hour — arraigned the Council for not giving him early information of their proceedings," which he had only heard of from Miss Plumtree, a lady acquaintance of Mr. Opie. Despite misgivings by ten of those present, there was a unanimous vote that Barry should not be given a copy of the charges against him.

The Barry affair was now a favorite topic of discussion in London society. Artists and patrons, critics and courtiers took sides. They laughed or winced at Barry's jibe: "They mean to immortalize me." They winced or laughed at his exchange with Lady Inchiquin. He would get his revenge, Barry told her, by republishing West's first discourse to the Academy. "How," Lady Inchiquin asked on cue, "can you propose to print such stuff?" Barry: "So that the public might know what is going on in the Academy." Bourgeois said that Barry deserved to be expelled because of his "avowed democratical opinions." He had said a republic was the proper government for art to flourish under, and he had commended the principles of the French revolutionary artist Jacques Louis David and of Mary Wollstonecraft, author of *Vindication of the Rights of Women*. Opie publicly defended Barry, lamenting, "What a thing it would be for landscape painters, an inferior branch of the art, to prosecute an Historical Painter of distinguished merit, and an author!" Northcote agreed, though he felt that the Council proceedings had been "just and moderate in the greatest degree, and West's conduct such as does him high honour."

The members met on the evening of April 15 to consider the committee's report and recommendations. (The foreign-born members — Loutherbourg, Zoffany, Bartolozzi, and Fuseli — did not attend, probably out of delicacy.) Barry, Farington reported, "came in before 8 — with much *bravura* and indifference, and soon called to the President to *take the chair* as the room was hot and the business should go forward. Little notice was taken of what he said." George Dance, as senior member of the committee, read the report, which took thirty-five minutes. All the members observed "the most respectful silence" except Barry, who from time to time broke out with "Bravo!" and "That's false!" and "That's not all!" The report, Farington thought, "had a manifest effect on him; he changed color and the latter part he heard with his eyes closed." The report ended with two recommendations: that Barry should be dismissed as professor of painting, and that he should be either expelled or suspended, according to the vote of the members.

William Tyler moved that the recommendations be put to a vote. Barry exchanged some "sharp remarks" with Dance, left his chair, put on his hat and greatcoat, and said if a copy of the charges were refused him he would leave the meeting; he did not wish to be a member of a Society that could act in such a manner. He removed his hat when called upon to do so, but after a few more exchanges he departed and did not return. Tyler's motion that Barry be removed from his professorship was passed twenty-one to three, Nollekens, Northcote, and Opie voting against. Lawrence put the question: Should the committee's final resolution, that the members vote on whether to expel or suspend Barry, be approved? It was approved nineteen to four. A ballot was then taken; thirteen were for expulsion, nine for suspension.

Westall and Hoppner, much disturbed at the small majority for expulsion, suggested that a second ballot be taken. Lawrence and Copley supported the proposal, but West ruled against it. Every step that had been taken, he said, was agreeable to the laws of the Academy and should be maintained. The meeting broke up at 1:00 A.M.

West, accompanied by John Yenn (the new treasurer) and John Richards (the secretary) set out at seven that morning for Windsor, arriving in time for an audience with the king at eleven. His Majesty, they discovered, was already thoroughly familiar with everything that had happened at the Academy. He read the committee's report, said it was very well drawn up, asked the names of the authors, and considered what would be proper for him to do. West observed that since His Majesty's signature created an Academician, his signature would be needed to confirm the decision of the Academy to expel a member. The king said he would do as he did with privy councillors; he wrote the word *expelled* beside

Barry's name, drew a line through the name, added an approval of the Academy's resolution, and signed it "G.R." He then handed a speech to West and asked him to convey it to the Academicians as a message from His Majesty. He felt pain that a member should by his conduct have made it necessary to put the laws in force against him. He also felt pain that the members who supported the laws and good order should have been under the disagreeable necessity of applying the laws to preserve it. He approved the proceedings of the Council, of the committee, and of the General Assembly.

Farington wrote a formal letter of dismissal and expulsion for Richards to sign and send to Barry. Fuseli, reading it, wondered if it was exactly right to say, "His Majesty is graciously pleased to . . . strike your name from the roll of Academicians." West allowed that it sounded odd, but he had already showed it to the king and did not dare change it.

Henry Fuseli was named to fill the vacant post of professor of painting. There was some grumbling about a foreigner being appointed to the staff, but West said stoutly, "That might have been a consideration before he was elected an Academician, but being one, he is entitled to any situation."

Barry's sorrow at being expelled from the Academy, if any, was assuaged within six weeks when the president of the Royal Society of Arts awarded him a gold medal and a purse of 200 guineas for his distinguished contribution to the arts, during the presentation of which the Society members cheered him to the rafters. He also enjoyed writing his version of the dispute with the Royal Academy, where, he said, "scum and offal direct and govern." He worked hard for the next six years designing pictures that he never painted. A public subscription was raised that would have paid him an annuity of £100, but he died in poverty in 1806 a few days before the first payment would have been made. He lay in state in the Great Room of the Royal Society. No member of the Royal Academy attended the funeral at St. Paul's, though two young Academy students, David Wilkie and Benjamin Robert Haydon, made a point of being present.

The diploma picture Barry submitted to the Academy in 1773, *Medea Making her Incantation after the Murder of her Children*, was returned to him with his letter of expulsion. Like most of his other paintings, it is now lost.

18

The Broken Laws

The charge of the Academy being governed by a Cabal and Combination requires to be noticed ... The exertions made by the members who propagate these reports are extraordinary ... The gentlemen are determined to break the Cabal, the gentlemen are determined to destroy the Combination. Ridiculous resolutions! Vain declarations! Do they suppose they can prevent men who regard and esteem each other from assembling together and from communicating their sentiments? Besides, how unreasonable! Do not they associate together? And long may they do so undisturbed, *and unenvied.* Let them be content.

JOSEPH FARINGTON,
in an address
to the Royal Academy,
January 14, 1800

*I*N MAY 1796 John Hoppner told Farington a rumor he had heard: West was "much straitened for money ... and his bills remain long unpaid." The rumor was true. Somehow the subject came up subsequently in a conversation with Farington (in whom everyone seemed to confide) and West talked quite frankly about his financial problems. He still received his £1000 annuity from the court, he said, but the king was so far behind in his payment for the pictures for the Windsor Chapel that "the bulk of his fortune," £15,000, "is in the King's hands." His Majesty, he added "is shy when money is touched upon." He had succeeded Richard Dalton in 1791 as surveyor (restorer) of the king's pictures, for which he was paid £300 a year. He had been earning £400 to £500 a year from the sale of his prints, but the war with France had virtually ended that market. He had cut back sharply in his expenditures; he no longer used the house in Windsor, though he still paid the £34 annual rent, and he had reduced his servants from six to three, retaining only a man and two maids. In these ways he had lowered his annual expenditures from £1600 to £1200. Mrs. West, he said, "manages with great frugality." He had to continue painting and to search for new patrons; the only alternative was to sell his collection of old masters.

In June 1797 West wrote the king begging payment of £2000 of the total sum owing him. Mr. Coutts, his banker, he said, had threatened to sue him if he did not pay that amount within a certain date. He would not have found it necessary to entreat His Majesty, he added, "had my great plan of publishing my own works" not been destroyed by the war. The king's steward asked for an account of all the pictures West had painted for the king from the 4th of October 1780 to the 4th of April 1797. West supplied it, and in July he wrote "with a grateful heart" to thank the king "for the generous relief granted me in the recent business with Mr. Coutts."

His problems were compounded by the demands of those who were dependent on him. He was educating one of his brother Thomas' girls. He was generous when an American nephew, John L. Clarkson, a child of his sister Rachel's unfortunate marriage, visited him in London and somehow cheated him out of a considerable sum of money. ("I should have been obliged to you and my other friends," he wrote his brother William, "had you, when Clarkson first came to this country for the avowed principle to plunder me under the mask of relationship, that you had communicated to me that character of him you must then have known, and which has since been transmitted to me — but not till the breach of honor and honesty was made by him on my benevolence.") His own two sons, moreover, were not only improvident but extravagant. The marquis of Townshend, "at the particular nomination" of H.R.H. the duke of Gloucester, offered West a commission, a cornetcy in the Second Dragoon Guards "without purchase," for his older son, but West, with expression of the deepest gratitude, rejected it. He could not provide the annual payment and supplementary income Raphael would need to live with the other officers in a suitable manner. "From a conversation I have recently had with some military gentlemen," he wrote, "I find the expense attending the appointment [is] such that my pecuniary situation will not admit of, without having recourse to His Majesty" for payment of money owing him, which he was not willing to do. Raphael complicated matters in 1797 by marrying Maria Siltso, who was (in Farington's words) "a country girl, daughter of a farmer near Salisbury, to the great mortification of his father and mother."

(Raphael presumably met her while accompanying his father on visits to William Beckford's castle there.) In January 1800 West had "accommodations" against him of £500.

West twice tried to achieve a financial coup in speculative projects with John Trumbull. As an American, as John Jay's secretary, and later in a quasi-diplomatic post as commissioner for settling shipping disputes between Britain and the United States (at £1500 a year), Colonel Trumbull was able to visit and travel in France. Obviously, such a person had opportunities for gain not open to those with less freedom of movement. One such opportunity was that of buying up old masters from distressed owners in France and, by being clever, getting them across the channel for resale in England. Trumbull needed capital for such a venture, and West supplied part of it as his partner.

Trumbull went to Paris in 1795 and there bought about 100 paintings through Judge J. B. P. Lebrun, husband of the painter Elisabeth Vigée-Lebrun. They arrived at London shortly after Trumbull's return and were delivered to the customs house quay by a lighter. (The London docks were not built until 1805.) The customs house was closed, it being August 12, the birthday of the Prince of Wales, and the lightermen, finding no one to receive them, made their barge fast with a chain to one of the posts and went off to the nearest pub. It was near low water, and when the tide came in that evening the boat, its bow held down by the chain, filled with water, and the wooden crates containing the pictures floated out. A watchman eventually saw them drifting down the Thames, gave the alarm, and effected a rescue.

Unaware of all this, Trumbull went next morning to pay the duty on his property and found the watersoaked crates laid out on the quay, the pictures badly damaged, some of them possibly beyond repair. He at once had them transported "to the extensive rooms of my friend, Mr. West." On learning that the insurance company could not be held liable, "I passed the remainder of the season in repairing, as well as I could, the damage they had sustained." Ninety-one of the salvaged pictures were placed on sale at two auctions. Farington had a private view three days before the first sale at Christie's in February 1797 and found the collection "inferior to what I expected." The prices bid were about one-fourth what the partners had hoped for, and West and Trumbull had to buy in twenty-five of the works, including some of the most highly valued. (A face-saving rumor had it that West was buying for the king.) Trumbull and West still had some of the pictures fifteen years later, and they were still trying to dispose of them at auction.

The following year a group of investors promised Trumbull one-fourth of the profits if he would go into France, buy brandy, and get it safely to England in his own name. He spent eight months on the undertaking and invested £80,000. The expected profit was wiped out when an Irish sea captain carrying 429 pipes of "Cogniac brandy" anchored his ship improperly at Guernsey Roads. He did so without advice of a pilot and without knowing that the harbor basin at ebb tide would be dry. The tide went out, the ship fell over with a tremendous crash, and both ship and cargo were destroyed. Again the underwriters could not be held responsible.

On his trips to France, Trumbull saw much of Thomas Jefferson, who offered him the post of his private secretary at £300 a year, "which is paid by the public" and "will not take a moment of your time from your present pursuit." But, wrote Jefferson, "whether you accept or not, be so good as to keep it a secret till the moment of its execution, unless you choose to mention it to Mr. West under the same injunction, for the purpose of consulting with him."

West's second venture with Trumbull was in the purchase and resale of American land. In partnership with Henry Drinker and Dr. Enoch Edwards, both of Philadelphia, he invested £1278 in a tract on the west bank of the Susquehanna River in Pennsylvania, paying six shillings an acre to Supreme Court Justice James Wilson. He bought a second tract of some 25,000 acres, at three shillings an acre, on the Genesee River in northwestern New York, apparently in partnership with Trumbull. He and Trumbull worked for some months to sell the second tract to William Beckford. Beckford's reluctance was overcome, and negotiations were concluded in the summer of 1798, when he signed an agreement to buy a township, 23,340 acres, at ten shillings an acre. "It is considered," Farington wrote, "a monstrous price."

In the meantime, the West family had made a momentous decision. Raphael was to go to America with his bride, settle permanently on the Genesee tract as a farmer, and oversee and improve the American lands. He sailed in August 1800. William Dunlap, Raphael's one-time companion and fellow student, writing in his massive history of American art, re-enters the story at this point: "Of all creatures my friend Raphael was the least fitted for the task of a pioneer in America. Born and educated in London...he was a stranger to the appearance of the untamed forest, where only the Indian footpath gave token of the presence of man." The young Wests spent some months at Big Tree on the Genesee River, the home of James Wadsworth, educator and land speculator, from whom the Genesee tract had been purchased. Raphael made sketches of the country and sent tracings back to his father. It became apparent that the venture in America was a mistake.

> Disappointed, discouraged, and home-sick, Raphael gladly broke
> from the Big Tree prison to return to the paternal home in New-
> man Street. On his way he visited me in New York. His anger
> was kindled against Wadsworth, who, like a true American, saw
> in the wilderness the paradise which was to grow up and bloom
> there, but which was invisible to the London painter, and if pos-
> sible, still more so to his London wife. "Would you believe it,
> Dunlap, as I sat drawing by a lower window, up marched a bear,
> as if to take a lesson!"

He last saw Raphael in the winter of 1802.

> His wife and himself were on a cold day surrounded by snow in
> a sleigh, and going to embark when I bade them adieu. Even the
> prospect of England in the distance could not cheer his English
> wife; and I felt for a moment that for a husband to bring a wife
> from London to America . . . was as certain a source of misery to
> both husband and wife as ingenuity could devise.

Raphael returned to England eager to impart a store of opinion and
information about America and Americans. The Quakers were the
most estimable people in the country. Of the others, the better sort,
in degree, were so occupied with thoughts of gain that their minds
were engrossed by it. The lower order of people cheated whenever
they could, and did so without shame, considering it a proof of
adroitness. Manners were better in the large towns than in the
country, where the settlers were rude and troublesome and would
enter your dwelling without ceremony and take all the liberties of
domestic familiarity.

Raphael also brought back the discovery that "a set of swindlers
[in America] were endeavouring to impose on Mr. Beckford," and
he conveyed this information to Beckford just as he was about to
pay his father and Trumbull for the Genesee tract. Beckford
thanked Raphael and canceled the purchase agreement. Raphael
did not stay long at Newman Street; he took up residence near
Sunning Hill, where he hunted game, occasionally painted a small
picture, and called upon his father for support as needed.

West's financial troubles were eased by the increasing number of
commissions he was getting from William Beckford. He had commitments, in fact, for nine historical, religious, and allegorical subjects, on the understanding that his charges would not exceed £1000
a year. Beckford admired West's preliminary drawings for his subjects and wished him to make the finished works as much like the
drawings as possible. Unlike the king, Beckford esteemed the

furious "Bedlamite" pictures from the *Book of Revelations*, with what he called "their mire and blood." Beckford's affinity with West's work — he commissioned seventeen pictures altogether — has baffled West's unfriendly critics, for he had discriminating taste and one of the most sophisticated minds of his time. He bought Mantegna and Bellini when those artists were considered crude and unimportant "primitives"; he almost alone praised Blake's illustrated books; and of William Turner's later work he made the perceptive, if sardonic, remark, "One must be born again to understand his pictures." Farington assumed that Beckford "leans to West because of his situation with the King," but the association continued after it was known that West was out of favor. Beckford once observed that West was "always Commander-in-Chief of the front page of the newspapers."

West frequently made the eighty-five-mile trip to Fonthill, sometimes with Raphael, often with James Wyatt, Beckford's architect, and at least once with Turner, who was doing a series of water color scenes for Beckford.[1] Visiting artists and architects stayed at Fonthill House, considered the finest edifice in western England. On these trips West learned more about the extraordinary man who was now his patron. The immense family fortune came from sugar plantations in Jamaica. Beckford's father had twice been lord mayor of London; his godfather was William Pitt, the Earl of Chatham. He had been educated at home by tutors, taking piano lessons at five from eight-year-old Wolfgang Mozart, learning the principles of architecture from Sir William Chambers, and drawing under the guidance of Alexander Cozens. He was close to being a child genius, but he confessed to West that he considered his private education "injudicious," for at a public school he would have had useful checks on his conduct and would have been exposed to making his own way among others. In 1780, at age twenty, he produced a satirical book on art, and three years later an account of his travels on the grand tour so personal that his mother persuaded him to recall it and destroy all but six copies. At age twenty-three he wrote, in French, in three days and two nights, *The History of the Caliph Vathek*, which is still recognized as a minor classic. In May 1783 he married Lady Margaret Gordon, who two years later died in

---

[1] On a trip to Fonthill in January 1797, West, William Turner and Ozias Humphry left London in a post chaise early in the morning. They dined at Hartford Bridge and continued on to Andover that evening, arriving there at 12:30 A.M. The inn was filled with soldiers and there were no beds, so they sat up all night in chairs by the fireplace. They left at five that morning, stopped to inspect Stonehenge, and arrived at Fonthill by midday.

Switzerland with the birth of her second daughter. He did not remarry. In 1797 he attempted through private diplomatic negotiations to end the war with France. He was informed from Paris that England might have peace if the government privately paid £6000 to "certain persons" and £1 million publicly to the French Directory. When he passed on the offer to the English government, offering to pay the £6000 bribe himself, his conduct was condemned and he was told that by corresponding with His Majesty's enemies he had made himself liable to indictment for treason.

Beckford's annual income in the 1790s was estimated to run between £100,000 in bad years and £170,000 in good. He was assembling at Fonthill House one of the best collections of art in England and had already amassed one of its finest libraries — some 600 choice manuscripts and 6000 volumes. These included the library of Edward Gibbon, bought in its entirety at Lausanne. In 1791 he retained James Wyatt to design and build Fonthill Abbey, an enormous neo-Gothic structure on which he was to spend £273,000 and in which he intended eventually to live. "Some people drink to forget their unhappiness," Beckford said. "I do not drink. I build." The abbey was a subject of rumor, gossip, and intense curiosity throughout England. People talked of the 260-foot tower; of the two enormous entrance doors, each 40 feet high, rising to a pointed arch, swinging on hinges that weighed a ton; of the Great Western Hall with its coffered ceiling 70 feet high; St. Michael's Gallery, 112 feet long with an uninterrupted 307-foot vista through other galleries; the wall, 7 miles long, 17 feet high, topped by spikes, that surrounded 520 acres of "flowering wilderness." They talked of the Revelation Chamber, a room with a floor of jasper and walls five feet thick, with recesses to hold coffins, where West's pictures from the *Apocalypse* were to be hung and Beckford's sarcophagus was to be placed opposite the door, to be viewed through a wire grating. All this was read and talked about, but very few people saw it, for no one was allowed past the gate at Fonthill without a permit from the owner, and very few wished to have it known that they were a guest of William Beckford.

In the second year of his marriage, Beckford had paid a visit to Powderham Castle, where he was apprehended in what appeared to be a homosexual act with the sixteen-year-old son of the house, William Courtenay, his friend of seven years. Sodomy was a capital offense in England, and Beckford fled to the Continent with his wife under a storm of censure in the press and in society. He returned to England in 1787 and secluded himself at Fonthill. His daughters were taken from him to be reared by their godmothers; he was allowed to write but could not see them. Socially he was ostracized; when he had appeared at a banquet in Salisbury a number of the guests rose and walked out. He did not subject himself again to such treatment. A few important people let it be known that they would have no objection to meeting him socially, but he ignored their overtures; he refused to be received again into society by steps and degrees.

Beckford was charming company when he wished to be; he was lively and witty, a good linguist, an excellent storyteller and singer, and a talented mimic, especially of the affectations of Britain's ladies of fashion. He talked with West from time to time about his "situation." He could never forgive himself, he said, for two actions he had taken. He had gone to Lord Courtenay's castle in the autumn of 1784 against the advice of his mother, who told him there were persons there who wished to injure his reputation and reduce his importance. And he had allowed himself, against his inclination, to be persuaded to flee with his wife to the Continent to avoid the scandal.

Curiosity about Fonthill and Beckford was so great that West's stock rose with his ability and willingness to describe a wonder almost no one else had seen. Indeed, with his entrée to Fonthill and his association with the mysterious caliph who ruled it, he was given a new power to confer small favors. He obtained permission, for example, for Henry Hope, another of his valued patrons, to visit the abbey-under-construction, and Beckford's consent to see him. ("You will be pleased with his conversation," he wrote to Beckford, explaining regretfully that he could not accompany him on the visit because he had a touch of the gout and Mrs. West, plagued with ill health, "is so low in spirits I cannot leave her.") In 1799 Beckford bought from the collection of Prince Altieri two pictures by Claude of Lorrain, then considered the greatest of landscape painters. When he placed the "Altieri Claudes" on view at Grosvenor Square, West distributed private tickets to a number of persons he wished to please, including Farington. He represented Beckford in a number of sales, purchases, and negotiations. (Dr. Thomas Monro, principal physician to Bethlehem Hospital, seeing Beckford at an auction with West, took him to be, by his appearance, a picture dealer.) West was Beckford's agent at the sale of the collection of the duke of Orleans in May 1799, and "owing to some bungling," failed to buy for him several pictures for which he would have paid any price. Nicholas Williams, Beckford's estate manager, wrote West that his employer was "angry and unforgiving because of your inattention." West was cleared of blame, however, and by August he was again received by Beckford.

In September 1799, West left Fonthill to spend some days at the country seat of Charles Howard, eleventh Duke of Norfolk ("Jockey of Norfolk"), and then to make a tour down some fifty miles of the River Wye with the duke and a party of his friends, from Monmouth to Tintern Abbey to Chipstow and on to Oxford. In a three-page account of the trip sent back to Fonthill, West gave a detailed description of the countryside, the estates he visited, and the titled persons whose guest he was. ("Lord and Lady Harcourt's friendly attention to me was very marked and highly gratified to my feelings.") The tour was a pleasant one, he reported, and attended with much satisfactory information, but nothing "gave me more pleasure than to find that the persons whose names I have mentioned are friendly to Mr. Beckford and rejoice in his great achievements in the fine arts at Fonthill."

West, in full enjoyment of Beckford's hospitality, conversation, and £1000 annuity, convinced himself that his patron was innocent of the charges against him. He told Farington what had really happened at Powderham Castle, as he heard it directly from Beckford's mother. Beckford had gone there to see Charlotte, Lady Loughborough, Courtenay's married aunt, with whom he was having an affair. They were discovered when young Courtenay, carrying a letter from Lady Charlotte to him, carelessly or intentionally delivered it to the wrong person. Beckford was so enraged that early next morning he went to Courtenay's room, locked the door behind him, routed the young man out of bed, and proceeded to horsewhip him. Courtenay screamed. His tutor came to the door and, finding it locked, summoned the family. Beckford was accused of buggery and forever thereafter suffered persecution founded on injustice and falsehood. "I could not but feel the improbability of much of the story," Farington wrote, "it not at all agreeing with many other authenticated circumstances, and being in itself difficult to give credit to... You see the character is irregular by looking at his countenance; there is a twist in his look." Beckford, Farington felt, was malevolent and had an evil heart. Beckford's mother told West that her son was too proud to do what was prudent and more than anything else would have removed suspicion from him: to go to Covent Garden and surround himself with the women there.

In assuming that his patron and host was not a practising homosexual, West, like a century of Beckford's biographers, overlooked or ignored a great deal of evidence to the contrary. The most obvious signs were the nature of the male staff at Fonthill House, the presence of visiting young boys, and the attendance of his companion, best friend, and pensioner, Gregorio Fellipe Franchi, Lisbonborn, ten years younger than Beckford. In his letters to Franchi and in his journals, Beckford used code names for himself and those around him.[2] His staff bore such names as Doll, the Calf, the Turk, and Bijou. Richardson, his valet, was Madame Bion. In describing himself when in pursuit of boys, Beckford used the code name Barzaba.

West and James Wyatt, who were in accord on so few things, agreed that the whole Academy, not just a few artists like themselves, should benefit from Beckford's largesse. Wyatt proposed at one of the meetings that Beckford should be given an invitation to the annual exhibition dinner. There was a dead silence. West volunteered that Mr. Beckford meant to patronize the arts and should be aided in that worthy objective. More silence. If the invitation was sent, he added, it would be considered as a compliment and would not be accepted. A member asked, why then should it be sent? Another asked, what would they do if he *did* accept? The subject was dropped. A few days later West took up the matter privately with Westall and Lawrence. Both evidently felt that the Academy had enough troubles; they wanted no noble lords or patrons rising and leaving the banquet hall. No action was taken and no invitation was sent.

Bourgeois told Farington indignantly in April 1799 that West and Wyatt were going to invite Nicholas Williams to the annual dinner. Williams was a respectable family man, but he was Beckford's steward, and an invitation to Williams was a kind of recognition of Beckford. Farington took the matter to West, who said he would discuss the matter with Wyatt. Dinner invitations were very much in demand, and Farington and West had both, from time to time, exhorted their colleagues to give their tickets, not to their friends, but rather to those persons in "elevated situations" whose presence would distinguish the Academy table. Nicholas Williams was not invited.[3]

West sent a message on December 2, 1799, to the members of the Academy Council; he was incapacitated with an attack of gout and would not attend the general meeting on December 10, at which officers for the coming year were to be elected and medals given to the students. Since he would not be present and there would be no presidential discourse, he recommended that the meeting be held

---

[2] First revealed in 1957 in *Life at Fonthill* by Boyd Alexander, custodian of the Hamilton-Beckford Papers in Scotland. (Beckford's elder daughter married the tenth duke of Hamilton.)

[3] Though Beckford was shunned by English society, West and Wyatt, as professional artists, could associate with him without being suspected of approving his sexual conduct.

in the Council Room and as privately as possible. The Council members decided otherwise, and they asked Thomas Banks to tell this to Mr. West. Banks called to say that the general meeting would be held in the Exhibition Room and as publicly as possible, since it was desired to distinguish the most meritorious students and make an impression on the minds of the others. Mr. Wilton, the president's deputy, he said, would preface the delivery of the medals with a talk on the purpose of giving them. Banks returned to the Council to report that Mr. West "was recovering surprisingly and had no doubt of being able to attend the General Assembly on Tuesday next, and would draw up an address to be delivered previous to giving the medals." There was some merriment at this news; Banks was congratulated on his cure for the gout and for some days was addressed as "Dr. Banks."

To all appearance, the December 10th meeting was a routine one. West was re-elected to another term. Robert Smirke, Jr., eighteen, won the gold medal for architectural drawing, though it was felt his father must have helped him.[4] Four members — Banks, Nollekens, Yenn, and Daniell — were elected to the Council for the year 1800, replacing four whose term had ended.

Thomas Daniell, fifty, was a new Academician who had spent ten years in India and was working on a massive folio, *Oriental Scenery*. He had been elected ten months earlier at the same time as Henry Tresham, forty-four, who had come to London from Dublin in 1775, studied and worked fourteen years in Italy, and was now a history painter and clerk of the works at Buckingham House. Tresham had become an Associate in 1791, five years earlier than Daniell, and so was senior to him. Tresham, however, was not named to a Council seat. He was passed over because he gave some indication that he was another difficult Irishman. For example, he had no sooner been inducted than he took a strong stand against a plan for regulating the schools that a carefully chosen committee had developed and that West and most of the other Academicians supported. Election of Tresham would give a dissident group four of the eight Council seats instead of a manageable three. And so those in charge named Daniell and skipped Tresham. It was a decision routinely taken, but it was to have unfortunate consequences for West, Farington, and the Royal Academy.

The first rumbles of trouble were recorded in Farington's diary on Christmas Day 1799: "Shee called. Tresham has complained to

---

[4] Robert Smirke, Jr., later designed the British Museum.

him of not being elected one of the Council for next year. Hoppner has also been very violent complaining of proceedings in the Academy." Two days later Farington called on Hoppner and learned from him that there was a growing movement to contest the Council election. Tresham had drawn up a memorial to the king on the violation of a law of the Academy in not naming him, and Beechey had presented it to the king. The king had asked Wyatt if it was true that a cabal was running the Academy, and Wyatt said there was. The king was told, "West acts through timidity, being fearful of the Cabal." Farington wrote:

> West I called on and told him what I had heard (but not from whom), all except about his timidity which, Mrs. West being present, I declined. West judges that the King will wait to see him and when the subject is mentioned he shall ask His Majesty whether the elections for years past have not been proper, and whether the Academy is not in a flourishing condition. These sufficiently disprove any improper conduct.

The Academy was indeed in a flourishing condition. The spring exhibition had set a record for receipts (£3753) and for admissions (almost 60,000). It was natural for the responsible officers to feel they had done what was best for the Academy and that the king would approve their conduct. The fact remained, however, that they had broken a rule of the Academy. Seats on the Council were not elective. The constitution clearly called for the eight seats to be filled by rotation among all members, with no one reoccupying a seat until all other members had served. By this means it was intended that no dominant group of the membership could control the Council by the force of its majority vote in the General Assembly. But the Council for the year 1800 had members on it who had been elected, and elected out of turn, by a dominant group. It had members who were serving a second, third, or fourth term, while there was at least one Academician — Henry Tresham — who had not served at all. To be sure, the rule had been skirted for some years on this point, but that was simply because no member, until now, had ever challenged the violation.

To some, the issue seemed (and may seem to us) to be small and unimportant, but it was, in its way, a grave constitutional question, and it was an issue that opened a violent struggle for control and power in the Academy. The dusty documents recording the struggle — the letters, pamphlets, minutes, memorials, and diaries — are at once amusing and painful because of the intensity of long-stilled emotions; but the pages still burn with the fierce passions and rivalries, the shouted words, the triumphs, anger, and anguish of the men involved.

The Farington-West "cabal" made the first move, calling a special meeting of the members to discuss whether the last election of Council was legal. West was called upon as president and a founding member to express his opinion on the matter. He spoke for ten minutes and concluded, not unexpectedly, that law and usage corresponded and the election was legal. Farington spoke for forty-five minutes "in a strong manner" and was so pleased with what he said that he copied the most eloquent passages into his diary. Mr. Tresham, he said, in addressing a letter to the president and then taking it to the king before it could be acted on, had treated the Academy with contempt. "Persons most acquainted with Mr. Tresham openly aver that His Majesty will annul the election. It may be so and the Academy must submit to His Majesty's determination. But if Mr. Tresham under such circumstances and by such means is authorized to take his seat in the Council, I am one who would not wish to be placed by his side." Tresham declared that Mr. West had ignored his letter and in so doing "had not treated him in a manner becoming a president nor with the civility of a gentleman."

Copley disavowed the authority of those (that is, West) who had framed the Academy's laws. It was *"the height of corruption to allow the law to be expounded by those who made it,* because they might explain it wrongfully for certain purposes." Lawrence and Hoppner said his statement was absurd.

William Beechey said he was never so ill treated as he had been at the last Council meeting. He had been very ill treated, in fact, ever since he was elected into the Academy, and he intended to avoid the company of those who treated him so ill.

Between one and two in the morning, after several hours of angry debate, Farington obtained approval of two documents he had prepared for West to submit to the king. One was a list of precedents culled from Academy records on the way Council members had always been chosen. The other was an address resolving that no one should take Academy affairs to the king except those authorized to do so. Copley was the lone dissenter.

West carried the two documents to Buckingham House, meeting Yenn and Richards there. The prize student pictures had been delivered to a waiting room, and the king, queen, and princesses inspected them, commenting most favorably on Smirke's drawing. The king, remarking that he was himself "a little of an architect," regretted that England's magnificent Old School was out of favor. The Adam brothers, he said, had "introduced too much neatness and prettiness." The ladies departed, and in a lull in the conversation West asked the king to accept two papers he had brought from the Academy. The king, West observed, "seemed to be under a palpitation when he took the papers." He read the address and said the Academy was perfectly right in resolving that only authorized persons should take matters to the king. He read the list of precedents, looked up, mentioned Tresham's memorial, and quoted the Academy law directing that seats on the Council should go in rotation, and first to those who had not served. He asked West for his opinion. West cited usage and precedents and expressed the view that members should be elected. But if the usage had been contrary to Academy law, the king said, was that a reason why it should continue to be so? There was a pause. The king said he supposed it would be best for him to write the Academy on the matter. He signed his approval to the election of the other officers but drew his pen through the names of Banks, Yenn, Nollekens, and Daniell, writing under them, "The Law declaring the Academicians shall serve in rotation, which, from a Memorial from Mr. Tresham, seems not to have been attended to. George R."

Tresham's victory in the king's decision to annul the Council election was received with consternation, not only by the "cabal" but also by members aligned with neither faction. The king had not before asserted his authority in such a way, and they had come to assume that the Academy made its own rules and decisions. The king's action was a blunt reminder that it did not. In the agitated and alarmed debates that followed, Farington introduced a moderate note. They would respond to His Majesty's communication with profound respect and grateful acknowledgment, and they would pass a resolution for the records that would exonerate them from any future supposition that they had acted improperly. In their anger, some talked of dissolving the Royal Academy Club, which was beyond the king's authority, and of forming another where admission was by ballot only. In this way they would indicate their feelings to the king, and "members would not have to associate with other members whose conduct disgusts them."

The crisis was meliorated a few days later when West had another meeting with the king. In a "quite confidential" conversation lasting two hours, with no other persons present, he found that His Majesty "appeared desirous that the Academy should not feel that he intended any reflection on their conduct in annuling the Council." He carried this happy news to Farington, Smirke, and Daniell, "with which they were much gratified." They decided that dissolving the Academy Club was probably not now a proper measure.

In the next two general meetings there was, Farington wrote, "much loose conversation — many speakers." West read the king's message with a brave show of satisfaction; it proved, he said, that His Majesty's favor had not been withdrawn. Lawrence "animadverted severely" at members who took their complaints privately to the king. Beechey objected to the severity of Lawrence's language. Copley said the Academy had disgraced itself by not rescinding the election as soon as the law was pointed out. West read a defense against Tresham's charges that he had acted unbecoming a president and not with the civility of a gentleman; he said he would leave his case to the consideration of the members and, appointing Wilton to take over the meeting, stalked from the room. Bourgeois and several others objected to his departure as improper. Farington said his departure was an act of delicacy. Lawrence went out and brought West back to the chair. Tresham allowed that his expressions had been improper, but he refused to give up that Mr. West had in fact so behaved to him. After "long and tedious arguments" it was decided to pass a resolution declaring that Mr. West "had acted with propriety both as a President and as a Gentleman in all that related to that transaction."

Despite the quarreling and hard feelings, the business of the Academy went forward. West developed the technique of adjourning Council meetings to a nearby coffee shop when certain delicate or controversial matters were to be discussed, so that they would not be entered on the minutes as Academy business. He consulted Farington on a thorny problem: what to do about two pictures of stark naked women submitted by Richard Cosway and John Opie for the 1798 exhibition. (They decided they would paint drapery over appropriate parts in water color, which the artists could later wash off without harm to the pictures.) And about this time West, Thomas Banks, and Cosway performed a practical scientific experiment in an effort to remedy a deficiency every painter of the human figure was aware of.

In pictures of the Crucifixion, artists had used both living models and dead bodies, but neither, obviously, was an accurate or honest representation of the appearance of a person in transition from life to death on the cross. Since an actual crucifixion of a live model was impossible in England, the three men concluded that if they could affix to the cross a body still warm with recent life, they would come much closer to the action of a crucified figure. They posed the problem to Dr. Joseph Constantin Carpue,[5] surgeon,

---

[5] Dr. Carpue (1764–1846), surgeon to the York Hospital, Chelsea, and member of the Royal College of Surgeons, became a pioneer in the restoration of missing

anatomist, and lecturer on surgery, and proposed that he procure such a body for them. He entered into the experiment with enthusiasm. He went to the surgeon general of the armed forces, who agreed to give them the warm corpse of James Legg, a pensioner of Chelsea Hospital who was about to be hanged for murdering Ensign William Lamb, one of his comrades. It is not known whether Mr. Legg or his family was consulted beforehand, but the moment the body was cut down from the gallows it was turned over to Dr. Carpue and the three artists, who at once nailed it naked to a wooden cross and transported it, presumably in an upright position, to an undisclosed workshop, where the sculptor Thomas Banks, assisted by West and Cosway, very skillfully made a cast. This was deposited in the Academy schools, where it was much admired by the students. It reposes today in the Royal Academy Life Class at Burlington House, Piccadilly.

Beckford and Nicholas Williams seem to have held no ill will against West for not being asked to the Academy dinners, for in December 1800 they invited him to a truly exceptional Christmas week entertainment at Fonthill, where the guests, Beckford said, were to spend "a few comfortable days of repose, uncontaminated by the sight and prattle of drawing room parasites." Fonthill Abbey, though it was still unfinished and uninhabited, would be opened for a reception for the first time. The honored guests were to be Beckford's cousin, Sir William Hamilton, the diplomatist, archeologist, and art collector, a charming and accomplished man now entering his dotage; his wife Emma Hamilton, whom he had, in a literal sense, bought from his nephew; and Rear Admiral Lord Nelson, who, having left his wife, was living in a modified *ménage à trois* with the Hamiltons. Nelson had recently won the great victory over the French at the Nile, and he was about to be promoted to vice admiral of the Blue,[6] but because of his scandalous private life the king had snubbed him on his return to England, and the official and social world was treating him coolly.

James Wyatt and Henry Tresham were also of the company, as were Madame Banti, born Briggitta Giorgi (a powerful soprano who had just completed a successful engagement in France), several French émigrés, several Portuguese noblemen, and Dr. John Wolcot,

---

noses, an art carried out in India, where noses were commonly cut off as a punishment. In 1816 he published *An Account of Two Successful Operations for Restoring a Lost Nose from the Integuments of the Forehead*. In an improved method he used the integuments of an upper arm.

[6] One of the three divisions of the navy, the Red, White, and Blue Squadrons.

the notorious "Peter Pindar." Wolcot had abused West unmercifully; he had accused Hamilton of manufacturing his own Etruscan vases; and in "A Lyric to Sir William Hamilton" he had suggested that, in view of his lordship's advanced age, Lady Hamilton might return to her career as a prostitute on Cockspur Street. Beckford, however, was amused by Wolcot's talents as a satirist, entertainer, and storyteller, and apparently his guests felt no rancor on this occasion, or at least none is recorded.

The guests assembled on Saturday, December 20. Nelson and the Hamiltons were met at the gates of the estate by a thirty-piece band which, to the strains of *Rule Britannia*, escorted them through a double line of Fonthill Volunteers to the marble steps of Fonthill House. There they were greeted by Beckford and a large number of other guests, West among them. A squad fired a salute, the band played *God Save the King*, and Admiral Nelson, with his empty sleeve and his eye patch, inspected the Volunteers. After dinner at six, according to an account in the *Gentleman's Magazine*, "A variety of vocal pieces were finely executed by Lady Hamilton in her expressive and triumphant manner, and by Banti with all her charms of voice and Italian sensibility."

The guests spent three days dining and drinking, talking (Emma Hamilton spoke Italian like a native and French fluently), listening to music, making excursions over the vast grounds (though never to or near Fonthill Abbey), and seeing the pictures, library, and objects of art. At five o'clock on Tuesday evening, they took their assigned places in a long fleet of carriages and began a winding forty-five-minute drive to the abbey (though it was actually only ten minutes' distance). They drove through two lines of Fonthill Volunteers holding lighted torches, past lanterns hung in the trees, while the band played solemn marches, and drum rolls sounded from the hilltops. Beckford loved theatrical effects, and he had retained Philip James de Loutherbourgh, R.A., a former associate of the magician-alchemist Alessandro di Cagliostro, to plan and direct the lighting. The first evidence of his work was an illuminated flag of a vice admiral flying from a 50-foot staff atop the 260-foot abbey tower.

At the immense doorway Beckford had stationed one of his retinue, a dwarf. (The local gentry were affronted that Beckford had a dwarf in his household, and doubly so that he was a *French* dwarf with the name Pierre Colas de Grailly and two nicknames: Narribus and Pierrot.) The guests dined at a 52-foot refectory table in the Oak Parlor "in one long line of silver dishes, in the substantial custom of ancient Abbeys, unmixed with the refinements of modern cookery." After dinner they went to St. Michael's Gallery, the staircase being lighted "by certain mysterious living figures at different intervals, dressed in hooded gowns and standing with large wax torches in their hands." Following an inspection of the galleries to the accompaniment of solemn airs played by concealed musicians, the guests partook of spiced wine and confectionary served in gold baskets and then took seats in one of the large rooms. Lady Hamilton entered in a Roman costume, holding a golden urn. As Agrippina Bearing the Ashes of Germanicus, she performed one of her celebrated *tableaux vivants*, pantomiming the attitudes and expressions of grief, courage, nobility, supplication, anger, and revenge. Some of the company shed tears. Beckford later remarked that she performed "greatly to her own satisfaction," and added that she really should have portrayed Cleopatra. Her performance on this occasion may have suffered somewhat owing to the fact that she was eight months gone with a child by Admiral Nelson.[7] The company returned to Fonthill House around midnight, where they were served yet another supper.

Farington heard accounts of the brilliant party from several sources. Lady Hamilton, he said, "is bold and unguarded in her manner, is grown fat, and drinks freely." In his letter of thanks sent from Newman Street, West wrote:

> When I reflect on the progress, which the combination of arts have made, directed by true taste, since I first rode on the ground on which the Abbey stands — I am lost in admiration — and feel that I have seen a place raised more by magic, or inspiration, than the labours of the human hand. This is the sensation which the examination of that elegant edifice produced on my feelings; and when the part which remains to be finished is accomplished, must raise a climax of excellence without an example in the European world — and to give an immortality to the man whose elegant mind had conceived so vast a combination of all that is refined in Painting, Sculpture, and Architecture.

---

[7] It was their first child, a daughter named Horatia Nelson Thompson, born in well-kept secrecy on January 30, 1801.

19

Paris: 1802

I am going to make you long to be in Paris. Benjamin West and
his son Ben are here, and Opie and his wife . . . and Kemble of
the Drury Lane Theatre. I have not seen West; only knew of his
coming last evening . . . He and Ben are coming to breakfast this
morning.

JOEL BARLOW from Paris,
to his wife in London,
September 1802

ENGLAND WAS in desperate straits after nine years of war with
France — with the Convention until October 1795, the Directory until November 1799, and now with Napoleon Bonaparte, First
Consul of the Republic. Ireland was in revolt again, sailors of the
fleet had mutinied against brutal treatment, and the army had
suffered terrible losses, 40,000 men, in the West Indies. King
George had been attacked in the streets and his coach destroyed.
Prices had risen and stayed up after the bad harvest of 1795; the
king issued a proclamation urging everyone to use the utmost
economy in bread and flour; and to curb the habit of eating quan-
tities of fresh bread at every meal, bakers were prohibited from
selling bread until it had been twenty-four hours out of the oven.
In the financial crisis of 1798, the Bank of England suspended payments in specie. The Pitt government imposed an income tax in
that year, and even a tax on powder. (It ended forever the wearing
of white wigs and powered hair.) A pro-Bonaparte peace party was
demanding an end to the war with France at almost any cost.

Bonaparte had introduced new concepts into international politics and ways of waging war. His victorious armies, swelled by
universal conscription, imposed huge demands for money and supplies on the conquered and occupied countries. He was admired

and supported by thoughtful people even in the countries he was fighting, even by some political leaders in the United States, including President Jefferson. He rewarded men for achievement (except for members of his own family) and honored them for merit without regard to their birth or rank, and he had, after all, controlled the Revolution, reconciled the church, recalled the émigrés, and made many improvements in the French economy. He was progressing in his "Continental System" — in his grand program to unify Europe under one currency, a common tariff system, a uniform code of law, and a single ruler.

The last opponent that stood in the way of Bonaparte's conquest of Europe was Britain. He had a plan to end that opposition: He would send an army of 150,000 men across the Channel in oared barges and gunboats, embarking on a windless day when the British home fleet could not move to attack it. Britain lived under the constant threat of invasion; two unsuccessful attempts, indeed, had already been made. Semaphore telegraphs (an invention borrowed from the French) were erected and beacon fires prepared on every hilltop to warn of a French landing. Volunteer militia drilled and trained throughout the island. The Royal Academy contributed £500 to the war effort, and there was talk of recruiting a company of artists to defend the homeland. Joseph Farington, fifty-six, joined the St. Pancras Volunteers. When a Mr. Le Jeune, a stockbroker, was appointed a major, Farington wrote in his diary, "The whole of the military business of this parish appears to be in low hands."

The Royal Navy was supreme on the seas in the summer of 1801, the French army was supreme on the Continent, and the war was at a stalemate. Bonaparte decided to negotiate a truce in order to obtain a respite, raise capital, rebuild his navy, and consolidate his conquests before proceeding to liberate England and the rest of the Continent. His representatives signed preliminary peace terms in London in October 1801, to the wild rejoicing of the populace in both London and Paris, and they signed the Treaty of Amiens — "the Experimental Treaty" — in March 1802.

Great numbers of English at once began to stream across the Channel to visit a Paris they had not seen in ten years. They stood in the very spots in the Place de la Concorde, the Place du Trône and the Place de la Grève where the guillotine had cut off the heads of Louis XVI, Marie Antoinette, Madame du Barry, Madame Roland, the sister, mother, and grandmother of the marquise de Lafayette, Lavoisier, the duc d'Orleans, Danton, the twenty Girondist deputies, Robespierre and, in the space of two days, the ninety-two leaders of the Commune. They stared at Bonaparte's veterans in their dashing uniforms, studied the Parisian women, admired the parades and the firework illuminations that came on every evening at ten. They compared the pleasure gardens — Tivoli and Frascati — with their own Vauxhall and Ranelagh, visited an industrial exhibition in the great square of the Louvre, tested the restaurants, opera, and theaters (Talma, the leading tragedian of France, was playing). They went to the Tuileries, the Pantheon, high mass in Notre Dame, and the shops, cafés, gaming houses, and the stalls for blacking shoes, each with a covered seat and a newspaper to read while waiting. They stood on tiptoe at public functions to see Bonaparte's generals and, if they were lucky or privileged, actually beheld the man who was being hailed as the greatest figure of the age. Among themselves they argued endlessly about what had really happened to these people who had thrown off the shackles of church and nobility. Was their condition better or worse than it had been under the king? How did it compare with what Englishmen had at home?

The most eager-eyed of all the visitors streaming into Paris were the English artists, for Bonaparte had been assembling the choicest works of art from all the conquered countries. The *Apollo Belvedere* was there, its fig leaf removed, the *Laocoon,* the *Dying Gladiator,* the bronze horses and the winged lion of St. Mark's, Raphael's *Transfiguration* and his *Madonna della Sedia,* Titian's *Entombment,* Veronese's *Marriage at Cana* and *Feast at the House of Levi.* Cardinal Albani's palace had been stripped of its treasures. Pope Pius VII saw 100 of his best pictures taken to adorn the Louvre (75 were eventually returned). Many of the stolen works, unfortunately, were not on view, for they were in the private possession of Bonaparte's various generals. There was remarkably little protest from the artists of the world at this monstrous thievery. John Flaxman tried to mount a campaign to stop the French from looting Rome, "The University of the World," but he found few supporters. He wrote two strong letters to the London *Courier* and a pamphlet in which he denounced the French artists who had petitioned their government to remove works of art from Rome. He read the pamphlet in manuscript to Henry Fuseli, who, though he abhorred the French and their larcenous conduct, advised Flaxman that the Academy might, at most, pass a resolution but could not prudently sponsor a campaign. Flaxman called on West and asked for Academy backing, but West (he complained) kept him waiting a half hour in a room without a fire, complimented him on his two letters, and said it would be improper to interfere with the French. The visit was short. He did not seem, Flaxman said, to comprehend the matter on a large scale.

A dozen or more Academicians departed for Paris in August and early September. Farington made the trip in the remarkably good time of only three days, carrying with him a special diary for this trip and a supply of Dr. James's Powders. He was still depressed over the death in February 1800 of his wife Susan, "the best, the most affectionate, the most amiable of women." ("My spirits continue to be oppressed without ceasing, sometimes to a degree which I can scarcely support.") He traveled with three companions: Fuseli, an Academy student named J. Halls, and James Moore, a surgeon, brother of General Sir John Moore. Fuseli, who hoped the six-week excursion would not cost him more than sixty pounds, was out of spirits from the time he departed, because he hated to leave England. Cosway, Opie, Flaxman, and Hoppner took their wives. Martin Shee traveled with his friend Samuel Rogers, the wealthy banker, art collector, scholar, social lion, and poet. (Shee and Rogers both lived to the middle of the century, long enough to marvel at the ease and comfort with which one might make the same journey to Paris in only twelve hours.)

West obtained from Beckford a list of contemporary French artists and of collections of old masters in Paris. He called on the French minister in London to obtain letters to high officials in his country, and on Lord Hawkesbury, foreign secretary, for letters to the British representative in Paris.[1] He set out on Monday, August 16, with his son Benjamin and his valet, James Dyer. In his baggage he carried a version of his small unframed picture *Death on the Pale Horse*, which he intended to hang in an exhibition of modern artists scheduled to open at the Louvre on 15 Fructidor (September 1). At Calais he fell in with John Flaxman and his wife and traveled with them the rest of the journey, spending a full day in Amiens and on August 22 arriving in Paris, where they took an *appartement* at the Hôtel de Marigny in the place du Louvre. West told his colleagues that Flaxman was the best informed of the English artists in his field and Mrs. Flaxman was "a very well informed woman of great sense and prudence."

West went with his son and his servant to the Prefecture of Police, where they turned in their English passports and were issued French passports of security to be carried at all times. Each was interrogated as to name, nationality, profession, place of abode, and length of stay, and each was described: height, color of hair, eyes and eyebrows, and shape of forehead, nose, mouth, chin, and face. The room was full of clerks busily working on passports for French

---

[1] West later maintained that he consulted the king about the propriety of making the trip and that it was the king who directed that letters be furnished him.

citizens who wished to leave or extend their stay in Paris. "What would an Englishman think," Farington wrote a week later on undergoing the same experience, "if he were told that he could not come to London or quit it without leave from his government on pain of imprisonment?"

West then called on various persons to leave his letters and his card. The government, he was told, knew of his arrival, intended to pay him "every mark of distinguished attention," and would help him and his friends to get access to collections of art, including several that were closed. In the course of the week he was visited at his hotel "by all the most distinguished French statesmen, and he had the honour of being invited to dine with them successively." Among his callers was Dominique Vivant Denon, artist and archeologist, once a favorite of Louis XV, the author of a recently published two-volume work on Egypt that contained 141 of his drawings. He was director of fine arts and Bonaparte's special advisor on which works of art to confiscate in the various conquered countries. Another was François André Vincent, historical painter, president of the French National Institute, and Bonaparte's special advisor on which works of art to confiscate in Spain. Denon or Vincent explained to West the great service to humanity that was being performed in placing these art works where they would be safe, appreciated, and seen. They told him of the "grand system of national decoration designed by Bonaparte . . . by which he expected to leave such memorials to posterity as would convince the world that his magnificence was worthy of his military achievements." West, who admired Bonaparte both as an apostle of liberty and for the favors granted to artists, was completely captured by these "extensive views" and "superb schemes" — by this realization of the neoclassical ideal of a "universal museum." He agreed to inspect and report on the sculptures and the nearly 1000 pictures brought to Paris from Italy. There were rumors that the *Laocoon* had been mishandled and broken in transit, that the *Apollo Belvedere* was a copy fobbed off on the French committee that was collecting art in Rome, and that the pictures had been harmed in being removed and spoiled by unskillful cleaning. It was expected that Mr. West would lend the authority of his position and his familiarity with the Italian works to an impartial examination of the truth of these rumors. He would be admitted to inspect any of the works of art at any hour of the day or night.

When he took his *Pale Horse* to the exhibition in the Salon at the Louvre, he was invited to choose the place where he wished it to hang and was told that a frame would be prepared for it. The picture created considerable excitement among French artists, one of whom said that "the attempt was hardy" and was the only successful presentation of such a difficult subject since the time of Rubens. Jacques Louis David stood before it for some time and then observed that it was a caricature of Rubens. West said that French artists, meaning David, were merely painting statues.

Farington and his party arrived on August 30, registered at the Hôtel de Marigny, and the next day had tea in West's apartment; Opie, Daniell, the Flaxmans, and Monsieur Vincent were among the company. The next day Farington had eleven of his English friends to dinner. During the evening West expressed astonishment at the amazing improvement in agriculture in the country between Calais and Paris since his two earlier visits. He "seemed to imagine," Farington said, "that the Revolution had been the principal cause of it." Edmund Garvey, who had also been in France before 1789, observed that the improvement had been gradual, as in other countries, and had been by no means forwarded by the Revolution. West was not chastened. A few days later he declared that the people of Paris appeared to be in a much better state since the Revolution. On his two earlier trips, he had found the streets of Paris crowded with fine coaches, with servants in rich liveries, two, four, or six of them standing behind on footsteps raised above each other, and religious processions moving in every direction, but the mass of the people abject and ragged. Now, he said, there appeared to be "but one order of people, a middle class, as they may be called."

West was delighted to see Robert Fulton, his one-time student, Elizabeth West's favorite among all the young Americans who frequented her husband's studio. Fulton had been a promising student in the years 1787–1794. ("Painting requires more studdy than I at first imagened," he had written to his mother, and "Mr. West and me are on a very familiar footing and when he is in town pays me much attention which is extremely agreeable as we live near each other.") He had painted several subjects from English history, visited Powderham Castle to do a portrait of Beckford's former friend, Viscount Courtenay, exhibited at the Academy, and seemed to be fairly launched on an artistic career. But Fulton's real interest came to be practical mechanical inventions, for a number of which he obtained British patents. He developed and tried to sell a grandiose plan for a network of inland canals in which a system of raising and lowering a train of small boats by inclined planes would have eliminated large boats, large canals, and locks. When the British government showed no interest in his plan, he had gone to France in 1797 with letters of introduction and hope of finding support for his work. There he met Joel Barlow, another American, another West friend; they developed such a warm friendship that Fulton moved into the Barlow's household and lived with them for the next seven years. (Joel and Ruth Barlow called him "Toot.") It was at the Barlows that West met with his friend Fulton, talking over a breakfast, telling each other the developments of the past half dozen years. West went to inspect Fulton's inventions, promised to give Barlow a catalogue of his works to be used in a book Barlow was writing, and, at Barlow's request, gave his observations on "the revolution which he had brought about in art within the last 30 years by his having broken the ancient shackles and modernized the art."

Barlow's years in Paris had cooled the revolutionary ardor that had caused him to write *Advice to the Privileged Orders*, for he had watched the bloody work of the guillotine, had seen innocent friends carried away for execution, and was with Thomas Paine when the police came to arrest that hero of two revolutions. In 1795 he had successfully carried out a dangerous diplomatic mission for the United States, going as American consul to Algiers to negotiate a treaty with three Barbary states and obtain release of more than a hundred Americans being held for ransom. French government-consolidated securities rose rapidly with Bonaparte's victories, and Barlow, having put all the money he could raise in that investment, found himself with a handsome fortune. He used some of it to finance Fulton's work.

When French officials showed no interest in canals with inclined planes, Fulton had offered them a new project, his "plunging boat." This was a craft that sailed on water but, when its sails and mast were struck, could submerge and proceed under water, propelled by a hand-turned screw and pushing an explosive charge that, it was hoped, would blow up somebody's warship. For two years he had conducted experiments on the Seine with models, and in the spring of 1800 he built and launched at Le Havre a vessel named *Nautilus*. He established certain scientific facts: His water ballast and moveable fins would submerge the *Nautilus*; a magnetic compass pointed as correctly under water as on the surface; he could achieve a speed of two and a half miles an hour and plunge to a depth of 25 feet; use of candles for light consumed air needed to breathe, but a very small watertight window would admit enough light for him to count the minutes on his watch; and by use of 1 cubic foot of compressed air in a copper globe, a crew of four could remain submerged as long as four hours and twenty minutes.

Barlow worked his way up through the marine bureaucracy to obtain a commission for his friend to blow up one of the British battleships that were blockading the French coast. Both men were pacifists and abhorred the thought of taking human life, but they were driven by the higher spirit of scientific research and by the sure knowledge that their terrible weapon would end the war between France and Britain and perhaps put an end to naval warfare forever. The *Nautilus* set out on its deadly mission, Fulton at the controls, two men turning the propelling machine, but agents had alerted the British, who withdrew their ships beyond range. Fulton later did succeed in sinking a French sloop anchored in the harbor of Brest for the experiment, but Bonaparte still was not interested, though he had sent observers to watch the event. At the time they told this story to West, Fulton and Barlow were both outraged at Bonaparte; he had just contrived to have himself named first consul for life. Barlow said with the bitterness of a betrayed republican, "Bonaparte has thrown back the progress of civilization and public happiness about one age." Fulton was now consumed by a new undertaking, that of propelling a surface vessel by the power of a steam engine. He was already making experiments on the Seine with the wealthy Robert R. Livingston of New York, who had arrived the previous November as minister to France, and who held a monopoly for steam navigation on the waters of his state, if and when steam navigation was developed. The statesman Talleyrand met Fulton at a dinner at Livingston's, listened to his recitation of ideas and inventions, and remarked to a friend that it was distressing to hear a man who was young, brilliant, and quite crazy.

West spent much of his time in Paris in the art galleries. He said he had never felt better and was sleeping unusually well, and he commonly arrived an hour or more before the doors opened, using his special position to gain admittance, returned following the afternoon meal, and remained after the doors had closed. He finished his report on the condition of the Italian art brought to Paris, read it aloud to Farington, including a preface on the greatness and high value of the collection, and turned it over to a translator. He attested that the works of art had been transported in a prudent and proper manner and that they were in as good condition as they had been when he saw them in Italy.

The English artists were scattered about Paris, but he encountered all of them in his tours of the galleries. Hoppner, he learned, detested Paris and the French but could scarcely sleep at night for thinking of the great works of art he had seen that day. Farington was keeping separate notebooks in which to write observations on each school of painting, beginning as early as Mantegna and several other "Gothic" artists. Maria Cosway was at home in Paris, for she had lived there before the Revolution, when she had been wooed by Thomas Jefferson, widower. (John Trumbull had introduced them to each other and since served in their exchange of letters.) Now she was copying a Titian in water color. One day she took Benjamin West on a round of picture-seeing and then to the residence of her friend, Letitia Bonaparte, the mother of Napoleon, who was unwell and could receive only Maria.

When he saw Correggio's *St. Jerome*, West climbed on a stool to examine it more closely, explaining to his companion, the banker Sir Francis Baring, that he had copied the picture in Parma in 1763 and had "formed himself on it." Farington, the actor John Kemble, Thomas Erskine (chancellor to the Prince of Wales) and Erskine's grown son called on West one morning and went with him through the dark, dirty hallways of the living quarters of artists in the Louvre. They were admitted to the apartment of the venerable artist Jean P. G. Viennet, once the president of the former French Academy, "who showed us many historical studies he had made at different periods of his life." West then led them to the exhibition gallery, where, at their request, he lectured Mr. Kemble and Mr. Erskine on what to look for in the pictures, both men making marginal notes in their catalogues as they progressed around the gallery. They were ignorant of art, Farington said, so that such assistance made the pictures more interesting to them.[2] Erskine may have been a little distraught during West's lecture, for "he had a sore on his mind" — he was upset at a slight he had received on being introduced to Bonaparte at a reception. Bonaparte had hardly more than nodded to him, asked him, *"Êtes-vous légiste?"* — Thomas Erskine, a leader in the House of Commons, the most highly paid barrister in Britain!

On another occasion West was in the gallery with the Whig statesman Charles James Fox when they encountered Fuseli. West introduced the two. Fox thought Fuseli's conduct was a bit odd and later asked Farington: Was there political animosity? Farington explained: Fuseli had not much liked "the conciseness of West's manner" in making the introduction.

When the English met in the streets, in the galleries, at tea and at dinners, they exchanged experiences and observations. Everyone agreed that the streets of Paris were narrower and harder to walk on than those of London, that the smells were often intolerable, and that London's public walks and parks were incomparably finer and greener. Paris, it was felt, was grander, but London was

---

[2] Erskine ten days earlier had asked Hoppner to point out to him the beauties of Titian's *Death of St. Peter Martyr*. Hoppner replied that if Mr. Erskine was not already sensible of them, it was not in *his* power to help him, for it required an education like learning Greek to understand the beauties contained in a picture.

more convenient; or, as Martin Shee put it, "London to live, Paris to look." Everyone was conscious of the large number of men in military uniform and of a corresponding lack of any evidence of civil power. Farington marveled that the monuments to heroes of the Revolutionary Wars contained the names of corporals and even of private soldiers. He visited the Champ-de-Mars and was pleased to report that among the prodigious number of captured flags there, perhaps as many as 1800, he could find only two that were English — "a small number when compared with those of France which may be seen in England." Fox told of attending the opera and of seeing the Italian ambassador sitting with his hands over his ears. There was much talk of Parisian women. Opie said he had seen many more beautiful women in walking from Berners Street to the end of Oxford Street than in all Paris in the fortnight he had been there. Young Robert Smirke saw but few such complexions as were common in England. Farington agreed there was less beauty, "but in form, and more particularly in carriage, the French women cannot be looked upon without much interest."

It was remarked that no one used the address *citoyen* outside of government offices, and that Parisians laughed when the English tried it. Some attention was paid to a new and strange dance in triple rhythm called the "walse," in which the partners kept turning around and around. Several of the artists saw Jean Greuze, seventy-seven, taking a lonely walk, his fame and his pictures now almost forgotten. Old Monsieur Viennet appeared at a dinner in the court dress of a past era, wearing so much lace that Fuseli said he looked like a baby. David was seen frequently but no one met and talked with him, which was a matter of regret to Flaxman, who had intended publicly to refuse to meet the notorious Jacobin, an aide to Robespierre, an artist who had voted for the death of the king and had been heard to say that 500,000 more heads should have passed under the guillotine. The British artists did not admire David's work, thinking the composition labored and artificial, the coloring "without union," and the principal characters nothing but common Academy figures. They were astonished at the uniformity of the pictures the French were painting and felt that viewed at a little distance they might all have been painted by the same hand and out of the same pot. It was to be expected, Fuseli said, that the British painters were in a better state; they were beginning their art and the French were at the end of theirs.

There was scandalized talk about the young countess of Oxford, one of the most beautiful women of her time, whose portrait by Hoppner in the 1797 Academy show had drawn much attention. She was being attended in Paris by Arthur O'Connor, the Irish revolutionary, a member of the United Irishmen, who was agent in France for Robert Emmet's rebellion.[3] (Children of the countess of Oxford, a member of the Harley family, were known as "the Harleian Miscellany," because their fathers were a mixed lot.) The English reported to each other on side trips they had taken. West told of a visit to the villa of General Murat, who had married Bonaparte's youngest sister. Farington inspected Madame Recamier's chateau in her absence and rode out to Versailles, which he found was very much run down; the Petit Trianon, favorite residence of the late queen of France, was being rented out at £300 a year as a place of public entertainment. Farington and West together visited the progressive school for the deaf and dumb being operated by the Abbé Roche-Ambroise Sicard, and they took a two-day excursion that included a tour of the state-owned Gobelin tapestry manufactory in the faubourg St. Marcel. Young William Turner reappeared after an absence of several weeks to tell of a strange expedition. He had traveled to Lyon (four days) and thence to Grenoble (one day) and into Switzerland, where he did what few artists had cared to do before him. He sketched and painted the mountains below Mont Blanc, the rocks and precipices, the wide 80-foot falls at Schaffhausen; and instead of finding them gloomy and repellent, he declared that they were "romantic and strikingly grand."

The chief object of attention and gossip was not women, nor art, nor artists; it was Bonaparte, the conqueror of Italy, the grand monarch of France, the pacificator of Europe. Everyone wished to see him, to be in the same room with him, by whatever right or stratagem. On August 18, before the arrival of most of the artists, William Beckford had infuriated his fellow Englishmen by obtaining a place in Bonaparte's official procession of thanksgiving to celebrate his birthday, his new title of "First Consul for Life," the restoration of peace, and the anniversary of the restoration of religion. Thomas Phillips, the portrait painter, scored a success when he obtained a letter from the archbishop of Lyon, Bonaparte's uncle, and used it to get into the monthly public dinner given on the day the first consul reviewed the Paris garrison. Phillips told his spellbound audience that when Bonaparte was served anything, he did not raise his head until he had eaten it, and that before he

---

[3] Emmet appeared in Paris the following month and became convinced in a meeting with Bonaparte that the Peace of Amiens would be of short duration and that a French invasion of England might be expected the following August. After an uprising in Dublin that miscarried, Emmet was hanged for treason in September 1803.

did raise his head he looked around under his eyebrows. Martin Shee managed to get into the Presence Chamber of the Consular Palace, where he saw Bonaparte distributing medals to the prize winners in the industrial exhibition. He stood for one hour and twenty minutes within six feet of Bonaparte "without any other person intervening to obstruct my view ... This long and complete view of Bonaparte is a favour which no other strangers, however high their rank, have been able to obtain." His figure, Shee felt, was not very good, but his face was "handsome, sedate, steady and determined." Kemble, whose countenance closely resembled Bonaparte's, observed that the lower part of his face was often smiling and always agreeable, but that his eyes never smiled or indicated pleasure. Fox told his friends that on being introduced to Bonaparte, he found him "easy and desirous to please without effort." In one particular only did he notice the manner of a man who acted as a superior; Bonaparte sometimes put questions and did not wait for the answers before he asked other questions. Mr. and Mrs. Hoppner had obtained a card to the head porter of the Palace of the Tuileries, and they took Farington with them to see the first consul's private apartment in his absence. They saw busts of Charles James Fox and Lord Nelson in one of the bedchambers. Farington got a good view of Bonaparte at the monthly grand review in the Place du Carousel. ("I thought his general appearance better than I expected ... He was dressed in blue, much more plain than his officers, which gave him additional consequence ... He looked much like a lieutenant of our Navy.") Of the grand review one month later he wrote

> The troops were passing before him in a state of the highest display, and the most exact order, with trumpets and musick, which had a very military effect ... He did not pay the least attention to the troops but confined himself [to petitions that had been given him]. When these were disposed of ... he looked at the troops as they passed but without any seeming interest or closeness of observation. It was more like a man waiting for a ceremony to be over which occupied little of his regard.
>
> ... I noticed that he picked his nose very much — sometimes took snuff, and would take off his hat and wipe his forehead in a careless manner. I also remarked that some of the officers occasionally spoke to him, *without his having addressed them,* and seemed only to be making such remarks as persons who are on an easy footing do to each other ...
>
> Bonaparte entered the Palace ... and passed me so close that I could have touched him. His eye having glanced upon strangers, when he came opposite to me he looked me full in the face.

Each visitor had his story to tell of seeing Bonaparte, but West was the only English artist who actually met and conversed with him. It happened when a government official told him that he should hurry to the Salon, for the great man was about to make a visit there and would honor Mr. West by stopping to look at *La Morte sur le Cheval Pâle*. He was standing nearby when the entourage came into the gallery and made its way to his picture. Bonaparte studied the work for a moment and asked the name of the artist. The minister of the interior brought West forward and introduced him. Bonaparte acknowledged the introduction in French. (He spoke no English.) West replied in Italian, explaining that he did not know French well enough to speak to him in that language. Bonaparte hoped (in Italian) that Mr. West had found Paris agreeable. West said he had found Paris very agreeable. Bonaparte expressed his approval of the picture. West thanked him. The entourage moved on. West, at a signal from the minister, followed along, the French dignitaries and artists making a place for him. They walked through the exhibition of drawings and models, descended the fine staircase of the Louvre, and entered the Gallery of Statues. Bonaparte stopped at the *Apollo Belvedere*. Someone remarked that Apollo required Venus. Bonaparte replied that Venus would soon attend him, for she was on her way. (The *Venus dei Medici* had been appropriated from the Uffizi Palace in Rome and was being shipped from Palermo to Marseille.) Though Bonaparte looked at a number of the works of art, West felt (as Farington had) that he was not deeply interested and that his mind was elsewhere. West made small drawings of Bonaparte, three-quarter length, and of his carriage.

A few days later, when West gave a large luncheon party, he was disappointed that Fuseli and several other Academicians did not accept his invitation. He mentioned it to Farington and discovered that once again he was in bad repute with his colleagues. The artists had taken "much umbrage," Farington said, that West had not told them that Bonaparte was to attend the exhibition, so that they might have seen him at close range and in a convenient setting. West sighed and explained that the notice he received was so short that he had not had time to tell anyone.

It was a time of teas and dinners and "conversations" exchanged among the Parisians and the British artists. Vivant Denon gave a dinner that Farington found "very handsome, in the French manner." The fourteen administrators of the Paris museums tendered a "fraternal banquet" at the Hôtel de Marigny at which West and Kemble were the guests of honor. Lavelle, the father of the secre-

THE BATTLE OF LA HOGUE, 1778. The picture marks the victory of the British over the naval forces of Louis XIV in 1692. On the king's order, West was taken to Spithead to watch several warships maneuver and fire broadsides while he made notes and sketches. The *Morning Post* praised the picture but deplored the undignified conduct of some of the combatants, including the sword-brandishing English Rear Admiral George Rooke. *National Gallery of Art, Andrew W. Mellon Fund, 1959.*

A detail from THE BATTLE OF LA HOGUE. William Williams, West's first teacher in Philadelphia, posed for the half-naked seaman in the boat.

John Passmore the Younger: BENJAMIN WEST'S PICTURE GALLERY, ca. 1828. West's two feckless sons spent some £2000 they did not have to build West's New Gallery, designed by John Nash. The gallery was considered a model for the most advanced concepts in displaying and lighting pictures. *Wadsworth Atheneum, Hartford, Ella Gallup Sumner and Mary Catlin Sumner Collection.*

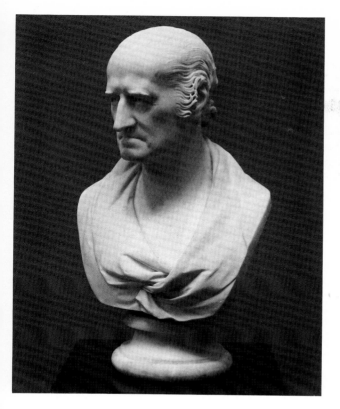

Sir Francis Legatt Chantrey: BUST OF BENJAMIN WEST, 1818. In April, 1814, at a gathering of some 150 artists, patrons, and royal visitors, Thomas Lawrence remarked that West's features showed "a strength of character and expression" seen in no others. *Royal Academy of Arts.*

George Dance: THOMAS LAWRENCE, West's successor in 1820 as president of the Royal Academy.

SELF-PORTRAIT, 1819. West's last self-portrait, painted in his eighty-first year shortly before his death. *National Collection of Fine Arts, Smithsonian Institution.*

tary of the Central Museum of Arts, read a long poem composed in English especially for the occasion, calling West "the Vien of the Thames," after the eighty-six-year-old painter and teacher, David's master, Joseph Marie Vien, and containing the lines:

> *Go West divine, where Thames in grandeur rolls,*
> *Waft the new hopes that spring from Gallic souls . . .*
> *O West! where'er we own thy wondrous mind,*
> *It breathes a sacred lesson to mankind.*

Farington discharged some social obligations with a dinner. "After our French visitors had left us," he wrote, "we had some stout English conversation." West and his friends, apparently on the introduction of Joel Barlow, were taken up by Miss Helen Maria Williams, a leading hostess among those with advanced political ideas. An Englishwoman, she had visited Paris in 1788 and stayed to become a French citizen and to join the Revolution as a friend of the leading Girondists and an intimate of Madame Roland.[4] At her salon West met the notorious Lady Oxford, her constant escort, Arthur O'Connor, and other assorted fugitive Irish revolutionaries.

West responded with a large "public breakfast" on Sunday, September 26. He gave it, he wrote later in an autobiographical note, "to make a proper return of their civilities and to maintain with becoming dignity his station." Some forty guests began to arrive between twelve and one — persons he described as "of great eminence in arts and science with their wives and friends, as well as those of marked abilities whom the fine arts had attracted to Paris . . . The entertainment was truly elegant." Farington and Shee were the only other Academicians present. At three o'clock thirty-seven of the guests adjourned to another room and sat down to what Farington described as "a very elegant cold collation, served up in a very handsome manner, with the best wines, champagne, etc." West sat between the two most beautiful women in the room: Madame Vigée-Lebrun on his left and beyond her Joel Barlow; and Lady Oxford on his right, beyond her Arthur O'Connor. ("Such an association," Farington wrote, "does not pass unremarked.") Farington sat between Jean Antoine Houdon, the

---

[4] Miss Williams was the author of a novel, *Julia* (made into the play *The Lady of Lyons* by Bulwer Lytton) and of several political works explaining and justifying the French Revolution. She was imprisoned by Robespierre and narrowly escaped the guillotine. She was living with John Hurford Stone, a disciple of Dr. Joseph Priestley who was now a political refugee. She lies buried beside him in the Père Lachaise Cemetery.

famous sculptor, and John Kemble, the famous tragedian.[5] Helen Maria Williams sat beside Thomas Erskine (who had distinguished himself defending Thomas Paine in London). John Stone, her protector, sat beside Mrs. Barlow. Farington was much taken by Madame LaHarpe, whose Swiss husband was tutor to the young emperor, Alexander I of Russia; her countenance was "sweet and interesting, her manner modest, easy and natural, yet with an air of refinement" — in strong contrast "to the *assured* vivacity of Madame Le Brun and the too-affected and laboured civilities of Miss H. Williams." A Mr. Brown was there from America, undoubtedly Charles Brockden Brown, disciple of Mary Wollstonecraft, friend of Joel Barlow, and author of America's first novels.

Michael Torcia, an Italian novelist who had lived two years in England, said that anyone who wished to be a man should go to England for three or four years, because "that country exhibits a model for mankind." He called across the table to Erskine to inform him that he resembled the bust of Demosthenes. Erskine said he doubted there was a resemblance, but if his features were similar to those of that champion of liberty, he hoped they would never change. This response was greeted by applause, both when it was spoken and when it was translated into French. Joel Barlow, Farington observed, was tall and bony, "his countenance ill-favoured but his look thoughtful and shrewd." With others, Farington said, he had "proved to the world the danger of endeavouring to carry visionary theories into practice, at the risk of all the horror of bloodshed and confusion." The breakfast ended at five o'clock and the company separated. Farington was committed to go next day to see the pictures of Madame Vincent, who, West said, painted better than Madame Lebrun.

Thomas Erskine left Paris for home on October 8, happy that he had been presented again to Bonaparte, who this time conversed with him for a while through an interpreter and so healed "the sore on his mind." Farington and his party began their return the same day, traveling in a diligence that made six miles an hour and was more roomy than a coach. To carry them the forty miles from Rouen to Dieppe, they hired a cabriolet, which cost an exorbitant four guineas and was "the most uneasy, jolting conveyance that can be imagined." A heavy rain began to come down. Halls, the young Academy student, had to sit on the roof and suffered most, "but he was young and could endure." Fuseli, whose temper was

---

[5] In his diary that night Farington, as was his custom, drew a diagram showing the place of each guest at the two tables.

already "feverish" from the misery of having his limbs imprisoned and his body jolted, now found that he was wedged into a corner where a steady stream of water leaked from the roof and down his shoulder. "The postillions stopped," Farington wrote, "at the uproar among us ... France was never so denounced before. The extremity of [Fuseli's] fury left us nothing to say, and to laugh would have been dangerous." They waited a day and a half for a fair wind for England. When he stepped ashore from the packet at Brighton, Farington knew he had come from disorder to order, from confusion to convenience, from subjection to freedom. "All appeared appropriate and substantial, and every man seemed respectable because his distinct and proper character was consistently maintained. What must be the nature of that mind that would not feel grateful that it was his lot to be an Englishman?"

West and his son left Paris at five in the morning on October 4, four days before Farington and Erskine, concluding a six weeks' visit. He was buoyed up by one great success of his trip. His main purpose in going to Paris had been to obtain help for young English artists who would now be traveling there to study; and he had come to a happy agreement with French museum administrators that "any young man who comes recommended to them by the President of the Royal Academy of London, will be admitted to all the advantages granted to French artists for the purpose of study."

The agreement was without effect, for the Peace of Amiens lasted only six more months. Bonaparte, fortified by 60 million francs received from the United States for the Louisiana Territory, made demands on the English that he knew to be unacceptable: to curb the attacks on him in the British press and to expel the French refugees in their country. He had annexed Elba and much of Northern Italy during the truce. In February 1803 he reoccupied Switzerland. On March 13 he publicly insulted the British ambassador. He began maneuvers that led to the occupation of Hanover, ruled by George III. When Britain declared war in May and seized two French ships, Bonaparte arrested every British male in France between the ages of eighteen and sixty as prisoners of war — tourists, traders, and Benjamin West's art students. The last of them were freed ten years later, after the battlefields of Europe had been littered with 500,000 French corpses.

20

"A Matter of Passion and Contest"

I believe no other people hate, envy and despise one another like painters.

JAMES NORTHCOTE
September 11, 1778

WEST PREPARED a formal "memorandum" for the king on his trip to Paris. He had gone there, he wrote on October 15, 1802, out of a sense of duty as head of the Royal Academy and with two objectives: to see what art works had been brought to the Paris galleries, and to determine on what footing professional men could be permitted to study them. He was happy to inform His Majesty that the assembled art works were in perfect condition, that the French officials had treated him with great liberality, and that the galleries were now open to the youth of England with the same advantages as those enjoyed by French students.

Very soon after his return from Paris, he learned that the king and the court were fully informed of his other activities — of his friendship with American radicals, his association with Irish revolutionaries, his praise of improved conditions in France, his meeting with Bonaparte. The rumor spread that Bonaparte had assigned him an apartment in the Louvre. From time to time His Majesty inquired of visitors, "Who were the artists that went to France?" though he knew their names very well. "The King's mind," a nobleman told his artist friends, "is prejudiced against those members of the Academy who have been to Paris, as being democratical." The king was surely informed when West dined in December with General Antoine-Françoise Andréossy, French ambassador in London, and heard that after the dessert a bust of Bonaparte was placed on the table. (It was, said a Major Rennel, who was there, "like singing God Save the King."] West's adversaries in the Academy, who were about to launch a first major effort to take control from what they called the Prevailing Party, had been making effective use of his addiction to "French principles."

West, in fact, had been so perturbed by charges made against him that on April 5, 1802, some four months before leaving for Paris, he had addressed a poignant letter to the king in which he sought to bring the charges into the open and to expose those who were making them. There was a plan, he wrote, "laid to degrade the profession of which I am at the head (sanctioned there by your Majesty) and to lessen me in the good opinion of your Majesty, your family, and the country."

> I have been recently told by one of the great movers of that plan that, "he knew your Majesty had disgraced me and that he believed it was owing to my politics and want of loyalty." My reply to this positive assertion was that such an event was unknown to me; that there must be some mistake, as the King was ever gracious to me on my approaching his presence; that if his mind was thus impressed towards me it must be owing to some cause of which I was ignorant and unconscious of having given any offence . . .
>
> If any unfavourable impression has been made on your Majesty's mind towards me, the greatest favour you can grant will be to signify what are the causes which have produced them that I may stand acquitted or condemned, or that those who have with so much confidence asserted my disgrace may be made sensible of their error.
>
> Would your Majesty be graciously pleased to permit me to give an account of what has been my language and conduct for the last thirty years respecting my attachment to your Majesty, your illustrious family, and this country?

Not wishing to press on the king's time and goodness, he asked if he might make that statement to any one or two persons the king had confidence in. He suggested the earls of Harcourt or Leicester, or others more private, such as Dr. John Fisher (soon to be bishop of Exeter) or the Reverend C. de Guiffardière (a French Protestant minister, one of the court preachers). "Or will your Majesty be graciously pleased to *signify to me at the present moment* that I have nothing to apprehend from the *malignant intrigues of those* who have sought my ruin in the completion of their plans?" There is no record of any response made by the king or his courtiers.

On February 19, 1803, West received a stern letter from five disaffected Academicians. The Academy's laws, they said, called for the Council to have the *entire* direction and *management* of all the business of the society. The Council had deviated from the law on January 15 when it asked the General Assembly to appoint a Committee of Inquiry to study a possible increase in pay and allowances of certain officers. Such matters were the Council's responsibility, and it had no authority to delegate such power to the Assembly. The five members — Sandby, Cosway, Rigaud, Beechey, and Tresham — formally requested the president to summon a Council meeting to reconsider its action.

West was perplexed and alarmed; he took the letter to Farington and asked his advice. He felt he should comply with the request, he said, as it seemed to be an attack of some kind, one designed to implicate him in an improper action. What did Mr. Farington think? Mr. Farington, who thought that Mr. West was being timid, advised him to do only what seemed best for himself. He concluded from the letter that those who were trying to take over control of the Academy now felt they had a majority on the Council and meant to show it by refusing to receive the report of the Assembly-appointed Committee of Inquiry. Lawrence and Smirke were called into the discussion, and they persuaded West to refuse to summon the Council on a technical point. He agreed, Lawrence drafted the letter of denial, and, to improve the hour, West "showed us his process of painting which he prefers to all former modes he had adopted."

Whether the four men realized it or not, they were now joined in a battle between those who were running the Academy and those who intended to run it. The rebels, led by Copley, were basing their attack on a constitutional issue: Who was to rule — the eight-man Council, or the forty members of the Assembly? A by-law did indeed say that the Council "shall have the entire direction and management of all the business of the society." The Council's decisions, however, had to be approved by the Assembly. Which of the two held the ultimate authority? What were the rights of the members in relationship to their executive body? The questions had never been tested.

The new Council for 1803 was evenly divided: It had four rebels (Copley, Wyatt, Bourgeois, and Yenn) and four adherents to the party in power (Ozias Humphry, Charles Rossi, John Soane, and William Turner). Humphry, however, was ill and often absent, Turner was erratic in his vote, and Soane was giving indications that he might defect. The rebels had decided to make their challenge in the Council, where Tresham two years earlier had won the victory on rotation of members that now promised to give them control of both the new Council and the Academy. First, they would demand that the controlling power be shifted from the Assembly to the Council. The party in power, of course, would refuse. Then they would demand that the issue be taken to the king, where they were confident that they would have enough influence to obtain a ruling in their favor. They would show that the party in power was not only by-passing the Council, but was evading it by use of special committees staffed with their friends and adherents.

West called a meeting of the Council on March 4, 1803 for the sole purpose of hearing the report of the Committee of Inquiry on pay increases. The four rebel councilmen refused to hear it. After a long debate, a vote was taken; it produced a three-to-three tie. (Yenn abstained, because an increase in his salary as treasurer was involved.) When West cast the deciding vote in favor of hearing the report, one of the rebels whipped out a prepared protest, read it aloud, and with his three colleagues walked out of the Council Room. West called in Farington and the six other committee members who had been waiting some four hours in a side room and told them their report could not be received, because he now had no quorum in the Council.

West received a letter on March 6 from Copley and his three colleagues requesting him to go to the king, "accompanied by the proper officers according to the laws of the Academy," and learn His Majesty's opinion on the conflict between the Council and the Assembly. If Mr. West declined to do so, they would go directly to the king themselves.

John Opie presided over a meeting of the General Assembly on March 12, West being seriously ill with influenza. All the rebel members were absent. The seventeen members who were present expressed "strong disapprobation" of the four councilmen and, on a motion of Hoppner and Shee, voted to call a meeting devoted solely to deciding what should be done about their rebellious conduct.

On March 19, with Opie again in the chair and the rebels absent, the members voted unanimously to censure the four councilmen "for conduct that was disrespectful of His Majesty."

At this point, before the conflict could be brought to a conclusion, two new developments brought West and Copley, the main Academy antagonists, to a violent and highly visible personal collision. Both developments had to do with pictures they entered in the 1803 exhibition.

Copley had accepted a commission in the summer of 1800 to paint the family of Sir Edward Knatchbull, eighth baronet of the name, member of Parliament for Kent. The canvas was to contain

Sir Edward with several hunting dogs and dead game birds, his ten children, and his two deceased wives somehow represented. Sir Edward thought the picture might be painted in a month; he was quite alarmed when Copley told him he hoped to complete it within a year. Sir Edward made an advance payment of £750. There was no mention of what the total cost would be.

Copley spent much of that autumn at the Knatchbull mansion at Mersham Hatch, near Ashford in Kent, making sketches and portraits for a canvas that would be 18 feet wide and 12 feet high. He was much pleased with "the hospitable and polite reception" he received from the Knatchbulls. Sir Edward was polite but mystified at the ways of artists. Mr. Copley, he later told West, spent ten days of his time at Mersham trying to decide whether a certain wall in the house would hold the picture, and he "seldom began to paint before 11 or 12 o'clock, appearing to be a very long time in setting his pallet."

Copley was a notoriously slow worker, but a series of unusual events delayed completion of *The Knatchbull Family* far beyond his one-year estimate. Norton, the second son, was away for extended periods on naval service. Sir Edward married again in April 1801, this time choosing twenty-year-old Mary Hawkins (he was forty-five), and he asked that she be included in the picture, which, of course, required considerable rearrangement and repainting of the other figures. An eleventh child arrived in 1802, and it too joined its half brothers and half sisters in the canvas.

The Knatchbull picture was of special importance to Copley, and he worked hard on it. For one thing, he needed the prestige of another triumph, for his portrait commissions were lagging and his recent history pictures had won only moderate success. For another, he had suffered a run of bad luck over the past ten years and was seriously short of money. His George Street establishment was expensive and times were hard for all artists during the unending war. Like West, he had lost heavily in the declining sale of engravings on the Continent. He had suffered a grievous loss of time, money, and reputation in 1801 when he refused to pay Jean Mari Delattre £650 for what he believed was an inferior engraving of his *Death of Chatham*; Delattre sued and collected £650 and his court costs, though West, testifying for Copley, told the jury the engraving was "utterly destitute" of correctness in the likenesses. When the Council ruled in 1799 that Copley owed the Academy £24 for tickets to the king's birthday dinner he had received as a steward, he signed a sixty-day note for the amount. When Trumbull pressed him for payment of a £50 loan he had made thirty months earlier,

Copley was affronted at the request and said he could not pay.

West told Farington that in the course of painting the Knatch-bull picture, Copley

> frequently applied to him for his opinion upon it, saying there was no other so good. He said that when he first saw the picture the figures appeared like so *many pokers,* there being nothing to *mass* and *unite* them. The composition was too much for Copley who did not know what to do with it. He (West) recommended to him to introduce the large mass of *red* in the *center* which gave vigor and effect to the whole.

Copley finished *The Knatchbull Family* at the end of 1802, but on April 2, six days before the sending-in day for the exhibition, he asked the Council for additional time, giving as his reason the concern he felt for the safety of so large a picture. The extension was granted by a margin of one vote. Eight members at once wrote a formal protest and sent it to West, who forwarded it to the Council with a strong letter of his own. Two years earlier, he pointed out, the Council had quite properly refused Lawrence a similar indulgence for his portrait of the Princess of Wales, though the princess herself had joined in the request.

When the Assembly took up the matter a few days later, with Copley present, West was absent, but a letter from him was read aloud; he sharply opposed the decision to grant additional time and, mentioning Copley by name, he censured the four rebel councilmen who had voted for it. The Assembly responded by voting a motion that the four had acted contrary to the interests of the Academy, whereas Turner, Soane, and Rossi were entitled to thanks "for having endeavoured, as members of the Council, to maintain the usages and regulations of the Academy." The meeting, Farington was pleased to write, ended "happily and effectually . . . obliging Mr. Copley to comply with the general opinion, and asserting the authority of the General Assembly" over the Council. Copley gave in and agreed to send in his work at once.

He delivered the picture even though after weeks of trying he still did not have Sir Edward's permission to place it on exhibition. There had been gossip about the picture and its problems, with derisive comment on the representation of Sir Edward's two earlier wives, whom Copley showed as angels peering down from heaven on the third, and one may surmise that the gossip and comment were conveyed to Lady Knatchbull by her friends. Scarcely had the picture been hung when Copley and President West each re-

ceived a letter from Sir Edward: The picture had been sent to the
Academy without his knowledge or consent and it must be immediately withdrawn from the exhibition. Copley made the hu-
miliating request at the next Council meeting. He had written to
Sir Edward, he explained, and asked his permission, and, receiving
no answer, assumed there would be no objection. The secretary
read a letter from Mr. West on the matter: The picture could not
be withdrawn, for the Hanging Committee had completed its work
and the catalogue was ready for the printer. Permission was given,
nevertheless, to withdraw the picture. The catalogue was revised
and the Hanging Committee went back to work to fill a very large
blank space on a wall of the Great Room.

The Knatchbull episode, in the meantime, had attracted so much
attention that the king commanded Copley to take *The Knatchbull
Family* to Buckingham House for a royal viewing. West saw him
waiting there beside his picture when he went to learn His Majesty's pleasure about visiting the exhibition.

Copley's next step was to send Sir Edward a bill for 1800 guineas,
with a credit shown for the £750 already paid.

The Knatchbull affair was interwoven with a second and more
serious development in the conflict between West and Copley.

In October 1802 West had begun work on *Hagar and Ishmael in
the Wilderness,* a picture he intended for the spring exhibition.
It was a Biblical subject, a favorite of artists — the story of Hagar,
the Egyptian concubine, the mother of Ishmael, Abraham's oldest
son, who, through the jealousy of Abraham's wife Sarah was driven
with her child into the wilderness, where an angel saved her from
death. He had painted the subject in 1776 and sold it to Viscount
Cremorne, who bought it because the young Ishmael bore a strong
resemblance to his own son. When his son died, Lord Cremorne,
distressed at seeing the figure that recalled him, disposed of the
work to another collector, from whom West bought it. Seeing it
again after several decades, he decided to "reconsider and repaint"
the work. It was an oil-on-canvas 76 by 54–1/2 inches in size. He
erased the angel and painted a new one with a different placement,
pose, and facial expression, altered the face of Ishmael, introduced
new dress, and changed the background. In the lower left corner he
painted "B. West 1803." He did not bother to paint out the "B. West
1776" in the lower right.

Copley was working on the acceptance and rejection of pictures
submitted for the spring exhibition when he came upon West's
Hagar and Ishmael. He recognized the work, for it had hung in the

1776 Academy exhibition, the first in which he had participated after arriving in Europe. He checked the 1776 catalogue and found the work listed. It was a serious breach of Academy rules and ethics to submit a work that had already been exhibited. West had placed in Copley's hands the means by which he might be humiliated, as Copley had been humiliated in recent years. Perhaps West might even be driven from his position of power in the Academy.

West was well enough on April 14 to attend and take the chair at a Council meeting. Part way through the session, a messenger delivered an envelope for Mr. West. It was from his wife and it contained an article from that day's *Morning Post*, reprinted in the evening *Courier*. It accused him of deliberate intent to defraud:

> The Hanging Committee of the Royal Academy has been exposed to the most distressing dilemma ... It happened that among the productions of art lately sent to Somerset House, was a large historical picture from the pencil of the President ... This picture was immediately recognized and challenged by one of the members of the Council. He stated that it was ... publicly exhibited in the year 1776. Upon the front, however, of the picture was written in strong characters, according to the usual practice of the artist, his name, together with the date, 1803; and, upon the *faith of this inscription*, it was determined that the performance should be received.
>
> Some doubts, however, still remaining, the catalogues were inspected, and it was found that a painting, descriptive of the same story, had been exhibited by Mr. West in 1776. This led to a second and more minute examination of the picture; the result of which was, that the date 1776 was discovered in an obscure corner *imperfectly obliterated*. The Members of the Council, indignant at this deception, regarded each other for some time in silent astonishment.

The heavily ironic close mocked West's lack of a formal education:

> At length it was resolved, that the Secretary should write to the President, requesting him to withdraw the performance. To this letter, no answer has yet been received. It is said, however, that the President, who is a *scholar* as well as a painter, meditates a concise and classical reply. *Haec decies repetita placebit*,[1] will be sufficiently expressive of the just confidence which he feels in the merits of the picture.

---

[1] This [picture] having been renewed ten times will be pleasing.

There is no record of what West did or said on the evening of April 14 after reading this attack, but the following day he prepared for the Council a temperate letter of protest and explanation. He admitted that *Hagar and Ishmael* had been exhibited in 1776, though he had forgotten the fact, and said he was aware that it was contrary to the laws of the Academy to submit a picture that had already been exhibited. He told of the changes he had made in the work, "so that in every respect it is a new picture."[2] The fact that he did not erase the earlier date, he pointed out, was proof that he had not acted with any intent to deceive the Council, but rather in the full expectation that it would be viewed as a new picture. He understood that the Council members, seeing the earlier date, could not have done otherwise than reject the picture. Unfortunately, the secretary had not written him as instructed. Had he done so, "you would have received my answer and the business would undoubtedly have been adjusted to our mutual satisfaction." But the secretary's "unaccountable neglect" had kept him "in a state of ignorance for six days," at a time when he was confined to his home by illness. He relied on the justice of the Council members and trusted they would give the picture a place in the present exhibition.

In response to West's protest, John Soane, attempting to act as a peacemaker, prepared what he thought was a conciliatory letter for the press and gave it to his fellow councilmen to approve. With Copley in the chair, they proceeded to "correct" it. John Richards, the secretary, described the situation in a letter to West:

> I know not whether I am capable of writing to be understood; I am so unwell — so perplexed — foiled, and deranged in our proceedings on a business I consider myself engaged to see completed.
>
> Those gentlemen here today have been wrangling the greatest part of it, and have but just now come to a Resolution, that a Council be summoned for tomorrow evening, which I have assured them I cannot do without your direction, but will, by having your direction. Pray Sir, let me have your answer.

Soane's revised letter, signed by Copley as deputy chairman, Soane, Bourgeois, Turner, Rossi, and Humphry, appeared in *The True Briton* the same day:

---

[2] X-rays of *Hagar and Ishmael* by the Metropolitan Museum of Art, and comparison with a drawing made as a study for the original version (in the Victoria and Albert Museum), verify that West made the changes he described.

The Council of the Royal Academy feel themselves compelled to notice a paragraph in the *Morning Post* of yesterday, of an unwarrantable kind, levelled at the President and at the Royal Academy at large. [A summary of the first part of the Hagar story followed.]

The Secretary was directed to communicate the circumstances immediately to Mr. West, in writing, which, in the hurry of preparing for the exhibition, he omitted to do; and it is to be observed that the first intimation Mr. West had of the paragraph [in the *Post*] was through the medium of an evening paper (the *Courier*), sent to him at the Royal Academy yesterday evening, being the first time his health had permitted him to attend since the picture was sent for the exhibition.

The newspaper referred to states, "The members of the Council, indignant at the deception, regarded each other with silent astonishment." This circumstance the Council positively deny. The illness of the President naturally suggested itself to the Council as the cause of the mistake — a mistake which deprives the exhibition of the picture, as the usual practice of the Academy expressly forbids the second exhibition of any picture whatever.

It is necessary to observe that Mr. West states that he is in the habit of altering and repainting his pictures, adding the date of the year in which the alterations are made. Upon this principle the picture of *Hagar and Ishmael* has been altered, and, in a great degree, repainted, and the name and year added.

Farington, of course, recognized that this subtly adverse explanation hurt more than it helped. "The charge has done great harm to West," he wrote, "and the *exculpation* has confirmed it. A statement of great folly."

West had not mentioned in his protest to the Council the action he resented the most. "Who," he asked wrathfully, "was the member who divulged to the *Morning Post* what passed in Council concerning the picture and its dates?" The members-at-large took up this question, and it became a part of the Academy's larger struggle between the Council and the Assembly. In the next several weeks these developments took place.

April 19: The *True Briton* identified Copley as the "industrious man" who discovered that *Hagar* had already been exhibited and gave the story to the *Post*. (It happened to be the day on which Copley obtained permission to withdraw *The Knatchbull Family*.) Copley asked the editor to retract the story; the editor refused but offered to run any statement Copley cared to make.

April 21: The Council, on a motion of Sir Francis Bourgeois, reaffirmed its decision to reject *Hagar* as an inadmissible picture.

April 25: West, returning to the Assembly for the first time in a month, made two warm statements. With Copley in the audience, he assailed a member (unnamed) who had "deranged and embarrassed" the Academy by removing a picture from the Great Room after it had been hung for the exhibition, thereby making it unlikely that the catalogue could be produced in time for the opening. And he told his side of the *Hagar* story — of the "malignant statements" in the papers, the effect on the minds of the public, the unaccountable six-day delay in notifying him that his picture had been thrown out. "Had I sent it," he declared, "to be inspected by artists who were competent to judge without prejudice, they would have seen *that it was a new picture. It is not the rejection of the picture that I complain of — but the malignant principles and shameful neglect attending the rejection.*" He called for an investigation: Which member or members had revealed confidential Academy business to the *Morning Post*? A little before midnight the meeting adjourned until the next evening. At this Assembly John Flaxman acted as secretary in place of Richards, who was "debilitated."

April 26: With twenty-four members present, including Copley, West read his statement again. There was "strong speaking" against the rebels by Flaxman and Shee and a recommendation that the eight members of the Council should "vindicate their characters" by taking an oath that they had not leaked the information to the *Post.*

April 27: In an unprecedented third consecutive daily Assembly meeting, sixteen members unanimously approved a Farington-Flaxman resolution exonerating the president from the charges made in the *Post.* On the same day a letter to *The True Briton* signed "Candidus" compared Copley's action on *The Knatchbull Family* to West's on *Hagar and Ishmael,* greatly to Copley's disadvantage. It charged that Copley had known for several months that Sir Edward would not permit his picture to be exhibited; that Copley sent it to the Academy despite this knowledge and contrary to Sir Edward's express injunction; and that at one time he declared himself to be the owner of the picture, though he was unwilling to reaffirm the claim.

April 28: Richards sent a press release to the *Post, Courier, Herald, Times,* and *True Briton* declaring that in the opinion of the General Assembly Mr. West "had in no respect acted with the least intention to depart from the rules and usage of the Academy," as alleged in many *anonymous* statements. Sir George Beaumont told Farington, "Much is said against West for his supposed deception about his picture."

May 3: The Assembly voted unanimously (the rebels being absent) that the members of the Council "be called to exonerate themselves from the accusation which lays upon them" by signing a declaration of innocence. On the same day Copley sent a letter to West asking whether he had complied with the request of the four Council members on March 10 that he learn His Majesty's opinion on the Council-Assembly conflict. They had allowed him extra time to do this, he said, because of his ill health.

May 4: West replied to Copley. He did not intend to learn His Majesty's opinion on the matter because (1) the Committee of Inquiry had acted under the Council, and the Council could receive or reject its report; (2) the committee no longer existed; (3) his attendance on His Majesty must be made by a decision of the Assembly or the Council and not by the request of one or more individual members.

May 9: West received a letter from John Soane as a kind of notice that he had gone over to the rebels; he deplored that the Assembly was breaking the law by taking away the independence of the Council.

May 12: At an Assembly boycotted by the rebels, Rossi read a declaration of innocence he and Flaxman had prepared. After some objections were answered and alterations made, Humphry, Rossi, and Turner signed. They were officially praised for their conduct and exonerated "fully from any imputation of suspicion" in a resolution that was distributed to every Academician.

Farington told Shee that he now felt "an unwillingness to subject myself to that exposure which the members are now liable to from communicating to newspapers." Shee told him that if he, Farington, "was to quit the Academy it would not stand three years."

May 14: West told Farington that he was not willing to go to any more Council meetings "under the circumstances that he stands to some members of it."

May 24: Humphry, Turner, and Rossi did not attend a scheduled meeting because the agenda dealt only with unimportant matters; West was laid up with the gout. Copley presided and, ignoring the agenda, he delivered a ringing declaration of rights. The Council, he said, had "the sole direction and management of the business of the Academy"; they were "not responsible collectively or individually to the General Assembly for anything they do as councilmen." The Council approved his declaration. The plan was to keep the vote a secret, confirm it, as required, at a second meeting to be held two days later, and then order West to carry it to the king for his sanction.

May 26: West asked Farington to call on him. He had learned about the rebel plan (presumably from Richards) and he asked what he should do. If the declaration was confirmed at a second Council meeting, Farington said, West would become involved in great difficulties, for if he did not take it to the king, the rebels would, and the king would probably support them. In his opinion, West should postpone the Council meeting until further notice and should refuse to sign the Council minutes. The question raised by Copley's declaration was one of such great importance that it should be referred to the General Assembly. The whole membership could then consider it — and the conduct of those who proposed to smuggle it in secrecy to the king.

May 28: West wrote to Copley to inform him and his colleagues that he had suspended meetings of the Council until further notice. The resolution they had passed, he said, was without any previous notice and without knowledge of the other Academicians. He held it a duty he owed to the station he filled, therefore, to place it before the entire membership.

May 30: A historic meeting of the Assembly was attended by nineteen members and boycotted by the ten others who were in opposition. West recounted the action taken by the Council six days earlier. The members held that the Council's view of its own supremacy was "monstrous and inconsistent with the laws of the Academy," and they resolved unanimously that the conduct of Copley, Wyatt, Bourgeois, Yenn, and Soane "has rendered it expedient to suspend *pro tempore* the said members from their functions as Councillors of the Royal Academy."

June 9: The five suspended members notified West that they were presenting a memorial on their suspension to the king. West so notified the Assembly. Farington began to prepare a voluminous countermemorial to the king from the Assembly.

The issue was now out of the control of the two conflicting groups and in the hands of the king and his advisors. In choosing to take part in this affray, the king opened himself to distress and agitation and increased the intensity of the struggle for control. It is clear now that he would have been wiser if he had stayed apart from the Academy's affairs and allowed the members to resolve their problems, for better or worse, among themselves. Instead he chose to adjudicate the differences; he instructed the lord chancellor to look into the matter and give him an opinion. During the long weeks and months of waiting, the adversaries could do little but watch each other and try to present themselves to the king and his counsel in the best possible light. Farington was pessimistic; he believed "the King is in the hands, as it may be said, of those who oppose us." Dance declared that if the king should decide "to support the few members of Council who go about him and oppose his own laws, it would be most becoming to *quit the Academy.*" West said he was in a state of perfect ease; he was satisfied that the Assembly was doing what was proper and that he had acted as it became him to do.

The Council held no meetings. When the adversaries otherwise came together in meetings, they sat apart from one another, and when they saw each other they were silent. Cosway was the only rebel member with whom West was still on speaking terms. The Assembly appointed a watchdog committee (Farington, Hoppner, Lawrence, and six others) to observe what went on and to "recommend such measures . . . as the occasion shall require." West had proposed that they consult some eminent lawyer "on the nature of our Academical constitution, so that we may fully know what ground we stand on." Farington had opposed the idea because it might be represented to the king as questioning his authority, but at the end of June a lawyer was chosen, and Farington and Hoppner called on him with a portfolio of Academy documents. In the lawyer's opinion, the king could deprive the society of its building but could not touch the funds or deprive the members of their diplomas. He advised the officers to send nothing to the king in the form of a question for his decision, but rather to proceed confidently as the group that was acting within the law to defend the society from attempts to endanger its existence. The king, he observed, had derived a great deal of credit from the Royal Academy at very little expense.

Samuel Pepys Cockerell, whose maternal grandfather was the nephew and heir of the diarist Samuel Pepys, and who was an architect and a candidate to become an A.R.A., asked Farington about the stories of disunion in the Academy. "It is," he was told, "a matter of passion and contest."

West saw the king at Windsor on July 7 and found him in an exceptionally "agreeable disposition of mind." He asked the king if he had been informed that there was some difficulty among the members. The king indeed had heard. It was proper, West said, that he should inform His Majesty that there was a contest of power between the Council and the Assembly. Jealousy, he added, was the cause of the dispute. Some members were active, able, and zealous. Some were indolent or had little competence in business, and they were envious of the others because of the influence they had in the society. The king expressed a fear that the Academy would be injured by it. West assured him that there was no danger

— the interests of the Academy were attended to. If the Council got beyond control, they might expend the money of the society or do other improper things, but it would be a duty of the General Assembly to attend to and prevent that. The king asked if long speeches were not frequently made. West smiled and answered, "Yes, and when they cause the sittings to be protracted to twelve and one o'clock, it is rather fatiguing." The visit ended without any indication of which way the king inclined in the Academy conflict.

Farington's watchdog committee recommended on July 21 that the suspension of the five Council members be extended through the remainder of their terms and that others be appointed to take their places. The Assembly unanimously adopted the recommendation, and it reaffirmed an earlier decision to give another £500 to a fund being collected by Lloyds for the war against France — a donation the rebel councilmen claimed was illegal because it had not been made or approved by the Council. West was instructed to present both resolutions to His Majesty for approval.

He left for Windsor on August 6 with Richards, carrying the two recent resolutions: an address and report to the king that Farington had prepared and all the loyal members had signed (Mrs. West read and approved of it); and a long letter of his own to the king. His letter, which Farington edited for him, began, "In the year 1767 Your Majesty was pleased to notice my efforts in historical painting"; it picked up speed part way through with a blast at "those who willfully or ignorantly act in opposition to the interest of the society"; and it ended in a crescendo with "Awful as I feel my situation to be while the Academy is thus circumstanced, I have endeavoured to act in that manner which has appeared to me to be the most prudent, and with that integrity without which I should be unworthy of the notice of Your Majesty and of the confidence of the Academy." When Farington delivered his edited version of the letter to West, he said that he was prepared for the worst news that West could bring back, for he was convinced that much intrigue had made an unfavorable impression on His Majesty's mind. West agreed; he would not be surprised if the king should say, "What! What! The Council should be paramount!" and turn on his heel.

The king was to receive them in the Queen's Lodge. When West and Richards were shown into the waiting room, they found Copley and Bourgeois sitting there. No conversation took place, and in about ten minutes Bourgeois rose and walked out, and shortly thereafter Copley followed him. (They returned from Windsor, West later learned, without having seen the king.) His Majesty was friendly and talked with them for two and a half hours. West delivered his documents. The king looked at a few pages. He said they were voluminous, that it would require some time to look through them, and that he would consult high legal authority before he made up his mind on them. He then took up West's letter and read through it; on coming to Copley's quoted declaration of rights he said it was "curious." As West reported the next day to Farington and as Farington faithfully recorded: "This opened a conversation, and His Majesty's mind by degrees got into a very good train. The King had an apprehension that there was a disposition to *Anarchy* in the Academy. This West denied and Richards concurred. West dwelt most upon the necessity of maintaining *the laws,* and showing the danger of allowing the Council to be irresponsible." West's *Hagar and Ishmael* came up and the king forced Richards to say who had taken the lead in that matter. Richards named Copley and Bourgeois. The king said, "It was an ill-natured action."

When the vote of £500 to the public subscription was mentioned, the king asked, "Should it not have originated in the Council?" "It was clear from the circumstances," Farington wrote, "that His Majesty had received papers from the opposition." Politics was touched upon. The king said he regulated himself under two principles. The first was that of a superintending Providence and a reliance on religion. The other was that as king he would never seek to extend the power of the throne, or permit the Constitution to be weakened by allowing the privileges of the throne to be entrenched upon. Under these beliefs, he said, "he looked calmly upon the agitated world and laid his head upon his pillow each night with the composure of a child."

West said to Farington that he did not believe there was a better heart in the country than that of the king. "I asked him what he thought of his understanding. He said he was ready in business and attentive to communication, but he *wanted direction in deciding.* I asked what impression is now on his mind as to the result of the present business. He said he certainly left Windsor with a favorable hope as to the issue of it." Farington was not so optimistic. "My apprehensions still continue," he wrote, "that His Majesty's prejudice is against us, and that it will be felt and will influence the authority to which he refers the matter."

21

The Struggle for Power

West is an American, and Copley is an American, and you are an Englishman, and if the Devil had you all I should not care.

KING GEORGE III
to William Beechey,
November 1804

*I*NVASION on a gigantic scale seemed certain in the summer of 1803. The French assembled 175,000 men and a fleet of small boats at Boulogne, and a corps of 117 guide interpreters who spoke and wrote good English. England, the last nation resisting Bonaparte's program to master Europe, mustered 300,000 volunteers to repel France's trained conscript army. All grades of English society were patriotically joining or forming military units, and the members of the Royal Academy, caught up in the enthusiasm, met to discuss how they might serve. On July 29, under the impassioned urging of Martin Shee, they resolved to form their own Military Corps of Artists. The Society of Engravers, swallowing their long resentment at being denied membership in the Academy, offered to unite with the artists in common resistance to tyranny. Committees from the two organizations met. Shee read a plan he had drawn up for organizing the corps. He was not content to resist the threat of invasion from Boulogne. He envisioned, rather, a corps of students, Associates, and Academicians to be equipped and uniformed at their own expense and to be unrestricted in their mission; they might be dispatched on any military service, domestic or foreign, in which the government felt their prowess would be needed. The rumor spread that he planned to induce the Home Office to send the Artists' Corps to Ireland to quell what remained of the Irish rebellion against England.

A discussion followed Shee's reading. He agreed to read each article again separately, while those present made observations. A motion was made that only Academicians should serve on the committee chosen to "direct the business," but Farington and Lawrence obtained a vote that engravers might also serve. Someone proposed that only Academicians should hold the rank of captain or higher. Farington made a counterproposal: Before anything else was decided, they should determine whether those who were appointed captains would really do their duty. There was a pause. Hoppner had said on the way to the meeting that the troubles he foresaw were so great that he would not be able to participate with any spirit. Smirke now said there were major difficulties in Shee's plan. The expense of uniforms, for example, would be greater than many of the artists could afford. The trouble of a command would be more than he would care to undertake, though he might do it. Farington, with unaccustomed optimism, concluded that all the captains would do their duty, and Shee's plan was adopted unanimously. No vote was taken on whether to limit captaincies to Academicians, or on whether to accept the engravers.

At a joint meeting of the two societies several days later, Farington found "a manifest want of spirit in the business." Shee "spoke with some warmth" in expressing his disappointment at the lack of zeal in a time of national crisis. "He made several remarks which I was afraid might be repeated to the disadvantage of the Academy and therefore endeavoured to do away with their possible effect." At this meeting the Academicians politely declined the engravers' offer to unite, and on August 5, 1803, they voted that formation of a military corps of artists would be "inexpedient." Shee did succeed in raising a body of artists at large, but the Home Office declined to accept them, saying there were already too many volunteer units. Shee then signed up as a private in the corps of Bloomsbury Volunteers, which was made up chiefly of lawyers, called itself "The Devil's Own," and never took the field, even to drill in Hyde Park or to march on Hampstead Heath. With Lord Nelson's victory over the French fleet off Cape Trafalgar in October 1805, the need for volunteer units to resist invasion came to an end.

The zeal of the members of the Academy to fight among themselves, however, was still strong. Throughout a summer and autumn in which the members waited for the king's decision on the suspension of the five councilmen, the rebels did not attend Academy meetings; but when they were encountered they were seen to have pleased expressions and a confident manner. Bourgeois told Nollekens, "You will soon have a whipping." There were many rumors. There would be no spring exhibition in 1804. The king intended to keep the rebellious councilmen in office for another year. No, he was planning to reorganize the Academy on a different footing and appoint another president. On the contrary, he had decided to take a desperate measure and quash the Academy altogether, establishing another organization in its place.

West was dining with his friends at the Academy Club early in November when he was called out to receive a letter. It was from Yenn, and it was a somewhat peremptory relay of a command from the king to be present with Treasurer Yenn and Secretary Richards at Windsor next Sunday morning between 8 and 9 o'clock. West returned to the table with a long face, showed the letter, and said, "All is up." The others agreed that such a message delivered by one of the suspended councilmen was probable evidence that the rebels had won. West met with Farington to discuss the forthcoming audience. He was determined, he said, to speak out to the king if necessary, to ask to have the whole of his conduct investigated, and if the opportunity presented itself, to tell the names for the first time of those who had been causing trouble. He told Farington that if anything happened to him, Lawrence would be the proper man to succeed him as president. "His ability in art," West said, "when compared to others is as fifty to five." Farington read aloud to him the accumulation of memorials and addresses they had submitted to the king and coached him in what he should say. He cautioned West to be very careful not to assent to anything that might be proposed as regulations — not until it could be carefully considered.

West and Richards arrived at Windsor about 5:30 Saturday evening, November 12. They were at dinner when Yenn (accompanied by Wyatt and Tresham) arrived and in an undeclared truce among enemies, joined them at the table and spent the evening together. The king received West, Richards, and Yenn next morning in his apartment at the Queen's Lodge. He asked West how his health was and observed that since they were both growing old, they must expect some of the effects of aging. He had a communication he wished Mr. West to make to the society and, so that Mr. West might not say too much or too little, as might happen if it were conveyed verbally, he had committed it to writing. He handed Richards a paper and ordered him to place it in the Academy archives. The president should have a copy but no one else. He then ordered Richards to read it aloud. Richards seem puzzled at the writing. The king said, "Take out your assistants." Richards looked at him inquiringly. West said, "Your glasses, Mr. Richards." The king: "Aye, aye, your glasses. They are what we must all have recourse to."

West's mind seems to have wandered during the reading, or to have been distracted; perhaps he was preoccupied with the precariousness of his own position as president. When the reading was completed and in the pause that followed, he spoke only of a part of the paper that "leaves me unprotected as president." After what he had experienced in the Council concerning his picture *Hagar and Ishmael*, he said, he could have no security except that afforded by His Majesty. The king replied, "That was the most ill-natured action that I ever heard of, to take such advantage of you being on your sickbed, and I wish my sentiments on it to be publicly known." His situation, West said, had been very unpleasant these past months. If any other person could be proposed to fill his office to the satisfaction of His Majesty and the society, he would that moment resign. The king said, "No, no. All parties concur in wishing you to remain in it, nor can any other be proposed so proper. You have had my friendship and shall continue to have it, and make yourself easy."

The next day, still flushed with pleasure at this commitment given with John Yenn present, West reported on the meeting to his group of Academicians. He had not yet received his copy of the king's paper, he said, but he thought it contained nothing very unpleasant for the society. Farington questioned him closely and at some length, bearing down on the one main point: What was the king's decision on the suspension of the five councilmen? "By degrees," he said, "we discovered that the suspended members had obtained a full decision against us." Indeed, when Farington, West, and some others went over the king's paper the next day, they found that the five had been reinstated as councilmen and that all reference to their suspension was to be expunged from the minutes.

The defeat was total, the humiliation complete. The thwarted majority spent their evenings debating what course to follow. "Many opinions were given of our situation," Farington wrote, "but nothing concluded." Again: "The evening passed unprofitably — nothing done." The king's letter was read at a general meeting, with its strong closing plea for harmony, and a quarrel broke out at once over who should answer it: Assembly or Council. Copley complained that he had asked Richards for a copy of the letter in order to answer it but had been refused; on this complaint he and his colleagues walked out of the meeting. The majority took advantage of their departure to pass a unanimous vote for a proposal worked up by West, Farington, and Dance. They had decided, after hours of discussion, to interpret the king's order to mean that he wished *everything* about the Council-Assembly quarrel to be expunged from the records. In that way they would at least erase the Council's minutes as well as their own, with its attacks on the Assembly, Wyatt's charge about the improper use of committees to by-pass the Council, and Copley's "monstrous" resolution asserting the Council's supremacy.

On December 4, however, the king, meeting with West, Yenn, and Richards, declared that he had *not* meant to order deletions in the Council's minutes. There had been an understandable misinterpretation of his order, he said — everybody makes mistakes — and so he would send another letter to make his meaning perfectly clear. West spoke up with a force not commonly used in addressing monarchs. His Majesty, he said, wished to restore harmony in the society, but he could not do it unless he drew a line that would satisfy the general body as well as the Council. If a middle course was not pursued, the Academy would fall. The king said, "I am sorry to hear you say so." West declared that a sense of duty to His Majesty and to the society urged him to say it. He felt for the existence of the Academy from having been one of its firmest supporters, and he wished to prevent anything that might create a perpetual disunion. The king "seemed embarrassed" and replied, "I will consider of it." A few days later Richards received a sealed letter from the king that spelled out exactly what he was to restore to the minutes. West, summoning up the spirit of Lexington and Concord, called it "very tyrannical." Richards, busy with scenes he was painting for a new opera at Covent Garden, asked for and got an extension of time to make the changes.

The struggle for power had now taken on a new dimension. The quarrel had originally concerned an interpretation of the Academy's laws, with West and his supporters technically in the wrong. Now the issue had broadened to become the right of the institution to govern itself. For some thirty years the members had thought of themselves as an autonomous, independent body. A faction comprising not more than one-fourth of the members had imposed its ideas by persuading the king and his advisors that its interpretation of the laws was correct. Now an order had been received that challenged the Academy's right to self-government and, in Farington's words to Lawrence, degraded the institution by denying its authority.

Richards read the king's second letter aloud at the next general meeting and then, as was the custom, immediately read it a second time. It was received on both readings with profound silence, and there was no move to return the usual address of thanks to the king.[1] Over the next few weeks there was talk among the majority that they should refuse to send pictures to the next exhibition. Shee opposed making any changes at all in the minutes. Smirke also called for a firm stand against the king's order. Opie was violent for resistance. Flaxman "flamed out" that they should make a strong remonstrance and then turn in their diplomas. Hoppner was "very violent" that no stand had been taken; Lawrence told him that if a stand had been taken, he, Hoppner, would have been one of the first to flinch. Hoppner went away angry, saying that he had done with the Academy and "with all unions to carry measures."

Farington, in what was probably his finest hour, advocated a policy of moderation, patient acceptance, and procrastination — "to submit to the necessity and wait for better times," and he won West, Smirke, and Lawrence to agree with him. He reasoned with the "wild and inconsiderate disposition of some members," meaning Dance, Shee, Hoppner, and Flaxman. "Wisdom and experience," Shee confessed, "are speaking to rashness and folly." Farington applied precise logical analysis to the proposal to contend against the king's will. It could not be done, he said, without breaking away from the Royal Academy.

> The consequence would be that a part would remain ... who would have the support and countenance of the King, and though at first their efforts would be weak in exhibitions, yet they would soon collect the rising genius, and in a few years the Academy would be filled up again, whilst those who might secede would in the course of nature lessen into nothing, as they would possess neither wealth or honors to offer as temptations.

After their first elation, the rebels were finding little satisfaction in their success. They had won all the victories, but the party in power was still in power and its leaders were still running the Academy. They had, moreover, adopted a maddening new tactic: Instead of quarreling with them in the customary manner, they kept saying calmly that His Majesty wished to have harmony and that the opposition's proposals would be against that royal command. And on January 1, 1804, only a few weeks away, four new

---

[1] Sir Francis Bourgeois' distress at this breach caused mixed indignation and amusement. George III detested Bourgeois as "that white-faced man ... an insignificant man ... a foolish man" and gave him no entrée at court, but Bourgeois lamented the cold manner in which His Majesty's order was received. "With silence!" he exclaimed. "What shall I say to the King upon it?"

councilmen would be taking office. All were conservatives, and one was their archenemy, Joseph Farington.

On December 23 West went to Windsor with the list of new officers for 1804, telling his colleagues grimly before he left, "If the King strikes any names on the list ... he would speak his mind to him." The king was affable. He read the names aloud, observed that it was a strong list, and signed his approval. He had no doubt, he said, that Mr. West "would go on more smoothly with the new Council than he had lately done"; thus he laid to rest the rumor that he would keep the rebel councilmen in power for another year.

On the day after Christmas, John Soane launched a new rebel attack in the Council. All business and elections conducted in the Academy after May 30, he declared, and throughout the illegal suspension of the five councilmen, were null and void and must be reconsidered. He offered a resolution to that effect. West refused to accept it; it would be directly contrary, he said, to His Majesty's desire for harmony. The resolution, nevertheless, successfully passed a first reading.

West adjourned the Council to December 28 and at once went to Farington to express his concern. Soane's resolution would certainly pass a second Council reading, and "it would lay them open to a severe punishment by the enemy." This, Farington said, ought not to be allowed to happen. Mr. West should stop it. How, West asked, could he do that? He could do it, Farington said, by postponing the next Council meeting two more days, from Wednesday to Friday, and then from Friday until further notice. This would bring them to the New Year weekend, and then the new Council, controlled by men of proper spirit, would take over. "This sunk deep into his mind," Farington wrote, "and he said he would go to the Academy to [tell] Richards, which he did." For the next week West stayed at home with the curtains drawn. Soane came storming to 14 Newman Street, but West "had himself denied to everyone as *out of town.*"

Elizabeth West celebrated the New Year by writing some sparkling verses:

> *The clock struck twelve! — the hour is past,*
> *And Cop . . y now has breathed his last.*
> *Thou Genius, who presides o'er Art,*
> *Create anew his envious heart.*
> *Drive Hatred, Malice from within,*
> *Blot from his face that ghastly grin;*
> *Becalm S . . nes temper, Y . nn and W . . tt,*

And boasting Knight, disposed to riot.
From henceforth let no passions rude
Among thy Votaries e'er intrude.
To Arts polite, their names give place,
All liberal Art, their names disgrace . . .
    Then for joy that they're out, let merry bells ring,
And hail the New Year with God Save the King!

The new Council met on Tuesday, January 3. Copley and Wyatt were not present, their terms having expired. "The complexion of the meeting," Farington wrote, "was very unpromising." Soane and Bourgeois looked "high and furious," and neither side spoke to the other before the meeting began. Soane at once brought up his proposal of the previous meeting, but West interrupted him to read a paper of his own in which he hoped in obedience to His Mayesty's command "there should be no reiteration of the late unpleasant business" that "had been hastily proposed and inconsiderately adopted." He then declined to allow Soane to read his proposal "as it related to a business which should not out of respect to His Majesty be entered upon." Soane finally gave up; he put his papers in his pocket and sat down. Farington successfully moved that the resolution of the late Council be expunged from the minutes, "and so the business ended."

At his December 23rd meeting with the king, West had presented the names of five members eligible for appointment as keeper to replace Joseph Wilton, who had died in November. The candidates were the painters Smirke, Fuseli, and John Francis Rigaud and two sculptors, Edward Burch and Thomas Banks. The king read the names aloud and said they were all able men, but no one, unfortunately, would ever equal George Moser, the first keeper, who had been zealous as well as able. He expressed neither preference nor disapproval of any of the five names, though Banks was known for his "democratical opinions" and had once been arrested on a charge of high treason.

West and Farington reviewed the five names to choose the person best fitted to run the schools and manage the students. In consultation with others they eliminated Rigaud because of his fierce temper and because he was of the opposition party. West felt that Fuseli, though a brilliant writer, artist and linguist (he spoke and read English, French, Italian, Spanish, Danish, Dutch, German, Greek, Latin, and Hebrew), was "not proper to superintend education," presumably because of his arrogance, profanity, and heavy accent. Burch, at seventy-three, was too old for the post. Banks was old (sixty-eight) and had suffered for his political views, but he was highly regarded for his sculptures — Westminster Abbey had a number of his works — and for his beneficent influence over other English artists. Banks, however, had recently experienced an extraordinary misfortune. He had paid a visit to his native county, Gloucestershire, and there found in the church records that he was much older than he supposed himself to be. When he returned to London he had suddenly aged and "seemed like a person whose senses were benumbed." And so the party in power chose to support Robert Smirke in the February election. He was fifty-one, a product of the Academy schools, an Academician since 1793. When she learned of his nomination, Elizabeth West was delighted and immediately set off to solicit the vote of her friend Mary Moser Lloyd.

The choice of Smirke had unhappy consequences. The opposition decided to support Rigaud, and the matter expanded into still another bout in the struggle for power and control in the Academy.

William Beechey began the rebel campaign by informing the king that Smirke had been heard to say in 1793, when the Queen of France was beheaded, "The guillotine might well be employed upon some more crowned heads." As the queen's portrait painter, Beechey was often with the royal family and he was making the most of his opportunities. He told Nollekens (who told West) that information he had supplied had caused the king to hold "such an opinion of West that he would never more have anything to do with him."

Mrs. West's call on Mary Lloyd on behalf of Smirke was followed by a solicitation from a more august person. It came from the Princess Elizabeth, the third of the king's daughters, and she asked Mrs. Lloyd to vote for Rigaud. The princess had said she was "sick and tired of hearing of the Royal Academy," and with her sisters she had come to detest Mr. West as a weak man. When an Academician who was painting their portraits told the princesses, "Whoever goes down his gallery will allow that he is a great artist," one of them replied, "Then he must be keeping his best works at home." Princess Elizabeth had decided that Mr. West and his friends were being disrespectful to the crown in opposing two Academicians — Yenn and Wyatt — who had her favor and that of His Majesty.

Farington campaigned in a gentlemanly way for Smirke. Humphry told him Smirke was not suitable for the office because he had never been to Italy. Hoppner declared that if Smirke was elected keeper, he would go over to the opposition and never again exhibit at the Academy. Beechey told Nollekens that if he did not vote for Rigaud, "he would repent it on his death bed."

To the sore disappointment of his supporters, Rigaud did not receive the eighteen sure votes they had expected, and Smirke was elected keeper by a comfortable margin. The elections result was delivered to the king, but weeks passed without his approval. West asked Smirke to take over the duties of the position, but he declined to serve until his election had been approved by His Majesty. Beechey's wife began to whisper at dinner parties, "The King will not sign Smirke's election, but do not mention it, for Beechey would murder me if he knew I had told it."

On February 12, five days after Smirke's election, the king had suffered a recurrence of his illness. Dr. Willis was not summoned this time, though the queen wished it, for two of his sons, the dukes of Kent and Cumberland, had sworn to their father that "in the event of its being the will of Providence that he should again be afflicted... we should use every means in our power to prevent anyone of the Willis family from being placed about him." Instead of Willis there came Dr. Samuel Simmons, physician to St. Luke's Hospital for Lunatics, who at once put the king into a straitjacket. Despite this treatment, he recovered his senses within ten days, his mind being fairly clear and his memory fairly good, and complained of the way he had been treated by "that horrible doctor," Simmons.

An unsigned forty-eight-page pamphlet appeared in February 1804 that made something of a stir with an intimate account of the Academy troubles. It was titled *A Concise Vindication of the Conduct of the Five Suspended Members of the Council of the Royal Academy,* and it paid a glowing tribute to the wisdom and courage of the opposition and lashed out in terms of the highest indignation at the "excess of indecency and outrage... the flagrant act of usurpation... the interested and mischievous projects... the gross illegality and violence" of the prevailing party. By this account, West was "held in a state of complete subjection" by Farington, "the avowed and open leader of the party." West showed Farington a copy of the pamphlet the day it was published, remarking that he and Mrs. West were "much gratified that it was a very flimsy performance." Farington agreed with West that they should make no answer.[2]

---

[2] John Landseer, an engraver, wrote a twenty-eight-page rebuttal titled *A Concise Review of the Concise Vindication*... in which he charged that West had been "publicly traduced and villified by the basest insinuations" and stressed the injustice of the Council majority, "invested with arbitrary and uncontrollable power," dictating to the entire forty-man Assembly.

The author was known to be Copley's son, John Singleton, Junior. After completing his studies at Cambridge, where he was second wrangler and fellow of Trinity, he had spent a year in America, where he attempted to get more money for the property his father had sold on Beacon Hill. Having seen the United States at first hand, he returned to England to announce, to his father's relief, that he was completely cured of democracy. Young Copley had decided to drop his law studies and make a career in the church, but his father persuaded him to continue with the law, and early in 1804 he was called to the bar at Lincoln's Inn. One of his first cases — in a long and distinguished career in which he was to become successively a member of Parliament, solicitor general, attorney general, master of the rolls, lord chancellor, chief baron of the Exchequer, and leader of the opposition — was that in which he represented his father in a suit to collect payment for *The Knatchbull Family.*

When that picture was completed in 1803, Sir Edward Knatchbull had asked what price Mr. Copley put upon it. (He had decided he would pay as high as £1200 if he had to.) Copley told him of the loss he had sustained in the suit brought against him by the engraver Delattre. Sir Edward observed, not unreasonably, that it was not *his* responsibility to make up that loss. When Copley asked for 1800 guineas, Sir Edward had said the figure far exceeded his expectations; he would pay £1400 but no more. Copley refused that amount, and both sides, accordingly, prepared for a lawsuit. As the trial date approached, Sir Edward deposited his offered payment with the court, making it 1400 guineas rather than pounds. When Lady Knatchbull begged her husband not to permit a hearing in an open court, the lawyers arranged for private arbitration proceedings.

The first of the sessions was held on March 1, 1804, in the chambers of James Burrough, a magistrate acting as referee. Copley testified on the many hours he had spent on a difficult work with many changes. Beechey testified that since he had received £1000 for painting the king with his seven sons, Knatchbull's picture with three wives and eleven children was worth at least £1800. Sir Edward testified on Copley's dilatory work habits, complained that the picture had been hung in the Academy and shown to the king without his permission, and said that Copley had painted his two former wives as angels against his wish; he had merely suggested that they be shown as portraits in the background of the picture.

The second day's hearing began at 2 P.M. in West's studio. Burrough, the referee, questioned West, who said he felt 1200 guineas would have been a very handsome price and 1400 guineas "a princely price" for the picture. West had recently painted a large portrait group of the family of Henry Hope of Cavendish Square, Amsterdam banker, merchant, and art collector who had fled Holland and taken up residence in London. Burrough asked him the size of that picture and the price he charged for it. West replied that it was 9 feet wide, 6 feet high, and contained nine portraits, some of them nearly whole length. He had given Mr. Hope an estimate of £470 before starting work, but Mr. Hope had sent him 500 guineas, which he acknowledged to be a very liberal act. Burrough then asked how much he had received for the large hunting piece he had painted for Lord Seaforth. West said he received 800 guineas for it and thought himself very handsomely paid.

Copley, Junior, then questioned West. He observed that Mr. West had charged the king £29,000 for pictures painted for him. Had Mr. West regulated those charges by the same scale as the Hope and Seaforth pieces? Judge Burrough instantly rose and expressed his astonishment that Mr. Copley, being a barrister, should ask so improper a question as that relating to the king. West said that he would not have replied to the question. He closed his testimony by saying that he judged the amount of work put into the Knatchbull group and its proper price by comparing it to the charge Copley made for a single whole-length portrait: 120 guineas. On that basis he had arrived at 1400 guineas as ample payment.

The hearing continued through the afternoon and into the evening. West left at five o'clock, explaining that he was to dine with the bishop of Durham, and the bishop, who was a punctual man, never waited dinner for anyone beyond 5:30. Lawrence and Shee were waiting to testify in support of Sir Edward when he departed. Judge Burrough said he was setting out to ride his circuit the next day; he would close the business that evening and write his "declaration" while he was away.

The Copley-Knatchbull hearing, though not public, was the subject of London gossip for several days. Shee said that he very much approved West's testimony, and that the evidence of West and Lawrence together was extremely damaging to Copley's case. West said there was only one person to whom the king had revealed that £29,000 figure, and he would certainly tell His Majesty that the person (presumably either Wyatt or Beechey) had divulged it to another. Young Copley, he said, appeared to be "a chip off the old block . . . his father's *double, refined,* a pretty promise of a lawyer." Lawrence "reprobated" Copley's conduct in the whole Knatchbull affair, and the Academicians to whom he was talking agreed that he "had done more injury to the arts, and to the character of artists, than any other man of his time."

Unfortunately, there seems to be no record, in Farington or elsewhere, on whether Judge Burrough ruled in favor of Knatchbull or Copley. Three years later, in August 1807, the two men were at least on speaking terms, for Copley and his wife rode to Kent to see *The Knatchbull Family* properly hung in the house at Mersham. He had painted out the two wives in the sky, and Sir Edward said he was pleased with the picture (though he may have been silently disappointed that his two latest children, numbers thirteen and fourteen, and his two grandchildren could not be added). Some years later the canvas was cut apart and the various individual portraits distributed among members of the family.

On March 26, Farington urged West to speed up the king's confirmation of Smirke as keeper. He wished to do so, West said, but he was helpless; he had to wait until Braun, the king's head page, sent word that the king would see him. He then brought up a subject that weighed heavily on his mind. He told Farington that he wished to hang *Hagar and Ishmael* in the Academy exhibition in April. He was still smarting under the dishonor of having it banned the year before, and to exhibit it would be a measure of vindication.

He made the proposal at the next Council meeting, and after a long discussion obtained the approval he sought. Yenn told Farington that Copley no longer wished to bar the picture. West worked at last-minute changes on *Hagar* in the Council Room. The critic of the *Monthly Magazine* wrote, "The President has gained his point, and triumphed over his opponents by exhibiting his picture ... *having first made such alterations* as are a salve for his own conscience."

There were many stories in the summer and autumn of 1804 that the king had come to dislike West, would never see him again, publicly or privately, and intended to accept his resignation. Tom Smith of the London *News* told a friend, who told Farington, "that the King once said to him that when he conversed with West, if West set out with one opinion and discovered that the King differed from him, '*like a true American he would creep from one shoulder to the other* behind his back and then appear to be of the same opinion with the King.' " Most of the stories originated with William Beechey, who was accused of prejudicing the mind of the king against a number of other Academicians, but whose special hatred of West was based on an extraordinary incident that was indeed unforgivable, if true. West, he charged, had told the king that Beechey's wife was not really his wife, and of course was therefore an improper person to be received by the queen. This had forced Beechey to show papers to prove his marriage. If the king had not been involved in the matter, he said, he would have felt it necessary to follow West to the end of the world to demand satisfaction of him (that is, to fight a duel). West apparently never deigned to explain, deny, affirm, or defend himself against Beechey's charge.

The day before the 1804 exhibition opened, West went to Somerset House, but on learning that Copley and Beechey were above stairs, he refused to go up. At the annual dinner in honor of the king, Bourgeois arrived early and began to rearrange the place cards so as to group the opposition members together at the foot of the table. To Farington, who made him stop, he explained "how disagreeable it would be to them to be near West." Beechey told Smirke in January 1804 that the king "has a contemptible opinion of West." In February he said he had spent three hours with the king and much of their talk was about West. The king, he said, called West "an ungrateful dog." Bourgeois passed this story on to Northcote, who, despite his low opinion of West, refused to believe it; the king did not talk that way. Beechey told Farington that the king "had long expressed great dislike of West, whose name he seldom mentioned without a degrading epithet"; that the king "had often declared that West was unfit to be president of the Royal Academy"; and that the queen and princesses all disliked him and "never spoke of him but with disgust." Farington gave him the lie; he told Beechey what the king had said in the presence of Richards and Yenn — that "West had his friendship and should [continue to] have his friendship." Beechey "expressed astonishment at it and allowed he could not reconcile it with what he himself had heard."

Despite the king's promise, West had reason to fear that he was indeed out of favor — a calamity for him both as the king's historical painter and as president of his Royal Academy. In November 1803 he had called on the king at the Queen's Lodge at Windsor and was told by a page, "who spoke with friendly feelings, that *he was not to come there.*" While waiting for the king to approve Smirke's appointment as keeper, he went to the chapel at Windsor "and so placed himself so that the King must see him, so that if His Majesty desired it he might send for him, but no message came. He also went upon the Terrace, but the King did not notice him. The Queen and Princess Elizabeth did in a slight manner." Beechey was obviously now the artist favored by the royal family. West was subjected to the peculiar misery of one whose royal patron ignores him.

Beechey had scored a striking success with a series of portraits of the royal family that were hung at Windsor Castle in what was known as "the Beechey Room." Now he ranked with Lawrence and Hoppner, all three charging the top price of fifty guineas for a head-and-shoulders. In 1798 he painted what was considered his finest work: a large picture showing a review of cavalry, with the king, the Prince of Wales and the duke of York in the foreground, surrounded by a brilliant red-coated staff on horseback. The king "at the express intimation of the Queen," knighted him the following year — the first painter after Reynolds to be so honored. Beechey assured his colleagues at the Academy that the new title would not make any difference, he would not alter his conduct to them.[3]

Something went wrong, however, in the autumn of 1804, for Beechey suddenly and unexpectedly lost the king's favor. One story was that he overcharged the king on some frames; another had it that he painted a replica of his portrait of the king (for which he had charged the king 120 guineas) for the bishop of Chester for 50 guineas, which incensed His Majesty when he learned of it. He said that Beechey did not understand color (the red in the coats in the cavalry review picture had begun to fade) and that he wanted no more of his pictures.

On hearing this, Beechey, anxious to explain, "placed himself in the King's way" — in one version of the story, in Windsor Castle while repainting the officers' coats. The king advanced on him in a passion, refused to allow him to speak, and blurted out that West was an American, and Copley was an American, and Beechey was an Englishman, and that if the Devil had them all he should not care. On leaving he was heard to say to those about him, "He would throw himself in my way and I am glad I have given it to him."

According to one eyewitness, Beechey stepped back into the crowd, took out his snuffbox, and said calmly, "I have had enough to last me a lifetime." According to another, Beechey was so overcome by this terrible denunciation that he staggered into the first apartment that was open, which happened to be that of a maid of honor, where he fell upon a sofa and fainted away. According to still another — the version West liked to tell — Beechey in his

---

[3] Beechey's was the only artist's wife in London who did any considerable amount of entertaining.

fright ran to the queen, who also gave him such a cold reception that it caused him to faint or to have some sort of fit. Beechey had brought this upon himself, West added, by his imprudent behavior, having made both the pages and the equerries his enemies. Hoppner told the story to the Prince of Wales, who had an attack of laughing that lasted ten minutes.

The firsthand stories of the unkind things the king said about Benjamin West continued — Tresham was the chief purveyor — but they came no more from Sir William Beechey, Knight.

22

The Hollow Triumph

Called on Edridge. He was at Mr. Long's at Bromley near a week and on Sunday last Mr. Pitt dined there and no other company. There was a good deal of conversation about art and it appeared that Mr. Pitt and Mr. Long were strongly impressed with an opinion that members of the Royal Academy as a body are a very discontented set of men.

JOSEPH FARINGTON,
Diary, September 7, 1805

WEST CALLED on Farington on Saturday morning, November 17, 1804, to say that he was leaving that afternoon for Windsor to see the king. He had written three times to the king's head page and to Lord Chancellor Eldon asking for an audience but had been put off with apologies. Now he would go to Windsor on official business, accompanied by John Richards and carrying three Academy documents that needed signatures. He would present only two of these, he said, but if he saw His Majesty in a proper disposition for it, he would raise the third, Smirke's election as keeper, and try to bring that issue at last to a conclusion.

Perhaps, Farington suggested, they should wait until they heard from the lord chancellor (with whom they had been conferring) in the hope that he might have favorably influenced the king's mind on the Smirke election. West thanked him but said the business of the Academy could wait no longer. He now believed there was no hope at all for Smirke. The opposition members, Farington warned, were reportedly declaring that the king would never again see West privately and probably would refuse to see him officially. He wished West to be prepared for such a possibility. He had the fortitude for it, West replied; he would face whatever might happen.

He had acted faithfully to the king both as a subject and as a servant, and he defied any man to impeach his moral character.

He had also been told, Farington said, that the papers West had given the king censuring the conduct of certain members had been turned over to the opposition and would be charged against him at the Academy.[1] West said he did not fear them. Farington asked: Had the Privy Purse paid his quarterly allowance? It had been paid, West replied, and the receipt sent to the king. West had spoken quite frankly to Farington about his financial problems, and now he revealed that he had been looking over his property and considering how to convert his collection of pictures and his own works into money for subsistence. For himself, he said, he was indifferent to what the king might do, but he was concerned for his own family. His wife had had two strokes, and though she was recovering well, she now seldom left the house.[2] Both of his sons were relying on him for some support. Benjamin had recently married a beautiful young lady, Miss Mary, the only daughter of Edward Dickinson of Perthall. Her father had opposed the match, having other plans for her, but he was now reconciled; West himself admired his second daughter-in-law as "a very fine young woman." If he were ten years younger, he said, and without such family responsibilities, he would return to America. He was sure that much might be done there, as the people had a strong disposition to the arts, and it would be easy to encourage a spirit of rivalry between areas of the country. Trumbull would settle in New York and he in Philadelphia, and they would "raise the spirit as high as it could be." He had received much encouragement from the king over the past thirty-two years, but he had also learned how much apprehension and difficulty there was in that relationship. If he were to live those years over again, he would depend on the public for support rather than on any individual person in a high position.

The two men talked for an hour before West left for Windsor. Farington probably did not mention an ominous remark Lawrence had made to him a few days earlier about the problem of defending their friend West against attack. If the king allowed the opposition

---

[1] Tresham tried to win over Henry Thomson, newly elected R.A., by saying that he was authorized at the next Academy meeting "to bring forward papers to show that West had calumniated members of the Academy to the King, and endeavoured to establish a prejudice in His Majesty's mind against their characters. This . . . was a violation of the privilege of his office [and] an act of malice, and as such was cognizable by the Academy."

[2] "As to my health it is very indifferent, and so lame that I can scarcely crawl about, but thank God my spirits bear me out, or all would soon be over." Mrs. West to Sarah Trumbull, February 6, 1805.

to produce evidence that West had "calumniated" members and caused a prejudice against them in the king's mind — or if the charge was made that he had lost the king's confidence and the king allowed it to stand — then a defense could hardly be conducted without reflecting on His Majesty.

West faced a new difficulty in trying to see the king, for there were days when his illness returned unexpectedly and his mind and manners were not steady enough for him to hold an audience. It was known throughout the court that the queen was frightened by the king's conduct. She appeared in public with him only on formal occasions and she again refused to be alone with him. The Princess Elizabeth or one of her attendants slept with her behind a locked door and a woman servant slept in an adjoining room. Pitt and the lord chancellor, wishing the king and the royal family to appear in as normal a state as possible, made a strong remonstrance to the queen, but she insisted she would not place herself in a situation where she felt there was a risk of physical harm. She was seen to show "great peevishness and tartness of behaviour to the King." His vision was failing and he had almost lost the sight of his right eye because of a cataract. Despite his afflictions he was generally cheerful and considerate of those about him.

West and Richards were at breakfast on Sunday morning when a page brought word that the king would receive them at four o'clock. West, who had not had an audience with the king for more than ten months, found him aged in appearance, emaciated, and stooped. He was wearing laced stockings because of a swelling in his legs. West felt that he had never been more affectionately received. The king talked about his health, about an excursion he had recently made to Weymouth, and of the bracing effect of the sea air. He asked about West's health and about the progress of Richards' scene-painting at Covent Garden. Turning to West's portfolio of papers spread before him, he twice read and then signed the document raising the salaries of the Academy's servants — an action, he said, which he very much approved. The Academy was right, he said, in granting a pension to its old servant John Withers. In signing Henry Thomson's diploma as an Academician, he remarked that the name had been written in very well. He then took up Smirke's election as keeper and read it.

West did not know it, but the lord chancellor had presented the same document some months earlier. On that occasion the king, in an agitated state, had so scribbled over it that he took it away with the hope "that by procrastination the King's mind might be in a better state on the business." Now the king looked up from the paper with displeasure. He had made up his mind on this paper six months ago, he said. He had let his opinion be known and he had not expected it to be brought before him again. He drew his pen through Smirke's name, wrote "Rejected, must proceed to a new election," signed his name, and began to talk of other matters. He escorted West and Richards through several rooms to show them alterations being made, doing so, West said, in what seemed to be great good humor and "in the most easy and friendly way that could be." The audience ended when a baron from Hanover, His Majesty's other realm, appeared with a bundle of documents to be signed. Going down the hill from the castle, Richards exclaimed, "Give me your hand, Mr. West! This has been a most grateful visit. When I went in to the King I was so alarmed for what might follow that a straw might have turned me over. But I was full of admiration at your coolness." The opposition members, he said, would soon be surrounding him "to pick his eyes" on the events of the meeting. He would tell them all they would care to know of what had passed.

On hearing West's account of the visit, Farington advised him to be on his guard, for he had learned that the opposition meant to overthrow him and install Wyatt as president. He had heard a rumor that fourteen of them had resolved to assemble, proceed to the Academy, declare that they were continuing an adjourned meeting, and nominate a member to fill the president's chair. West asked Farington to do him the favor of breaking the unhappy news to Smirke.

Farington at once grasped the deeper significance of Smirke's rejection. "I told Lawrence," he wrote in his diary, "that after this act of the King it became me to look to myself and fully to consider what it would be for me to venture my name up to the King as a member of Council and auditor — with the chance of the King doing the same against me as he had done to Smirke." No man would be safe; an enemy might make up a mischievous story against him for the purpose of having the king remove him from office.

West, Farington, and Lawrence reviewed the names of possible candidates for keeper and, overlooking earlier objections, settled on Henry Fuseli. Farington and Lawrence called on him, told him in confidence what had happened, and asked if he still wished to become keeper and would run against Rigaud. He replied that he did and would. His two callers left to begin a quiet campaign to solicit votes.

West reported the king's decision on Smirke at the next general meeting. The opposition now insisted that the king had not only canceled Smirke's election but had also told West and Richards that he wished Rigaud to be elected — a claim that both men swore was not true. In an altercation between Bourgeois and Farington, Bourgeois asserted that when the king's private wishes could be known, the Academy was bound to agree with them. Farington drove to the heart of that dangerous proposition:

> I showed the ill consequences which must arise from establishing a precedent of such a nature . . . I replied that His Majesty had wisely resolved to make the elections *free* that he might thereby collect the real judgment and opinion of the members. That His Majesty could only know characters from report, whereas the professional talents — the morals — the manners — the industry — the general fitness of men for particular offices was intimately known to the members from their habits of association and intercourse . . . I told them that such proceedings as were now proposed would eventually lead to *mandates* which would in fact throw the whole power over the Academy into the hands of some person who might influence a future sovereign.

In succeeding days, Bourgeois argued that the president of the Academy ought not to be a painter, as it excited jealousy in other painters. Cosway said the king should appoint all the Academy's permanent officers. Copley said he did not approve of Wyatt as his party's candidate for president, because he was an architect. Bourgeois promised Fuseli a raise in his salary as professor of painting to £100 a year if he withdrew his candidacy as keeper. Cosway complained that the majority in the Academy carried all the decisions and won all the votes. Fuseli asked him, "Is it otherways in the House of Commons? Can it be otherways in any free society? Will not there always be differences of opinion among a number of persons, and will not the majority carry and decide the question?"

Lawrence dined with Farington on Monday evening, December 10; they were joined after dinner by Dance and Daniell and went together to Somerset House for the annual meeting and election of officers for 1805. Thirty-two of the forty members were present. The time had come at last for the open battle to be joined on the floor of the chamber. Tresham rose after the reading of the minutes to declare that he had much to say on the subject of the election of officers, and since he had charges to bring against the president, perhaps Mr. West should quit the chair. The members decided he should stay. They were assembled, Tresham began, to choose a proper person to serve as president of their institution. Mr. West had not done his duty as president, and he no longer had His Majesty's confidence. It would be highly improper, therefore, to re-elect him. It was necessary that the member filling the chair should have the king's confidence, and James Wyatt was that person. He therefore proposed Mr. Wyatt to the General Assembly for election to the presidency.

He was able to prove, he went on, that His Majesty wished a man other than West to be president. There was a member present who had a message from His Majesty that he was commanded to deliver on that subject. He called on John Yenn to give that message. West described the scene in a letter to John Trumbull:

> This threw the General Assembly into great agitation, and most of the members called on Mr. Yenn to inform them, [what] *were the commands he bore from His Majesty;* but Mr. Yenn not rising — I then addressed him — by saying, that if he bore a message from His Majesty — I would answer for myself — and for most of the members that His Majesty's message would be received by them with the most profound respect and attention. He therefore had but to make it known. The General Assembly repeated my words — which brought up Mr. Yenn with much agitation — when he declared that he had no message from His Majesty — the King had not commanded him to deliver anything respecting the elections of that night. The speeches which followed that declaration of Mr. Yenn you may easily imagine, for most of the members were on their feet at once.

Farington's diary fills in some details of this startling upset. Before Tresham had called on Yenn to deliver the coup de grâce to West, Farington rose to point out the danger of admitting reports that came so indirectly to the Academy, by-passing communication through the proper officers. Lawrence then put the question to Yenn: "Do you have authority to convey His Majesty's wishes to the Academy?" Yenn replied that he did not have such authority, and he was not permitted to use the king's name, but he did have *discretionary power* to repeat what the king had said to him on filling the presidency.[3] Various members asserted they would never accept any message given to them under such peculiar circumstances. The election was called for. Wyatt received seven votes, West twenty. There were three blanks; they were cast, West surmised, by some of Wyatt's party "who took the alarm when they found that Mr. Yenn had no message."

West spent two hours the following Sunday with the lord chancellor and gave him a polite warning. Smirke's rejection, he said,

---

[3] Yenn later explained that the king had told him he "had no objection to his name being used *if it were done with delicacy.*"

had been kept out of the papers, but if the king rejected his re-election as president it would be publicly noticed and he would have to defend himself and his character.

The new election of a keeper was to be held on December 24. The opposition swore that the king would accept no other keeper than Rigaud, and that he would draw his pen through the name if Fuseli was elected; furthermore, if he consented to receive West at all, he would refuse to sanction his re-election as president. Farington told Lawrence that the newer and younger members should now make up their minds what to do: whether to submit to what might be imposed upon them, or to resist. If the king refused West, Lawrence said, Farington should accept the presidency, for he had the confidence of most of the members and would excite no jealousy. Farington disagreed; he was not of sufficient professional importance for the office, and he felt further that "there was great reason to believe that other things against particular members were to be expected, and . . . I looked upon myself to be the first after Smirke." He and Lawrence met for tea with Dance, Opie, and Thomson and after much conversation came to an extraordinarily bold decision:

> Should the King interfere in any way to affect the privilege of election [of a Keeper] on Monday next, that Opie should rise and propose an *adjournment* and a *remonstrance*, to be presented to His Majesty, and that Lawrence should second it: and that should the King still persevere, that the whole of our side of the Academy should resolve to absent themselves from all public meetings and to refrain from exhibiting, that it be seen and felt what the Academy is, and what the factious members are.

The election of a keeper took place as scheduled. Fuseli defeated Rigaud by twenty votes to thirteen, and West braced himself for still another trip to Windsor with his official papers and a walk up the hill to a perilous audience with the king. He took Richards with him, again ignoring Yenn, the treasurer (which caused Yenn to mutter that this was "a smuggled business.") Farington was at Newman Street when West left, and he stayed to talk for a while with Elizabeth West. In the forty years of their marriage, she told him, she had only once seen Mr. West intoxicated, and she never had seen him in a display of anger. He had been so devoted to drawing when young, she lamented, that every other part of his education was neglected.

The king received them in the afternoon. He was alone, standing before a fire, when they entered. West bowed; the king advanced toward him. The weather, he said, was very cold; he had been out that morning but was glad to be back in a warm room. He began to talk about pictures and pointed to a portrait of George I, his great-grandfather. He had recently rescued it from a storage room and hung it, because it pleased him more than the one painted by Sir Godfrey Kneller. He valued the portrait, he said, because George I was a good man.

Richards, in the meantime, had been nervously laying out his papers on a table. West explained what they were. The king took up the election of officers and holding it up read the names of West, the re-elected president, Council, visitors, and auditors. He remarked that it was a strong Council, took a pen, and signed the document. He next took up the election of Fuseli as keeper. He advanced toward West and said, "Fuseli is a man of genius." West replied, "He is a very able man." The king went toward the window, took up a pen, came back to West, and asked, "You think Fuseli is an able man?" West replied, "He is not only an able man in his profession, but he is distinguished as a literary character and known to all Europe."

The king went to the table and signed the document. He then began to talk about the castle and his intended improvements. He would show them what he had done, he said, advising Richards to carry his portfolio with him so he would not have to return for it. He led them through various apartments "and conversed with all the cheerfulness and familiarity that he could do." He asked if George Dance had given any lectures lately. West said he had not because he was so busily engaged in architectural work about the great docks. He was, the king said pleasantly, a clever man. A little later he dropped a remark that led West to conclude that he was "very sick of all the French who are in this country." On reaching a descending stairway he said, "Now you must find your way out as well as you can."

West later said he had known from the first that all would go well, for the king's expression was one of kindness and ease, and he felt he was being received as a brother and friend. Now he stepped forward to thank the king and to say some words (not divulged) in a low voice. The king went down a few steps, turned, and asked West to follow him. The two men went into an apartment and stayed for some time. West was fond of gossip and he loved to impart inside information that others had not heard, but he seems never to have revealed the content of that conversation, other than to say that the king "spoke upon a subject quite different from any he had heard before touched upon," and that at times the king wept. West returned to Richards and went with him to the inn, where they passed the evening "with great comfort." The audience had lasted three and one-half hours. West pledged Richards to silence on what had happened at Windsor, and he himself told the story to only a few confidants who were sworn to secrecy.

West's notice of a general meeting called for January 2, 1805, was cryptic. Copley called on Fuseli and begged him for information. He supposed from the tone of the summons either that West had succeeded and meant to have a triumph by a sudden disclosure, or that the king had not decided on the keeper's place and had sent back the names of Fuseli and Rigaud to be reconsidered. Fuseli volunteered no information. Copley said he had not voted for Fuseli, but he would not be sorry to see him win. He felt that Rigaud was "a man of unpopular manner," and confessed sadly that he himself was not popular.

Twenty-six members were present at the general meeting, including the rebels Copley, Bourgeois, Rigaud, Soane, and Tresham. West began by recalling the events of the election on December 10, which "was attended by circumstances the most unprecedented that ever occurred on that occasion since its formation." The charge had been made that the president had not done his duty as head of the Academy; that he no longer had the king's confidence; and that a member bore His Majesty's command to substantiate what was said about the president. Following that meeting, he had gone to Windsor with the secretary and laid the official papers before His Majesty. It was "with a lively sense, flowing from a feeling heart," that he could reveal that his reception, first as president and secondly as Mr. West, "was marked by all that was gracious and benign during the several hours he had the honour to be in His Majesty's presence." He now presented to the members the documents bearing His Majesty's signature, approving the choice of those elected to the several offices. "I must confess," he wrote to Trumbull, "I never saw an opposition so crushed, or a majority act with more becoming moderation and dignity."

Farington rose and delivered a moving tribute to West. He expressed satisfaction that their actions had been approved by the sovereign, and he was convinced that the hearts of most of the Academicians would be warmed by grateful sensations.

> Sir, I now beg leave to say a few words which more immediately relate to yourself. It happened that I came into the profession to which I belong at a very early age, which enables me to say that I remember your arrival from Italy, and in a short time after, at the age of 25 or 26, you produced works of such merit as to cause you to be ranked with the first men of your profession. In a few

years after, you were known to be employed with a few others in planning and forming this institution . . . The catalogues of the exhibitions will show that from that period, 36 years ago, you have exerted yourself professionally in a singular manner to maintain and support the credit of the Royal Academy.

He recalled that when it pleased God to take from them the great man, Sir Joshua Reynolds, one sentiment prevailed on who should be his successor.

In that situation you have remained 14 years. Your professional abilities entitled you to be placed in it — those abilities which, however they may now be appreciated . . . will be still more highly rated at a future period. But other considerations operated in your favor. Your long standing in the art; your age, which . . . made you appear as a father, are causes why you have held your rank without exciting jealousy. Thus honorably distinguished, it was natural for you to hope that you might conclude a life of great professional labour, in ease and tranquility.

In that expectation he had been disappointed and had suffered many mortifications. He had been charged with neglecting the duties of his office.

You have also experienced a treatment that is remembered with much more sorrow. It has been declared to your face, before this Assembly, that you *had lost the confidence of your Sovereign;* and a solemn pledge was then given by a member under the penalty of suffering merited contempt, that it should *then be proved.* It was not done; and this night you have had the happiness to lay before us a full confutation of that unfounded assertion.

Having been a witness to all that passed on these occasions, I should think I acted towards you with cold indifference were I not to express the satisfaction I now feel, and my hope, that, assured of the protection of . . . the most beloved of monarchs, you may pass the remainder of your days unmolested, and possessing what blessings this world can afford, go to your grave in peace and security.

Bourgeois attacked Farington for his speech, declaring that he had not always felt that way about Mr. West, but he was cried down. Tresham attempted to exculpate himself from blame, but Lawrence and Flaxman quoted back to him the charges he had made. He turned to Yenn for support, but Yenn (as Farington saw it) "slunk out of the room and was seen no more." Shee, in "an animated speech," said that Tresham appeared to have been only

the hod carrier of his party and so might be forgiven; he called
Tresham a friend and suggested that he relieve himself by making
an apology to Mr. West for what he had done. Tresham admitted
that he had been led into assertions that were now refuted and said
he was willing to make or second a motion complimentary to Mr.
West. Farington opposed the offer; Mr. Tresham's sentiments were
now as fully known as they could be by a motion, and it would be
better that nothing of that nature should appear in the minutes, as
it could not but imply that there had been a question of West's performance. There was then a suggestion that those most active in
the opposition should be censured by a formal vote. West opposed
it. He did not wish the record to show such disgraceful events. His
triumph, and the triumph of his friends, lay in the king's signature
on the documents. His opponents should be left to retire unnoticed
with their own thoughts. He recommended to them and to all
members the prosperity of the arts and the Academy. The meeting
broke up before eleven. Farington, Smirke, Daniell, and Nollekens
accompanied West to his home and there passed happy hours before separating.

Elizabeth West wrote an exultant letter to the Trumbulls on her
husband's victory.

> Oh, that I had you here for a few hours to whisper in your ears
> the complete triumph His M-----y has given Mr. W. over those
> dirty d-gs of the R.A., whose malicious endeavours have been to
> ruin him. They hoped for a time, they even boasted, that their
> purpose was effected, when His M-----y ... confirmed the late
> elections. This seemed to be (by the party) unexpected, and was
> to their great confusion and dishonour. Thus let such wretches
> fall, to rise no more as respected men; 'tis thought they never can.

"His Majesty," West wrote to Trumbull, "has ... by a single act
placed all those vipers who have been endeavouring to sting and
drive me from my chair of the Royal Academy for some years under
my feet ... You will see that the Institution is in the hands of His
Majesty, and myself, and friends."

On recovering from his mauling at the general meeting, Tresham
told his friends that the last word had not been said about West's
loss of the king's confidence. West, he insisted, had happened to
visit the king at a lucky hour when His Majesty was angry at
Wyatt's neglect of his architectural work at Windsor Castle. It was
in that mood and at that hour that he signed West's election, without being aware of what he was doing. Farington remarked that no

dependence was to be placed on what Tresham said, "other than there was no doubt but that he would keep the Academy in trouble if he could."

There were rage and bitterness in the rebel camp, not only at their defeat but at their blunders that had made it possible. Bourgeois spoke freely to Fuseli, who reported the conversation to Farington. He "laid great blame upon Yenn, who he said had brought Tresham and him into such a situation that 'Mr. Farington, Mr. Lawrence and Mr. Shee run over them like mud.'" Bourgeois showed Fuseli a copy of a letter Tresham had written to Yenn, which, Fuseli said, "was little short of a challenge." Bourgeois was on his way at the time to meet Wyatt at the White Horse Cellar, the meeting place of the rebel club, where they "intended to consider Yenn's conduct."

The rebels, nevertheless, rallied and regrouped to attack again. Whether or not they consciously intended to do so, they followed a strategy that was irresistible: They made the Academy so unpleasant that members less sturdy than they, less passionately committed to retain power than they were to seize it, were reluctant to attend. Most of the members were devoted to the institution. It was their club and meeting place, their trade union, their main social outlet, the source of good fellowship among artists of widely different backgrounds. It was the means by which bristly personalities from the farms, slums, provinces, and foreign countries smoothed the edges of their manners, overcame class distinctions, and rose in their profession. It was also the center of gossip — which patrons were buying, who demanded constant repainting, who bargained down the price, who never paid, which duke or earl kept an artist waiting for hours while his time and the good light were wasting. All this was being lost, and to some of the forty artists it was a personal and professional tragedy.

Farington expressed his disgust on January 10 at the never-ceasing prospect of trouble, and a few weeks later he wrote of "passing the most unpleasant evening I ever did in the Royal Academy in the midst of party spirit and *personal attack* and sneering remarks." Hoppner "expressed great dissatisfaction with the Academy and went to it against his will." Smirke declined to accompany Farington to a general meeting, as the Academy was "a place he never entered but with a disagreeable feeling." Only ten members were present at that meeting, the bare number required for a quorum. "To such a state," Farington wrote, "is the Academy reduced, more divided than ever."

West gave a private dinner late in January at Newman Street, sent in from a tavern, for the officers and Council members, inviting everyone but Yenn. He presided at the Academy's annual dinner in April, sitting between the Prince of Wales and the duke of Somerset. He hung eleven pictures in the spring exhibition, including *The Deluge, Mary Magdalene at the Sepulchre, The Expulsion from Paradise, The Eagle Bringing the Cup of Water to Psyche, The Blind Belisarius and the Boy,* and *Cranford Bridge.* More works were sent to the 1805 exhibition than in any previous year, and some 1500 of them were rejected. In an unprecedented gesture, West withdrew three of his pictures to give a chance to younger artists. He invited other painters of reputation to follow his example, but none appears to have done so.

West was giving serious thought in the autumn of 1805 to resigning the presidency. Smirke advised him that "he saw nothing but what was difficult and disagreeable attached to his continuing in the chair . . . having such a set of men as now opposed him to deal with. West was silent." Five of his supporters — Shee, Hoppner, Opie, Thomson, and Stothard — had gone over to the opposition on a relatively minor disagreement,[4] and on July 19 Farington recorded the ominous words, "The two sides of the Academy were equal in number." On September 11, West told his colleagues that Wyatt had ruined the Academy. On November 4, in an extraordinary move, he sought out Wyatt and had with him a long, private, and frank conversation. He described it for Farington:

> West said to him that however the matter had been improperly handled by Tresham and Yenn on 10th December last, it was evident that the King had talked with Yenn respecting his (West's) being continued as president . . . He wished to know with certainty His Majesty's sentiments. He was willing to quit the situation.
>
> Wyatt replied that no person was so fit to fill the chair . . . as he (Mr. West) was — that there had been a confederacy formed consisting of Hoppner, Shee and Opie — that it had been proposed to fill the chair by the members in rotation — and that Hoppner should be the first president; but it was afterwards felt that Beechey would not concur in that proposal, and it was judged best to place Wyatt in the chair the first year and Hoppner the second year.
>
> He added that there was a decided determination among them to oppose Lawrence being appointed. Wyatt appeared to be very

---

[4] Fuseli wished to hold his old position as professor of painting in addition to serving as keeper, and West and Farington unwisely supported him. They later persuaded him to withdraw his candidacy for the professorship.

little disposed to the triumvirate, and called one of them "a little devil." [5]

On the evening of November 28, West attended a meeting of the Council and while there signed an Associate diploma for the brilliant young sculptor Richard Westmacott. It was his last act as an officer of the Academy, for he had now definitely decided to resign his position within the week. He told Lawrence, Dance, Smirke, and Farington; Dance wished to resign from the Academy as a gesture of support and protest, but West dissuaded him. (He compromised by resigning as professor of architecture.) Farington called on West and asked permission to put up his name for re-election, but West replied that "he would not continue as president for £1000 a year." He "perceived that West's mind was fully made up ... and under all circumstances I could not advise him against it." He talked to Mrs. West on leaving, and when she expressed her regret that her husband was "being troubled with the feuds of the Royal Academy," he concluded that she had not yet been told of the resignation.

West decided not to take his letter personally to the king but rather to send a copy to Windsor to be delivered at noon on the day of announcement, December 2. He labored over the letter and then gave it to Dance and Farington, who found it "very prolix and under the circumstances ill-judged." They rewrote it for him, and he sent it to be read at the Academy. He was, he said, the only survivor of the four artists who had the honor of presenting to His Majesty a plan for an Academy. After the death of that eminent master, Sir Joshua Reynolds, without solicitation on his part he was unanimously elected to the chair.

> I have now, during a period of fourteen years, endeavoured assiduously to perform the duties of that distinguished situation to the best of my abilities, and I have a consolation in reflecting that I have rendered some aid to its formation, and contributed everything in my power to its prosperity.
>
> Thirty-seven years are nearly completed during which time I have never failed to exhibit my works in the Royal Academy; but whatever may have been my exertions, or whatever my wishes for the welfare of the institution, the occurrence which took place on 10th December last, and subsequent circumstances, have determined me to withdraw from the situation of President of the

---

[5] Wyatt probably was referring to John Hoppner.

Royal Academy. I shall retire to the peaceful pursuit of my profession, and I hope that my present declination will afford you
sufficient time to consider of the choice of my successor.

The election, presided over by the veteran Paul Sandby, was attended by only twenty-one members. West, ill with "gout all over,"
could not be present, and Farington did not choose to go. Wyatt,
the only candidate, received the votes of seventeen of the twenty-
one members. The election, according to Northcote, was "quickly
over" — so quickly that he and Shee, talking below stairs, were too
late to vote when they went up to the meeting. Though he had
recently joined the coalition against West, Shee made a point of
seeking out Wyatt to tell him he would have spoken in favor of
West's re-election if he had been present. Fuseli, who had hoped
that West would remain in office, was certain that he would have
been re-elected if all his supporters had been present.[6] Farington
told him he had resigned the chair when he might have kept it, the
opposition amounting in reality to only thirteen persons.

West's letter of resignation was given to the press, which printed
it widely; most of the comment was friendly, with scathing denunciation of the treatment he had received. The news, however, was
overshadowed by celebration of Nelson's splendid victory over the
French and Spanish fleets off the coast of Spain at Trafalgar, by the
mourning for his death in battle, and by the shocking reports of
Bonaparte's victory over the Austrians and Russians at Austerlitz.

---

[6] Many art historians and biographers of artists writing on this period have
tended to draw unwarranted conclusions when they come upon unfriendly comments made by one artist about another; the conclusion being that the first artist
hated and was a lifelong enemy of the second. The assumption ignores the capacity people had then, as they have today, to hold favorable and unfavorable
opinions at the same time about another person, and to shift from enemy to
friend and from friend to enemy with changing circumstances and the passage
of time. Fuseli is consistently depicted as an inveterate enemy of West who had
nothing but contempt for his art and his person. The evidence lies in a number
of statements Fuseli made about West. But Fuseli also at the same time, and
without being egregiously inconsistent, praised West on occasion, expressed
gratitude for his support, in his classroom lectures was eloquent on the bold
originality of some of his works, notably *The Death of Wolfe*, and wished him
to be re-elected president in 1805.

23

To Stumble, Fall, and Rise Again

I told him the Academy now saw what they had lost by causing West to resign, from which time I had scarcely been near the place.

JOSEPH FARINGTON
to John Hoppner,
November 8, 1806

*O*NE COULD ASSUME that in the spring of 1806 the sun had set on the career of Benjamin West. He had enjoyed a phenomenal success, but now, in his sixty-eighth year, he was reeling under an accumulation of reverses that would surely finish him as an artist if not as a man. He was confined to his home throughout a three-month illness, his wife was an invalid, his sons were a burden and a disappointment. He had been driven from the presidency of the Royal Academy, to which he had devoted decades of labor, and the Academy was controlled by his adversaries. The king, his patron, the source of his power, prestige, and much of his income, was ailing and no longer accessible to him, and those in power at the court thought of him as an admirer of England's enemy, Bonaparte. The works he exhibited had lost favor; Sir George Beaumont, the patron and collector, spoke with regret of "the violent prejudice which prevails against the pictures of West. His drawings are allowed to have merit, but his pictures are spoken of with disgust." When Farington called on West on May 11, he found him "very thin and much broken in appearance," and "his pronunciation affected, perhaps from loss of teeth." His physician, Sir John Macnamara Hayes, said in July, "His personal appearance has much changed in the past twelve months . . . He is become more *bony* and his flesh has fallen in."

A more grievous blow came with the cancellation of the pictures for the Revealed Religion Chapel at Windsor Castle, which West had intended as the crowning achievement of his career. Five years earlier, in August 1801, when the king suffered the brief attack of his illness, he had received an order from the queen, through James Wyatt, to suspend work on the pictures. He wrote a graceful letter to the king on that occasion, lamenting that the suspension, if permanent, "will be ruinous . . . — a damp in the hope of more exalted minds in the refined departments of painting."

> Animated by your commands, gracious Sire, I renewed my professional studies and burnt my midnight lamp to attain and give that polish [to] Your Majesty's chapel which has since marked my subsequent scriptural pictures . . . I have been . . . zealous in promoting merit in [the] three branches of art . . . The ingenious artists have received my professional aid and my galleries and my purse have been open to their studies and their distresses.

He had received no answer. On the king's recovery he sought out and obtained an audience and found that the king had never seen his letter, nor was he aware that the chapel pictures had been stopped. "Go on with your work, West," the king said. "Go on with the pictures, and I will take care of you."

Complaints were heard thereafter, some of them attributed to the royal family, that "West's work never has an end." There had certainly been a great delay, West admitted, but he pointed out that "it was the King's desire the work should proceed slowly to make the expense easier to him." In May 1804, Wyatt had proposed to the king that all West's revealed religion pictures be placed in the theater room at Hampton Court. And then in June 1805 the king himself sent word to West, again through Wyatt, to stop work on the chapel pictures. Of the thirty-five pictures planned, some twenty-eight were completed, a number of others existed as finished oil sketches or preliminary drawings, and all had been "composed." West continued the work for a time at his own expense, but in John Galt's words, the cancellation "rendered the studies of the best part of the artist's life useless, and deprived him of that honourable provision, the fruits of his talents and industry, on which he had counted for the repose of his declining years." He poured out his feelings in a lecture to the students of the Royal Academy:

> If you expect either honour or profit by spending your days and nights in endless labour, that you may excel in the department of

historical painting, you will be miserably deceived, as I have been . . .

You *must* live. You cannot live by historical painting. Do you sigh for riches? Turn the whole bent of your mind — expend all your anxious and laborious hours in becoming fashionable painters of vacant faces. Are you not equal to this? Then design vignettes for books of travel and novels, or subjects for engravers of calico rollers, or daubings upon china ware.

A document was circulated at this time revealing that West had received no less than £34,187 from the king for works he had executed by royal command, and the inference was drawn that he had unfairly amassed a fortune at the king's expense. Indignation subsided, however, when West countercirculated a list of the pictures he had painted with their prices and showed that the amount represented recompense for work done over a thirty-three-year period. Someone made the point that £34,000 was no more than what a moderately successful portrait painter would have earned in a third of a century; someone else observed that the government had offered Francesco Bartolozzi £400 a year simply not to leave England. (He went to Lisbon in 1802 to become head of the Royal Academy there.) West brought up the matter in a conversation with Farington and Smirke in which he asked what they thought of the charge he had made the king for his *Crucifixion* "intended for one end of the chapel at Windsor, the size 36 feet high by 28 feet wide, and containing near seventy figures, many of them colossal in size, [for which] he had charged only 2000 guineas."

West had to seek new sources of income from his painting, but he was hampered in what he might do by his conviction that he must not solicit portrait commissions. "The department of art I have maintained," he wrote to the official in charge of the king's privy purse, "and the station I have the honour to hold under His Majesty, is too dignified to submit to commonplace painting in this country, where my pencil has attained celebrity in the most exalted class of art." In July 1804 he wrote to the owner of the house he rented in Windsor that he could not pay the three years' rent due; he had been disappointed in payments of notes that were owing him. He therefore enclosed a draft for £65.6.0 on Coutts, his banker, dated three weeks later, and his note for £34.13 payable in October. He tried to sell some of his treasured old masters, but he was unwilling to lower their market value by accepting less than inflated prices. When a prominent collector offered to buy one of his pictures but demurred at the figure asked, West offered to sell it at less on condition that the amount be kept a secret. The collector was offended and refused to enter into such an agreement; when word of the attempted transaction reached the art community, West was criticized for unbecoming conduct. He expressed his philosophy on sale of his pictures when he said, "If it is worth their while to offer me that sum to have it, it is worth my while to keep it."

One would indeed assume that the sun had set on the career of Benjamin West, but the assumption would be mistaken. He recovered from his illness and began to enjoy his freedom from the time-consuming, energy-draining labors of running the Royal Academy. By withdrawing himself, he told Farington, he had secured his own comfort. "He could now wake in the morning without the unpleasant consideration of having those people to meet in the evening; to him it had been a happy release." He had found no difference, he said, in the respect and attention paid to him. If the king were to ask him to return to the chair, he would beg to decline. When Farington had commented in May on West's broken appearance, he attributed it to his close confinement at home, but also to "much professional application." West, indeed, was working night and day on a picture he hoped would be so sensationally successful that it would "show the Academy what they had done in causing the author of it to withdraw himself, and an architect to be placed in his room."

He was painting the death of Lord Nelson, killed off Cape Trafalgar on October 21, 1805, by a bullet in his spine. As soon as that news reached London on November 6, a race began among artists to be the first to produce a commemorative picture, sculpture, or monument. Lord Hawkesbury, secretary of state for foreign affairs, sent the king's command to the Royal Academy "to consider the best mode of perpetuating the memory of Lord Nelson." The Corporation of the City of London offered £500 to the sculptor who designed the best monument for the Guildhall. Richard Westall, Arthur William Devis, and William Turner were known to be working on Nelson pictures. A printseller named Thomson engaged Copley, agreeing to pay him £1200 for a death scene and the right to engrave a print by public subscription. West signed a partnership agreement with the engraver James Heath. He would paint a companion piece to *The Death of Wolfe* and pay Heath 1200 guineas to make the engraving; they would then publish it jointly, sharing the expenses and the profits equally.

West's claim to the subject was better than most. George Ticknor, a young Boston scholar who was spending four years traveling and studying in Europe, recorded it in 1815 on a visit to 14 Newman Street. As West told the story, he was sitting beside Nelson at a "large entertainment." Nelson, talking to Sir William Hamilton, expressed regret that as a youth he had never acquired a taste for art and the ability to discriminate between good and bad pictures. "But there is one picture whose power I do feel," he said, turning to West. "I never pass a paint [print] shop where your *Death of Wolfe* is in the window without being stopped by it." West acknowledged the compliment. Why, Nelson asked, had West painted no more like it? "Because, my Lord," West replied, "there are no more subjects. But I fear your intrepidity will yet furnish me with another such scene, and if it should, I shall certainly avail myself of it." "Will you? Will you, Mr. West?" Nelson poured champagne, touched glasses with him, and said, "Then I hope I shall die in the next battle."

Nelson died in the cockpit[1] of his flagship *Victory*, but West chose to paint the death scene on the quarterdeck against a background of fighting ships, fallen rigging, swirling flags, and smoke of battle. There was, he said,

> no other way of representing the death of a Hero but by an *epic* representation of it. It must exhibit the event in a way to excite awe and veneration, and that which may be required to give superior interest to the representation must be introduced — all that can show the importance of the Hero. Wolfe must not die like a common soldier under a bush; neither should Nelson be represented dying in the gloomy hold of a ship, like a sick man in a prison hole. To move the mind there should be a spectacle presented to raise and warm the mind, and all should be proportioned to the highest idea conceived of the hero. No boy . . . would be animated by a representation of Nelson dying like an ordinary man. His feelings must be roused and his mind inflamed by a scene great and extraordinary. A mere matter of fact will never produce this effect.

Though he changed the scene to suit his higher purposes, West was painstaking in his effort to paint the details accurately. He studied the accounts of the action and of Nelson's death, and he questioned the officers and seamen from the *Victory* who came to his studio to tell their stories and pose for their portraits. Thomas Goble, who was on the *Victory* and became secretary of the Fleet when his predecessor was killed early in the battle, offered him continu-

---

[1] A space below the waterline in a warship, occupied by the quarters of the junior officers and used as a dressing station for the wounded during an action.

ing technical advice. Nelson is shown in full uniform at a moment just after he received his mortal wound. Officers and seamen stand or kneel in attitudes of concern or grief. Men are still firing; some are waving their hats as a signal of victory. Nelson is supported by the ship's chaplain and the purser, while Dr. Beatty, the surgeon, massages his chest. Nelson has reached out to clasp the hand of Captain Hardy, who (somewhat prematurely) reads from a paper listing the nineteen ships taken from the French and Spanish. In the right foreground a seaman kneels at Nelson's feet, while another stands wringing his hands — figures that recall the contemplative Indian and the anguished grenadier in *The Death of Wolfe*. Some sixty-five figures are shown in all, perhaps half of them recognizable portraits of men who were there. It was a remarkable feat for an artist to research and paint such a picture in less than six months, and especially so for one sixty-eight years old who was working through a prolonged illness.

West was the first on the market with his picture. Copley sprained his painting arm in a fall and seems not to have finished his work; Devis produced his a year later. West did not send his *Death of Nelson* to the Academy exhibition that spring; he did not, in fact, hang a picture there at all. (It was his only absence in thirty-seven years.) Instead he showed the work in his own gallery, displaying with it his *Death of Wolfe* and *Battle of La Hogue*, both borrowed for the occasion from Lord Grosvenor. He sent out 6500 cards of invitation, underscoring his disdain of the Academy by opening on the same day as the Academy's exhibition. In less than two months some 30,000 people visited his house and paid a fee to see the three pictures. They "behaved extremely well," he said, and neither stole nor damaged his property. Visitors approached *The Death of Nelson* with awe and reverence and men removed their hats.

West's triumph was sweetened when the queen sent word to him that she wished to be listed as one of his subscribers to the Nelson print. He made the most of her request to see the picture by advertising in the newspapers that *The Death of Nelson* could not be seen on May 15 "as it is to be sent to the Queen by her command." He met the king on taking the picture to Buckingham House, but nothing is known of their conversation except that the king took West to a window to show him his eyes; the sight of one was nearly gone and the other could see in only one direction.

In the midst of his resounding success, West began a second interpretation of the death scene called *The Apotheosis of Lord Nelson*, this one intended for the king's monument to Nelson in St.

Paul's. He designed a large three-part memorial which, he said, used all "three branches of art that constitute the Academy" — painting, sculpture, and architecture. For it he painted an extravagantly allegorical picture in which *Victory* takes the body of the hero, like a dead Christ, from the arms of *Neptune* and presents it to *Britannia*. Flaxman won the St. Paul's commission; West exhibited his picture at the Academy show in 1807 and allowed it to be used as a frontispiece in a biography of Nelson. He then completed a third interpretation in 1808 in which he placed the death scene in the "gloomy hold" of the *Victory* with only nine persons present. This too was used as an illustration in the biography. When Heath's engraving after the first *Death of Nelson* was completed in 1811, West hung it with the original in the Academy exhibition of that year.

West's hopes were now directed at a new organization he had helped to found during his last months as president of the Academy: the British Institution for Promotion of the Fine Arts. Its promise, he told Farington, was so great that the Royal Academy would soon become "a mere drawing school."

The British Institution grew out of a passionate belief West shared with others that Britain must have a national gallery of the fine arts. James Barry, Flaxman, Desenfans, Opie, Shee, and a dilettante-collector-author named R. Payne Knight had written, declaimed, and expostulated on the theme that the lack of such a gallery was a national disgrace. In Paris in 1802 West had preached to Sir Francis Baring and Charles James Fox of the need for a national museum of painting, and Fox had assured him, "If ever I have it in my power to influence our government to promote the arts, the conversation that we have had today will not be forgotten." Later in London, West made his appeal to two men in government, Sir Charles Long and Sir Abraham Hume, and Long attempted to win Pitt's support for an art subsidy. Pitt had no interest in the arts and took no action before his early death in 1806; Fox, when he finally entered the government, died before he could make good on his promise. In the spring of 1805, however, Thomas Bernard, a philanthropist, the driving force behind the Foundling Hospital, drew up a plan for founding the British Institution with financing by private subscribers. Nearly £8000 was subscribed by 125 persons, including one duke, five marquesses, fourteen earls, two viscounts, nine barons, seven baronets, two bishops, four ladies, twenty-two Members of Parliament, five clergymen, and twenty-two private gentlemen, bankers, and merchants. The directors, none of whom, by design, were artists, bought John Boydell's bankrupt Shakespeare Gallery at 100 Pall Mall and remodeled it to suit the Institution's purposes.

In his last months as Academy president, West had invited a committee to his home to hear Bernard's proposal. Farington, Lawrence, Smirke, and Beaumont were among those invited; Shee and Hoppner were furious that they were not. Bernard explained that the British Institution would accept and buy pictures for a national gallery, offer "a new venue in London" where artists could exhibit their works for sale, award prizes for new pictures, and provide rooms where for the first time in England temporary loan exhibitions of old master paintings could be displayed. The committee asked West to approach the king, explain the plan, and obtain his agreement to serve as a patron. West saw the king, satisfied him on some objections he voiced, and on May 16, 1805, wrote: "On the conduct of myself in this business, I hope Your Majesty will find it, and the plan, congenial with the patronage and protection of the fine arts in the establishment of the Royal Academy." The two institutions, he said, had very different objectives. The Academy had been formed for the instruction of pupils, and the British Institution would encourage artists who had arrived at maturity in their professions. The king approved the plan within two weeks.

The first exhibition of 250 selected pictures by living artists opened in the Institution's British Gallery on February 17, 1806, admission one shilling. (Portraits were excluded.) West exhibited 15 works, placing on them such high prices and so many conditions of sale that it appeared he did not wish to part with them. (They were, for example, not to be resold by the purchaser, and no prints from them were to be made.) Hoppner called the show "the puke of the Royal Academy exhibition" and tried to have a rule passed that no Academician might send a work to the British Institution that he had not previously exhibited at the Academy.

Various paintings were given to the Institution's British Gallery to form the first important public collection of art in England. That summer it exhibited a small but select group of old masters lent by its subscribers, open only to painters and students of painting. One of the lenders was Sir George Beaumont, who on occasion would send a new purchase to hang for a while in West's gallery, where members and students of the Academy might see it. Another lender was John Julius Angerstein, who had arrived from Russia as a boy around 1750, became a broker and underwriter, and founded the modern Lloyds of London. With West as his advisor, he had been collecting pictures for some six years, buying only the choicest masterpieces, most of them from broken collections in revolutionary Europe. Angerstein's gallery was always open to members of the Academy.[2]

West's success in helping to found the British Institution and the respect shown him by those who were its subscribers probably had influenced his decision in the autumn of 1805 to resign as Academy president. He tended to speak thereafter of the new organization in a proprietary manner that annoyed his friend Farington. At a dinner given by the students of the British Institution, Farington wrote

> West was the only member of the Academy present and was flattered by [Valentine] Green[3] in a speech, on which West commented and said it had brought tears into his eyes. He went on and assumed to himself the credit of having occasioned the establishment of the British Institution . . . *I* might with as good a right claim the merit of being the author of it, for I was present, with Mr. West, when Mr. *Bernard* the real author of it, read his proposal for forming it. To such lengths does West's self-love carry him — to expose himself to be confuted by many.

The art historian W. G. Constable, writing in 1924 on "The Foundation of the National Gallery," was more generous: "An honourable exception to the indifference and selfishness of the members of the Royal Academy was the attitude of Benjamin West; and for him must be claimed no inconsiderable share in urging upon public authorities the need for action." Constable adds that Sir Charles Long, later Lord Farnborough, who was close to West, was among those primarily instrumental in bringing about the founding of the British Institution and its British Gallery, out of which developed England's National Gallery.

West was pleased at being relieved of the toil and turmoil of the Royal Academy's affairs, but he must have been pained by what was taking place in Somerset House in his absence. It was to be expected, of course, that the quarrels among the members

---

[2] Angerstein's pictures were sold to the government in 1824 for £57,000, and, with works given by the British Institution, they formed the nucleus of the collection of Britain's National Gallery of Art, founded in that year. Of the thirty-eight Angerstein pictures purchased, all but five or six have withstood the critical tests of time and added knowledge as works of genuine merit and aesthetic value. There were, among others, five choice Claudes, Hogarth's *Marriage à la Mode*, works by Poussin, Titian, Rubens, Rembrandt, Vandyke, and David Wilkie (the only living artist), and the second largest picture in the National Gallery, still number one in the catalogue, S. del Piombo's *Raising of Lazarus*.

[3] Engraver, first keeper of the British Institution, and West's neighbor on Newman Street.

(for some of which he had once been held responsible) would continue apace. Shee and Edmund Garvey exchanged words on where their pictures were to be placed in the 1806 exhibition and on which other pictures were placed beside theirs; as did Westall and Lawrence, and Hoppner and Lawrence, and Hoppner and Shee, and Hoppner and Garvey. Mrs. Fuseli quarreled with the Academy's housekeeper, telling her, a gentlewoman, that she was really only the Academy's sweeper. The Academy Club was dissolved and then reconstituted in another location with Wyatt's party in control. Tresham and Wyatt, West learned from Beckford, no longer associated with each other. Beechey announced that he never again would speak to Tresham. Wyatt appointed Hoppner his deputy, but Hoppner resigned after a few weeks and declared he was going to call a general meeting "to enquire into the cause of the delay in opening the exhibition." (Flaxman said if such a meeting was called, he would go to be amused.) Richards told West that when he now went to Windsor with the officers, the king signed the papers without a word and did not enter into any conversation with them. Mrs. West wrote to the Trumbulls on September 29, 1806:

> Mr. Wyatt was elected for 1806, since when all business has been at a stand, the President never having made his appearance. Hoppner, thinking himself better qualified for the Chair, accepted the office of deputy, but they soon disagreed and abused each other in their own style. Mr. W., as he says he will, retires to the peaceful pursuit of his profession, and has in his picture, *The Death of Lord Nelson*, given a proof of what he can do when his mind is fully occupied in the peaceful pursuit of his subject. The picture gives general satisfaction: Mr. West admitted by ticket to see the picture at our house, and I believe the number that came could not be less than 30,000 who have seen it.

It was soon apparent to the other Academy officers that Wyatt was not a competent president, and it became evident to the members-at-large during the 1806 annual dinner and exhibition. Both had to be postponed one week because Wyatt had not yet seen the king — "his old habits of delay," Farington wrote, "thus operating." (The invitations could not be sent out until the king had been consulted.) Wyatt finally reported that His Majesty declined to attend the exhibition, since he could see the pictures only imperfectly, and it would pain him to go. The reason was a valid one, but it was recalled that West had always persuaded His Majesty to honor the Academy with a visit. Since the king would not attend, the princesses also declined.

The dinner (which neither West nor Farington attended) was sent in from Freemason's Tavern, and the diners complained that the food was cold and not good; the proprietors gave as their excuse that they had no place to dress it, as Mrs. Fuseli refused to allow them to use the Academy's great kitchen. Wyatt gave the toasts in so low a voice that he could not be heard. The Prince of Wales mocked him by asking him to say, "as loud as he could," that His Royal Highness drank the healths of the noblemen and gentlemen present — a remark that Sir George Beaumont thought was either impertinent or foolish. "Wyatt was a sad president at the Great Dinner," Farington reported. "It might truly be said that he fell below West in his manner of communicating to the company what he had to say." The £300 dinner bill, he added, "was enormous ... Many of the charges were shamefully extravagant and unreasonable. Such has been the management under the new government of the Academy!" Receipts of the exhibition were down because of the week's delay, and the Council reprimanded Fuseli for his inattention during the arrangements.

Farington was not an unprejudiced observer, but other members were equally strong in their censure of the new government. James Boaden, editor of the *Oracle,* observed as early as May 5, "Those members who made Wyatt president are now dissatisfied with him." When Farington asked him why, Boaden replied, "Because he does not take notice enough of them." Wyatt presided at the king's birthday dinner in June, and William Porden, a fellow architect, found him "very dull in the chair." Garvey complained that Wyatt neglected Academy business, did not answer notes from Richards, and did not attend meeings. Henry Thomson "expressed great dislike of Wyatt being president." Wyatt was away from London, Farington wrote, for a stretch of five months, "trifling away 13 weeks of it at the Marquess of Hertford's." He was a heavy drinker and had a habit of falling asleep in his place at the few meetings and Academy lectures he did attend. He did not keep appointments. He was given to bursts of intensive and effective application, but these were followed by periods of irresponsible indifference. Beechey and Cosway lamented to a friend that they had had high hopes when Wyatt was elected, believing that great reforms would follow, but they were disappointed in his conduct.

Since re-electing Wyatt was out of the question, there was much talk in the summer and autumn of 1806 of choosing his successor. Of the two leading aspirants, Hoppner had a manner considered offensive by many members, and Lawrence was felt to be cold, distant, and reserved. In any case, each lived in terror at the thought that the other might become president. Smirke preferred

Dance, but Dance was an architect and the painters wanted a painter to be president — if they could find a painter acceptable to the other painters. The new duke of Gloucester, the king's nephew (known as "Silly Billy") laid a wager of five guineas in the city that Bourgeois, Beechey, or Loutherbourgh would be chosen, though none was seriously considered in the Academy. Northcote contributed the remark that if a mere portrait painter was to be elected, it would be the first instance of a painter of dolls being president of an academy of painting. Henry Hope of Cavendish Square said in company that it would be advisable to have for president "a person not professional, but a man of distinction," and he named Sir George Beaumont. His recommendation was considered to be pushing and unbecoming in a nonmember.

On September 14, 1806, Edmund Garvey uttered the unthinkable: He wanted to bring back West.

The idea spread. A member recalled that West, unlike Hoppner and some others, spoke favorably of other artists. Flaxman said he would be willing to vote for West, despite his indecision and other defects. He thought that re-electing him would be an appropriate compliment to him after the gross treatment he had received. Thomson preferred Hoppner, despite his "intemperate and offensive conduct to most of the members," but he felt that under the circumstances it would be best to bring West back, though he did not like him. Farington told the members, "West, in all the conversations I had with him . . . declared that nothing should induce him again to accept that office."

In the autumn of 1806, Farington quietly began taking measures to bring West back to the presidency. He was no doubt moved by a desire to regain his lost power, but respect must be paid to the motives he expressed to Lawrence: to keep the presidency from being degraded and the Academy thrown into confusion by a fight for the office.

Hoppner, apparently acting on behalf of the remnants of the shattered opposition, called on Farington on November 6. It was impossible, he said, to go on with Wyatt; the Academy, unsupported by its members, would fall. He had come to learn which candidate they could agree to support. Farington said that the members now saw the consequences of having driven Mr. West from the presidency. For himself, he had scarcely been near the Academy since Wyatt took office ten months earlier. In his opinion, the best possible course to prevent jealousy and dissension was to return West to office.

Hoppner went away and called again two days later. He agreed to support West, but he opposed sending a deputation to solicit him to return. Farington concurred: West should not be elected unless the members knew privately beforehand that he would accept the office. He should not be given the opportunity to refuse it publicly.

Consultations were held among Lawrence, Thomson, Dance, Westall, Smirke, and Flaxman. Farington repeated his doubt that West would accept the office. Mrs. West was very ill, and she certainly would not wish her husband to subject himself again to troubles that had made them both unhappy. Farington, nevertheless, was authorized to tell West that he would have strong support if he agreed to accept.

West took two weeks to make up his mind. George Dance was a gentleman, he said, a man of sense and a man of business, and would make a good president, even though he was an architect. He spoke of the indignities he had received as president and of the abhorrence he felt for some of the members. His tranquil life would be disturbed if he took the office. On the other hand, if he did return, it would enable the members "to make a proper representation" for history of the circumstances of his resignation and of what had taken place with Wyatt in the chair. If he did take office again, he could not think of holding it for more than one year. He would agree, he said at last, to serve for one year if the members felt it would restore order and would enable them "to make a proper exposition of the state of the Academy." He expressed the hope that the court would order him to complete the pictures for the Chapel of Revealed Religion, even though Wyatt had changed the design of the building.

"I was now authorized," Farington wrote on December 3, one week before the election, "to communicate his consent to accept the chair, and that I should give him information of what might pass upon it."

Given these tidings, the members took another look at the faults and virtues of Benjamin West as P.R.A. There was resentment at what was surely a forgivable sin: He had recently told the students of the British Institution that he considered the respect and attention they paid him to be the greatest honor he had ever received. Smirke reported the revival of an old complaint: Dr. Hayes, West's physician, had lately spoken to him of the "excessive indiscretion of West, situated as he was with the King, in speaking as he did of the state of Europe and his partiality to Bonaparte." Dr. Hayes himself was thought to be partial to Bonaparte, but he said of West, "He talks in such a way as cannot be agreeable to the feelings of Englishmen, and he ought to be advised to the contrary." Smirke suggested that Farington was the proper person to convey such advice. Farington told Smirke, "West certainly had not an *English mind,* and is kept to this country only by the income he receives from the King and by his sons having married here." But the members recalled that West was a painter of great themes, not of mere portraits; he spoke well of other artists; his presence in the chair excluded other candidates less desirable; he paid attention to his presidential duties; and in all the years he was in office the exhibition was on time and the food at the great dinner was properly cooked and served while it was still warm.

The election was to be held on December 10, 1806. That morning Wyatt sent a letter of resignation as president to be read at the meeting, adding in it, "The best thing the members can do will be to re-elect Mr. West." On the first ballot, Beechey received one vote, Hoppner one vote, Loutherbourgh four, and West sixteen. On the second ballot, Loutherbourgh received four votes, West seventeen, with one abstention. West was declared the new president.

Farington called on him the next morning and found that Lawrence and Westall had already been there to tell him of his election. West was "very well pleased with all that has been done." He did not know how the king would take it, he said, but if His Majesty should strike his pen through his name, he would not be uneasy about it, but would leave the matter up to the members. The queen and Princess Elizabeth, he thought, were so much dissatisfied with Wyatt that the queen, at least, would be pleased to hear of his re-election. In January he called on the king, who received him "like a brother." Friends at court told him that the king had expressed satisfaction at his return but had said he did not think West would accept.

West received letters of congratulation "from many distinguished persons, expressing the pleasure they felt." Several members who had voted against him approached to make their peace. John Soane came up to his chair at an Academy dinner to compliment him on his victory, and John Yenn did the same at the first meeting of the new Council. West did not outwardly glory in his triumph. When Paul Sandby called at Newman Street to express his satisfaction, West "spoke prudently to him." The two of them, he said, were of the small number of original members remaining, and they should do whatever they could for the benefit of the institution. Ozias Humphry made his apologies to Farington, who told him that the experiment had now been tried and it had showed what the Academy could be reduced to in consequence.[4] Thomson told Farington

---

[4] Farington followed his account of the visit with, "Humphry's father a barber at Honiton and his mother manufactured lace and sold spirits by *retail.*"

that he now "reprobated" the conduct of the party he had served and that henceforth in his voting he would join with "*the respectable part of the Society.*" Copley wearied Samuel Woodforde, R.A., with long complaints of the Academy's activities and said he did not intend to go there again; he "spoke of the disrespect shown to a man of his reputation, and that he should keep from the Society till they should require him to go." West sent his son Raphael to call on Desenfans to demonstrate that he bore no ill will toward him. Desenfans responded to the overture by asking for a complete reconciliation and by making West one of the trustees in charge of his art collection. "No man," West told Farington, "could appear to suffer greater anxiety and distress of mind . . . proceeding from reflecting upon his own conduct." West and Bourgeois met at an Academy dinner and were so "sociable" with each other that it was commented on. (Desenfans died a few months later, leaving his collection to his friend Bourgeois, who in 1811 left it and £12,000 to the Gallery of Alleyn's College of God's Gift at Dulwich — Dulwich Gallery in south London.)

West resumed the duties of the presidency on January 1, 1807. When "Jan" Opie died in April, in his forty-fifth year, West represented the Academy at the funeral.[5] (Fuseli declined to go, because he had once attended a funeral in a chilly cathedral, caught cold, and lost five teeth as a result.) At that year's annual dinner West sat between the Prince of Wales and the duke of Kent. The dinner was well managed, the food was hot and on the table by six P.M., the toasts could be heard, and the exhibition opened next day on schedule.

At an Academy dinner three months earlier, the first West had attended since his re-election, Caleb Whitefoord, the Craven Street wine merchant, diplomatist, wit, and art patron, rose and asked leave to make a few remarks. The president, he said, had given a number of excellent toasts that evening, but there was one toast he could not give. He, Whitefoord, therefore wished to give it. He proposed, "The Health of the President of the Royal Academy." The toast was drunk, and it was followed by a crescendo of applause, prolonged over several minutes.

---

[5] Opie was buried in the crypt of St. Paul's in a perpendicular position, but by accident, with his head down and his feet up. The undertaker sought out the chief mourner, asking if Mrs. Opie should be informed and if the coffin should be reversed. The chief mourner, a relative who had never liked Opie, replied, "Oh, Lord, no! Leave him alone. If I meet him in the next world walking about on his head, I shall know him."

The Era of Good Feeling

Mr. West, to whom I was soon introduced, received me with the greatest kindness. I shall never forget his benevolent smile when he took me by the hand: It is still fresh in my memory . . . His gallery was open to me at all times, and his advice always ready and kindly given.

WASHINGTON ALLSTON
1779–1843

WEST'S PLEASURE in his Academy triumphs was checked when Elizabeth West's "paralytic complaint" became worse. In May 1807 she lamented to Farington that Mr. West could not afford to send her to Bath for a cure. Any notion that her husband was rich, she said, was unfounded. He had never invested a shilling in the public funds, and *"she could say more."* His easy temper had caused him to allow his sons to be brought up improvidently. They could contribute nothing to lessen his expenses.

West somehow obtained money for the trip to Bath and set out with Elizabeth in July, believing this to be her only hope for recovery. They traveled the hundred miles (normally a sixteen-hour journey) in a private carriage, accompanied by Mrs. Thomas Banks, now three years a widow, who had been engaged to attend Mrs. West, and by Mary Moser Lloyd, R.A., who went along as a friend. West intended to stay only long enough to get his wife settled, perhaps a fortnight, but he changed his mind and spent some three months at Bath. He kept the carriage and every morning rode out on excursions to make sketches, hiring two or four horses as the distance might require. He was in raptures over the beauty of Bath and the country for twenty miles around, concluding that there was nothing in the world superior to their variety of landscape and noble scenes; the finest large, square rocks for a painter he had ever seen; worked-out quarries that were now most picturesque and romantic; roads with occasional pools and streams of water falling alongside from the hills. Except for the Tivoli falls, he said, the countryside around Rome itself was not to be compared with that of Bath.

At William Beckford's request he rode the twenty-five miles to Fonthill and spent three days there. Beckford was in financial trouble. He revealed that he had spent £242,000 in building Fonthill Abbey, of which at least £30,000, he felt, was a waste caused by James Wyatt's negligence and inattention. Wyatt had encased the timbers of the abbey in a new material called compo-cement, which he said would last forever but which had deteriorated so badly that the tower had to be dismantled in 1806 and rebuilt in stone. (It collapsed again in 1825.) He had been swindled by rapacious agents in Jamaica, he was plagued with lawsuits over his plantations, and the price of sugar had collapsed. To settle claims against him, he had sold his estates in Bedfordshire and at St. Pancras for £74,000, which left the Fonthill property, good for £10,000 a year, as his main source of income. He had sharply reduced his scale of living, selling his carriages and horses and discharging the grooms. The building of the abbey, nevertheless, went on. He had just moved into the south wing and was making it his residence. Fonthill House had been dismantled and most of its contents sold at auction; the materials were being used to complete the abbey. He wished Mr. West to assist him in disposing of a number of his pictures and drawings.

The Wests returned to London early in November. Elizabeth West had suffered from bathing in the springs but had so benefited by drinking the waters that West thought she might survive the winter. She was no longer speaking to Mrs. Banks and Mrs. Lloyd, having had "a certain difference" with them at Bath. Farington, calling on the Wests, found them together in their "little room," where West was touching with white chalk a painting called *Prince Bladud Discovering the Medicinal Virtues of the Bath Springs*. He had "strong marks of age in his countenance" but seemed to have lost none of his power as an artist. When Farington drank tea with Mrs. West several months later, "she complained much of the state of the world, of bad servants, etc., and said that were it not for Mr. West she would wish herself out of the world." She suffered from nervous and bilious ailments, said she had begun to use glasses too soon, and lamented, "My sight depends on the state of my nerves, which are at times intolerably bad." Dr. Hayes opined that West's painting was bad for her, as the smell of white paint brought on her frequent paralytic complaints. West, he said, did not seem to be affected by what might happen: "He feels only for the present."

Relations between England and the United States had been bad from March 1801, when the pro-British Federalists were supplanted by the pro-French Republicans. They became worse in October 1807 with an attack on Britain in President Jefferson's message to Congress, followed in December by an Embargo Act (1807) and a Nonintercourse Law (1809) that attempted (unsuccessfully) to interdict trade with the warring nations and produced a movement in New England to secede from the South. Despite the tensions and the threat of war, however, and all through the five years of the Academy dissension, West's American School had flourished; young Americans had continued to come to England and to 14 Newman Street in search of artistic instruction. Rembrandt and Rubens Peale, two of the seventeen children of West's favorite pupil some thirty-five years earlier, arrived in 1802 with a letter to West from their father and advice from President Jefferson on how to conduct themselves among class-conscious Europeans. They also brought with them the skeleton of a mammoth, one of two they had helped their father to unearth near Newburgh, New York. (They joked that Rubens, the younger brother, was in charge of the mammoth, while Rembrandt, who was twenty-three and had with him a wife and two children, was in charge of Rubens.) To display the monster they rented the old Royal Academy quarters at 118 Pall Mall, redecorated it in green baize, and mounted the bones on a pedestal. Rembrandt lectured to audiences on the mammoth but, tiring of this, wrote a descriptive leaflet titled *An Historical Disquisition on the Mammoth or Great American Incognitum, an Extinct, Immense, Carnivorous Animal whose Remains Have Been Found in North America*. He dedicated this work to Sir Joseph Banks, president of the Royal Society, whose portrait he painted and who obtained for him admission to the British Museum without being run through as one of a group and introduced him to important people in the scientific world. One of these was his countryman Robert Fulton, who, having returned from France to England, was trying to sell his plunging boat to the British Admiralty.

Rembrandt's real purpose in going to England was to study under West. Following his father's edict that "anyone can learn to paint," he had studied art from the age of eight and at seventeen had painted a portrait of President Washington from life (three sittings of three hours each, beginning at 7 A.M.). West, he said, "received me affectionately and kindly directed my studies in his gallery," introducing him to Thomas Lawrence and Washington Allston, an American pupil who had arrived a few months earlier. Rembrandt attended classes at the Royal Academy and showed two pictures in the 1803 exhibition, one of them a portrait of himself holding a tooth of his mammoth. Rembrandt and West were among the first to make lithographic drawings, and it is quite likely that West introduced him to that new art, or at least gave him instruction in it.

The mammoth was an international sensation; it was the first time man had laid eyes on that animal of the Pleistocene epoch, and for a time the Pall Mall showroom was crowded. But then interest flagged, perhaps because Londoners were once again preparing themselves for an invasion by Bonaparte, and so the brothers took their skeleton to the provinces, vainly hoping to recoup their losses and pay their mounting debts. Back in London, when they were unable to sell the mammoth, West advised them to return home. He would, he said, either go with them or follow soon after; he intended to begin a new career in America. (This was at the height of his troubles at the Academy.) "I did not suppress my conviction," Rembrandt wrote, "that he could not find encouragement for the employment of his pencil in History" in the United States. West was not pleased at having an illusion shattered by one he must have known was speaking the truth. Rembrandt suggested innocently, however, that Mr. West could do very well if he enlarged his "spirited composition" of *Death on the Pale Horse* and took it around various American cities as a traveling exhibition. The master, Rembrandt recollected, was "mortified with the idea of descending to such means of getting money.... Mild as was his temper, and pale his complexion, his countenance suddenly became flushed, and he replied, 'I will thank you *never* to name that subject again!' " [1]

The Peales returned alone to Philadelphia in the autumn of 1803. They were still in debt, but they ingeniously persuaded their largest creditor, a bookseller in the Strand, to go with them to America, where they would pay him and he could use the money to set himself up in the New World. Rubens painted still-life subjects in a primitive manner, but because of bad eyesight specialized in museum

---

[1] Rembrandt Peale followed his own advice in 1820. He mounted a traveling exhibition of his massive allegorical picture, *Court of Death*, 24 by 13 feet with twenty-three life-size figures, printed 100,000 colored engravings at $1 each, and cleared almost $9000 in thirteen months.

management. Rembrandt, on his way to a remarkable career in art, science, and self-promotion, instructed his sixty-two-year-old father in the new realism in painting and inspired him to take up again his brush and palette. Charles Peale wrote to his old teacher in London that he felt he would now produce better work than ever. Rembrandt was again in Europe in 1808 and present in Paris at a great moment in American art. "When I was painting the portrait of the celebrated David," he wrote in his *Reminiscences,* "David asked me, 'why it was that all the best painters in London were Americans.' I replied, 'Not all.' He added, 'West, Copley, Trumbull, Allston.' "

Washington Allston, who would come to be known as America's first full-fledged romantic artist, arrived in June 1801, a handsome and engaging twenty-one-year-old artist from Charleston, South Carolina. With him came Edward Greene Malbone, a New Englander, a self-taught painter of miniatures, a classmate of Allston's at Harvard. They took rooms together at 51 Upper Titchfield Street, Marylebone, and set out to learn what they could of art and life in London. Allston went to Somerset House, made a drawing of the Academy's plaster *Gladiator,* and submitted it to West, to whom he had managed an introduction. West was astonished when Allston told him it was his first drawing at the Academy and complimented him on the correctness of his eye and on preserving not only the form of his subject but also its facial expression, which few students thought to do. He signed papers sponsoring Washington Allston as an Academy student on October 3, 1801.

Fuseli gave Allston the student's numbered and dated ivory wafer and asked him if he intended to make a career as an artist. "I mean to be an artist," he replied, "if industry will make me one." Fuseli inquired, "In what branch of the art?" Allston replied, "History." Fuseli said, "If I have any skill in physiognomy, you have more than industry on your side. But you have come a great way to starve." Allston replied, "I have a certain patrimony." "Ah," said Fuseli, "that makes a difference."

Allston had left America "strongly prejudiced" against West's work — a feeling he later attributed to the inferior quality of the engravings he had seen. To a young friend in Charleston he wrote:

> You will no doubt be surprised that among the many painters in London I should rank Mr. West as first. I must own I myself was not a little surprised to find him such . . . But when I saw his gallery and the innumerable excellences which it contained, I pronounced him one of the greatest men in the world. I have

looked upon his understanding with indifference, and his imagination with contempt, but I have now reason to suppose them both vigorous in the highest degree.

He was overwhelmed at his first sight of *Death on the Pale Horse*: "A more sublime and awful picture I never beheld. It is impossible to conceive anything more terrible . . . and I am certain no painter has exceeded Mr. West in the fury, horror and despair which he has represented in the surrounding figures."

Malbone, in the meantime, had shown West his miniatures, and West expressed a high opinion of his talents, gave him free access to his gallery, and showed him "marked and friendly attentions." Malbone wrote to an American friend, "Yesterday was the first time he had seen . . . my painting; today he condescended to walk a mile to pay me a visit, and told me that I must not look forward to anything short of the highest excellence. He was surprised to see how far I had advanced without instruction." After examining a miniature portrait of Allston done by Malbone — water colors on ivory — West declared, "I have seldom seen a miniature that pleased me more."

Malbone drew for a short time at the Academy, contrived to see every old master that was available for viewing in London, and shocked Allston by asserting that they held no interest for him — he preferred the work of Thomas Lawrence. He stayed in England only five months. West urged him to stay longer, assuring him he had nothing to fear from the competition, but he returned to Charleston in December, giving as his reason family matters that required his attention, though there was cause to believe he felt he could learn nothing more to his advantage in Europe. He died of tuberculosis in 1807, only thirty years of age. West never forgot his lost protégé; four years later he said to James Monroe, special minister to Britain, "I have seen a picture painted by a young man of the name of Malbone, which no man in England could excel." In 1808 an American visitor showed West several Malbone portraits in miniature. West asked the favor of retaining them for a while; when the time came to give them up, he said he could hardly bear to part with them; he considered them invaluable.

Allston showed three pictures in the 1802 Academy exhibition, one of them, curiously enough, in the Hogarth style. The following year he traveled to Paris with the American artist John Vanderlyn, going by way of Holland. He spent the next four years on the Continent, much of the time in Rome. There he became a friend and companion of Washington Irving, whom he almost converted from a writer to a painter, and of the poet Samuel Taylor Coleridge, whose portrait he painted and who gave him a golden rule of aesthetics: Never judge a work of art by its defects.

In 1805 the pictures commissioned for the Shakespeare Gallery by the late John Boydell were sold at auction. Robert Fulton bought two of West's works: *Ophelia before the King and Queen* (125 guineas) and *King Lear in the Storm at the Hovel on the Heath* (205 guineas). "Mr. West has been retouching my pictures," Fulton wrote to Barlow on the eve of his departure for America, adding the rather inappropriate comment, "They are charming." Fulton had been engaged for several years in trying to blow up the French fleet with his automatic torpedoes, but he failed. His friend West was much embarrassed; he had been alerting his colleagues that *"within ten days"* they would hear of some extraordinary development in the war. Despite the failure, the British government, in an arbitrated settlement, paid Fulton the very large sum of £15,000 for his services, most of which he had already spent. "My situation now," he wrote to Barlow, "is, my hands are free to burn, sink and destroy whom I please, and I shall now seriously set about giving liberty to the seas by publishing my system of attack." He left all his pictures and prints behind for a safer crossing in the spring, and he made "a complete set of drawings and descriptions of my whole system of submarine attack, and another set of drawings with description of the steamboat. These with my will I shall put in a tin container, sealed, and leave them in care of General Lyman," the American consul. He carried with him a Boulton-Watt steam engine.

Mrs. West gave Fulton a letter to the Trumbulls, recommending him as "one of my adopted sons." West made a farewell present of a picture — a portrait of himself in the act of painting his wife. Fulton placed this with *Lear, Ophelia,* and several other pictures in Philadelphia's new Pennsylvania Academy of the Fine Arts (founded 1807). In doing so he launched a campaign to induce the city to buy West's entire collection of his own work, portraits excluded, for £15,000. It was, he assured the city fathers, "a sum inconsiderable when compared with the objects in view and the advantages to be derived from it ... [It was] the most extraordinary opportunity that was ever offered" to the lovers of art. The name he suggested for the establishment that would hold the collection was the Westinian Gallery. As an added inducement he sent along a plan for raising the money by sale of fifty dollar shares to the citizenry, and he intimated that West himself would come to

Philadelphia to live. The venerable George Clymer, merchant and civic leader, declined the offer with the observation, "You have counted too much upon our public spirit."

From time to time West received letters from Fulton describing his other activities in America. In December 1807 he read to Farington from such a letter: Mr. Fulton had "invented and established a *Passage Boat* to be navigated by steam *only*. It goes from Albany twice a week and carries seventy passengers, and in less time by fifteen hours than the boat which carried the mail."

On January 9, 1808, West dined with William Waldegrave, Lord Radstock, an art-collecting admiral. In the evening Sir Francis Bourgeois sent around his carriage to carry Mr. West home. This good deed was another of many evidences of the blessed peace that had fallen upon the Royal Academy. When John Fisher, Bishop of Salisbury, asked Farington "how matters went on at the Royal Academy," he replied that "all had gone on well since Mr. West returned to the chair, and that there was no longer any dissension." West was re-elected in 1808 with only token opposition from Beechey, Hoppner, and Sandby (one vote each), and in 1810, with Copley, Beechey, and Yenn voting, he was elected unanimously, twenty-two to nothing, with no abstentions. Yenn was "very cordial" to Farington, declaring that they were both growing old and should be kind to one another. West said that Martin Shee, on becoming a Council member, paid much attention to him, occasionally walking home with him as far as his door, thus seeming indirectly to apologize, West thought, for having turned against him in the late months of his Academy troubles. When Shee published a volume of poems titled *Elements of Art* (praised by Byron in *English Bards and Scotch Reviewers*), West called on him and acknowledged the manly and able manner in which he had maintained the cause of art and artists.

There were, to be sure, still Academy problems. John Soane created an unpleasantness when he criticized in one of his lectures young Robert Smirke's design of the new Covent Garden Theater, citing it to his students as one of "some obvious instances of bad taste . . . in the building of a newly constructed public edifice." The unpleasantness heightened when Soane made a public issue of it when the Council ruled that no Academy professor might comment on the work of living artists, and especially not when the artist was a member of the Academy. And West still drew adverse criticism on occasion. His presence at a dinner given by Academy students and his delivery there of a set speech were condemned as being very improper. After a dinner given by the marquess of Stafford, at which West had been present, there was laughter "at the false pronunciation of one of the party notorious for it. He pronounced phalanx *flanks*." James Lowther, Earl of Lonsdale, talked frankly to Farington about West, observing that he had a great deal of information. Farington replied, "If the manner in which he expresses his information was better than it is, he would be justly estimated much more highly than he now is." Lonsdale said that his deficiency in that respect could be felt by persons who were not competent to judge of his real knowledge. Farington agreed: The criticisms about him were upon deficiencies which a school boy might notice and remark upon.

The Academy, however, had fewer and less serious problems, and the complaints leveled at West were milder, fewer, and less unkind. They were countered, moreover, by stories told about him that were pleasant and had a note of affection for one who has endured and survived. While on a fishing party organized by Sir Anthony Carlisle, surgeon, in the neighborhood of Carshalton, West announced that he was making a sketch of the participants thus amusing themselves. When they came to look at the finished work, they found that he had made himself the principal figure and that all the others were standing around looking at him. When the Arranging Committee rejected a model of Apollo by a sculptor, Peter Turnerelli, West persuaded them to reconsider: It was, he said, a commission from a country gentleman to be executed in marble and Turnerelli might lose £1500 if it should be rejected.

The good feeling was reflected in a dinner given in May 1809 by Farington. West arrived late, "having been prevented from dining by Mrs. West's indisposition."

> The party was sociable and joyous, and made more so by my producing a sketch made by Mr. West at my table, May 24, 1784, when he, Sir G. Beaumont, Mr. Bowles, and Mr. Hearne dined with me. It was made for the purpose of showing us the composition of the picture of St. Peter Martyr by Titian. This excited warm feelings of recollection, and Sir George expressed a desire that our meeting should be continued at each other's houses, and it was agreed to, and our next meeting was appointed to be at Dance's.
>
> On the back of the sketch of St. Peter Martyr, Dance wrote, in addition to what had been written by me on the 24th of May 1784, that "The same party dined together at the same table, May 15, 1809 with the addition of the Honble. Augustus Phipps and George Dance," and to this we each added our signatures . . . All

seemed very happy, and Sir George, on going away, said to me,
That when he dined with me something occurred to make our
meetings singularly pleasant.

In 1810 West came to the end of the long story of William
Williams, his first teacher of art in Philadelphia, of whom he said,
"Had it not been for him I never should have become a painter."
In November of that year, at the request of an acquaintance, he
wrote a long letter about Williams that is a key document today
in his own history as well as that of William Williams.

The acquaintance was Thomas Eagles, a well-to-do Bristol merchant, an amateur painter, a classical scholar. Five years earlier,
in 1805, West had called by invitation at Eagles' London residence.
His host was out, and while waiting for him to return, West leafed
through an unsigned bound manuscript he found on a table, titled
"Mr. Penrose: The Journal of Penrose, Seaman." He was astonished
to recognize it as the work of William Williams, who during their
time together in Philadelphia had regaled him with the same Robinson Crusoe-like story of his shipwreck on the coast of Nicaragua
and the two years spent there among the Rama Indians. West
learned from Eagles that he had befriended and helped Williams
in Bristol in 1780 and, when a vacancy occurred in Bristol's Merchants' and Sailors' Almshouse, obtained a place for him among the
thirty-one inmates. Williams lived there pleasantly for five years,
supported by a weekly stipend of three shillings.

On Williams' death in 1791, Eagles said, he found that he had
inherited the painter's possessions: several portraits of his deceased
family; a checklist of 187 canvases he had painted in Philadelphia;
a manuscript titled "Lives of the Painters" (the one West had read
as a boy); and the manuscript of an autobiographical narrative of
the adventures of "Mr. Penrose." Eagles did some editing of the
manuscript and between 1791 and 1805 had been trying unsuccessfully to place it for publication. He and West marveled at the
coincidence of their common friendship with this man, Eagles
questioning West at length, taking notes as they talked. With this
new information about Williams, he renewed his attempts to find
a publisher, again unsuccessfully. Then, in 1810, he asked West to
write a full account of his association with Williams, intending to
use it to validate Williams' story. West did this on November 10
in a 2100-word letter that throws as much new light on his own
career as it does on Williams'. In 1815, thanks largely to West's
testimony, the retitled *Journal of Llewellin Penrose, a Seaman*, as
edited by Thomas Eagles, was published by John Murray in a four-

volume edition of 1000 copies. The book was dedicated to Benjamin West.[2]

Interest in Williams has grown in the past several decades, both as a painter and as the author of what appears to be, in date of composition (before 1791, perhaps before 1760), the first novel by a colonial American — the first American novel. The piece-by-piece re-creation of Williams' career and study of his pictures has received the fruitful attention of a half dozen scholars. The leading authority on Williams, David Howard Dickason, calls West "the star witness of the case."

The year 1811, in which he turned seventy-three, was West's *annus mirabilis*, the most productive of his later career.

He shared top honors with Thomas Lawrence at the Academy exhibition that year. One of his two pictures, *Omnia Vincit Amor*, an allegory that contained Venus, Cupid, a lion, and a horse, was described by a reviewer as "an exquisite production, equally distinguished for its conception and its execution." His other picture was the first large *Death of Nelson*, painted in 1806, shown privately at Newman Street in that year, and since that time in the hands of Charles Heath, the engraver. The print was exhibited and placed on sale at the time of the 1811 showing, six guineas for an early impression, three for a later one.

Receipts for the exhibition were the highest in the Academy's history, excepting only for those in 1780, and the exhibition dinner was an outstanding success. "No meeting of the Academy on this annual occasion," Farington wrote, "ever went off in so marked a manner, nor did there ever before appear so much cordial warmth for the prosperity of art." The Prince of Wales, since February 6 the prince regent, attended with his brothers, the dukes of Clarence and Kent. Following the dinner the prince regent commented on the poor light in which the pictures were shown after sundown and promised to install a huge chandelier in the main gallery.

The names of West and Copley were coupled in Anthony Pasquin's review of the exhibition and coverage of the annual dinner in the *Morning Herald*. After some critical observations on the pictures, Pasquin engaged in a flight of literary fancy more amusing than most of his writing. He passed the entrance to the galleries at

---

2 Williams' original manuscript, a stronger work than Eagles' edited version, was published in 1969 by Indiana University Press, David Howard Dickason, editor.

Somerset House, he said, just as the dinner was beginning. Waiters were carrying up the tureens of turtle soup; rich odors of roasting turkeys and capons ascended from the kitchens in the lower regions. Fascinated, he lingered and watched at the door until a guard drove him away. At home he fell asleep in his chair and dreamed that he was back in the banqueting room. The tablecloth had just been removed and the American minister was proposing a toast: "May the Statesmen of Britain and the United States be ever in a State of Harmony."

This was drunk with three times three [cheers], after which the Minister called upon his fellow-citizens, Messrs. West and Copley, to sing their favourite descriptive travelling duet, with which they complied, after a few vocal experiments and preparatory hems:

THE PRESIDENT

From Philadelphia's broad-brimmed race
Who vanity have undone,
I took my easel on my back
And crossed the seas to London!

Lord, how I marvelled as I passed
The streets with Uncle Goodin,
For here we saw the men and girls
As thick as hasty pudding.

(Chorus of R.A.'s dancing)

Yankee doodle, doodle do,
Yankee double dandy,
A perpendicular line is straight
But beauty's line is bandy.

JOHN SINGLETON COPLEY, ESQ.

From Massachusetts rebel state
When loyalty was crying,
I ran on shipboard here to paint
Lord Chatham who was dying.

Then I hung up the House of Peers
(Though some were quite unwilling)
And gave the group to public view
And showed them for — a shilling.

(*They sing together, hand in hand*)
Let David paint for hungry fame
And Wilkie subjects funny,
Let Turner sit and study storms
But *we* will paint for money.

This charming duet was terminated by a *pas de deux* in high style between the minstrels.

West's major success in 1811 — indeed, one of the greatest of his career — came with the exhibition of his *Christ Healing the Sick in the Temple*. The picture developed from a flattering letter he had received in 1800 from the managers of the Pennsylvania Hospital in Philadelphia, asking for the gift of a painting to be used in raising money "for the relief of maniacs and sick poor." Instead of sending one of the unsold classical or religious pictures from his studio, he promised a new work, a picture 16 feet long and 10 feet high illustrating verses 14 and 15, chapter 21, of St. Matthew: "And the blind and the lame came to him in the temple, and He healed them. And when the chief priests and scribes saw the wonderful things that He did, and the children crying in the temple, and saying, Hosanna to the Son of David, they were sore displeased." Extensive correspondence followed on the light and dampness of the room in which the picture would be shown. Hospital officials solemnly consulted Gilbert Stuart and Charles Willson Peale to determine "the best situation." Joseph Wharton, referred to in the correspondence as "thy friend," took part in the negotiations. West, however, did not finish the work, with its fifty-odd figures, some of them life-size, for ten years. Early in 1811 he exhibited it at the gallery of the British Institution, planning thereafter to ship it to Philadelphia. The picture created something of a sensation. People lined up for blocks to be admitted to the British Gallery. The common greeting in London was not a comment on the weather but the query, "Have you seen the picture?" At a dinner at Lawrence's in May (West being absent), the conversation was on West's picture. Farington reported, "The exaggerated praise of it which is so much kept up in the newspapers was thought disgusting."

When interviewed by the press, West let it be known that in painting *Christ Healing* he had been influenced and inspired by "those sublime sculptures" the earl of Elgin had brought from Greece. In his repeated statements and his public position on the greatness of the Elgin marbles, West became a central figure in the major art controversy of his time — one that roused passions, ruined reputations, produced a furious national debate in the years 1806–1816, and in our own time still has significance.

West's first association with Thomas Bruce, seventh Earl of Elgin, came in 1799, when his lordship, newly appointed minister to the Ottoman Empire, asked West to recommend a painter to accompany him to Constantinople. Elgin planned to have professional drawings and plaster casts made of the sculptures in Athens, then under Turkish rule. West recommended William Turner, twenty-four, but Turner declined the post when he learned that Elgin would claim the artist's entire artistic output, expected him to give drawing lessons to Lady Elgin, and refused to pay the £400 yearly salary and expenses he demanded. (Elgin offered £30.) An Italian, Don Tito Lusieri, was chosen.

In Athens Elgin discovered that the marble sculptures of the Parthenon were being looted — used in other buildings, burned for lime, and carried away piecemeal by the first wave of European visitors to Greece. He obtained an order from the Turkish government that gave him permission to remove, collect, and transport the sculptures to England. The first fifty cases, weighing 120 tons, arrived in London in 1804; the sculptures were laid out or stacked in a large shed Elgin built behind a house he rented at the corner of Piccadilly and Park Lane. In June 1807, when he permitted a few artists and connoisseurs to view the pieces, the response was one of excitement, wonder, and dispute. West spent three weeks in the shed that autumn studying and drawing the marbles. During that time, he told Farington, "all those feelings which had possessed him when he first went to Rome [were] again excited in him. His morning walk to Lord Elgin's in Park Lane gave him spirits, and the gratification he felt while among those wonderful works of art was in the extreme." He arranged for Academy medal winners to be admitted to the Park Lane shed, and he undertook to write passes for others who wished to view the marbles.

Other artists — notably Flaxman, Nollekens, and Benjamin Robert Haydon — were also excited by Elgin's treasures. Haydon, twenty, a young man of strong opinions and great promise, expressed an enthusiasm that verged on the fanatic. He made Fuseli go with him to Park Lane; Fuseli strode around the shed exclaiming, "De Greeks were godes! De Greeks were godes!" He took his friend John Keats to see them, and Keats wrote an immortal sonnet. Haydon had preceded West by several months as the first to study and draw the marbles, and he had come to feel a proprietary claim as the first to discover and really understand their beauties. He described a meeting with West:

> While I was drawing there, West came in and, seeing me, said with surprise: "Hah, hah, Mr. Haydon, *you* are admitted, are you?

I hope you and I can keep a secret." ... He did not draw the
marbles and study their hidden beauties. He merely made a set
of rattling compositions, taking the attitudes as models for his
own inventions. This was not doing what I had done, investigating their principles deeply and studiously. West derived little
benefit from this method, while in every figure I drew the principle was imbibed and inhaled forever.

The dealers and collectors of London were less enthusiastic than
the artists about Lord Elgin's treasure. These figures were totally
different from the accepted models of Greek beauty and perfection;
they were quite unlike the *Apollo Belvedere* and the other Greco-
Roman works praised by Winckelmann. They were large, vigorous,
masculine; they had muscles and veins; they showed emotion and
strain. If these were actually what West called them — "the perfection of art, where nature predominated everywhere and was not
resolved into and made obedient to a system" — then the aesthetic
standards on what constituted ideal beauty, grace, and elegance in
classical art had ceased to be valid. It followed that the "classical"
pieces in English private collections and dealers' shops were no
longer of the highest order either as works of art or as investments.

The campaign to preserve the prestige of existing collections
and to ruin the Elgin marbles (and, if necessary, Lord Elgin as well)
was led by R. Payne Knight, a wealthy member of the Dilettanti
Society, a founding governor of the British Institution, author of
a book on phallus worship (recalled), and dictator of aesthetics
as the author of *An Analytical Inquiry into the Principles of Taste*.
Knight greeted Elgin — while the cases were still unpacked — with
the words, "You have lost your labour, my Lord Elgin. Your marbles
are overrated. They are not Greek. They are Roman of the time of
Hadrian."

Before Elgin had left for Turkey, he had asked for government
support for his undertaking and been refused. He proceeded with
his own money on a project far larger than he had ever dreamed,
borrowing at very high interest rates. In 1809, back in England, he
conceived the idea of selling the marbles to the government, and
in 1810 he offered them for the amount he had paid out: £62,440.
He produced a well-written pamphlet in that year explaining his
action as one taken to save the sculptures from certain destruction.
In it he printed a supporting letter West had sent him in February
1809:

I had the singular good fortune, by your Lordship's liberality, to
select from the first productions of sculpture which ever adorned
the world in that department of art; which neither Raphael nor
any of the distinguished masters had the advantage to see, much

less to study... I may therefore declare with truth, my Lord, that I am the first in modern times who have enjoyed the much coveted opportunity, and availed myself of the rare advantage of forming compositions from them, by adapting their excellences to poetic fiction and historical facts...

West suggested that the Academy print his letter, but Farington, in consultation with others, quietly objected. "This letter," he said, "had too much *self* in it to be proper for publication in the Academy Annals and was also too incorrect. I told Hoare I thought West might write a letter addressed to the Academicians on this subject which by management might be kept free from self-panegeryck, and that I would speak to him about it." The following year, the government having failed to act on his proposal, Elgin brought out an improved second edition of his pamphlet, adding a second letter from West: "It is... my devout wish that [the sculptures] should rest in the capital of this empire: and that their resting place should be as accessible as possible to public inspection, in order to impart ...a true notion of what is classical in art. Such a deposit would... be of infinite advantage of young artists."

Haydon, of course, was furious at West for claiming to be the first to make use of the Elgin marbles in art, and he made fierce marginal notations on West's letters in his copy of Elgin's pamphlet. Payne Knight was furious at West for his high praise of the marbles. The French were furious at everyone that the marbles had not gone to the Louvre. A fourth furious outcry was now heard from one who was not concerned with the West-Knight battle over the aesthetic quality of the sculptures, nor whether they were Greek or Roman, nor with the amount that should or should not be paid to Lord Elgin. George Gordon, Lord Byron, had used Elgin's painter, Lusieri, as his guide in Greece, and he had availed himself of the added convenience of the fifteen-year-old brother of Lusieri's wife or mistress, Nicolo Giraud, with whom he had a passionate relationship of five years' duration. While in Greece, he decided that Elgin was a plundering criminal whose removal of the Parthenon sculptures was a shameful spoliation of one of the treasures of Greece, the country he loved most. In *The Curse of Minerva* (1811) and in five stanzas of Canto II of *Childe Harold's Pilgrimage*, Byron flayed Elgin alive as, among other things, a "filthy jackal" and "a bastard of a brighter race."[3] In *Minerva* he also struck out at

---

[3] In other writings he called him a cuckold and said he had the pox (syphilis). Elgin had sued his wife for divorce for acknowledged infidelity with a friend of theirs, and he had contracted a skin disease in Turkey that ate away part of his nose.

"hireling artists" whose "noblest gusto" was to sell and make "the state receiver of his pilfered prey." And then:

> Meantime, the flattering, feeble dotard, West
> Europe's worst dauber, and poor Britain's best,
> With palsied hand shall turn each model o'er
> And own himself an infant of fourscore.

The lines have dogged West down to this day; they are almost invariably quoted in any analysis of West's career and work, and seldom with recognition or acknowledgment that the comment was merely a by-blow of a motivated assault on Lord Elgin.

The British government considered Elgin's offer to sell and debated the price he asked. Payne Knight advised that Elgin should not be paid more than £15,000 for inferior sculptures, and he recommended that an act be passed prohibiting him from selling them out of the country (that is, to Bonaparte). Elgin, though he was in financial straits, refused. There was an impasse for the next five years.

When the exhibition at the British Gallery closed and the time came for West to send *Christ Healing* to the Pennsylvania Hospital, the patrons of the British Institution were so disturbed at losing a masterpiece that they organized to rescue it. The prince regent and thirty-nine other persons subscribed 3000 guineas to buy the picture, marking it as the beginning of the national gallery West had worked so hard to create.

West confessed that he was in "a predicament." He needed the 3000 guineas, but the work was pledged to America. He found a solution in a judicious compromise. He agreed to sell but reserved the right to paint a copy for the hospital. He sent the news to Philadelphia, promising to paint an even better version with more figures and without delay. He then had 300 impressions of a crown-size bronze medal struck at Birmingham, honoring the patrons of the British Institution. One side carried West's bust in profile done by young Francis Chantrey; the other gave the names of the forty subscribers with an inscription. One medal was struck in gold and presented to the prince regent. The British Institution responded by collecting five guineas from each of its patrons and commissioning Nollekens to produce a marble bust of West "as a testimony of respect."

The 3000 guineas paid for *Christ Healing the Sick* was an unheard-of sum, and some observers thought the Institution's patrons had taken leave of their senses.[4] The patrons' financial acumen, if not their artistic judgment, was validated when within a year the picture earned the Institution £9300 in admissions at the door and in £5 subscriptions for an engraving.

He must have felt bitterness mixed with a sense of vindication when he received a letter in May relaying to him, by command, His Majesty's congratulations on the success of *Christ Healing* — especially since his £1000 annual stipend and his engagement as history painter to the king had been discontinued in December 1810. The king's message, West replied, gave him inexpressible joy. The union of feeling in favor of the picture was "a proud circumstance to his professional sensibility." His greatest gratitude, however, was due His Majesty for the friendly aid that had enabled him "to gain that point in art which is now sanctioned by the gentlemen and noblemen of the British Institution." He then permitted himself a restrained expression of his bitterness at the injustice he felt had been done him:

> Had the great work of my life on Revealed Religion . . . not been checked some years past, that work by this time would have been of the same class in art with the one now exhibiting . . . And had it been completed, it would have marked itself as worthy of His Majesty's protection as a Christian and a patriot King, and all Christendom would have received it with affection and piety. But, though checked, my zeal for its completion has not abated or damped my studies for its dignity and honorable termination, although I have never been able to ascertain what was to be its subsequent situation, since the place for which it was intended has been appropriated to other purposes.

West's success with *Christ Healing* inspired other artists to emulate him. John Trumbull painted two scriptural pictures and exhibited them at the British Institution in the hope (unrealized) that they would achieve acclaim, a prize, and a sale. He had returned to England in 1808, having had bad luck in a four-year stay in New York and Boston, and was having equally bad luck in London, despite what William Dunlap described as "strenuous efforts to attract popular attention." When war broke out between Britain and the United States in 1812, Colonel Trumbull, his earlier war record remembered, was treated somewhat coolly. This was ironic, for he

---

[4] With one possible exception in 1854, this was the highest fee paid to any living painter in any country before the year 1860.

had ended his friendship with Jefferson because of his pro-French
foreign policy, despised "Mr. Maddison" and his war, and thought
of Bonaparte as the anti-Christ. Trumbull had cut himself off from
West; he had, in Farington's words, taken umbrage over a trifle and
had concluded that West was no longer disposed to show him respect or to forward his interest. (Trumbull had carried to England
several sketches of Niagara Falls, intending to have a panorama
made of them for public exhibition. He accused West of subtly
influencing popular opinion against him and his proposal.)

Copley also set to work on a scriptural subject in the hope of
recouping his fading fortunes. He had suffered burning humiliations in these later years. He had asked the king to appoint him
treasurer of the Academy to succeed Chambers and had been ignored. He had called on George Granville, Marquess of Stafford,
president of the British Institution, and asked to paint his portrait.
When Stafford declined, Copley explained that he wished to paint
it without charge. Stafford replied that if he sat to Mr. Copley he
should certainly pay his usual price, but he had no desire to have
another portrait. Copley had waited with John Yenn in an apartment of the palace, and when the king entered it with his courtiers,
he asked if he might speak to His Majesty in private. The king replied, "Whatever you have to say you may speak here." Copley
humbly requested that His Majesty would sit to him for a portrait.
The king exclaimed, "Sit to you for a portrait? What do you want
— to make a show of me?" and went off indignantly.

Mrs. Copley wrote to her daughter in Boston in 1811:

> Your father has now almost finished a picture of the "Resurrec-
> tion," which is much liked. Indeed, it makes me melancholy
> when I see his rooms so full of pictures that are highly spoken of,
> and I think with how much perplexity they were produced. We
> are, indeed, revolving what change we can make, and whether to
> quit George Street . . .
>
> You will hear of Mr. West's success; it has been great. The
> picture which he has painted . . . interests the feelings of all
> classes, and the Institution which has purchased it, at great price,
> has availed itself of this work, which is generally much ap-
> plauded, to give an éclat to their establishment, and perhaps to
> prevent the censure which would have followed if they had let
> the picture go to America unnoticed.

Copley's *Resurrection* (now unlocated) was hung in the 1812 Academy exhibition, where it attracted virtually no attention or comment.

The two men, of course, had no social contact and scarcely spoke to one another at Academy functions. West was astonished, therefore, when in March 1808 Copley called at his home to seek a favorable position at the Academy exhibition, a space above the fireplace, for one of his pictures. He called again a year later to demand an extension of time for another picture. This was a large equestrian portrait of the Prince of Wales which he was painting without a commission in the hope that the prince or some other collector would buy it.

In the autumn of 1811 West began to design a Biblical work even larger than *Christ Healing*, 17 by 22 feet, titled *Our Saviour Brought from the Judgment Hall by Pilate to Caiaphas the High Priest*, commonly called *Christ Rejected*. Farington marveled that he should undertake a work of this magnitude at such an advanced age. West "smiled and made light of it." He said, "When the principal points shall have been finished up to their proper force, all the other parts of the picture will go off expeditiously. It is upon a few points the eye fixes, and these having been attended to, the business is in great measure done."

"On the Highest Pinnacle"

I have heard Constable say that under some disappointment, I
think it was the rejection at the Academy of a view of Flatford
Mill, he carried a picture to Mr. West, who said, "Don't be dis-
heartened, young man, we shall hear from you again. You must
have loved nature very much before you could have painted this."

CHARLES ROBERT LESLIE,
*Memoirs of the Life
of John Constable*, 1845

IN THE YEARS 1810 AND 1811 West had a new generation of
American artists under his tutelage in five attractive, spirited,
talented young men: Charles Bird King, Washington Allston,
Thomas Sully, Samuel Finley Breese Morse, and Charles Robert
Leslie.

King, a native of Rhode Island, had been studying under West
since his arrival in England in 1805 in his twentieth year. Sully
described him as "the most industrious person I ever met . . . with
qualities of heart and correctness of conduct rarely equalled for
purity or usefulness." King limited himself to four hours sleep each
night, and at meals he always read "some instructive book."

Sully arrived in July 1809, a twenty-six-year-old Philadelphian
who had studied the pictures in Peale's Museum and had once been
allowed to see Stuart paint a portrait. When seven merchants contributed $200 each to send him to study under West, on the promise
that each would receive a copy of an old master, he gave $1000 to
his wife for her subsistence and sailed for London with what was
left. He presented a letter of introduction to Charles Bird King,
who had a room with Mrs. Bridgen, a widow at 2 Cleveland Street,
Buckingham Place. King asked him, "How long do you intend
staying in England?"

"Three years, if I can."

"And how much money have you brought with you?"

"Four hundred dollars."

"Why, my good sir, that is not enough for three months." King said that his own funds were almost gone and that he wished to stay another year or two. Samuel Lovett Waldo, another American studying under West, had been rooming with him and had recently returned home. Bird suggested that Sully move in with him and that they buy a stock of potatoes, live on bread, milk, and potatoes, conceal it from Mrs. Bridgen, keep her happy with a little present now and then, "and work like merry fellows." Sully agreed. Years later Mrs. Bridgen told a visiting American of Mr. King, the young man who, instead of going into the good bed that had been made up for him, "used to strip off the bedclothes, wrap himself up in them, and throw himself with his whole length on the floor, that he might have it to say that he slept on a board and lived on potatoes while pursuing his studies. At last we persuaded him, as the cool weather came on, to sleep in a bed like other folks."

King took Sully to the Royal Academy and registered him for examination at the school. (As the students read the book and saw "from Philadelphia," each was heard to exclaim, "Another American!") He went with Sully when he called at 14 Newman Street. West was working on *Christ Healing the Sick*, but he stopped to give a warm welcome to an artist who came from Philadelphia with a letter from such a distinguished citizen as the Quaker lawyer William Rawle. "I can't teach you," he said, "until I know what you can do. Paint a head and show it to me." Sully returned a few days later with a portrait of King. West found "an indecision in expressing the anatomy of the head, which indicated a want of confidence" in his knowledge of the bone structure; he advised the young man to study osteology.

West obtained permission for Sully to visit private collections of old masters, but the restrictions on viewing hours and on copying were such that he could not possibly make the seven copies he was obliged to send back to his patrons. In desperation he decided to go to France, which as an American he could do, and where the policy on copying old masters was more liberal. He consulted West on the decision, who said, "I understand that your object on your return is portrait painting."

"Yes, sir."

"Then stay in England. My collection, old and new, is at your service. There are specimens of the ancient masters and of the moderns. Take them as you want them, and come to me for advice when you want it."

Sully labored for eight months on the copies, painting his choice of West's pictures in his own room by day, drawing at the Academy until it closed at 8 P.M., copying anatomical engravings after class to learn osteology, earning a little money by copying a half dozen landscape paintings owned by the Penns, and living all the while on potatoes, milk, and bread. During this time he came under the influence of Thomas Lawrence, the artist who affected him most deeply in England. In the meantime, West sent off a letter on November 3 to a friend in Philadelphia in praise of Mr. Sully, who, "now studying painting under my directions," would have to return to Philadelphia sooner than he should because of his "slender means." Could not his friends unite to give him one more season? The letter was printed in Philadelphia's *Port Folio* but it produced no help. Sully was forced to leave for home in March 1810, having been in England less than nine months. He finished his seventh copy one week before he sailed.

Washington Allston returned to England in August 1811 after an eleven-year absence. On his first trip he had brought Edward Malbone with him; now he was accompanied by his wife[1] and a twenty-year-old pupil named Samuel F. B. Morse, one year out of Yale, whose father was a Congregational minister and a noted geographer. The Allstons took an apartment at 49 London Street; Morse took a room close to Allston's friend, Charles Bird King, in Fitzroy Square, an artists' quarter.

West was astonished at the progress Allston had made since his first stay in England and was unreserved in his praise of the work he now began to produce. He called at Allston's home to see a large Biblical subject, *The Dead Man Revived by Touching the Bones of the Prophet Elisha,* and after studying it had only one suggestion: to introduce one more figure. "This," he said, "reminds me of the fifteenth century. You have been studying in the highest school of art. There are eyes in this country that will be able to see so much merit." *The Dead Man Revived* won the gold medal and the 200 guinea prize at the 1813 British Institution show; and Sir George Beaumont, having eyes to see its merit, took up Allston and gave him a commission.[2]

Samuel F. B. Morse wrote to his parents a few days after his arrival:

> I was introduced to Mr. West by Mr. Allston and likewise gave him your letter. He was very glad to see me and said he would render me every assistance in his power.

---

[1] The sister of the Unitarian clergyman William Ellery Channing.

[2] Of this picture, John Canaday wrote in December 1975, "[It] may well be the greatest American painting of the first half of the nineteenth century. And it is one of the fine paintings of its period by international standards as well."

At the British Institution I saw his famous piece of *Christ Healing the Sick.* He said to me, "This is the piece I intended for America, but the British would have it themselves; but I shall give America the better one." . . . A sight of that piece is worth a voyage to England of itself.

The encomiums which Mr. West has received on account of that piece has given him new life, and some say he is at least ten years younger. He is now likewise about another piece which will probably be superior to the other. He favored me with a sight of the sketch, which he said he granted to me because I was an American. He had not shown it to anyone else . . . The subject is *Christ before Pilate.* It will contain about fifty or sixty figures the size of life.

Mr. West is in his seventy-fourth year (I think), but to see him you would suppose him only about five-and-forty. He is very active; a flight of steps at the British Gallery he ran up as nimbly as I could . . . I walked through his gallery of paintings of his own productions. There were upward of two hundred, consisting principally of the original sketches of his large pieces. He has painted in all upward of 600 pictures, which is more than any artist ever did, with the exception of Rubens, the celebrated Dutch painter. Mr. West is so industrious now that it is hard to get access to him, and then only between the hours of nine and ten in the morning. He is working on eight or nine different pieces at present, and seems to be more enthusiastic than he ever was before.

Morse's letters to his family introduce into the London art scene of 1811–1815 the first voice clearly identifiable as American in idiom and style. He prowled about the city; he went to the Covent Garden Theater to see John Kemble and old Mrs. Siddons in her last stage performances; traveled ten miles to Epsom to see the horse races; walked four miles to Hackney to join a crowd of 300,-000 to watch "the ascension of a Mr. Sadler and other gentlemen in a balloon"; visited St. Bartholomew's Fair to observe an earlier-age Ferris wheel; obtained a pass from West to see Lord Elgin's Greek marbles; and described all he saw with enthusiasm, perception, and an informal, almost modern tone. He went to St. James's Palace to see and laugh at those who attended the queen's drawing room in their old-fashioned attire:

It was a singular sight to see the ladies and gentlemen in their court dresses; the gentlemen were dressed in buckram-skirted coats without capes, long waistcoats, cocked hats, bag-wigs, swords, and large buckles in their shoes; the ladies in monstrous hoops, so that in getting into their carriages they were obliged to go edgewise. Their dresses were very rich.

I had a sight of the prince regent as he passed in his splendid state carriage, drawn by six horses. He is very corpulent. His pictures are good, but he is very red and considerably bloated.

Morse took instruction from both Allston and West; Allston joked that he would have a battle with Mr. West if he did not give up all pretensions to Morse as a pupil. Morse found West "friendly and liberal to me . . . He appears quite attached to me, as he is, indeed, to all young American artists. It seems to give him the greatest pleasure to think that one day the arts will flourish in America . . . For the first, to economize, he told me a way of preparing common paper to paint on, instead of canvas, which will be a great saving of expense to me." Morse was happy to be able to repay the master by posing for the hands of the Saviour in *Christ Healing.*

Morse worked two weeks on a finished drawing of the *Farnese Hercules,* intended for his application to the Royal Academy school. Allston told him it would undoubtedly get him admitted, as it was better than two-thirds of those generally offered, but advised him to draw it again and remedy some defects in the handling of the chalks. West put on his glasses and carefully scrutinized the work. "He told me," Morse wrote home, "that it was an extraordinary production, that I had talents, and only wanted knowledge of the art to make a great painter." But West added, "Very well, sir, very well. Go on and finish it."

"It *is* finished," Morse replied.

"Oh, no," West said. "Look here, and here, and here," pointing to unfinished details that Morse had missed. Morse devoted several more days to a careful reworking and submitted the result to West, who studied it, praised it, and said, "Very well, indeed. Go on and finish it."

"Is it not finished?" Morse asked.

"Not yet. See, you have not marked that muscle, nor the articulation of the finger joints."

Morse spent several more days retouching and reworking his drawing, returned with it to Newman Street, and again met with the advice, "Very clever, indeed," and, "Go and finish it."

"I cannot finish it," Morse said in despair.

"Well," West replied, "I have tried you long enough. Now, you have learned more by this drawing than you would have accomplished in double the time by a dozen half-finished drawings. It is not numerous drawings, but *the character of one,* which makes a thorough draughtsman. *Finish* one drawing and you are a painter."

A few months after Morse was settled, there appeared in London still another American student, this one only sixteen years old, a bookseller's apprentice who was believed to be a child prodigy in drawing. Charles Robert Leslie had taken his first painting lessons from Sully shortly before leaving Philadelphia. Like others before him, he was being given two years under West by contributions from a group of well-disposed citizens. Leslie spent several days at the London Coffee Shop on Ludgate Hill, where he was ill for a time and very unhappy, and then settled in lodgings on Warren Street, Fitzroy Square — "two desolate-looking rooms up two pairs of stairs." He dutifully presented a letter from Sully to West and "was kindly received." He presented another from Sully to Charles Bird King, who introduced him to Allston and Morse. He was suffering a severe case of homesickness. "I was solitary," he said, "and began to find that even in London it was possible to be unhappy. My new acquaintances, Allston, King and Morse were very kind, but still they were *new acquaintances.* I thought of the happy circle round my mother's fireside, and there were moments in which ... I could have been content ... to return immediately to America." He learned, however, that Morse felt very much as he did, and Morse found that Leslie's "thoughts of art agree perfectly with my own." In January 1812 they took rooms together on Great Titchfield Street, still at Fitzroy Square. They ate their meals at Mrs. Bridgen's or, when in company, at the York Chop House in Wardour Street, worked at the Royal Academy in the evenings, and painted in their rooms during the day, beginning with portraits of each other in costumes. Leslie wrote his sister, "I have lately been made a student in the Academy ... I have now access to the library every Monday, beside the privilege of wearing my hat in the Academy, and coming in with a greater swagger than before."

Allston, three minutes' walk away, called every day. "We meet by turns at each other's rooms," Morse wrote home, "and converse and laugh"; and years later, "We all lived together for years in the closest intimacy." Coleridge sometimes joined them, and Benjamin Haydon, and John Howard Payne, the American actor, playwright, and composer of songs, who in Boston in 1809 had played Hamlet, the first American actor to do so. Morse wrote to his parents on January 30: "Leslie and myself sleep in the same room armed with a pair of pistols and a sword and alarms at our doors and windows." They did so, he explained, because "very horrid attempts at robbery and murder have been very frequent of late in all parts of the city, and even so near as within two doors of me in the same street, but do not be alarmed."

West gave Leslie letters that got him unhindered access to the British Museum and to the Elgin marbles. In Leslie's words, "He

lent me pictures to copy, allowed me to paint in his home, and
spent a great deal of what was to him of the greatest value, his time,
in directing my studies." Leslie's first attempt at a large composition was *Saul and the Witch of Endor,* a subject West suggested to
him.

> He came often to my room while I was engaged in it and as-
> sisted me very greatly in the arrangement of the composition,
> effect, etc. By his advice I sent it to the British Institution for
> exhibition, but as it was too fresh to varnish, the directors
> thought it unfinished and turned it out.
>
> Feeling very disappointed, I went to Mr. West for consolation,
> and I received it. He desired me to bring the picture to his house.
> I did so, and by his advice varnished it in his large painting room.
> He then told me he would show it to some of the directors of the
> institution, most of whom visited him frequently. In a few days
> I had the satisfaction to receive a note from him, telling me he
> had sold it for me to Sir John Leicester, one of these very di-
> rectors.

The payment was 100 guineas.[3]

In the course of his studies, Leslie became a friend and then a
companion of John Constable, an Academy student. The son of a
prosperous miller in Sussex, Constable had come to London in 1799

---

[3] Charles Robert Leslie (1794–1859) returned to the United States in 1833 to
teach drawing at the U.S. Military Academy, stayed only a few months, and
went back to England, where he had a brilliant career. He introduced a new
style of painting: genre scenes ("cabinet pictures") illustrating subjects from the
classic English authors, painted in clear bright light and sharp detail. He became
the Royal Academy's professor of painting in 1847.

Charles Bird King (1785–1862) returned to the United States in 1812 and had a
successful career in Washington, D.C. On a commission by the Indian Department, he painted a series of portraits of American Indians visiting Washington.
Though many were destroyed in a fire at the Smithsonian Institution, those that
survived are now considered a precious national treasure.

Samuel F. B. Morse (1791–1872) was broken-hearted to find there was no future
in history painting in the United States. He settled in New York, painted some
fine portraits, served as a founder and first president of the National Academy
of Design, and led a revolt against the do-nothing policies of the American Academy of Fine Arts and its long-time president, John Trumbull. Morse ended his
career as a painter after he invented the electromagnetic recording telegraph, for
which he developed the Morse Code. He introduced the daguerreotype into the
United States, engaged in reactionary nativist and anti-Catholic agitation, and
died a rich man, internationally honored for his scientific discoveries.

Thomas Sully (1783–1872) was without a rival as a portrait painter in America
after the deaths of Gilbert Stuart (1828) and Charles Willson Peale (1827). He
painted some 2000 portraits, came to be known as "The Sir Thomas Lawrence of
America," and died in his eighty-ninth year — the last of West's coterie of students.

against his father's will, intending to study under West and at the Royal Academy schools. He did an altar piece in West's manner, and some portraiture (two guineas each, three if painted with a hand), and landscapes, his chief interest. His work, however, was uncertain, clumsy, and badly drawn, and he improved with painful slowness. He did not become West's pupil, though West did help and advise him from time to time. Leslie (who became his friend's biographer) wrote, "Constable acknowledged many obligations to the amiable President of the Academy, in whom every young artist found a friend; but the greatest was one which possibly affected the whole course of his life." In the spring of 1802, when Constable was twenty-six, his friend Dr. John Fisher, rector of Langham, afterwards bishop of Salisbury, obtained for him the offer of a position as drawing master at the new Royal Military College at High Wycombe. Constable made on-site drawings for General William Harcourt and was offered the post. He consulted Farington, who had been his advisor since his arrival in London, and Farington counseled him not to accept a situation that would divert him from his artistic career. Constable then talked with Sir George Beaumont, who seems to have advised him to take it, since he lacked the application necessary to be a good artist.

Now thoroughly perplexed, uncertain about his future and his abilities, worried about offending Dr. Fisher, perhaps having already accepted the offer, Constable went to West, told him the whole story, and asked his opinion. West saw in Constable what almost no one else saw in 1802: the promise of a major talent. He advised most strongly against accepting the post; if he did it would mean giving up all hopes of artistic distinction. Dr. Fisher was an admirer of West's work and West knew him well; he offered to convey the refusal. He did so, and in such a way that Constable neither offended Dr. Fisher nor lost his friendship. "Had I accepted the situation offered," he wrote to a friend a few days later, "it would have been a death-blow to all my prospects of perfection in the art I love."

In April 1812, Constable wrote to his intended, Miss Maria Bicknell:

> I met Mr. West in the street the other day — he stopped to speak to me, and told me he had been much gratified with a picture (the Mill, etc.) which passed the Council at the Academy. He said it had given him much pleasure and that he was glad to find I was the painter of it. I wished to know if he considered that mode of study as laying the foundation of real excellence. "Sir," (said he) "I consider that you have attained it."

Charles Leslie described another occasion on which West was able to help the artist. When his picture *Flatford Mill* was rejected at the Academy, Constable, downhearted, took it to West, who encouraged him in the words the artist would most want to hear.

> He then took a piece of chalk and showed Constable how he might improve the chiaroscuro by some additional touches of light between the stems and branches of the trees, saying, "Always remember, sir, that light and shadow *never stand still.*" Constable said it was the best lecture, because a practical one, on chiaroscuro he ever heard.
>
> Mr. West at the same time said to him, "Whatever object you are painting, keep in mind its prevailing character rather than its accidental appearance ... and never be content until you have transferred that to canvas. In your skies, for instance, always aim at *brightness,* although there are states of the atmosphere in which the sky itself is not bright. I do not mean that you are not to paint solemn or lowering skies, but even in the darkest effects there should be brightness. Your darks should look like the darks of silver, not of lead or of slate." This advice was not addressed to an inattentive ear.

Constable came to detest West's history painting, but he was forever grateful to West for the help he received. He said of West that "in his own room, and with a picture before him, his instructions were invaluable."

Constable was overjoyed in 1810 when he sold his first landscape (to an earl for thirty guineas), and he began to hope that he might be elected an Associate of the Academy, which, he told Farington, "would have a great effect upon his father's mind by causing him to consider his situation more substantial." Constable's mother, on the other hand, had none of her husband's doubts of their son's artistic abilities and future success. She came to London in April 1811, saw *Christ Healing the Sick,* and wrote to her son:

> I am glad ... that I have seen Mr. West's picture — of which I think highly ... but I speak from my own judgment of the performance, and have pleasure in the idea that your representation ... of the infant in your Brantham altar piece is much more delightful to my eyes ...
>
> With my present sight, I can perceive no cause or just impediment that you should not in due time, with diligence and attention, be the performer of a picture worth £3000.

Constable exhibited in that year *A View Near Dedham, Essex,* a picture that revealed, suddenly and almost fully developed, what he was striving to achieve: "Light — dews — breezes — bloom — and freshness; not one of which has yet been perfected on the canvas of any painter in the world." The picture was hung very low in the anteroom of the Academy, and Constable, "in much uneasiness of mind," called on Farington to say despondently that this was proof that he had fallen in the opinion of the members. Farington encouraged him by reporting that "Mr. Lawrence had twice noticed his picture with approbation."

Sir George Beaumont had known Constable as a boy in Sussex and was friendly to him in London, received him in his homes, but declined to buy his work or to take it seriously as art. Lady Beaumont (one of whose side interests at the time was studying the postulates of Euclid) thought the young man was weak. Both she and Sir George "reprobated" the use of green in landscapes, holding firmly that "a good picture, like a good fiddle, should be brown," and "there ought to be a brown tree in every landscape." Sir George told Hoppner sadly that "he would give anything to see an accomplished landscape painter arise." He waged "a continual cry" against the landscapes of Turner (who was too strong to be hurt by it), and he opposed (and hurt) a new school of English painters who were using water colors as a medium. Sir George told Farington and the company at a dinner that West was "an excellent judge of art, but that he often dealt out lavish and immoderate praise upon modern works"; he was especially disapproving of West's praise of a Turner seascape. West, in turn, was so disturbed by Beaumont's attacks that he spoke to him formally about the harm he was doing in "criticizing the works of young artists and praising one artist at the expense of another." Sir George replied that "it was not his fault that the artists did not paint better."

On the way home from an evening Council meeting on August 18, 1813, West pointed out to his companions the house, No. 19 Bedford Street, Covent Garden, where he first lodged on his arrival from Italy in August 1763, just fifty years earlier. Farington and Robert Smirke, Junior, were with him, and they decided to commemorate the anniversary by forming a party to drive two days hence to Shooters Hill and there to dine at the inn where West had his first dinner in England. Accordingly, Farington, Lawrence, and Smirke, Senior, went to 14 Newman Street on August 20 and began the commemoration by congratulating Mrs. West on Mr. West's safe arrival at Dover on that date in 1763. "She was seated in a chair in a paralytic state," Farington wrote, "but looked fuller in person and face than when I saw her last. Her voice was difficult to understand when she spoke; it was a husky effort. Her appetite good — free from pain — and slept well." The men set off in a coach-and-four, with Raphael West now one of the company, and proceeded to Greenwich. West and Lawrence were stiff and sore on the journey, for in returning at midnight recently from a dinner party their carriage had overturned. West's right arm was so badly bruised that he could paint in only one direction and it pained him when he was in bed. He had not bothered to see a doctor but was applying sweet oil and hartshorn to it. Lawrence was much bruised about the face. He said it was remarkable to see West's tranquillity on the occasion; "he did not appear to be at all agitated, but gave the best advice he could to Lawrence to prevent ill effects from his bruise."

At Greenwich they stopped for a tour, going first to see "the basso relievo executed at Coade's manufactory from a design by Mr. West, in honor of Lord Nelson, in the pediment of a portico.[4] The figure of Brittania eleven feet high; women figures 8 feet high." They proceeded to the hospital chapel and looked at West's *St. Paul's Shipwreck* over the altar. Their fellow Academicians Henry Thomson, William Owen, and Robert Smirke, Jr., met them, making a company of seven, and they went on to the inn at Shooters Hill, where a table had been reserved and the dinner ordered.

The conversation turned naturally to "the state of artists in this country compared with what it was when Mr. West arrived in England, in respect to their personal manners and the degree of estimation in which they were and are held." West said that in fifty years they had become "a different description of men — so much more decorous in their deportment and in their reception in society." The Royal Academy, he thought, had done much in giving dignity to the arts. The name of Sir Joshua Reynolds came up, and Lawrence said that he could justly assert that Mr. West had maintained more personal dignity in the society than Sir Joshua had done. Smirke, Senior, agreed. Northcote's *Life of Reynolds*, published earlier that year, was discussed and condemned as "vulgar and made up by compiling from others."

They had coffee and tea after dinner and talked until eleven, when they returned to London together. "Mr. West," reported Farington, "desired that it might be considered to be his dinner, which domestic circumstances prevented his giving at his own house, and he paid the bill."

---

[4] Coadestone was an artificial composition stone newly and successfully introduced at this time, much used in monumental statuary. West had made himself ill in November with a week of heavy physical exertion in the installation of the monument.

On June 6, 1814, this unusual advertisement appeared in the *Morning Herald* and several other newspapers:

> THE FINE ARTS. *Mr. West's picture of Christ rejected by Caiaphas, the High Priest and Jewish people, now in the Great Room, formerly the Royal Academy, 125 Pall Mall, was by the members of the Royal Academy seen on the 1st inst.; by the Noblemen and Gentlemen of the British Institution on the 3rd; by the Bishops, Ministers and Judges on the 4th, and on Thursday the 9th will open at twelve o'clock for public inspection.*

The picture — 361 square feet of canvas — was "enriched with a splendid frame after the model of the Gate of Theseus at Athens." Three attendants were present to collect the one shilling admission fee, protect the picture, and sell a pamphlet identifying the cast of characters: Christ in a purple robe, crowned with thorns, hands bound, standing in a public square before the governor's palace in Jerusalem; the Roman Pontius Pilate; the richly dressed High Priest Caiaphas, his arms raised, leading the cry of condemnation; Mary Magdalene, fallen in despair on the cross; Mary the Mother supported by the disciple John; Peter weeping in repentance; the murderous Barabbas at the portal of the prison; the wife of Pilate in the gallery, stricken by foreboding; Roman soldiers holding the standard of the emperor Tiberius; a vast multitude surrounding these subjects — some eighty faces in all. Critics called the picture "the crowning work" and "the finest production of his genius." One wrote in a long and rhapsodic review: "The work is most indubitably the grandest performance of modern times, and irrevocably fixes the painter on the highest pinnacle of the temple of fame. Long may he flourish in his green old age, setting a high example to the British School, of perseverance, correctness, elegance and piety!" The Reverend Sydney Smith — he who was considered the wittiest man in England and who had asked the famous question, "Who reads an American book, or looks at an American painting, or a piece of American sculpture?" — the Reverend Mr. Smith, on looking at it, said simply, "I can preach you no better sermon than this picture."

In the first four months of the showing, an average of 470 people a day — 59,000 in all — came to marvel and admire. Farington went to see the picture on October 10 and found 80 persons present, who "appeared to be impressed with much awe by the subject. It was like a small congregation in a church." West told him that he had been offered and had refused 8000 guineas for the work. A later newspaper account — one suspects that it was planted — said that buyers had approached Mr. West with offers of 10,000 guineas, or 7000 guineas plus a sum equal to the profits of the first season's exhibition.

West hung the small study for *Christ Rejected* at the next Academy show. Sir George Beaumont declared that no other work in the gallery had "so much in it of the true quality of high art." No other artist since the time of Le Brun, he said, could be compared with Mr. West.[5]

Not everyone agreed. Criticizing the picture was almost like blaspheming the Christian religion, but Charles Long, the paymaster general, openly expressed great contempt for it and thought it a very poor performance. Beaumont felt that the printed description sold at the gallery was perhaps creating criticism because it arrogated so much in favor of the picture. William Hazlitt, artist *manqué* turned journalist, had just signed up to write articles for *The Champion*, and he wrote his first on *Christ Rejected*. Everyone agreed it was an excessively severe onslaught, but everyone read it with interest and Hazlitt became instantly famous.[6] His words, "He is only great by the acre," clung to West forever after. Crabb Robinson, the journalist, barrister and diarist, thought the review "an admirable criticism . . . a bitter and severe but most excellent performance," and he read it aloud to Flaxman at early tea. Flaxman, he recorded, "was constrained to admit the high talent of the criticism, though he was unaffectedly pained by its severity; but he was himself offended by West's attempt to represent this sacred subject."

West told Farington in March 1814 that his wife did not expect to live through the spring. She was in no pain. Her articulation was so imperfect that he could scarcely understand her. For several years he had found it difficult to leave her, as she was always apprehensive she should die during his absence. For himself, he never had pains in his head or stomach and was troubled only by long and severe fits of the gout, which he got if he drank port. He felt

---

[5] Charles Le Brun (1619–1690), cofounder of the French Academy of Painting and Sculpture, the Academy of France at Rome, and of the Gobelins factory, "first painter" to Louis XIV, dominated French art during his lifetime.

[6] A typical passage: West made Joseph of Arimathea look like "a respectable elderly country gentleman in the gallery of the House of Commons, listening to a speech of Lord Castlereagh's; — James the Less is a pert yeoman's son, thrusting himself forward to see a trial at Guildhall, or the honours of an election dinner; — St. Peter is a poor old man who has had his goods distrained for rent; — Mary Magdalene would do for one of the sprawling figures, Ceres, Juno, or Minerva, that we see at the head of ships of war."

he might reasonably expect three more years, to the age of eighty, in which he could continue to practice his profession. Farington dined with West at the end of July, marveled at the amount and quality of the food served, and "had much conversation," but did not see Mrs. West.

She died on December 6, 1814. Farington called on West "and sat for some time." West wondered if, as president of the Academy, he should invite the Council members to attend the funeral. Farington advised that "the funeral should be respectfully carried out but in a private manner." Elizabeth Shewell West was so buried on December 15. Her last wish was that she might lie in a grave near her husband. She was buried in the crypt of St. John's Chapel at the northeast end of St. John's Woods Road.

A long obituary notice read, in part:

> She was charitable to all, but virtue and talents in distress had a prior claim on her bounty ... Though she was not blind to her own endowments, yet when they were mentioned in her presence, she would turn from the speaker in modest distress. When she indulged her poetic fancy in delineating living characters, it was to cherish virtue, or gently admonish, but never to wound the feelings of a friend for the sake of displaying her wit. Such were some of the amiable qualities which won the love of all to whom she was known.

26

The Final Years

The dinner went off very well — the mutton excellent. The evening was made somewhat dull by the slowness with which Mr. West gave the toasts; the intervals were too long . . . Lawrence accompanied me home and drank tea with me. He remarked that in observing the profiles of the faces of those who sat in a long line before him, that he was struck with that of Mr. West, the President, as having in it a strength of expression and character such as he saw in no other face.

JOSEPH FARINGTON,
Diary, April 30, 1814

THE LAST FIVE YEARS of West's life, 1815–1820, were full and busy ones, especially so for a man progressing from his seventy-seventh to his eighty-second year. He entertained, traveled, and gave many hours to his painting, with productive results. He was re-elected president of the Academy five more times without serious opposition, as he had been every year since 1806, when he replaced Wyatt in the office. Benjamin West, Junior, and his wife and son moved into 14 Newman Street to run the household, leaving their home in Staffordshire. West told Farington that he was not accustomed to household problems, since Mrs. West had managed everything. "An artist," he said, "should be free from all domestic cares and be left wholly to his profession." Farington developed a liking for the young couple, and especially for the new Mrs. West, who was pretty, vivacious, and passionately addicted to social gossip, some of which Farington recorded in his diary. ("Lord Chancellor Eldon is not yet reconciled to his daughter who married Mr. Repton.")

An extraordinary thing happened at the Academy exhibition

dinner on April 27, 1815. The prince regent had fulfilled his promise to West and installed in the Assembly Room a two-ton bronze chandelier with thirty-two lamps that was raised and lowered with a windlass; it was much admired during the dinner. Walter Scott was there, the poet and novelist who two months earlier had published *Guy Mannering,* his second romance, and he described the affair in a letter to a friend: "Old West presided, and was supported by Jockey of Norfolk [the duke of Norfolk] on one side and one of the Royal Dukes on the other." A few preliminary toasts had been drunk when a loud cracking noise was heard overhead. The huge bronze chandelier began to descend slowly on the transfixed diners. Gradually it came down to a serving table on which stood a quantity of bottles and goblets and inch-by-inch crushed it and all the glass. "What was very odd," Scott wrote, "the chain, after this manifestation of weakness, continued to hold fast; and we, I think to the credit of our courage, continued our sitting. Had it really given way ... it must have broke the floor like a bombshell and carried us all down to the cellars of that great national edifice. A fine paragraph we should have made!"

Receipts for the 1815 exhibition reached a record-breaking £5255, a total that was not attained again for many years.

At a dinner of the Artists' Benevolent Fund at Aldersgate on May 25, those present spoke highly of the manner in which the prince regent's brothers, the dukes of Kent and Sussex, conducted themselves. They placed Mr. West between them at the head of the table and each, in a speech "tending to conviviality," eulogized the arts. Dr. John Willis, the king's doctor, complimented West on the address he made. "I felt some pain for you when you began to speak," he said, "but in a little time you spoke with so much effect that I and all about me were highly gratified."

On this same day the House of Commons voted 331 to 92 to resume the war against Bonaparte, who had abdicated his throne in April 1814 but escaped from the island of Elba and was now again in Paris and in power. Englishmen were filled with despair and anger at having to do again what had already cost so much wealth and so many lives. Robert Smirke, Senior, spoke bitterly on May 25 of the pain it gave him in this critical period to hear biased sentiments in favor of Bonaparte, "notwithstanding his atrocious conduct." He had on this account, he said to Farington, "avoided intercourse with several persons so inclined, though in other respects he was disposed to think well of some of them. He mentioned Dr. Hayes and Benjamin West as of the number always ready to think favourably of Bonaparte, and said it was most extraordinary that men who professed themselves advocates for liberty should be so warped in their opinions." Farington did not disagree with Smirke on Bonaparte; he considered him "one of the most malignant and remorseless tyrants that ever existed."

Bonaparte was defeated at Waterloo in June, the victory costing the allies 22,000 men killed and wounded, the French 40,000. Under the terms of the 1814 peace treaty the French had been permitted to keep their *Musée Napoléon*, but this time, when several of the allies entered Paris, they took back all they could find of the art that had been stolen from them; it was then decided that the art taken from Italy and Spain should be returned as well. When they saw the art works carried away, the French were outraged and indignant.[1]

West's activities during these last years are seen in the letters he wrote and received, in a few newspaper stories and official documents, but chiefly through the eyes and the daily entries of the diarists of the time — the ever-watchful Joseph Farington; John Quincy Adams, the American minister to Great Britain; and Benjamin Haydon, the young student who said of himself, "I was always burning for distinction." Haydon spent a long evening in July 1815 looking over West's portfolio of drawings by Raphael and Michelangelo. He was still angry at earlier injuries he felt he had received from West; but he was grateful to him for behaving with such "grandeur of soul" in the Elgin marbles controversy, and more strongly for a call West made at his home the year before to see his *Judgment of Solomon*. He recorded the visit in his autobiography:

> He said there were points in the picture equal to anything in the art. "But," said this good old man, "get into better air; you will never recover with this eternal anxiety before you. Have you any resources?" "They are exhausted." "D'ye want money?" "Indeed I do." "So do I," said he; "they have stopped my income from the King, but Fauntleroy is now arranging an advance, and if I succeed, my young friend, you shall hear. Don't be cast down — such a work must not be allowed to be forgotten." This was noble of West.
>
> Such is the lot of High Art in England. West — whose *Wolfe* had immortalized his name and his country, President of the Academy, cut off suddenly from his means of existence . . . with-

---

[1] Pope Pius VII offered to give the English prince regent the Vatican's sculpture taken to France, including the *Apollo Belvedere*, in return for his help in recovering the other art works. The regent refused and instead paid the cost of returning all the pieces to Rome.

out a guinea; I without a shilling . . . and the venerable old President promising to [help me] if his bankers helped him!

In the course of that day down came from West £15, with the following characteristic letter:

> Newman Street,
> February 17, 1814

"Dear Sir:

The business was not adjusted in time for me to draw out money from my bankers before five o'clock this day, or I would have sent it to you; but I hope the enclosed draft of tomorrow's date will be adequate to keep the wolfe from your door, and leave your mind in freedom in exercising your talents of acquiring excellence in your profession of painting, of which you have a stock to work on."

On July 25, 1815, a Select Committee of members of the House of Commons began to take testimony on whether to buy the earl of Elgin's Greek sculptures. West was requested to appear to testify, but he declined, citing his age and health, and asked the members to meet with him in his house. They refused. West then wrote out answers to a long list of their questions. He placed the marbles "in the first rank of dignified art," said they appeared to be "more than human work," and urged the government to buy them from Lord Elgin "as likely to be of great service to the arts."

August 7: Five artists, meeting at the request of the master of the Mint, went to West's house to discuss with him a medal to commemorate the defeat of Bonaparte at Waterloo. (West called it "a victory over a rapacious enemy.") They chose Flaxman to make the design.

September 7: West departed on a ten-day visit to the Isle of Wight that extended to three months, staying with his friend John Nash at East Cowes Castle.[2] An Academician who saw him there reported on "the great attention paid to West by many families, and of the hospitality with which he has been treated, and of the good effect this excursion appears to have had on his constitution. The ladies had been particularly attentive to him, and everything flat-

---

[2] John Nash, a leading architect of the Regency period and the "Picturesque" movement, much favored by the prince regent, had just begun his complete redesign of Brighton Pavilion (1815–1822) at the time of West's visit. Nash and West were working together on a design for a Waterloo monument in a competition.

tering was done." Mr. Nash seldom had fewer than twenty persons present at dinner.

September 9: John Singleton Copley died in his seventy-seventh year in his home on George Street. He was buried at the parish church in Croyden in the tomb belonging to the family of the former governor of Massachusetts, Thomas Hutchinson. He was deeply in debt, had been living for some time on money begged from his son-in-law in Boston, and left his estate, in his widow's words, "in a very unpleasant and involved condition."

November 27: West attended a dinner given for Antonio Canova by diplomat William Richard Hamilton (formerly Lord Elgin's secretary). Haydon wrote in his diary, "West was there, but his bad Italian annoyed us all."

December 1: West presided at a dinner given in the Council Room of the Academy in honor of Canova, of whose modesty and talents even the terrible-tempered Henry Fuseli approved. When West later introduced Canova to the students at an Academy lecture on anatomy, a reporter wrote, "The attention paid by Mr. West to Mr. Canova was liberal and enlightened."

While in London, Canova inspected the Elgin marbles, pronounced them the work of Phideas, declared that he had never before seen such sculptures at such a height of perfection, and said it would be a sacrilege to restore them.[3] With his reputation as the first of living artists, Canova's authority was such that his pronouncement settled the controversy between artists and patrons, and between Benjamin West and R. Payne Knight, over the merits and the provenance of the marbles. (Knight was labeled "an ignorant, presumptuous connoisseur" in the Academy; he is remembered today for that appellation and for the great collection of coins, gems, and bronzes he willed to the British Museum. As an ultimate mark of disapproval, the Academicians did not invite him to their exhibition dinner the following April.) Lord Elgin, his life ruined by his sculptural marbles, was paid £36,000 for his collection, all of it being turned over to his creditors.

On April 25, 1816, Benjamin West, Junior, remarked to Farington on the great change that had taken place in his father. Until lately he had been most industrious in the practice of his art, but for some months past he had become indolent and had done nothing. He

---

[3] Restoration would require cutting into the original pieces. Sir George Beaumont recommended that the Elgin marbles be restored, as the mutilated fragments "excite disgust rather than pleasure in the minds of people in general, to see parts of limbs and bodies, stumps of arms, etc."

"seemed to be acting like a young man who had a life to pass rather than as one who in common reckoning, at 77 years of age, had little remaining of time he could presume upon." Raphael said his father at times was irritable, quite unlike himself, for he had never seen him out of temper but once.

In May, Farington dined with twelve other members of the Academy Club, which had been reconstituted in February 1813. On the way home with a group, he heard a member say, "How very agreeably the Club meetings go on." Smirke said the club was now like a family.

John Galt's *The Life and Studies of Benjamin West, Esq., President of the Royal Academy of London, Prior to his Arrival in England* (the first volume of his biography), was published in London and Philadelphia in this year. Dr. Hayes, West's physician, thought the account of West's early life was well written. Flaxman said the incident of the young untutored West drawing his niece in the cradle before he had seen a picture was "fabulous" — that is, impossible to believe. Maria Edgeworth, the novelist, a woman who (Farington observed) put questions rather abruptly and received answers like one who comprehended them quickly, asked Farington at a dinner party if he had read the book. "She said, 'It is a curious account,' and she put it to me as a question, whether I gave credit to it, and whether I supposed that Mr. West furnished the matter for it. I told her I concluded he did. She asked me whether Mr. West received observations (criticisms)."

West addressed the Academy on July 1 to announce that he intended to present a bronze medal to each member "as a memorial respecting himself." His bust would be on one side, done by an ingenious young medalist, and the names of the forty Academicians on the other. (The presentation of such medals on special occasions was not uncommon.) On receiving his medal, Henry Fuseli wrote an acknowledgment in which he referred to himself in the third person: "Though conscious of his own inferiority and too far advanced in life to consider it an incentive to future exertions, he feels proud in considering it as an unequivocal testimony of esteem and a flattering pledge of friendship from the President of the Royal Academy and the Prince of British Art." In his thanks Flaxman went beyond what was normally required for such a gift. The likeness of Mr. West was striking, it was "the best head that has been engraved in Europe since the Fifteenth Century," and he would always "preserve it with affectionate care and regard." But its great attractions were "that it presents before me in the most lively manner the excellent President of the Royal Academy for twenty-five years, the Patriarch of painting in our days, the exemplary character of private life, and the man whose kindness and benevolence I have experienced ever since I have had the honor of being known to him, which is now nearly half a century."

Earlier in 1816, the directors of the American Academy of Fine Arts in New York, at the suggestion of Samuel Waldo, one of West's former students, collected $2000 with which they persuaded Thomas Lawrence to paint a full-length portrait of West, "that [American] artists might see what constituted a work of art in that branch of painting." Trumbull, as president of the American Academy, ignored his quarrel with West long enough to write him as a friend to request that he sit to Lawrence. He was painted full-length and life-size, in the act of lecturing the students on his theory of color. When he saw the portrait in New York, William Dunlap felt that it showed West taller than his 5-foot, 8-inch height, but he admired the likeness. To Trumbull he remarked with pleasure on the fine resemblance. Trumbull replied, "Yes, it has precisely his jesuitical expression." When the Pennsylvania Academy wrote to West saying that they too wished to have a full-length portrait, West obtained Lawrence's permission to copy the head, as an approved likeness, and to add the figure himself. Dr. Hayes spoke to Farington on Lawrence's portrait. It was so ably managed, he said, "that though it indicated sufficiently the advanced age of Mr. West, there was nothing in the appearance to excite pain from a look of decay; whereas . . . one cannot look at Mr. West now without a painful feeling from seeing so much manifestation of age and decay, particularly his sunk in mouth."

On July 5 of this year West met John Quincy Adams among 300 guests at a ball held at the John Penn mansion. They inspected the original *Penn's Treaty* together and "had much conversation" with each other. Adams called on West in August and was shown his work-in-progress, the large version of *Death on the Pale Horse*, which West said he hoped to complete by next spring and which he said "must be in the terribly sublime style." On another call Adams took his wife and children and met "a company of ladies and gentlemen" who were at 14 Newman Street to see West's pictures. Among the visitors were Francois Joseph Talma, the French tragedian, and Mlle. George (Marguerite-Joséphine Weimer), a principal of his cast, whom Adams had known in St. Petersburg. They all went to the British Museum with West and "saw the whole collection of its curiosities." West's enthusiasm, Adams wrote, is all concentrated upon the Elgin marbles, and he was impatient until we were among them . . . A horse's head Mr. West says [is] the most perfect sample of art that he ever saw." The museum closed at four and all the visitors were told to leave, but an exception was made for Mr. West and his company, and they stayed another hour. West later gave one of his bronze medals to Mr. and Mrs. Adams, "my two American friends."

On November 4, Barenger, an engraver, called on West and found him painting *Death on the Pale Horse.* He was using his left hand, his right being "wrapped up with the gout.[4] Dr. Hayes condemned West's practice of going to his painting room between ten and eleven in the morning and remaining there till between five and six without taking any refreshment. This, he warned him, "caused inanition."

At the opening of the Academy exhibition on May 3, 1817, the Great Room was for the first time lighted by gas, the burners being fitted to the prince regent's chandelier. At the annual dinner, over which West presided, one of the guests was a Mr. Hamlet, a goldsmith, who had been invited because he had generously lent his *Bacchus and Ariadne* by Titian to the Academy school. He was aggrieved when he found himself at a table where the other diners were three Associate Members and seven musicians and singers who were to perform after the cloth was removed.

On Saturday evening, June 28, West attended the first dinner given by the gallery at Dulwich College for the president and officers of the Royal Academy and other guests "on the occasion of an inspection of the pictures on or about St. Luke's Day in each year."[5] In what must have been a curious confrontation of old adversaries, he sat beside John Singleton Copley, Jr. — now Mr. Serjeant Copley, an officer at law acting for the king in his courts. Whatever West's opinion of this once "pert" young man, Copley was now a man of charm, humor, and liberal views who on June 16 had so distinguished himself in a difficult court case that he was being talked of as a future lord chancellor of England.

---

[4] It is commonly stated that the large *Pale Horse* was painted by Raphael West as an enlargement of his father's small sketch. This appears to be an assumption without evidence to support it. West was seen a number of times by various persons working on the picture. On September 8, 1815, Raphael talked to Faringdon on the subject: "He spoke of the assistance he gave his father in tracing on large canvases the subjects for which his father made sketches, who when he comes to paint finds every form in its place, but nothing more than a general outline, a space for him to fill up agreeable to his own ideas. Thus all the tedious and dry business of preparation his father is relieved from, besides the fatigue of doing it." Raphael West, it may be noted, was not one to understate his contribution to his father's work.

[5] Under the terms of the will of Sir Francis Bourgeois, the president of the Academy was authorized to inspect Dulwich Gallery once each year and choose a picture from the collection for the students to study at the Academy. Mrs. Desenfans made a bequest of £500, plus plate and linen, to entertain the president and other members of the Academy on the day of the inspection.

July 16: A committee formed to draw up plans for commemorating the Academy's fiftieth anniversary in 1819 asked Farington to prepare a history of the society, to be kept in the library as an unpublished private record. Beechey warned the committee that West would try to make the history suit his own views. Henry Thomson said that West "still continues to propagate that the commemoration . . . will be as a compliment to him."

July 18: West, Farington, Beechey, and five others dined at John Penn's. On the way, West said that more than 120,000 persons had gone to see *Christ Rejected.*[6] He said that he expected to complete *Death on the Pale Horse* by September 1. Farington said he had heard that West lost much time by allowing himself to be interrupted by persons calling on him. West replied that, on the contrary, "the conversations he had on such occasions were a relief to his spirits and enabled him to proceed with more vigor." Farington noted that he drank several glasses of wine and partook of everything that was served: giblet soup, fish, venison, roast fowls, custard, and ice cream.

August 15: West shipped his second version of *Christ Healing the Sick* to the Pennsylvania Hospital in the care of an artist-friend, sending it in the name of Elizabeth Shewell West. It was placed in a separate building erected partly for that purpose; proceeds from the exhibition (twenty-five cents admission, ten dollars for a life ticket) soon paid the cost of the building and earned a profit of some $15,000 — enough to pay for an additional wing that held thirty patients.[7]

November 8: West gave out a number of cards to a private showing of his completed *Death on the Pale Horse* at the Pall Mall gallery, but because of the death of Princess Charlotte, the only child of the prince regent and his estranged wife, the Princess of Wales, the doors were not opened. (Princess Charlotte and her baby died in childbirth. Sir Richard Croft, the attending physician, committed suicide.)

November 11: Constable was not elected an A.R.A., but for the first time since he put up his name in 1810 he received votes, and he let it be known that he was "well satisfied with the good disposition shown towards him in the election." He was defeated

---

[6] If they each paid a shilling, the gross income to West was £6000.

[7] The picture now hangs in the lobby of the Hospital's Elm Building, where it still produces income in the form of a thirty-five dollar fee for permission to reproduce it.

nineteen to five by a sculptor named E. H. Baily and fifteen to eight by a painter named Abraham Cooper.

West let it be known that he would read a lecture to the students on the afternoon of December 10 when he gave out the gold and silver medals in the Great Room. There was mild consternation among the members at the announcement, a dozen of whom were present on the occasion. The gold medal (it weighed a half pound and was the first given out in eight years) went to young Joseph Severn for his *Una and the Red Cross Knight in the Cave of Despair.* His intimate friend John Keats had accompanied him to Somerset House a few days earlier to see the picture and had told Severn that he was delighted with it. He admitted that he had no knowledge of the art of painting, but he felt, after an inspection of the other pictures, that Severn's was the best, and if it did not win the gold medal it would be the most honorable of failures.

West's lecture was on his theory that the order of colors in a rainbow was the proper arrangement in a historical picture. Lawrence reported in some surprise, "He spoke nearly one-half hour and *extempore,* and with great self-possession, also with a readiness of delivery beyond what had been before heard from him."

When the Pall Mall gallery reopened in December, this time with a showing of both *Christ Rejected* and *Death on the Pale Horse,* John Keats went to study the second work. "It is a wonderful picture," he wrote to a friend, "when West's age is considered; but there is nothing to be intense upon; no women one feels mad to kiss; no face swelling into reality. The excellence of every art is its intensity, capable of making all disagreeables evaporate, from their being in close relationship with Beauty and Truth ... In this picture we have unpleasantness without any momentous depth of speculation excited, in which to bury its repulsiveness."

December 17: Mrs. Benjamin West, Jr., wished to see *Much Ado About Nothing* at the Covent Garden Theater. West obtained the use of John Angerstein's box and took her and Farington to dinner and then to the play. He was in high spirits, Farington saw, at having completed *Death on the Pale Horse.*

By February 1818, Raphael West's financial situation was so poor and his creditors so importunate that he was forced to appeal again to his father for help. From Staines (twenty-eight miles from London) he sent a three-page letter, enclosing a note he had received from Mr. Mills, his landlord, to whom he owed £64, two years' past-due rent for the house he was living in. Mr. Mills demanded his money. Raphael requested "by return of post you will have the goodness to inform me what answer I am to give to Mr. Mills." He also chose that occasion to send his father "the amount of my other bills for housekeeping, etc., many of which are *of very long standing.*" The list contained thirty-two tradesmen and service people and totaled £556 16s.

Raphael wrote again to his father one month later. An attorney had called on him that morning about £8 2s. owing Mr. Richards, a carpenter, who was now bankrupt, and had told him the bill *should be immediately paid.* Raphael told the attorney he had no money in the house but would write his father at once. In his letter he named four other creditors who were pressing him the hardest — Mrs. West's shoemaker, the music master, the writing master, and the landlord at his former residence in Farnham, whose rent was four years past due. He said he had written to Mr. Mills "to inform him of your proposition of paying him the two years rent . . . by a note to be made payable in six weeks." He ended his letter, "I remain, my dear Father, as I ever have been, your unoffending and affectionate son."

February 25: Farington dined with the Wests at 14 Newman Street, young Mrs. Benjamin West sitting at the head of the table. West showed him a picture about 18 feet wide of Lord Clive, the British statesman and general, "accompanied by General Carnack [John Carnac] etc., receiving a paper of agreement from the Nabob." He was painting it for India House and was to make a replica for the Clive family.

March 18: Farington told Lawrence that West intended to hang his picture of Lord Clive over the fireplace in the Great Room for the annual exhibition, and Lawrence must now decide where to place his portrait of the duke of Wellington. On March 25 Lawrence agreed to give up the fireplace position and to group his six pictures in another part of the gallery. On April 3, however, Smirke and Farington called on West and persuaded him to let Lawrence have the fireplace position. Ten days later the Hanging Committee put West's *Clive* over the fireplace.

May 1: The Princess Elizabeth, West's severest critic, now grown "extremely corpulent," one of the six spinster sisters in what was called "the Windsor nunnery," called at the exhibition with a royal party of thirteen persons. West attended her on a ninety-minute tour of the galleries.

May 16: At a Saturday night party given by a Mr. Seddons in Russell Square, West was seen to be in high spirits at 2 o'clock in the morning. A few months earlier he had attended the British Institution exhibition accompanied by two ladies.

Farington dined at 14 Newman Street on June 2 with the two West sons, their wives, and the Raphael Wests' fourteen-year-old daughter, Maria — their only child. West was ill with an upset stomach:

> He was in bed and in a weak state, but he cordially held my hand and talked with his usual recollection. I told him of the large exhibition receipts, and we both remarked upon the increasing public feeling for works of art. I spoke to Mrs. B. West about the cause of his indisposition. She . . . said that in her opinion it was owing to his indulging too much in the use of *butter,* for when she has given him what is the usual quantity he would call for more.

West took a special delight in his granddaughter Maria. William Dunlap wrote of her: Washington Allston and Charles Robert Leslie "were one day waiting in Mr. West's large painting room to see him, when the door opened, and a young girl of about fifteen came bounding in, but stopped suddenly on seeing strangers, blushed and ran out. We both thought we had never beheld anything so lovely. Mr. West entered soon after, and we asked him who the beautiful creature we had just seen was. He told us, she was his granddaughter, and added, 'She is a little Psyche.' "

Washington Allston, after a seven-year stay in England, sailed for Boston in September 1818. In 1814 his *Uriel Seated in the Sun,* an enormous foreshortened figure nearly twice the size of life, had won a British Institution award of £150 and Lord Stafford had immediately bought it. Allston became an Associate Member in 1818, and he was being hailed as the one man who might raise English art to the level of the sixteenth century. There was even serious talk — though Allston was an American — that he should succeed West as president of the Academy; the alternative was Lawrence, who was, after all, only a "face painter." But Allston's wife had died suddenly in 1815, and her death left him shaken and ill. His patrimony was exhausted in 1818 and he was homesick for his native country.

He took with him his nearly completed scriptural picture of enormous size, *Belshazzar's Feast,* which he considered the great work of his life. Stuart saw it in 1820 and condemned the perspective. Allston attempted to change the composition, ignoring one of the strongest of West's precepts: that it was better to begin a picture anew on another canvas than to make major alterations in it. He worked on it at intervals, unhappily and unsuccessfully, leaving it unfinished at his death in 1843.[8]

November 17: Queen Charlotte, mother of thirteen discontented children, grown sullen and crabbed in her last two decades, died at Kew in her seventy-fourth year. She was buried in the Royal Chapel at Windsor. Care of the king was entrusted to Frederick, Duke of York, his second son. The king was buried beside Charlotte fourteen months later.

In January 1819, Thomas Lawrence wrote a long and affectionate letter to West from Vienna. ("Your high reputation makes enquiries after you frequent, from persons of the highest consideration.") He was traveling about the Continent at the prince regent's command, painting full-length portraits of the leading sovereigns, statesmen, and generals of the coalition that had defeated Bonaparte; the prince had given him a knighthood to raise him a little closer to the level of the exalted personages he was painting. (He carried a number of pictures with him as evidence of his capacity.) After the defeat of Bonaparte, a proposal conceived by the *Weekly Messenger* and approved by the Royal Academy had been submitted to the prince regent: The great figures of the coalition should be painted, each by a different British artist, and placed in a special gallery built to hold them, "the execution of the whole to be under the advice of Mr. West." The plan was "frustrated" by Thomas Lawrence, and the prince was persuaded to commission a single artist to paint all the portraits, the artist being Lawrence. The prince further ordered that a Waterloo Gallery be built on Horn Court inside the walls of Windsor Castle — on the area where George III had once planned to place his chapel for West's pictures of revealed religion.

April 17: Sir George Beaumont called on West, who was ill, and sat a half hour with him. Beaumont said that West, though feeble, seemed to be very clear in his intellect.

July 3: West wrote to Phillips, the auctioneer at Pall Mall, that he wished to sell some of his old masters. Phillips told Lord Egremont, who called on West and looked at several pictures. He could not persuade West to give him a sale price. West's own small cabinet pictures — his preliminary sketches in oil — were much sought

---

[8] It is often said that he virtually stopped painting after he returned to the United States, but E. P. Richardson has pointed out that Allston, "a subjective artist . . . the first American painter whose art was an exploration of the visions within his own mind," produced at least forty works after 1818, including some that are "most appealing to modern taste . . . his landscape reveries."

after, but he would not sell them. Since 1797 he had been saving these "to sell at once, which may contribute to make an independence for others."

July 20: West and Farington signed a testimonial on the superior qualities of a black lead pencil that was being manufactured and marketed by a Mr. Pethers.

September 3: In a conversation with Farington, West spoke bitterly of "the little encouragement given to him and to historical painting in general." He had tried the nobility of the country, he said, and he had tried the wealthy gentlemen, and "he knew them. They partook of the common character of the people of whom Bonaparte justly said, 'They are a nation of shop keepers.' " He had expressed this opinion, he said, in a recent letter to America.

In an admirable exhibition of tolerance and self-restraint, Farington changed the subject. He spoke to West "of the injury he does to his pictures long since painted, by touching upon them with fresh colour which would not assimilate with the old colour." West replied that in eleven or twelve years the colour would harmonize. "The remarks I made on this point," Farington wrote, "were pressed upon me by Sir Thomas Lawrence and by Benjamin and Mrs. West, who thought me the most proper person to speak to him."

December 8: John Constable called on Farington to thank him for his aid in getting elected an Associate Member of the Academy over thirty-seven other candidates.

December 10: At its annual meeting and election of officers for the coming year (1820), the Royal Academy marked its fiftieth anniversary with a special program. West and George Dance were the last of the founding members still alive, and West was the oldest member, save only for Joseph Nollekens, who, older by one year, was worth £200,000 but was living like a miser. Angelica Kauffmann had died in Rome in 1807, buried in what was virtually a state funeral, attended by more than one hundred ecclesiastics in the habits of their orders, the pall supported by young ladies dressed all in white, some of her best pictures borne on the shoulders of the mourners. Many other members were gone, including most of the adversaries of the great struggles of 1798–1806. James Barry in 1806, a few weeks before he was to have received an annuity. Ozias Humphry in 1810, one of six deaths in that year. Hoppner in 1810, after a long illness, leaving rooms full of unfinished portraits, which his son was completing. John Richards, the secretary, in 1810, of a paralytic affliction, leaving an illegitimate child without provision and a widow destitute. John Rigaud in 1810 of apoplexy. James Wyatt in 1813, killed by a blow on the head in a carriage accident, leaving a huge load of debt and one of his female servants large with child. (West had ruled that he should not be given a Royal Academy funeral.) Francis Bourgeois in 1811, buried beside Noel Desenfans in Dulwich Chapel. Henry Tresham in 1814, and John Copley the following year. John Yenn was alive but in a state of imbecility and was being replaced as treasurer.

During the year 1819 West painted what he knew would be his last self-portrait. He used oils on a composition board about 32 by 25 inches in size. He showed himself half-length, seated with a square of paper on his drawing board, a crayon holder in his right hand. He wore a formal white stock, a loose orange painting gown, and a beautiful, incongruously stylish high beaver hat with a flared brim. He gave the face in the mirror an unsparing look and painted an honest portrait of the face that looked back: one large ear under a tuft of brushed gray hair, cheeks with the creases of old age, the enlarged, elongated nose of extreme old age, frosty eyebrows, and a penetrating look in the eyes, the level gaze of a man beyond fear and illusion. This was a picture that might have been painted as a manifesto: as an answer to those critics who were saying that he could not paint small pictures and was great only by the acre; as a means of confusing those who said he painted history pictures only because he could not paint portraits; as a defiance to those who were to mock his lifework in the decades to come.

27

A Windy Night, a Rainy Morrow

Students of the history of "Taste" have long been puzzled by the real savagery of the judgments passed by cultivated people when they are discussing the style that has just gone out.

JOHN STEEGMAN,
*The Rule of Taste —
From George I to George IV,*
1936

JOSEPH FARINGTON received a message from Henry Thomson at 9 A.M. on March 11, 1820, that Mr. West had died shortly after midnight. Thomson then called to discuss the election of a new president. Flaxman came to say that he wished to deliver a tribute to Mr. West at an Academy meeting. "Mr. West," he said, "has perhaps done less for the Academy and taken more to himself than he might have done, but he has done a great deal, and allowance might be made for his vanity." George Dance formally announced the death of the president at a General Assembly meeting of the Academy two days later.

Sir Thomas Lawrence wrote from Paris, "I found in the papers the sad event of the death of Mr. West, the most profound judge of art and one of its ablest professors that Europe has had for centuries, and a humane kind-hearted man."

Arrangements were made to bury Benjamin West in St. Paul's Cathedral, the fee being £150, but the bishop of Lincoln, dean of St. Paul's, refused his permission, because Mr. West's parents were Quakers and there was no proof that he had ever been baptised. Henderson, the Wests' attorney, went to see the bishop and in the course of the conversation learned that objection had been raised

by "an artist or a friend of the arts." Finding that the bishop was
determined to support the objection, and concluding that he was
"bigotted," Henderson went to Sir William Scott, judge of the court
at Doctors' Commons, who regretted the bishop of Lincoln's stand
but declined to become involved, because he might be called upon
to act in the matter as a judge. John Fisher, bishop of Salisbury,
fearing the current widespread unrest and rioting among the populace, declared that Lincoln's decision would have "bad consequences in raising a great spirit of opposition in all the different
sects." He informed the bishop that he had often seen Mr. West at
church in Windsor; that he had been married in London at St.
Martin's Church; that his children were baptised and attended "our
Protestant church"; and that Mr. West had a seat in Fitzroy Chapel.
The bishop of Lincoln was not satisfied; he must see a baptismal
certificate. Henderson applied to Dr. Adam, an attorney, who (Farington said) declared "that proof of baptism was not necessary
where it was shown that the individual conformed to the usages of
the Church and remarked on the evil of such precedent of objection
as it might be used by country clergymen, and of the cry that would
be set up by all *Dissenters*. The Bishop then said he would refer it
to the Prebend and soon after he granted leave for the interment."
West was buried with much pomp and circumstance on March 29,
nineteen days after his death, near Christopher Wren, John Opie,
James Barry, Joshua Reynolds, and Dr. Thomas Newton, his early
patron.

The next day Sir Thomas Lawrence was elected president of the
Royal Academy, receiving twenty-one votes of the twenty-three
cast, Flaxman and John Jackson receiving one each. Joseph Farington wrote on that date: "After the election I returned to Sir
Thomas's with Dance, Smirke and Thomson. Westall had preceded us. We had tea and conversation."

Benjamin West left everything to his two sons: an estate with
an estimated worth of £100,000, which included the house on Newman Street, its contents, all works of art, rights in his engravings,
no cash, and pressing debts of £11,000. On April 14, ten people met
at dinner at Newman Street "regarding the best mode of proceeding
for the disposal of West's property." The two sons and their wives
were there, the oldest grandchild, Henderson the attorney, Fauntleroy the banker, and Farington, Smirke, and Lawrence. The sons
decided that Benjamin, Junior, would continue to live in the house
for a time. They would first sell the collection of prints, drawings,
and paintings by other artists. As a money-making proposition they

would mount an exhibition of their father's works, keep it open "as long as it may be attractive," and then dispose of everything by public sale, after which Benjamin would move back to the country.

James Christie was retained to manage the sale. He printed a thirty-two page catalogue, in one copy of which the sons, for their private guidance, marked the price they expected to receive on each major piece; their agent would bid in any object that did not meet its price. Farington told Henderson that they were estimating the values of the pieces at far too high a figure.

The drawings realized very good prices, the prints sold "indifferently," and the old master paintings did poorly. The sons swore they would never again "suffer the anxiety attending such sale," but rather would sell only by private contract. Raphael confessed to Farington that the sale "had gone off very badly"; Henderson, who collected all the receipts as payment against debts, told him it produced only £6999 in actual bids. Many of the pictures were bought in against Christie's advice and against the wishes of Henderson, whose main concern was to pay off the bonded debt to Fauntleroy. (It was later discovered that Henderson was also solicitor for Fauntleroy's firm, Marsh, Sibbald and Company.)

Raphael, fearing their inheritance would be "reduced by driblets," wished for a speedy disposal of everything they owned; he talked of holding a lottery, "reckoning that many tickets would be sold in America." The bankers sent the Wests a notice that they must dispose of the old masters immediately at whatever sacrifice and give them the proceeds. At this point Raphael retired to the village of Staines, and Benjamin, with extraordinary lack of good sense, proceeded to build an addition to the Newman Street house in which to exhibit the pictures painted by their father. It was designed by John Nash, a room 70 by 43 feet set down in the garden, and contained the most advanced methods of displaying and lighting pictures, to be known as "West's New Gallery." Benjamin said the cost was £1500, but Farington believed it to be closer to £2000. A near neighbor, a coachmaker, formally objected to having a wall raised next to his property. Lady Beaumont asked Farington in some concern about the West boys and their new gallery; he replied that he had not been consulted, had no knowledge of it, and had advised them to keep their expectations moderate. On April 4, 1821, Messrs Marsh, Sibbald and Company refused to advance any more money on the project.

West's New Gallery, nevertheless, opened in May. It was greeted with much acclaim, both as an exhibition room and for its pictures, which for the most part were reviewed with respect and sometimes with reverence. There were almost 100 works, including a piece called West's first picture, *Seascape with Cow*, painted as a child in Pennsylvania, and his last picture, *Boys with Grapes*, painted late in 1819. The critic of the *Morning Herald* wrote, "While we are before the pictures and under their fascinating influence, we conceive we have never before seen so great powers exerted in art. And it is not until we are removed from their influence that we can acknowledge an inferiority in West to any other painter whatever."

Dr. Hayes said it was a fine display. Smirke spoke well of the general effect and said that West's pictures had never looked so good, though he regretted that *Penn's Treaty* and the pictures from the royal collection were not shown, "as those now exhibited had been much seen." He doubted that the public would be attracted in sufficient numbers to produce a large profit. Farington called, found fifty people in the gallery, and congratulated Benjamin on the high reports he had heard of the exhibition. Benjamin was in good spirits; he said the duke of York had been to the gallery and that within another two weeks the public would be aware of it and would come in large numbers. Farington sent his servants, Mary and Sarah, to see the pictures, "which afforded them much gratification." Beaumont said he feared the gallery would prove a disappointment; he and Nash both felt that Newman Street was "too far removed from the great line of communication" in London to be visited by large numbers. A few weeks later the Benjamin Wests called on Farington to ask his advice. The crowds had dwindled. What did he think of hiring people to carry placards in the streets advertising the exhibition? Farington advised against it.

In December of that year, having just turned seventy-four, Farington visited his brother at Didsbury, near South Lancaster. On Sunday, December 30, he rose at ten minutes after eight. It was a moist morning, the wind from the west, the thermometer reading 44-1/2 degrees at noon. He attended morning and afternoon services at the Didsbury Church, sitting in the gallery in his brother's pew, speaking to Mrs. George Phillips, Mr. and Mrs. Fieldin, and Mr. Birleg. He made those entries for the day in his diary late that afternoon and went back to the evening service. In descending the stairs from the gallery, his hands holding a hat, umbrella, and prayer book, his feet encumbered by heavy overshoes, he slipped, fell, plunged down the flight of stairs with great speed and force, and struck his head a heavy blow on the paved floor of the church.

On the last page of Farington's diary his niece wrote, "Mark the uncertainty of this life!! ... The vital spark was gone. He — neither looked, spoke, moved — or breathed again."

The intimate record of the West family ended with the closing of Farington's diary. The further efforts of the sons to realize something from their father's works appear only in official records and fragmentary gossip. Some 95,000 people visited West's New Gallery in its first year, but the novelty of an unchanging exhibition wore off and the crowds and the gate receipts dropped. Thomas Lawrence spoke of this to the students at the Academy. Mr. West, he said, was "the one popular painter of his country." He had produced a series of compositions from sacred and profane history that were profoundly studied and executed with easy power. They were not only superior to any former productions of English art and surpassed contemporary merit on the Continent, but were unequaled at any period below the schools of the Caracci.

> It is now more than three years that we have witnessed at his own residence an exhibition of the accumulated labours of this venerable and great artist — whose remains were honoured with a public funeral, and whose loss was felt as a national calamity — totally neglected and deserted! the spacious rooms in which they are arranged, erected in just respect to a parent's memory, and due attention to the imagined expectations of the public, as destitute of spectators as the vacant halls of some assembly.

Inevitably there was family dissension. When Raphael sold the Bartolomeo drawings to Thomas Lawrence in 1824 for 800 guineas, Benjamin protested that he had not been consulted or informed. Raphael replied, "I am sorry to perceive you seem suspicious that something is intended to be hid from you, as no secrecy of any kind is intended." Benjamin wrote to say that he would answer the letter after he had consulted his solicitor. Raphael wrote in the same year to the president of the Pennsylvania Academy of the Fine Arts offering the large *Death on the Pale Horse* and fifty smaller pictures for £15,000. The Academy knew it would be impossible to raise so much money and declined. In February 1825 the sons tried to sell the entire collection to the British government for the newly established National Gallery. The government, however, had just expended a large sum to buy the pictures John Julius Angerstein had collected under the guidance of West and Lawrence, using them as the nucleus of the new gallery, and it had no interest in the Wests' offer. On April 12, 1826, "feeling deeply impressed with the conviction that the works of their father should find their final resting place of destiny in his native country," the sons wrote to the Speaker of the House of Representatives of the United States. "No country," they assured him, "ever yet had such an opportunity

of commencing a truly National Gallery as now presents itself."
They listed 150 pictures with their dimensions, including *Pale
Horse, Christ Rejected, Death of Wolfe, La Hogue, Hagar and Ishmael, Angelica and Medoro, Kosciuszko,* and eleven original designs
in chiaroscuro for the Windsor Chapel pictures. Their price was
only £40,000. The letter was read at the second session of the nineteenth Congress, tabled, printed as HR Document No. 8, and forgotten. The sons began to give their father's pictures as surety for
loans.

On January 7, 1828, Raphael wrote a desperate letter to the
marquess of Lansdowne, secretary of state for home affairs, who
had presented for him a memorial to His Majesty George IV, "containing a representation of the distress into which I am reduced."
If, he said, "I were not an intruder at the table of my relatives I
know not how I should be able to sustain myself." He described
his father's loyal service to His late Majesty from 1769 to 1810 and
told of the fifty-six West pictures painted for him in those forty-one
years. He asked his lordship to thank the king for his benevolent
and munificent offer to restore to the West family all the pictures
painted for the king's chapel at Windsor. He observed, however,
that the pictures would be taken up as security for redeeming the
mortgage on the Newman Street property, and that if they were
not so taken, they would only be an addition to the number of pictures they already had and were unable to sell. Thus they "will
not be to me of that assistance which I am so much in need of at
this moment."

> When I consider that all the labour of my father's arduous life
> has proved in vain for leaving a support for his family, and that
> the prime of my life has passed away endeavouring to assist him
> in the subordinate but necessary part of all the great works he
> was engaged in for His late Majesty — whereby I lost the oppor-
> tunity of acquiring a knowledge of some profession that might
> now have enabled me to provide for myself, my wife, and my
> daughter, I must confess I cannot help feeling that my situation
> is most adverse and unfortunate, not having the smallest degree
> of derivable income.[1]

---

[1] John Singleton Copley, Jr., now lord chancellor and Baron Lyndhurst, exerted
himself to persuade the government to buy some of the large pictures left by
West but was not successful. He then offered Raphael a post, the best for which
he was qualified, but Raphael felt it was not a sufficiently eligible one and declined to accept it.

The sons held a three-day sale on the premises in May 1829 under the management of the auctioneer George Robins. According to the *Morning Post* it "has produced a greater degree of public excitement than any event connected with the Fine Arts . . . since the founding of the Royal Academy." The sale included all or nearly all the King's Chapel pictures returned by George IV, called "these precious gems" in Mr. Robins' advertising. Despite the public excitement, the thronged gallery, and the fashionable bidders, the prices were far below what West might have received in his lifetime, and the sale realized only a disappointing 19,137 guineas, of which at least 5000 guineas was phantom money used to buy in pictures, including *Christ Rejected* and the large *Pale Horse*. The chapel pictures were bought legitimately by Henry Bone, the enamel miniature painter, who was acting for Joseph Neeld, a wealthy M.P. from Wiltshire. The house, grounds, and new gallery were sold last in one lot; they brought 4800 guineas.[2] Fauntleroy was dead by this time, having been hanged for embezzling his clients' funds, and it is possible that the Wests actually received some of the money from the Robins sale. Both Raphael and Benjamin, however, later appealed twice to the Royal Academy for financial assistance, which was given.

The one unqualified success of the Robins sale was the catalogue, which sold for half a crown and was in such demand that it went into five printings. The title page contains these words:

> In West's gallery, almost all the British and foreign nobility — all the great and honored of the age — for half a century were used to assemble; and here were first discussed, and by enlightened leaders of public taste, those measures which awakened the rulers

---

[2] The chapel pictures stayed at Grittleton House, Neeld's residence at Chippenham, until 1962, when they were offered for sale at Christie's. Six were bought for Bob Jones University by an anonymous donor. They are hanging today, with a seventh of the set, in the university's War Memorial Chapel at Greenville, South Carolina.

The Newman Street property was bought in 1832 by the "Irvingites" — a religious sect known as the Holy Catholic Apostolic Church. The purchaser was Edward Irving, who had loved and almost married Jane Welsh before her marriage to Thomas Carlyle and who had been expelled from his parish church in Scotland. The Irvingites were given to apocalyptic sermons and prophetic utterance. The Newman Street Church was their main place of worship in London. The house was standing as late as 1914, when the exhibition gallery was known as St. Andrews Hall, scene of concerts, rehearsals, and other performances. The site is now occupied by a post office warehouse.

of the state to a sense of the national importance of the culture of the Fine Arts. Hence, no site is more sacred to Science and Arts than this Gallery, which, fondly familiar to the memory of three generations, almost from infancy, is about to close forever upon this last display of the genius of its venerable Founder.

Epilogue:
The History
of a Reputation

As we move forward in time, the black patch of bad taste moves after us, separated from us always by an almost constant number of years. There is, in short . . . a gap in appreciation, and everything that falls into this gap is labelled for a while as bad taste.

JAMES LAVER,
Taste and Fashion,
London, 1937

THE OVERTURNING of standards in art after 1830, the changes in accepted fashion, taste, and attitude, were such that no artist grounded in the eighteenth century was secure in his reputation. Victorians attacked, mocked, and then ignored the art of their fathers. Family attics and dealers' storerooms were crammed with unfashionable, unsalable portraits by Gainsborough, Romney, Hoppner, Beechey, Lawrence. A pedigreed Hoppner portrait in an 1881 sale was bought by the auctioneer for £22 3s. A portrait of David Wilkie by Beechey sold in 1860 for £33 12s. When C. Edwards Lester wrote *The Artists of America* in 1846, he stubbornly included West, Trumbull, and Stuart, though everyone except a few artists advised him to pass them over in silence, "since sketches of these old painters will carry with them little interest for general readers."

The *British Press* had decreed in 1821: "His [West's] reign in fine taste is now perfectly established. The carpings of jealousy and the shades of professional and unmerited obloquy are gone." It was mistaken. The decline of West's prices, popularity, and reputation was faster and steeper than that of any of his contemporaries. An *Annunciation* for which he had received £800 from a provincial church was sold at auction in 1860 for £10. "West's paintings command only furniture prices," Samuel Redgrave wrote in 1874 in his

Dictionary of Artists. "His work is now scoffed at and his works are put out of sight," Henry B. Wheatley wrote in 1897 in *Historical Portraits.* There were jokes about the generosity of the National Gallery and the country lords who disposed of their West pictures by depositing them in the provincial museums.

The position of West in English-American art was unique, for he was the object, not merely of inattention and neglect, but of adverse criticism more intense and prolonged than that directed at any of his colleagues. Critics attacked him with an eagerness that is astonishing in its vindictiveness. "He is unsparingly censured where he fails," Martin Shee said in 1832, "and is allowed little credit where he has succeeded. He is tried, not by his merits, but by his defects, and judged before a tribunal which admits only the evidence against him." John Ruskin wrote in *Modern Painters* (1853): "English art, as far as I know, has never yet produced an historical picture. West is too feeble an artist to permit his designs to be mentioned as pictures at all — otherwise his *Death of General Wolfe* might have been named as an approximation of the thing needed." Walter Thornbury, a biographer of Turner, said in "West, the Monarch of Mediocrity," a chapter in his *British Artists from Hogarth to Turner* (1861): "This old pig-headed painter, sitting in his gallery in Newman Street, calmly waiting for Death to bring him a crown of immortality, was an incarnation of vanity almost sublime in his self-confidence." Various critics damned West for various crimes: for having been too successful too early and too easily; for overestimating his own power and attempting to embody ideas and sentiments beyond the reach of his natural abilities; for holding a high opinion of his own work ("He looked upon himself as a sacred being and the Founder of British Art"); for having no passions; for never having endured a trying ordeal that presumably would have improved his character and therefore his art. West was attacked — one might say, revenge was taken — for accepting commissions from King George III that should have gone to Joshua Reynolds or James Barry or Richard Wilson ("Barry might starve in his Castle Street den; Wilson die broken-hearted; nothing ruffled the calm serenity of West's vanity.") In 1905 Frederick Eaton, secretary of the Royal Academy, collaborating on a history of the institution, agreed with an earlier critic that West's personality was "utterly colourless," and with the charge that in company, "by observing a prudent silence, he gained a reputation for latent wisdom, which he would have sacrificed had he been loquacious." (Farington would have been puzzled, and Smirke and Flaxman amused, by that attribution of taciturnity.)

West was unfortunate in having no writer after John Galt to prepare a full-scale biography and a *catalogue raisonné* — no single-minded competent scholar to serve as his advocate in the old rivalries that were revived, discussed, and judged when his contemporaries published their memoirs or had their biographies written. As John Ruskin sought to enhance Turner by denouncing Constable, so biographers and critics tended to make points for their own artist by ridiculing West. Few defended him in the long stretch of years from 1820 to 1938.

The Georgian artists began to return to favor around 1910, when tastes changed and scorn was directed at Victorian styles, fashions, and attitudes. English portraits, landscapes, and genre scenes painted before 1830, even a few neoclassical history pictures, attracted new interest. American buyers coming into the art market raised the prices for what had now become eighteenth- and early nineteenth-century old masters.

Benjamin West did not share in the revival. For the next half century, well into the 1950s, the criticism continued. Now he was condemned for faults and sins conceived by twentieth-century taste. He was damned for painting subject pictures that told a story and pointed a moral; for always painting pictures of enormous size; for persuading John Copley to go to England, where he painted pictures that were inferior (it was then thought) to those he had painted in Boston; for not being as good an artist as Copley; for having ruined Trumbull and Allston by making them paint in his own image.

In 1936: "As much as his pupils admired him, none of them could make good pictures without denying in some way his teaching ... They did not acquire solid draftsmanship, modelling and respect for what they saw."

In 1940: "West's fatal influence molded three generations of artists ... As a portrait painter, West was *quantité négligeable* ... Let it be said emphatically: John Singleton Copley, not Benjamin West, occasioned the revolution of history painting."

In 1950: "It was West's own shallowness of mind which inflated the drama [of *Penn's Treaty*] into melodrama and thinned out the sentiment to sentimentality ... A general judgment based upon the whole of West's work must be a general censure."

In 1959: "There presided, from the presidential chair of the Royal Academy, an artist who, while susceptible to some of the changes around him, was singularly unapt to understand their meaning and implications."

A number of critics did allow, somewhat condescendingly, that

West's work reflected and typified the spirit of his age. All but a few conceded that he was generous and kind to young students, and especially to American students, of whom he had a large number. ("If a bad painter, he was a good man.") This concession demonstrated that the critic was being utterly fair and impartial. "In recent times," E. P. Richardson observed in 1956, "no American artist has been more scornfully denigrated."

Somehow, West refused to vanish under these attacks, though the critics slew him over and over again, and with such sustained fury that James Thomas Flexner wondered, "If they are convinced West is so insignificant, why do they expend so much hatred in lambasting him?" When John Walker and Magill James produced their *Great American Paintings from Smibert to Bellows* (1943), West was very much alive and present. He painted three of the included works (*Death of Wolfe, Penn's Treaty, Guy Johnson*); he appears as the main figure in another (Matthew Pratt's *American School*); and his former students painted twenty-one others (Charles Willson Peale, Rembrandt Peale, Earl, Stuart, Trumbull, Mather Brown, Allston, Sully, and Morse). Thus in some degree was West connected with 25 of the 104 pictures chosen. By the middle of the twentieth century, moreover, West began now and then to be praised in language that had not been heard from serious, sophisticated critics for 130 years.

West's ability to stand and stay in the arena despite a century of battering scorn and ridicule is a curious episode in the history of taste. Aside from the quality of his art, which is a subjective consideration, how and why did he survive?

For one thing, it is apparent that the severest critics made charges against West that were clearly overstated or not in accord with the known facts. Not all his pictures, for example, were of enormous size; most had conventional dimensions, and one of his masterpieces was only 12 by 15 inches. Did he really have "a dull, careful, but tame and feeble mind" that simply "followed rules and receipts"? The words hardly describe an artist who constantly experimented with new styles, subjects, and techniques, or who discarded the sure formulas on which he had built a reputation, in order to break new ground. His twenty-odd American students who distinguished themselves as artists showed an extraordinary ability to resist his "fatal influence" and paint in their own widely differing individual styles, which is what West advised them to do.

For another thing, many of the severest critics of West's work were almost as scornful of the work of Fuseli and Allston, among others. When Fuseli and Allston were "rediscovered" in this century and crowned with laurels, one had to conclude that somebody had been wrong then or was wrong now — that the critics were simply following the prejudices of their time, or were laying too great importance on their own subjective responses. When Copley's English work was re-examined and upgraded a few decades ago, where did that leave those who had condemned West for drawing him to Europe? [1]

Many of West's critics, moreover, singled out one picture as an exception from his usual poor performances, and admitted (boldly or apologetically) that they had for it a particular admiration. Since they generally chose different works — *Kosciuszko, La Hogue, Death of Wolfe, Self-Portrait at Thirty-Two, Self-Portrait at Eighty-One, Thomas Mifflin, The West Family, Mrs. West and Child, King Lear, Edward the Third Crossing the Somme, Sir Guy Johnson, Dr. Enoch Edwards, Agrippina Bearing the Ashes, Queen Charlotte and Her Thirteen Children, The Peace Commissioners, Robert Fulton, Charles Willson Peale, Death on the Pale Horse* (sketch), *Penn's Treaty, Self-Portrait Painting Mrs. West, Paddington Passage, The Bathing Place at Ramsgate*, among others — the total number added up to a body of work that any artist might be proud of, both for volume and variety, and that no artist called worthless could possibly have produced.

Finally, the eight volumes of the Farington *Diary* published in the 1920s and the complete 7000-page typescript of the entire diary made available in 1951 reveal a Benjamin West who is altogether different from the commonly accepted figure — one far more complex, much more human and humane. A line-by-line reading of Farington's pages exposes a disturbing amount of creative imagination on the part of respected scholars and critics in pursuit of a viewpoint, with an appalling willingness to cite as fact some things they could not possibly have known — facts that are confuted in Farington. Allen Cunningham's picture of West traveling from London to Windsor with the sobriety and stateliness of a Quaker merchant going to church is obviously nonsense. Thornbury's description of West at his wedding ("They were married . . . gravely and calmly as Quakers should be, with no outburst of intemperate joy, and no visible demonstration of feeling") is revealed not only as invention but as mean and dishonest writing. The picture drawn by Hodgson and Eaton of West observing a prudent silence to gain

---

[1] "Copley's outstanding contribution to the history of art as a whole occurred in London." Frederick Cummings in Cummings-Staley, *Romantic Art in Britain*, 88.

a reputation for latent wisdom simply does not accord with the hours West spent in conversation with his friends, nor with his demonstrated fondness for gossip, anecdote, and curious information. The picture of West as heartlessly indifferent to the financial troubles of his fellow artists does not accord with the pains he took, with Farington, to set up the Academy pension system that gave them financial security.

If one were to try to name the year, the turning point, when West's reputation began its long, slow climb back to cultural respectability, the choice would have to be 1938, the 200th anniversary of his birth. It started with the long essay, "The American Work of Benjamin West," by the scholar-critic William Sawitzky. This was the first attempt to compile a descriptive listing of the artist's early "performances," and it identified twenty-two such works, some of them having that childlike primitive quality that carries an appeal beyond their actual artistic merit.

In that same year the Pennsylvania Museum of Art in Philadelphia held a bicentenary exhibition of West's works: a selection of sixty-four oils, thirty-one drawings, and five of the great engravings. Fiske Kimball, director of the museum, in his introduction to the catalogue challenged art professionals to form a new estimate based on West's actual historic importance and influence — importance not merely as the first American artist to achieve a European reputation, but also in the general evolution of European painting; influence not merely as the founder and teacher of the American School, but influence as well on both British and French painters "as a pioneer of European classicism and as a founder of romanticism in figure painting." The exhibition was a solid success, widely and seriously reviewed in the art journals, in some magazines and newspapers of general circulation, and in the bulletins of those other museums that had sent their West pictures to be shown in Philadelphia.

1938 was also the year in which James Thomas Flexner finished his *America's Old Masters,* the first section of which, eighty pages in length, is a biographical study and critical appraisal of West. (The other masters are Copley, Peale, and Stuart.) It was the first long piece on the artist written by a discerning mind, and the closest West had yet come to having a proper biography. Flexner described West's career as "perhaps the most successful ever achieved by an American artist."

Critical opinion showed a marked shift in West's favor after 1938. A counterattack began in 1940 when Oskar Hagen, a particularly dogmatic art historian, delivered a harsh and furious attack on

West in his *Birth of the American Tradition in Art*, repeating all the familiar charges and adding a few fresh ones of his own. A new development then occurred: For the first time in more than a century, West had an advocate. Parker Lesley of the University of Minnesota, in the *Art Bulletin* of September 1940, delivered a scholarly, detailed, and devastating defense of West in a ten-column review.

In 1942, the Metropolitan Museum's A. Hyatt Mayor declared in an address to the American Philosophical Society: "Through engravings the *Death of Wolfe* helped [Antoine Jean] Gros to find the formula for his Napoleonic battle paintings, which were impressive forerunners of romanticism . . . What Sir Charles Holmes said of Copley applies equally well to West and Trumbull, that had he 'been French, he would have been famous as the forerunner of the Romantic Movement.' "

Kurt M. Semon, writing in 1945 in the *American Collector* on West's drawings, said, "We find a fluid line of great ability and assurance."

Oliver Larkin wrote in 1949 in his seminal *Art and Life in America*, "There was a deep humanity in West . . . His *Regulus* had shown his pioneering mind, for it was neoclassical fifteen or twenty years before the Frenchmen Vien and David."

E. P. Richardson, in his writings in 1955–56, cited West's "monumental powers," described his "usual facility and sensitiveness to new impressions," and declared, "In his quick absorption of new ideas and his ability to make an effective display of them at once, he was very American." And he posed a pertinent question: "Why was it legitimate for Raphael to paint *Jacob's Dream* or for Rembrandt to paint *Belshazzar's Feast* but not legitimate for a romantic artist [that is, Allston or West] to do so if he wished?"

1960: Princeton University's Robert Rosenblum wrote in the *Art Bulletin*: "Thanks to a handful of brilliant articles, mainly by European scholars, an awareness of Benjamin West's crucial importance to the revolutionary currents of Western art in general, rather than to American art in particular, has filtered down to even the most parochial writings on American painting . . . In an analysis of late eighteenth century art, West's role can hardly be overestimated . . . His work offers a major reflection of pictorial trends for half a century. Moreover, his tremendous stature transcended Anglo-American boundaries . . . It is all the more surprising, then, that no full-length study of West has replaced John Galt's essential but unreliable biography of 1820."

1961: England's Gerald Reitlinger, in his *Economics of Taste*, found West "an incredibly able and versatile painter who invented the English battle picture in modern dress" and "was to reform the English subject picture just as Reynolds ten years earlier had reformed the English portrait." Some of West's classical works done in the 1760s, he said, "foreshadow the extreme classicist French style of Jacques Louis David. In fact, they look like paintings of the French Revolution period." He was "a man capable of that extremely original little picture, the *Kosciuszko in London* of 1797, which looks for all the world like the work of a Pre-Raphaelite . . . He practiced "a style of simplicity which seems to anticipate the Pre-Raphaelites by more than two generations."

1964: Charles Mount, artist and biographer, wrote in his life of Gilbert Stuart: "West spread through England and the world classic lore and classic arts, an awareness of both, and a classical taste."

1965: Allen Staley, in "The Landing of Agrippina" in the Philadelphia Museum of Art *Bulletin*: "His fresh approach to his subjects made him a stylistic innovator of immense influence."

1966: Neil Harris in *The Artist in American Society*: "The only innovation made by the early American painters — and it was a considerable one — involved the entry of particularity into history painting . . . Benjamin West's introduction of modern uniforms into his *Death of General Wolfe* caused a sensation in England." Scotland's David Irwin wrote in *English Neoclassical Art* in the same year: West "gradually developed a highly successful personal style. He could brilliantly portray, for example, some of George III's children with a freshness comparable to Zoffany's, or sensitively paint his wife and child as a Raphaelesque Madonna . . . In some of the smaller paintings he [produced] some of the more interesting medieval subject-pieces of the century."

The most widely read modern critic writing on West was probably John Canaday of the New York *Times*. He expounded qualified but penetrating praise of the artist in his reviews and in his books *The Lives of the Painters* and *Mainstreams of Modern Art*. West, he said, "when he was trying the hardest, could be laughably bad . . . But West was also a sensitive and original artist . . . In his relaxed moods he painted with great fluency, with tenderness and with true fervor as well as technical bravura . . . He was a prophet of two major nineteenth-century revolutions — of romanticism . . . and of realism . . . He anticipated all the tempestuousness and emotionalism of the great French romantics, Géricault and Delacroix, before either of them was born."

"It is not a bad record for a man," Mr. Canaday concluded, "to have been a pioneer classicist and a prophet of realism and romanticism."

In the 1970s a curious thing happened: The praise of West ceased, and so did the censure. Major articles on West, to be sure, continued to appear. West, in fact, enjoyed a revival of interest. He was given considerable space in the new catalogues and art histories; his pictures during the Bicentennial Year were widely displayed. He was featured in the Philadelphia Museum's *Three Centuries of American Art* and in the large exhibition *Towards Independence, 1750–1800* mounted by the Yale University Art Gallery and the Victoria and Albert Museum. The Pierpont Morgan Library held a definitive exhibition of his drawings in 1975 and in Ruth S. Kraemer's catalogue produced an important new work on West. But the recent writings on West and his work contain scarcely a quotable passage of approbation or disparagement. The content is factual, the manner scholarly.

The change is significant in the history of the reputation of Benjamin West. There is no satisfaction now in lambasting West, no shock value in insulting him. And there is no longer the same need to defend West from abuse by unfriendly critics, nor does praise of a West picture elicit surprise. For the first time in a century and a half, West, for better or worse, stands simply as one artist among other artists, to be judged calmly, rationally, on his merits. The pronouncement of *The British Press* in 1821 has finally come true: "The shades of unmerited obloquy are gone."

West was washed back and forth by the changing tides of taste. In his lifetime he rose with remarkable speed to "the highest pinnacle of the temple of fame," and within a few years after his death he sank to an artist's hell that is worse than obscurity or neglect — to be unrelentingly denounced and ridiculed. Now, restored to grace, he can be accepted simply for what he is and was and did. As an artist who had known the best and the worst, West would have welcomed that — or at least would have submitted to it with professional grace.

Various contemporary critics have called for a dispassionate appraisal of West and his work. Such an appraisal might begin with the acknowledgment that he was an able craftsman and a superior draughtsman; that he painted some good, honest, and important pictures; and that he explored new paths and introduced new subject matter in art. He helped a king to found a brotherhood of painters, who twenty-seven times elected him their presiding officer. He helped to raise the level of British art and artists throughout the fifty-year span of the Golden Age of British Art. As a teacher and champion of the young he had no peer; no one has ever matched him in the number and quality of the pupils who passed through his studio to become outstanding artists. With John Copley, John Trumbull, and Washington Allston he broke the confining pattern of the early American portrait tradition to bring American art into contact with the culture of Europe. Not many artists have achieved such a career or have made such a contribution in their time.

Acknowledgments
Appendices
Notes and Sources
Bibliography
Index

Acknowledgments

$\mathcal{I}$ WISH first to express my profound thanks for being permitted to use and quote extensively from the diary of Joseph Farington, R.A. which by the permission of Her Majesty the Queen is available in holograph and transcript at Windsor Castle, in transcript at the British Library, and in microfilm of the transcript in libraries around the world. I am also deeply indebted to the Royal Academy of Arts in London for giving me access to its library, minutes books, scrapbook, catalogues, and correspondence collections; and to the Historical Society of Pennsylvania in Philadelphia for permission to quote from its extensive store of Benjamin West material.

I also wish to thank the following institutions and their staff members who helped me in my research. At the Friends Historical Library at Swarthmore College: Dr. J. William Frost, Director; Jane A. Rittenhouse, Assistant Director; and Martha A. Connor, Librarian. At the American Philosophical Society, Philadelphia: Carl F. Miller, Assistant Manuscript Librarian. At the Pierpont Morgan Library, New York: Felice Stampfer, Curator of Drawings and Prints At the Henry Francis du Pont Museum, Winterthur, Delaware: Charles F. Hummel, Curator; Frank H. Somer III, Head of Libraries; Elizabeth H. Hill, Librarian; and E. McSherry Fowble, Associate Curator. At the American Archives of Art, Washington, D.C.: Beverly H. Smith, assistant in 1974 to the Deputy Director. At the Beinecke Library, New Haven: Marjorie G. Wynne, Research Librarian.

And in Great Britain: at the Royal Academy, Constance-Anne Parker, Librarian, and Sarah Boys-Stones, Assistant Librarian. At the National Portrait Gallery, London: Richard Ormond, Assistant Keeper. At the Royal Archives, Windsor Castle: Sir Robin Mackworth-Young, Librarian, and Jane Langton, Registrar. At the National Registrar of Archives, Edinburgh: D. M. Hunter, Registrar, and Hazel Horn. At the National Army Museum, London: M. Harding. At the Royal Society of Arts, London: D. G. C. Allan, Curator. At the Coram Foundation for Children, London: J. G. B. Swinley, Director and Secretary. At the Sir John Soane Museum, London: Sir John Summerson, Director. At the British Library Department of Prints and Drawings: Peter Moore, Executive Officer. At Alleyn's College of God's Gift (the Dulwich Art Gallery): D. G. Banwell, Bursar. At Coutts and Company, Bankers, London: M. V. Stokes, Archivist. At the Lord Chamberlain's Office, St. James's Palace, Sir Oliver Millar, Surveyor of the Queen's Pictures.

Also these other institutions: the Victoria and Albert Museum; the Fitzwilliam Museum, Cambridge, England; the New York Public Library; and the New-York Historical Society.

In the course of working on this biography I was given help and scholarly courtesies by many other persons in many other places. I should like to thank those who answered queries and supplied information: Beverly Carter, Secretary, The Paul Mellon Collection, Washington, D.C.; Edmund P. Pillsbury, Director, and Joan M. Friedman, Assistant Research Librarian of the Yale Center for British Art and British Studies, New Haven; George L. McKenna, Registrar and Associate Curator, William Rockhill Nelson Gallery of Art, Kansas City; Kneeland McNulty, Curator of Prints, Drawings, and Photographs, Philadelphia Museum of Art; Edwin Wolf II, Librarian, The Library Company, Philadelphia; Martin I. Yoelson, Chief of Interpretation, Independence National Historical Park, Philadelphia; and Celeste Walker, on the editorial staff of the Adams Papers at the Massachusetts Historial Society, Boston.

I am grateful to Calvin Tribble of Washington, D.C., who expressed the need for a biography of Benjamin West and urged that it be written.

Dr. Charles Coleman Sellers of Carlisle, Pennsylvania, the leading authority on Charles Willson Peale, his ancestor, gave me good advice and steered me into several productive research channels. William B. Henry of Greenwich, Connecticut, and Mary Henry Stites of Nazareth, Pennsylvania, answered my questions and supplied valuable information on their ancestor, West's early patron, William Henry of Lancaster. John S. Kebabian of Scarsdale, New York, kindly photographed with a hand-held camera some documents that were inaccessible to me. Thomas C. Pears III of Pittsburgh, Pennsylvania, called my attention to an unpublished 1784 letter from Benjamin Franklin to Benjamin West. Helen L. Harriss of Pittsburgh, Mrs. Joseph A. Estes of Lexington, Kentucky, and Mrs. Leonard Le Blanc of La Habre, California, supplied me with genealogical information on the West family. Richard T. Frick, Jr., of New York City, and Harry Ward, Executive Assistant, Bob Jones University, Greenville, South Carolina, were also helpful. In London, Jean Agnew, Research Assistant of the Royal Commission on Historical Manuscripts, Chancery Lane, directed me to valuable West-Beckford letters in the duke of Hamilton's collection at the Scottish Record Office in Edinburgh; and Margaret Sisam of Buckinghamshire, England, gave me information about her ancestor, William Allen.

It is a pleasure to acknowledge my debt of gratitude to Stephen S. Bank of London, historian and research consultant. Throughout the work on this biography he served as my researcher and representative in Britain, and when it was finished he twice read the manuscript, instructed me in English protocol and use of titles, and called my attention to a number of factual errors. I also wish to thank Mary Abu-Shumays of Pittsburgh, who in 1977 and early 1978 performed spot research assignments in the final rush to prepare the manuscript for publication.

I was fortunate in having available to me at close hand the help of an extraordinary complex of five fine libraries and research facilities grouped in the university center in Pittsburgh: the main branch of the Carnegie Library; the Henry Clay Frick Fine Arts Library, Henry L. Hillman Library, and Darlington Library of Rare Books, all three part of the University of Pittsburgh; and the Historical Society of Western Pennsylvania. I wish to thank them and their staffs, especially the following. At Carnegie: Anne W. Gordon, Librarian in charge of the Fine Arts Division; Rachel George, Head of the Reference Library; Michael Marino, Reference Librarian in charge of interlibrary loans; and Anthony A. Martin, Director, who in 1974 kindly procured for me the seven microfilm reels of the Farington diary — the second set to enter the U.S. library system. At the Frick Fine Arts Library, Elizabeth G. Booth, Director; and at the Historical Society, Helen Wilson, Librarian, and Ruth Salisbury, Archivist.

I should like to express my thanks publicly to H. J. Heinz II, who generously made a personal gift to help defray the cost of a month-long research trip to London.

Finally, I offer my profoundest thanks and gratitude to two special people. One is Joyce Hartman, my editor at Houghton Mifflin, who in 1973 suggested this subject to me and read the several drafts with critical and creative discernment. The other is my wife Zita, who with a sharp ear listened to each chapter read aloud when it was written and helped me to pound and polish the words in each successive revision.

ROBERT C. ALBERTS

APPENDIX I

John Galt's Biography of West as a Source

ANYONE WHO WRITES about Benjamin West begins with John Galt's two-volume *Life, Studies and Works of Benjamin West, Esq. . . . Compiled from Materials Furnished by Himself*, 1816 and 1820. For more than a century and a half it has been the only full-length biography of West. The framework of the story is there, set down for the first time, and a debt is owing to John Galt for having written it.

In using Galt, however, the writer faces the problem of what to do about a number of episodes that seem exaggerated, doubtful, or untrue. Even the most unlikely of these must be mentioned for the record. West presumably told these stories to Galt, and they must be examined for what they may reveal about an event or about West himself. Yet their validity can seldom be determined, and to carry on a continuing argument with John Galt soon becomes tedious.

William Dunlap, who studied under West for three years in the 1780s and wrote a sixty-three-page account of his life in 1834 (much of it based on Galt), called Galt "a most injudicious biographer." He blamed him for "the puerilities of the performance and absurd tales" that West, he felt, could never have given him, naming, among others, the Quaker preacher's sermon that so affected West's pregnant mother. (See page 9.) Writers on West have echoed that criticism ever since, generally in the course of paraphrasing and using Galt's material. They have been torn between an author's desire for a good story and a scholar's regard for accuracy.

Galt was a journeyman writer-for-hire from the time he left Scotland in 1804, in his twenty-fifth year. He wrote such commissioned articles as he could get, reviews, political pieces, an unproduced tragedy in blank verse, travel essays, and a biography of Cardinal Wolsey. Finding few editors or publishers interested in his work, he undertook two business ventures and failed in both. He traveled on the Continent for two years (1809–11) and in 1815 took a post as secretary and fund raiser (at £300 a year) for the Royal Caledonian Asylum, a charity established by the Highland Society of London for the children of Scottish soldiers and sailors. It is not known how Galt met West or whose idea it was to write a West biography. Galt averred in 1820, "I have enjoyed his frankest confidence for many years." He described their method of work: "The whole materials were derived from him, and it may be said to have been all but written by himself. The manuscript of the first part he carefully corrected; the second was undertaken at his own request when he was on his deathbed, and nearly all the last proof in the printing submitted to him . . . The manuscript had long previously been read by him. My custom was, to note down those points which seemed important in our own conversations, and from time to time to submit an entire chapter to his perusal; afterwards, when the whole narrative was formed, it was again carefully read over to him."

Galt's approach to "the whole materials" was essentially that of a writer of romantic fiction. There is evidence that suggests he fastened on a number of true but relatively minor incidents told him by West and used his creative imagination to develop them into major episodes.

Despite his romantic approach to biographical writing, several points may be made on Galt's behalf at this late date. Most of his factual material checks out routinely. Some of the vague and suspect references on West's younger days, moreover, have now been examined and validated. In 1952, James Thomas Flexner, assisted by E. Marie Becker, reference librarian of the New-York Historical Society, set out to investigate those early associates and patrons who are called in Galt's biography, in the annoying eighteenth-century custom of ignoring first names, "Mr. Pennington, a merchant of Philadelphia," "Mr. Wayne, a gentleman of the neighborhood," and so forth. In every instance the facts fell into place, with each name identifiable as a person who was unmistakably present at the proper time and place, each with the imprimatur of dates of birth and death after a correctly spelled patronym. (See pages 11–17.) With this development, Galt's credibility rating rose several points on the scholar's exchange.

I have been able to validate in a similar way the names of three persons involved in West's voyage to Italy in 1760. According to Galt, the vessel carrying West, John Allen, and Joseph Shippen was chased into Gibraltar by a French privateer. At Gibraltar a Commodore Carney boarded the ship, examined its papers, and was about to confiscate ship and cargo as being engaged in illicit trade in wartime. But he exclaimed, throwing down his pen, "I am much affected by the situation in which I am now placed. This valuable ship is the property of some of my nearest relations, and the best of friends that I ever had in the world," and he passed the ship without inquiring into its destination. It is, of course, a dubious utterance, an unlikely story, and an even more improbable coincidence. No naval officer of the period named Carney, moreover, appears in *The Commissioned Sea Officers of the Royal Navy, 1660–1865*. The thought occurred: Could Carney be West's or Galt's phonetic spelling of another name? There is indeed a Captain Michael Kearny in the record of appropriate date and service. A re-examination of the Shippen Papers reveals that the Allen-Shippen vessel was seized; that the English captain who came aboard had a brother at Perth Amboy, New Jersey; that he had seized an American brig in Gibraltar one week earlier for illicit trading; and that he was holding it while he sent to London for a clear command decision on his right to make such confiscations. Kearny's lack of firm authority to seize vessels of the American colonies explains his willingness to allow the Allen-Shippen vessel to pass. Two other naval officers who were hospitable to the young Americans on the convoyed voyage across the Mediterranean are identified in Galt as Captain Meadow and Captain Pownell. *The Commissioned Sea Officers* shows they were Captain Charles Pierrepont Medows and Commodore Philemon Pownall.

Several of the important Galt stories about West's younger years may now be tested, since they were told in two separate accounts: once in 1816 by Galt in his biography; once again in 1810 in a recently discovered letter West wrote to Thomas Eagles, the Bristol merchant. One episode is that in which West meets William Williams, his first teacher in art (pages 12–13). West's 1810 letter to Eagles gives a straightforward factual account of the meeting and the relationship. Galt's 1816 account, obviously based on similar material given him by West is flamboyant and immoderate in a manner designed to reflect credit on young West. West had also told Eagles in 1805 of an incident (recorded by Eagles) in which Williams showed him a *camera obscura* and how to use it in drawing barnyard animals. West thereupon made one for himself, using an old pair of spectacles given him by his father. As Galt told the same story, however, West, at age sixteen, discovered the principle of the camera on his own and built one. These two examples of Galt's use of material that West gave him furnish a guide for appraising some of Galt's other extravagances.

The question arises: Why did West accept and approve romanticized, inaccurate stories about himself? There is no firm answer — only a choice of possibilities. He may simply have liked what he read. Or he may have been so dominated by Galt as the author that he was unwilling to demand major changes in a long manuscript. He may have asked for and obtained so many changes (of which we are, of course, unaware) that he could not bring himself to ask for more. He was almost seventy-eight when he read the first volume and was in his eighty-first year when he saw the second, and at such an advanced age he may not have been able to read with the sustained attention and hard thought the subject required. Or he may simply have lacked the literary sophistication to understand the tone, the appearance, the effect of what Galt wrote — the harm done him, for example, by some of Galt's immoderate praise. It is worth noting that West did not correct in volume two the date of his marriage to Elizabeth Shewell, which Galt gave as 1765 instead of 1764, or of Elizabeth West's death, given as 1817 instead of 1814. Both errors have been repeated and compounded down through the decades, and by some of those who have been severest in their criticism of Galt's inaccuracies.

Neither West nor Galt was responsible for one of the most dubious of the West legends, that of the midnight elopement of his bride-to-be (pages 65–67). It was created by other persons several decades after West's death. Nor were they responsible for two of the most egregious errors frequently repeated in the writings on West. One was that he served in 1758 in General Forbes' frontier army that took French Fort Duquesne (occasionally it is General Braddock's army in 1755). That error arose from misreading Galt's perfectly clear text. The other error was that George III said to West, on receiving a copy of the American Declaration of Independence, that he hoped the Americans would be happy in their new state and that they would not change it for a worse. He wished them no ill. The statement was made eight years later when George III received from his ministers the speech he was to make in 1782 acknowledging American independence; the error arose from a misinterpretation of West's words by his young pupil, Samuel F. B. Morse, or perhaps his editor. (See pages 142–43.)

Galt's text indicates that West did not see the much-quoted embarrassing passage that Galt used in the concluding pages of volume two: "As an artist he will stand in the first rank. His name will be classed with those of Michelangelo and Raphael; but he possessed little in common with either. As the former has been compared to Homer, and the latter to Virgil, in Shakespeare we shall perhaps find the best likeness to the genius of Mr. West."

One more point may be made. Whatever its exaggerations and inaccuracies, there is nothing in John Galt's biography as improbable, as incredible, as the actual course of Benjamin West's career.

APPENDIX II

The Controversy over Contemporary Costume

THE STATEMENT has been made a number of times in this century that Benjamin West was the first painter to show modern military heroes clothed in their regulation uniforms instead of in the Greek or Roman garments required in the eighteenth century in serious works of art. The claim is overstated, and the predictable result has been that every few years or so a new young art historian or critic announces the discovery that West had been preceded by this, that, or another artist in use of contemporary dress — that in fact Edward Penny and George Romney had painted the dying General Wolfe in his British uniform several years before West. A valid claim can be made that West did indeed introduce a new element in his use of contemporary costume in *The Death of Wolfe* and that in so doing he worked a revolution in history painting; but the claim must be expressed and understood in precise terms.

The controversy over costume between two schools of British artists in the second half of the eighteenth century, and between Joshua Reynolds and Benjamin West as the leading protagonists, had a real point; it was an important issue that was seriously debated. The Reynolds school held that the use of contemporary dress rather than classical costume was improper for the Grand Style of painting — that it would degrade academic art and bring ridicule down upon the recently formed Royal Academy. (Neither the Penny nor the Romney picture was of a scale, composition, or importance to be considered as Grand Style. Penny was a painter of genre scenes; Romney was a young student.) Out of this artistic conviction rose the opposition to West's use of "boots and britches" in his *Death of Wolfe.* As the German critic Edgar Wind put it in 1939, "The Academicians . . . feared that the presentation of heroic death in everyday dress would destroy respect for the hero in the spectator and deprive the latter of that feeling of reverence and astonishment, that sense of the extraordinary and marvelous, with which he ought to approach heroic deeds." West risked derision, loss of reputation, and withdrawal of the king's patronage by holding to the position that he should paint Wolfe and those around him as they actually appeared at the scene. West, said Edgar Wind, "supplied the controversy with a test case." His contribution, as described by the critic Charles Mitchell, was to introduce new subject matter into historical painting, and to introduce it deliberately within the academic framework of the Grand Style.

Despite his concession in 1771 that West was right, Reynolds was not converted to the use of contemporary dress in historical pictures or even in portraits painted in the Grand Style. He continued to dress his matrons in flowing gowns and to depict them as performing some classical ritual — as Psyches, Dianas, Junos, the Graces, the Fates. In his *Seventh Discourse* (1776), he said: "He, therefore, who in his practice of portrait painting wishes to dignify his subject, which we will suppose to be a lady, will not paint her in the modern dress, the familiarity of which alone is sufficient to destroy all dignity. He ... dresses his figure something with the general air of the antique for the sake of dignity and preserves something of the modern for the sake of likeness." He used the Grand Style most effectively in his portrait of the actress Sarah Siddons. Charles Mitchell wrote of this picture in 1950: "He showed both by precept and example how a portrait could be raised to a historical level by generalising faces and dress to correspond with the elevation of the stylistic model. Thus, in his famous portrait of Mrs. Siddons as the Tragic Muse he pitched historical portraiture as high as it could go. He took his composition from one of the prophets in Michelangelo's Sistine ceiling, with brooding Michelangelesque figures, transformed into shapes of Pity and Terror, standing behind the enthroned actress. But this was still portrait, not history. Accordingly, Reynolds drastically idealised the face (as one sees by comparing it with Mrs. Siddons' much more angular and individual features in Gainsborough's portrait in the National Gallery), and he transposed the drapery into a more or less Venetian style." (For his part, Gainsborough declared in a letter about this time, "Nothing can be more absurd than the foolish custom of painters dressing people like scaramouches and expecting the likeness to appear.")

The debate on costume continued through the rest of the eighteenth and well into the nineteenth century, with the sculptors resisting the introduction of contemporary costume long after the portrait painters had capitulated. On his first trip to London in 1786, Thomas Jefferson discussed with American artists there the propriety of having the sculptor Houdon show General Washington in modern dress and hair style rather than in the Roman manner. Washington had mildly opposed "a servile adherence to the garb of antiquity" and a bust of himself in a Roman toga. "I should ... scarcely have ventured to suggest ... some little deviation in favor of the modern custom," he wrote to Jefferson, "if I had not learned from Colonel [David] Humphreys [his wartime aide, later secretary of the legation in Paris under Franklin] that this was a circumstance hinted in conversation by Mr. West to Houdon. This taste, which has been introduced in painting by Mr. West, I understand is received with applause and prevails extensively." Jefferson replied, "I was happy to find ... that the modern dress of your statue would meet your approbation. I found it strongly the sentiment of West, Copley, Trumbull and Brown, after which it would be ridiculous to add that it was my own. I think a modern in an antique dress as just [as much] an object of ridicule as an Hercules or Marius with a periwig and chapeau bras."[1] Jefferson, however, changed his mind thirty years later; when instructing Canova on carving a statue of Washington, he said, "As to the style of costume, I am sure the artist and every person of taste

---

[1] A compressible three-cornered silk hat.

in Europe would be for the Roman. Our boots and regimentals have a very puny effect."

In 1795, at an Academy Council meeting called to discuss the terms of a competition for a statue of Lord Cornwallis, West argued for modern dress, using much the same reasoning he had used with Reynolds and Archbishop Drummond twenty-five years earlier. He was opposed by the sculptors Thomas Banks and John Bacon and the painter Henry Fuseli, among others. Bacon said a statue of dress in the period "would appear disgusting" in twenty years. Fuseli said it would be "absurd" and would "totally prevent the artist from expressing the extent of his ability." The sculptors prevailed, and the statues and busts in antique or semiantique costume continued for several more decades. Turnerelli, West's friend and neighbor, placed George III on an English horse in a Roman toga (the work is in the Soane Museum); Ceracchi showed Washington in a Roman toga with short curly locks; Horatio Greenough put him in a suit of armor; and Canova solved the problem by sculpting a statue of Bonaparte showing no clothes at all. In the end, of course, West's ideas prevailed. The last vestige of "generalized" dress in portraits or busts after 1850 was the academic gown.

The revolution in history painting worked by *The Death of Wolfe* had an effect that carried past the borders of England and beyond the decade in which it was painted. Richard Muther, writing his *Geschichte der Malerei* in 1893 described it best:

> If West . . . represented the General and his soldiers in their regulation uniforms, it seems at the present no more than the result of healthy common sense, but at that time it was an artistic event of great importance, and one which was accomplished in France after the work of several decades. In that country Gérard and Girodet still clung to the belief that they could only raise the military picture to the level of the great style by giving the soldiers of the Empire the appearance of Greek and Roman statues. Gros is honored as the man who first ceased giving modern soldiers the air of the antique. But the American Englishman had anticipated him by forty years . . . [West's pictures] forecast the realistic programme for decades to come and indicated the course of development which leads from Gros onwards.

A modern critic wrote in 1948: "West's historical contribution . . . had nothing to do with the introduction of contemporary costume into the painting of contemporary events." That denial, echoed by a few others in degree, is a development of our own century. No artist or critic of West's period, even among those who disliked him the most, ever made such a statement. In affirmative terms, Joseph Baretti said before 1790, "The Art and the Artists are greatly indebted to Mr. West for having been one of the first who opened the eyes of the English to the merits of modern Historical Painting, and excited in them a desire of seeing it flourish in this happy island." Joel Barlow declared in the notes to his *Columbiad* in 1807, "He rendered himself conspicuous for the boldness of his designs, in daring to shake off the trammels of art so far as to paint modern history in modern dress . . . The engraving from his *Wolfe* has been often copied in France, Italy and Germany, and it may be said that in this picture the revolution in painting really originated. It would now be reckoned as preposterous in an artist to dress modern personages in Grecian or Roman habits, as it was before to give them the garb of the age and country to which they belonged." A London article on West in 1805 said, "An axiomatical truth of painting has been established by the labours of Mr. West, that the dress of a picture has no influence over the passions of the mind . . . This innovation has been extensive and undisputed, and no painter in Europe is now bold enough to dress his figures in a picture contrary to the costume of the age and country in which the event he delineates took place." Articles on West in the British *Port Folio, La Belle Assemblée,* and the *Analectic Magazine and Naval Chronicle* made similar statements, all with variations on the now-familiar theme, "No painter in Europe is now bold enough to dress his figures in a picture contrary to the costume of the age and country in which the event he delineates took place." It is of some interest that West drafted this statement himself — it appears in his hand in rough form among his papers in Philadelphia — and gave it to Barlow, to the author of the 1805 article, and perhaps to others. It is of more importance that there is no record that anyone of that period denied it was true.

Anthony Pasquin probably spoke the definitive word on the subject. He was West's severest and most prejudiced critic. He wrote in 1796, "His best labours in general appear to me to be but the happiest efforts of a sign painter of the first order." But he had written in 1786: "Mr. West deserves much commendation for his boldly undertaking to group an historical fact in modern habits, an attempt which originated with him in this country."

Notes and Sources

CITED SOURCES are keyed to the text by page number and an identifying phrase, and to the Bibliography by the last name of the author or editor, with the appropriate page number of the work referred to: In some instances, in the absence of an author or editor, the title of the volume, publication, or manuscript collection will be given. Where two or more works by the same author are listed in the Bibliography, the source is indicated by the name of the author and a short title. These variations, however, should be noted:

1. Citation of William Dunlap means his *A History of the Rise and Progress of the Arts of Design in the United States* unless otherwise indicated.

2. Citation of John Galt means his *Life, Studies and Works of Benjamin West* unless otherwise indicated.

3. Because Charles Coleman Sellers wrote two biographies of Charles Willson Peale and both are cited, the work intended is identified by its year of publication (1947) or (1969).

4. For ease of reference, William T. Whitley's two two-volume works on the history of British art from 1700 to 1830 are treated as a single work and are identified by I, II, III, IV.

5. Both the Windsor transcript of the full Farington diary and the eight volumes of Greig's printed abridgment of the diary are cited. All the published material is of course also in the Windsor transcript; citations of the published volumes are given simply because of their greater accessibility to the reader. Because of unscholarly liberties Greig took in telescoping and paraphrasing Farington's original text, those using the material may wish to check quoted matter against the Windsor transcript or the holograph diary.

6. Activities at the Royal Academy, especially in Chapters 15 and 20–23, are most often supported by references to Farington's diary and not always by reference to the minute books of the Academy's Council or General Assembly. The minute books obviously exist, and obviously they record the activities described on the dates indicated.

The following abbreviations identify other sources.

AAA   Archives of American Art

APS   American Philosophical Society

BM   British Museum (including British Library, Print Room, and Manuscript Division).

DAB   *Dictionary of American Biography*

DNB   *Dictionary of National Biography*

EB   *Encyclopaedia Britannica* (eleventh edition)

Far.   Farington *Diary,* published Volumes I to VIII
Far. Mss.   Farington diary transcript at Windsor Castle
HSP   Historical Society of Pennsylvania
LC   Library of Congress
NYHS   New-York Historical Society
NYPL   New York Public Library
PAFA   Pennsylvania Academy of the Fine Arts
PMHB   *Pennsylvania Magazine of History and Biography*
RA   Royal Academy
SRO   Scottish Record Office
V and A   Victoria and Albert Museum and Library

Introduction   Pages xiii–xvi

PAGE

xiii   "First great success story." Kramer, "West Recalled."
xiii   "Like a work of fiction." Van Devanter, "Self-Portraits," 764.
xiii   Most popular painter. J. T. Smith, *Nollekens,* II, 385.
xiii   First effective school. E. P. Richardson, *Painting in America,* 77.
xiii   Adaptation of Galt. Henry E. Jackson.
xiv   Flexner on need for a biography. *Old Masters,* 344.
xiv   Hilton Kramer: "astonishing." "West Recalled."
xiv   John Canaday on shift in values. "A Hodgepodge."
xiv   "Long-neglected works." Canaday, "Peculiar Innocence."
xv   Farington mss., 7261 pages. The typescript shows 8261 pages, but cites an error of 1000 pages in numbering, jumping from 4,666 to 5,667.

Chapter 1.   *The Death of Kings*   Pages 1–6

1   Epigraph on West as teacher. Dunlap, I, 87.
1   King to West: "When I die." Whitley, III, 306.
1   Sons kept news from father. Ibid.
1   Servants in mourning. Ibid.
1   West's exhibit closed. Rollins, 192.
1   St. Paul's tolled. Far., VIII, 241.
2   West: "The King is dead." Dunlap, I, 75.
2   Tended to forget Mr. Dance. Far. Mss., 7599.
2   Assumed Royal Academy celebration in his honor. Far. Mss., 7276.
2   Talked of retouching pictures. Ibid., 7708.
2   *Pale Horse,* "my great work." HSP, letter to William Carey, no date.
2   Designed *Peter's Denial.* Dunlap, II, 313.
2   Jane Porter and worn brushes. Whitley, III, 310.
2   West did not consult sons. Far. Mss., 7630.
2   Mrs. West, Jr.'s "many particulars." Ibid., 7631.
2   Sons felt West's mind wandering. Ibid., 7736.
2   Dr. Baillie's fee. Ibid., 7726.
2   Charged king 30 guineas. Brooke, 385–86. The king's medical expenses since January 1812 had averaged £35,000 a year.

2 West complained. Far. Mss., 7698, 7700.

2 "Decay is natural." Ibid., 7708, 7678.

3 Galt called with galleys. Ibid., 7721.

3 Farington called. Ibid., 7620.

3 West's diet. Ibid., 7725.

3 Royal Academy officers agreed on Lawrence. Ibid., 7696.

3 J. T. Smith the last caller. J. T. Smith, *Nollekens*, II, 378–79.

3 Lawrence: "a national calamity." Ibid., II, 385.

3 Cast taken of West's hand. Whitley, III, 310. It was long preserved in the picture gallery of Sir John Leicester as an "unostentatious but feeling memorial of Mr. West's genius."

3–4 Elegy. AAA, Micro Roll 52, "A Tribute of Respect to the Memory of Benjamin West, Esq." No signature.

4 Farington urged public funeral. Far. Mss., 7738.

4 Funeral. J. T. Smith, *Nollekens*, II, 378–83; Galt, II, 244–51; Far., VIII, 244–46, Mss., 7736–53; B. R. Haydon, *Autobiography*, 337; R. Rush, 281–85; Whitley, III, 306–7; Dunlap, I, 87. The body lay in state in the Life Academy room to the right of the ground-floor antechamber at Somerset House. Edmonds the undertaker charged the Royal Academy £221, the West family £694. Far. Mss., 7744; V & A "Press Cuttings," V, 1216.

4 Leslie's description. Sandby, I, 284.

4 Surrogates sent. *Annual Register*, 1820, p. 87.

4 Comparison with Reynolds' funeral. Far. Mss., 7753; B. R. Haydon, *Autobiography*, 337.

4 Henderson's bill. Far. Mss., 7979.

5 Fauntleroy hanged. *DNB*. He had been a partner in his father's bank, Marsh, Sibbald and Co.

5 Hunt on West. Rollins, 192. He used the phrase "wretched foreigner" in his libel of the prince regent, for which Leigh Hunt and his brother John, rather than promise to stop maligning the prince, served several comfortable years in jail.

5 Hunt's newspaper on West. Ibid. The article was signed with the initials R. H.

5 Farington returned home. Far. Mss., 7753.

5 Wellesley asked to conduct service. B. R. Haydon, *Autobiography*, 337.

5 Galt: "an impressive manner." Galt, II, 249.

5 West's baptism. See Chapter 27.

6 Twentieth-century painter-critic. Albert Rosenthal, 43.

Chapter 2. *"A Fire in My Breast*   Pages 7–16

7–8 West family. Hart, "Family," 1–10; Stern, 81 et seq., 142; Dunlap, I, 36; Furthey-Cope, 761; Galt, I, 1–5; G. Smith, *Delaware*, 512–13.

8 Married in 1720. "Data on the West Family," a ms. at the Friends' Library, Swarthmore College, Pa., by Kate D. West, January 5, 1922.

8 West not a Quaker. Hart, "Family," 3, 7.

8 John West's tavern in Chester. Ashmead, 369.

8 Pearson settled Springfield. Ashmead, 713; Galt I, 3.

8 West born in Swarthmore house. This has been questioned, but

Thomas Sully visited this house in 1810 at West's request and made a drawing of it for him. Ashmead, 725.

8–9   John West's tavern in Darby-Springfield. Furthey-Cope, 761.

9   Preacher's prophecy. Galt, I, 6–9; Dunlap, I, 35–36.

9   Hawthorne. *Biographical Stories*, 145–55.

9   Ward-Sartain picture. *Art Journal*, 1863, p. 218. Sartain's engraving appears in Carson, with a picture of the Swarthmore house and a West drawing of his father.

9   Modern children's books. Marguerite Henry and Wesley Dennis, *Benjamin West and His Cat Grimalkin*, 1947; Dorothea J. Snow, *Benjamin West, Gifted Young Painter*, 1967.

10   West drawing niece. Galt, I, 9–10. Flexner in "Neo-Classicism," 8–9, points out that young West could not have grown to age seven in a Pennsylvania German community without having seen pictures in various forms. West told Nicholas Biddle in 1807 that his father disapproved of so much time spent in drawing, until some of the old Quakers told him the talent was a gift from God, whose will was not to be contradicted. Wainwright, 111.

10   Indians present in Eastern Pennsylvania. Barton, 337.

10   Indians supplied paint. Galt, I, 18.

11   West and cat. Galt, I, 19–20.

11   John West's inn at Newtown Square. Ashmead, 649; Stern, 142.

11   Penington. Flexner, "Neo-Classicism," 9–10; *DAB*; Galt, I, 21–22; J. F. Watson, I, 444; Dickason, "Unpublished Letter," 130.

11   "Grevling" engraving. Galt, I, 21. The edited ms. of the catalogue of a HSP exhibition of West's work held in November 1910 says that the engravings were after Guercino, giving no source for the statement. See Evans, 110–11.

11   West's first picture. Dunlap, I, 40; Galt, I, 22–24.

12   "Most grateful to my feelings." Dickason, "Unpublished Letter," 130; Galt, I, 25–26.

12   Shoemaker. Flexner, "Neo-Classicism," 10; Dickason, "Unpublished Letter," 130; Galt, I, 27–28.

12   "Palpitation of joy." Dickason, "Unpublished Letter," 130.

13   West and two books as companions. Ibid., 131.

13   Fresnoy quotations. Du Fresnoy, 310–13.

13   Jonathan Richardson quotation. *The Theory of Painting*, 17.

14   West and schoolfellow. Galt, I, 29–31.

14   Isaac Wayne. Flexner, "Neo-Classicism," 13; Galt, I, 32; Dunlap, I, 38.

14   Dr. Morris first patron. Flexner, "Neo-Classicism," 14; *PMHB* XVIII (1894), 219–22; G. Smith, *Delaware*, 513; Galt, I, 32.

14   Log school house, Newtown Square. Ashmead, 641.

14   Mr. Hide, teacher. Far., II, 88. The time, place, and nature of Hide's teaching are not given, other than that he taught West "when a boy." He was one of a group of five foreigners in London who in the 1730s "made up a little academy for drawing from a living model by lamp light," hiring a room for the purpose in Gough Square, Fleet Street. The academy attracted Hogarth's attention, and it became St. Martin's Academy, a forerunner of the Royal Academy

of Arts. Hide may be an unrecognized and unacknowledged missing link in young West's artistic education.

14 Samuel Flower. Flexner, "Neo-Classicism," 14; Galt, I, 32–34.

15 Clarkson. Flexner, "Neo-Classicism," 17–18; Galt, I, 38.

15–16 West and Williams. Dickason, *Williams*, 10, 19–29, 230, "Unpublished Letter," 130–31.

Chapter 3. *The Practising Artist*   Pages 17–28

17 George Ross. *DAB*; Flexner, "Neo-Classicism," 19.

17 "Celebrity enlarged." Galt, I, 35.

18 Identifiable portraits. Sawitzky, "American Work," 437.

18 William Henry. F. Jordan; Kulp, 516–19; Tinkcom, 381–83; *DAB*; Galt, I, 35–37; Sawitzky, "American Work," 448–49.

18–19 *Death of Socrates.* Wainwright, 111; Flexner, "Neo-Classicism," 19–21, 23–24; Van Devanter, "Socrates." The picture was carefully restored in 1962–63 by Bruce Etchison, art conservator. It is the only known American work on which West put his signature. Sawitzky in "American Work" named the owner of the picture but apparently did not see it and listed it among West's "unlocated paintings."

19 West told Nicholas Biddle in 1807 that he painted a sign at Lancaster of "a drove of oxen." While there has been general conjecture that West painted commercial signs (in Philadelphia and New York) this appears to be the only hard evidence that he did so. Wainwright, 111; Dickson, *Jarvis*, 26.

19 William Smith. *DAB*; Galt, I, 37–40, 44–45, 71–72, 84–85.

20 Special college course. Galt, I, 44–45.

20 Smith introduced four young men. Ibid., 38–40.

20 Fishing parties. Ibid., 40. West was all his life an ardent fisherman.

20 Godfrey. *DAB*; E. Robins, 326.

20 Drawing of Hopkinson. Semon, 7, 19.

20–21 West and Dr. Morris. *PMHB*, XVIII (1894), 219–22; West to Morris, July 25, 1769 and July 20, 1798.

21 West drilled alongside militia. Galt, I, 61–62. A misreading of Galt has led a number of writers, beginning with Cunningham in 1834, to say that West saw military service with General Forbes in the 1758 expedition to capture Fort Duquesne. Some have said that West saw service with General Braddock in 1755. It was his brother Samuel who saw service on the frontier.

21 Samuel West a captain. Galt, I, 63.

21–22 Philadelphia. *Historic Philadelphia*; J .F. Watson, I, 174–77, 187, 189, 198, 207, 383–84, II, 264; Burt, 84, 85, 87, 94, 102.

22 Dunlap on West's appearance. Dunlap, I, 48, 87.

22 Physician's report. Zorgniotti, 703.

22 Courtier on West. Angelo, I, 361.

22 Saw George Washington. Far. Mss., 1750.

22 Acquainted with William Howe. Galt, II, 27. I have been unable to establish that Howe was in Philadelphia before April 1760.

23 The "Philadelphia Salute." Button, 354.

23 Supposed author of poem. Hastings, 102; Hornberger, 343–51. The

obscure 1758 poem by "Lovelace" has an uncanny resemblance in word and thought to Lord Byron's "She Walks in Beauty," written decades later.

23 Wollaston's influence. Sawitzky, "American Work," 440–44.

24 Fee 5 guineas. Galt, I, 70.

24 Painted Dr. Smith as a present. Henderson, 344.

24 West's portraits. Sawitzky, "American Work," 438 et seq.

24 Made a drawing of Elizabeth Shewell. Far. Mss., 2248.

24 Wayne introduced Miss Shewell. Carson, 307.

24 Shewells were prosperous. Sawitzky, *Pratt*, 69.

24 Trial of Suzannah. Galt, I, 72–73; Dunlap, I, 44. The picture has disappeared. Dunlap, who saw it, said that West "made ample use of a print on the subject."

24 Portrait of Sally Franklin. Franklin *Papers*, VII, 278, VIII, 92. No portrait of Sally by West or Hesselius is known to exist.

24 Thomas Mifflin. *DAB*; Sawitzky, "American Work," 457–58.

24–25 William Allen. *DAB*; L. B. Walker; Klein, 102–103; Henderson, 329–331; J. F. Watson, I, 208. A portrait of William Allen formerly attributed to West is now thought to be by Robert Feke. Letter to the author, December 1, 1977, from Martin I. Yoelson, Chief of Interpretation, Independence National Historical Park, Philadelphia.

25–26 West in New York. Sawitzky was unable to find a single portrait in or near New York attributable to West. He favors the supposition, therefore, that West's stay in New York was less successful and of shorter duration than Galt said. "American Work," 439–40.

25 West self-portrait. *PMHB*, VI (1882), 495; Van Devanter, "Self-Portraits"; Hart, "Family," 5, 6.

25 Elizabeth Steel. *PMHB*, VI (1882), 495. The son-in-law's name was Thompson Westcott.

25–26 West on New York. Galt, I, 76–85.

26 Shippens' business venture. According to Galt (I, 84), Messrs. Jackson and Rutherford wrote to William Allen from Leghorn to say that the harvest in Italy was bad and to ask him to send a cargo of wheat and flour. Galt was mistaken. In a letter to Jackson and Rutherford written April 5, 1760, seven days before the *Betty Sally* sailed, Allen discussed only the shipment of sugars by the partners. L. B. Walker, 41. This and some of the other letters of the Italian period appear in E. P. Richardson's "West's Voyage."

26 Allen on vice and luxury. Klein, 103; HSP, Allen letterbook, Allen to David Barclay and Sons, July 20, 1761.

26 Allen on Col. Shippen, sober, virtuous. L. B. Walker, 38, Allen to David Barclay, March 10, 1760.

26 Smith called on Allen. Galt, I, 84–85.

26 West met William Henry. Tinkcom (382) says that West gave Henry a portrait of himself on departure that deteriorated beyond recognition.

27 Letters of introduction. West seems to have obtained letters from two Jesuit priests who had befriended him. See Van Devanter, "Holy Family." Their friendship supports James Flexner's thesis on West: Galt "attempted to exemplify the theories of Rousseau by demonstrating that West had been an untaught child of nature, who

painted spontaneously out of natural genius which society had not spoiled. The picturesque view thus given of his early years has been repeated from book to book until it became an American legend . . . [In fact], since he was about nine years old, the boy had been the petted favorite of remarkable people . . . Rarely has a youthful prodigy been encouraged by so many brilliant and well-informed men." "Neo-Classicism," 7, 26.

27 "Some love passages." Rodenbough, 255.

27 Allen to Jackson and Rutherford. L. B. Walker, 40–42.

27 E. P. Richardson's thesis. *Painting in America*, 71, 89, 146.

27 Edward Shippen accompanied his brother. Edward later became the father-in-law of Benedict Arnold.

27 fn Fifty Guineas equal to about £1000. Reitlinger, III, 17.

Chapter 4. *An American in Italy*   Pages 29–40

29 Allen on West's finances, epigraph. L. B. Walker, Allen to D. Barclay and Sons in London, August 10, 1761.

29 "Strong gales of wind." HSP, Col. Joseph Shippen from Gibraltar to his father, May 16, 1760; Klein, 103.

29 John seasick, others "hearty and well." HSP, Col. Shippen to brother, May 11, 1760, Col. Shippen to father, May 16, 1760; Klein, 103.

29 Did not tell underwriters about pirates. Balch, 185, Charles J. Shippen to his father, September 17, 1760.

29 Chased in to Gibraltar. HSP, Col. Shippen to father, May 16, 1760, Col. Shippen to brother, May 11, 1760.

29–30 Captain Kearny incident. HSP, Col. Shippen to father, May 16, 1760; Galt, I, 88–89. Galt called him Commodore Carney. In a letter to Barclay, August 25, 1760, William Allen said he had heard that the cargo had been condemned because it had been bought in Haiti, and that he would "seek for justice . . . even to the dernier resort." (Richardson, "West's Voyage," 13.) Jensen in *Maritime Commerce*, 63, says the Leghorn venture was in flagrant violation of British commercial policies. For further comment on this episode, see Appendix I.

30 Convoyed across Mediterranean. Galt, I, 90; Klein, 103; HSP, Col. Shippen to father from Leghorn, July 4, 1760; *Commissioned Sea Officers.*

30 Quarantined at Leghorn. Balch, 184, Charles J. Shippen at Philadelphia to father, September 17, 1760; HSP, Col. Shippen to father, July 4, 1760, Col. Shippen to brother, July 4, 1760.

30 Rutherford and Jackson hospitality. Galt, I, 91; Klein, 104; HSP, Col. Shippen to father, July 4, 1760.

30 "Benny" West. HSP, Col. Shippen to father, July 13, 1760.

30 Description of Leghorn. HSP, Col. Shippen to father, July 13, 1760; Piozzi, 178.

30 fn On return voyage. HSP, Col. Shippen at Leghorn to father, July 13, 1760, Edward Shippen to father, November 27, 1760; Col. Shippen's orders to captain, July 13, 1760; Klein, 103.

31 Arrival at Rome. Galt, I, 91–94, 101; Mead, 64, 142, 313–14.

PAGE
31 Thomas Robinson. Galt, I, 102; *DNB.*
32 Crispigné. Galt, I, 102; *Gentleman's Magazine,* February, 1818, p. 187. John Fleming (in *Robert Adam,* 377) suggests that Crispigné may have been the same person as Daniel Crispin, who befriended West in Rome. Robert Rutherford spelled the name Crispin and Crespin.
32–33 Cardinal Albani. Galt, I, 91, 103–4; L. Lewis, 11, 149–50; Leppmann, 203–5; Andrieux, *Rome,* 383; Fleming, "Drawings," 164; Casanova, VII, 182–83; Northcote (Ward), 154. Lesley Lewis holds that it is incredible that Albani was so naive as to think West might have been colored or had the education of a savage (p. 182).
33–34 Apollo Belvedere episode. Galt, I, 104–6; Richardson, *Allston,* 42; Leppmann, 165; Ettlinger, "Winckelmann," xxxiii; Boswell, 84. West related the episode in or before 1796 to Anthony Pasquin, who revealed it in his *The Royal Academicians* (p. 75), almost twenty years before Galt used it.
34–36 Eighteenth-century Rome. Galt, I, 95–99; Mead, 270–331; Andrieux, *Papal Rome,* 11–25, 183; Andrieux, *Rome,* 366–67; Gwynn, 156; Smollett, 226; Northcote (Hazlitt), 200, 237; Northcote (Ward), 176; *British Artists in Rome;* Piozzi, 212; Far., I, 123.
36 West on strangers in Rome. Galt, I, 97.
36 High Mass at St. Peter's, many beggars. Ibid., 109–12.
36 Batoni episode. Dunlap, I, 51, as retold by Allston; Far., I, 126, VII, 284–85; Northcote (Ward), 174–75; Gwynn, 141. West told this story many times to many people with slight variations. I have synthesized the different versions.
36–37 Gavin Hamilton. Galt, I, 114–18; *DNB; British Artists in Rome;* Irwin, "Gavin Hamilton"; Cummings-Staley, 44–47; Waterhouse, *Three Decades;* Irwin, *Neo-Classical Art,* 113–16. The picture of Dawkins and Wood appears in Irwin, *Neo-Classical Art,* plate 17. Among many other antique sculptures, Hamilton excavated *The Wounded Amazon,* now in the Metropolitan Museum of Art; and *The Towneley Venus,* now in the British Museum. He bought for resale Raphael's *Ansidei Madonna* and Leonardo's *Virgin of the Rocks,* both in London's National Gallery.
37–38 Villa Albani. Fleming, "Drawings"; Leppmann, 213–15; R. Peale, *Italy,* 155–57; L. Lewis, 200–201; Piozzi, 285, 288; Casanova, VII, 321; Boswell, 77. The Villa Abani, started in 1743, was the largest construction project of its time, and the last palace to be built in the city in the grand manner. It is now the Villa Torlonia and, owned by the Torlonia family, is the only eighteenth-century museum in Italy that is preserved today virtually unchanged. Tedious negotiations are required to see it.
38 Mengs' Parnassus. Fleming, "Drawings," 168; Honour, *Neo-Classicism,* 31; Leppmann, 215–16.
38 West said his drawings excited little attention. *Georgian Era,* "Painters," 87. As Galt told the story, West informed Robinson he could not produce a sketch for Mengs because "he had never learned to draw." The statement is unlikely.
38 West aware of his deficiencies. *Annual Register,* 1820, p. 1166.
38–39 Robinson portrait episode. Galt, I, 119–22.

PAGE

38–39 fn   Jenkins. *British Artists in Rome;* Far., I, 125; Marle, IB; F. H. Taylor, 483–84.

38–39 fn   Dance. *DNB; British Artists in Rome;* Far., IV, 257.

39   West's illness. Galt, I, 113, 123–24; *Public Characters,* 526–28; Zorgniotti; Du Pont Winterthur Museum, West to Joseph Shippen, May 11, 1762; Balch, lxix–lxxii, West to Col. Shippen, September 1, 1763; Far., V, 46–47; *Annual Register,* 1820, p. 1166; Wainwright, 111.

39   West and John Dick. Galt, I, 124. Dick had been British consul at Genoa and became Sir John Dick. He is identified as one of the keyed figures in Zoffany's *The Tribuna of the Uffizi.*

39–40   Col. Shippen to West from Rome. PAFA, September 17, 1760. It is contained in AAA Micro Roll 50, Nos. 779–781.

40   West's *Savage Chief.* Barlow, 180.

40   Samuel Powel among West's supporters. Barton, 336.

40   Benjamin Franklin on West. Franklin *Papers,* X, 233, Franklin in Philadelphia to Mrs. Stevenson in London, March 25, 1763.

Chapter 5. *"The American Raphael"*   Pages 41–56

41   West's statement on leaving Italy. Galt, I, 149.

41   "The most glorious productions." *Public Characters,* 527.

41   West's study of art works. Kraemer, 80–81, Plates 3, 107; Galt, I, 107, II, 127–28; drawings at Friends' Library, Swarthmore College; West sketchbooks at Royal Academy; Far., I, 125.

41   "State of high excitement." Galt, I, 113.

42   West shocked by what he saw. Galt, I, 96, 110–11, 146, 147; *La Belle Assemblée,* 9.

42   "Graces of the human character." Galt, I, 146.

42   Mengs incidents. Casanova, VII, 192–93; Leppmann, 252–53; Northcote (Ward), 175; Goldwater-Treves, 244–45. There is no clear record that West ever met Winckelmann. He seems to have been away from Rome while West was there (Snyder, 40), but Nicholas Biddle, after a conversation with West in 1807, wrote, "Mengs and Winckelmann were at Rome when West was." Wainwright, 112.

43   Mengs "my favorite master." Balch, lxix, West to Col. Shippen, September 1, 1763.

43   Among the few in Mengs circle. *British Artists in Rome,* Intro, unnumbered.

43 fn   Waterhouse theory. Waterhouse, *British Contribution,* 59, 61, et seq.

43–44   West: "to assist the reason." Galt, I, 157.

43–45   Neoclassical theory. I am indebted to L. D. Ettlinger, Arnold Hauser, Hugh Honour, Wolfgang Leppmann, Judy Marle, Richard Muther, Geraldine Pelles, E. P. Richardson, Martin D. Snyder, and Robert Rosenblum. Their works are cited in the bibliography.

44   Winckelmann, imitation of the Greeks. Leppmann, 113.

44   Laws of beauty. Ibid., 276–78.

44   "Noble simplicity." Ibid., 113; Winckelmann, 72.

44   Passion should not be shown. Far. Mss., 485, Flaxman to Farington, 1795.

45   "A whole intellectual climate": Ettlinger, "The Role of the Artist," 218. "A new attitude": Denvir, "Revolution in Painting," 349. A

protest against the rococo: Hauser, 632. A *risorgimento* of the arts: Honour, "Neo-Classicism," 14.

45   E. P. Richardson, the dream of Greece and Rome. *Painting in America*, 86.

45   Honour: "It does not matter very much." "Neo-Classicism," 15.

45–46   Mengs' advice to West. Galt, I, 122.

46–47   West's illness. Zorgniotti; Nannoni; Galt, I, 123–25; *Public Characters*, 526–28; APS, Rutherford to Col. Shippen, April 22 and June 21, 1763; Balch, lxix, September 1, 1763; Du Pont Winterthur Museum, West to Col. Shippen, May 11, 1762. Because of passages in Galt (I, 123) and in the first extended biographical note on West (*Public Characters of 1805*, p. 526), it is commonly said that the first cause of West's illness was a kind of emotional disturbance, a feverish oppression of mind caused by the constant excitement of his new life and the conflict between his sober upbringing and the novelties and grandeur of Rome. Nicholas Biddle wrote in 1807, "When I went to Rome, said West to me, such was the effect which a sudden passage from a little town on the Delaware to the mistress of the world, and such the enthusiasm for his art, that his mind was overwhelmed by it. After six weeks of anxious days and sleepless nights, he was obliged to go to Leghorn out of reach of the arts to recover his enthusiasm. After his mind had become tranquil, he again returned to Rome, but the ardor of his mind instead of being diminished became greater by enjoyment and after seven months he was obliged again to leave Rome and abstain from study." (Wainwright, 111.) There is, however, nothing at all in Dr. Nannoni's careful and complete clinical case history on West to suggest such emotional disturbance; the illness was purely physical. I am unable to account for West's apparent misreporting of his own illness some forty years later. It is possible he did so because the fashion of the first decades of the nineteenth century placed a value on deep emotional feelings and extreme sensibility openly expressed.

46   "I can bear pain." Far., V, 46–47.

46   Made frame for bed. *Public Characters*, 528; Galt, I, 125; Far., V, 47.

47   Lodged deplorably. Du Pont Winterthur Museum, West to Col. Shippen, May 11, 1762.

47   Horace Mann and other visitors. *Public Characters*, 528; Galt, I, 125; Balch, lxix, West to Col. Shippen, September 1, 1763.

47   Visited Boboli Gardens. *Public Characters*, 528.

47   "Slowly picking up." Balch, lxix, West to Col. Shippen from London, September 1, 1763.

47–48   Angelica Kauffmann. Manners-Williamson; Hartcup. West met her in Florence. Far., I, 189. The inscription on the back of the Kauffmann portrait of West in the National Portrait Gallery, London, reads, "Mr. West — drawn in Rome by Angelica Kauffmann 1763." The only recorded meeting of the two, however, was in Florence. The inscription may have been added years later.

48   She set her cap for West. Peale, "Autobiography," quoted in Sellers, *Peale* (1969), 64.

48   Fire broke out in gallery. Balch, lxx, West to Col. Shippen, September 1, 1763.

PAGE

48 "Favourable opportunity." Ibid.

49 Henry Matthews. Ibid.; Galt, I, 126; *Public Characters*, 528; APS, Rutherford to Col. Shippen, April 22, 1763.

49 Sixty pounds from John Allen. L. B. Walker, 47, Allen to D. Barclay and Sons, August 10, 1761.

49 Withdrew last £10. Galt, I, 128.

49 Three hundred pounds credited to West by William Allen and Hamilton. APS, Rutherford to Col. Shippen, April 22 and June 21, 1763; L. B. Walker, Allen to D. Barclay and Sons, October 10, 1762, p. 51.

49 Jackson and Rutherford did not disapprove. Balch, lxx, West to Col. Shippen, September 1, 1763.

49 Bologna. Galt, I, 129; Gwynn, 170.

49 Method of copying Guido Reni. Dr. Morgan, *Journal*, 76–77; Piozzi, 128.

50 Venice. Andrieux, *Papal Rome.*

50 Painted Lady Northampton. APS, Rutherford to Col. Shippen, April 22, 1763.

50 Murray's "particular kindness." Balch, lxx, West to Col. Shippen, September 1, 1763.

50 Ladies joked about Philadelphia. Dr. Morgan, *Journal*, 117.

50 West painted Murray. APS, Rutherford to Shippen, April 22, 1763.

50–51 Lady Mary on Murray. Montagu, *Letters*, III, 127, 137, 140, 151, 242, 247, 264, 282.

51 Casanova on Murray as a libertine. IV, 136, 138, 155, 160, 179, et seq.

51 Lady Mary on Murray's sister. Montagu, *Letters*, III, 147.

51 Joseph Smith. F. H. Taylor, 446–48; APS, Rutherford to Col. Shippen, April 22, 1763; *George III, Collector*, 3.

51 Richard Dalton. F. H. Taylor, 446, 448, 481; APS, Rutherford to Col. Shippen, April 22 and June 21, 1763.

52 West finished *Venus*, arrived Rome in January 1763. Balch, lxix–lxxi, to Col. Shippen, September 1, 1763.

52 Angelica Kauffmann. Irwin, *Neoclassical Art*, 52; Manners-Williamson, 14; J. T. Smith, *Nollekens*, I, 285–86; Far., IV, 257–58, VII, 65; *Age of Neo-Classicism*, 377.

52 Albani sold drawings. Flemings, "Drawings," 164–67; Leppmann, 240–41.

53 Vittoria (or Vittiuccia). Leppmann, 240. She appears in Mengs' *Parnassus* as the Muse of Memory, holding her ear.

53 West concentrated on Raphael. Galt, I, 106, 131.

53 Studied cameos with Wilcocks. Galt, I, 131. Galt spells the name incorrectly as Wilcox.

53 Abbé Grant. Galt, I, 138–42; Pottle, 509. Grant was a supporter of the Jacobite claimants to the throne of Great Britain. James Boswell thought him "an excellent, obliging, hearty character"; a British secret agent in Rome reported that he "served the Pretender, assisted the English who came to Rome, and spied on both." (Pottle, 509.)

53 West's health good. APS, Rutherford to Col. Shippen, April 22, 1763.

53 Copied *Herodias*. APS, Rutherford to Shippen, June 21, 1763; Balch, lxxi, West to Col. Shippen, September 1, 1763.

53–54 *Cimon and Iphigenia*. Galt, I, 142. Painted it for the king. APS,

       Rutherford to Col. Shippen, April 22 and June 21, 1763.
54   *Angelica and Medoro.* Galt, I, 142; *Public Characters,* 529.
54   West elected to academies. Galt, I, 144.
54   "The American Raphael." Whitley, I, 197.
54   Letter from his father. Galt, I, 143.
54   Letter of regret from Dalton. APS, Rutherford to Col. Shippen, June
       21, 1763.
54   Italy to England by sea. S. Rogers, *Italian Journal,* 75.
54   Dread of being laid up. Balch, lxx, West to Col. Shippen, September
       1, 1763.
54   William Patoun. Galt, I, 143–44; Whitley, I, 196; *Public Characters*
       529; Balch, lxi, West to Col. Shippen September 1, 1763; APS,
       Rutherford to Col. Shippen, June 21, 1763. Galt says that Wilcox
       [Wilcocks] produced Dr. Patoun, but the letters indicate it was Dan-
       iel Crispin.
54–55 Rutherford, a touch of weariness. He wrote to Col. Shippen on
       April 22, 1763: "He keeps me much in the dark, for you know with
       how much difficulty he handles the pen . . . I shall desire him to give
       you ample information of all his proceedings hitherto and what he
       intends to do hereafter, but I will not engage to his performing it
       very punctually." West indeed handled the pen with much diffi-
       culty. To his friend Peter Thomson in Philadelphia he wrote on
       February 23, 1772, "I don't like writing — it's as difficult to me as
       painting would be to you. Every man in his own way. I could as
       soon paint you a description of things on this side the water as
       write." Hart, "Family," 13.
55   Jenkins letter to Wilson. Constable, *Wilson,* 41.
55   Arrived Florence June 1, 1763. APS, Rutherford to Col. Shippen,
       June 21, 1763.
55   West in Leghorn. Ibid.
55   West's copies. The three pictures were Titian's *Venus,* Mengs' *Holy*
       Family, and Annibale Caracci's *Death of Adonis.* The copy of
       Guido's *Herodias* had not yet arrived in Florence. All four pictures
       arrived safely. HSP, Col. Shippen to Rutherford, June 28, 1764.
55   West asked favor of Shippen. Balch, lxxii, September 1, 1763.
55   Letters of recommendation for England. APS, Rutherford to Col.
       Shippen, June 21, 1763.
55   Drew last £150. Ibid. West had lived on £100 a year during his three
       years in Italy. Copley, *Letters,* 191.
55   Kept hat on before the duke of Parma. The story is generally told
       in the sense that West played the part of a Quaker because he felt
       it was expected of him. Galt, however, wrote (I, 145) that West fol-
       lowed what he thought was the practice of the court in London.
55   Route followed. Far. Mss., 8116; *Public Characters,* 529–30.
55   Did not attend salon. Bizardel, 5.
55–56 Robert Mackinlay to West. HSP, April 13, 1789.

Chapter 6.   *A Fine View of London*   Pages 57–68

57   Powel to Roberts. *PMHB,* XVII (1894), 37.
57   Dover to London. Far., VII, 197; *Gentleman's Magazine,* July 1820,

p. 76; American *Port Folio,* No. 3, 1810, "A Citizen of Philadelphia [Benjamin Rush] to Benjamin West," January 24, 1810, p. 232.

57   First night at White Bear Inn. Walford, IV, 208.

57   Called first on Coutts. Far. Mss., 7206.

58   Moved to 19 Bedford Street. Far., VII, 197.

58   Patrons in London. Galt, II, 4; *PMHB,* XC (1966), 221; Balch, lxxii, West to Col. Shippen, September 1, 1763. Allen was staying in Bath, but West's letter indicates they met in London.

58   Powel's tour. Dr. Morgan, *Journal,* 24–25, 218–19.

58   "Joy and triumph." Dunlap, I, 54.

58–59   Wilson. DNB; Dulwich Gallery, 99; Rutter, 21, 96; Constable, *Wilson,* 38, 39; *Georgian Era,* IV, 66–68; Cummings-Staley, 32–33; Angelo, I, 256–57.

58   Young Farington. Far., III, 94, VII, 181; Rutter, 24; Constable, *Wilson,* 39, 115, 137–38.

59   West's tour. Galt, II, 5; *Public Characters,* 530.

60   Attended St. Martin's. *Public Characters,* 533.

60   Patoun introduced him to Reynolds. Galt, II, 5.

60   General Monckton called. *Annual Register,* 1168.

60   Wilson and Reynolds urged West to exhibit. Galt, II, 6; *Public Characters,* 532; *Annual Register,* 1820, p. 1168.

61   Juliana Penn. See Coleman.

60–61   Skating episode. Galt, II, 26–31; Whitley, I, 220; Whitley Papers, 1681, Item 3; Dunlap, I, 61; Button. I have been unable to identify "Dr. Hewitt."

61   Allen to Chew. *PMHB,* April 1966, 211.

61–62   "Waste of genius" on portraits. Dunlap, I, 84, West to C. W. Peale, 1809.

62   Consulted Allen and Smith. Galt, II, 10.

62   Moved to Castle Street. Far., VII, 197.

62   Hogarth. Wheatley, *Hogarth's London.* West made the comment in praising Hogarth's book, *Analysis of Beauty.*

63   Exhibition of 1760 was crowded. Whitley, I, 171.

63   1764 works of poor quality. Ibid., 197. The first exhibition had been held in 1760 by the six-year-old Society of Arts, later the Royal Society of Arts. The Society of Artists, later the Incorporated Society of Artists (1761–1791), an offshoot of this institution with which West became involved, continued the exhibitions. They should not be confused with the Royal Society of London, founded 1660, an institution with scientific interests.

63   Walpole on West's paintings. Ibid., 196.

63   Eulogy in *Public Advertiser.* Ibid., 197; Von Erffa, "Early Years," 7.

63   Would blush to call him Raphael. BM, Whitley Papers, 1667, Item 6, *Public Advertiser,* May 2, 1764.

63   Dr. Markham. *DNB;* Galt, II, 6, 7.

63   Burke's brother. Galt, II, 7.

63   Marquis of Rockingham. Ibid., 9, 10; *DNB.*

64   Colonel Shippen to Rutherford. HSP, June 28, 1764.

64   Matthew Pratt. Sawitzky, *Pratt.* The editors of the Philadelphia Museum's *Philadelphia: Three Centuries of American Art* conjecture (p. 86) that Pratt's presence on the journey to England probably

      meant that he had known West in Philadephia. C. W. Peale called Pratt "a mild and friendly man." APS, autobiography, typescript, 101.

64   Miss Shewell's Almanak. Von Erffa, "Early Years," 9. A member of the West family gave the Almanak to Professor Helmut von Erffa, who presented it to Princeton University Library.

64   Betsy delivered a letter from Dr. Smith. Hastings, 138.

64   John West on changes in London. Leslie, *Recollections,* 40; Dunlap, I, 58.

64   Marriage register. It is reproduced in Huish, 329.

64   Pratt on wedding. Sawitzky, *Pratt,* 19.

65   Thomas F. Shewell letter. *PMHB,* XXXII (1908), 376–77. He wrote it to Brigadier General T. F. Rodenbough (ret.), a Shewell descendant. See Stowe, 23–25.

66   C. H. Hart scoffed at elopement story. In an exchange of letters with Rodenbough. *PMHB,* XXXII (1908), 377.

67   Pratt painted Elizabeth's parents. Sawitzky, *Pratt,* 11, 68–70.

67   West wrote to his brother in care of Joseph Shewell. Hart, "Family," 15. On December 13, 1766, Dr. William Smith, provost of the College of Philadelphia, wrote to Francis Hopkinson in London, "The little picture West did for me was drawn when I had just got out of an eleven weeks' fever, and you will tell him I have now a little more complexion, as well as health, which I beg him to supply also to the piece, with a dash or two of his brush, that I may send for it. I wrote him by his bride and did everything he expected of me in that affair, but he has never been kind enough to send me a line." (Hastings, 138.) Unless we conclude that Dr. Smith was also part of the legendary elopement party, he presumably meant that on his return to Philadelphia he had encouraged Elizabeth Shewell to make the journey to England.

67   Franklin called on Wests. Franklin, *Papers,* Franklin to his wife, XII, February 9 and 14, 1765, pp. 43, 63, and XIV, May 23, 1767, p. 167.

67   West and the Shewells. On July 25, 1787, he wrote to his brother William in America, "I hope Stephen Shewell will act with dispatch and honor in terminating the account between him and his sister [Elizabeth Shewell West], respecting that property she left in her mother's hands, which from motives of delicacy I never drew. This conduct of mine, united with the assistance I have given his daughter [Mrs. Isaac Hunt] and grandchildren in this country (which amounts to much more than the original property left in his hands), I was in hopes would have been felt by him as a mark of esteem of mine that connection which on my part has ever been honourable and friendly, and I must say, merits other returns than those which I have received." On one of the very few times the critic Anthony Pasquin had a good word to say of West, he publicly praised him for marrying without receiving a dowry and for supporting his father. Hart, "Family," 19–20; Pasquin, *Memoirs,* 75.

68   Pratt on honeymoon, became his student. Sawitzky, *Pratt,* 19.

68   "No secrets or mysteries." Dunlap, *Diary,* 542–43.

68   Reynolds concealed painting supplies. Mount, 50.

Chapter 7. *"In Britain's Bosom"* Pages 69–82

PAGE

69 Peale to Bordley. Sellers, *Peale* (1969), 57.

69–72 Life in England and London. Wages: M. D. George, *London Life,* 164–65; Scott, 171. Washable cotton: M. D. George, *London Life,* 60. Stockings: ibid.; W. S. Lewis, *Tours,* 97. Witchcraft: Kronenberger, *Kings,* 94. Few consulted stars: Burton, 257. Orphanages: M. D. George, *London Life,* xiii; Plumb, 78. Child labor: Cobban, 298. Hospitals: Kronenberger, *Wilkes,* 110; Brander, 92. Could not force deportation: Marshall, 248. 14,000 black slaves: M. D. George, *London Life,* 134. (They were freed in 1772.) Birmingham to London: Brander, 152. Mail coaches: Brander, 160. New road for livestock: Margetson, 7. (It is now Euston Road.) Paving act of 1762: W. S. Lewis, *Tours,* 51; Moritz, 32. Casanova shocked: W. S. Lewis, 34. Cows in parks: Moritz, 29. Parks reserved for adults: Chancellor, 82. Best lighting: Moritz, 36; W. S. Lewis, *Tours,* 53. George III: Brooke; Millar, *Pictures, Text,* Text, xi; *George III, Collector.* Marine chronometer: Cobban, 118.

71 Dr. Johnson's pension. Several writers have claimed that West persuaded George III to give Dr. Johnson the pension. West, however, was in Italy when the pension was granted in 1762.

72 Raphael West born April 8, 1766. HSP, West family records.

72 A director of St. Martin's Lane Academy. Whitley, I, 195.

72 A director of Society of Artists. Sandby, I, 43.

72 West-Wilson as hanging committee. Dunlap, I, 66.

72 Smith, *Ohio Indians.* Only the London edition has West's engravings.

73 Ramsay. He spent much of his career making replicas of the official portrait of the young king. Nollekens did some 200 repetitions of his busts of Fox and Pitt the Younger. Margetson, 97.

73 Reynolds, 2½ hours. Whitley, I, 280. Davies, *English Society,* 42.

73 West would have ranked with masters. Roberts, "Mrs. Barrington."

73 West, no future in history painting. *Journal of the AAA,* IV, No. 1 (January 1964), West to John Green, September 10, 1771.

73 Share classical tradition. Evans, 10.

73 Great crowd of the year. Charles Landis attributed the remark to Reynolds in 1926 ("Benjamin West," 246), and others have since repeated the unlikely attribution. Landis gave no source and I have been unable to find any. Leslie and Taylor, (I, 263) quoted the statement in *Reynolds* in 1865 without attributing it to Reynolds.

73–4 *Pylades and Orestes.* Northcote, *Reynolds,* I, 142.

74 Mr. Geddes bought. *Annual Register,* 1820, p. 1169.

74 Verses by "An Impartial Hand." Whitley, I, 212.

75 Delanoy. Dunlap, I, 161, 250.

75 Hopkinson. Hastings, 103, 132, 137, 141.

75 West's gift to the Library Company. Correspondence with Edwin Wolf II, Librarian, The Library Company, March 4, 1977.

75–8 Peale. Sellers, *Peale* (1947), I ,74–86; *Peale* (1969), 5–74; H. W. Sellers, 262.

78–82 West and Copley. Copley, *Letters,* 35–66; Prown, 47–51; Amory,

17–19; Dunlap, I, 103–30; A. Cunningham, *Lives*, "Copley," 164–66; Whitley, I, 214–19. The correspondence exchanged between Captain Bruce and Copley, and between West and Copley, is found in Copley, *Letters*. Two undated letters are found in Cunningham that do not appear in Copley.

78 fn First picture for export to Europe. Frankenstein, 60.

81 fn "Every part of a picture must work." Ibid., 63.

Chapter 8. *The Visible Instrument*   Pages 83–98

83 Robert Drummond. *DNB*.

84–7 Drummond and West. Galt, II, 11–13, 20–22; *Public Characters*, 533; *Annual Register*, 1169.

84–6 *Agrippina*. The first trial version, inscribed "B. West/1766," is reproduced in the present work. The finished version is at Yale University Art Gallery. The reader is referred to the Allen Staley article listed in the Bibliography for an informative commentary on this picture. He identifies West's sources, compares West's *Agrippina* with Gavin Hamilton's, and analyzes the changes made in the finished version.

85 Flexner on *Agrippina*. "American School," 65.

85 Allen Staley. 17.

85 Frederick Cummings. Cummings-Staley, 98–99.

85 E. P. Richardson. *Painting*, 88.

86 Robert Rosenblum. *Transformations*, 43.

86 3000-guinea campaign. Galt, II, 13, 20; A. Cunningham, *Lives*, "West," 31.

86 George III. Brooke; *George III, Collector*. One of his drawings, *View of Syon House*, was exhibited at the Queen's Gallery, Buckingham Palace, in 1974–75.

87 King's interest in *Agrippina*. Galt, II, 22–26.

87 Visit by Barnard. Galt, II, 23. This was probably Francis Barnard. See Brooke, 214.

87 Peale on West's departure. Sellers, *Peale* (1969), 63; APS, Peale autobiography typescript, 95.

87 fn Dalton promised preferment. Robert Rutherford, writing to Colonel Shippen, told of "all the favors Mr. Dalton has promised him from the King, or from several English gentlemen who during their stay in Italy seemed to be very fond of his performances." (APS, June 21, 1763.) The article on West in *Public Characters*, however, written in part by Raphael West, says specifically (533) that the king obtained his "first knowledge of Mr. West" with Dr. Drummond's introduction.

88 Buckingham House (also known as the Queen's House). *George III, Collector*. Actually, it was the royal family's London residence.

88 West's visit to the king with *Agrippina*. Galt, II, 24–26; Sellers, Peale (1969), 63–64; Far. Mss., 722.

89 Peale posed for Regulus. Sellers, *Peale* (1969), 64.

90 West, king, and *Regulus*. Ibid., I, 64; Galt, II, 25–26, 33; Dunlap, I, 60.

90 Fifty sketches for *Regulus*. Prown, 255.

PAGE

94–5 West, king, Kirby incident. Galt, II, 38–41; Northcote, *Reynolds*, I, 167. Galt wrote that Kirby died soon thereafter from the shock, but in fact he lived until 1774. He resigned the unhappy post of president of the Society of Artists on June 15, 1770.

94 Royal Academy quarters. The building stood on the site of the present United Services and Royal Aero Club.

96 No needlework, etc. Lamb, 10; V and A "Press Cuttings," I, 113.

96 Admission charge. Preface to catalogue for 1769 exhibition.

96 Reynolds a timid speaker. Northcote, *Reynolds*, I, 178; Hudson, 28–29; Hilles, 33–34.

96 Would keep out troublemakers. Paul Sandby to Sawrey Gilpin, December 13, 1770, in Soane Museum Royal Academy manuscripts. (There is a typed copy in the Royal Academy Scrapbook.)

96–7 Moser appropriated equipment. Hutchison, *History*, 48, *Homes*, 7; Whitley, I, 234–35; *Conduct of the Royal Academicians*; RA, H. C. Morgan, Academy schools manuscript, 15, 16; Leslie-Taylor, I, 305–6.

97 Dalton excluded Strange. Far., VII, 139; Wornum, *Lectures*, 21–23. Francesco Bartolozzi, the King's Engraver and a favorite of Dalton, was admitted as a full foundation member, which added to Strange's anger. Strange, a line engraver, condemned Bartolozzi's "stippling" and "dotting."

97 Dalton sold print-warehouse. Strange, 71–73.

97 Chambers excluded Stuart and Adam. Waterhouse, *Three Decades*, 61, 69; *Age of Neo-Classicism*, 485; A. T. Bolton, 161.

97 Chambers to Swedish authorities, Hudson, 95.

97 Chambers dominated Reynolds. Ibid., 94–95; Whitley, I, 249; Far., III, 31.

97 Chambers told king of Reynolds' hesitation. Far., III, 32.

97 Reynolds excluded Romney, Pine, Benjamin Wilson. Waterhouse, *Three Decades*, 58, 61, 68, 69; Wornum, *Lectures*, 23. For an interesting assessment of Reynolds' character, see Wilenski, 135–42, and Sir Walter Scott's *Journal*, II, 177.

97 Reynolds was promised a knighthood. Whitley, I, 251; Strange, 99.

97 Reynolds charged with duplicity. Whitley, I, 251–52.

97 Reynolds made knighthood a condition. *Georgian Era*, "Reynolds," 70; Strange, 99.

98 Every breast glowed. English *Port Folio*, January 1810, West to Peale, September 19, 1809.

Chapter 9. *A Star Ascendant*   Pages 99–112

99 West to Green. *Journal* of the AAA, IV, No. 1 (January 1964), 11.

99 "Ingenious Mr. Peale." Dunlap, I, 137; C. C. Sellers, *Peale* (1969) 57.

99 Peale in London. C. C. Sellers, *Peale* (1947), I, 74, 84, 85 (1969), 60, 63, 64; APS, Peale autobiography typescript, 34, Peale account book; H. W. Sellers, 264.

100 Kauffmann popularity, relationships with Dance and Reynolds. Hartcup, 38; Far., VII, 65; Hudson, 137–40.

100 Peale refused to remove hat. H. W. Sellers, 264.

100 Peale and Kauffmann. C. C. Sellers, *Peale* (1969) 64.

PAGE
100 Count de Horn. Manners-Williamson, 29–33; *DNB*.
100 Peale lonely and poor. C. C. Sellers, *Peale* (1947), I, 85 (1969), 58; APS, Peale autobiography typescript, 34; Briggs, 71.
101 West gift to Peale. C. C. Sellers, *Peale* (1969), 74.
101 Dynasty of art. Gerdts, 5.
101 Peale's gift of portrait to West. C. C. Sellers, *Peale* (1947), I, 110; APS, Peale to Bordley, May 20, 1771.
101 1769 R.A. exhibition. Hutchison, *History*, 55–56; Whitley, I, 258; Northcote, *Reynolds*, I, 184; *Royal Academy*, Holme, RX.
101 Walpole, "brilliant route." Whitley, I, 258.
101 *Venus and Adonis*. It hangs in the Carnegie Institute's Museum of Art in Pittsburgh.
101 Twenty-one West pictures at Society of Artists. Graves, *Society of Artists*.
101 Four hundred twenty pounds for *Regulus*. Millar, *Pictures*, Text, 131.
102 Garrick and Regulus. Angelo, I, 360.
102 Zuccarelli-Zoffany exchange. Angelo, I, 361. Zoffany, whose work has lately risen in critical esteem, has been cited as the only artist of the period who made more money than West. Reitlinger, I, 499.
102 Entertainment on king's birthday. Northcote, *Reynolds*, I, 186, 188.
102 Reynold's threat to resign. Hutchison, *History*, 51.
102 Country house at Hammersmith. One visiting American family called it "a villa." HSP, Thomas Combe, Jr., to Sally Combe, August 17, 1770.
102 West to Dr. Morris. *PMHB*, XVIII (1894), 220, July 25, 1769.
102 James Dyer. Whitley, I, 281.
102 Mrs. West's reading, poetry, spaniels. HSP, Dr. C. Pears to West, December 28, 1812; Hunt, I, 21. For a sample of the poetry, see pages 296–97 of this biography.
103 Benbridge. Stewart, 13–19; Rutledge, 8–10.
103 West to Hopkinson. NYPL, July 20, 1770.
104 *Death of Wolfe*. Mitchell, "Wolfe" and "History Picture"; Wind, "Revolution," and "Penny"; Webster; Galt, II, 46–51; Addison; Dunlap, I, 64; Clements Library.
104 Romney denied second prize. Mitchell, "Wolfe," 30; Romney, 45–48.
104 Reynolds and the Grand Style. See Appendix II.
105 West's "quotations." Mitchell, "Wolfe," 31; Larkin, *Art and Life*, 63.
105 Whereabouts of Barré, Monckton, etc. Webster, 68–69.
106 fn West's offer to paint anyone for £100. Todd, "Imaginary Indian," 43.
106 King disapproved. Galt, II, 46.
106 West-Drummond-Reynolds episode. Galt, II, 46–50.
108 West to Peale on Wolfe. APS, June 21, 1770. West's six-month illness would explain why he exhibited only two pictures in the 1770 show: *Leonidas and Cleombratus* and the charming rondel portrait of his wife and son.
108 Old Somerset House. Hutchison, *History*, 62, *Homes*, 7–8; Whitley, I, 273–76.

PAGE
108   1771 exhibition. Whitley, I, 281–83; Hutchison, *History*, 57.
108 fn   Affirmation of Galt story. English *Port Folio*, February 11, 1804, "Notes Relative to the Paintings of Mr. West," 46.
109   Pitt and Garrick on *Wolfe*. Whitley, I, 282.
109   Englishmen were ready for *Wolfe*. Charles Mitchell develops this idea in his "Wolfe," 29.
109   Walpole on *Wolfe*. Graves, *R.A. Contributors*, VIII, 212.
109   Grosvenor paid £400. Ibid.
109   King's chagrin. Galt, II, 50.
109   Indian and moccasins. Dunlap, I, 64; Clements Library, unnumbered.
110   Woolett and Boydell. *DNB*; Webster, 67; Mitchell, "History Picture," 921, "Wolfe," 32–33.
110   Treaty "pledged and never broken." J. F. Watson, I, 134.
110   Composition of *Penn's Treaty*. Neumeyer, Mendelowitz, Wright-Tatum. It has been said that West based the composition of the picture on Masaccio's *The Tribute Money* in the Brancacci Chapel in Florence. One can look long and searchingly without seeing any significant resemblance.
110–11   West's collection of Indian garments. Larkin, *Art and Life*, 63. This is the only reference I have seen to such a collection.
111   West's purpose. Brinton, 114–15, West to Darton, February 2, 1805.
111   Walpole on *Penn's Treaty*. Graves, *R.A. Contributors*, VIII, 212.
111   Opie on *Penn's Treaty*. Far., II, 220.
111   Admired for emotional reasons. Drake, 373; Burroughs, *Limners*, 75–76.
111   Widely reproduced. Brinton, 99–100, 128–33.
111   Roger Fry detested. Ellen Starr Brinton (p. 99) quotes Virginia Woolf: "Even in the 19th century almost the only picture to be found in a Quaker household was an engraving of *Penn's Treaty with the Indians* — that detestable picture, as Roger Fry called it later."
111   W. F. Craven and F. B. Tolles quotations. Tolles, 119.
111   Canaday. *Mainstreams*, 240–41, *Lives*, II, 613.
112   Franklin godfather. APS, Franklin to his wife, August 22, 1772.

Chapter 10.   *"The American War"*   Pages 113–126

113   Verplanck to his brother. Dunlap, I, 110.
113   Copley apology to West. Copley, *Letters*, 97–98.
113–14   West to Copley. Ibid., 116, June 16, 1771.
113–14   West to a Bostonian. Ibid., 118–119, 143. He was Shrimpton Hutchinson.
114   A visitor to London. Ibid., 182.
114   West advice to Copley on trip. Ibid., 190–93, 194–97, January 6, 1773.
115   Copley in Boston. Prown, 86, 91–93; Copley, *Letters*, 1773–1774; Amory, 26.
116–17   Copley in London. Amory, 27, 28, 30; Copley, *Letters*, 225–27, 236–37, 239; Prown, 245–46; Whitley, I, 276.
117   Disappointed in old masters. Copley, *Letters*, 340.
117   Painting a composition. Ibid., 226.

118–19 Copley and Carter episode. Dunlap, I, 112–13; Cunningham, *Lives*, "Copley," 167–70; Copley, *Letters*, 227; Amory, 30–31.

118 "I feel half a Frenchman." Copley, *Letters*, 242.

119 Gavin Hamilton. Amory, 41.

119 Decision to stay in England. Ibid., 37, 43.

119 Hamilton: "Better than West." Copley, *Letters*, 340.

120 Copley to wife on the war. Amory, 57–58.

120 Almost 800 miles in sixteen days. Ibid., 64.

120 Regretted loss of casts. Ibid., 54.

120 Greenwood delegated by Society of Artists. Prown, 260.

120 West obtained commissions for Copley. Amory, 13; Dunlap, I, 126.

120 14 Newman Street. Huish, 330; Walford, IV, 466; Wheatley, *London*, II, 594; Far. Mss., 7777; J. T. Smith, *Rainy Day*, 37; Thornbury, *Turner*, I, 39.

121 Copley not a West pupil. Charles Merrill Mount, in his biography of Gilbert Stuart (1964), holds that Copley worked for a time in West's studio as his assistant. I can find no solid evidence of this. (Mount, 56, 57, 64, 337.)

121 West on painting "vacant faces." *Analectic*, VIII, 49.

122 King called him Benjamin. Whitley, II, 44. Whitley quotes the sculptor Peter Turnerelli, who was West's neighbor and protégé.

122 King would spend a half day talking with West. Hunt, I, 23.

122 West sympathetic to American cause. Hunt, I, 101; C. C. Sellers, *Peale* (1969), 113; Trumbull, 69; Einstein, 306.

122 West to Peale on "present commotions." LC, Peale Papers, February 10, 1775.

123 West gave information to king. Galt, II, 71; Einstein, 306; Mount, 80.

123 West to king on war. Far., I, 278–79.

124 Curwen on "these conceited islanders." Curwen, 36, 37, 51, 90, 91.

124 Isaac Hunt. Hunt, I, 17, 18, 21, 23; Leary.

124 Samuel Shoemaker. *PMHB*, II (1878), 35–39.

124 West's house in Windsor. He signed a "running lease" with the Reverend Samuel Sewell and obtained the king's permission to extend a kitchen on royal property adjoining. When he gave up the house in November 1809, he removed the extension. HSP, West to Sewell, November 24, 1809.

125 Illustrations for Duché's sermons. Neill, 71.

126 Cathcart episode. Silliman, 164–65; Einstein, 306–7; Far., I, 279.

Chapter 11. *The American School: 1777–1781* Pages 127–143

127 Stuart on West. J. H. Morgan, *Stuart*, 84.

127 Wharton posed for *La Hogue*. HSP, Wharton to West, December 20, 1809.

127–28 Wharton-West-Stuart meeting. Dunlap, I, 174; Dunlap, *Diary*, 690; J. Stuart, 642.

128 Stuart hoped to study under West. J. Stuart, 642.

128 Stuart in London. Dunlap, I, 170–75; J. Stuart, 642–43; Mount, 42–46, 50; J. H. Morgan, *Stuart*, 87.

128 West's "kindness and attention." J. Stuart, 643.

PAGE

136 fn   Stuart on drawing. J. H. Morgan, *Stuart*, 85.

137   Stuart completed a West portrait. Dunlap, I, 178. Dunlap says the portrait West had been painting was that of the king, which had to be ready for a diplomat to take with him to a new post. West, however, did not paint such portraits; that was the province of Allan Ramsay's studio.

137–41   Trumbull's arrest and confinement. Trumbull, 63–72; Dunlap, I, 352–55; Dunlap, *Diary*, 736; Whitley, II, 109–10; Jaffe, 47–52; Far. Mss., 3502; Sterling Library, Trumbull to father from Amsterdam, July 13, 1781.

139   Major André. It was generally felt that Trumbull's arrest was in retaliation for André's execution as a spy, but no one has found hard evidence to that effect. Dunlap, I, 353.

139 fn   "Just possible that Trumbull was involved." Jaffe, 50.

139–40   West's meeting with king. Trumbull, 69–70; Dunlap, I, 353–54. Trumbull wrote, "Mr. West came to me immediately with this message."

140   West called on Germain and Thompson. Sterling Library, Trumbull to his father, July 13, 1781.

141   £400 bond. Trumbull, 72.

142   Galloway not consulted. Einstein, 373–74.

142   King intended to abdicate. Brooke, 221, 239–40; W. Smith, I, 105.

142   King wished West to accompany him. Far., II, 178. West told William Smith, Loyalist refugee, on July 12, 1784, that the King's decision was made when his son, the Prince of Wales, joined the political opposition.

142   West, king, and acknowledgment of American independence. Far., VII, 191; Prime, 34; Dunlap, I, 69.

142–43   West and Copley in gallery. Einstein, 349.

143   Elkhanah Watson. E. Watson, 176; Amory, 463.

Chapter 12.   *The Peace Commissioners*   Pages 144–160

144   John Adams' recollections. III, 150.

144   Academy paid own way. Hutchison, *Homes*, 12; Lamb, 11.

144   "Monument of taste and elegance." Baretti, 4.

144   Walpole on R.A. opening. XXIX, H.W. to William Mason, May 19, 1780.

144–45   Rooms of the Royal Academy. Hutchison, *Homes*, 8–14; Lamb, 11; Baretti; Whitley, I, 348–49; "Somerset House: The Fine Rooms," a 20-page mimeographed pamphlet distributed at Somerset House at an exhibition in the autumn of 1977; Lipman.

145   "On the line." Whitley, *Stuart*, 47; G. D. Leslie, 75. The "line" was a horizontal ledge eight feet from the floor. Favored pictures were hung with the tops of their frames touching the line.

145   Downman, "my beloved teacher." Whitley, II, 67–68; Hardie, I, 144; Hutchison, *History*, 67. There is a Downman portrait of West at the National Portrait Gallery, London.

145 fn.   Downman's high prices. Far., II, 258n; Whitley, II, 213.

145   Gainsborough and Hanging Committee. Hutchison, *History*, 67–68. His demand was that his group portrait, *The Three Elder Princesses*,

be placed three feet below the line. His two letters are in the R.A. scrapbook.

146   "Picture mania." Whitley, II, 71.

146   Northcote: "patron of the arts." Northcote, Reynolds, I, 182.

146   King ignored son's portrait. Whitley, II, 80.

146   Reynolds' pictures deteriorated. Hudson, 248; Tinker, 18; Far., III, 297, V, 183. In 1805, West served on a committee of seven to consider the restoration and repair of the two major pictures by Reynolds owned by the Society of Dilettanti. Watkin, Hope, 15.

146   Reynolds and lady's hands. Northcote, Reynolds, II, 267.

146   Reynolds, Gainsborough, and Wilson. Constable, Wilson, 52. There are several variants on this story.

146   Wilson and the Falls of Terni. Rutter, 19.

147   Wilson: "Do they draw?" Far., V, 278; Constable, Wilson, 55.

147   Wilson would not distress the king. Constable, Wilson, 49–50. There are three versions of this story. Wilson held, despite all his poverty and misfortune, that posterity would value him as one of the great and original masters of his time. West was one who was inclined to agree. He owned Wilson's Convent on the Rock, which he said was "colored equal to Cuyp . . . and in parts like Titian," and he praised his attempts to achieve atmospheric effects before such attempts were commonly recognized or admired. "No man's pictures," West said, "were more finished . . . He made all his points to bear upon each other with great judgment." Far. Mss., 649, 1435.

147   Nollekens. J. T. Smith, I, 361, 397.

147   Stuart's portrait of West. Whitley, Stuart, 27; Dunlap, I, 180.

147   "You must steal his eyes." Mount, 69.

148   Walpole: "Very good." Mount, 72.

148   Stuart: "fame by a single picture." Whitley, Stuart, 31.

148   West advised to set out on own. Dunlap, I, 182.

148   Stuart and N. Dance. Dunlap, I, 180; Whitley, Stuart, 41.

148   Mrs. Hoppner on Stuart. Dunlap, I, 191.

148   Chronicle on West and Stuart. Whitley, Stuart, 30.

148   Stuart painted Lord Grantham. Mount, 76.

148   Mather Brown. J. H. Morgan, Stuart, 6–8; Whitley, Stuart, 18; Flexner, Stuart, 29; Gardner-Feld, 108–9; Coburn, 252–54.

149   Trumbull's return. Dunlap, I, 356; Trumbull, 83, 84.

150   Peale to West on state of arts. APS, April 9, 1783.

150   West to Peale, congratulations. AAA, June 15, 1783.

150   West's second letter to Peale. Hart, "Family," 11–12, August 4, 1783.

150–51   Peale to West on uniforms. APS, August 25, 1783.

151   Peale to West suggesting subjects. APS, December 10, 1783.

151   The Peace Commissioners. J. Adams, III, x–xi. See also Arthur S. Marks.

151   Adams and Jay posed in London. Marks, 24, 25.

151   Adams-Jay visit to Queen's Palace. J. Adams, III, 150. Young John Quincy and William Bingham, Philadelphia merchant, were with the group. AAA, West to John Adams, November 6, 1783.

152   Copley-Adams-Mansfield incident. J. Adams, III, 150.

152   Painted Laurens. Marks, 25.

152   Franklin to West, query on visiting London. American Book Col-

lector, September 1971, report on a sale of rare books and autographs held at the Swann Galleries, New York. The Franklin letter, No. 3118, brought $2100.

152 Whitefoord brought letter and bust. APS, West to Franklin, April 28, 1782. Marks (p. 28) believes the bust was a plaster cast of Jean Jacques Caffieri's terra cotta bust of Franklin of 1777. See also APS, Whitefoord to W. T. Franklin, June 30, 1784.

152 Joseph Wright. Hart, "Portrait of Dr. Franklin," 322, 328–33. West's letter to Pierre as he wrote it in French appears in *PMHB*, XXXII (1908), 17.

152 Temple Franklin. At the "great desire" of William Franklin, his Loyalist father, Temple also sat to Stuart, who, he wrote to his grandfather in Paris, "is esteemed by West and everybody, the first portrait painter now living; he is moreover an American . . . He is astonishing for likenesses. . . . I heard West say — 'that he *nails* the face to the canvas.' By which he meant I believe to express not only that the resemblance of the person was perfect — but that his colouring did not change; a fault common to some of the first painters in this country — and particularly to Sir Joshua." APS, November 9, 1784.

153 West's call on J. Q. Adams. J. Adams, III, xi.

153 West abandoned American Revolution project. He painted one other picture on the subject: *Reception of American Loyalists by Great Britain in 1783*. The picture is known only in Henry Moses' album of engravings of West's pictures in outline. Hart, "Family," 12.

153 Trumbull copied *La Hogue*. Trumbull, 87; Sizer, *Works*, 94.

154 Trumbull's call on Reynolds. Trumbull, 86–87.

154 Trumbull's *Warren* and *Montgomery* painted in West's studio. Ibid., 89.

154 West's advice to Trumbull. Ibid., 88–91.

155 Antonio di Poggi. Ibid., 91.

155 West's dinner party. Mrs. West's Account Book, Friends Library, Swarthmore College, February 16, 1785.

155 Copley, *Death of Chatham*. Prown, 276–80, 283, 286; Whitley, I, 355–58; A. Cunningham, *Lives*, "Copley," 172–73.

156 Chambers to Copley, "raree show." Whitley, I, 357.

156 Twenty thousand paid to see Copley's picture. Whitley, I, 357, III, 169; Prown, 284.

156 West gave up *Death of Chatham*, Whitley, I, 355–56; Prown, 280–81. Whitley says West was working on the picture with the king's approval.

156–67 *Three Youngest Daughters*. Dunlap, I, 126; Prown, 31, 315–16. Martha Amory, Copley's granddaughter, wrote, "He was indebted for the commission to West, who, on being consulted by George III as to a good artist for his children's portraits, warmly recommended Copley." Amory, 13.

157 Copley won *Siege of Gibraltar*. Prown, 311–12.

157 Proposed St. Paul's project. Whitley, I, 293; Meyer, "Chapel," 247; Galt, II, 14; W. B. Taylor, II, 176–77; Northcote, *Reynolds*, I, 305–6, 308–9.

158–60 West, King, and Chapel of Revealed Religion. "Anecdotes of Artists," 27; Northcote (Ward), 154–55; Galt, II, 52–56; Dunlap, I, 65; Meyer, "Chapel," W. Smith, I, 21; Dillenberger.

Chapter 13.   *Life at 14 Newman Street*   Pages 161–178

161   Reynolds, two painters cannot be friends. Northcote, *Reynolds*, II, 238.
162–64   Dunlap's career. Dunlap, I, 243–311.
161   Dunlap calls on West. Ibid., 255–56.
164   Dunlap ordered to go home. Canary, 19.
164–65   Raphael West. Dunlap, I, 258, II, 146–47; Papendiek, I, 278–79; Whitley, *Stuart*, 27; Gardner-Feld, 30; Far. Mss., 256.
165   Small, elegant garden. Hunt, I, 100.
165   House cost £1600 a year. West's account book at HSP shows total expenditures of £5174 from July 1810 to June 1812, with frequent withdrawals of sizable amounts marked "to yourself" in West's handwriting.
165   Stuart on West's establishment. Dunlap, I, 66.
165 fn   West gave room to abolitionists. Dunlap, I, 57.
166   Leigh Hunt at Newman Street. Hunt, I, 100–103.
166–67   Dunlap and West's instruction. Dunlap, *Diary*, 542–43.
166–67   Smith on West. J. T. Smith, *Nollekens*, II, 369. Smith, keeper of prints at the British Museum, considered West "the founder of historical engraving in England." Ibid., 377.
167   Northcote on West as teacher. Northcote (Ward), 153–54.
167   Mather Brown. Whitley, II, 98–100; Malone, 62; Page Smith, 643, 671, plate 17.
168   Stuart at zenith. Herbert, 237–38; Whitley, *Stuart*, 64; Dunlap, I, 93; Flexner, *Distant Skies*, 60; J. Stuart, 644–45.
168   Stuart stole West portrait. Dunlap, I, 194.
168   If Stuart had stayed. Whitley, II, 96.
168   West to Ambassador Jackson on Stuart. Dunlap, I, 212. That Stuart felt himself to be on good terms with West after leaving Britain is indicated by his act in asking a very considerable favor of West in 1796. See Alberts, 290–93, 512.
171   Elizabeth West grew American corn. Rodenbough, 257; Stowe, 25.
172 fn.   Copley: "a bed of tulips." Pasquin, *Memoirs of Academicians*, 137.
172–78   Hoppner-West affair. Whitley, II, 39–52; A. Cunningham, "Hoppner," *Lives*; McKay-Roberts; *DNB*; C. C. Sellers, *Wright*, 132–33, 149–50, 174; Dunlap, I, 135.
173   Hoppner on West's pictures. *Morning Post*, May 2, 9, 11, 1785.
173   *Post* critic on Hoppner's pictures. *Morning Post*, May 9, 1785.
173   "Mr. Hoppner deserves our thanks." R.A. Scrapbook, SB/67a; Whitley, II, 39.
174   Hoppner to West. R.A. Scrapbook, SB/67a; Whitley, II, 39–42.
174   Hoppner's childhood and parentage. C. C. Sellers, *Wright*, 133, 258; Papendiek, I, 232; BM, Cromarty Mss., 240; Pasquin, *Memoirs*, 91; McKay-Roberts, xv. Hoppner's son, Belgrave Hoppner, denied emphatically that his father was George III's natural son, declaring that

PAGE

his father had been born one month after his parents arrived in England. (Cromarty, 249.)

174 fn King did not recognize Hoppner. Far., I, 104.

175 Patience Wright's house. Pasquin, *Memoirs*, 92.

175 West introduced Mrs. Wright to king, shared sittings. C. C. Sellers, *Wright*, 51, 57.

175 Hoppner lost favor. Papendiek, I, 232; Sellers, *Wright*, 149–50; BM, Cromarty Mss., 247, 256, 269.

175 Mrs. Hoppner's lawsuit. McKay-Roberts, xiv.

175–77 Hoppner's charges against West. *Morning Post*, July 2 and 4, 1785. Belgrave told his father's biographer in 1869 what he had heard: "At a very early age [Hoppner was 24], in consequence of his marriage without King George the Third's consent, to my mother, and at the instigation of Mr. West, he was turned out into the streets with a half crown in his pockets; West's hostility to him being thought the more iniquitous because he pretended to be the friend of my grandmother [Patience Wright], an American like himself, and the reason he assigned for it being that the younger Hoppner was an idle fellow who would never do anything while the King supported him, and until he was forced by necessity to exert himself." (Whitley, II, 42–43.) Mrs. Papendiek wrote, "Mr. West, the friend of no one who might possibly interfere with his success, pronounced Hoppner as the possessor of a talent too inferior for Royal notice, and he left Windsor with blighted hopes. (Papendiek, I, 232.)

177 Hoppner's ill health. Far., I, 84; McKay-Roberts, xxix.

177 Hoppner "the most spiteful person." S. Rogers, *Table Talk*, 208.

177 Peters-Hoppner exchange. Whitley, II, 44–46.

178 Academicians observed Copley's opposition. Farington wrote on April 18, 1804 (Mss., 2624): "Loutherbourg told me he saw Copley's disposition 20 years ago, at the General Meeting, by his manner to West. He had no doubts of counteracting him."

Chapter 14. *The Painter's Eye* Pages 179–193

179 Fanny Burney and the queen's jewels. Burney (1892), II, 35.

179 King on Octavius. Brooke, 266.

179 Robert Strange. Far., I, 276; Whitley, I, 307–10; Millar, *Pictures*, Text, 130. West had introduced Strange to the king, despite the fact that Strange had long been under a cloud as an active Jacobite.

180–81 West and knighthood. Far., I, 276; Galt, I, 2, II, 189–90; Dunlap, I, 73. Joan, the daughter of Roger, Lord de la Warre, married Sir Thomas, Baron West (whose father had also fought at Crecy). Their son Reginald became the 6th Baron de la Warre.

181 Miss Burney on West. Burney (1842), I, 498, II, 531.

181 Standing in the Queen's presence. Queen Charlotte forbade her sons to sit in her presence, and she kept Sarah Siddons standing during a long reading until she became faint. The prince regent caused surprised comment in 1816 when he told Thomas Lawrence to sit in his presence during a conversation. Far., VIII, 83.

181 Ramberg. West, "True Taste"; HSP, letter to West from Windsor, no date.

181 fn　Queen tired of jewels. *George III, Collector*, 11, 12.

182　West observation on court. Northcote (Hazlitt), 242, 292; Dunlap, I, 69.

182　Painted Windsor Park. Kraemer, xi, introduction by Charles Rys-kamp. Contemporary critics spoke favorably of West's few land-scapes. George Robins' 1829 auction catalogue quoted Gains-borough, "West understands the very anatomy of forest trees."

183　King noted changes made in pictures. Angelo, I, 198–99.

183　King liked gossip. Brooke, 297–98.

184　Houghton Hall appraisal. Reitlinger, I, 21–25; Walpole, XXIV, 441.

184　Pleasure designing new chapel. Galt, II, 56.

184　West in Paris. J. Q. Adams, *Memoirs*, I, 16, 19. "Mr. West" is no-where in J. Q. Adams' diary identified as *Benjamin* West, though C. F. Adams, editor of the *Memoirs*, so listed him in the index in volume 12. In kind response to my query in 1977, Celeste Walker of the Adams Papers staff informed me that an unpublished entry in John Quincy's diary (March 14, 1785) reads, ". . . Mr. West of Phila-delphia arrived from London." Three other unpublished entries (April 15, 16, 18, 1785) refer to Mr. West's right hand, "afflicted with an inflammatory rheumatism." On November 4, 1816, Farington wrote that a caller on Benjamin West found him painting with his left hand, his right being "wrapped up with the gout." In November 1795 in London, John Quincy again met "Mr. West of Philadelphia." The evidence indicates that the "Mr. West" in Paris in 1785 and in London in 1795 was Benjamin West the painter.

185　West's Titian. W. Smith, II, 4, 5; Whitley, II, 31–33; Page Smith, 643, Miss Abigail Adams to John Quincy Adams, September 24, 1785; BM, Whitley Papers, 1670–73, 1693.

185　Greenwich Chapel competition. Prown, 319; Whitley, II, 48; BM, Whitley Papers, 1674, BM, Anderdon catalogues, 1786, p. 84. Ad-miral Sir Hugh Palliser, governor of Greenwich Hospital, was West's close friend and fishing companion. BM, Whitley Papers, 1688.

185–6　Copley's trouble with Gibraltar. Prown, 322–336.

186　Desenfans suit. Whitley, II, 87–88; Whitley, *Gainsborough*, 276–81.

186–7　The painter's eye. Northcote (Hazlitt), 292; Whitley, *Gainsbor-ough*, 276.

187　Gainsborough funeral. Whitley, *Gainsborough*, 308–9. Miss Mar-garet Gainsborough presented the Academy with one of her father's romantic landscapes, and the Academy gave her a two-handled sil-ver cup, designed by West, in thanks. Gainsborough's last lineal descendant presented the cup to the Academy in the 1960s. *Country Life*, March 4, 1965, with picture of the cup.

187–8　West and Reynolds offered counsel. Whitley, *Gainsborough*, 314–15; Reitlinger, I, 76.

188　West and the king's "madness." Whitley, II, 73. That this intimate detail of the king's illness appeared in a newspaper, presumably re-vealed directly or indirectly by West, certainly harmed him at court and with the royal family.

188　No earlier indication of mental trouble. See Brooke, 337–38, and Macalpine-Hunter on the rumored illness in 1765.

188–90 King's illness. Brooke, Chapter 8; Macalpine-Hunter; Papendiek, II, 6, 12, 68.
189 West several times with king. Far., II, 170–71.
189 King's payments stopped. Hart, "Family," 20, West to William West, February 14, 1789.
189 West supporting half brother's family. Ibid., 3, 20–25, West to William West, February 14, 1789, February 13, 1793, and September 18, 1796; Beinecke Library, West to Henry Finck, March 16, 1797. Thomas West was gravely ill and his two daughters were destitute several years before he died on December 25, 1792. West's father had died in October 1776.
190 Reynolds denied space to others. Whitley, II, 102, 140.
190 Reynolds dictating from "golden chair." Hilles, Literary Career, 266.
190 fn Theory that king chose West because of unsound mind. See Thornbury, British Artists, II, 128; Barker, Critical Introduction, 25.
191 Quarrel over professor of perspective. Gwynn, 211–18; Whitley, II, 125–27; Hudson, 215–21; Northcote, Reynolds, II, 251–60; Hilles, 174–77, 259–76. Reynolds' candidate was Joseph Bonomi. Henry Fuseli received the appointment.
191 West, king, and Tyler. Hudson, 216; Far., II, 179.
191 Reynolds and Chambers. Northcote, Reynolds, 251–54; Hudson, 217, 221; Hilles, 174–76; Hodgson-Eaton, 43; RA, Assembly minutes, I, July 2, 1791, p. 264.
192 Floor beam cracked. Hilles, 182; Northcote, Reynolds, II, 262–63; Hudson, 222. Reynolds ignored the tremor in the floor and the meeting continued in situ.
192 Reynolds named West his deputy. Northcote, Reynolds, II, 285.
191 West behaved well in crisis. European Magazine, September, 1794, p. 166.
191 West thought Reynolds wrong but ill-treated. Far. Mss., 1450.
192 Reynolds' funeral. Whitley, II, 155–56; Hudson, 228–29; Hodgson-Eaton, 168–69; Far., I, 143; RA, Assembly minutes, I, March 3, 1792.
192–93 Reynolds' pictures. Reitlinger, I, 9.
193 Copley sought presidency. Prown, 337.
193 West elected 29 to 1. Richard Cosway received the single vote.

Chapter 15. Benjamin West, P.R.A. Pages 194–209

194 West would wear hat. Whitley, II, 161–62. The gesture was not unknown. Sir Joseph Banks, president since 1778 of the Royal Society of London for Improvement of Natural Knowledge (which also had quarters in Somerset House) had been wearing his hat at assembly meetings.
194 West's inaugural address. In his emphasis on the benefits of British art to British manufactures, West was playing to a favorite conviction of the king. See Wainwright, 113. His speech to the Academicians and his first discourse to the students were published together in 1793 by Thomas Cadell, printer to the Royal Academy, price five shillings. Students who won gold medals for their performances

were presented with specially bound copies of Reynolds' and West's discourses.

194 Ordered gowns for porters. Lamb, 25.

195 Boswell speech. Whitley, II, 174–75.

196 Exhibition receipts. Hodgson-Eaton, 170.

196 King at exhibition. Whitley, II, 79–80; Angelo, I, 356.

196 Boswell's songs. Whitley, II, 175–76.

197 Academy statistics. Lamb, 24; Hodgson-Eaton, 170; Hutchison, *History*, 74.

197 Traveling fellowships for students. They were discontinued during the years 1794–1818.

197 Mrs. Hogarth a beneficiary. Sandby, I, 262.

197 "A permanent monument." Hodgson-Eaton, 171.

198 West's bifocal glasses. He had hyperopia and presbyopia and wore "divided glasses" when he painted, having started to do so in the 1790s. They were made for him by Samuel Pierce, who described them as 30 inches focus (+1.33 diopters) in the upper half and 12 inches (+3.33 diopters) in the lower, representing a +2.0 diopters bifocal addition. Levene, 141–156.

198 Lady Inchiquin complained. Far. Mss., 1019.

198 Women embarrassed. Whitley, I, 348–49; Prown, 276; Silliman, 206. A vast amount of time was spent in Council meetings discussing how to place the enormous Farnese Hercules in such a way that it would cause the least offense. The Pennsylvania Academy introduced separate attendance of the sexes at its antique statue gallery. Miller, 106.

198 Lawrence petitioned. Far., I, 44.

198 Students threw bread. Ibid., 129–30.

199 Reynolds and the High Style. "To judge by the pictures which Reynolds chose to exhibit at the first Royal Academy Exhibition, he must have been obsessed at this moment — almost to the point of near lunacy — with trying to impose his own notions of grandeur upon the rising national school." Waterhouse, *Three Decades*, 71.

199 "Virtue indispensable." "He [Fuseli] sputters with contempt whenever he encounters the current assumptions of the age, that the man of genius is by nature necessarily virtuous, or that there is any need for him, *qua* artist, to be so." E. C. Mason, 188.

199 Twenty-fifth anniversary dinner. Far., I, 17, 22, 23, 27, 29, 31, 32, Mss., 88, 92B.

199 Anniversary medal. Far., I, 60; Hutchison, *History*, 75.

200 Lady Inchiquin complained. Far., I, 42.

200 Hoppner defeated. Ibid., 40.

200 Opie's appearance, pronunciation of name. Smith, *Nollekens*, II, 286, 289; Far. Mss., 1446, 2358.

200–203 Contentions among Academy members. Fuseli and Lawrence: Whitley, II, 177. Northcote and Hoppner: Far., I, 41. Nollekens angry about busts: Far. Mss., 157. Yenn and Soane: Far., I, 79. Opie on Beechey: Ibid., 85. Northcote and Hanging Committee: Far. Mss., 336. Copley on architects: Ibid., 412. Barry versus Dance and Tyler: Far., I, 107, Mss., 409. Council versus Chambers: Far. Mss., 499.

Richards versus Copley: Ibid. Hoppner versus Lawrence: Far., I, 142. Beechey demands pictures back: Far. Mss., 581. Hoppner and Fuseli: Ibid., 591–92. Northcote alarmed: Ibid., 585. Yenn's verses on Soane: Ibid., 648. Hoppner versus Flaxman: Far., I, 184. Fuseli versus Barry: Far. Mss., 918. Beechey versus Humphry: Ibid., 942. Yenn versus Farington: Ibid., 930–31. Beechey resigned: Whitley, II, 207. Fuseli and Col. Smith: Far. Mss., 1171. Garvey on Richards: Ibid., 1274. Barry on Cosway: Ibid., 1280. Northcote excluded from office: Ibid., 1454. Hoppner threatened to withdraw: Far., I, 267.

202   Sandby: "Friends and brothers in art." Sandby, I, 253. Paul Sandby's nephew William, who wrote the first history of the Royal Academy (1862), was generous in his praise of West. For examples: He had "a quiet and gentle temper, extreme courtesy and forebearance, and a natural dignity of manner"; and, "His perfect command of temper, his uniform courtesy of manner, and above all, his real kindness of heart . . ." (I, 249, 285.)

203   Farington quarrel with West. Far. Mss., 164–67.

203   Farington biography. Far., I, v–x, Mss., Reel VII, 36–37; Roe; Rutter; Hardie, I, 182–88.

204   Barry and Northcote on Farington. Far., I, 147; Northcote (Ward), 165; Hardie, I, 184–85.

204   Farington's height. Far. Mss., Reel VII, addenda, 117. He was 5 feet, 11 3/4 inches tall.

204   West: "Charges not founded." HSP, May 21 (?25), 1794, West to Farington.

204 fn   Farington began diary. Far., I, 1.

205   Farington avoided West. Far. Mss., 171, 173, 325.

205–209   Bromley affair. Far., I, 26, 42–43, 99, Mss., 68, 134–36, 140–42, 153, 163–65, 177, 222, 252, 1450; Knowles, I, 182–86; Prown, 338; BM, Whitley Papers, 1677; Bromley, I, 56–63, II, iii–xlii; Pasquin, Liberal Critique, 30; F. C. Mason, 278–79; Sandby, I, 252; RA Assembly minutes, I, 309–28.

205   Bromley on Fuseli as libertine. Knowles, I, 182–84.

205   Bromley praised West. Bromley, I, 56–63.

205   Fuseli on Bromley's book. E. C. Mason, 278–79.

206   Copley on Bromley, "treason against the arts." Bromley, II, xxviii.

206   Copley's motion on Bromley's book. Pasquin, Liberal Critique, 30.

206   Members should read it first. Ibid.

206   West: King owned book. Ibid.; Far. Mss., 103.

206–207   Bromley on Fuseli and Copley. Bromley, II, iii–xvii, xxviii–xli.

207   Copley: Information came from West. Far. Mss., 222. Copley threatened to resign from the Academy if Bromley's book was not removed from the library. (Ibid., 105.)

207   Copley defeated. Far. Mss., 129; Pasquin, Liberal Critique, 30.

207   February 20 meeting. Far. Mss., 134–36.

207   Resolution approving Fuseli. Knowles, I, 186.

208   Farington on Bromley's letters. Far. Mss., 140, 153.

208   Bromley praise of West. Bromley, II, xxxii.

208   Farington and Bourgeois warned West. Far. Mss., 59, 165.

208 fn   Farington-West quarrel. Ibid., 165.

209   "A little burst of genius." Gwynn, 242.

PAGE

of Somniator," an allegory published in the *Annals of Fine Arts*, 1818. West as Nestor, is addressing a deputation from the French Academy, which has come to try to discover the principles on which the Greeks executed their figures:

> "Phidias, you see, Sir, studied nater, on the — on the principles I painted my great picters — yes, Sir, I painted my great picters — of Christ Rejected, and Christ Healing the Sick. Yes Sir Phidias and I, Sir, you see Sir, looked at nater Sir, with the same eye you see gentlemen. There is but two eras of art in the world, gentlemen, you see, Sir — Phidias was one of 'em — gentlemen — you see Sir, and — and, and I — I — this here — here age, as you see this here era, that is, you see *my* era, is gentlemen another — you see Sir, and now gentlemen, you see Sir — I would advise 'ee when you draw 'em, that is, gentlemen, you see, the Elgin Marbles, that is, you see, the works of Phidias — not to make accurate finished drawings, as H-yd-n did, from 'em, that all their hidden excellence might be investigated; but to make compositions from 'em, as I did, without studying their hidden excellence at all, you see, Sir."
>
> Sir Th-m-s L-wr-nce rose, and said, "Exactly so!"

218 Farington: No notice was taken. Far. Mss., 258–59.
218 Yenn on "Hack, Hack." Far., I, 83.
219 King maligned. *Annual Register*, 1820, 703.
219 Critical insults. Her Majesty's nose, Lord Spencer disgusting: Whitley, II, 131, 215. Mr. Knight repulsive, "meretricious performance": Pasquin, *Liberal Critique*, 28, 29. On Westall: Sandby, I, 254. On Barry: Irwin, *Neoclassical Art*, 41.
219 fn Yenn caught in a lie. See page 311 of this biography.
220 John Williams ("Pasquin"), lounging pickpocket. Whitley, II, 214.
220 Pasquin attack on Cosway. R. and S. Redgrave (1886 ed.), 540–41.
220 Attack on Copley. Prown, 339.
220 No dependence on hereditary power. Pasquin, *Liberal Critique*, 11.
220 Wolcott-"Pindar" on West's knighthood. Pindar, II, 538. Williams-"Pasquin" was charged with blackmailing and terrorizing actors through his dramatic criticism, and he fled to the United States to avoid paying the damage claim against him. West, in a singular act of forgiveness, gave him advice on where to settle.
221 Boydell's Shakespeare Gallery. West was one of seven persons who met at Boydell's in 1786 and conceived the idea of commissioning the paintings for and publishing an illustrated edition of Shakespeare's works. The gallery opened in 1789 with 34 pictures by 18 leading artists. Far., I, 236.
222–23 Kosciuszko. Far., I, 209–10; Cummings-Staley, 103.
222–23 Romanticism. E. P. Richardson, quoting Washington Allston, wrote in 1948: "Romanticism reopened the mind to the voices of our consciousness from beyond the range of reason, to 'those intuitive powers which are above and beyond both the senses and the understanding.'" E. P. Richardson, *Allston*, 49.
222 fn Kosciuszko gave West picture to Jefferson. Constable, *Collecting*, 12.
222–23 *Death on the Pale Horse*. Carey; Kimball; Kimball-Marceau, 11; American *Port Folio*, No. 6, 1811, p. 455, et seq. Robert Rosenblum holds that West was influenced by John Hamilton Mortimer's drawing, *Death on a Pale Horse*, exhibited at the Society of Artists show

in 1775. (*Art Bulletin*, March, 1960, p. 78.) West's 1783 drawing is at the Royal Academy. The first oil sketch of 1787 and the third oil sketch of 1802 are at the Philadelphia Museum of Art; the second, dated 1796, is in Lord Egremont's collection at Petworth House, Sussex. The very large finished picture is at the Pennsylvania Academy of the Fine Arts.

223　Kimball. Kimball-Marceau, 11.

223 fn　Delacroix on West. Trapp, 55, 88, 109.

224　Northcote mortified. Far. Mss., 589; Graves, *R.A. Contributors*, V, 386.

Chapter 17.　*The Venetian Secret*　　Pages 225–239

225　Blake: "What has reasoning to do?" Erdman, *Blake Poetry and Prose*, 636.

225–32　The Venetian Secret. The only important source of information on the story of the Provises and their color discovery is Farington's diary, 53 unpublished manuscript pages of which (between 859 and 1052) contain indexed references in 1797 to the Provises and their process. Despite some hundreds of words on the process itself (including a copy of the formula in the Royal Academy Library, about half of it in Farington's hand), there is unfortunately no clear explanation of what the painter was supposed to do, or why, or with what results. West said that the successful use of the process required mastery of two points that had puzzled him and all other imitators of Venetian coloring: they were the ground on which the painting was to be made, and "the dark color, ground tint, for which asphaltum, etc., are substitutes." Use of the process, he said, required new disciplines that not every artist could practice. If adopted, the process would do away with the palette, replacing it with pots of color.

A feature of the Provis method was the use of Antwerp blue. Whitley points out that Antwerp blue is a preparation of Prussian blue, and that Prussian blue was not invented until 1710, some 135 years after Titian's death. See Whitley, II, 211, and John Gage, "Magilphs and Mysteries," in *Apollo*, July 1964, pp. 38–41, which has on its cover a caricature of the affair by James Gillray.

229 fn　West's praise of Blake. Erdman, *Blake: Prophet*, 403; Far., I, 141.

232　Bourgeois' advice to Tresham. Far. Mss., 1770.

233　West and Farington drew together. Far. Mss., 554–55, 581, 586, 1195, 1844, 1985.

233　Members attacked Farington. Yenn and Beechey were strongest in their opposition. Beechey described him as "Warwick the King Maker." Far., I, 147, Mss., 930–32, 943–44, 971, 1731, 1735. A critic wrote on May 8, 1792, "Though Mr. Farington has more authority in the Academy than any other member, and from majesty of appearance and haughtiness of behaviour can terrify his puny competitors into *violent* obedience, we speak our opinions." Far., I, vi.

233　West good and interesting company. See, for example, Far., I, 225, 276, 278–9, II, 103–4, 242, IV, 240, Mss., 1489.

233 Governor of Foundling Hospital. It is now the Thomas Coram Foundation for Children.

233 Dr. Hays' "electric fire." Far. Miss., 1559, 1568.

233 West pioneer in lithography. *EB*, 14th ed., "Lithography"; Kraemer, 35.

233 Negotiations on war taxes. Far. Mss., 1181, 1187.

233 Chambers' obscure records. Far., I, 106; *La Belle Assemblée*, 151.

234 "Indecent behaviour of students." Far. Mss., 1576.

234 Monuments in St. Paul's. HSP, Vansittart to West, Dec. 12, 1801, Wyatt to West, April 20, 1798.

234 West and Orleans collection. Far. Mss., 1411, 1428, 1447.

234 Academy pension plan. Far. Mss., 628, 693, 698, 738, 793, 1116.

235 Barry and Copley opposed pensions. Far. Mss., 820–21, 872, 1087, 1662; Barry, II, 501.

235 Farington: Changing presidents would bring trouble. Far. Mss., 2115–16.

235 Barry reproached Burke. Barry, I, 230–31.

235 Reynolds hated Barry. Far. Mss., 1518; Whitley, I, 292–93.

235 Miss Cockings on Barry. Whitley, I, 375; information obtained from D. G. C. Allen, curator, Royal Society of Arts, in October 1977.

236 fn Adelphi paintings "finest achievement." *British Artists in Rome*, "Barry," unpaginated.

236 Barry's "brutal behaviour" to West. Far. Mss., 1269, 1411, 1428, 1447, 1465–66, 1479.

236 "Mercenary cabal." Wornum, *Lectures*, 44.

236 Meeting at Wilton's. Far. Mss., 1475.

236–37 Wilton's letter of complaint against Barry. It is printed in full in Hutchison, *History*, 78–9. See RA, Council minutes, III, 15–17, Assembly Minutes, II, 46–47, 55–58.

237 Council meeting, March 16, 1799. Far. Mss., 1488, 1517.

237 Assembly meeting, March 19, 1799. Ibid., 1493–95. The first page of West's prefatory remarks in his own hand is at HSP. Barry's defense is given in full in Barry, II, 626–41.

237 "They mean to immortalize me." Far. Mss., 1519.

237 Barry would republish West's discourse. Ibid., 1545.

237 Bourgeois on Barry's "democratical opinions." Ibid., 1498.

237 Opie and Northcote defended Barry. Ibid., 1482.

237 "West's conduct does him high honour." Ibid., 1483.

237–38 Expulsion meeting, April 15, 1799. Whitley, II, 228–29.

238 West to see king. Far. Mss., 1526, 1530–32, 1534.

239 Farington wrote expulsion letter. Ibid., 1532, 1538.

239 West defended Fuseli. Ibid., 1586.

239 Royal Society award to Barry. Whitley, II, 229.

239 "Where scum and offal direct." Far. Mss., 1540.

239 No Academician went to the funeral, Haydon and Wilkie present. J. T. Smith, *Nollekens*, I, 349; Olney, 34. West was prescient enough to see David Wilkie's promise from the first. "Never in my life," he said, "have I met with a young artist like Wilkie. He may be young in years, but he is old in the expression of his art. He is already a great artist . . . I consider him an honour to his country." In 1810 he negotiated with the prince regent to commission Wilkie to paint one

of his genre scenes, Wilkie to name the subject, the price, and the time required. The result, *Blind-Man's-Buff*, so pleased the prince that he commissioned a sequel to it, *The Penny Wedding*. Millar, *Pictures*, Text, xxxvii, 137–38; Gower, *Wilkie*, 28; Wainwright, 110.

239   Barry's pictures lost. Irwin, *Neo-Classical Art*, 40, 41.

Chapter 18.   *The Broken Laws*   Pages 240–257

240   Rumor of West's financial troubles. Far., I, 225–26, Mss., 1173–74.

241   Asked £2000 of the king. Aspinall, *George III*, II, letter 1575, undated, letter 1589, July 26, 1797. The huge 1797 ledger in the Coutts and Company archives in London shows that West at this time owed £100 on a note and £2000 on a bond. It also shows that Raphael West from time to time borrowed £10 or £25 on his father's account.

241   West educating niece. Beinecke Library, West to Henry Fincke, March 16, 1797; HSP, West to "Dear Madame," June 25, 1799.

241   Cheated by Clarkson. HSP, West to William West, February 13, 1793.

241   Raphael's army commission. Far. Mss., 383–84; LC, West to the Earl of Pembroke, January 13, 1796.

241   Maria Siltso, mortification of Wests. Far. Mss., 1361.

242   West's accommodations of £500. Ibid., 1741.

243   Trumbull, West, and French old masters. Far., I, 163, 192, Mss. 1482; Trumbull, 188–91, 294–95.

243   Trumbull and brandy. Trumbull, 190–91.

243   Offer of secretary's post. Jefferson, XV, 144, Jefferson to Trumbull, May 21, 1789; Trumbull, 157.

243   West, Trumbull, and American land. Far., I, 251, Mss., 1173–74, 1188, 1895, 1229, 1246, 1361–62, 1483; Trumbull, 86, 306–8; HSP, West to Enoch Edwards, July 27, 1794; West to Henry Drinker, April 1, 1796, August 27, 1796; West to [?], September 29, 1808; Raphael West to [?], February 23, 1825; undated statement of West's heirs.

243   Beckford signed agreement to buy. Far. Mss., 1361.

243   "A monstrous price." Far., I, 251.

243–44   Raphael West in America. Far., II, 113, Mss., 1226, 1616; Kraemer, 97; Dunlap, II, 144–48.

244   Beckford canceled land purchases. Far. Mss., 1783; HSP, West to [?], September 29, 1808. This letter makes it clear that Raphael was to have settled permanently in the United States.

244   Raphael retired to Sunning Hill. Far. Mss., 1226.

244–46   Background on Beckford. Alexander, Chapman, Melville, M. F. Rogers, Jr., *EB*, *DNB*.

244   West's commissions £1000 a year. Far. Mss., 1401.

244   Beckford preferred West's drawings. Ibid., 1115.

245   Beckford on Turner. Alexander, *Wealthiest Son*, 250.

245   Leaned to West because of king. Far. Mss., 1096.

245   "Commander of front pages." Alexander, *Life*, 231.

245   Regretted his private education. Far., IV, 242.

245 fn   Trip to Fonthill. Williamson, 183.

246   Negotiations with France. Far., I, 217, 219–20, 225, Mss., 1401.

PAGE

246 Fonthill Abbey. Only the northeast end is still standing.

246 West's pictures for the apocalypse. Far. Mss., 1401.

247 Beckford to West on his "situation." Ibid., IV, 242–43.

247 Hope's visit to Fonthill. SRO, West to Beckford, August 2, 1809.

247 West and Altieri Claudes. Whitley, II, 225; Far., I, 269, Mss., 1545; Alexander, Life, 56.

247 Dr. Monro thought him a picture dealer. Far., II, 118. Monro was the physician who administered to the mental troubles of Mary Anne Provis, purveyor of the Venetian Secret. Gage, 41.

247 West in trouble over Orleans sale. Far. Mss., 1610–11; HSP, Williams to West, May 26, 1799.

248 Excursion on River Wye. Far. Mss., 1644; SRO, West to Williams, September 30, 1799; HSP, West to Beckford, October 7, 1799.

248 West believed Beckford innocent. Far., I, 237, IV, 243, Mss., 1141, 1489.

248 Farington: "improbable . . . bad heart." Far., I, 187, IV, 243.

248–49 Life at Fonthill. Alexander, Life, 28–29, 34, 41, 48.

249 Proposal to invite Beckford. Far., I, 282, Mss., 1000, 1028, 1520.

249–50 West, gout, and December 10, 1799, meeting. Far. Mss., 1682, 1684, 1686. West in fact did not attend the meeting. Smirke, in what apparently was sincere concern for his health, persuaded him not to leave his house in bad weather. Ibid., 1689.

250 Smirke, Junior, had help. Ibid., 1689.

250 Council-Assembly contest for control. Far., I, 283, 286, 287, Mss., continuing entries between pp. 1704 and 1770. The contest, of course, is covered in the Assembly and Council minutes books.

251 Academy flourishing. Whitley, II, 232.

252 Special meeting, January 14, 1800, West and Farington spoke. Far. Mss., 1728–36.

252–53 West to king with Council papers. Ibid., 1736–38, 1740.

253 Talk of dissolving Academy Club. Ibid., 1742, 1745.

253 King, no reflection on conduct. Ibid., 1744.

254 February 4 and 8 meetings. Ibid., 1745–48, 1759–61, 1765–66.

254 Cosway, Opie, and naked ladies. Ibid., 1232.

254–55 West and the crucifixion. Whitley, IV, 34; H. C. Morgan thesis on R.A. schools, 62–63.

254 Dr. Carpue. DNB; Thorwald, 70–71, 76–79.

255–57 Christmas at Fonthill. Far., I, 307; Chapman, 272–73; Melville, 234–36; Beckford, II, 111–127; Fothergill, 394–97; Gentleman's Magazine, March, April 1801, pp. 266–68, 297–98; Oman, Nelson, 416–17; Alexander, Wealthiest Son, 162–63; SRO, West to Williams, January 5, 1801. A picture of Emma Hamilton as Agrippina, surrounded by three children, has been "tentatively attributed" to West. See Burlington Magazine, June 1976; Country Life, May 27, 1976. West's relationship to Beckford is made clearer in the correspondence in the Scottish Record Office. West wrote on May 12, 1801, to express his thanks for help that Beckford had given, probably in some financial crisis: "Did I permit another day to elapse without expressing to you that I felt your friendship on that occasion more than in any other instance that has occurred since I have [had] the satisfaction of being known to you, would be depriving myself of the first of all gratifications, which is that of acknowledging a favour." Beckford's friendship in the arts, he said, had contributed more to his professional happiness than any other he had met with in England, save only the friendship he had received from the king. He wished to say that the "abatements" made by Beckford in his last bill coincided perfectly with his own wishes, although they placed him under many difficulties. He hoped it was understood that in all settlements made between them, "if there was any part of my account not exactly meeting your wishes, to strike your pen through the article or price and it would be to me perfectly satisfactory."

Chapter 19. *Paris: 1802*   Pages 258–273

258   Barlow to his wife. C. B. Todd, 202.

259   Jefferson admired Bonaparte. LC, Jefferson Papers, Jefferson to Madison, June 15, 1797, Jefferson to Thomas Randolph, January 11, 1798.

259   Farington and St. Pancras Volunteers. Far., II, 141.

260   Looted art. There is an account of the French depredations in F. H. Taylor.

260   Flaxman campaign. Far. Mss., 898–99, 918.

261   Farington to Paris. Far., II, 1–6, Mss., 8098–8110.

261   Death of his wife. Far. Mss., 1796, 1798–99.

261   John James Halls. A man of many parts, Halls exhibited 108 pictures at the Royal Academy and wrote several books. Far., II, 1.

261   Fuseli hoped not more than £60. Ibid., 2081.

261   West got list from Beckford. SRO, West to Beckford, August 7, 1802.

261   West obtained letters. Galt, II, 177.

261   West traveled with Flaxmans. Far. Mss., 8157.

261   West to Prefecture of Police. Far., II, 9–10, Mss., 8122, 8238–39. I have used Farington's account of a procedure required of all foreign visitors.

261 fn   Consulted the king. *Gentleman's Magazine*, March 20, 1820, p. 277. See also a three-column letter dated April 12, 1820 in the *Observer* (available in the V and A "Press Cuttings," 1235), signed by "A Friend to the Truth." He claimed to have had "a close intimacy of more than twenty years" with West and described a conversation between West and the king, quoting the king's words in approving the journey.

262   West received distinguished attention. Galt, II, 178–79; *Gentleman's Magazine*, March 20, 1820; HSP, West to Foubert, October 25, 1802.

262   Denon and Vincent on Bonaparte's art plan. Galt, II, 179–80.

262   West's report on looted art. Far. Mss., 8157, 8234.

262–63   *Death on the Pale Horse*. Far., II, 7, Mss., 8113, 8159. Smirke told West that David had really spoken well of his picture and admired the execution of it. Ibid., 2105.

263   West on improvement in agriculture. Ibid., 8116.

263   On improvement in Paris. Far., II, 21.

263   Robert Fulton. Dickinson, 13, 15, 16; Woodress, 210–17; C. B. Todd, 176–81. Fulton carried a letter of introduction from West to Barlow. West's nephew, David Morris, had married Fulton's sister.

263   Barlow. Woodress, 139, 154, 190; C. B. Todd, 202; EB; DAB.

PAGE

264 Submarine would stop war. Woodress, 212–13.

265 Barlow on Bonaparte. Woodress, 216.

265 Fulton and Livingston, Talleyrand. Ibid., 228–29; Lee, 303.

265 West's good health. Far. Mss., 8118.

265 Report on looted art. Ibid., 8234.

265 Hoppner detested Paris. Far., II, 20, 25.

265 Farington's notebooks. Far. Mss., 8166.

265–66 Maria Cosway. Ibid., 8177; Earland, 188.

266 West lecture to Baring. Far. Mss., 8160.

266 Visit to Viennet. Ibid., 8207.

266 Erskine, "sore on his mind." Ibid., 56–57.

266 West offended Fuseli in introducing Fox. Far. Mss., 8152, 8178. In his chapter on West published in 1834, Allan Cunningham told a West-Fox story that has lastingly harmed West's reputation (*Lives*, 52). West was in the company of Fox, who was famous in France as the antiwar, pro-French Parliamentary leader. "He [West] certainly had a very lofty notion of himself, and his account of the stir which he excited in Paris marks a mind amiably but extravagantly vain. 'Wherever I went,' he said, 'men looked at me, and ministers and people of influence in the state were constantly in my company. I was one day in the Louvre — all eyes were upon me; and I could not help observing to Charles Fox, *who happened to be walking with me*, how strong was the love of art, and admiration of its professors, in France.' " Cunningham gave no source for the story, and its truth seems doubtful.

266–67 The sights of Paris. Far., II, 18, 23, 25, Mss., 2088, 8179, 8189; Shee, I, 244.

266 fn Hoppner rebuffed Erskine. Far., II, 23.

267 Farington and monument. Far. Mss., 8171.

267 Only two captured British flags. Ibid.

267 Fox saw Italian ambassador. Far., II, 27.

267 On Parisian women. Ibid., 7, 8, 21, 23.

267 No one used "*citoyen.*" Far. Mss., 8108.

267 "Walse Dance." Far., II, 22–23.

267 Saw Jean Greuze. Ibid., 33.

267 Viennet looked like a baby. Ibid., 29.

267 Flaxman and David. Ibid., 26–27; Honour, *Neo-Classicism*, 163–64.

267 David wanted 500,000 more heads to roll. He said it to John Trumbull in 1797. Trumbull, 224.

267 English did not like David's work. Far., II, 17, 46, Mss., 8119, 8176, 8200.

267 Uniformity of French pictures. Far. Mss., 8116, 8236.

267 Fuseli: French art was at its end. Ibid., 8160.

267–68 Countess of Oxford and Arthur O'Connor. Far., II, 34, 36, 37. Mss., 8164, 8197.

268 Harleian miscellany. Priestley, 43.

268 Murat's villa, Versailles, Gobelin factory. Far. Mss., 8233, 8181, 8208–9.

268 Turner and mountains. Far., II, 43, 44.

268 Beckford in Bonaparte's procession. Alexander, *Wealthiest Son*, 24, on August 18, 1802.

PAGE

268–69 Comments on Bonaparte. Far., II, 8, 31, 37, 38; Shee, I, 245–47.

269 Hoppners to Bonaparte's apartment. Far., II, 19–20.

269 Farington on Bonaparte. Ibid., II, 7, 53–55.

270 West and Bonaparte. Ibid., 31, 37, 73; HSP, Meredith Papers. "Joshua B. Bacon Memo," February 2, 1817.

270 West sketched Bonaparte's carriage. Kraemer, 73.

270 Artists took umbrage. Far., II, 37.

270 Vivant dinner. Far. Mss., 8190, 8234, BM, Whitley Papers, 1676.

271 "Stout English conversation." Far. Mss., 8149.

271 Helen Maria Williams. Far., II, 6, 15, 33, 37, Mss., 8135. West and Barlow went together to one of Miss Williams' parties at which there were 50 guests.

271 West's "public breakfast." Far., II, 33–36, Mss., 8204. HSP has a rough draft in West's handwriting giving an account of the affair, in the third person, as though for a press release.

271 "Such an association does not go unnoticed." Far. Mss., 8197.

272 Erskine received by Bonaparte. Far., II, 57.

272 Farington's return trip. Ibid., 57–62.

273 West's return trip. Far. Mss., 8258.

273 West arranged for young artists. Ibid., 8234. A note in Farington's diary, not in Farington's hand, reads: "In the autumn of 1802 Mr. West visited Paris and as it was the year of the Exhibition of the French artists he took over his picture . . . Death on a White Horse which was also exhibited there. He staid about six weeks and took no small pains to make himself conspicuous and contrived to meet the Chief Consul and converse with him of which he seemed not a little proud when he returned. Yet it may be questioned whether this conduct was much to his credit."

273 Imprisoned English artists. John Ramsey, an English art student, a prisoner at Verdun, addressed a letter to the president and the Council asking them to apply to the French government to free him. Farington moved that a certificate be sent him stating that he had been an Academy student. RA, Council minutes, III, September 24, 1804; H. C. Morgan thesis on R.A. schools, 94–95.

Chapter 20.   *"A Matter of Passion and Contest"*   Pages 274–289

274 Northcote on artists. Whitley, II, 310.

274 West report to king on Paris trip. Aspinall, *George III*, IV, 54, No. 2668, October 15, 1802.

274 Rumor Bonaparte gave him an apartment. V and A "Press Cuttings," IV, 1235.

274 King: "Who were the artists?" Far., II, 67, 118.

274–75 West dined with Andréossy. Far. Mss., 2123.

275 West asked king to investigate his loyalty. Aspinall, *George III*, IV, 22–23, No. 2611, April 5, 1802.

275–76 Letter from five Academicians. A facsimile appears in *Royal Academy*, Holme, R ii.

276 West consulted Farington. Far. Mss., 2186, 2188.

276 West's painting process. Ibid., 2189. "Middleton sends him a canvas

with a slight sized ground passed over it. Over this Mr. West passes another sized ground made up to a tint which he prefers, something of a light buff when dry. On this he sketches the outline with charcoal, and then corrects and improves the outline by drawing in the whole with water color. He then brushes off the charcoal and passes over the whole surface of the canvas with linseed oil. After which he wipes the surface with a cloth that no *quantity* of oil should remain. He then proceeds to wash in with colour mixed with linseed oil . . . the whole of his subject, but begins with laying a *slight body of colour* on his lights, and afterwards proceeds to finish.

"The absorbing power will allow of repetitions of colour mixed with linseed oil only, but where drying oil is mixed with the colours that power ceases. So that he only uses drying oil when he glazes with thin colours at the last. He puts a little turpentine with the linseed oil which he uses to render it more limpid."

277   March 4, 1803 Council meeting. Far. Mss., 2197; HSP, West to Council, no date.

277   Copley to West, March 6, 1803. Far. Mss., 2200–1. The letter appears in facsimile in *Royal Academy,* ed. by Holme, R iv.

277   March 12 and 19 meetings. Far. Mss., 2202, 2207.

277–80   Knatchbull affair. Far., II, 196, Mss., 2201, 2215, 2218, 2226, 2237, 2245; Prown, 360–71; Amory, 183, 184, 187, 189, 223, 236–8; Whitley, III, 52–53; RA, Council minutes, III, 189..

278   Knatchbull told West. Soane Museum, diary, 2201.

278   Delattre affair. Far. Mss., 1986; Prown, 290–91; Amory, 222; *Morning Chronicle,* July 3, 1801; *Morning Post,* July 3, 1801. Delattre's print after Copley's Chatham was published in London in 1820. Jules Prown, Copley's biographer, says it is as bad as Copley claimed.

278   Copley owed £24. Far. Mss., 2103.

278   Trumbull loan to Copley. Prown, 310.

279   Copley asked West's advice. Far. Mss., 2548.

279   Copley's troubles with picture. Far. Mss., 2218, 2245; Prown, 365, 367, 368; Whitley, III, 52–53. There is a detailed account of Copley's appearance before the Council in Sir John Soane's papers, once in his diary for April 1803, and again in the minutes he kept for himself of the several Council meetings.

280   *Hagar and Ishmael* affair. RA, Council minutes, III, 185–89, 197–98; Far. Mss., 2226–27, 2234–51; Whitley, III, 54–56; Prown, 367; Fineberg, 97; Gardner-Feld, 28–29; HSP, West to George III, November 20, 1803.

281   Mrs. West sent clipping. Far., II, 92.

281   *Morning Post* article. April 14, 1803.

282   West's temperate letter. HSP, West to Council, April 16, 1803.

282   John Richards lament to West. HSP, April 16, 1803.

282 fn   Metropolitan Museum X-rays. Gardner-Feld, 29.

282–83   Soane's conciliatory letter. Far., II, 92, Mss., 2226. It appears in full in Sandby, I, 264–65.

283   Farington on harm of Soane's letter. Far., II, 92, Mss., 2226–27.

283   *True Briton* identified Copley. Far. Mss., 2229.

283   Hagar rejected again. Far. Mss., 2231; HSP, Richards to West, April 22, 1803.

PAGE

284 West's warm statement, Richards "debilitated." Far. Mss., 2234, 2235; RA, Assembly minutes, II, 215.

284 West exonerated. Far. Mss., 2236, 2245. He personally delivered the resolution on his exoneration to the king.

284 "Candidus" on Copley. *True Briton*, April 27, 1803.

284 Richards sent press release. HSP, April 28, 1803.

284 Beaumont to Farington on Hagar. Far. Mss., 2237.

285 Councilmen should exonerate themselves. Far. Mss., 2243.

285 Copley to West: Had he complied? Ibid., 2244; R.A. Scrap Book, 92b, Copley to West, May 3, 1803.

285 West to Copley: Did not intend to comply. Far. Mss., 2245; HSP, May 4, 1803.

285 Soane to West. Far. Mss., 2248; HSP, May 7, 1803.

285 Statement of innocence. Far. Mss., 2248–51.

285 Farington unwilling to subject himself. Far., II, 97.

285 West unwilling to go to Council. Far. Mss., 2253.

285 Copley's resolution. Ibid., 2264–65, 2270.

285–86 West asks Farington's advice. Ibid., 2264–65; Soane's minutes of Council meeting, May 24, 1803. West signed the minutes only after Dance and Richards crossed out Copley's resolution.

286 West to Copley. HSP, May 28, 1803.

286 Suspension of five Council members. Far. Mss., 2270–71, 2282; HSP, Richards to West, March 13, 1803. Richards' notice to members, March 15, 1803. The ten opposition members who boycotted the general meeting were Beechey, Bourgeois, Copley, Cosway, Rigaud, Sandby, Soane, Tresham, Yenn, and Wyatt.

286 Farington pessimistic. Far. Mss., 2284.

286 West in a state of ease. Ibid., 2297.

286 Dance: "Quit the Academy." Ibid., 2282.

286 Adversaries did not speak. Ibid., 2358, 2447, 2464, 2490, 2681.

287 Watchdog committee. Ibid., 2275–76.

287 Consulted a lawyer. Ibid., 2270–71, 2297, 2300, 2307–8.

287 Farington to Cockerell. Ibid., 2396.

287 West saw king, July 7, 1803. Far., II, 121–22.

288 Suspension of members extended. Far. Mss., 2330–31, 2338.

288 Mrs. West read and approved Farington report. Ibid., 2339.

288 West's letter to king. Ibid., 2346; HSP, undated, marked "A True Copy." The letter is printed in full in Landis, 139–41.

288 West and Farington pessimistic. Far. Mss., 2348.

288 West saw the king. Ibid., 2352–54, 2356, 2358–60. Farington recorded West's account in two separate tellings. A version in West's hand is in HSP, August 7, 1803.

Chapter 21. *The Struggle for Power*   Pages 290–305

290 George III's rebuff of Beechey. There are slight variations in three versions quoted by Farington. One ends, "...I should not inquire after you." Far., III, 18, 43, 250.

290 French massed on Channel. Oman, *Napoleon*, 153.

290–91 Military Corps of Artists. Far. Mss., 2338, 2342, 2344, 2404; Shee, I, 257–65; Sandby, I, 269.

PAGE

291 Rebels did not attend meetings; Bourgeois, "You will have a whipping." Far. Mss., 2394, 2417.

292 Rumors. Ibid., 2385, 2405, 2430.

292 West: "All is up." Ibid., 2420–21. Yenn apologized to West the next day for the "shortness" of the note he sent, saying he had only acted on the king's order and "upon his soul" did not know what decision the king had made.

292 West and Farington discuss audience with King. Ibid., 2423, 2425–26.

292–93 West with king, November 12, 1803. Far., II, 167–68; D. E. Williams, I, 247–49.

293 West's report to colleagues, "total defeat." Far., II, 167–68, Mss., 2429.

293 Debate on what course to follow. Far. Mss., 2429–34.

293 King's letter read at general meeting of November 21, 1803. Ibid., 2433–34.

293 Copley denied a copy of king's order. Ibid., 2435.

294 Majority decided to expunge everything from minutes. Ibid., 2434, 2437, 2444, 2446, 2448.

294 West with king, December 4, 1803. Ibid., 2452–53, 2455.

294 King's "very tyrannical order." Ibid., 2460; RA, Council minutes, III, 209–10, 214–15, 218–19, Assembly minutes, II, 255–69. Copley's famous resolution, cut out of the Council minutes by Richards, is neatly taped back in the minutes book, as ordered by the king.

294 Farington: "degraded the institution." Far. Mss., 2450.

294 King's letter received with silence, December 10 meeting. Far. Mss., 2463, 2468.

295 Talk of resisting the king's orders. Ibid., 2430, 2447, 2464, 2488.

295 Farington advocated moderation. Ibid., 2429, 2432, 2457–58, 2460, 2461, 2465, 2467, 2488.

296 West to king, December 23, 1803. Far., II, 177–78, Mss., 2476.

296 Soane's attempt to cancel all business. Far. Mss., 2481–83, 2490–91.

296 Farington advised West not to summon Council. Ibid., 2483.

296 West stayed home. Ibid., 2484.

296 Mrs. West's verses. Ibid., 2487.

297 Council meeting. Ibid., 2490; RA, Council minutes, III, 232. The minute of December 26, 1803 is crossed out but is readable.

297 West gave king five candidates. Far., II, 177.

297 Thomas Banks, treason. DNB; Far., III, 54.

297 Review of candidates. Far., III, 54, 55, Mss., 2510. Banks died within the year. West was so upset at receiving the news that he at once adjourned the Academy meeting over which he was presiding.

298 Mrs. West campaigned for Smirke. Far. Mss., 2436, 2530.

298 Beechey, Smirke, king, guillotine. Ibid., 2836; Fineberg, 114.

298 Beechey to Nollekens on West. Far. Mss., 2698.

298 Princess Elizabeth. Far., II, 183, Mss., 2510.

298 Humphry: Smirke not suitable. Far., II, 189.

298 Hoppner opposed Smirke. Ibid., 189, Mss., 2528, 2533.

298 Beechey on Smirke. Far., II, 189.

299 Smirke elected, declined to serve. Ibid., Mss., 2529, 2558, 2562.

299 Beechey's wife: "King will not sign." Far. Mss., 2665, 2698.

299 Recurrence of king's illness. Brooke, 376–78.

299 West thought *Vindication* very flimsy. Far. Mss., 2507, 2513–14.

300 Young Copley "cured of democracy." Far., II, 197, Mss., 1798–99.

300–302 Knatchbull hearing. Far., II, 196–97, Mss., 2547–48, 2558–61, 2572, 2580, 2635, 2641. As the trial date approached, Knatchbull deposited his offered payment with the court. Copley withdrew the money, and for a time it was thought that his action had ended the proceedings.

301 West on £29,000. Far. Mss., 2572.

301 West on young Copley. Far., II, 197; Prown, 371.

301 Lawrence "reprobated" Copley. Far. Mss., 2544.

302 Winner of Knatchbull-Copley suit not known. Jules Prown conjectures that Copley won, since Farington did not record the verdict and the quantitative weight of testimony was on his side. Dunlap (I, 128) quotes a source as saying that Copley Junior won the Knatchbull case for his father, his first as a lawyer, but Dunlap said of the story, "I fear it is too good to be true."

302 Copley hung picture at Mersham. Amory, 288; Prown, 371; Far., V, 2.

302 Picture cut apart. Prown, 363.

302 Farington to West on Smirke. Far., II, 216.

302 West on exhibiting *Hagar*, Copley not opposed. Far., II, 216, Mss., 2598, 2603, 2624.

302 West worked on *Hagar*. Far., II, 226, Whitley, III, 70–71.

302 West "like a true American." Far. Mss., 2771.

303 West, Beechey, and Beechey's wife. Far., III, 23, 33.

303 West would not go above stairs. Far. Mss., 2632.

303 Bourgeois rearranged place cards. Ibid., 2680.

303 Beechey on king's "contemptible opinion" of West. Far. Mss., 2515.

303 Beechey: West "an ungrateful dog." Far., II, 192–93.

303 Farington doubted Beechey's story. Far., III, 33.

303 West was turned away from Queen's Lodge. Far. Mss., 2438.

303 King did not notice him. Far., II, 281.

304 Hoppner, Lawrence, Beechey charged 30 guineas. Far. Mss., 1252.

304 Beechey's knighthood. Millar, *Pictures*, Text, xxii; Whitley, II, 217, 219.

304 Beechey loses favor. Far., III, 18, 23, 42, 43, 62, 250.

304 Tresham now carried stories about West. Ibid., 14, 17.

304 fn Beechey's the only artist's wife who entertained. Whitley, III, 157.

Chapter 22. *The Hollow Triumph*   Pages 306–320

306 "A very discontented set of men." Far., III, 104.

307 West planned trip to Windsor. Ibid., 14, 17, 18, Mss., 2814, 2828, 2866–67.

307 West's financial problems. Far., II, 282, Mss., 2455.

307 West admired daughter-in-law. Far. Mss., 2425, 2582.

307 Would return to America. Far., II, 245. Copley also talked of his desire to return to America, but Mrs. Copley would not leave England. Far. Mss., 412.

307 Sorry did not paint for public. Far. Mss., 2663.

PAGE

307 fn Tresham tried to win Thomson. Far., III, 17.

307 fn Mrs. West to Sarah Trumbull. HSP, February 6, 1805.

307–8 Lawrence on defending West. Ibid., 2817.

308 King's illness. Far. Mss., 2824; Brooke, 329, 377–79.

308–9 Audience with king. Far., III, 21, Mss., 2542, 2818, 2822, 2828, 2833.

308 Lord chancellor withheld Smirke paper. Far. Mss., 2803, 2861, 2866–67.

309 Farington's advice. Far., III, 22, Mss., 2820.

309 Farington on deeper significance. Far. Mss., 2837.

309 Farington and Lawrence to Fuseli. Far., III, 21, Mss., 2819.

309–10 General meeting, November 20, 1804. Far. Mss., 2826–27, 2834, 2854.

310 Bourgeois and Cosway on choosing a president. Far. Mss., 2837, 2847.

310 Copley disapproved Wyatt. Ibid., 2829.

310 Bourgeois promised Fuseli £100. Ibid., 2847.

310 Cosway and Fuseli discussion on majority rule. Ibid., 2837.

310–11 General meeting, December 10, 1804. Far., III, 31, Mss., 2850–53.

311 West to Trumbull on meeting. February 6, 1805, Sterling Library, Yale. The entire letter is printed in the Yale University *Library Gazette,* January 1951.

311 Farington filled in details. Far., III, 31, Mss., 2850–53.

311 West two hours with chancellor. Ibid., 2861.

311 fn Yenn explained: "If done with delicacy." Far. Mss., 2929.

312 Opposition swore king would not approve. Far., III, 14, 17, 18, Mss., 2834–35, 2837, 2847.

312 Farington: Younger members should decide. Far., III, 34.

312 Lawrence: Farington should be president. Ibid.

312 Farington felt he would be censured next. Far. Mss., 2809.

312 Decision to rebel. Ibid., 2860–61.

312 Yenn: "A smuggled business." Ibid., 2895.

312–13 Audience with king, December 28, 1804. Far., III, 37.

312 Mrs. West on husband. Far., III, 36.

314 Copley's call on Fuseli. Far. Mss., 2876.

314–16 General meeting, January 2, 1805. Far., III, 40–42, Mss., 2879–84.

314 West to Trumbull on meeting. Sterling Library, February 6, 1805.

316 Mrs. West to Sarah Trumbull. HSP, February 6, 1805.

316 Tresham: King not aware. Far. Mss., 2894–95.

317 Farington on Tresham. Ibid., 2895.

317 Rage in rebel camp. Ibid., 2929.

317 Farington's disgust. Far., III, 44, Mss., 3037.

317 Hoppner's "great dissatisfaction." Far. Mss., 3043.

317 Smirke declined to go to Academy. Far., III, 99.

317 Farington on state of Academy. Far. Mss., 3043.

317 West's private dinner. Ibid., 2907.

318 West withdrew three pictures. Whitley, III, 88.

318 Smirke's advice to West. Far. Mss., 3014.

318 Five supporters went over to rebels. Far., III, 85, Mss., 3009, 3037.

318 West: Wyatt has ruined Royal Academy. Far., III, 105.

318 West's parley with Wyatt. Far. Mss., 3117.

318 fn Persuaded Fuseli to withdraw. Far. Mss., 3038.

PAGE
319 West's resignation. Far., III, 127–30.

319 Mrs. West on Academy feuds. Ibid., 128.

319 Farington concluded Mrs. West did not know of resignation. He was mistaken. She wrote to the Trumbulls, "Mr. W. after this very gracious reception [from the king] could not think of resigning the chair, besides it might have been assigned as a reason by those sons of falsehood, that it was a ratification of the *truth of their assertions;* however, he determined it should be only for [one] year. NYPL, September 29, 1806.

319 Did not deliver letter to king. Far., III, 128.

319 Dance and Farington rewrote letter. Ibid., Mss., 3117.

319–20 His letter of resignation. Far., III, 128, Mss., 3128, 3133. The manuscript letter, December 2, 1805, is at the HSP. It is printed in full in Landis, along with a letter on the resignation from West to John Timmons, a friend, in which he wrote: "The unpleasant circumstances arising from a party spirit in the Academy, commenced in the last years of my worthy predecessor: they rendered the station of the chair as unpleasant to him as they have to me, but notwithstanding the professional warmth of passion I was in hopes a patient steadiness on my part . . . would have the good effect to subdue those animosities." HSP, West to Timmons, December 22, 1805.

320 1805 election of Wyatt. Far., III, 130, 132, Mss., 3122, 3126. The General Assembly minutes do not show the number of votes cast for the candidates.

320 Letter of resignation praised. Far. Mss., 3128, 3133.

Chapter 23. *To Stumble, Fall, and Rise Again* Pages 321–335

321 Farington to Hoppner. Far. Mss., 3490.

321 Beaumont on West's pictures. Far., III, 187.

321 West broken in appearance. Far., III, 273, Mss., 3276, 3279.

322 Chapel cancellation in 1801. Galt, II, 193–98; Far., II, 170, Mss., 2430. West's 1801 letter is printed in full in Galt.

322 Chapel cancellation in 1805. Far. Mss., 3004A.

322 Statistics on chapel pictures. Galt, II, 194; Meyer, "Chapel," 247–50; Dillenberger.

322 Rendered artist's life useless. Galt, II, 193.

322 Bitter statement to students. *Analectic*, VIII, 47–48.

323 West was paid £34,187. Galt, II, 200; Sandby, I, 264.

323 Bartolozzi was offered £400. Far. Mss., 6093.

323 West to Farington on *Crucifixion*. Ibid., 2853.

323 House in Windsor. HSP, July 20, 1804.

323 Sale of old masters. Far., III, 181.

324 West's philosophy on selling. BM, Whitley Papers, 1689, Far. Mss., 1026.

324 "Happy release." Far., III, 227, 269.

324 No difference in respect paid. Far. Mss., 3503.

324 Would decline to return. Far., III, 165, 226.

324 Hawkesbury on Nelson. Ibid., 131.

324 City of London payment. Ibid., 159.

PAGE

324 Other artists painting Nelson. Ibid., 137, 138, 159, 272; Mitchell, "Nelson," 269.

324 West and Heath engraving. Mitchell, "Nelson," 267; Far., III, 127, 272, IV, 150.

324–25 Ticknor on West-Nelson meeting. Ticknor, I, 63.

325 West philosophy on painting Nelson. Far., IV, 151.

325 West's painstaking effort. Mitchell, "Nelson," 267.

326 Copley sprained arm, Devis a year later. Amory, 281; Mitchell, "Nelson," 269.

326 West's exhibition of *Nelson.* Far., III, 226, 227, 269, IV, 150.

326 Queen asked to see picture. Far., III, 276; BM, Whitley Papers, 1679.

326 West saw king. Far., III, 270.

326 West's second Nelson, the *Apotheosis.* Mitchell, "Nelson," 272. A number of writers have mistakenly assumed that it was this second version, the *Apotheosis,* that West exhibited so successfully in 1806 in his private gallery. Farington's account of the first picture exhibited, however, which he saw in West's home on July 8, 1806, clearly establishes that the picture was the first "epic representation." The confusion has arisen from the fact that the first picture, though painted, signed, and dated in 1806, was not exhibited at the Academy until 1811. (It is now at the Walker Art Gallery, Liverpool, England.) In 1812 the governors of Greenwich Hospital erected a huge bas-relief monument in artificial (Coade) stone of West's *Apotheosis.* It occupies one of the pediments of the King William Block. The National Maritime Museum at Greenwich has the paintings *The Apotheosis of Nelson* and the small *Death of Nelson* in its Nelson Room.

327 Illustrated a Nelson biography with 2nd and 3rd versions. It was Clark and McArthur's *Life of Nelson,* 1809.

327 West and British Institution. Constable, "Foundation," 166–68; Far., III, 79, et seq.; Galt, II, 185; Hutchison, *History,* 85; A. Cunningham, *Lives,* "West," 53; Dunlap, I, 83. A strong faction at the Royal Academy, including Farington, opposed the British Institution because it was clearly a rival, because its emphasis on old masters might harm sales of modern artists, and because it was run by connoisseurs, not artists. It did indeed break the domination of the Royal Academy over British art.

327 West to Baring and Fox in Paris. Galt, II, 180–84.

327 West to Long and Hume on British Institution. Ibid., 182. Constable, "Foundation," 171.

327 British Institution subscribers. W. B. Taylor, II, 222.

328 Meeting in West's home. Far., III, 73.

328 West to king on British Institution. HSP, May 16, 1805; Far., III, 79–81.

328 British Institution exhibition. Far., III, 127, 137, 150; Hutchison, *History,* 85.

328 West's condition of sale. Far., III, 189.

328 Hoppner: "Puke of the Royal Academy." Ibid., 168.

328 British Institution exhibition of old masters. Hutchison, *History,* 85.

328 Beaumont sent pictures to West's gallery. Boase, 22.

328 Angerstein. Far., III, 23; Whitley, III, 62; G. Martin, May 1974. p.

24. In 1813 the British Institution showed a large number of pictures by Joshua Reynolds in the first commemorative exhibition of works by an individual artist held in England.

329   West assumed credit for founding British Institution. Far., IV, 227.

329   Constable was more generous. Constable, "Foundation," 171.

329   Sebastian del Piombo's *The Raising of Lazarus*. This was for many years the showpiece of the National Gallery. West called it "the finest picture in the world, exquisitely colored." Despite his admiration, he was charged with "severely manhandling" the work by repainting the entire surface (later the entire figure) of Lazarus. The accusation was made by John Landseer, A.R.A., an engraver, the father of Sir Edwin Landseer. West is still being routinely charged with the desecration. While it is impossible to determine the truth of the accusation, West's strong opposition to retouching and repainting old masters is a matter of record. On April 8, 1807, West and Farington went to a dealer on Oxendon Street to see Titian's *Bacchus and Ariadne*. Farington wrote: [West] "said the picture was really in fine preservation, but it was mortifying to see that Burch the picture dealer had *been putting colour upon it,* in many parts. Upon the sky with ultramarine and had stippled colour upon parts of the flesh. He said if the picture was his he would take off the whole that *Burch had done.*" In 1838 a knowledgeable reviewer of Gustav F. Waagen's *Works of Art and Artists in England* wrote, "Among the most atrocious destructions of late years was the flaying and dissection of two celebrated Claudes [formerly owned] by Mr. Beckford of Fonthill. West and Sir Thomas Lawrence called at the house of the distinguished 'flayer' to whom they had been entrusted to clean; the servant inadvertently showed them into a room where these exquisite pictures were — actually excoriated — the ground apparent in several places, the foliage in many parts totally obliterated, and all the surfaces forever destroyed. The *cleaner* entered the room. The mild, courtier-like Lawrence was for once enraged and exclaimed, 'I see, Sir, we have been where we were not wanted, and I am sorry — for this destruction — (pointing to the Claudes) will deprive me of my rest.' West, who was a man of great command of temper, stood as he was wont when angry, working his closed lips; then looking at the destroyer, he said, 'Sir, you deserve to have been flayed as you have flayed those pictures.' The conceited varlet replied: — 'Oh, gentlemen, it is nothing — all very easily put to rights.' 'Yes,' said West, 'when you can get Claude to come from his grave to do it, not before.' The two artists immediately left the house." (Reitlinger, I, 33; Whitley, II, 358, IV, 73–74; Far., IV, 116, Mss., 676.)

330   Quarrels among Shee, Garvey, Westall, Lawrence, Hoppner. Far., III, 182, 185–86, 201, 208, 211.

330   Mrs. Fuseli quarreled. Far., III, 255.

330   Academy Club dissolved. Far. Mss., 3150.

330   Tresham and Wyatt did not associate, Beechey did not speak to Tresham, Hoppner resigned as deputy. Far., III, 226, Mss., 3142, 3162, 3356.

330   Flaxman amused. Far., III, 226.

PAGE

330 Mrs. West scornful. NYPL, September 29, 1806.

330 King did not converse with Royal Academy officers. Far., III, 227.

330 Exhibition postponed, complaints on food and Wyatt. Ibid., 193, 201, 216, 255–56, Mss., 3257, 3285.

331 Dinner bill enormous, Fuseli reprimanded. Far., III, 303–04.

331 Dissatisfaction with Wyatt. Ibid., 216, 247, Mss., 3418, 3356, 3358, 3580.

331 Wyatt's career. DNB; Dale, 91, 99, 102, 103, 106.

331 Possibilities for president. Far., IV, 49, Mss., 3507, 3510.

332 Gloucester bet five guineas. Far., IV, 50.

332 Northcote, "doll painter." Ibid., III, 200.

332 Henry Hope's advice. Ibid., IV, 40.

332 Garvey wanted West to return. Ibid., III, 304.

332 West spoke favorably of other artists. Ibid., 266.

332 Flaxman for West, Thomson for Hoppner. Ibid., IV, 49, 50, Mss., 3520–21, 3507.

332 Farington said West would not accept. Far. Mss., 3361.

332 Farington to Lawrence on avoiding a struggle. Ibid., 3495.

332 Hoppner's call on Farington. Ibid., 3490, 3493, Far., IV, 43.

333 Mrs. West's illness. Far. Mss., 2620, 3500.

333 Farington authorized to solicit West. Ibid., 3495.

333 West's thoughts on returning to office. Ibid., 3499, 3503, 3517, Far., IV, 54.

333 Hoped to complete chapel. Meyer, "Chapel," 262–63.

333 Farington authorized by West. Far., IV, 54.

333 West to British Institution students. Far., Mss., 3524.

333 West and Bonaparte. Far., IV, 48–49.

334 Farington: West's mind not English. Ibid., 49.

334 West re-elected. Ibid., 57.

334 Farington call on West. Ibid., 59.

334 Queen dissatisfied with Wyatt. Ibid., 54.

334 King received West "like a brother." Far. Mss., 3577, 3581.

334 West congratulated. Ibid., 3535, 3577, 3581.

334–35 Humphry, Thomson, Copley. Ibid., 3536, 3556, 3558–59, 3570.

335 West and Desenfans. Ibid., 3728, Far., IV, 170.

335 West and Bourgeois "sociable." Far. Mss., 3741.

335 Bourgeois bequest. Hutchison, History, 85–86; Dulwich, xi, xiv–xv, xviii.

335 West reception at annual dinner. Far. Mss., 3566, 3570, 3700.

335 fn Opie's funeral. Far. Mss., 3661, 3684. In The Artist, April 25, 1807, West wrote one of his infrequent critical articles, in which he expressed the highest praise of Opie's work in well-phrased language. He is quoted in Earland, 17–18.

Chapter 24. The Era of Good Feeling Pages 336–355

336 Allston on West. Dunlap, II, 158–59.

336 Mrs. West's illness and lament. Far., IV, 133; Rodenbough, 267, Mrs. West to Elizabeth S. Swift, September 5, 1799.

336 To Bath in private carriage. Far., IV, 212.

336 West in Bath. Ibid., 211–12, V, 32, Mss., 3772, 3821, 3840–41.

PAGE

337   Visit to Beckford. Far., IV, 242–44.

337   Return from Bath. Ibid., 211, Mss., 3858, 4034.

337   Mrs. West's eyesight, illness from paint. Far. Mss., 3500; Roden-bough, 267–68, Mrs. West to Elizabeth S. Swift, September 5, 1799.

338   Rembrandt and Rubens Peale. Dunlap, II, 50–52; C. C. Sellers, *Peale* (1947), II, 147 et seq. (1969), 310; Lester, 205–08; *DAB*; Elam, 116.

339   Lithography. PAFA, *Portraits . . . by Peale*, 12; *EB*, 14th ed., XIV, 209; H. T. Wood, 305.

339   West angry. C. C. Sellers, *Peale* (1947), II, 169.

339   Peales took creditor to U.S. C. C. Sellers, *Peale* (1947), II, 169.

339 fn   Peale's *Court of Death*. Dunlap, II, 54; Lester, 209.

340   C. W. Peale resumed painting. C. C. Sellers, *Peale* (1969), 375; *PMHB*, IX, 1885, p. 131, Peale to West, December 16, 1807; APS, Peale to West, July 4, 1808.

340   Rembrandt Peale exchange with David. R. Peale, "Reminiscences," 23.

340   Allston, *Gladiator* to West. Dunlap, II, 158; Flagg, 46.

340   West sponsored Allston. RA, Mss. list of "Students Admitted to Draw."

340   Allston and Fuseli. Dunlap, II, 160; Flagg, 39.

340   Allston on West's painting. Flagg, 43.

341   West and Malbone. Dunlap, II, 18, 19, 25.

341   Malbone not interested in old masters. Tolman, 119; Flagg, 36.

341   Malbone felt he could learn nothing more. E. P. Richardson, *Allston*, 52.

341   West urged him to stay. Dunlap, II, 25.

341   West on Malbone in 1808. Dunlap, II, 19, 27.

341   Washington Irving and Allston. Cahill-Barr, 32.

342   Allston and S. T. Coleridge. Dunlap, II, 167.

342   Fulton bought two Wests. Dickinson, 200–1.

342   West on blowing up French fleet. Far., III, 3, 4.

342   Fulton, Mrs. West's "adopted son." NYPL, Mrs. West to Mrs. Trumbull, September 29, 1806.

342   Fulton to Barlow: "My hands are free." Dickinson, 199, 200.

342   Prepared extra set of drawings. Dickinson, 200.

342   West gave Fulton his self-portrait. Reigart, 44. He charged Fulton with investigating his land purchases in America with authority to sell if he so decided. HSP, West to [?], September 29, 1808; Friends Library, West to Fulton, September 29, 1806.

342   Fulton and Pennsylvania Academy. Reigart, 46–48; Dickinson, 201; *PMHB*, IX, 1885, "Correspondence of C. W. Peale," 122–23, 126–30.

343   George Clymer declined. Brumbaugh, 385–86.

343   Fulton's steam boat. Far., IV, 237.

343   Bourgeois sent carriage. Far., V, 1.

343   Farington: "All had gone well." Ibid., 8.

343   West elected unanimously 1810. Far. Mss., 4637.

343   Yenn cordial to Farington. Ibid., 3856.

343   Shee paid much attention to West. Far., V, 183.

343   Soane unpleasantness. Whitley, III, 163; Far., VI, 6, 18, 242, 244, 255, 262. For a defense of Soane's stand, see A. T. Bolton, 148, et seq.

PAGE
344 West speech to students. Far. Mss., 3870.
344 West's pronunciation. Ibid., 6319, Far., VII, 180.
344 West on fishing party. Far., V, 215.
344 West's help to Turnerelli. Far. Mss., 6071.
344 Farington's happy dinner. Far., V, 160.
343–46 William Williams. Dickason, "Unpublished Letter," 128–30, Williams, 188–202.
346 West's *Omnia Vincit Amor*. Whitley, III, 189.
346 Nelson print. HSP, Thomas Powell to West, May 11, 1809.
346 Second highest Academy receipts. Far., VII, 5.
346 Farington on successful 1811 Academy dinner. Far., VI, 264.
346 Prince regent at dinner. Whitley, III, 187–88; Far., VI, 264–65; HSP, notes on the prince regent's visit in West's hand. In a graceful speech delivered in an amiable mood, the prince addressed the president, "Distinguished Sir, as you are in the highest walk of art, every acknowledgement is due for those works within these walls and in the British Gallery." Following the dinner, he indicated that he would retain West as surveyor of pictures and ordered him to make a complete inventory of the royal collection. One result was *The History and Antiquities of Kensington Palace*, edited by Thomas Faulkner. West's recorded views on the various pictures he inventoried are revealing.
347 Pasquin's parody. Whitley, III, 168–69.
348 Pennsylvania Hospital and *Christ Healing*. It has been assumed that the hospital asked West for money and that he offered a picture instead, but the hospital minutes for September 1, 1800 show that the original request was for a picture. *Pennsylvania Hospital Bulletin*, VIII, No. 4 (1950–51). The lower part of the original picture was badly damaged in the great flood at the Tate Gallery in 1948.
348 "Have you seen the picture?" F. W. Haydon, II, 293.
348 Exaggerated praise was thought disgusting. Far., VI, 275.
348 West inspired by Elgin marbles. Evans, 93. West's earlier opinion of Elgin seems not to have been favorable. Nicholas Biddle wrote in 1807: "[West] agreed with me about Elgin, a sad barbarian who collected merely to sell and whose boxes are now lying in some corner in London." Wainwright, 114.
349 Elgin asked West to recommend a painter. St. Clair, 8.
349 West spent three weeks. Far., V, 130.
349 Arranged for medalists to see marbles. St. Clair, 218.
349 Gave passes to see marbles. One of West's passes is reproduced in Munby, 29.
349 Haydon took Fuseli. St. Clair, 171; B. R. Haydon, *Autobiography*, 395.
349 Haydon took Keats. St. Clair, 265.
349 Haydon met West at Park Lane shed. B. R. Haydon, *Autobiography*, 81, 98.
350 Controversy over artistic quality of marbles. St. Clair, 166–67, 173–77.
350 West: "The perfection of art." Far., V, 68.
350 Elgin's attempt to sell. St. Clair, 181, et seq.

PAGE

350 Payne Knight. St. Clair, 172–79.
350 West's letter to Elgin. W. R. Hamilton, *Memorandum*, Appendix, 47–56.
351 Academy rejected West's letter. Far., V, 122.
351 Haydon made furious notes. B. R. Haydon, *Autobiography*, 98, 141, *Diary*, I, 212.
351–52 Lord Byron. St. Clair, 164, 179, 187–201.
352 Sale of *Christ Healing* to the British Institution. Far., VI, 248, 252; Dunlap, I, 85.
352 West's medal for British Institution subscribers. Smith, II, *Nollekens*, 386–87.
352 Nollekens bust of West. Far., VI, 252, Mss., 5721.
352 fn Three thousand guineas highest price. Reitlinger, I, 67.
353 Earnings of *Christ Healing*. Far., VII, 1, 91.
353 King's congratulations, West's answer. HSP, West to H. Rowland, May 25, 1811. This is a draft of a letter, much emended, in West's hand. Rowland was in charge of the king's privy purse.
353 Trumbull's efforts. Dunlap, I, 374, III, 312.
354 Trumbull on Jefferson, "Maddison," Bonaparte. Trumbull, 172–73; Jaffe, 214, 227.
354 Trumbull quarrel with West. Dunlap, I, 372–73, *Diary*, 799; Far. Mss., 6343, 6351.
354 Three Copley humiliations. Far., II, 244, III, 250–51, Mss., 562.
354 Mrs. Copley to her daughter. Amory, 302–3.
354 No attention paid to Copley's *Resurrection*. Prown, 380.
355 Copley's calls on West. Far., V, 47, 135, Mss., 5963; Whitley, III, 146–47. Copley's equestrian portrait of the Prince of Wales was brutally ridiculed. His last call on West was made in November 1811, when he came several times to deplore the losses he had sustained in selling his Beacon Hill property for £7000. The spirit of building and improvement, he lamented, had since run in that direction, and it was now valued at £100,000.
355 West began *Christ Rejected*. Far., VII, 63.

Chapter 25. *"On the Highest Pinnacle"*   Pages 356–369

356 West's encouragement to Constable. Leslie, *Memoirs*, 14, 15.
356–57 On Sully in Philadelphia and London. Dunlap, II, 115–19, 261.
357 Mrs. Bridgen on C. B. King. Dickson, *Neal*, 54, 85, 86.
357 "Another American!" Dunlap, II, 123.
357 Sully and West. Dunlap, II, 118–26; Biddle-Fielding, 13, 18. For West's emphasis on learning the bone structure, see his lecture in Galt, II, 108–9.
358 West's letter to Philadelphia on Sully. Dunlap, II, 122.
358 West praise for *Dead Man*. E. P. Richardson, *Allston*, 105.
358 Beaumont took up Allston. Flagg, 89.
358 Morse to parents on West. Prime, 35–36.
358 fn Canaday on *Dead Man*. *New York Times*, December 28, 1975.
359 Morse's activities. Ibid., 45; Morse, I, 49, 52.
360 Allston would battle West over Morse. Ibid., 59.
360 Morse found West friendly. Ibid., 40.

PAGE

360 Saving by preparing common paper to paint on. Ibid., 57. For a painting 8 feet by 6½ feet, an artist paid almost £8 at this time for the canvas, almost £20 for the cheapest acceptable frame.

360 Morse, West, and the *Farnese Hercules*. Ibid., 40–41, 46.

360 Posed for hands. Ibid., 41.

361 C. R. Leslie. *Recollections*, 18–27.

361 Morse and Leslie. Ibid., 20–21; Prime, 41; Dickson, *Neal*, 54: Dunlap, III, 310.

361 Rooms on Great Titchfield Street. C. R. Leslie, *Autobiography*, 20, 21; Prime, 36.

361 Leslie entitled to swagger. Olney, 27.

361 "We all lived together . . ." Flagg, 88; Mabee, 29; Prime, 37.

361 Slept with pistols. Morse, I, 64.

361 West's help to Leslie. Dunlap, II, 243; C. R. Leslie, *Recollections*, 27.

361 Unhindered access to the British Museum. No more than ten persons were permitted to enter each hour, to stay no more than three hours. Besant, 447.

362 Constable. Far., II, 245; C. R. Leslie, *Memoirs*, 15; Beckett, IV, 18; Canaday, *Lives*, II, 612.

363 Constable and job offer. Beckett, VI, 6, 7; C. R. Leslie, *Memoirs*, 15–16.

363 Constable: "Would have been a death blow." Beckett, VI, 7.

363 Constable to Maria Bicknell. Beckett, II, 65.

364 West instruction on *Flatford Mill*. C. R. Leslie, *Memoirs*, 14, 15.

364 Constable detested West's history pictures. Beckett, VI, 107.

364 Sold first landscape. Far., VI, 88.

364 Wanted to become A.R.A. Far., VI, 78. In July 1807 Farington discouraged Constable from entering his name for A.R.A., knowing he would be passed over. (IV, 167.)

364 Mother to Constable. Beckett, IV, 62–63.

365 Constable on light, dew, and breezes. MacColl, 77.

365 Uneasy over placement of *Dedham*. Far., VI, 262.

365 The Beaumonts and Constable, Turner, and West. Far., I, 170, 229, II, 174, 182, 219, VI, 279, Mss., 353, 1497, 6095.

365–66 The expedition to Shooter's Hill. Far., VII, 197–99, Mss., 6383. West's bill for the dinner was £6-18s., with five shillings (3.5 percent) for the waiters.

367 Advertisement in *Morning Herald*. Whitley, III, 232.

367 Frame of *Christ Rejected*. Ibid.

367 Three attendants. Far. Mss., 7206.

367 Praise for *Christ Rejected*. J. Robinson; Henderson, 46; Whitley, III, 232.

367 Sydney Smith. Henderson, 46; Sydney Smith, review of *Statistical Annals . . . of the United States*, by Adam Seybert, in the *Edinburgh Review*, January, 1820.

367 Four hundred and seventy visitors a day. Far., Mss., 6616.

367 Farington: "Like a church." Ibid., 6614.

367 West refused 8000 guineas. Far., VII, 143; Whitley, III, 232.

368 Beaumont on small study. Far., VIII, 6.

368 Charles Long's contempt. Far. Mss., 6544.

368 Beaumont blamed printed piece. Ibid. West was conscious of and

embarrassed by the laudatory pamphlets on *Christ Healing* and *Christ Rejected* and wrote out a statement that he was not responsible for the work of William Carey, the worst offender. HSP, undated letter; Dillenberger, 120.

368 Hazlitt in *The Champion*. Far. Mss., 6544; Baker, 269; MacLean, 313; Hazlitt, XVIII, 28–34; Whitley Papers, 1680.

368 Robinson and Flaxman. H. C. Robinson, I, 433.

368 Mrs. West did not expect to live. Far. Mss., 6449.

368 Feared she would die with Mr. West absent. Ibid., 6016.

369 West's health good. Ibid., 6064, 6449.

369 Farington dined with West. Far., VII, 272.

369 Elizabeth West's death and burial. Far. Mss., 6641, 6644; *Analectic*, V, 1815, p. 524; Kent, 475. Her grave in the crypt cannot now be found.

Chapter 26. *The Final Years*   Pages 370–384

370 Benjamin Wests, Jr., moved in. Far. Mss., 6710.

370 Farington liked Benjamin Wests, Jr. Ibid., 7425, 7523. The Dulwich College Gallery in south London has a portrait by West of one of his daughters-in-law, presumably Mrs. Benjamin, with her child.

371 Walter Scott and chandelier. Whitley, III, 240–41; Far. Mss., 6070. Farington was present at the dinner but stopped his diary for some days after writing no more than a diagram of each table and its occupants.

371 Record-breaking 1815 exhibition receipts. Whitley, III, 246.

371 Dinner at Benevolent Fund. Far., VIII, 25, Mss., 6658.

371 Smirke on West's admiration for Bonaparte. Far., VIII, 3.

372 Farington on Bonaparte. Ibid., 237.

372 French were outraged at losing looted art works. F. H. Taylor, 574.

372 Haydon looks at West's drawings. B. R. Haydon, *Autobiography*, 253.

372 Haydon on West's grandeur of soul. Ibid., 79, 395.

372 West visits Haydon. Ibid., 194–95.

372 fn Prince regent and return of art works. Priestley, 143.

373 West's testimony on Elgin marbles. Far. Mss., 6875; *Report of the Select Committee*, 148–49, and "West" in index; J. T. Smith, *Nollekens*, I, 315–16.

373 Waterloo medal. Far., VIII, 29; HSP, West to Beaumont, September 20, 1815.

373 West on Isle of Wight. Far. Mss., 6756, 6790, 7333; HSP, Nash to West, December 30, 1816.

374 "Involved condition" of Copley's estate. Amory, 314.

374 Hamilton's dinner for Canova. Far., IV, 56, VIII, 46, 48; St. Clair, 152; B. R. Haydon, *Autobiography*, 265.

374 West, Canova, and students. Far., VIII, 47–48; Whitley, III, 252.

374 Knight a "presumptious connoisseur," not invited to dinner. Far. Mss., 6895; St. Clair, 260.

374 Benjamin and Raphael on their father. Far. Mss., 6905, 7064.

374 fn Beaumont favored restoration of marbles. Far., V, 72.

PAGE
375 Club meetings agreeable. Far. Mss., 6234, 6910.
375 First part of Galt's biography published. Far., VIII, 216, Mss., 7368; H. C. Robinson, II, 8.
375 West's 1816 medal. Far., VIII, 79, Mss., 6922; HSP, Flaxman to West, July 3, 1816; Morgan Library, Fuseli to West, July 10, 1816.
376 Samuel Waldo. In writing to Trumbull, September 30, 1806, from London, Waldo had said, "I have been highly favored with the instruction of Mr. West, whom I sincerely venerate and esteem." AAA, D5, 332–34.
376 Lawrence portrait of West. HSP, West to American Academy of Arts in New York, May 25, 1819; NYPL, Trumbull to West, September 8, 1819; Far., VIII, 88, 89; Dunlap, I, 71, 289, 373, II, 207, 208, 340; Lawrence Papers, R. A., Trumbull to Lawrence, January 24, 1818.
376 West and John Quincy Adams. J. Q. Adams, Memoirs, III, 386, 548, 552; Ford, 94, J. Q. A. to mother, September 28, 1816; Copley, Letters, 195.
377 Barenger found West painting with left hand. Far., Mss., 7034. I have been unable to identify Barenger.
377 Dr. Hayes' warning on overwork. Ibid., 7150.
377 First use of gas at Academy. Whitley, III, 271.
377 Mr. Hamlet aggrieved. Ibid., 271.
377 West and Dulwich dinner. Far., VIII, 135; Whitley, III, 253.
377 fn Raphael West's help to father. Far., VIII, 35.
378 Beechey and Thomson warn on West and 50th anniversary. Far. Mss., 7276, 7350.
378 Dinner at John Penn's. Ibid., 7205, 7206, Far., VIII, 140.
378 Christ Healing for Philadelphia. Du Pont Winterthur Museum, West to Samuel Coates, August 5, 1817, March 22, 1818; HSP, West to Sarah Wharton Robeson, August 5, 1817; Dunlap, I, 85–86.
378 Private showing of Pale Horse. Far., VIII, 167, Mss., 7256, 7269.
378 Constable well satisfied though defeated. Far., VIII, 149.
379 Keats and Severn. Birkenhead, 62–63.
379 West's lecture to students. Far., VIII, 154, Mss., 7276–77, 7282.
379 Keats on Pale Horse. Rollins, 192. Of Keats' comment, Sidney Colvin said in 1920, it is "worth whole treatises and fit, sketchy as it is, to serve as text to most of what can justly be discoursed concerning problems of art in relation to nature — of realism, romance, and the rest." Ibid.
379 West to theater. Far. Mss., 7271–72.
379–80 Raphael West's financial problems. HSP, Raphael West to father, February 24, March 25, 1818.
380 West, Lord Clive, and exhibition space. Far. Mss., 7334, 7352, 7359, 7363, 7368.
380 Princess Elizabeth at exhibition. Ibid., 7374.
380 Mr. Seddons' party; West seen with two ladies. Ibid., 7387, 7175.
381 Farington calls on West. Ibid., 7411–12.
381 West's granddaughter, "a little Psyche." Dunlap, II, 148.
381 Allston won award. Flagg, 130.
381 Talk that Allston should succeed West. Ibid., 135–36.
382 Lawrence to West from Vienna. Far., VIII, 215; HSP, January 16, 1819.

PAGE
382　Academy program pre-empted by Lawrence. Whitley, V and A "Press Cuttings," IV, 940; Garlick, *Loan Exhibition*, 10.

382　Beaumont calls on West. Far. Mss., 7585.

382　Sale of his pictures. Ibid., 1026, 7624.

382 fn　E. P. Richardson on Allston's American work. *Painting in America*, 143, 147; Allston, 3.

383　West testimonial for lead pencil. Ibid., 7570, 7633.

383　West bitter at English. Far., VIII, 228.

383　Constable elected A.R.A. Far., VIII, 236, Mss., 7673.

383　Hoppner's unfinished portraits. Far., VII, 238.

383　Richards' illegitimate daughter. Far., VII, 11.

383　West ruled on Wyatt's funeral. Ibid., 205, VIII, 178.

383　Yenn in a state of imbecility. Far. Mss., 7771.

383　Kauffmann funeral. V. and A. "Press Cuttings," I, 5; Smith, *Nollekens*, 287.

Chapter 27.　*A Windy Night, a Rainy Morrow*　　　Pages 385–392

385　"A windy night . . ." Shakespeare, Sonnet 90.

385　Steegman, "gap of appreciation." xxv.

385–86　Death and burial of Benjamin West. Far., VIII, 243–46, Mss., 7736, 7742, 7748. (See Chapter 1.) On a motion of John Soane, the 30 shillings billed to each Academician for the funeral expenses was paid out of Academy funds. RA, Assembly minutes, II, 317; V. and A. "Press Cuttings," IV, 1175, V, 1216.

385　Lawrence on West. RA, Lawrence Papers, No. 9, p. 5.

386　Lawrence elected P.R.A. Far., VIII, 245. He did not follow West's custom of wearing his hat at Academy meetings. He designed a medallion to be worn by the president on a gold chain. George IV made a gift of medal and chain to the Academy, and it is worn today.

386　Estate estimated at £100,000. Whitley, III, 311. West's will, leaving everything to his sons in 30 lines on one-half page, is in the probate book at the Public Record Office.

386　Debts of £11,000. Far. Mss., 7808.

386　Conference at Newman Street. Ibid., 7761, 7777.

386　Christie catalogue. AAA, Roll 52; Far. Mss., 7777.

387　Sons set prices too high. Far. Mss., 7763.

387　Sales went off badly. Far., VIII, 255, Mss., 7798, 7800, 7808, 7813–14, 7816.

387　No more auctions. Far., VIII, 255.

387　Henderson collected all receipts. Ibid., Mss., 7863.

387　Sons "bought in" against advice. Far. Mss., 7814.

387　Henderson also the bank's solicitor. Ibid., 7947.

387　Raphael feared "in driblets." Ibid., 7919.

387　Banker's stern notice. Ibid., 7947.

387　West's New Gallery. Ibid., 7814, 7886, 7919, 7947; Whitley, IV, 9–11; Whitley Papers, 1686; *Morning Herald*, May 25, 1821. The HSP has an 1822 gallery catalogue of the collection.

387　Lady Beaumont concerned. Far. Mss., 7939, 7942.

387　Marsh, Sibbald stopped credit. Ibid., 7946.

Epilogue: *The History of a Reputation*   Pages 393–402

PAGE

394 "Barry might starve." Ibid., 124.

394 "Utterly colourless." Hodgson-Eaton, 192.

395 "None of his students could make good pictures." Burroughs, *Limners*, 76.

395 "Fatal influence." Hagen, 116, 123, 133.

395 "Shallowness of mind." Barker, 203, 207.

395 "Singularly unapt to understand." Boase, 3.

395 "Bad painter . . . good man." Whitley, III, 312.

396 E. P. Richardson: "No artist more scornfully denigrated." *Painting in America*, 89.

396 Flexner: "Why so much hatred?" *Old Masters*, 94.

396 "Tame and feeble mind." Thornbury, *British Artists*, II, 101.

397 Allan Cunningham on West as a stately Quaker. *Lives*, "West," 45.

397 Thornbury on West's wedding. *British Artists*, II, 113–14.

398 Heartlessly indifferent to financial problems. Ibid., 124.

398 Flexner: "Most successful career." *Old Masters*, 19.

399 Parker Lesley on Hagen. 167–72.

399 Mayor on West. *Early American Painters*, 106–7.

399 Semon: "Fluid line." 6.

399 Larkin: "Deep humanity." *Art and Life*, 63.

399 E. P. Richardson on West. *Painting in America*, 89, 142–43; "Benjamin West"; *Allston*, 129.

399 Rosenblum: "West's crucial importance." *Art Bulletin*, 76.

399 Reitlinger: "Incredibly able." I, 66, 67, III, 376.

400 Mount: "Classic lore and arts." 50.

401 Staley: "Stylistic innovator." 19.

401 Harris: "Made the only innovations." 14.

401 Irwin: "Highly successful style." *Neo-Classical Art*, 96, 152–53.

401 Canaday. *New York Times*, May 19, 1968; *Lives*, II, 614.

Appendix I: *John Galt's Biography of West as a Source*   Pages 411–414

411 Dunlap: "Injudicious biographer." Dunlap, I, 34.

411 Galt and West relationship. Aberdein, 89–90; Gordon, 9–20; Pye, 132; Galt, II, 202, *Literary Life*, I, 190; *DNB*; *EB*. Flexner research. "Neo-Classicism," 9–19.

412 Validation of officers at Gibraltar. *Commissioned Sea Officers*; HSP, Col. Shippen to brother, May 11, 1760, to father, May 16, July 4, 1760.

413 West and Eagles. Dickason, "Unpublished Letter," 128–33.

413 Galt's clear text on war service. I, 63.

413 King and American independence. Prime, 34; Dunlap, I, 69; Far., VII, 191.

Appendix II: *The Controversy over Contemporary Costume*
Pages 415–418

415 Edgar Wind: "Academicians feared." "Revolution," 116, 117.

415 Mitchell, new subject matter, Mrs. Siddons. "History Picture," 918.

416 Gainsborough, absurd custom. Whitley, *Gainsborough*, 75, to Lord Dartmouth, April 18, 1770.

PAGE
416 Washington to Jefferson on dress. Jefferson, X, 186, August 1, 1786.
416 Jefferson to Washington. Mayor, "Painters in England," 108.
416 Jefferson to Canova. Ibid.
417 Lord Cornwallis statue. Far. Mss., 375, 380, 381.
417 Muther, *Geschichte der Malerei.* Quoted in Marceau, 6–7.
417 "West had nothing to do with . . ." R. Todd, "History Picture," 303.
417 Baretti. *European Magazine,* Sept. 1794, 163.
417 Barlow, *Columbiad.* 81.
418 1805 article on West. *Public Characters,* 538.
418 Articles on West. American *Port Folio,* July 1811, 257. *La Belle Assemblée,* 10; *Analectic,* VIII, 39.
418 Pasquin's final word. *Memoirs of the Royal Academicians,* 75.

ADDITIONAL NOTE

In the January 1978 issue of *The Pennsylvania Magazine of History and Biography* — too late for use in the text of this biography — Nicholas Wainwright published six annotated pages of newly discovered conversations held by Nicholas Biddle (1786–1884) with Benjamin West in London in 1807. Biddle, later to become a prominent statesman and Philadelphia banker, described West as "really a good old man, fond of talking of himself and like all the distinguished men I have ever seen, equally fond of flattery . . . He paints by candle light — immense industry."

On a visit with West to see the marquis of Stafford's collection, "the finest in England," West called Raphael the greatest of all painters; a marine piece by Turner was "the best piece in the whole gallery"; Turner "was a promising artist but has fallen off much"; Wilkie's faces "are expressive of feelings which evidently come from the bottom of the soul." At a dinner at James Monroe's, at which Biddle and Dr. Edward Jenner were present, West predicted that in a century America would be above all the world in the arts. England, he said, would never be famous in the higher department of arts, because "most English painters are obliged to earn their subsistence, so that before they reach the summit of their art they are wholly occupied in portrait painting and pleasing the people." He went on to tell Biddle that he would himself "have been reduced to the same necessity had it not been for the private patronage of the King, his public profits not being enough." West said it was he who had persuaded the Reverend Samuel Preston to bequeath his valuable library to the Library Company of Philadelphia in 1803. Henry Hope's collection of Dutch painters was good, "but the rest are not of any consequence, scarcely one . . . being the production of the person whose name is affixed to it." He praised the works of Velasquez and Murillo, which produced a footnote by editor Nicholas Wainwright: "West's taste and knowledge of painting are surprising. Neither Velasquez nor Murillo were well known in England until after the Peninsular War, when examples of their work found their way to England."

Other extracts from the conversations have been worked into the notes of this biography.

Bibliography

Manuscript Sources

The following manuscript sources were consulted in the writing of this biography.

In the United States

Historical Society of Pennsylvania, Philadelphia

The richest store of Benjamin West manuscript material is found here. At the heart of the collection are the pages of Galt's life of West, mounted separately in seven handsomely bound royal folio volumes, extra-illustrated with engravings of every portrait of the artist and with 313 letters or manuscripts in West's hand or bearing his signature. These folios were acquired in 1910 from one of West's descendants, who claimed that Benjamin West had prepared them himself. The documents include original drafts of several of his letters to George III; drafts of addresses to the Royal Academy; other papers pertaining to Academy business; and 532 letters by other persons, most of them addressed to West. Among the miscellaneous pieces in the HSP collection are lists of the people West invited to Academy affairs; admission tickets signed by him; lists of subscribers to his engravings; his check book on Coutts' Bank for 1790–1804; many documents on his American land purchases; eighty pages of J. H. Henderson's itemized charges for legal services, including collection of rents for West on property in London; and annotated catalogues of his exhibitions and sales. A number of West's letters in the collection are reassembled after having been torn into two pieces, which would seem to indicate rescue from a rubbish heap or a change in intention by the owner.

There is no known collection of West's private correspondence or family papers as such, but some of the letters at the HSP are highly personal, including those West sent to his brother William and to friends of his boyhood, and Raphael West's begging letters to his father. There are only a few letters here and elsewhere by Elizabeth West. An article in *Harper's New Monthly Magazine*, December 1867, refers to "her letters written to her friends at home — still in possession of the family — breathing only of the kindness of all she met and in particular of 'our gracious Queen Charlotte' "; but the article is a superficial one and these letters, if they existed as a collection, have never been found — nor do they sound like Mrs. West's extant letters. Judging by the one known example of her poetry (page 296) and her outspoken correspondence with Mrs. Trumbull in 1805 and 1806, the loss of her letters is a lamentable one.

The Society also owns two small West sketchbooks of his American years, containing 110 figure drawings, 46 engravings after his pictures, and four oil paintings, including his young Thomas Mifflin.

The Society's Shippen-Balch Papers and the William Allen letterbook contain the letters that are the prime source on West's trip to Leghorn and his three years of study in Italy and first months in England.

The American Philosophical Society, Philadelphia

In its Charles Willson Peale Papers, which includes the typescript of his autobiography, his letter books, and his account book, the APS has material of major importance in the West-Peale relationship. It also has six letters from West to Benjamin Franklin (1778, 1782, 1783, 1787, and 1789); two key letters (April 22 and June 21, 1763) from Robert Rutherford to Colonel Joseph Shippen; and an unpublished 141-page manuscript by the artist John Neagle, *Hints for a Painter with Regard to His Method of Study,* ca. 1818, which describes some of West's painting practices.

The Pennsylvania Academy of the Fine Arts, Philadelphia

The Academy owns a letter (September 17, 1760) from Colonel Joseph Shippen in Rome to West in Leghorn.

Friends Historical Library of Swarthmore College, Swarthmore, Pennsylvania

The Library has a unique possession in Mrs. West's account book and a useful one in a random collection of press clippings and exhibition reviews dating back to 1830. Its West letters include one to Robert Fulton (September 29, 1806), one to Francis Chantrey (May 19, 1819), and one to Thomas Sully (August 5, 1817). It has a collection of more than 200 West drawings in pencil, crayon, and sepia (both ink and wash), some of them major works. Among them are his portrait of Angelica Kauffmann made in Italy and his portrait of Beckford's dwarf made at Fonthill. West's collateral descendants have supplied genealogical information to the Library.

Henry Francis du Pont Museum at Winterthur, Delaware

The Museum has the original manuscript of William Williams' *Journal of Lewellin Penrose, a Seaman,* of peripheral interest in a West biography; two letters (August 5, 1817, March 22, 1818) from West to Samuel Coates, president of the Pennsylvania Hospital; and a choice, newly discovered letter (May 11, 1762) from West to Colonel Joseph Shippen — the only known letter written by West during his three-year stay in Italy. It appears in E. P. Richardson, "West's Voyage."

Library of Congress, Washington, D.C.

The Manuscript Division has three West letters: one (July 12, 1775) from West to his brother William; one (Feb. 10, 1775) to C. W. Peale on the American Revolution; one (1796) to the earl of Pembroke; and extracts from his remarks to the students of the Royal Academy on the Italian masters.

Archives of American Art, Washington, D.C.

The AAA (a bureau of the Smithsonian Institution) has an original letter (Sept. 10, 1771) from West to his boyhood friend in Philadelphia, John Green. It has on microfilm the West letters and documents owned in most of the other American archival collections. The microfilm can be obtained on interlibrary loan.

New York Public Library, New York
The Manuscript Division has seven West items, including a West letter to Francis Hopkinson (1770), one to Rufus King (1800), one to James Monroe (1804), and a copy of Mrs. West's letter of Sept. 29, 1806 to Mrs. Trumbull.

Pierpont Morgan Library, New York
In addition to its extraordinary collection of drawings by Benjamin West and his son Raphael, the Library has some twenty letters by, to or relating to West, including two letters from Joshua Reynolds to West (no date and April 7, 1789) and from Fuseli to West (July 10, 1816).

New-York Historical Society, New York
The Society has twenty-one West items, including a letter to West from James Monroe (May 18, 1816), from John Howard Payne (Dec. 24, 1814), two from Robert Fulton (Feb. 22, 1805, July 12, 1810), and Gilbert Stuart's famous plea for West's help in 1777.

Sterling Library, Yale University, New Haven
The Sterling is the repository of John Trumbull Papers, including his autobiography, which contain many West references and exchanges of letters. Two letters are West's report to Trumbull on Royal Academy affairs on Feb. 6, 1805 and Mrs. West's strong letter to Mrs. Trumbull of the same date. Among the manuscripts at the Sterling is J. T. A. Burke's *A Biographical and Critical Study of Benjamin West, 1738–1792*, an unpublished Master of Arts thesis at Yale, presented in 1937.

The Beinecke Rare Book and Manuscript Library, Yale University, New Haven
The Library has several letters by West, including one to Henry Finck (Mar. 16, 1797) on the aid he was giving to his half brother's children.

In Great Britain

The Royal Academy of Arts, London
The Academy has some 2000 letters of the Georgian period, which an archivist of the National Register of Archives, Royal Commission on Historical Manuscripts, has been arranging into separate Academy collections. Most of the letters and documents belong to the Thomas Lawrence Papers; the others are for Reynolds, Gainsborough, Chambers, Farington, Fuseli, Ozias Humphry, James Northcote, John Yenn, and the Society of Artists. Many contain material relevant to West. There is no collection of West Papers as such, but there are several dozen letters by West, most of them on routine Academy matters.

The minute books of the Academy Council and of the General Assembly, legibly written in large folios, are, of course, invaluable to anyone working on West, as is the bound Academy Scrapbook of miscellaneous letters and documents. A happy recent discovery in the Academy's papers is a record of the students admitted to the Life Academy, the date admitted, and their sponsor.

The Academy has two West sketchbooks for his years in Italy and for his 1802 trip to Paris. An unpublished thesis on its shelves is H. C. Morgan's "A History of the Royal Academy Schools, 1768–1836," two volumes, typescript, 1964, accepted for a Ph.D. degree by the University of Leeds.

The Academy has a copy of the twenty-six volumes of J. H. Anderdon's extra-illustrated Royal Academy catalogues. (See British Museum.)

Royal Archives, Windsor Castle

The Royal Archives, maintained in the Norman Keep, the Round Tower, contains twenty-eight letters from West to George III, Queen Charlotte, the prince regent, and officials serving them. The letters are on Royal Academy business, the pictures for the Chapel of Revealed Religion, and the stained-glass windows West designed for St. George's Chapel; but they often have a personal tone, since they relate to West's problems at court or with his colleagues in the Academy. The letters appear in full in Aspinall's published correspondence of the two Georges, except for the elaborate salutations and closings. They include Raphael West's begging letter to George IV in 1828.

Queen Charlotte's diary, of which two small volumes are preserved here (parts of the years 1789 and 1794), contains several casual references to West.

The great West treasure of the Archives is the vast manuscript diary (1793–1821) of Joseph Farington, West's colleague in the Royal Academy. The diary was discovered in 1921 in a mahogany box in the attic of one of Farington's collateral descendants. Farington had intended to destroy it, but instead left it to his three brothers. It was sold at auction in December 1921 (the auction was held in what had been Joshua Reynolds' house in Leicester Square); the *Morning Post* bought it for 110 guineas. The *Post* printed a part of the diary serially in 1922–23, and an abridgment, edited by James Greig, was published in eight volumes in 1922–28. Lady Lilian Bathurst, proprietress of the *Post*, presented the complete manuscript in 1924 to George V.

Sir Owen Morshead, the Royal Librarian at Windsor Castle, undertook the enormous task of transcribing and indexing the entire diary in typescript, though its small, difficult handwriting made it "a wearisome labour" to read and "sustained reading barely practical." The product is twenty-five volumes of the double-spaced Windsor transcript on 8- by 13-inch foolscap — 7261 pages, plus some 540 pages in separate diaries Farington kept on his travels in Belgium (1793), Scotland (1801), and France (1802); plus more than 200 pages of indexes. In an act of extraordinary scholarly courtesy and consideration, a marginal line was placed beside those portions of the transcript that were published in Greig's eight volumes. The transcript is prefaced by the generous words of the royal librarian, "This text may be used without restriction or acknowledgment for any bona fide quotation." The transcript is available to any purchaser on seven microfilm reels for forty-five pounds.

British Museum and Library, London

The Manuscript Department has eleven relatively unimportant letters by West. The Department of Prints and Drawings (Print Room) has on its open shelves a carbon copy of the twenty-five-volume Farington diary Windsor transcript (see above). The original Anderdon catalogues are here: a twenty-six-volume set of Royal Academy catalogues, extra-illustrated by James Hughes Anderdon with pictures, his annotations, reviews of the exhibitions, and miscellaneous letters, all assembled ca. 1850–75. Also "Mrs.

Cromarty's Notes Concerning Her Grandfather John Hoppner . . . Taken from Mama's Anecdotes and from Uncle Belgrave's Letters," no date.

William T. Whitley's "Notes on Artists" (The Whitley Papers) are also here: thirteen large volumes containing the research materials and sources used by Whitley (1858–1942) in writing his invaluable but unannotated four volumes on the history of British art, covering the years 1700–1830. There are 171 items on West under the "W" section.

Victoria and Albert Museum and Library, London
The V and A has in its archives one unimportant letter by West. It houses the valuable V and A "Press Cuttings from English Newspapers on Matters of Artistic Interest, 1686–1835" — six volumes of indexed miscellaneous newspaper and magazine clippings and "unbindable periodicals."

Scottish Record Office, Edinburgh
The SRO has an important body of unpublished letters exchanged between West and William Beckford or Beckford's steward, Nicholas Williams. These, the property of the duke of Hamilton, are in the Beckford Collection of Papers, Box 3/12. Ten of the letters were written by West.

Fitzwilliam Museum, Cambridge, England
The Museum has three commonplace West letters, one of them (May 5, 1816) introducing a Miss King and her two sisters to Vivant Denon in Paris and Antonio Canova in Rome.

National Portrait Gallery, London
The NPG has one West piece, a charming letter of advice from West (July 28, 1802) to Thomas Phillips, a young English protégé of West's who was visiting Paris. (He became a distinguished portrait painter and in 1824 succeeded Fuseli as professor of painting at the Royal Academy.)

Sir John Soane Museum, London
Soane's diary has a running commentary on Royal Academy people and affairs through most of the years of West's presidency. In two separate notebooks he kept his own minutes of the Council meetings for 1803 and 1812. The 1803 diary and minutes throw some new light on the quarrels of that year. The Museum also has eleven letters or documents on Royal Academy affairs.

The Thomas Coram Foundation for Children, London
The Foundation (formerly the famous Foundling Hospital) has several West letters and a number of references to West in its archives, mostly relating to a picture (*Suffer Little Children to Come Unto Me*) he painted for the Hospital.

The Religious Society of Friends, London
The Society has three letters by West, one (February 23, 1816) to an unknown recipient asking for a loan of £500 for his oldest son, Raphael, who then would be better able to help his father in a work in which he was engaged.

PRINTED SOURCES

Aberdein, Jennie W. *John Galt.* London: Oxford University Press, 1936.

Adams, John. *Diary and Autobiography* (The Adams Papers), Vol. III, edited by Lyman H. Butterfield. New York: Atheneum, 1964.

Adams, John Quincy. *Memoirs,* edited by C. F. Adams, Vols. I, III, VI. Philadelphia: Lippincott, 1874.

————. *Writings.* Edited by W. C. Ford, 7 vols. New York: Macmillan, 1913–17.

Addison, Agnes. "The Legend of West's 'Death of Wolfe.' " *College Art Journal,* November 1945.

Africa, J. Simpson. *History of Huntingdon and Blair Counties.* Philadelphia: Everts, 1883.

The Age of Neo-Classicism. (The Fourteenth Exhibition of the Council of Europe.) London: The Arts Council of Great Britain, 1972.

Alberts, Robert C. *The Golden Voyage: The Life and Times of William Bingham, 1752–1804.* Boston: Houghton Mifflin, 1969.

Alexander, Boyd. *England's Wealthiest Son: A Study of William Beckford.* London: Centaur Press, 1962.

————, ed. and trans. *Life at Fonthill, 1807–1822, with Interludes in Paris and London: From the Correspondence of William Beckford.* London: Hart-Davis, 1957.

Amory, Martha Babcock. *The Domestic and Artistic Life of John Singleton Copley, R.A.* Boston: Houghton Mifflin, 1882. Facsimile Reprint. New York: Da Capo Press, 1969.

Analectic Magazine and Naval Chronicle, Vols. VII and VIII. Philadelphia, 1815 and 1816.

Andrieux, Maurice. *Daily Life in Papal Rome in the Eighteenth Century.* Translated by Mary Fitton. New York: Macmillan, 1968.

————. *Rome.* Translated by Charles L. Markmann. New York: Funk and Wagnalls, 1968.

————. *Daily Life in Venice at the Time of Casanova.* Translated by Mary Fitton. New York: Praeger, 1972.

"Anecdotes of Artists of the Last Fifty Years." *Library of the Fine Arts,* Vol. IV. London, 1832.

Angelo, Henry. *Reminiscences.* 2 vols. London, 1828.

The Annual Register. London, 1820.

Antal, Frederick. *Hogarth and His Place in European Art.* London: Routledge and Kegan Paul, 1962.

Ashmead, Henry Graham. *History of Delaware County, Pennsylvania.* Philadelphia, 1884.

Aspinall, A., ed. *The Letters of King George IV, 1812–1830.* 3 vols. Cambridge: At the University Press, 1938.

————. *The Correspondence of George, Prince of Wales, 1770–1812.* 8 vols. New York: Oxford University Press, 1963–71.

————. *The Later Correspondence of George III.* 5 vols. Cambridge: At the University Press, 1968.

Baigell, Matthew. *A History of American Painting.* New York: Praeger, 1971.

Baker, Herschel. *William Hazlitt.* Cambridge: Harvard University Press, 1962.

Balch, Thomas, ed. *Letters and Papers Relating Chiefly to the Provincial History of Pennsylvania.* Philadelphia: Crissy and Markley, 1855.

Bardwell, Thomas. *The Practice of Painting and Perspective Made Easy.* London, 1756.

Baretti, Joseph. *A Guide through the Royal Academy.* London, no date (probably 1781).

Barker, Virgil. *A Critical Introduction to American Painting.* New York: Whitney Museum of Art, 1931.

————. *American Painting: History and Interpretation.* New York: Macmillan, 1950.

Barlow, Joel. *The Columbiad: A Poem.* 2 vols. Philadelphia, 1807.

Barry, James. *The Works of James Barry, Containing His Correspondence . . . His Lectures.* Edited by E. Fryer. 2 vols. London: Cadell and Davis, 1809.

Barton, Benjamin Smith. "Mr. West" (under "Historical Notes"). *Pennsylvania Magazine of History and Biography* IX, no. 3 (1885).

Beckett, R. B., ed. *John Constable's Correspondence,* Vols. II, III, IV, VI. London: Her Majesty's Stationery Office, 1962–68.

Beckford, William. *Memoirs.* 2 vols. London: Skeet, 1859.

Bell, Clive. *Landmarks in Nineteenth-Century Painting.* London: Chatto and Windus, 1927.

Besant, Walter. *London in the Eighteenth Century.* London: Black, 1903.

Biddle, Edward, and Mantle Fielding. *The Life and Works of Thomas Sully.* Philadelphia: Wickersham Press, 1921.

Birkenhead, Sheila. *Against Oblivion: The Life of Joseph Severn.* New York: Macmillan, 1944.

Bizardel, [Mr.] Yvon. *American Painters in Paris.* Translated from the French by Richard Howard. New York: Macmillan, 1960.

Boase, T. S. R. *English Art, 1800–1870.* Oxford University Press, 1959.

Bolton, Arthur T., ed. *The Portrait of Sir John Soane, R.A.* London: Frome and London, 1927.

Bolton, Theodore. "A Portrait of Benjamin West Painted by Himself." *Art in America.* October 1920.

Boswell, James. *Boswell on the Grand Tour: Italy, Corsica and France.* Edited by Frank Brady and Frederick A. Pottle. New York: McGraw-Hill, 1955.

Brander, Michael. *The Georgian Gentleman.* Farnborough: Saxon House, 1973.

Briggs, Berta. *Charles Willson Peale: Artist and Patriot.* New York: McGraw-Hill, 1952.

Brinton, Ellen Starr. "Benjamin West's Painting of Penn's Treaty with the Indians." *Bulletin of the Friends' Historical Association* XXX, No. 2 (1941).

British Artists in Rome 1700–1800. London: Greater London Council, 1974.

Broeder, Frederick Den. "Notes on Works of Benjamin West in the Collection." Storrs: Museum of Art, University of Connecticut, *Bulletin* I, No. 1 (1972).

Bromley, Robert Anthony. *A Philosophical and Critical History of the Fine Arts.* 2 vols. London: 1793–95.

Brooke, John. *King George III: A Biography of America's Last Monarch.* New York: McGraw-Hill, 1972.

Brooks, Alfred Mansfield. "West's Drawings." *Art Bulletin,* September 1925.

Brumbaugh, Thomas B. "The Pennsylvania Academy's Early Days: A Letter of George Clymer to Robert Fulton." *Pennsylvania Magazine of History and Biography,* July 1968.

Buchan, W. *Memoirs of Painting, with a Chronological History of the Importation of Pictures by the Great Masters into England Since the French Revolution.* 2 vols. London, 1824.

The Builder. An Illustrated Weekly Magazine for the Architect, Engineer, Archaeologist, Constructor and Artist, conducted by George Godwin, London. XI, No. 534, April 30, 1853. (On Joseph Neeld's display of West's revealed religion pictures at Grittleton House, Wiltshire.)

Burgess, John Anthony Wilson, and Francis Haskell. *The Age of the Grand Tour.* New York: Crown, 1967.

Burke, Edmund. *A Philosophical Enquiry into the Origins of Our Ideas on the Sublime and the Beautiful.* London, 1757.

Burney, Frances (Madame d'Arblay). *Diary and Letters.* Edited by Charlotte Barrett. 4 vols. London: Vickers and Son, 1842.

―――. *Diary and Letters.* 3 vols. London: F. Warne, 1892.

Burroughs, Alan. *Limners and Likenesses: Three Centuries of American Painting.* Cambridge: Harvard University Press, 1936.

―――. *John Greenwood in America, 1745–1752: A Monograph.* Andover, Mass.: Addison Gallery and Phillips Academy, 1942.

Burt, Struthers. *Philadelphia: Mr. Penn's Holy Experiment.* London: Rich and Cowans, 1945.

Burton, Elizabeth. *The Pageant of Georgian England.* New York: Scribner's, 1967.

Butterfield, Herbert. *George III and the Historians.* New York: Macmillan, 1959.

Butterfield, Lyman H. *The Letters of Benjamin Rush.* 2 vols. Published for the American Philosophical Society. Princeton University Press, 1951.

Button, Dick. "The Art of Skating." *Antiques,* February 1973.

Byron, Lord (George Gordon). *English Bards and Scotch Reviewers.* 1809.

―――. *The Curse of Minerva.* 1811.

———. "To Dives." 1811.

———. *Childe Harold's Pilgrimage, A Romaunt.* Canto II. 1812.
> Three of the Byron works have
> reference to Lord Elgin's marbles.
> "To Dives" is on William Beckford.

Cahill, Holgar, and A. H. Barr, Jr. *Art in America: A Complete Survey.* New York: Reynal and Hitchcock, 1935.

Canaday, John. *Mainstreams of Modern Art.* New York: Holt, Rinehart and Winston, 1959.

———. "The Peculiar Innocence of Benjamin West." *New York Times,* May 19, 1968.

———. *The Lives of the Painters.* 4 vols. New York: Norton: 1969.

———. "A Hodgepodge of 19th-Century 'Bad' Paintings: Not So Bad as They Used to Be?" *New York Times,* July 28, 1974.

Canary, Robert H. *William Dunlap.* New York: Twayne, 1970.

Carey, William. *A Critical and Analytical Review of "Death on a Pale Horse."* London, 1817.

Carson, Hampton L. "The Life and Works of Benjamin West — An Address Delivered before the Historical Society of Pennsylvania." *Pennsylvania Magazine of History and Biography* XLV, No. 4 (1921).

Casanova de Seingalt, G. C. *History of My Life.* Translated by Willard R. Trask. 5 vols. New York: Harcourt Brace, 1966–70.

Chalmers, Alexander, ed. *The General Biographical Dictionary,* Vol. XXXII. London, 1817.

Chancellor, E. B. *The Eighteenth Century in London: An Account of Its Social Life and Arts.* London: Batsford, 1920.

Chapman, Guy. *Beckford.* London: Cape, 1937. (2nd ed., with a new preface, 1952.)

Cheney, Sheldon. *A World History of Art.* New York: Viking, 1937.

Christ Rejected, From the Original by Benjamin West, Engraved on Steel by John Sartain. Also a Sketch of the Life of Benjamin West. Philadelphia: William M. Bradley, 1871.

Christie, Ian R. "The Age of George III" and "The Age of the Prince Regent." In *Connoisseur's Guides,* Edwards-Ramsey, eds.

Clements Library. *The Death of Wolfe.* Bulletin 17. Ann Arbor: William L. Clements Library of American History, University of Michigan, 1928.

Cobban, Alfred, ed. *The Eighteenth Century: Europe in the Age of Enlightenment.* London: Thames and Hudson, 1969.

Coburn, Frederick A. "Mather Brown." *Art in America* XI (1923).

Coleman, James, compiler. *A Pedigree and Genealogy Notes . . . of the . . . Family of Penn.* London: privately printed, 1871.

The Commissioned Sea Officers of the Royal Navy, 1660–1815. Edited by David B. Smith and the Royal Naval College, 3 vols. London: printed by the British Admiralty, 1954.

Comstock, Helen. "Benjamin West and His Times." *Connoisseur,* October 1950.

Comstock, Helen. "Benjamin West and the Neo-Classical Style." *Connoisseur*, January 1962.

The Conduct of the Royal Academicians while Members of the Incorporated Society of Artists. London, 1771.

The Connoisseur. "Benjamin West's Portrait of the Hay-Drummond Family." November 1932.

Constable, W. G. "Foundation of the National Gallery." *Burlington Magazine*, April 1924.

————. *Richard Wilson*. London: Routledge and Kegan Paul, 1953.

————. *The Painter's Workshop*. London: Oxford University Press, 1954.

————. *Art Collecting in the United States*. London: Nelson, 1964.

(Copley, John Singleton.) *The Letters and Papers of John Singleton Copley and Henry Pelham, 1739–1776*. Edited by Guernsey Jones. Boston: Massachusetts Historical Society, 1914.

(Copley, John Singleton, Jr.) *A Concise Vindication of the Conduct of the Five Suspended Members of the Council of the Royal Academy*. London, 1804.

Crook, J. Mordaunt, and M. H. Port. *The Surveyorship of James Wyatt, 1796–1813*, Vol. VII of *The History of the King's Works*. London: Her Majesty's Stationery Office, 1973.

Cross, Wilbur L. *The Life and Times of Lawrence Sterne*. 2 vols. New Haven: Yale University Press, 1925.

Cummings, Frederick. "Phideas in Bloomsbury: B. R. Haydon's Drawings of the Elgin Marbles." *Burlington Magazine*, July 1964.

Cummings, Frederick, and Allen Staley. *Romantic Art in Britain*. Detroit Institute of Art and Philadelphia Museum of Art, 1969.

Cunningham, Allan. *Lives of the Most Eminent British Painters*. 5 vols. London: Murray, 1830–39.

Cunningham, C. C. "Benjamin West's Picture Gallery." Wadsworth Atheneum *Bulletin*, April 1956.

Curwen, Samuel. *Journal and Letters*. Edited by George A. Ward. New York and Boston: C. S. Francis, 1842.

Cust, Leonard, and Sidney Colvin. *History of the Society of Dilettanti*. London: Macmillan, 1898.

Dale, Anthony. *James Wyatt, Architect, 1746–1813*. London: Basil Blackwell, 1936.

Davies, Randall. *English Society of the Eighteenth Century in Contemporary Art*. London: Seeley, 1907.

DeLancy, Edward F. "Chief Justice William Allen." *Pennsylvania Magazine of History and Biography* I, No. 2 (1877).

Denvir, Bernard. "Benjamin West, Innovator and Romantic." *Antiques*, December 1956.

————. "Benjamin West and the Revolution in Painting." *Antiques*, April 1957.

————. "Painting and Sculpture" [Regency Period]. In *Connoisseur's Guides*, Edwards-Ramsey, eds.

A Description of the Picture, "Christ Healing the Sick in the Temple." Philadelphia, 1817.

Dickason, David H. "Benjamin West on William Williams: A Previously Unpublished Letter." *Winterthur Portfolio,* No. 6 (1970).

————. *William Williams: Novelist and Painter of Colonial America.* Bloomington: Indiana University Press, 1970.

Dickinson, H. W. *Robert Fulton, Engineer and Artist; His Life and Works.* London: Lane, 1913.

Dickson, Harold E. *Observations on American Art: Selections from the Writings of John Neal.* University Park: Pennsylvania State University, 1943.

————. *John Wesley Jarvis: American Painter, 1780–1840.* New York: New-York Historical Society, 1949.

————. *Pennsylvania Painters.* University Park: Pennsylvania State University, 1955.

————. *Arts of the Young Republic: The Age of William Dunlap.* Chapel Hill: University of North Carolina, 1968.

Dictionary of American Biography. Edited by Allen Johnson and Dumas Malone, 20 vols. New York: Scribner, 1928–36.

Dictionary of National Biography. Edited by Sir Leslie Stephen and Sir Sidney Lee, 63 vols. London: Macmillan, 1885–1900.

Dillenberger, John. *Benjamin West: The Context of His Life's Work, with Particular Attention to Paintings with Religious Subject Matter.* San Antonio: Trinity University Press, 1977.

Drake, Thomas E. "William Penn's Experiment in Race Relations." *Pennsylvania Magazine of History and Biography,* October 1944.

Du Fresnoy, Charles-Alphonse. *The Art of Painting.* Translated into English by William Mason, with annotations by Sir Joshua Reynolds. York, 1778.

Dulwich Gallery. *Catalogue of the Pictures in the Gallery of Alleyn's College of God's Gift at Dulwich.* Dulwich, 1926.

Dunlap, William. *A History of the Rise and Progress of the Arts of Design in the United States.* Introduction by James Thomas Flexner. Edited by Rita Weiss. New York: George P. Scott, 1834. Facsimile Reprint (3 vols.). New York: Dover Publications, 1969.

————. *Diary, 1766–1823.* 3 vols. New York: New-York Historical Society, 1930.

Dunning, Brian. "American History Painters in London." *Country Life,* April 4, 1968.

Earland, Ada. *John Opie and His Circle.* London: Hutchinson, 1911.

Edwards, Edward. *Anecdotes of Painters Who Have Resided or Been Born in England, with Critical Remarks on the Productions.* London, 1808.

Edwards, Ralph. "George III as Collector." *Apollo,* August 1974.

Edwards, Ralph, and L. G. Ramsey, eds. *The Connoisseur's Complete Period Guides.* New York: Bonanza, 1968.

Einstein, Lewis. *Divided Loyalties: Americans in England During the War of Independence.* Boston: Houghton Mifflin, 1933.

Elam, Charles H., ed. *The Peale Family: Three Generations of American Artists.* Detroit: Detroit Institute of Art and Wayne State University Press, 1967.

Erdman, David W. *Blake: Prophet Against Empire.* Princeton: Princeton University Press, 1954.

———, ed. *The Poetry and Prose of William Blake.* New York: Doubleday, 1965.

Ettlinger, L. D. "Taste and Patronage: The Role of the Artist in Society." In Alfred Cobban, ed., *The Eighteenth Century.*

———. "Winckelmann." In *The Age of Neo-Classicism.*

The European Magazine and London Review, September 1794.

Evans, Grose. *Benjamin West and the Taste of His Times.* Carbondale, Illinois: Southern Illinois University Press, 1959.

Farington, Joseph. *The Farington Diary.* Edited by James Greig, 8 vols. London: Hutchinson, 1922–28. See Farington under manuscript sources.

Faulkner, Thomas. *History and Antiquities of Kensington . . . and a Descriptive Catalogue of the Collection of Pictures in the Palace, from a Survey Taken by the late Benjamin West, P.R.A.* London, 1820.

Fielding, Mantle, and Edward Biddle. *Life and Works of Thomas Sully.* Philadelphia: Wickersham Press, 1921. Reprint. New York: Kennedy Graphics, 1970.

Fineberg, Alexander J. *The Life of Joseph Mallord William Turner, R.A.* Oxford: Clarendon Press, 1939. 2nd ed. 1961.

Fisher, George P. *Life of Benjamin Silliman.* 2 vols. New York: Scribner, 1866.

Flagg, Jared B. *Life and Letters of Washington Allston.* New York: Scribner's, 1892. Facsimile Reprint. New York: Da Capo Press, Library of American Art, 1969.

Fleming, John. "Cardinal Albani's Drawings at Windsor." *Connoisseur,* November 1958.

———. *Robert Adam and His Circle.* Cambridge: Harvard University Press, 1962.

Flexner, James Thomas. *America's Old Masters: First Artists of the New World.* New York: Viking, 1939. Revised edition. New York: Dover Publications, 1967.

———. "The Amazing William Williams." *Magazine of Art,* November 1944.

———. *American Painting: First Flowers of Our Wilderness.* Boston: Houghton Mifflin, 1947.

———. "The American School in London." *Bulletin of the Metropolitan Museum,* October 1948.

———. *John Singleton Copley.* Boston: Houghton Mifflin, 1948.

———. *That Wilder Image: The Painting of America's Native School.* Boston: Little, Brown, 1950.

———. "Benjamin West's American Neo-Classicism." *New-York Historical Society Quarterly,* January 1952. (Reprinted in a slightly abridged form in Flexner's *America's Old Masters,* revised edition.)

————. *The Light of Distant Skies, 1760–1835.* New York: Harcourt Brace, 1954. Reprint. New York: Dover Publications, 1969.

————. *Gilbert Stuart: A Great Life in Brief.* New York: Knopf, 1955.

————. *Nineteenth Century American Painting.* New York: Putnam's, 1970.

Forbes, Gerritt van Husen. *Life of Benjamin West, the Great American Painter, Written for Children.* New York, 1837. (The American Antiquarian Society, Worcester, Massachusetts, has one of the few known copies.)

Ford, Brinsley. "A Portrait Group by Gavin Hamilton." *Burlington Magazine,* December 1955.

Fothergill, Brian. *Sir William Hamilton: Envoy Extraordinary.* New York: Harcourt Brace and World, 1969.

Frankenstein, Alfred Victor. *The World of Copley.* New York: Time-Life Books, 1970.

Franklin, Benjamin. *The Papers of.* Edited by Leonard W. Labaree. 20 vols to date. New Haven: Yale University Press, 1959 —.

————. *The Writings of.* Edited by Albert Henry Smythe, 10 vols. New York: Macmillan, 1907.

Frost, J. William. *The Quaker Family in Colonial America: A Portrait of the Society of Friends.* New York: St. Martins Press, 1974.

Fry, Roger. *Reflections on British Painting.* London: Faber and Faber, 1934.

Fulton, John E. and Elizabeth H. Thomson. *Benjamin Silliman, 1779–1864: Pathfinder in American Science.* New York: Henry Schuman, 1947.

Furthey, J. Smith, and Gilbert Cope. *History of Chester County.* Philadelphia, 1881.

Gage, John. "Magilphs and Mysteries." *Apollo,* July 1964.

Galt, John. *The Life, Studies and Works of Benjamin West, Esq., President of the Royal Academy of London. Composed from Materials Furnished by Himself.* 2 vols. London: Cadell and Davies, 1816–1820.

————. *The Progress of Genius, or, Authentic Memoirs of the Early Life of Benjamin West, Esq., Abridged for the Use of Young Persons by a Lady.* Boston, 1831.

————. *Literary Life and Miscellanies.* 3 vols. London, 1834.

Gardner, Albert Ten Eyck. "Beckford's Gothic Wests." *Bulletin of the Metropolitan Museum of Art,* October 1954.

————. "West's Legacy." *Bulletin of the Metropolitan Museum of Art,* March 1966.

Gardner, Albert Ten Eyck, and Stuart P. Feld. *American Paintings: A Catalogue of the Metropolitan Museum of Art.* Vol I: *Painters Born by 1815.* New York: Metropolitan Museum of Art, 1965.

Garlick, Kenneth. *Loan Exhibition of Paintings by Sir Thomas Lawrence,* London, 1951.

————. *Sir Thomas Lawrence.* London: Routledge and Kegan Paul, 1954.

Gentleman's Magazine. December 1800; March, April 1801; July 1803; March, July, August 1820; July 1829.

George, Eric. *The Life and Death of Benjamin Robert Haydon.* Oxford University Press, 1948.

George, M. Dorothy. *English Social Life in the Eighteenth Century.* London: Sheldon, 1923.

———. *London Life in the Eighteenth Century.* London: Kegan and Paul, 1925. New York: Harper and Row, 1964.

George III — Collector and Patron. London: The Queen's Gallery, Buckingham Palace, 1974.

The Georgian Era: Memoirs of the Most Eminent Persons Who Have Flourished in Great Britain. 4 vols. London, 1834.

Gerdts, William H. Introduction to *American Cornucopia: 19th Century Still Lifes and Studies.* Pittsburgh: Hunt Institute for Botanical Documentation, 1976.

Gifford, William. *The Baviad and Maeviad.* London, 1811.

Gillray, James. *Fashionable Contrasts: Caricatures by.* Edited by Draper Hill. London: Phaidon, 1966.

Goldstein, Carl. "Towards a Definition of Academic Art." *Art Bulletin,* March 1945.

Goldwater, Robert, and Marco Treves, compilers and eds. *Artists on Art from the 14th to the 20th Century.* New York: Pantheon, 1945.

Goodrich, Lawrence B. *Ralph Earl: Recorder for an Era.* Albany: State University of New York, 1967.

Gordon, Ian A. *John Galt: The Life of a Writer.* Edinburgh: Oliver and Boyd, 1972.

Gower, Ronald Charles Sutherland Levison. *Sir Thomas Lawrence.* London: Goupil, 1900.

———. *Sir David Wilkie.* London: Bell, 1902.

Graham, Richard. "Benjamin West, American Romantic: A First One-Man Show in Philadelphia on His Bicentennial." *Art News,* March 19, 1938.

Graves, Algernon. *Dictionary of Artists Who Have Exhibited Works in the Principal London Exhibitions of Oil Paintings from 1760 to 1893.* London: H. Graves, 1901.

———. *Royal Academy of Arts: A Complete Dictionary of the Contributors and Their Work from Its Foundation in 1769 to 1904.* 8 vols. London: Henry Graves, 1905–06.

———. *The Society of Artists of Great Britain, 1760–1791; The Free Society of Artists, 1761–1783; a Complete Dictionary of Contributors and Their Works.* London: Bell and Graves, 1907.

———. *The British Institution, 1806–1867. A Complete Dictionary of Contributors and Their Work.* London: Bell, 1908.

———. *A Century of Loan Exhibitions, 1813–1912.* 5 vols. London: A. Graves, 1913–15.

Green, Samuel M. *American Art: A Historical Survey.* New York: Ronald, 1966.

Gwynn, Stephen. *James Northcote: Memorials of an Eighteenth Century Painter.* London: Unwin, 1898.

Hagen, Oscar. *The Birth of the American Tradition of Art.* New York: Scribner's, 1940.

Hamilton, William Richard. *Memorandum on the Subject of the Earl of Elgin's Pursuits in Greece.* London, 1809; revised edition 1811.

Hardie, Martin. *Water-Colour Painting in Great Britain.* Vol. I: *The Eighteenth Century.* Vol. II: *The Romantic Period.* London: Batchford, 1966–67.

Harris, Neil. *The Artist in American Society: The Formative Years, 1790–1860.* New York: Braziller, 1966.

Hart, Charles Henry. "Autobiographical Notes of Matthew Pratt, Painter." *Pennsylvania Magazine of History and Biography.* XIX (1895).

———. "Benjamin West's Family: The American President of the Royal Academy Not a Quaker." *Pennsylvania Magazine of History and Biography* XXXII, No. 1 (1908).

———. "An Original Portrait of Dr. Franklin Painted by Joseph Wright." *Pennsylvania Magazine of History and Biography* XXXII, No. 3 (1908).

Hartcup, Adeline. *Angelica: The Portrait of an Eighteenth-Century Artist.* London: Heineman, 1954.

Haskell, F. *Patrons and Painters: A Study in the Relations Between Italian Art and Society in the Age of the Baroque.* London: Chatto and Windus, 1963.

Hastings, George E. *The Life and Works of Francis Hopkinson.* Chicago: University of Chicago Press, 1926.

Hauser, Arnold. *The Social History of Art.* London: Routledge and Kegan Paul, 1951.

Hawthorne, Nathaniel. *Biographical Stories for Children.* Boston: Tappan and Dennet, 1842.

Haydon, Benjamin Robert. *The Autobiography and Journals.* Edited by Malcolm Elwin. London: MacDonald, 1950.

———. *The Diary of.* Edited by Willard Bissell Pope. 2 vols. Cambridge: Harvard University Press, 1960.

Haydon, Frederick Wordsworth, ed. *Benjamin Robert Haydon: Correspondence and Table Talk, with a Memoir by His Son.* 2 vols. London: Chatto and Windus, 1876.

Hazlitt, William. *Complete Works.* Edited by P. P. Howe. 21 vols. New York: AMS Press, 1967. (Vol. 18.)

Henderson, Helen W. *The Pennsylvania Academy of the Fine Arts and Other Collections of Philadelphia.* Boston: Page, 1911.

Herbert, J. D. *Irish Varieties of the Last Fifty Years.* London, 1836.

Hibbert, Christopher. *George IV, Prince of Wales.* London: Longman, 1972.

Hilles, Frederick W., ed. *The Literary Career of Sir Joshua Reynolds.* New York: Macmillan, 1956.

Hind, Arthur M. *A History of Engraving and Etching from the 15th Century to the Year 1914.* Boston: Houghton Mifflin, 1923. Reprint. New York: Dover Publications, 1962.

Hirsch, Richard. *The World of Benjamin West.* Allentown, Pa.: Allentown Art Museum, 1962. Catalogue of the 1962 exhibition.

Historic Philadelphia, from the Founding until the Early Nineteenth Century. Philadelphia: American Philosophical Society, 1953.

Hodgson, John E., and Frederick A. Eaton. *The Royal Academy and Its Members, 1768–1830.* London: Murray, 1905.

Hofland, T. C. *A Visit to London,* Vol. IV. London, 1814.

Honisch, Dieter. *Anton Raphael Mengs und die Bildform des Frühklassismus.* Recklinghausen: Bongers, 1965.

Honour, Hugh. *Neo-Classicism.* Harmondsworth: Penguin, 1968.

———. "[Georgian] Painting and Sculpture." In *Connoisseur's Guides,* Edwards-Ramsey, eds.

———. "Neo-Classicism." In *The Age of Neo-Classicism.*

Hornberger, Theodore. "Mr. Hicks of Philadelphia." *Pennsylvania Magazine of History and Biography* LIII, No. 4 (1929).

Howe, A. P. *The Life of William Hazlitt.* New York: R. R. Smith, 1930.

Hudson, Derek. *Sir Joshua Reynolds: A Personal Study.* London: Geoffrey Bles, 1958.

Hudson, Derek, and Kenneth W. Luckhurst. *The Royal Society of Arts, 1754–1954.* London: Murray, 1954.

Huish, Marcus B. *The American Pilgrim Way in England.* London: Fine Arts Society, 1907.

Hunt, Leigh. *Autobiography with Reminiscences.* 2 vols. New York: Harper, 1872.

Hutchison, Sidney C. *The Homes of the Royal Academy.* London: Royal Academy, 1956.

———. *History of the Royal Academy, 1768–1968.* London: Chapman and Hall, 1968.

Irwin, David. "James Barry and the Death of Wolfe in 1759." *Art Bulletin,* December 1959.

———. "Gavin Hamilton, Archeologist." *Art Bulletin,* June 1962.

———. *English Neoclassical Art: Studies in Inspiration and Taste.* London: Faber and Faber, 1966.

Isham, Samuel. *The History of American Painting.* New York: Macmillan, 1905; new edition with supplemental chapters by Royal Cortissoz, Macmillan, 1936.

Jackson, Henry E. *Benjamin West: His Life and Works: A Monograph.* Philadelphia: Winston, 1900.

Jaffe, Irma B. *John Trumbull: Patriot-Artist of the American Revolution.* Boston: New York Graphics Society, 1975.

Jefferson, Thomas. *Papers.* Edited by Julian P. Boyd. 19 vols. to date. Princeton: Princeton University Press, 1950. (Vols. 8, 10, 12, 13, 15.)

Jensen, Arthur L. *The Maritime Commerce of Colonial Philadelphia.* Madison: State Historical Society of Wisconsin for the University of Wisconsin, 1963.

Jordan, Francis, Jr. *The Life of William Henry.* Lancaster, Pa., 1910.

Jordan, John. *Colonial Families of Philadelphia.* 2 vols. New York: Lewis Publishing Company, 1911.

————. *Encyclopedia of Pennsylvania Biography.* New York: Lewis Publishing Company, 1916.

Kent, William. *The Encyclopedia of London.* London: Dent, 1937, reissued 1951.

Kielmansegge, Count Frederick. *Diary of a Journey to England in the Years 1761–62.* New York: Longmans, Green, 1902.

Kimball, Fiske. "Benjamin West au Salon de 1802: La Mort sur le Cheval Pâle." *Gazette des Beaux Arts* VII (June 1932).

Kimball, Fiske, and Henri Marceau. *Benjamin West, 1738–1802.* Philadelphia: Pennsylvania Museum of Art, 1938. Catalogue of the exhibition of that year.

Klein, Randolph Shipley. *Portrait of an Early American Family: The Shippens of Pennsylvania across Three Generations.* Philadelphia: University of Pennsylvania Press, 1935.

Knapp, Oswald G. *An Artist's Love Story: Told in the Letters of Sir Thomas Lawrence, Mrs. Siddons, and Her Daughters.* London: Allen, 1904.

Knowles, John A. *The Life and Writings of Henry Fuseli.* 3 vols. London, 1831.

Konody, Paul George. *The National Gallery.* Edited by Thomas Leman Hare. New York: Dodge, 1923.

Kraemer, Ruth S. *Drawings by Benjamin West and His Son Raphael Lamar West.* New York: Pierpont Morgan Library, 1975.

Kramer, Hilton. "Benjamin West Recalled in Art." *New York Times,* May 3, 1975.

Kronenberger, Louis. *Kings and Desperate Men.* New York: Knopf, 1942.

————. *The Extraordinary Mr. Wilkes.* New York: Doubleday, 1974.

Kulp, George B. *Families of the Wyoming Valley,* Vol. II. Wilkesbarre, 1889.

La Belle Assemblée, or, Bell's Court and Fashionable Magazine, Vol. IV. London, 1808.

Lamb, Walter R. M. *The Royal Academy.* London: Alexander Maclehose, 1935. London: Bell, 1951.

Landis, Charles I. "Benjamin West and the Royal Academy." *Pennsylvania Magazine of History and Biography* L, Nos. 2, 3 (1926).

[Landseer, John.] *A Concise Review of the Concise Vindication of the Conduct of the Five Suspended Members of the Council of the Royal Academy.* London, 1804.

Larkin, Oliver W. *Art and Life in America.* New York: Rinehart, 1949.

————. *Samuel F. B. Morse and American Democratic Art.* Boston: Little, Brown, 1954.

Laver, John. *Taste and Fashion from the French Revolution until Today.* London: Harrap, 1937.

Law, Ernest. *Historical Catalogue of the Pictures in the Royal Collection at Hampton Court.* London: G. Bell, 1881.

Leary, Lewis. "Leigh Hunt in Philadelphia: An American Literary Incident of 1803." *Pennsylvania Magazine of History and Biography,* July 1946.

Lee, Cuthbert. *Early American Portrait Painters.* New Haven: Yale University Press, 1929.

Leppmann, Wolfgang. *Winckelmann.* London: Gollancz, 1971.

Lesley, Parker. Review of *The Birth of the American Tradition of Art*, by Oscar Hagen. *Art Bulletin*, September 1940.

Leslie, Charles Robert. *Memoirs of the Life of John Constable.* London: Longmans, Brown, Green and Longmans, 1845.

———. *Autobiographical Recollections.* Edited by Tom Taylor. Boston: Ticknor and Fields, 1860.

Leslie, Charles Robert, and Tom Taylor. *Life and Times of Sir Joshua Reynolds, with Notices of Some of His Contemporaries.* 2 vols. London: Murray, 1865.

Leslie, George Dunlap. *Inner Life of the Royal Academy.* London: Murray, 1914. Facsimile reprint. New York: B. Blom, 1971.

Lester, Charles Edwards. *The Artists of America: A Series of Biographical Sketches.* New York: Baker and Scribner, 1846.

Levene, Dr. John R. "Benjamin Franklin, FRS, Sir Joshua Reynolds, FRS, PRA, Benjamin West, PRA, and the Invention of Bifocals." Royal Society of London, *Notes and Records*, 1971–72.

Levey, Michael. *Rococo to Revolution: Major Trends in Eighteenth-Century Painting.* New York: Praeger, 1966.

Lewis, Lesley. *Connoisseurs and Secret Agents in Eighteenth Century Rome.* London: Chatto and Windus, 1961.

Lewis, Wilmarth Sheldon. *Three Tours Through London in the Years 1748, 1776, 1797.* New Haven: Yale University Press, 1941.

———. *See for Yourself.* (Chapter on Ralph Earl.) New York: Harper, 1971.

Lipman, Sonia, and Vivian Lipman. "The Strand Block of Somerset House, Part One, The Royal Academy." *History Today*, August 1977.

Liscombe, R. W. "The Commencement of Real Art." *Apollo*, January 1976. (On the Elgin marbles.)

Locquin, Jean. "Le Retour à l'Antique dans l'Ecole Anglaise et dans l'Ecole Française avant David." *La Renaissance de l'Art Française et des Industries de Luxe* V (1922).

Lucas, E. V. *A Wanderer in Rome.* New York: Doran, 1926.

Lynes, Russell. *The Art Makers of Nineteenth Century America.* New York: Atheneum, 1970.

Mabee, Carlton. *The American Leonardo: A Life of Samuel F. B. Morse.* New York: Knopf, 1943.

Macalpine, Ida, and Richard Hunter. "Porphyria and King George III." *Scientific American*, July 1969.

MacColl, D. S. *Nineteenth Century Art.* Glasgow: Maclehose, 1902.

McCoubray, John W. *American Art: Sources and Documents.* New York: Prentice-Hall, 1965.

———. "Painting." In *The Arts in America*, Wright-Tatum, eds.

McKay, William, and W. Roberts. *John Hoppner, R.A.* London: Colnaghi, 1909.

MacLean, Catherine MacDonald. *Born Under Saturn: A Biography of William Hazlitt.* New York: Macmillan, 1944.

McQuinn, A. D. *A Description of the Picture "Christ Rejected by the Jews." Synopsis or Mental Plan of the Picture.* Philadelphia, 1830.

Malone, Dumas. *Jefferson and the Rights of Man.* Boston: Little, Brown, 1951.

Manners, Lady Victoria, and G. C. Williamson. *Angelica Kauffmann, R.A.: Her Life and Works.* London: Brentano, 1924.

Marceau, Henri. "Benjamin West, Esq., of Newman Street, London." *Parnassus,* April 1938.

Margetson, Stella. *Regency London.* New York: Praeger, 1971.

Marks, Arthur S. "Benjamin West and the American Revolution." *American Art Journal.* November 1974.

Marle, Judy. *Neo-Classical England.* Arts Council of Great Britain, London, 1972. Catalogue for the English section of the Council of Europe's exhibition, "The Age of Neo-Classicism."

Marshall, Dorothy. *Dr. Johnson's London.* London: Wiley, 1968.

Martin, Gregory. "Founding of the National Gallery in London," *Connoisseur,* nine issues, April–December 1974.

Martin, Sir Theodore. *Life of Lord Lyndhurst.* London: Murray, 1883.

Mason, Eudo C. *The Mind of Henry Fuseli: Selections from His Writings with an Introductory Study.* London: Routledge and Kegan Paul, 1951.

Mason, George C. *The Life and Works of Gilbert Stuart.* New York: C. Scribner's Sons, 1879.

Mayor, A. Hyatt. "Early American Painters in England." *Proceedings of the American Philosophical Society,* No. 1 (1943).

————. *Giovanni Battista Piranesi.* New York: Bittner, 1952.

Mead, William Edward. *The Grand Tour in the Eighteenth Century.* Boston and New York: Houghton Mifflin, 1914. Reprint. New York: B. Blom, 1972.

Mechlin, Leila. "Early American Portrait Painters." *Connoisseur,* March 1924.

Melville, Lewis. *Life and Letters of William Beckford.* London: Heinemann, 1910.

Mendelowitz, Daniel M. *A History of American Art.* New York: Holt, Rinehart and Winston, 1960.

Meyer, Jerry D. "Benjamin West's Chapel of Revealed Religion: A Study in Eighteenth-Century Protestant Religious Art." *The Art Bulletin,* June 1975.

————. "Benjamin West's 'St. Stephen Altar Piece': A Study in Late Eighteenth-Century Church Patronage and English History Painting." *Burlington Magazine,* September 1976.

Millar, Oliver. *Gainsborough.* New York: Harper, 1949.

————. *Pictures in the Royal Collection: Later Georgian Pictures,* Vol. I, Text; Vol. II, Plates. London: Phaidon, 1969.

Miller, Lillian B. *Patrons and Patriots: The Encouragement of the Fine Arts in the United States, 1790–1860.* Chicago: University of Chicago Press, 1966.

Mitchell, Charles. "Benjamin West's 'Death of General Wolfe' and the Popular History Piece." *Journal of the Warburg and Courtauld Institutes*, January–June, 1944.

———. "The History Picture in English Art." *The Listener*, May 25, 1950.

———. "Benjamin West's 'Death of Nelson.'" *Essays in the History of Art Presented to Rudolf Wittkower*. Edited by Douglas Fraser, Howard Hibbard, and Milton J. Levine. London: Phaidon, 1967.

Montagu, Lady Mary Wortley. *The Complete Letters*, Vol. III, edited by Robert Halsband. Oxford: Clarendon Press, 1967.

Montgomery, Charles F., and Patricia E. Kane. *American Art, 1750–1800: Towards Independence*. Published for Yale University Art Gallery and the Victoria and Albert Museum. Boston: New York Graphics Society, 1976.

Morgan, Charles H., and Margaret C. O'Toole. "Benjamin West: His Times and Influence." *Art in America*, December 1950. Catalogue of a West exhibition at Amherst College.

Morgan, Eileen. *Sir Joshua Reynolds, P.R.A.* Plymouth, England: The Plymouth Corporation, 1973.

Morgan, Dr. John. *Journal . . . from the City of Rome to the City of London in 1764. Together with a Fragment of a Journal Written at Rome, 1764, and a Biographical Sketch*. Philadelphia: Lippincott, 1907.

Morgan, John Hill. *Early American Painters*. New York: New-York Historical Society, 1921.

———. *Gilbert Stuart and His Pupils, Together with the Complete Notes on Painting by Matthew Harris Jouett from Conversations with Gilbert Stuart in 1816*. New-York Historical Society, 1939. Facsimile reprint. New York: Da Capo Press, 1969.

Morgan, John S. *Robert Fulton*. New York: Mason, Charter, 1977.

Morris, Richard B. *The Peacemakers: The Great Powers and American Independence*. New York: Harper and Row, 1965.

Moritz, C. P. *Journey of a German in England in 1782*. Translated and edited by Reginald Nettel. Berlin: F. Maurer, 1785. New York: Holt, Rinehart, 1965.

Morse, Edward Lind, ed. *Samuel F. B. Morse, His Letters and Journals*. 2 vols. Boston: Houghton Mifflin, 1914.

Moses, Henry. *The Gallery of Pictures Painted by Benjamin West . . . Engraved in Outline by H. Moses*. [London: 1811.]

Mount, Charles Merrill. *Gilbert Stuart: A Biography*. New York: Norton, 1964.

Munby, A. N. L. "Letters of British Artists of the XVIIIth and XIXth Centuries." *Connoisseur*, March 1947.

Muther, Richard. *The History of Modern Painting*. 4 vols. London: Henry, 1895–96 (3 vols.). London: Dent, 1907.

———. *The History of Painting from the Fourth to the Early Nineteenth Century*. Translated from the German by George Kriehn. 2 vols. New York: Putnam's, 1907.

Myers, Albert Cook. "Benjamin West's Mother Sarah Pearson, and Her Family." *Bulletin of the Friends' Historical Association* XVIII (Autumn, 1929).

Nannoni, Dr. Angelo. *Memorie Di Chirurgia* (*per Servire Alla Formazione del Secondo Tomo del Trattato Sopra La Semplicità del Medicare I Mali Curabile Coll' Adjuto della Mano*). Siena, 1774. (See Zorgniotti, Dr. Adrian W.)

Neill, Edward Duffield. "Rev. Jacob Duché: The First Chaplain of Congress." *Pennsylvania Magazine of History and Biography* II (1878).

Neumeyer, Alfred. "The Early Historical Paintings of Benjamin West." *Burlington Magazine,* October 1938.

Nicolson, Benedict. *Joseph Wright of Derby: Painter of Light.* Published for the Paul Mellon Foundation for British Art. London: Routledge and Kegan Paul, 1968.

Nicolson, Harold. "The Romantic Revolt." *Horizon,* May 1961.

Northcote, James. *The Life of Sir Joshua Reynolds.* 2 vols. London, 1819.

———. *Conversations* [with William Hazlitt]. London, 1826. Vol. II of Hazlitt's *Complete Works.* London: Dent, 1930–34.

———. *Conversations* [with James Ward]. Edited by Ernest Fletcher. London, 1830. London: Methuen, 1901.

Norton, Mary Beth. *The British-Americans: The Loyalist Exiles in England 1774–1789.* New York: Little, Brown, 1972.

Noszlopy, George T. "A Note on West's 'Apotheosis of Nelson.' " *Burlington Magazine,* December 1970.

Novak, Barbara. *American Painting of the Nineteenth Century.* New York: Praeger, 1969.

Oberholzer, Ellis Paxton. *Philadelphia: A History of the City and Its People.* 4 vols. Philadelphia: Clark, 1912.

O'Donoghue, Freeman. *Catalogue of Engraved British Portraits . . . in the British Museum.* 4 vols. British Museum, 1914.

Olney, Clark. *Benjamin Robert Haydon: Historical Painter.* Athens, Georgia: University of Georgia Press, 1952.

Oman, Carola (Lenanton). *Nelson: A Biography.* New York: Doubleday, 1946.

———. *Napoleon at the Channel.* London: Hodder and Stoughton, 1947.

Orpen, Sir William, and Frank Rutter. *The Outline of Art.* Revised edition by Horace Shipp. London: Bookplan, 1967. First published in New York and London: Putnam's Sons, 1923–24.

Painting in England 1700–1850. From the Collection of Mr. and Mrs. Paul Mellon. London: Royal Academy of Arts, 1964. Catalogue of a Royal Academy exhibition, 1964–65.

Park, Lawrence. *Gilbert Stuart: An Illustrated Descriptive List of His Works.* 4 vols. New York: Rudge, 1926.

Papendiek, Mrs. Charlotte Albert. *Court and Private Life in the Time of Queen Charlotte: Mrs. Papendiek's Journals.* 2 vols. London: Bentley, 1887.

"Pasquin, Anthony." (John Williams). *The Royal Academicians: A Farce.* London, 1786.

———. *A Liberal Critique on the Present Exhibition of the Royal Academy.* London, 1794.

"Pasquin, Anthony." *Memoirs of the Royal Academicians.* London, 1796.

Peale, Charles Willson. "Extracts from the Correspondence of Charles Willson Peale Relative to the Establishment of the Academy of the Fine Arts, Philadelphia." *Pennsylvania Magazine of History and Biography* IX, No. 2 (1885).

Peale, Rembrandt. *An Historical Disquisition on the Mammoth or Great American Incognitum, an Extinct, Immense, Carnivorous Animal Whose Remains Have Been Found in North America.* London, 1803.

———. *Notes on Italy.* Philadelphia: Carey and Lea, 1831.

———. "Reminiscences." *The Crayon Magazine* I, No. 2 (January 10, 1855).

Pelles, Geraldine. *Art, Artists and Society: Origins of a Modern Dilemma — Painting in England and France 1750–1830.* New York: Prentice-Hall, 1963.

Pennsylvania Academy of the Fine Arts. *Catalogue of an Exhibition of Portraits by Charles Willson Peale and James Peale and Rembrandt Peale.* Philadelphia, 1923.

Pennsylvania Magazine of History and Biography XXXV, No. 2 (1911). "The West Collection of the Historical Society of Pennsylvania."

The Penny Magazine. "West's Pictures in the National Gallery." London, June 23, 1838.

Philadelphia Museum of Art. *Philadelphia: Three Centuries of American Art.* Catalogue of an exhibition April 10–October 10, 1976. In two parts.

Phillips, Hugh. *Mid-Georgian London: A Topographical and Social Survey of Central and Western London about 1750.* London: Collins, 1964.

Phillips, John Marshall. "Ralph Earl, Loyalist." *Art in America,* October 1959.

Pilkington, M. *A Dictionary of Painting.* Edited by Henry Fuseli. London, 1805.

"Pindar, Peter." (John Wolcot.) *The Works of Peter Pindar, Esq.* 2 vols. Dublin, 1795.

Piozzi, Hester Lynch. *Observations and Reflections Made in the Course of a Journey Through France, Italy and Germany.* Edited by Herbert Barrows. London: 1789. Ann Arbor: University of Michigan, 1967.

Plan of an Academy for the Better Cultivation, Improvement and Encouragement of . . . the Arts of Design. London, 1755.

Plumb, John Harold. *England in the Eighteenth Century.* Harmondsworth: Penguin, 1950.

The Port Folio. London, 1800.

The Port Folio. Philadelphia, 1804, 1809, 1810, 1811, 1816, 1823.

Pottle, Frederick A. *James Boswell: The Earlier Years, 1740–1769.* New York: McGraw-Hill, 1966.

Praz, Mario. *On Neo-Classicism.* London: Thames and Hudson, 1969.

Price, Frederick Newlin. *Benjamin West: An Address.* Swarthmore: The Benjamin West Society and Swarthmore College, 1938.

Priestley, J. B. *The Prince of Pleasure and His Regency.* New York: Harper and Row, 1969.

Prime, S. Irenaeus. *The Life of S. F. B. Morse.* New York: Appleton, 1875.

Prown, Jules David. *John Singleton Copley.* 2 vols. Vol. I: *In America;* Vol. II: *In England.* Published for the National Gallery of Art, Washington, D.C. by Harvard University Press, 1966.

Public Characters of 1805, Vol. VII. London, 1805.

Pye, John. *The Patronage of British Art.* London: Longman, Brown, 1845.

Quennell, Peter. *Hogarth's Progress.* New York: Viking, 1955.

———. "Magpie's Nest in a London Mansion." *Horizon,* November 1963. (Sir John Soane's Museum.)

Raikes, Thomas. *A Portion of the Journal Kept by Thomas Raikes, Esq. from 1831 to 1847: Comprising Reminiscences of Social and Political Life in London and Paris During That Period.* 2 vols. London: Longman, Brown, Green, Longmans, and Roberts, 1858.

Raimbach, Abraham. *Memoirs and Recollections.* London: F. Shoberl, Jr., 1843.

Redgrave, Samuel. *A Dictionary of Artists.* London, 1874.

Redgrave, Richard, and Samuel Redgrave. *A Century of British Painters.* London: Smith, Elder, 1866. Revised edition, edited by Ruthven Todd. London: Phaidon, 1947.

Reigart, J. Franklin. *The Life of Robert Fulton.* Philadelphia: C. G. Henderson, 1856.

Reitlinger, Gerald. *The Economics of Taste.* Vol. I: *The Rise and Fall of the Picture Market, 1760–1960;* Vol. III: *The Art Market in the 1960s.* New York: Holt, Rinehart and Winston, 1961, 1970.

Report from the Select Committee of the House of Commons on the Earl of Elgin's Collection of Sculptured Marbles. London, 1816.

"*Revealed Religion: Paintings by Benjamin West.*" Greenville, S.C.: Bob Jones University, 1963.

Reynolds, Sir Joshua. *Discourses Delivered to the Students of the Royal Academy.* London: Printed for the Royal Academy of Arts, Macmillan, 1924.

———. *Letters.* Collected and edited by F. W. Hilles. Cambridge: Harvard University Press, 1929.

———. *Portraits.* Edited by Frederick W. Hilles. Yale Edition of the Private Papers of James Boswell. New York: McGraw-Hill, 1952.

Richardson, Edgar Preston. *The Way of Western Art 1776–1914.* Cambridge: Harvard University Press, 1939.

———. *American Romantic Painting.* New York: Weyhe, 1944.

———. *Washington Allston: A Study of the Romantic Artist in America.* Chicago: University of Chicago Press, 1948.

———. "Benjamin West," in *The One Hundred and Fiftieth Anniversary Exhibition of the Pennsylvania Academy of the Fine Arts.* Philadelphia: 1955.

———. *Painting in America: The Story of 450 Years.* New York: Crowell, 1956.

Richardson, Edgar Preston. "William Williams: A Dissenting Opinion." *American Art*, Spring, 1972.

———. "West's Voyage to Italy, 1790, and William Allen." *Pennsylvania Magazine of History and Biography*, January 1978.

Richardson, Jonathan. *The Connoisseur: An Essay on the Whole Art of Criticism as It Relates to Painting*. London, 1719.

———. *An Essay on the Theory of Painting*. 2d ed. London, 1725. Facsimile reprint. London: Scolar Press, 1971.

Roberts, William. *Sir William Beechey*. London: Duckworth, 1907.

———. " 'Mrs. Barrington,' by Benjamin West, P.R.A." Victoria and Albert Museum, *Art Monologues*, 1920.

Robins, Edward. "Some Philadelphia Men of Letters." *Pennsylvania Magazine of History and Biography* L, No. 4 (1926).

Robins, George. *A Catalogue Raisonné of the Unequalled Collection of Historical Pictures and Other Admired Compositions of Benjamin West, Esq. Sold by George Robins in the Gallery at Newman Street, May, 1829*. London, 1829.

Robinson, Henry Crabb, *Diary, Reminiscences, and Correspondence*. Edited by Thomas Sadler. 3 vols. London: Macmillan, 1869.

Robinson, John. *A Description of, and Critical Remarks on the Picture of "Christ Healing the Sick in the Temple."* Philadelphia, 1818.

Rodenbough, Theodore Francis. *Autumn Leaves from Family Trees*. New York: Clark and Zugalla, 1892.

Rodenbough, Theodore Francis, and Charles Henry Hart. Exchange of letters on the claimed elopement of Elizabeth Shewell West. *Pennsylvania Magazine of History and Biography* XXXII, No. 3 (1908).

Roe, F. Gordon. "Joseph Farington, 'Dictator of the Royal Academy,' " *Walker's Quarterly*, No. 5 (1921).

Rogers, Millard F., Jr. "Benjamin West and the Caliph: Paintings for Fonthill Abbey." *Apollo*, June 1966.

Rogers, Samuel. *Recollections of the Table Talk of*. New York: Appleton, 1856.

———. *The Italian Journal*. Edited by J. R. Hall. London: Faber and Faber, 1956.

Rollins, Hyder Edwards. *The Letters of John Keats 1814–1821*. Cambridge: Harvard University Press, 1958.

Romney, Rev. John. *Memoirs of the Life and Works of George Romney*. London, 1830.

Rosenblum, Robert. "Benjamin West's 'Eagle Bringing the Cup to Psyche': A Document of Romantic Classicism." Princeton University *Art Museum Record* XIX (1960).

———. Review of "Benjamin West and the Taste of His Times," by Grose Evans. *Art Bulletin*, March 1960.

———. "Gavin Hamilton's 'Brutus' and Its Aftermath." *Burlington Magazine*, January 1961.

———. *Transformations in Late Eighteenth Century Art*, Princeton University Press, 1967.

Rosenthal, Albert. "Two American Painters: West and Fulton." *Antiquarian*, July 1929.

Rowland, Benjamin, Jr. *The Classical Tradition in Western Art*. Cambridge: Harvard University Press, 1963.

Royal Academy of Arts. *Catalogues of the Royal Academy of Arts, Illustrated with Original Drawings, Autograph Letters and Portraits in the Possession of Edward Basil Jupp*. London: 1858.

————. *The Royal Academy from Reynolds to Millais*. Edited by Charles Holme. London: Studio, 1904.

————. *The First Hundred Years of the Royal Academy, 1769–1868*. London: Royal Academy, 1951.

————. *Treasures of the Royal Academy*. Introduction by Sidney C. Hutchison. London: Royal Academy, 1963.

————. *Catalogue of the Bicentenary Exhibition, 1768–1968*. London: Royal Academy, 1968.

Rudé, George. *Hanoverian London 1714–1808*. Berkeley: University of California Press, 1971.

Rush, Benjamin. *Autobiography*. Edited by George W. Corner. Published for the American Philosophical Society by Princeton University Press, 1948.

Rush, Richard. *Memoranda of a Residence at the Court of London, 1819–1825*. London: R. Bentley, 1845. Philadelphia: Lea and Blanchard, 1845.

Ruskin, John. *Modern Painters* in *The Works of John Ruskin*. Edited by E. T. Cook and Alexander Wedderburn. Vol. V of 39 volumes. London: G. Allen, 1903–12.

Russell, John. "The Royal Academy." *Horizon*, May 1962.

Rutledge, Anna Wells. "Henry Benbridge." *American Collector*, October 1948.

Rutter, Frank. *Wilson and Farington*. New York: Stokes, 1923.

St. Clair, William. *Lord Elgin and the Marbles*. London: Oxford University Press, 1967.

Sandby, William. *The History of the Royal Academy of Arts, with Biographical Notices of All Its Members*. 2 vols. London: Longman, Green, Longman, Roberts and Green, 1862.

Sartain, John. *The Reminiscences of a Very Old Man, 1808–1897*. New York: Appleton, 1899.

Sawitzky, William. "William Williams, the First Instructor of Benjamin West." *Antiques*, May 1937.

————. "The American Work of Benjamin West." *Pennsylvania Magazine of History and Biography*, October 1938.

————. *Matthew Pratt: A Study of His Work*. New York: New-York Historical Society and Carnegie Corporation, 1942.

————. *Catalogue Descriptive and Critical of the Paintings and Miniatures in the Historical Society of Pennsylvania*. Philadelphia: Historical Society of Pennsylvania, 1942.

————. *Ralph Earl, 1751–1801*. New York: Whitney Museum, 1945.

Sawitzky, William, and Susan Sawitzky. "Two Letters from Ralph Earl, With Notes on His English Period." Worcester Art Museum *Annual* VIII (1960).

Schmid, F. *The Practice of Painting.* London: Faber and Faber, 1948.

Scott, A. F. *Every One a Witness: The Georgian Age, an Anthology.* London: Martin, 1970.

Scriven, Edward. *Elements of Drawing in a Series of Examples Extracted from Pictures Painted by and in the Gallery of Benjamin West,* Esq. London, 1821.

Sellers, Charles Coleman. *Charles Willson Peale, Artist of the Revolution.* 2 vols. Philadelphia: American Philosophical Society, 1947.

———. *Portraits and Miniatures by Charles Willson Peale.* Philadelphia: American Philosophical Society, 1952.

———. "The Pale Horse on the Road." *Antiques,* May 1954.

———. "Rembrandt Peale, Instigator." *Pennsylvania Magazine of History and Biography,* July 1955.

———. *Charles Willson Peale.* New York: Scribner's, 1969.

———. *Patience Wright, American Artist and Spy in George III's London.* Middletown, Conn.: Wesleyan University Press, 1976.

Sellers, Horace Wells. "Charles Willson Peale, Artist Soldier." *Pennsylvania Magazine of History and Biography* XXXVIII, No. 3 (1914).

Semon, Kurt M. "His Sketches Reveal the Scope of Benjamin West's Work as an Artist." *American Collector,* May 1945.

Shee, Martin Archer. *The Life of Sir Martin Archer Shee by His Son.* 2 vols. London: Longman, Green, 1860.

Sherman, Frederick Fairchild. "The Art of Benjamin West." *Art in America,* April 1918.

———. *Early American Portraiture.* New York: privately printed, 1930.

———. *Early American Painting.* New York: Century, 1932.

Shoemaker, Samuel. "A Pennsylvania Loyalist's Interviews with George III." *Pennsylvania Magazine of History and Biography* II, No. 1 (1878).

Silliman, Benjamin. *A Journal of Travels in England, Holland and Scotland.* Boston, 1805.

Sitwell, Sacheverell. *Conversation Pieces.* London: Batsford, 1936.

———. *Narrative Pictures: A Survey of English Genre and Its Painters.* London: Batsford, 1937.

Sizer, Theodore, ed. *The Works of Colonel John Trumbull, Artist of The American Revolution.* New Haven: Yale University Press, 1950.

———. "A Portrait of the Mysterious Sarah Trumbull." *Winterthur Portfolio* II (1965).

Smith, George. *History of Delaware County, Pennsylvania.* Philadelphia: H. B. Ashmead, 1862.

Smith, H. Clifford. *Buckingham Palace: Its Furniture, Decoration and History.* London: Country Life, 1921.

Smith, John Thomas. *A Book for a Rainy Day, or Recollections of the Events of the Years 1766–1833.* London: 1861; Methuen, 1905.

————. *Nollekens and His Times.* 2 vols. London, H. Colburn, 1828. New edition, edited by Wilfred Whitten. New York and London: John Lane, 1917.

Smith, Page. *John Adams.* 2 vols. New York: Doubleday, 1962.

Smith, Dr. William. *Historical Account of the Expedition against the Ohio Indians, in the Year MDCCLXIV. Under the Command of Henry Bouquet, Esq.* Philadelphia and London, 1766.

Smith, William. *The Diary and Selected Papers of Chief Justice William Smith, 1784–1793.* Edited by L. F. S. Upton. 2 vols. Toronto: Champlain Society, 1963.

Smollett, Tobias. *Travels Through France and Italy.* Introduction by Osbert Sitwell. London, 1766. London: Lehman, 1949.

Snyder, Martin D. "The Icon of Antiquity." In *The Usefulness of Classical Learning in the Eighteenth Century,* Susan Ford Wiltshore, ed. American Philological Association, 1975.

Soby, James Thrall. *Contemporary Painters.* New York: Metropolitan Museum of Art, 1948.

Soby, James Thrall, and Dorothy C. Miller. *Romantic Painting in America.* New York: Museum of Modern Art, 1943.

Sparks, Esther. " 'St. Paul Shaking Off the Viper': An Early Romantic Series by Benjamin West." Chicago Art Institute *Museum Studies,* No. 6 (1971).

Specimens of Polyautography ... Impressions Taken from Original Drawings. London, 1806.

Stacey, C. P. "Benjamin West and 'The Death of Wolfe.' " National Gallery of Canada *Bulletin,* No. 4 (1966).

Staley, Allen. "The Landing of Agrippina at Brundisium with the Ashes of Germanicus." Philadelphia Museum of Art *Bulletin,* Nos. 287–288, Fall-Winter, 1965–66.

————. "Drawings by Benjamin West and His Son Raphael Lamar West." *Master Drawings,* Autumn, 1975. Review of the catalogue by Ruth S. Kraemer, Pierpont Morgan Library.

Steegman, Francis. *The Rule of Taste from George I to George IV.* London: Russell and Russell, 1936.

Stern, Cyrus. *Our Kindred.* Part II: *The Stern and West Record Ancestry and Genealogy.* West Chester, Pa., 1885.

Stewart, Robert G. *Henry Benbridge: American Portrait Painter.* Washington, D.C.: National Portrait Gallery, 1971.

Stowe, Walter Herbert, ed. *The Life and Letters of Bishop White.* New York: Morehouse, 1937.

Strange, Robert. *An Inquiry into the Rise and Establishment of the Royal Academy of Arts.* London, 1775.

Gilbert Stuart: Portraitist of the Young Republic. Washington: National Gallery of Art; Providence: Museum of Art, Rhode Island School of Design, 1967.

Stuart, Jane. "The Youth of Gilbert Stuart" and "Anecdotes of Gilbert Stuart." *Scribner's Monthly,* June 1876 and March 1877.

Sully, Thomas. *Hints to Young Painters*. Introduction by Faber Birren. Philadelphia: J. M. Stoddart, 1873. New York: Reinhold, 1965.

Summerson, John. *Georgian London: An Architectural Study*. New York: Praeger, 1962.

Sunderland, John. *John Constable*. London: Phaidon, 1971.

Tate Gallery. *Henry Fuseli: 1741–1825*. Catalogue of the 1975 exhibition. Foreword by Norman Reid; chapters by Gert Schiff and Werner Hoffmann. London: The Tate Gallery, 1975.

Taylor, Francis Henry. *The Taste of Angels: Art Collecting from Rameses to Napoleon*. Boston: Little, Brown, 1948.

Taylor, William Benjamin. *The Origin, Progress and Present Condition of the Fine Arts in Great Britain and Ireland*. 2 vols. London: 1841.

Thornbury, George Walter. *British Artists from Hogarth to Turner*. 2 vols. London: Hurst and Blackett, 1861.

———. *The Life of J. M. W. Turner*. 2 vols. London: Chatto and Windus, 1862.

Thorwald, Jürgen. *The Century of the Surgeon*. London: Pantheon, 1956.

Ticknor, George. *Life, Letters and Journals*. Edited by George S. Hillard. 2 vols. Boston: J. R. Osgood, 1876.

Tinkcom, Harry Marlin. "Sir Augustus in Pennsylvania." *Pennsylvania Magazine of History and Biography*, October 1951.

Tinker, Chauncey Brewster. *Painter and Poet; Studies in Literary Relations of English Painting*. Cambridge: Harvard University Press, 1939.

Todd, Charles Burd. *Joel Barlow*. New York: Putnam's, 1886.

Todd, Ruthven. *Tracks in the Snow*. London: Grey Walls Press, 1946.

———. "Benjamin West versus the History Picture." *Magazine of Art*, December 1948.

———. "Imaginary Indian in Europe." *Art in America*, July 1972.

Tolles, Frederick B. "The Culture of Early Pennsylvania." *Pennsylvania Magazine of History and Biography*, April 1957.

Tolman, Ruel Pardee. *The Life and Works of Edward Greene Malbone, 1777–1807*. New York: New-York Historical Society, 1958.

Tomory, Peter. *The Life and Art of Henry Fuseli*. New York: Praeger, 1972.

Trapp, Frank Anderson. *The Attainment of Delacroix*. Baltimore: Johns Hopkins Press, 1971.

Trumbull, John. *The Autobiography of Colonel John Trumbull, Patriot-Artist, 1756–1843*. Edited by Theodore Sizer. New York and London: Wiley and Putnam, 1841. New Haven: Yale University Press, 1953.

Tuckerman, Henry T. *Book of the Artists: American Artist Life*. New York: Putnam, 1867.

Turberville, A. S. *Men and Manners in the Eighteenth Century*. New York: Oxford University Press, 1926.

Universal Magazine of Knowledge and Pleasure. London, 1805.

Valentine, Alan. *The British Establishment, 1760–1884. A Biographical Dictionary of Eighteenth Century Personages*. Norman: University of Oklahoma Press, 1970.

Van Devanter, Anne C. "A Holy Family Attributed to Benjamin West." *Antiques*, November 1970.

―――. "Benjamin West and His Self-Portraits." *Antiques*, April 1973.

―――. "Benjamin West's 'Death of Socrates.'" *Antiques*, September 1973.

Von Erffa, Helmut. "Benjamin West Reinterpreted." *Antiques*, June 1962.

―――. "Benjamin West's 'Death of Socrates.'" *Antiques*, April 1973. *Journal*, Spring, 1969.

―――. "Benjamin West at the Height of His Career." *American Art Journal*, November 1973.

Waagen, G. F. *Works of Art and Artists in England*. 3 vols. London, 1838. Facsimile Reprint. London: Cornmarket Press, 1970.

Wainwright, Nicholas, ed. "Conversations with Benjamin West." In "Notes and Documents," *Pennsylvania Magazine of History and Biography*, January 1978.

Walford, Edward, and Walter Thornbury. *Old and New London*. 7 vols. London, New York, and Paris: Cassell, Petter, and Galpin, 1872–78. (Thornbury produced the first two volumes, Walford the others.)

Walker, John, and Macgill James. *Great American Paintings from Smibert to Bellows*. New York: Oxford University Press, 1943.

Walker, Lewis Burd. *The Burd Papers: Extracts from Chief Justice [William] Allen's Letter Book*. Pottsville: privately printed, 1897.

Walpole, Horace. *The Yale Edition of Horace Walpole's Correspondence*. Edited by W. S. Lewis, et al. 36 vols. to date. New Haven: Yale University Press, 1937 —. (Six or seven volumes still to come, plus a six-volume index.)

Ward, George Atkinson, ed. *The Journals and Letters of the Late Samuel Curwen, an American in England*. Boston: Little and Brown, 1842.

Waterhouse, Ellis Kirkham. *Painting in Britain, 1530 to 1790*. Harmondsworth: Penguin, 1953.

―――. "The British Contribution to the Neo-Classical Style in Painting." *Proceedings of the British Academy* XL (1954).

―――. *Gainsborough*. London: Hulton, 1958.

―――. Review of "Benjamin West and the Taste of His Times," by Grose Evans. *Burlington Magazine*, November 1960.

―――. *Three Decades of British Art, 1740–1770*. Philadelphia: American Philosophical Society, 1965.

―――. *Reynolds*. London: Kegan Paul, Trench, and Trubner, 1941. London: Phaidon, 1973.

Watkin, David. " 'The Hope Family' by Benjamin West." *Burlington Magazine*, December 1964.

―――. *Thomas Hope and the Neo-Classical Ideal*. London: Murray, 1968.

Watson, Elkhannah. *Memoirs: Men and Times of the Revolution, Including Journals of Travels in France and America from 1777 to 1842*. New York: Dana, 1856.

Watson, John Fanning. *Annals of Philadelphia and Pennsylvania in Ye Olden Times*. Philadelphia: Whiting and Thomas, 1857. Philadelphia: Lippincott, 1870.

Watts, Harvey M. "West: The Real Father of the American School." *Arts and Decoration*, December 1921, January 1922.

———. "The Benjamin West Exhibition at the Art Alliance, Philadelphia." *Art and Archeology*, January 1922.

Webster, J. Clarence. *Wolfe and the Artists: A Study of His Portraiture*. Toronto: Ryerson, 1930.

Wehle, Harry B. *Samuel F. B. Morse: American Painter*. New York: Metropolitan Museum of Art, 1932.

West, Benjamin. *A Discourse Delivered to the Students of the Royal Academy . . . December 10, 1792*. London, 1793.

———. Letters to the Earl of Elgin in W. R. Hamilton's *Memorandum on the Subject of the Earl of Elgin's Pursuits in Greece*. Edinburgh, 1810.

———. "The Sources of True Taste: Benjamin West's Instructions to a Young Painter for his Studies in Italy." Edited by Franziska Forster-Hahn. *Warburg and Courtauld Institutes Journal*, XXX (1967).

West's Gallery. *Catalogue of Pictures and Drawings by the Late Benjamin West*. London, 1824.

West, Raphael Lamar, and Benjamin West, Jr. *Letter to the Speaker of the House of Representatives of the United States*, April 12, 1826, HR Doc. 8, 19th Cong., 2d sess., December 11, 1826.

Westcott, Thompson. "West's Auto-Miniature." *Pennsylvania Magazine of History and Biography* VI, No. 4 (1882).

Wheatley, Henry B. *London Past and Present*. 2 vols. London: Murray, 1891.

———. *Historical Portraits: Some Notes on the Painted Portraits of Celebrated Characters of England, Scotland and Ireland*. London: G. Bell and Sons, 1897.

———. *Hogarth's London*. London: Constable, 1909.

Whitley, William T. *Thomas Gainsborough*. London: Smith, Elder, 1915.

———. Vol. I. *Artists and Their Friends in England, 1700–1799*. London: Medici Society, 1928. Facsimile reprint. New York: B. Blom, 1968. II. Volume two of the above. [III] *Art in England: 1800–1820*. Cambridge University Press, 1928. [IV] *Art in England: 1820–1835*. Cambridge University Press, 1930.

———. *Gilbert Stuart*. Cambridge: Harvard University Press, 1932. Facsimile reprint. New York: Da Capo Press, 1969.

Wilenski, R. H. *English Painting*. London: Faber and Faber, 1933.

Williams, D. E. *The Life and Correspondence of Sir Thomas Lawrence*. 2 vols. London, 1831.

Williams, William. *The Journal of Llewellin Penrose, A Seaman*. Edited by John Eagles. 4 vols. London: Murray, 1815. 1969 edition, introduction and notes by David Howard Dickason. Bloomington: Indiana University Press.

Williamson, George C. *Life and Works of Ozias Humphry*. London: John Lane, 1918.

Wilmerding, John. *The Genius of American Painting*. New York: Morrow, 1973.

Winckelmann, Johann Joachim. *Writings on Art*. Edited by David Irwin. London: Phaidon, 1972.

Wind, Edgar. "The Revolution of History Painting." *Journal of the Warburg Institute*. October 1938.

———. "Penny, West, and 'The Death of Wolfe.'" *Journal of the Warburg and Courtauld Institutes* X, Nos. 3 and 4 (1947).

Wood, Henry Trueman. *The History of the Royal Society of Arts*. London: Murray, 1913.

Woodress, James. *A Yankee's Odyssey: The Life of Joel Barlow*. Philadelphia: Lippincott, 1958.

Wornum, Ralph. *Lectures on Painting by the Royal Academicians Barry, Opie and Fuseli*. London: H. G. Bohm, 1848.

———. *The Epochs of Painting Characterized: A Sketch of the History of Painting*. London: J. Murray, 1859.

Wraight, Robert. *Hip! Hip! Hip! R.A.: An Unoffical Book for the Royal Academy Bicentenary, 10 December 1968*. London: Frewin, 1968.

Wright, Louis B. and George Bishop Tatum. *The Arts in America: The Colonial Period*. New York: Scribner's, 1966.

Zorgniotti, Dr. Adrian W. "Benjamin West's Osteomyelitis: A Translation." *Bulletin of the New York Academy of Medicine*, August, 1973. (See Nannoni, Dr. Angelo.)

NEWSPAPERS CITED

British Press, April 27, 1803.

Courier (London), April 4, 1820.

Examiner (London), June 10, 1821; May 10, 1824.

Gazetteer (London), May 21, 1771.

London Globe, March 11, 1820.

London Times, April 15, 1789; May 12, 1806; March 13, 1820; May 11, 1824.

Morning Chronicle (London), March 17, 1783; May 7 and 18, 1785; May 2, 1786; July 3, 1801; April 30, 1810; July 23, 1811; October 18, 1811.

Morning Herald (London), February 4, 1764; February 27, 1786; April 17, 1787; November 27, 1788; May 3 and 8, 1792; March 12, 18, 25, and 31, April 17 and 19, May 15 and 26, July 9, August 4, September 13, 1794; April 30, 1810; June 6, 1814.

Morning Post (London), May 2, 9, 11, July 2, 4, September 20, 21, 23, 28, November 17, 1785; January 5, 1786; January 13, April 14, 1789; February 24, 1791; July 3, 1801; April 13 and 14, 1803; April 28, 1804; May 20, 22, 23, and 30; June 23, 1829.

Public Advertiser (London), April 20, May 2, 1764; October 17, 1776; November 18, 1785; May 1, 1786; May 26, 1789.

St. James's Gazette (London), April 26 and 28, 1785.

The True Briton, April 27, 1803.

Index